17th Edition

# HIGHER EDUCATION LAW IN AMERICA

- Freedom of Speech
- Copyright Law
- Employment
- Athletics
- Hazing
- Cheating
- Privacy Issues
- Discrimination

Center for
Education & Employment Law
CEEL

Center for Education & Employment Law
P.O. Box 3008
Malvern, PA 19355

> "This publication is designed to provide accurate and authoritative information in regard to the subject matter covered. It is sold with the understanding that the publisher is not engaged in rendering legal, accounting or other professional services. If legal advice or other expert assistance is required, the service of a competent professional person should be sought." *-from a Declaration of Principles jointly adopted by a Committee of the American Bar Association and a Committee of Publishers and associations.*

**Library of Congress Cataloging-in Publication Data:**

Higher Education Law in America. 17th ed.
        p.  cm.
    Includes index.
    ISBN 978-1-944331-00-9 (pbk.)
    1. Universities and colleges – Law and legislation – United States.
    I. Center for Education & Employment Law.
    KF4225 .H54 2000
    378.73–dc21

                                                            00-055074


ISBN 978-1-944331-00-9

Cover Design by Amy Jacoby

Other Titles Published
By Center for Education & Employment Law:

*Deskbook Encyclopedia of American School Law*
*Deskbook Encyclopedia of Employment Law*
*Deskbook Encyclopedia of Public Employment Law*
*Keeping Your School Safe & Secure: A Practical Guide*
*Legal Update for Teachers: The Complete Principal's Guide*
*Private School Law in America*
*Students with Disabilities and Special Education*

# TABLE OF CONTENTS

# CHAPTER FIVE
## Employment

# CHAPTER SIX
## Employment Practices and Labor Relations

## CHAPTER SEVEN
### Employment Discrimination

## CHAPTER EIGHT
### Intellectual Property

## CHAPTER NINE
### Liability

TABLE OF CONTENTS

**CHAPTER TEN**
**University Operations**

**CHAPTER ELEVEN**
**School Finance**

**APPENDIX A**

## TABLE OF CONTENTS

**APPENDIX B**

# INTRODUCTION

*Higher Education Law in America* provides an encyclopedic compilation of federal and state court decisions in the area of college and university law. We have reviewed hundreds of federal and state court decisions involving higher education law and have included the most important ones in this deskbook. The chapters have been arranged topically, and the cases have been presented in an easy-to-use manner.

Each chapter contains explanatory passages at the beginning of each section to help you develop an overall understanding of the legal issues in that particular area. The case summaries have been written in everyday language, and at the start of each case is a brief note highlighting the holding or the significant issues discussed within. Further, the case summaries themselves contain boldface type to emphasize important facts, issues and holdings.

We feel that *Higher Education Law in America* will help you understand your rights and responsibilities under state and federal law. It has been designed with professional educators in mind, but also has tremendous value for lawyers. We hope you will use this book to protect yourself and to gain greater wisdom and understanding. Hopefully, we have succeeded in making the law accessible to you regardless of your level of understanding of the legal system.

Carol Warner
Editor
Center for Education & Employment Law

# ABOUT THE EDITORS

James A. Roth is editor of *Legal Notes for Education* and *Special Education Law Update,* and a co-editor of *Students with Disabilities and Special Education Law.* He is a graduate of the University of Minnesota and William Mitchell College of Law, and is admitted to the Minnesota Bar. Mr. Roth is an adjunct faculty member at Hamline University, St. Paul, Minnesota, and an adjunct program assistant professor at St. Mary's University of Minnesota, Twin Cities Campus.

Thomas D'Agostino is a managing editor at the Center for Education & Employment Law and is the editor of *Higher Education Legal Alert.* He is a co-author of *Keeping Your School Safe & Secure: A Practical Guide.* He graduated from the Duquesne University School of Law and received his undergraduate degree from Ramapo College of New Jersey. He is a past member of the American Bar Association's Section of Individual Rights and Responsibilities as well as the Pennsylvania Bar Association's Legal Services to Persons with Disabilities Committee. Mr. D'Agostino is admitted to the Pennsylvania Bar.

Curt J. Brown is the Editorial Director of the Center for Education & Employment Law. Prior to assuming his present position, he gained extensive experience in business-to-business publishing, including management of well-known publications such as *What's Working in Human Resources, What's New in Benefits & Compensation, Keep Up to Date with Payroll, Supervisors Legal Update,* and *Facility Manager's Alert.* Mr. Brown graduated from Villanova University School of Law and graduated magna cum laude from Bloomsburg University with a B.S. in Business Administration. He is admitted to the Pennsylvania Bar.

Carol Warner is the editor of *EducationTechNews.com* and two monthly newsletters: *School Safety & Security Alert* and *Legal Update for Teachers.* She is also a contributing editor for *HigherEdMorning.com* and *Higher Education Legal Alert.* Before joining the Center for Education & Employment Law, she was an editor for two employment law newsletters: *What's Working in Human Resources* and *What's New in Benefits & Compensation.* Carol is a graduate of The New York Institute of Technology and holds a Bachelor of Arts in English with an emphasis in professional writing.

Elizabeth A. Wheeler is editor of the monthly newsletter *Private Education Law Report* and the *Private School Law in America* deskbook. She's also a contributing editor for the newsletters *Higher Education Legal Alert* and *School Safety & Security Alert.* A graduate of Macalester College and Capital

University Law School, she's a member of the Massachusetts bar. Before joining the Center for Education & Employment Law, she was a legal editor for a South Boston publisher, where she edited employment law and education law newsletters.

# How to Use Your Deskbook

We have designed *Higher Education Law in America* in an accessible format for both professional educators and attorneys to use as a research and reference tool toward prevention of legal problems.

## Research Tool

As a research tool, our deskbook allows you to conduct your research on two different levels – by topics or cases.

### Topic Research

◆ If you have a general interest in a particular **topic** area, our **table of contents** provides descriptive chapter headings containing detailed subheadings from each chapter.

➢ For your convenience, we also include the chapter table of contents at the beginning of each chapter.

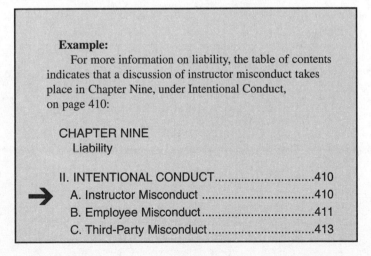

**Example:**
For more information on liability, the table of contents indicates that a discussion of instructor misconduct takes place in Chapter Nine, under Intentional Conduct, on page 410:

CHAPTER NINE
  Liability

II. INTENTIONAL CONDUCT..............................410
  A. Instructor Misconduct ....................................410
  B. Employee Misconduct....................................411
  C. Third-Party Misconduct................................413

◆ If you have a specific interest in a particular **issue**, our comprehensive **index** collects all of the relevant page references to particular issues.

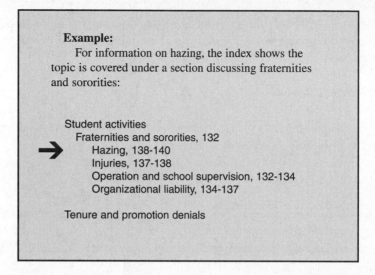

**Example:**
For information on hazing, the index shows the topic is covered under a section discussing fraternities and sororities:

Student activities
Fraternities and sororities, 132
→ Hazing, 138-140
Injuries, 137-138
Operation and school supervision, 132-134
Organizational liability, 134-137

Tenure and promotion denials

*Case Research*

◆ If you know the **name** of a particular case, our **table of cases** will allow you to quickly reference the location of the case.

**Example:**
If someone mentioned a case named *Godinez v. Siena College,* looking in the table of cases, which has been arranged alphabetically, the case would be listed under section "G" and would be found on p. 428 of the text.

**G**

Glover v. Jackson State Univ., 389
→ Godinez v. Siena College, 428
Goldman v. Wayne State Univ., 167
Gonzaga Univ. v. Doe, 49, 51
Gonzales v. North Carolina State Univ., 85
Goodwin v. Creighton Univ., 95

✓ Each of the cases summarized in the deskbook also contains the case citation, which will allow you to access the full text of the case if you would like to learn more about it. See *How to Read a Case Citation,* p. 523.

◆ If your interest lies in cases from a **particular state**, our **table of cases by state** will identify the cases from your state and direct you to their page numbers.

**Example:**
If cases from California are of interest, the table of cases by state, arranged alphabetically, lists all of the case summaries contained in the deskbook from that state.

**CALIFORNIA**

Adoma v. Univ. of Phoenix, Inc., 259
Alpha Delta Chi-Delta Chapter v. Reed, 184
Ass'n for a Cleaner Environment v. Yosemite
Community College Dist., 449

✓ Remember, the judicial system has two court systems — state and federal court — which generally function independently from each other. See *The Judicial System,* p. 519. We have included the federal court cases in the table of cases by state according to the state in which the court resides. However, federal court decisions often impact other federal courts within that particular circuit. Therefore, it may be helpful to review cases from all of the states contained in a particular circuit.

## Reference Tool

As a reference tool, we have highlighted important resources which provide the framework for many legal issues.

◆ If you would like to see specific wording of the **U.S. Constitution**, refer to **Appendix A**, which includes relevant provisions of the U.S. Constitution such as the First Amendment (freedom of speech and religion) and the Fourteenth Amendment (which contains the Equal

# How to Use Your Deskbook

Protection Clause and the Due Process Clause).

 If you would like to review **U.S. Supreme Court decisions** in a particular subject matter area, our topical list of U.S. Supreme Court case citations located in **Appendix B** will be helpful.

The book also contains a glossary, which provides definitions of legal terms and certain statutes. The glossary can be found on p. 525.

We hope you benefit from the use of *Higher Education Law in America*. If you have any questions about how to use the deskbook, please contact Carol Warner at *cwarner@pbp.com*.

# TABLE OF CASES

# TABLE OF CASES

# TABLE OF CASES

# TABLE OF CASES

# TABLE OF CASES

# TABLE OF CASES

# TABLE OF CASES BY STATE

# TABLE OF CASES BY STATE

# CHAPTER ONE

## Student Rights

## I.  THE CONTRACTUAL RELATIONSHIP

*The relationship between private institutions of higher learning and their students is contractual. Contract terms are established by the written materials distributed over the course of a student's enrollment. Public institutions of higher learning are government entities which have constitutional due process obligations to provide students notice and an opportunity to be heard.*

### A.  Breach of Contract

◆ *The Fifth Circuit affirmed the dismissal of a student's tort claim that alleged a Texas university breached a contract.*

A student was notified he wouldn't be recommended for reappointment for his RA position the following year. Meetings with administrators to resolve the matter were heated. After a run-in with a fellow RA, the student was immediately fired. He went to administration and the university's chaplain to discuss his appeal. There, administrators and campus police discussed his behavior and the university's safety concerns. After the meeting, an officer

1

escorted the student to the university's mental health facility for an evaluation. He left without being evaluated. He lost the appeal for his RA position but was allowed to remain enrolled as a student – with certain restrictions in place. He then went to a dorm that he'd been ordered to stay away from. The next day, he was placed on mandatory administrative withdrawal. He sued, alleging a laundry list of complaints. The court dismissed the suit, and the student appealed a breach of contract claim. He claimed a "special relationship" exception applied, as he trusted university officers who encouraged him to seek mental health services and university administrators who expressed a desire to help him during the disciplinary hearings. The court wasn't swayed. **"Encouraging students to take advantage of resources ... and offering to help students struggling through disciplinary problems are all workday aspects of an administrator's job," so there was nothing special about the relationship**, it held. The ruling was affirmed. *Hux v. Southern Methodist University*, 819 F.3d 776 (5th Cir. 2016).

◆    *An applicant's decision to omit a critical fact during the admissions process voided his admission and negated a breach of contract claim.*

The student applied for admission to the college's LL.M. program. On his application, he said he was born in the Philippines and obtained a J.D. degree from the Novus University School of Law. At his admission interview, the director of the program told the student that a law degree from a school in the Philippines was fine, thus clearly indicating his belief that Novus was a school with a physical location in the Philippines. In fact, Novus operated only online. But the student didn't correct the program director's misconception. Months later, the school received the student's transcript and learned he attended an online program. It said no degree would be awarded because the student wasn't eligible for admission in the first place. The student sued, alleging breach of contract. The case reached a New York appeals court, which held a school can rescind a student's admission if the student's application included material omissions. Here, when the student submitted his application, he was essentially saying that he satisfied admission requirements – including the requirement that he attended a foreign law school with a physical location. **Because his admission was obtained falsely, the school had no contractual obligation to award him a degree**, the court said. The claim failed. *Salvador v. Touro College*, 139 A.D.3d 1 (N.Y. App. Div. 2016).

◆    *A university in Mississippi did not breach a contract with a medical student when it dismissed him based on his history of disciplinary issues, a state appeals court ruled.*

The student enrolled in a medical program and engaged in conduct that raised red flags. The promotion and matriculation committee met to discuss the student's conduct and set conditions for him. He failed to meet them. The problems continued, and the committee recommended dismissal. After his unsuccessful internal appeal, the student sued, alleging breach of contract. A chancellor granted judgment in favor of the school, and the student filed an appeal. A state appeals court affirmed the decision in the school's favor. It said the decision to dismiss the student was not arbitrary or capricious. Though he claimed the decision was arbitrary and capricious because the school did not precisely follow student handbook guidelines in connection with its pursuit of disciplinary proceedings against him, perfect compliance with the guidelines was not legally required. **All that was required was an informal give and take, and the student was provided with that**, the court said. As a result, the decision to dismiss the student from the school was affirmed. *Mahaffey v. William Carey Univ.*, 180 So.3d 846 (Miss. Ct. App. 2015).

◆   *A New York federal judge rejected breach of contract claims filed by a veterinary student who was expelled for violating the honor code.*

The student brought her dog to the school's animal clinic for treatment. She allegedly told clinic staff that the dog wasn't aggressive. But during the exam, it bit a fourth-year student. The clinic later determined the dog had bitten before. The student was charged with violating the honor code. At the hearing, veterinary board members expressed concerns about her professional judgment. The dean suspended the student for one year and said the board could decide whether to readmit her. After the suspension, the student asked the board to readmit her. It sent her a letter saying that she could return to classes – but said her return was conditional as it hadn't reached a final decision about her case yet. After a hearing, the board decided to expel her. She lost three years' worth of credits. Alleging $500,000 in damages, she sued the university for breach of contract based on the letter that informed her she could return to school. The court wasn't convinced the letter constituted a contract – but even if it did, there was no breach. **The board's approval was a clear condition of her permanent return to school, and that approval wasn't granted.** As she couldn't show the university breached a contract, her suit was dismissed. *Habitzreuther v. Cornell Univ.*, No. 5:14-cv-1229 (GLS/TWD), 2015 WL 5023719 (N.D.N.Y. 8/25/15).

◆   *An Ohio federal court ordered a university to issue the diploma of a student who alleged a breach of contract after he was dismissed.*

In medical school, the student performed well academically but had a few conduct issues on and off campus. He was arrested and charged with driving under the influence (DUI). The charges were pending for more than a year. The student did not tell the university immediately after the arrest. The student was convicted on the DUI charge a month before graduation. He was dismissed and was not awarded a diploma. The student sued, alleging a breach of contract as the school's handbook required students to report convictions, but not arrests. He argued he'd suffer irreparable harm if he didn't receive his diploma. He asked the court to order the university to issue the diploma. Noting the university acted arbitrarily in requiring more than the student handbook outlined, the court found the student was likely to win the breach of contract claim. It ordered the school to issue the student's diploma. *Al-Dabagh v. Case Western Reserve Univ.*, 23 F.Supp.3d 865 (N.D. Ohio 2014).

On appeal, the Sixth Circuit reversed the decision, holding the university properly dismissed the student because he failed to exhibit a requisite level of professionalism. In addition, **his argument ignored the fact that the school's**

**curriculum strongly emphasized the need for professional behavior**. The court's decision to order the school to issue the student a diploma was reversed. *Al-Dabagh v. Case Western Reserve Univ.*, 777 F.3d 355 (6th Cir. 2015).

◆   *An Ohio appeals court affirmed a decision that a lower court properly dismissed a student's breach of contract claim.*

To become a corrections officer, the student had to pass the corrections officer certification and take a course at a community college. She was taking the class when she injured herself during the self-defense portion. The student sued for breach of contract and negligence, alleging the school had a legal duty to provide safety mats and she was injured because that duty was breached. The court refused to grant pretrial judgment, and the school appealed. The appeals court reversed the call on the negligence claim, finding the defendants had state law immunity to it. The case returned to the trial court, which granted the defendants judgment without a trial on the contract claims, too. The student appealed, arguing "student performance objectives" in the textbook used in the training course required the college to provide safety mats. The text stated that "given a safety mat," the student would be able to demonstrate the maneuvers. **To recover for breach of contract, the student had to show a binding contract existed that required the school to provide her a safety mat. She didn't.** Crucially, the textbook was not written and distributed by the school. The court stated: "We reject any contention that a course textbook, not drafted or reviewed by a college, can somehow create a contractual obligation on the part of the college." So the decision for the school was affirmed. *Duncan v. Cuyahoga Community College*, 29 N.E.3d 289 (Ohio Ct. App. 2015).

◆   *An Oregon federal court rejected the breach of contract claim of a student who was dismissed from a mental health counseling degree program.*

In a small group session that took place as part of a residency, the student disclosed his "pedophilic sexual orientation." Afterward, he was dismissed from the program. He sued the university, accusing it of breaching its contract with him. He alleged that the student handbook formed a contract between the parties and that the university's decision to dismiss him violated the handbook's nondiscrimination policy. The court granted the university's motion to dismiss. **The court rejected the student's claim that the handbook created an enforceable contract between the parties as it included a disclaimer that specifically said it was not a contract.** Further, the dismissal did not violate the handbook's nondiscrimination policy, as the student did not even assert that "pedophilic sexual orientation" is a protected classification. So the claims were dismissed. *Gibson v. Walden Univ., LLC,* 66 F.Supp.3d 1322 (D. Or. 2014).

◆   *A Connecticut university's decision to expel a medical student didn't amount to a breach of contract.*

The student struggled academically. A handbook said students must pass step one of the U.S. medical licensing exam within three attempts and within six years of admission to the program. In the student's third year, he was put on academic probation. Afterward, he failed step one of the licensing exam twice. He was expelled. He appealed, and the program conditionally readmitted him. One condition was to make his final attempt at passing the exam by a specific date. The student missed that deadline – and was again expelled from the program. Nine months after the conditional deadline, the student passed the exam. He asked to be readmitted, but his request was denied. He sued for breach of contract, alleging the school expelled him for failing the step one exam twice when the handbook gave him three chances to pass. The court dismissed his claim, and the student appealed. The appellate court affirmed, saying **he was expelled for a pattern of poor academic performance capped the by the failure to meet a requirement of his conditional readmission**. *Morris v. Yale Univ.*, 63 A.3d 991 (Conn. App. Ct. 2013).

◆ *A private Mississippi college did not breach its contract with a law student who was expelled for plagiarism, a federal court decided.*

When the student turned in a paper, his instructor suspected plagiarism. The student admitted it and begged the school for another chance. He was suspended and returned to the school a year later on academic probation. He submitted another paper that did not include proper attribution. The school expelled the student. He sued, alleging the college was in breach of contract. He claimed the school breached its contract by failing to give him proper notice of the charges against him. He said this alleged failure deprived him of process he was due under the contract. The court noted that the school was a private institution, meaning that it was not required to meet constitutional due process requirements. **Students who are dismissed from private schools for academic reasons are not entitled to any type of due process hearing, the court explained.** Because the school's procedures were fundamentally fair and the expulsion decision was not arbitrary or capricious, the student's claim was dismissed. *Beauchene v. Mississippi College*, No. 3:12-CV-784-CWR-LRA, 2013 WL 5965698 (S.D. Miss. 11/8/13).

◆ *Finding students couldn't sue a university for breach of contract until it reached a final decision in ongoing conduct proceedings against them, a North Carolina appeals court dismissed the claim.*

Two fraternity brothers lived in two off-campus houses that shared a backyard with three other frat houses. After repeated noise complaints about loud music, the dean launched an investigation. One of the students received a citation for violating the city's noise ordinance. The dean referred the case to the undergraduate conduct board. It found the two students violated the student handbook and the city's noise ordinance. Both students were suspended for two semesters. The students appealed, saying the board violated its own policy by scheduling the hearing at a time when the students' advisors couldn't attend. The appellate board vacated the panel's decision and ordered a new hearing. In the meantime, the appellate board agreed the students could participate in commencement, but decided to put a hold on their transcripts and diplomas until the situation was resolved. The students sued, claiming the undergraduate conduct board's failure to follow outlined procedures amounted to a breach of contract. The judge dismissed the students' claims, explaining that **they couldn't validly sue the board for breach of contract until a final decision was reached in ongoing disciplinary matters.** *Samost v. Duke Univ.*, No. COA 12-635, 2013 WL 157-4421 (N.C. Ct. App. 4/16/13).

◆   *A New York university did not breach a contract by refusing to let a student complete his MBA degree studies after he was convicted of insider trading.*

While he was pursuing his MBA degree, the student worked as a certified public accountant. He was convicted of violating insider trading laws by providing material, nonpublic business information to his brother – a securities trader. But the student did not tell the university about his criminal activity. After he graduated, the university learned about the conviction and decided not to certify him as qualified for an MBA. In a federal court action, the student claimed the university breached an implied contract by not following its rules and procedures. Appeal reached the U.S. Court of Appeals, Second Circuit. It held **academic decisions are best left to educators**. Judicial review of such decisions is limited to a determination of whether the institution acted in good faith. Courts are not to disturb these decisions unless educators acted arbitrarily, irrationally, or in bad faith. In this case, the university disallowed the student's MBA certification on the basis of a bylaw making it the duty of each faculty member to determine standards of academic achievement for degrees.

As the student had admitted his crime, university faculty members had reasonably concluded his conduct was not befitting a member of the academic business community. The court held it could not be shown that the university acted arbitrarily, irrationally, or in bad faith. The judgment was affirmed. *Rosenthal v. New York Univ.*, 482 Fed.Appx. 609 (2d Cir. 2012).

◆   *A federal court of appeals affirmed the dismissal of a former student's breach of contract action against a New York medical school.*

After the student failed a required course, the medical school disenrolled him. As a result, he could not take a required medical licensing exam, and he sued for breach of contract. **Under New York law, an "implied contract" is created when a student is admitted to an institution.** Contract terms are created by the institution's written materials, and it must act in good faith when dealing with a student. On the other hand, the student must satisfy school requirements and follow its procedures. In this case, the student claimed the medical school fabricated his failing grade. A federal court found he presented no evidence from which a reasonable jury could conclude his grade was fabricated. In fact, he emailed his instructor to acknowledge the failing grade. On appeal, the U.S. Court of Appeals, Second Circuit, affirmed the judgment for the medical school. It held the student could not show a breach of contract based on fabricating a failing grade and dismissing him. *Dasrath v. Ross Univ. School of Medicine*, 494 Fed.Appx. 177 (2d Cir. 2012).

◆   *A New York court found no breach of contract based on a college's decision to expel a student who admitted setting a fire on campus.*

After the student admitted committing arson on campus, he was arrested and charged with criminal violations. The college expelled him, and he filed a state court action for breach of contract in which he said he had falsely confessed to arson. After the case was dismissed, the student appealed. **A state appellate division court explained that an implied contract is formed when a student is admitted to a higher education institution.** Students must comply with terms prescribed by the institution. Courts will not disturb the discipline unless there is evidence that the institution acted arbitrarily, or did not substantially comply with its own rules and regulations. In this case, the student failed to identify any specific contract terms were violated. He did not point to any internal rule, regulation or code that was not followed. To succeed on his breach of contract claim, there had to be a more specific showing with respect to what the college did to breach the contract. Since the student relied on vague assertions of breach and did not identify any rule, regulation or code that was violated, his breach of contract claim had been properly dismissed. *Jones v. Trustees of Union College*, 937 N.Y.S.2d 475 (N.Y. App. Div. 2012).

◆ *An Ohio court rejected a former student's breach of contract claim based on his dismissal from a medical college program.*

In his first year of medical school, the student failed two classes and his grade point average fell below 1.5. The school placed him on academic probation. After the student failed two more classes, he was dismissed. He claimed the school breached a contract by changing the sequence of his courses, refusing to let him remediate the failed classes, and refusing to let him register as a special status student. A state court found the university exercised professional judgment. On appeal, the Court of Appeals of Ohio found no breach of contract. Instructor permission was required for a student to enroll as a special status student, and a professor had denied the student's request to take the class via distance learning. As the lower court had found, the student failed to meet the conditions set for him, including raising his grade point average to at least 2.5, completing a particular course, avoiding outside employment without pre-approval, and attending monthly status meetings. There was evidence that he had violated these conditions. **There was competent evidence that the university exercised its professional judgment in good faith.** Rejecting all the student's arguments, the court held for the university. *Jefferson v. Univ. of Toledo*, No. 12AP-236, 2012 -Ohio- 4793 (Ohio Ct. App. 2012).

◆ *A federal district court rejected a breach of contract claim against a California university that dismissed a student from a psychology program.*

Due to poor performance, the university dismissed the student from a graduate clinical psychology child studies program. He waited more than two years after losing an appeal within the university to file a federal district court action for breach of contract. According to the student, the university breached a contract by falsely accusing him of program violations, failing to allow him to challenge the accusations against him, dismissing him, and refusing to refund his tuition. As the court explained, California law required the filing of actions based on breach of an oral or implied contract within two years. On the other hand, the time limit for filing a claim for breach of a written contract is usually four years. In support of his written contract claim, the student offered his application to the university, an admission letter, the university's general catalogue and a clinical training agreement. But the court held these documents did not prove there was a written contract, **as none of them "express[ed] the obligation sued upon." The catalogue did not say that the university was contractually bound and did not create any implied contract provisions.** The clinical training agreement addressed only site-based clinical training and did not address any conditions of enrollment or dismissal, or otherwise create a contract. As a result, the university was entitled to judgment. *Bazzi v. Antioch Univ.*, No. CV 11-00482 DDP, 2012 WL 123542 (C.D. Cal. 1/13/12).

◆    *A Pennsylvania nurse anesthesia student unsuccessfully claimed his university breached its contract with him by dismissing him from the program.*

A Pennsylvania university dismissed a nurse anesthesia student from the clinical portion of his program, stating he consistently needed help and was not at an acceptable level. The university nursing department chair said the student was insubordinate and gave patients medicines he had been told not to provide. Administrators said the student's performance in the clinical portion of the program imperiled patient safety. After being placed on probation, he filed an unsuccessful internal appeal and was dismissed from the program. In a federal court lawsuit against the university and others, the student alleged breach of contract, breach of the covenant of good faith and fair dealing, denial of due process and tortious interference with contract. The court held for the university, and appeal reached the U.S. Court of Appeals, Third Circuit.

**On appeal, the court held the relationship between private institutions and their students is a contractual one. Evidence showed the student's performance was deficient, and his deficiencies were documented.** His inability to assure administrators that he could work safely with patients justified dismissal and was consistent with terms of the student handbook permitting dismissal "if an error of commission or omission jeopardize[d] the safety and/or welfare of the patient." The court rejected the student's claim that he was denied due process by the refusal of his request to have counsel attend his internal appeal. Private institutions need not offer their students the constitutional due process protections that must be provided by public institutions. *Kimberg v. Univ. of Scranton*, 411 Fed.Appx. 473 (3d Cir. 2010).

◆    *A Pennsylvania public university had certain due process obligations to its students, but its student handbook did not constitute a binding contract.*

A student claimed she was unfairly dismissed from a clinical practicum for violating safety rules. She had to withdraw from another practicum and, instead of waiting a year to retake them, she completed the requirements at a private university. The student sued the State System of Higher Education for breach of contract, alleging the university did not follow the procedures set out in its handbook when it dismissed her from the practicum. After deciding the handbook constituted a binding contract between the parties, the state Board of Claims held it had no authority over state contracts to provide education.

On appeal, the Commonwealth Court of Pennsylvania held the claim was properly dismissed because the board lacked jurisdiction (authority) to hear the dispute. **But the board incorrectly found a public institution's handbook forms a binding contract with a student.** Instead, the court held the board lacked jurisdiction over the claim because the handbook was not a contract. While private institutions have a contractual relationship with students, Pennsylvania public institutions have a due process obligation to provide students notice and an opportunity to be heard. **The court held a public university handbook did not constitute a contract** and affirmed the decision. *Tran v. State System of Higher Educ.*, 986 A.2d 179 (Pa. Commw. Ct. 2009).

◆ *An expelled graduate student had no constitutional right to stay in the Indiana University School of Optometry.*

The student claimed two professors assigned him poor grades for purely arbitrary reasons and that a third professor refused to let him take an exam. As a result, the university did not allow him to take required clinical rotations. The student failed a clinical rotation and was dismissed from the program. He sued the university board and several employees in a federal district court, which dismissed the case. On appeal, Seventh Circuit found **students generally have no federal constitutional right to remain in a graduate institution**. An exception applies if the student can show an implied contract. But to claim an implied contract was formed, the student must identify some promise from the university that was not honored. This promise could be made in a catalogue or some other written material.

**The student said the promises he was relying on had been posted around campus in university bulletins and flyers.** But he did not specify what they were, instead claiming the specific promises would be unearthed during the pretrial investigation and information-sharing procedure called "discovery." As a result, the court held the case had been properly dismissed. Repeating language from the lower court decision, the court held that allowing the case to proceed without specific facts would "sanction a fishing expedition costing both parties, and the court, valuable time and resources." *Bissessur v. Indiana Univ. Board of Trustees*, 581 F.3d 599 (7th Cir. 2009).

◆ *Virginia's highest court rejected a claim by female students that a college for women that transitioned to a coeducational facility breached a contract.*

The college was a predominantly female institution until 2006, when its trustees decided to make it coeducational. A group of students sued the college in a state court, claiming the college breached a contract that included a promise of a four-year education at a women's college. They relied on an academic catalogue, which stated that the college offered "an education fully and completely directed toward women." The students claimed they chose the college specifically because it provided a single-sex environment. The college filed a motion seeking documentation on the existence of a contract to keep the college from going coed. The students produced letters of offers of admission, emails and other correspondence.

The trial court dismissed the complaint, and the students appealed to the Supreme Court of Virginia. On appeal, the students repeated their claim that a contract was formed when they accepted offers of admission, paid tuition and registered for classes. The court rejected the claims, explaining that **to be a legally binding contract, an agreement must be definite as to all terms, identify the subject matter involved, and state essential commitments and agreements relating to the subject matter**. The court found no language in any document indicating a clear promise by the college to remain predominantly female for the duration of their studies. As the students failed to prove the existence of a contract that would require the college to remain all-female while the students were enrolled there, the court affirmed the judgment. *Dodge v. Trustees of Randolph-Macon Woman's College*, 276 Va. 1, 661 S.E.2d 801 (Va. 2008).

◆    *The Supreme Judicial Court of Maine held a handbook reservation clause, which allowed a college to unilaterally change the terms of its handbook without notice to students, defeated a student's breach of contract claim.*

A college appeals board found a male student guilty of sexual assault. The board prohibited him from living in campus housing, eating in college dining halls, and being on campus after 11:00 p.m. It placed him on permanent disciplinary probation. The student sued the college in a state court for breach of contract. The court found the college did not breach any contractual obligation to the student and held for the college. The student appealed, arguing the college breached its contract because the decision by the college to allow the female student to appeal did not meet his reasonable expectations. He said the disciplinary process described in the student handbook did not authorize the female student's appeal to the dean's hearing board. On appeal, the Supreme Judicial Court of Maine held **a reservation clause in the handbook allowed the college to unilaterally change handbook terms without notice to the students**. As a result, the court affirmed the judgment for the college. *Millien v. Colby College*, 874 A.2d 397 (Me. 2005).

## B.  Fraudulent Misrepresentation

*In Byrd v. Lamar, 846 So.2d 334 (Ala. 2002), Alabama's highest court held a student could sue two university employees for intentionally trying to deceive him, where there was evidence he relied on their misrepresentations. In another Alabama case, a party could be held liable for fraud even where a misrepresentation was "made by mistake and innocently," if another party acted on the misrepresentation and suffered harm. See Craig v. Forest Institute of Professional Psychology, 713 So.2d 967 (Ala. Civ. App. 1997).*

◆    *Graduates of a Michigan law school failed to present evidence sufficient to proceed with their fraud-based claims against the school, a federal appeals court decided.*

Twelve graduates who did not secure desired employment sued the school in a federal district court, claiming violations of the state's consumer protection act, common law fraud and negligent misrepresentation. To support their claims, the plaintiffs relied on an "employment report and salary survey" that the school provided to prospective and current students. They said the school misrepresented info relating to the percentage of graduates employed and their average starting salaries. They claimed the stats provided in the report did not accurately reflect their real employment prospects upon graduation. The district court granted the school's motion to dismiss, concluding the state's consumer protection act didn't apply to the purchase of a legal education that is made to secure employment. The graduates appealed, and the U.S. Court of Appeals for the Sixth Circuit affirmed. **The court noted that the title of the challenged report included the words "salary survey," and statements from the report indicated it was based on responses from some graduates but not all of them.** There was no fraudulent or negligent misrepresentation because the graduates did not reasonably rely on the challenged information. The district court's ruling was affirmed. *MacDonald v. Thomas M. Cooley Law School*, No. 12-2066, 2013 WL 3880201 (6th Cir. 7/30/13).

◆   *A federal court allowed a class action to proceed against a New Jersey law school based on claims that it posted misleading and incomplete graduate employment information on its website in violation of state laws.*

In refusing to dismiss the case, the court acknowledged the different result in *Gomez-Jiminez v. New York Law School*. The court disagreed with the New York court's finding that persons could not have reasonably relied on the alleged misrepresentations and could have learned about employment prospects through the exercise of due diligence. Instead, the New Jersey court questioned whether a reasonable student looking to go to law school would consider that published data included non-law and part-time work. As a result, the court allowed consumer fraud claims based on New Jersey and Delaware law to proceed. In so doing, **the court held the students did not have to show they reasonably relied on a misrepresentation**. Instead, they had to show the law school knowingly concealed a material fact with the intent of having them rely on the concealment, causing a loss. *Harnish v. Widener Univ. School of Law*, No. 2:12-cv-00608 (WHW), 2013 WL 1149166 (D.N.J. 3/20/13).

◆   *No legal violation occurred in connection with a District of Columbia graduate student's failure to obtain a desired doctoral degree.*

A part-time graduate student at Howard University (HU) lost some credits due to a time lapse. Although HU had procedures to restore credits earned within 10 years, she did not follow them. After the student took a semester of leave, some of her old credits became permanently unusable and some more recently earned credits became unusable. Because the credits were not restored, she was dismissed from the program. The student sued, claiming breached a contract by failing to provide an adviser and allowing her to continue to register for courses after seven years, even though HU rules stated that students are to be dismissed after seven years in those circumstances. **Though the student claimed graduate school rules and regulations formed a contract, the court held they were simply a way for HU to communicate expectations to its students.** As there was no evidence that HU intended its rules to create binding obligations, the breach of contract claim failed. A constructive fraud claim was also rejected, as the student did not prove a confidential relationship with her adviser. *Mosby-Nickens v. Howard Univ.*, 864 F.Supp.2d 93 (D.D.C. 2012).

◆   *A federal district court denied a request to hold off on deciding a case filed against a California college until an appeals court had a chance to review it.*

A group of students claimed the college advertised "a quality education at an affordable price." However, they asserted they paid tuition rates that were among the highest in the country and that their degrees did not prepare them for anything but low-wage and low-skill jobs. Among the claims were breach of contract, negligent misrepresentation, fraud, breach of an implied covenant of good faith and fair dealing, and violations of state consumer protection laws. A federal district court held all claims should be resolved via arbitration except for the state consumer protection law claims. They could not be arbitrated because they sought to enforce a public right by blocking the college from deceiving other consumers. The college appealed the decision to deny its motion to compel arbitration with respect to the public injunctive relief claims. It then filed a motion asking the district court to hold off on deciding the public injunctive relief claims until after the appeals court had ruled on its appeal. After balancing the four factors utilized by courts when considering a request for injunctive relief, the court held a stay should be denied. **In the court's view, the public interest in promoting consumer protection justified a denial of the request to stay the proceedings**, and it did not find the college was likely to prevail on the merits of the case. *Ferguson v. Corinthian Colleges*, No. SACV 11-0127 DOC (AJWx), 2012 WL 27622 (C.D. Cal. 1/5/12).

◆    *A federal court dismissed a breach of contract claim against Harvard Extension School by an applicant who misrepresented the fact that he had already attended other institutions and held numerous degrees.*

The extension school's online application required applicants to list all prior colleges and universities attended – even if they did not want to transfer credits and even if they withdrew from a program. Not listing a prior institution attended was a serious enough misrepresentation to trigger disciplinary action. In a federal district court action by the applicant, **the court found no agreement between the parties, much less an agreement to accept him or award him a degree. There was no promise of enrollment or a degree as the applicant claimed**, but only "correspondence regarding certain course requirements." In addition, the court held "the decision to grant or deny admission to a student is a quintessential matter of academic judgment," that would not be "second guessed by the courts." *Getso v. Harvard Univ. Extension School*, No. 10 Civ. 4624, 2011 WL 135012 (S.D.N.Y. 1/13/11).

◆    *The Court of Appeals of Ohio rejected fraud claims by two students in a surgical technician program.*

At the time the students completed their classroom work, the college told them that no externship sites were available. When the students were finally placed in externships, both of them were asked to consider transferring into different programs. They both left the college and later filed a state court action against it for breach of contract, fraud and violation of a state consumer sales practices act. The students claimed the college knew it was enrolling more students than it could place in hospital externships. According to the state court of appeals, **the placement delay may have reflected poor planning, but it did not support a claim based on knowing or false representation**. On the other hand, the court reversed a lower court decision to reject claims under the state consumer sales practices act. To constitute a violation of the act, conduct does not need to rise to the level of fraud, negligence or breach of contract. In this case, a fact issue was present as to whether the college unfairly or deceptively represented that externships would be available during the final term of the program. The judgment was reversed in part, and the case was returned to the trial court for further proceedings. *Hacker v. National College of Business and Technology*, 186 Ohio App.3d 203, 927 N.E.2d 38 (Ohio Ct. App. 2010).

◆    *A Texas chiropractic student failed to convince a court that a college made misrepresentations about its graduation requirements.*

Among other requirements, the college required students to complete 10 trimesters of work. The student completed her 10 trimesters, but the college refused to award her a degree because she failed a clinical exit examination. According to the student, the college told her before she took the examination that her application for graduation had already been approved. She also said a college official told her before she took that examination that she should not worry about passing it. The student sued the college in a state court, raising a claim under a state consumer protection statute. She added claims for fraud, negligent misrepresentation and equitable estoppel. The court ruled for the college, and the student appealed. The Court of Appeals of Texas held all four of the claims had a common element of reliance, meaning she could not prevail unless she showed she relied on misrepresentations by the college. However, **the student did not show she relied on any alleged misrepresentation made by college officials and could not prevail on any of her claims**. As a result, the trial court judgment was affirmed. *Wood v. Texas Chiropractic College*, No. 01-07-00952-CV, 2008 WL 2854268 (Tex. Ct. App. 7/24/08).

◆   *A student did not show breach of contract or fraudulent misrepresentation by a college that accused him of selling copies of an upcoming examination.*

After an investigation and hearing, the college concluded the student had engaged in academic misconduct and dismissed him from the program. He sued the college for breach of contract, fraudulent misrepresentation, and fraudulent nondisclosure. The student filed a separate breach of contract claim against the teacher of the class in which he was accused of cheating. A jury ruled in his favor on the fraudulent misrepresentation claim against the college and awarded him $20,000 in damages. But the court set aside the verdict, and the jury found against the student on the breach of contract and fraudulent nondisclosure claims. On appeal, the Supreme Court of Missouri reversed the judgment on the breach of contract claim, and upheld the decision to set aside the fraudulent misrepresentation verdict. Any misrepresentation regarding the disciplinary hearings did not harm the student because he did almost nothing to prepare for them. **As the student did not show he relied on representations that the college would follow certain due process procedures at his appeal hearing, he could not prove fraudulent misrepresentation.** *Verni v. Cleveland Chiropractic College*, 212 S.W.3d 150 (Mo. 2007).

◆   *The Indiana Court of Appeals held a student had to show a university acted with a dishonest purpose in order to prove bad faith.*

An Indiana student who was pursuing a doctorate in economics received an "Unsatisfactory" grade in a thesis research course. Despite receiving an extension, the student did not complete tasks assigned by an economics policy committee, and he was dismissed from the program. After exhausting internal appeals, the student sued the university and a professor for breach of contract, negligence and defamation. A state court held the university's actions constituted academic judgment that it would not disturb, absent bad faith. It granted the student permission to assert a claim of bad faith, but then dismissed the amended complaint. On appeal, the state court of appeals held **courts do not rigidly apply contract law principles to education disputes, even though the relationship between students and educational institutions is contractual**. Courts recognize that implied contracts exist between students and universities, and the nature of contractual terms varies. To prove bad faith, the student had to show more than bad judgment or negligence. Instead, he needed to show the university acted with a dishonest purpose. As the amended complaint did not support such a claim, the court held for the university. *Gordon v. Purdue Univ.*, 862 N.E.2d 1244 (Ind. Ct. App. 2007).

◆   *A federal district court in New York refused to dismiss students' claims that a university engaged in deceptive business practices and breached a contract when it made changes to its drama program, including a change in its name.*

Current and former students sued the university, claiming the changes were deceptive business practices and in breach of contract. To address the contract claim, the court referred to a catalogue the university published every other year to promote the drama program. The catalogue included a policy relating to changes, which said course offerings, academic requirements, degree programs, tuition, fees and faculty were subject to change at any time.

**The court held "the relationship between a university and its students is contractual." It would be inappropriate to grant judgment to the students on the claim that the change in the name of the program was a breach of contract.** Although the catalogue clearly stated that degree programs were subject to change, it also emphasized the prestige and uniqueness of the program and promised students they would receive diplomas bearing the previous name. The court found a factual question as to whether the catalogue was likely to mislead a reasonable consumer and as to whether it fully disclosed the university's right to change the program name. *Deen v. New School Univ.*, No. 05 Civ. 7174 KMW, 2007 WL 1032295 (S.D.N.Y. 3/27/07).

### C. Educational Malpractice

*Courts have been reluctant to recognize educational malpractice claims. In* Leiby v. Univ. of Akron, *No. 2004-10094, 2006 WL 1530152 (Ohio Ct. App. 6/6/06), an Ohio court rejected a student's educational malpractice claim based on his contention that his diplomas were "worthless." It held Ohio does not recognize claims for educational malpractice, as they lack readily acceptable standards of care, cause or injury. Educational malpractice claims are further disfavored due to public policy considerations, such as increased litigation and judicial deference for academic decisions. In* Ross v. Creighton Univ., *957 F.2d 410 (7th Cir. 1992), the U.S. Court of Appeals, Seventh Circuit, found at least 11 states have rejected educational malpractice claims.*

◆   *A Missouri court rejected a claim asserting that a law school failed to act on a faculty irresponsibility complaint against a professor.*

A University of Missouri (UM) law professor cancelled some classes and changed the times and places for class meetings. A student then emailed her to object to an assignment and restrictions she placed on outside research. She forwarded his emails to the dean and the associate dean for academic affairs, stating that she found the emails threatening. The professor asked the deans to remove him from her class, alert police and begin an honor code investigation. The student withdrew from the professor's classes, filed faculty irresponsibility charges against her, and later filed a lawsuit against UM for breach of contract.

When the case reached the state court of appeals, it noted Missouri courts have not found a contractual relationship exists between a student and a higher education institution. Other courts have held brochures, policy manuals and other advertisements can form the basis of a contractual relationship. But to show a breach, a student must point to an identifiable contractual promise that was not honored. **Changing a class time did not mean the university failed to provide a guaranteed service.** The court also rejected a claim that failure to follow procedures in handling the faculty irresponsibility charge constituted a breach of contract. As this claim questioned "the reasonableness of the educator's conduct in providing educational services," the court found it was an educational malpractice claim that was not recognized in Missouri. As a result, the court held the case was properly dismissed. *Lucero v. Curators of the Univ. of Missouri*, No. WD 74768, 2013 WL 519460 (Mo. Ct. App. 2/13/13).

◆   *The Supreme Court of Connecticut recognized at least two situations where courts will entertain a claim for breach of a contract for educational services in* Gupta v. New Britain General Hospital, *239 Conn. 574 (Conn. 1996).*

A Yale University School of Medicine handbook granted students three opportunities to pass the U.S. Medical Licensing Examination before dismissal. **That was a distinct contractual promise independent of the medical school's obligation to offer a reasonable educational program.** As a result, a student who was dismissed after two unsuccessful attempts at passing Step 1 of the USMLE would receive a trial to consider his breach of contract claim. Breach of contract may be found if the educational program failed in some fundamental respect, like not offering any of the courses necessary to become certified in a particular field. *Morris v. Yale Univ. School of Medicine*, No. 05CV848 (JBA), 2006 WL 908155 (D. Conn. 4/4/06).

## II.  DISCIPLINARY ACTIONS

*Courts will not disturb disciplinary decisions unless the institution acted arbitrarily, or did not substantially comply with its own rules and regulations.*

### A.  Due Process

#### 1.  Hearings and Procedural Safeguards

*As noted in* Tran v. State System of Higher Educ., *986 A.2d 179 (Pa. Commw. Ct. 2009), this chapter, public institutions of higher learning are government entities with certain due process obligations to their students. The Due Process Clause of the Fourteenth Amendment requires state entities to provide notice and an opportunity to be heard when individual liberty or property interests are at stake. Due process includes the notion of fundamental fairness and notice and an opportunity to be heard at some point during disciplinary procedures. By contrast, private institutions have a contractual relationship with students and are not bound by constitutional requirements.*

*All institutions must comply with the procedural protections they promise to their students. A federal district court explained that informal procedures may minimize the risk of lawsuits in higher education disciplinary cases. These include: 1) use of an impartial decisionmaker; 2) providing notice of the charges and the evidence against the student; 3) an opportunity for the student to appear before the decisionmaker; 4) an opportunity for the student to suggest witnesses; 5) avoiding the imposition of sanctions against witnesses; and 6) permitting the student to either voluntarily accept discipline or the ruling of the decisionmaker.* A. v. C. College, *863 F.Supp. 156 (S.D.N.Y. 1994).*

◆    *Finding a student was unlikely to win his due process claims, an Ohio federal judge refused to order a university not to require him to attend a preliminary conduct meeting.*

Things got ugly after a student ended his relationship with a woman at a nearby university. She went to campus police at both universities to report that he was sexually harassing her. The student's university informed him it had received information alleging he'd violated three student conduct code provisions concerning stalking, sexual harassment and sexual exploitation. It asked him to come in for a preliminary conference to help determine whether charges were warranted. It warned that if he didn't, a disciplinary hold would be placed on his account. Instead of attending the meeting, the student sued, alleging due process violations. He asked for a court order to prohibit the university from requiring the meeting. To grant it, the court had to find, among other things, that he was likely to win his lawsuit. The claims weren't ripe – that is, things had not yet happened that could give him a valid legal claim. For example, **the university had not yet initiated "a true disciplinary process" against him**, the court explained. So it refused to order the university not to require the student to attend the preliminary conduct meeting. *Doe v. The Ohio State Univ.*, 136 F.Supp.3d 854 (S.D. Ohio 2016).

◆    *A suspended student was unlikely to win his due process claim, so a Pennsylvania federal judge refused to order a university to reinstate him.*

The student was accused of harassing a female classmate. The university warned him not to have direct contact with the woman and pursued disciplinary charges. It also told him that proposed sanctions would include a suspension, participation in counseling and participation in an online educational program. He signed a form acknowledging the allegations against him. Then, in spite of the warnings, he contacted her. The school placed him on interim suspension, and the student appealed. The sanctions were upheld on review. He sued, alleging due process violations. He asked the court to order the university to reinstate him. The court refused, finding he was not likely to win the case. The student alleged his due process rights were violated because he wasn't allowed to examine the evidence against him. But **students are not entitled to discovery as though they were involved in criminal or civil litigation**, the court said. The court pointed out that the student was advised of the charges against him and the allegations supporting the charges. Nothing more was required. The motion for an order to reinstate him was denied. *Howe v. Pennsylvania State Univ.*, No. 1:16-0102, 2016 WL 393717 (M.D. Pa. 2/2/16).

◆   *Finding due process requirements were met in connection with disciplinary proceedings, a New Jersey court upheld a university's decision to sanction students who engaged in cult-like behavior.*

A student attended a small gathering in a dorm room with a group of five others. The group told the student she was possessed by a spirit and placed her on "lockdown" in the dorm room. When she tried to escape, she was tackled and dragged back. Two students slapped her. After the lockdown, the group performed an exorcism on the student. She went to campus police. The school charged the students with violating student code provisions relating to assault, disorderly conduct and hazing. After a hearing, the school found the two students who struck the victim were responsible for assault and hazing. Both sought judicial review, alleging they were denied the requisite procedural due process. They said they were not given all the process outlined in the school's student handbook. The court rejected the claims. The students were provided with due process even if the handbook was not precisely followed, and they were not due more. **The students received notice of the charges and the hearing, and they were provided with copies of the police reports that were used as evidence against them.** Due process requirements were met, so the university's decision was affirmed. *Rockwell v. William Paterson Univ.*, 2016 WL 9902440 (N.J. Super. Ct. App. Div. 1/25/16).

◆   *A suspension from a university's corp of cadets didn't violate a student's right to due process, a Texas appeals court held.*

The student was a member of the university's corps of cadets (CC). In his junior year, he was suspended from the CC following disciplinary proceedings. He sued, alleging a violation of his due process rights. The court refused to dismiss the claim, and the university appealed. The appeals court dismissed the claim, finding the case was barred by sovereign immunity. Federal courts have held that students do not have a federal constitutional right to participate in extracurricular activities. Following that lead, **the Texas Supreme Court has ruled that students – including higher ed students – don't have that right** under the state constitution either. The university was entitled to immunity – so the claim failed. *Texas A & M Univ. v. Carapia*, No. 10-14-00280-CV, 2015 WL 3451609 (Tex. Ct. App. 5/28/15).

◆   *A federal district court in Idaho allowed the lawsuit of a student who said she was wrongfully labelled a "cheater" to proceed.*

The student claimed a university, university professionals and three professors violated her due process rights by assigning her a failing grade and calling her a "cheater" without allowing her to respond to the charge of academic dishonesty that was levied against her. The court granted an injunction, finding the student was likely to succeed on the merits of her claim. As a temporary remedy, it ordered the defendants to exonerate the student of all charges of academic dishonesty and refrain from taking punitive action against her based on such charges unless it provided due process and decided such action was needed. The defendants filed a motion to dismiss, arguing that the student failed to exhaust her administrative remedies and that her claims were barred by the Eleventh Amendment. The court determined that the issue relating to exhaustion of administrative remedies was moot because the injunctive relief it already provided called for the student to pursue administrative remedies. Thus, the court refused to dismiss the case on that basis. As to immunity, the court noted that the student conceded that her claims against the university were barred by the Eleventh Amendment because the university is an arm of the state. However, the court said **the student's claims against the university professors and officials were not barred by the Eleventh Amendment because they were based on an ongoing alleged violation of her federal rights**. A suit in which a plaintiff seeks prospective injunctive relief provides a narrow exception to Eleventh Amendment immunity, the court said. The student sought to require the defendants to provide her with due process before deciding whether to assign her a failing grade based on alleged cheating. This claim fell within the immunity exception, the court said. The defense motion for summary judgment was thus granted in part and denied in part. *Huntsinger v. Idaho State Univ.*, No. 4:14-cv-00237-BLW, 2014 WL 7149634 (D. Idaho 12/15/14).

◆   *No due process violation occurred when a Pennsylvania school suspended a student-athlete from the university's baseball team.*

Campus police received a tip about possible drugs in a dorm. The student – a baseball player for the university – denied having drugs in the room but admitted smoking marijuana earlier in the day. The student went to a disciplinary meeting related to the drug incident. There, a hearing officer told him a "limited punishment" would be recommended. He was given a "Disciplinary Incident Notification Form," which he signed. When the student went to practice, the coach told him he was suspended from the team for the rest of the academic year due to the marijuana incident. The student sued, claiming he was intentionally misled into signing the form. The lawsuit alleged a violation of his right to due process. It also asked for an injunction ordering the school to reinstate him on the team, as he would be removed from Major League Baseball's prospect list if he missed the season. The court denied the motion, explaining the handbook banned drug use and a separate student-athlete handbook made it clear that drug use could result in dismissal from the team. So the student was aware of the possible sanctions before his suspension. Further, **students do not have a constitutional right to participate in school sports**, and the student did not show he would suffer irreparable harm without the injunction, as there was no guarantee he would become a professional if he played on the school's team. *Mattison v. East Stroudsburg Univ.*, No. 3:12-cv-2557, 2013 WL 1563656 (M.D. Pa. 4/12/13).

◆   *A Colorado federal judge refused to put a stop to a university's disciplinary proceedings.*

While he was a teaching assistant at Western State Colorado University, Keifer Johnson entered into a sexual relationship with student Onna Gould. At some point during their relationship, Johnson sent Gould an explicit letter, outlining sexual acts he wanted to perform with her. The relationship ended. In July 2013, the school notified Johnson that he wouldn't be able to continue as a teaching assistant due to his relationship with Gould. During that conversation, the dean explained the school's policies relating to student conduct and Title IX obligations. In August 2013, the school charged Johnson with three violations of the school code – one of which was related to his "inappropriate relationship." After a hearing, Johnson was put on probation for a year. Meanwhile, Gould filed her own complaint with the university against Johnson the following day. She alleged Johnson forced himself on her sexually and frightened her. Based on the new complaint, the school met with Johnson again. He filed suit against the school, claiming a second hearing would violate his due process rights. He asked for a court order to stop the proceedings against him. Johnson argued a second hearing would violate his right to due process and unlawfully subject him to double jeopardy. The court rejected his argument for two reasons. **First, the issue of sexual harassment was never addressed in the first hearing. And second, the school was not aware of the alleged events giving rise to the second charge until after the initial hearing was completed.** Thus, the court rejected his claims and denied the motion for a preliminary injunction. *Johnson v. Western State Colorado Univ.*, No. 1:13-cv-0274, 2013 WL 6068464 (D. Colo. 11/18/13).

◆  *A Texas federal judge determined a university did not violate students' due process rights by changing its policy regarding whether they could retake exams.*

Students enrolled in a nursing program were given a handbook saying they couldn't graduate until they passed an exit exam. It also said students could retake the exam if they didn't pass on the first try. After the students enrolled, the school changed its policy on the retake, based on the advice of the state board of nursing. The updated policy stated the exam only accounted for 40% of the final grade and there was no opportunity to retake it. Seven students failed the exam and asked to retake it. Their request was denied, and they could not graduate. The students sued, claiming the school violated their procedural and substantive due process rights. The court explained that procedural requirements attached to a school's academic decisions are much less stringent than requirements that apply when a student challenges disciplinary decisions. **When it comes to academic decisions, procedural due process requires notification but not a hearing.** Because the school's decision was academic in nature and the students were given a right to appeal the denial of their request to retake the test, the students didn't state a valid procedural due process claim. Their substantive due process claims failed, as it is far from clear that students have a right to be free from arbitrary grading. As a result, both claims were dismissed. *Burnett v. College of the Mainland*, No. 3:12-CV-00310, 2014 WL 129668 (S.D. Tex. 1/13/14).

◆  *A men's rowing club could not challenge a university's decision to impose a suspension, a federal district court decided.*

The school's men's rowing club was a student organization. Only students were allowed to participate in training and competition. Nonetheless, the club had a practice of allowing a rowing team alumni or coach to participate when an insufficient number of current members were available to fill the boats. In mid-December of 2012, a rowing alumni and the club's assistant coach rowed in an event. Two days later, the club was suspended for failing to comply with training and competition rules. The club sued the university, claiming it was denied due process because the suspension was issued without notice or a hearing. The school filed a motion to dismiss. The court explained that the Constitution's due process guarantee generally does not protect a student's participation in extracurricular activities. It noted, however, that a protected property interest may be created if participation is conditioned on compliance with mandatory rules or disciplinary policies. The club argued that was the case here, pointing to the fact that the school was authorized to establish codes of conduct for its student organizations. The court rejected the argument, finding that **although the school could set conduct codes, nothing required it to do so**. Student participation in the rowing club was not protected by the Constitution's due process guarantee, the court concluded. As a result the school's motion to dismiss the case was granted. *Sacramento State Univ. Men's Rowing Club v. California State Univ.*, No. 2:13-cv-00366-MCE-EFB, 2014 WL 546694 (E.D. Cal. 2/11/14).

◆   *A university did not violate the due process rights of a student when it revoked her doctoral degree after finding she had plagiarized her dissertation.*

After the student received a doctorate in education, university officials began disciplinary action for plagiarism. She selected an informal conference with the school's dean to resolve the matter, after being told that if she did so, she was subject to the full range of sanctions authorized by the student code. According to the student, an associate dean told her the university had never revoked a degree through the informal route. But after a 45-minute conference, the dean considered the evidence and revoked the student's degree. It was found that the dissertation had 27 instances of plagiarism. In a federal action, the student sued the university for due process violations. Appeal reached the U.S. Court of Appeals, Sixth Circuit, which rejected her claim based on insufficient notice that her degree could be revoked. It held that the oral notice of this possibility, which she had acknowledged receiving, was sufficient. In the court's view, the fact that the associate dean told her no degree had been previously revoked was not problematic. **Since the court found the informal conference provided the student an adequate opportunity to present her case, the court held for the university.** *Jaber v. Wayne State Univ. Board of Governors*, 487 Fed.Appx. 995 (6th Cir. 2012).

◆   *No due process violation occurred when Temple University suspended a student who threatened a professor via email.*

While enrolled in a bachelor's degree program at Temple, a student claimed he received an unfair grade. He sent the professor an email threatening "a curse against [the professor's] life and family forever." Another email told the professor the student wanted "justice on [him] spiritually and physically" and warned him to "[c]ooperate to prevent things from escalating." In response to the emails, the university charged the student with student conduct code violations. After a hearing, the university suspended him, required him to attend anger management classes, and placed him on probation. The student sued the university in a federal court for due process violations. On appeal, the U.S. Court of Appeals, Third Circuit, explained that **due process requires officials to provide students facing suspensions notice of the charges, an explanation of the evidence, and a chance to present their side of the story**. In this case, the student received adequate due process. He received notice of the witnesses against him and was not wrongfully deprived of his right to confront the professor, who was not at the hearing. Instead, the court found "the emails spoke for themselves." The decision for the university was affirmed. *Osei v. Temple Univ.*, No. 1104033, 2013 WL 870376 (3d Cir. 3/11/13).

◆ *A Washington court held a student was properly dismissed from a nursing program after she admitted giving classmates prescription medications.*

When confronted, the student admitted giving classmates Flexeril and Ritalin. After meeting with a community college official, she was dismissed from the program. Instead of appealing, she filed a state court complaint against the community college for negligent dismissal, violation of her due process rights and related claims. The court ruled against her, and she appealed. The state court of appeals held her state-law due process claims were barred by her failure to exhaust available administrative remedies. By refusing to file an internal appeal with the school, she deprived it of the chance to correct any errors it may have made. With respect to her federal procedural due process claim, the student received all the process she was due. **When an institution bases a disciplinary decision on facts admitted by a student, no further hearing is needed.** Rejecting a claim that the student was entitled to "specific treatment" outlined in the student handbook, the court affirmed the judgment. *Buechler v. Wenatchee Valley College*, 298 P.3d 110 (Wash. Ct. App. 2013).

◆ *A Nevada student who was dismissed for plagiarism raised a viable due process claim, according to a federal district court.*

A professor accused the student of plagiarizing text in a draft dissertation. An academic integrity appeal panel held a hearing, but the student said she was denied an opportunity to have an advisor's assistance. The panel found the student committed academic misconduct and did not avail herself of multiple opportunities to correct the plagiarism. The panel recommended removing the student from her Ph.D. program. In a lawsuit against the university, she raised claims for breach of contract, negligence, infliction of emotional distress, defamation and due process violations. A federal court found the student claimed officials had prevented her return to school while also blocking her from admission to another institution. As this asserted a deprivation of her constitutionally protected property and liberty interests, the court held her case could proceed. **By alleging the lack of an advisor had prevented her from effectively representing herself at the hearing, the student made a valid claim** that university procedures violated her rights. *Gamage v. State of Nevada*, No. 2:12-cv-00290-GMN-VCF, 2013 WL 1182084 (D. Nev. 3/19/13).

◆ *A federal district court held Temple University's decision to expel a student could not stand because of the failure to provide him adequate due process.*

Temple police officers arrested and charged the student with aggravated assault on a police officer. Based on the incident, Temple charged the student with violating its code of conduct and instituted disciplinary proceedings. At the hearing, panel members received a hearing summary from one officer. None of the student's witnesses showed up. He asked for a continuance, which was denied. The officer testified but was not closely questioned. By contrast, the student's testimony was vigorously questioned, to the point of arguing. The panel refused to ask some of the questions he wanted to ask witnesses. At one point, a panel member told the student's attorney to "shut up." The panel took about 20 minutes to decide he was guilty, and it recommended expulsion.

The student sued the university and several officials for breach of contract, retaliation, and violation of his due process and equal protection rights. A federal court held the university violated the student's due process rights in several ways. The panel accorded the officer "significant respect" and did not closely question him, but the student was questioned in a confrontational and argumentative manner. **In the court's view, the university did not fairly review the recommendations of the hearing panel and the review board.** An official improperly met with a witness after the hearing. While the court found a due process violation, it held the university officials were entitled to qualified immunity. It ordered the student's reinstatement or a new hearing within 60 days. *Furey v. Temple Univ.*, 884 F.Supp.2d 223 (E.D. Pa. 2012).

◆ *A public university has adequate procedures for academic discipline if it provides notice of lack of progress and the decision is careful and deliberate.*

After a poor performance review, a medical student claimed an evaluating physician made a racist remark about her communication skills. The evaluator later denied this, and the program director met with the student to discuss her performance problems. Within weeks, he recommended placing the student on immediate academic probation with the requirement that she undergo a psychiatric evaluation as a condition of readmission. After failing her licensing examination a third time, the student was released from the program. She filed a federal district court lawsuit against the university and 15 individuals.

In pretrial activity, the court held that racially charged statements can be direct evidence of unlawful bias. However, the statement in this case did not qualify, because it was an "isolated and ambiguous" remark and the evaluator was not directly involved in the decision to put the student on probation. There was no due process violation, as the university had substantial documentation supporting its reasons for action. **A public university provides adequate procedures for academic discipline if a student has been fully informed of the faculty's dissatisfaction with the student's academic progress** and "the decision to dismiss was careful and deliberate." That was the case here. Under Sixth Circuit precedent, a formal hearing was not required for academic discipline, as academic decisions required an expert evaluation of cumulative information and were not readily adapted to judicial decisionmaking. The university and staff were entitled to judgment. *Peavey v. Univ. of Louisville*, 834 F.Supp.2d 620 (W.D. Ky. 2011).

◆ *Texas Tech University (TTU) did not violate a student's due process rights by expelling him after finding he had pointed a gun at a classmate.*

TTU initiated disciplinary proceedings based on information that the student had pointed a pistol at his ex-girlfriend at his off-campus home. TTU'S student conduct board advised him in writing of a hearing date with the factual basis of a complaint against him. The notice also specified the particular student code violations he was being charged with, named the board members, offered him a chance to challenge their partiality, and explained how he could submit his own evidence, call witnesses and get an advisor. At the hearing, the student presented his position but chose not to call witnesses. The board found he had pulled a gun on a fellow student. It expelled him from the university.

The student sued TTU and certain officials for violating his due process rights, but a federal district court held he received all the process he was due. On appeal, the U.S. Court of Appeals, Fifth Circuit, held **students who are subject to discipline by a public institution are entitled to notice of the charges, an explanation of the evidence supporting the charges, and an opportunity to tell their side of the story**. On the other hand, the court said students facing discipline are not entitled to an opportunity to secure counsel, confront and cross-examine witnesses, or call their own witnesses. Based on the record, the court held TTU provided him with more than the minimum process due under the Constitution, and it affirmed the judgment. *Willis v. Texas Tech Univ. Health Sciences Center*, 394 Fed.Appx. 86 (5th Cir. 2010).

◆ *Finding a two-year student suspension "arbitrary and capricious," a state court ordered the University of Minnesota to reconsider the discipline.*

The student was accused of sexually assaulting another student. No criminal charges were filed, but he was charged with a student conduct code violation. At a hearing, the Campus Committee on Student Behavior (CCSB) refused to consider evidence that the student would lose more than $200,000 in financial assistance if he was suspended. The CCSB found he had violated university rules and engaged in threatening, harassing or assaultive conduct, and decided he should be suspended for two years. An appeal committee found the student should have a new hearing because the exclusion of the financial evidence violated his due process rights. A university provost reinstated the CCSB's decision, and the student appealed to the state court of appeals. It noted **courts generally defer to university decisions involving student discipline**. But the decision in this case was held "arbitrary and capricious," because the university had no standards or guidelines for sanctions the provost could impose.

CCSB procedures required a fair hearing and required the committee to let accused parties offer relevant, reliable information. The excluded evidence was relevant and would have helped the CCSB make a reasoned decision. Finding the provost had relied on vague and unsupportable statements, the court ordered the university to hold a new hearing on the issue of sanctions. *Berge v. Univ. of Minnesota*, No. A10-131, 2010 WL 3632518 (Minn. Ct. App. 7/21/10).

◆ *Students at public institutions have a protected property interest in due process under the Fourteenth Amendment to the Constitution.*

In a Michigan case, the Constitution required less than the student code called for, and the university was not obligated to strictly abide by the code's provisions. A student was accused of stalking and harassing a professor. She received a hearing before a disciplinary board that found she violated the university statement of student rights and code of student conduct. At the hearing, the student was not allowed to cross-examine the professor. A hearing board ordered her expulsion. Appeal reached the Court of Appeals of Michigan, which held the student received notice of the hearing and a written statement outlining the charges against her. She was allowed to call witnesses, state her version of the facts and record the hearing. The university offered an appeal process, and the student was allowed to continue her studies. Even if the university did not technically comply with all the requirements of its student code, it provided due process in this case. **Nothing about the university's decision would have been made any more accurate or fair by adding the further procedural protections insisted upon by the student.** Since the steps the university took to provide due process were adequate, the court affirmed the decision for the university. *Lee v. Univ. of Michigan-Dearborn*, No. 284541, 2009 WL 1362617 (Mich. Ct. App. 5/12/09).

◆    *The U.S. Court of Appeals, Sixth Circuit, held an Ohio medical college did not violate a student's due process rights during his disciplinary hearing.*

The student was arrested for a felony drug crime. The college notified him by letter that it was suspending him until investigations and hearings on his drug charge were completed, and advised him of his right to an investigation. The student decided not to schedule an investigation until the pending criminal charges were resolved. The student was not permitted on campus until the completion of a disciplinary hearing. A few months later, the student pled guilty to a felony drug charge, then asked for a hearing. The college sent him a written notice to appear before its student conduct and ethics committee to answer questions about his arrest. The student was not entitled to be represented by an attorney at the hearing because the criminal proceedings had ended. However, the college allowed his attorney to be present. At the hearing, the officer who had arrested the student testified. The committee questioned the officer, but denied the student's attorney an opportunity to do so. The college expelled the student for violating its zero-tolerance drug policy. The student sued the college in a federal district court for due process violations.

The court dismissed the case. On appeal, the Sixth Circuit stated **the student's interest in pursuing an education was a protected property interest. Due process is flexible, and its basic requirements are notice and an opportunity to be heard. Additional procedures vary based on the circumstances of each case.** The court held the college provided the student sufficient notice of the disciplinary charges against him and the procedures that would follow. As college procedures were fundamentally fair, the judgment was affirmed. *Flaim v. Medical College of Ohio*, 418 F.3d 629 (6th Cir. 2005).

### 2. Private Schools

*Students at private institutions lack the due process rights available to students at public institutions. Private higher education institutions need only ensure they observe their own rules for student discipline and refrain from arbitrary, bad faith or unlawful actions. **When it comes to academic decisions by private institutions, court review is very limited.***

◆    *A South Dakota federal judge said a student wasn't likely to win his due process claim – so the judge refused to order a university to postpone his disciplinary hearing.*

The male student was enrolled in a private university when a female student accused him of rape. She called the police and filed a Title IX complaint with the university. Police arrested the student, and the school suspended him pending an investigation and adjudication of the complaint. He asked the school to postpone its proceedings until the criminal proceedings ended because the prosecutor could use anything he said at the disciplinary hearing against him at the criminal trial. But if he remained silent at the hearing, the school could interpret his silence as an indication of guilt – a presumption that isn't allowed under the Fifth Amendment at a criminal trial. The school refused to postpone the proceedings. The student sued, alleging a violation of his due process rights. He asked the court to order the school to put the proceedings on hold. It refused, finding the student was unlikely to win his suit. **His due process claims would fail because the university was a private school – not a state actor**, the court explained. *Tsuruta v. Augustana Univ.*, No. 4:15-CV-04150-KES, 2015 WL 5838602 (D.S.D. 10/7/15).

◆ *A private university provided an Oklahoma student adequate procedural protections to consider charges that she had cheated on her assignments.*

A University of Tulsa (UT) student was charged with academic misconduct because her work resembled that of a classmate. She met with an assistant dean, who explained the charge to her. The student also received a chance to discuss the charge with a professor and tell her side of the story. After a second offense, she received similar interviews and was warned in writing that a third offense would lead to dismissal. The student was charged a third time, and TU dismissed her. The student sued TU in a federal court. It observed that private institutions are not state actors and generally cannot violate the Constitution.

Given the student-university relationship, the Tenth Circuit requires private universities to afford certain protections in disciplinary proceedings. These include **notice and a hearing that gives a student a meaningful opportunity to participate**. When private schools provide these protections, federal courts in the Tenth Circuit will defer to their factual findings if they are supported by substantial evidence. Courts could only reverse a student dismissal that was arbitrary. Although the student argued she was not afforded adequate notice or hearings, the court disagreed and upheld the discipline. *Ye Li v. Univ. of Tulsa*, No. 12-CV-641-TCK-FHM, 2013 WL 352116 (N.D. Okla. 1/29/13).

◆ *A person who took an online human nutrition class was unable to pursue constitutional claims against a private institution with no state affiliation.*

The person made negative posts about his instructor and the university in response to assignments for students to discuss the effect of the class and the university on their post-graduation plans. He said he planned to "run ... without ever looking back" and to "get out of City U ASAP" following his graduation. The person said the nutrition course was a "flub" or a "fluff" course. The instructor was offended, and she told him he would be assigned a poor grade and brought before a disciplinary committee. He was also told not to have any contact with the instructor. The person sued the university in a federal district court, claiming violation of his speech and due process rights. The university sought dismissal, arguing it could not be held liable for constitutional violations because it is a private institution. **The court stated that constitutional claims against a private actor cannot succeed unless there is some nexus between**

**the challenged action and the state** that is so close that the action could "fairly be treated as that of the state itself." But the university did not exercise any powers usually reserved to a state. Nor did it act in concert with or with the help of state officials or act closely with a state. As the university was not a state actor and had no close connection with a state, the case was dismissed. *Becker v. City Univ. of Seattle*, 723 F.Supp.2d 807 (E.D. Pa. 2010).

◆ *A Tennessee court found evidence to support a jury verdict against an optometry college for dismissing a student in breach of their contract.*

In the student's third year of his optometry program, college faculty recommended he avoid dismissal for poor grades by voluntarily withdrawing and then reapplying. He did and was conditionally re-admitted with the requirement that he earn at least a C in every course. After receiving a D in one class and failures in two classes he was auditing, the student was dismissed. After some negotiations, the college president offered to revise his transcript to reflect withdrawal instead of a dismissal, and to write a letter of good standing. The student agreed, and the college sent the letter and revised transcript to other optometry schools at his request. However, the student was unable to transfer and sued the college in a state court for breach of contract and negligence.

A jury found that even though the college violated its own policies, it did not violate the withdrawal agreement with the student. On appeal, **the state court of appeals found the evidence supported the jury's finding that the college violated its policy when it dismissed the student for failing audited classes**. While the student argued there should be a new trial so he could further pursue his claims, the court found the verdict for the college was not inconsistent and was supported by the evidence. As a result, the court refused to disturb the verdict. *Rutherford v. Southern College of Optometry*, No. W2008-02268-COA-R3-CV, 2009 WL 5064972 (Tenn. Ct. App. 12/28/09).

◆ *A registered sex offender could not bring federal claims against a private Kentucky university and its staff because they were not state actors.*

In a federal district court lawsuit asserting violations of the U.S. and Kentucky Constitutions, the offender claimed the university and staff members wrongfully banned him from attending classes on campus. He acknowledged that he was subject to a state sex offender registration act, but he said he was in compliance with it. The offender claimed that in barring him from campus, the university failed to follow its own guidelines for student conduct and discipline.

The court explained that federal claims filed under 42 U.S.C. § 1983 may survive only against persons who acted with the authority of the state, or "under color of state law." **Private actors can be sued for constitutional violations only if their actions are "fairly attributable to the state."** The university was a private, for-profit corporation, and there was no indication it was publicly funded or that the state controlled its operations. The court held that as the offender failed to state a claim for violation of his rights under the Constitution, he could not proceed with his Section 1983 claims. *McGlothin v. Strayer Univ.*, No. 09-231-JMH, 2009 WL 1956463 (E.D. Ky. 7/6/09).

◆ *A federal court held a Maryland university did not breach a contract by interfering with a student's ability to complete his thesis.*

The student pursued a doctorate degree at a private university. He fulfilled the requirements for his degree except his thesis. Under a university policy, students were allowed a maximum of seven years from the date they enrolled to obtain a degree. The university extended the deadline for the student several times. After the last extension, the university denied the student further access to the office space. The student sued the university in a federal district court, alleging it breached a contract by sabotaging his ability to complete the thesis, among other things. He contended his enrollment in the university established an implied contract. **The court agreed that the relationship between a student and a private university is largely contractual in nature. Such a contract requires a university to act in good faith, and to act fairly.** There was evidence that the university reasonably accommodated the student above and beyond any reasonably imagined contractual requirement. Courts intervene into academic decisions only if a student completes all academic requirements and the school's refusal to grant a degree is "arbitrary and capricious." As nothing suggested the university acted arbitrarily, there was no breach of contract. *Onawola v. Johns Hopkins Univ.*, 412 F.Supp.2d 529 (D. Md. 2006).

The Fourth Circuit later affirmed the decision in a brief memorandum. *Onawola v. Johns Hopkins Univ.*, 221 Fed.Appx. 211 (4th Cir. 2007).

## B.  Academic Dismissals

*Courts have traditionally left grading policies to the expertise of educators and do not substitute their judgment for that of university faculty on academic matters unless faculty decisions are arbitrary and capricious, irrational, made in bad faith, or contrary to constitutional or statutory law. The Tennessee Court of Appeals held it was not equipped to review university academic policies.* Lord v. Meharry Medical College School of Dentistry, *No. M2004-00264-COA-R3-CV, 2005 WL 1950119 (Tenn. Ct. App. 8/12/05). In* Susan M. v. New York Law School, *556 N.E.2d 1104 (N.Y. 1990), New York's highest court restated the general rule that courts do not substitute their judgment for that of educators regarding degree requirements and academic dismissals.*

### 1.  Poor Performance

◆ *A dismissed nursing student wasn't likely to win his due process claim, so a Texas federal judge refused to order the university to reinstate him.*

The university had an attendance policy to ensure nursing students met state attendance requirements, which were required to take the licensing exam. The student had to work while attending school – so often arrived late or missed classes. Halfway through the year, he was ill but knew that missing a clinical session would put him over the limit of hours missed. He called the assistant coordinator of the program to ask if he could attend the clinical despite his illness in order to avoid violating the attendance policy. She said no, and the student was dismissed. The university offered to readmit him if he signed an agreement acknowledging he'd be dismissed if he missed one more hour of school. He refused to sign and filed a lawsuit asking the court to order the university to reinstate him along with his financial aid. He said the university actually dismissed him for a disciplinary reason "under the veneer of an academic dismissal" – so should have provided him notice and a hearing. But he wasn't likely to win that claim, as **U.S. Supreme Court and Fifth Circuit precedent support the court's conclusion that the attendance policy is academic as it "directly relates to one's fitness to practice the nursing profession."** He failed to show he was likely to win his suit, so the court refused to order the school to reinstate him. *Anyadike v. Vernon College*, No. 7:15-cv-00157-O, 2016 WL 107901 (N.D. Tex. 1/11/16).

◆   *A federal judge in Wisconsin found a university did not violate a student's due process rights by requiring her to retake a course that she failed.*

A student was enrolled in a social work program. An internship was required during the final semester. The student was placed at an agency to complete the internship – but she received a poor mid-term evaluation so the agency let her go. The school told her that because she was let go she would need to enroll for another semester so she could complete her internship. She completed the second internship and obtained her degree, although she paid for the additional semester under protest. She sued, alleging a due process violation. When it comes to poor academic performance, the court said, even the "ultimate sanction" of dismissal calls for only a minimal level of due process. Here, the student was not dismissed, but the school still met with her and provided a written explanation of its decision. Further, **the school's action didn't "shock the conscience" – because it allowed her to retake the course**. The case was dismissed. *Jarecki v. Univ. of Wisconsin-Eau Claire*, No. 14-cv-890-jdp, 2015 WL 2229231 (W.D. Wis. 5/12/15).

◆   *A former nursing student was unable to convince the Fifth Circuit she was dismissed for disciplinary reasons rather than academic inadequacy.*

The course requirements were clear: Students would fail if they did not maintain a 75 average or if they received three warnings during a semester. In one semester, the student received three warnings. The first was for failing to complete a hospital orientation in a timely manner, and the second was for being late to a clinical rotation. The third and final warning was for failing to provide proper care for a patient. She was dismissed, and her request for reinstatement was denied. She appealed the dismissal, and the school held three hearings affirming its decision. She sued, asserting a denial of her procedural and substantive due process rights. A district court granted a defense motion to dismiss on the basis of qualified immunity. The student appealed, arguing that her dismissal was disciplinary rather than academic, as the second warning was based on tardiness. The Fifth Circuit rejected that argument, explaining "absences and tardiness in the higher education context may relate to a student's ability to perform academically and professionally." The court noted **academic dismissals do not have the same stringent procedural requirements that disciplinary dismissals have. An academic dismissal requires only that the student be informed of the faculty's dissatisfaction with his progress and that the dismissal decision be "careful and**

**deliberate,"** the court explained. So the ruling was affirmed. *Perez v. Texas A&M Univ. at Corpus Christi*, 589 Fed.Appx. 244 (5th Cir. 2014).

◆    *Two former Texas law school students were unable to convince a federal court that they were wrongfully dismissed for earning poor grades.*

Texas Southern University dismissed the students for failing to maintain grade averages of at least 2.0. In a federal district court, they claimed their due process rights were violated because a professor did not adequately explain their poor grades. Under this theory, the students were deprived of a fair chance to appeal the grades. The court rejected this argument. It held **courts "strongly disfavor claims that require judges to second-guess judgments about the academic quality of a student's work."** There was no question that the students were dismissed for academic reasons and were given an oral hearing when they petitioned for grade changes. The grading at issue did not depart from academic norms, so the claims failed. *Chan v. Board of Regents of Texas Southern Univ.*, No. H-12-0325, 2012 WL 5832494 (S.D. Tex. 11/16/12).

◆    *There was no breach of contract when a community college followed its handbook in dismissing a student from a medical imaging program.*

During an examination, a college official corrected the student for not staying in an assigned area, not participating in the exam and making repetitive mistakes. A few months later, the college disciplined him for "failure to maintain a professional demeanor." After a third disciplinary incident involving "inconsiderate treatment and failure to perform," the student was placed on an academic readmission plan. Although he met its requirements and was readmitted to the program, he performed a lumbar spine procedure without supervision or permission, and was immediately and permanently dismissed from the program. In the student's action for breach of contract, a state court awarded the college judgment without a trial. On appeal, the state court of appeals found it well-settled under Ohio law that a contract is formed between a student and institution when a student enrolls, pays tuition, and attends class. This contract is typically found in a handbook, catalogue or other guideline.

**Case law precedent required a court to defer to a higher education institution's decisions** unless there was "such a substantial departure from accepted academic norms as to demonstrate that the person or committee responsible did not actually exercise professional judgment." See *Regents of the Univ. of Michigan v. Ewing*, 474 U.S. 214 (1985), this chapter. As the college followed its handbook procedures and did not depart from any accepted academic norm, the court upheld the judgment. *Tate v. Owens State Community College*, No. 10AP-1201, 2011 WL 2685664 (Ohio Ct. App. 7/12/11).

◆    *A federal court dismissed a Nevada dental-school student's due process claim based on the denial of his attempt to appeal an academic decision.*

The dental school twice suspended the student for failing examinations pertaining to Part I of the National Board of Dental Examinations, which are prerequisites to a fourth year of dental school. In his complaint, the student claimed the dental school could not suspend him without a hearing. When the dental school sought dismissal, the court issued an order clarifying that **the**

U.S. Supreme Court has held a formal hearing is only required for suspensions based on misconduct, not for academic suspensions. See *Board of Curators v. Horowitz*, 435 U.S. 78 (1978), this chapter. There was no need for a hearing unless the student could prove he was not fully informed of relevant academic requirements. Although the claim was dismissed, the court gave the student permission to allege facts supporting his theory that he was not fully informed of academic requirements. The court refused to dismiss a contract claim at this point, as he made out a preliminary case for breach of contract based on procedures in dental school handbooks and the state higher education code. *Salus v. Nevada ex rel. Board of Regents of Nevada System of Higher Educ.*, No. 2:10-cv-01734-GMN-GWF, 2011 WL 4828821 (D. Nev. 10/10/11).

◆   *A former Pennsylvania law school student was able to avoid dismissal of her challenge to her dismissal for deficient academic performance.*

After the law school informed the student she was not in good academic standing, she sought reinstatement and appealed to the school's academic rules committee. Her request was denied, and a federal court considered her claims of breach of contract, unjust enrichment and due process violations. According to the student, her professors did not evaluate her as required by a student handbook. She further claimed a dean who engaged in confidential conversations with her should not have presided at her hearing. But the court held none of these facts supported a due process claim. Evidence indicated **the law school notified the student that she had failed to remain in academic good standing, and provided her with an opportunity to appear before the academic rules committee**. As this was all the process she was due, her due process claim failed. As for the student's contract claim, she pointed to a handbook provision declaring that the academic rules committee must seek evaluations from each faculty member when a student sought reinstatement. The court decided that might be a sustainable claim, and gave her permission to amend her complaint to provide more specific information about her contract dispute. Finally, the court rejected a claim that the law school was unjustly enriched when it accepted her tuition and then dismissed her. *Bradshaw v. Pennsylvania State Univ.*, No. 10-4839, 2011 WL 1288681 (E.D. Pa. 4/5/11).

◆   *A New York medical student who was dismissed for poor academic performance failed to convince a court that he was entitled to reinstatement.*

In his third year of medical school, the student was dismissed from the program. He initiated a state court lawsuit to force his reinstatement. A trial court denied his petition, and he appealed. The court explained that **judicial review of academic decisions is limited**. Such decisions are not to be disturbed by courts unless they are arbitrary and capricious, irrational, made in bad faith, or contrary to constitutional or statutory law. In this case, the record showed the student's academic performance was deficient and he had failed a clerkship while he was on academic probation. As the university's decision to dismiss him was properly based on academic considerations, the decision to uphold the dismissal was affirmed. *Gilbert v. State Univ. of New York at Stony Brook*, 73 A.D.3d 774, 899 N.Y.S.2d 853 (N.Y. App. Div. 2010).

◆ *The dismissal of a student who failed to timely complete a thesis did not violate his due process or contract rights.*

The student received an unsatisfactory grade on a Ph.D. candidacy exam and did not timely complete his thesis. He continued to take classes for two years, after which he was "retroactively removed" from the program. The student sued the university and a committee chair in a federal district court for due process violations. The court held the claims against the university and the chair in his official capacity were barred by the Eleventh Amendment. **In a disciplinary context, due process requires that a student receive notice and an opportunity to be heard.** However, less is required for academic dismissals, where no formal hearing is required. The university easily met this standard when it notified the student he had failed the exam, told him he had violated rules regarding students who failed the exam, and met with him to tell him he had not timely completed his thesis. These actions more than satisfied due process requirements. The court also rejected a breach of contract claim.

On appeal, the U.S. Court of Appeals, Fourth Circuit, found no error in the district court's finding that the student was dismissed for academic, rather than disciplinary reasons. Removal from the program had been based on his failure to timely complete his thesis after he failed a candidacy exam. As a result, the court found the student ineligible to remain in the program. **Since he was removed for academic, rather than for disciplinary reasons, the district court properly found the decision was due a heightened level of deference and "subject to greatly reduced procedural requirements."** *Brown v. Rector and Visitors of the Univ. of Virginia*, 361 Fed.Appx. 531 (4th Cir. 2010).

◆ *The decision to dismiss a graduate student from a master's program was not a retaliatory response to a prior lawsuit he filed against the university.*

The student filed a second suit against the university, claiming he was dismissed in retaliation for the earlier suit. A state court ruled against him, and he appealed to the Court of Appeals of Massachusetts. It noted the lapse of more than two years between the time the first suit was filed and the time the student was dismissed. This gap indicated there was no causal connection between the two events. **The retaliation claim also failed because the student failed to show the university's reasons for dismissing him were pretextual.** There was no evidence that he was making progress toward completion of his degree. *Nguyen v. Univ. of Massachusetts at Boston*, 72 Mass.App.Ct. 1107, 889 N.E.2d 981 (Table) (Mass. App. Ct. 2008). Later, the Supreme Judicial Court of Massachusetts refused to review the student's appeal.

◆ *The District Court of Appeal of Florida held a university did not exercise its discretion arbitrarily by dismissing a student.*

The student attended a master's program in social work. After he received a failing grade in a field practicum course, the university dismissed him. The student was granted two unsuccessful appeals. He sued the university in a state court, alleging it denied him due process. The state court of appeal found no evidence to support the student's claims. **The court held university authorities have wide discretion in determining whether a student has met academic requirements. Courts will not interfere unless school authorities**

**acted in bad faith or exercised their discretion arbitrarily.** The student's field instructor indicated he needed improvement in 10 out of 38 areas evaluated. The field director also noted his difficulties with staff and clients at the agency where he performed his field practicum. The student's clients were unhappy with his performance and demeanor and did not want to participate in any more sessions with him. For all these reasons, the court of appeal held the university did not act in bad faith or exercise its discretion arbitrarily when it dismissed the student. It affirmed the judgment. *Karlan v. Florida Int'l Univ. Board of Trustees*, 927 So.2d 91 (Fla. Dist. Ct. App. 2006).

◆    *The Supreme Court of Alaska held a university did not violate a student's due process rights by dismissing him and denying him readmission.*

The student did not get along with a field instructor who supervised his field course work toward a social work degree. Although the field instructor did not recommend a failing grade, a faculty liaison professor assigned him an incomplete grade that was later changed to failure. An academic review panel upheld the grade, and the university later denied his reapplication. The student sued the university in the state court system, alleging due process violations for allegedly not following its own rules and failing to provide him with proper notice and an opportunity to be heard. The student added discrimination claims based on his gender and a disability. The court held the professor gave the student adequate notice of his academic deficiencies. She warned him several times about ongoing lateness and inferior work. The state supreme court affirmed the decision, agreeing that the university had provided the student with due process. **A person has no due process interest in admission to a professional school in the absence of dishonesty or publication of the reason for denying admission.** *Hermosillo v. Univ. of Alaska, Anchorage*, No. S-10563, 2004 WL 362384 (Alaska 2004).

◆    *The U.S. Supreme Court upheld a university's decision to dismiss a student from an advanced academic program based on poor performance.*

A student enrolled in the University of Michigan's "Inteflex" program – a special six-year course of study leading to both an undergraduate and medical degree. He struggled with the curriculum and failed the NBME Part I, receiving the lowest score in the brief history of the Inteflex program. The university's medical school executive board reviewed the student's academic career and decided to drop him from registration in the program. It denied his request to retake the NBME Part I. The student sued the university in a federal court, claiming due process violations. The evidence showed that the university had a practice of allowing students who had failed the NBME Part I to retake the test up to four times. The student was the only person ever refused permission to retake the test. Nonetheless, the court held that his dismissal did not violate the Due Process Clause. The U.S. Supreme Court agreed. The **Due Process Clause was not offended because "the University's liberal retesting custom gave rise to no state law entitlement to retake NBME Part I."** *Regents of Univ. of Michigan v. Ewing*, 474 U.S. 214, 106 S.Ct. 507, 88 L.Ed.2d 523 (1985).

◆    *Academic dismissals do not require the procedural requirements of* Goss v. Lopez, *419 U.S. 565 (1975). In disciplinary cases, officials need only provide notice of the charges and an opportunity to respond. Institutions have broader discretion in dealing with academic discipline than in misconduct cases.*

Several faculty members expressed dissatisfaction with a Missouri medical student's progress, and she was placed on probationary status. Faculty complaints continued, and a university council warned the student that absent "radical improvement," she would be dismissed. She was allowed to take a set of oral and practical examinations as an "appeal" from the council's decision.

Subsequent reports regarding the student were negative, and she was dropped from the program upon the council's recommendation. She sued the student in a federal district court for due process violations. Her case reached the U.S. Supreme Court, which held **she received all the process she was due**. The procedures leading to the student's dismissal, under which she was fully informed of faculty dissatisfaction with her progress, and the consequent threat to her graduation and continued enrollment did not violate the Fourteenth Amendment. **The court explained that dismissals for academic reasons do not necessitate a hearing before the school's decision-making body.** *Board of Curators v. Horowitz*, 435 U.S. 78, 98 S.Ct. 948, 55 L.Ed.2d 124 (1978).

## 2. Cheating and Plagiarism

*The Court of Appeals of Indiana has noted that courts use different paradigms to analyze the student-university relationship. In* Amaya v. Brater, *the court explained that Indiana has adopted the "most pervasive and enduring theory" – that the parties have a contract and that "catalogues, bulletins, circulars, and regulations" form the terms.*

*A New York decision recited the general rule that judicial review of academic discipline by educational institutions is very limited. In* Kickertz v. New York Univ., *924 N.Y.S.2d 310 (Table) (N.Y. Sup. Ct. 2011), the court held that if an institution "substantially complies" with its written guidelines, courts will not disturb its decisions.*

◆ *Alaska's highest court upheld a university's decision to dismiss a student and a lower court ruling that awarded $5,000 in attorneys' fees to the school.*

A Ph.D. psychology student was accused of plagiarism. She denied the charge, but after a meeting faculty members concluded she had plagiarized. She was required to write a paper about how and why it was judged to have been plagiarized. She submitted the paper, but the school said it failed to show an understanding of the issue. The school notified the student that it wasn't satisfied with the paper and she could be dismissed from the program. After a hearing, she was. She appealed, to no avail. Then she sued, saying she should have received more due process because the dismissal was disciplinary rather than academic. The lower court affirmed the dismissal and awarded the school $5,021 in attorneys' fees. Appeal reached the state's highest court, which affirmed the ruling for the school. It said **the school reasonably characterized the dismissal as academic rather than disciplinary**. The level of due process needed for academic dismissals is lower than the level needed for disciplinary ones. All that was needed was for the student to get prior notice of faculty dissatisfaction with her performance and the possibility of dismissal, together with a decision that was careful and deliberate. That standard was met, so the ruling was affirmed. *Richards v. Univ. of Alaska*, 370 P.3d 603 (Alaska 2016).

◆    *A California state appeals court negated a university's decision to dismiss a student who was accused of cheating on an exam.*

A chemistry professor accused the student of cheating on an exam, as 24 of 26 answers – including eight incorrect ones – matched those of an unidentified classmate, referred to as "Student X" in the suit. The professor consulted with a colleague experienced in statistical analysis, who said the chances of two students having eight matching wrong answers were a billion to one. The accused student was already on probation – so after this incident, he faced dismissal. He pressed the school to identify Student X. But it refused, and the student was dismissed. After two internal hearings, he sought judicial review. The case reached a state appeals court, which held the school violated its policy by refusing to identify Student X. One provision in the policy said students facing charges could submit the names and contact info of people who had knowledge relevant to the charge. Knowing where Student X sat during the exam was relevant, so **the refusal to supply the information violated the accused student's right to procedural due process**, the appeals court held. His defense was "unfairly crippled" by his inability to figure out where Student X sat during the exam, the court held. It directed the trial court to require the university to set aside the dismissal. *Dorfman v. Univ. of California, San Diego*, No. D065865 (Cal. Ct. App. 9/16/15).

◆    *A Massachusetts federal court rejected breach of contract claims filed by a law student who was reprimanded for plagiarism.*

The student submitted work that contained 23 instances of apparent plagiarism. After a hearing, a board issued a formal reprimand. She was allowed to graduate on time with her class, and a letter of reprimand was put in her file. She sued, alleging claims of breach of contract and defamation. The court rejected the student's argument that she didn't "submit" the work within the meaning of the handbook because she viewed it as a work in progress. The student also claimed the school breached its contract by failing to keep the hearing non-adversarial, but the court noted that nothing in the transcripts showed the proceeding was conducted in an adversarial manner. The court also rejected the student's claim that the school didn't meet the handbook's standard of "clear and convincing evidence" in her case. There was no dispute that the student handed in work that failed to include proper attribution, the court said. The board had enough evidence to determine she plagiarized, the court held. Finally, the court rejected the defamation claim, which was premised on the fact that her transcript said she was issued a letter of reprimand that said she committed plagiarism because the statement was true: She committed plagiarism within the meaning of the student handbook. A motion for pretrial judgment was granted. *Walker v. President and Fellows of Harvard College*, No. 12-10811-RWZ, 2014 WL 7404557 (D. Mass. 12/30/14).

◆    *A federal district court denied several claims raised by a student who was dismissed from a doctoral program after plagiarizing parts of her dissertation.*

After the student submitted a draft that she was set to defend, one committee member identified a provision of the dissertation that was taken from a source different from the one cited. The committee chair told the student he planned to recommend her removal from the program for plagiarism. At her request, the committee agreed to give her another chance. When she submitted a "corrected dissertation," it contained more plagiarism than the original. The committee recommended that the student be removed from the program. The student appealed the decision at three separate hearings – in front of an academic appeal board, a conduct hearing panel and an appeal board. All three affirmed the recommendation. She filed suit, asserting she was denied her due process rights because she was not provided with an adequate opportunity to dispute the plagiarism charges. The court rejected her claims, finding **the student received notice and multiple hearings**. Also, the student couldn't show there was no rational basis for the university's decision or that her dismissal was motivated by bad faith or ill will that had nothing to do with her academic performance. A defense motion for pretrial judgment was granted. *Gamage v. State of Nevada,* No. 2:12-cv-00290-GMN-VCF, 2014 WL 250245 (D. Nev. 1/21/14).

◆ *Deferring to a university's decision to dismiss a medical student for cheating, an Indiana court noted the university's duty to the public.*

An Indiana University (IU) medical school handbook provision prohibited cheating and the appearance of cheating. Three professors observed a student looking at a neighbor's exams, resulting in a dismissal hearing. A committee gave the student letters from the professors explaining their belief that he cheated. After the hearing, the committee determined that test proctors could distinguish between glances at a clock and glances at a neighbor's test. The committee recommended dismissal, and the student sued the dean and others in a state court for breach of contract. When the case reached the state court of appeals, it held **Indiana court review of academic decisions is limited to determining if the institution acted "illegally, arbitrarily, capriciously, or in bad faith."** The court refused to consider the student's arguments absent some evidence that IU had acted arbitrarily or in bad faith. Since he offered no such evidence, the court found IU medical school officials made a "rational determination arrived at after much deliberation." IU offered the student many opportunities to be heard and explain himself. As a result, UM was entitled to judgment. *Amaya v. Brater*, 981 N.E.2d 1235 (Ind. Ct. App. 2013).

◆ *A New York Appellate Division Court upheld Union College's decision to suspend a student who was caught cheating three different times.*

During his freshman year at Union, the student admitted plagiarizing a lab report in a biology class. He received a zero and did not challenge the penalty. Two years later, Union charged the student with two more acts of plagiarism. An internal committee found him guilty of the two charges. After exhausting his internal appeal rights, the student sought a state court order to annul the decisions. Appeal reached a state appellate division court, which explained that **court review of a disciplinary decision was limited to whether the college substantially followed its disciplinary rules and was based on a rational interpretation of the evidence**. The student admitted he had failed to properly cite material in his written assignment and also admitted collaborating with a partner to produce the report. Union guidelines would have allowed expulsion under these circumstances, and the court upheld its decision. *Shah v. Union College*, 97 A.D.3d 949, 948 N.Y.S.2d 456 (N.Y. App. Div. 2012).

◆    *A New York Appellate Division Court reinstated a state college's decision to dismiss a student from a nursing program for cheating.*

One of the student's classes required a position paper that made up 25% of the grade. After he submitted his paper, the instructor discovered it matched one submitted by a different student in an earlier semester. After disciplinary proceedings, the college dismissed the student from the program. He sued the college in a state court, which found dismissal was too severe a penalty. It instructed the college to reduce the discipline. On appeal, a state appellate division court explained that **a penalty imposed by a college is to be upheld unless it is shocking to one's sense of fairness**. That standard was not met in this case, because the student received notice that he could be dismissed. Despite this, he denied plagiarism and did not provide a plausible explanation for the similarity between his paper and the other student's. As a result, the court held the case should have been dismissed. *Idahosa v. Farmingdale State College*, 97 A.D.3d 580, 948 N.Y.S.2d 104 (N.Y. App. Div. 2012).

◆    *Vanderbilt University followed proper procedures and gathered enough evidence to support its decision to expel a student for cheating.*

The student correctly answered only one of 15 questions on a physics test. It was discovered that 13 of his answers matched those of a classmate who sat next to him but took a different version of the test. At a hearing, a university official stated that the chance of randomly matching 13 of 15 test answers with a classmate was less than one in two billion. A university honor council found the student guilty of cheating on the test. Following an unsuccessful internal appeal, he sued the university in a federal court. Appeal reached the U.S. Court of Appeals, Sixth Circuit. It first rejected an argument that the university lacked clear and convincing evidence of cheating. The student's answers were nearly identical to those of the classmate and could not be explained by his test notes. In the court's view, this adequately supported the cheating charge. **There was no breach of contract based on the university's appeal procedures and no violation of the university student handbook based on the official's statement.** The university handbook did not bar opinion testimony nor limit the type of testimony that could be offered. As a result, the university was entitled to judgment. *Anderson v. Vanderbilt Univ.*, 450 Fed.Appx. 500 (6th Cir. 2011).

◆    *An Ohio university did not breach a contract with a law school student who was suspended for violating its honor code.*

After an investigation, a university honor council found probable cause that the student violated the honor code by receiving test questions prior to an exam and then giving them to a classmate. A seven-student panel found the student violated five honor code provisions. In response to a three-term academic suspension, the student filed a federal action against the university. The case reached the U.S. Court of Appeals, Sixth Circuit, which held the university did not breach its contract by limiting the student's request to introduce certain evidence. This also defeated his claims for breach of the duty of good faith and fair dealing. In the court's opinion, none of the tort claims were viable. Nor was a claim for breach of a fiduciary duty. It held **a "fiduciary relationship" is not properly applied to the university-student relationship**. A negligence claim could not proceed because it was based entirely on an alleged breach of contract. As none of the student's claims had any merit, the court held for the university. *Valente v. Univ. of Dayton*, 438 Fed.Appx. 381 (6th Cir. 2011).

◆ *A California court denied a private law-school student's challenge to her discipline after a judicial board found she cheated on an assignment.*

In her final semester, the student submitted material she had found online for a group assignment. A few days before she was to graduate, the university notified her of an investigation for plagiarism and academic dishonesty. The student refused to "plea bargain," but two of her classmates accepted offers to admit wrongdoing for reduced penalties. A judicial board upheld the charges and voted to deny credit to the student for the class. She challenged her suspension in a state court for violating state Education Code Section 94367.

The section prohibited private universities from disciplining students based solely on speech that would be protected by the state and federal constitutions if it had occurred off campus. The court denied a request to halt additional penalties, and the student appealed. The state court of appeal explained that **Section 94367 covered only speech rights and created no right to seek redress from an institution**. Moreover, the punishment was not increased because of a letter to the dean. The letter explained that the suspension was justified based on her lack of remorse and other relevant reasons. As a result, the court denied the requested order. *Yu v. Univ. of La Verne*, 196 Cal.App.4th 779, 126 Cal.Rptr.3d 763 (Cal. Ct. App. 2011).

◆ *A New York court upheld a plagiarism charge against a student despite the inability of university officials to identify the source of the plagiarized item.*

A history professor concluded that the student had plagiarized a paper. The case was referred to a committee on academic honesty, which found the student had plagiarized the paper and recommended a one-semester suspension. After an internal appeal, a state trial court rejected the student's case. A state appellate division court later held that **identifying the source of plagiarism was not a prerequisite to a finding of plagiarism under the university academic honesty code**. Evidence supported the university's conclusion that the student used secondary sources in the paper. He submitted the paper just 10 days after he had selected his topic. The professor said the manner in which the paper linked complex documents suggested the analytical ability of a professional historian. The student received all the process he was due, and the university's decision was upheld. *Katz v. Board of Regents of the Univ. of the State of New York*, 85 A.3d 1277, 924 N.Y.S.2d 210 (N.Y. App. Div. 2011).

◆ *A University of Washington (UW) student who admitted that she doctored an exam failed to win a federal court order requiring her reinstatement.*

The court held that people who claim failure to accommodate a disability generally bear the burden of requesting accommodations. In this case, the student did not seek accommodations before disciplinary proceedings. **As the university had a legitimate, nondiscriminatory reason for suspending her** from the program, and she did not show that the charge of cheating was a pretext for disability bias, the court denied her request for a temporary restraining order against UW. *Blower v. Univ. of Washington*, No. C10-1506MJP, 2010 WL 3894096 (W.D. Wash. 9/27/10).

◆ *A New York court held a university did not act arbitrarily or otherwise improperly when it decided to expel a student for plagiarism.*

The student was repeatedly told to remove plagiarized portions of her master's thesis from drafts she prepared. Eventually, she was expelled for plagiarism. After a state trial court denied the student's request to set aside the expulsion, she appealed. A New York Appellate Division Court held **the school substantially complied with applicable procedures for dealing with students accused of plagiarism**. It was acceptable for the professor who reported the plagiarism to serve on a committee that considered the charges. It was also acceptable for an associate dean to serve on two committees that were involved in the expulsion decision. *Dequito v. The New School for General Studies*, 68 A.D.3d 559, 890 N.Y.S.2d 56 (N.Y. App. Div. 2009).

◆ *The Supreme Court of Vermont rejected a medical student's claim that a university violated state law by dismissing him for falsifying documents.*

In the student's fourth year of the medical program, a faculty member discovered he had falsely reported completing a rotation at another medical school. At a hearing of the committee on fitness, the student admitted lying about the rotation. The university later discovered he had engaged in other misconduct and had falsely reported at his hearing that he graduated *magna cum laude* from an undergraduate institution. It was further learned he had falsified reports of completing rotations at other schools and had impersonated an employee of his undergraduate institution. Based on this information, the college held a second hearing, where the student said his misconduct was caused by his disabilities.

The university dismissed the student, and he sued it in a state court. The case reached the state supreme court, which held the university had legitimate interests in enforcing its standards, protecting patients and producing students who could successfully practice medicine. As the student did not meet the medical school's essential eligibility requirements, his disability discrimination claims failed. His dishonesty and fraud were unacceptable, regardless of their cause. **It would fundamentally alter the nature of the medical school to require the school to accept dishonest behavior. Nor did the student timely meet his duty to seek an accommodation.** Accordingly, the decision for the university was affirmed. *Bhatt v. Univ. of Vermont*, 958 A.2d 637 (Vt. 2008).

◆ *An engineering student failed to convince a Florida court that a university failed to follow appropriate disciplinary procedures before expelling him.*

The student failed a required engineering class three times. While enrolled in the class for a fourth time, the course professor determined that his paper was missing after an open-book examination. The professor partially graded all the returned examinations and placed them in an envelope in his office. When he returned to his office later that day, he found the student's paper had been placed with all the others. The paper indicated an expected time of return but did not show the time it was actually handed in. Still, the professor left part of his examination ungraded, hoping the student would contact him to discuss the discrepancy. The student never contacted the professor about the exam. As the professor's suspicions were elevated, he arranged for the final examination to be videotaped. The tape showed the student receiving a note from another student during the exam. After the exam, the professor met with the student and later filed a formal complaint of academic misconduct against him. The university expelled the student, and he brought a state court action for due process violations. **The court held evidence showed the university provided adequate due process and followed appropriate disciplinary procedures before it expelled the student.** Since there was substantial evidence to support the charges of academic misconduct, the court affirmed the expulsion. *Colorado v. Florida Int'l Univ.*, 967 So.2d 372 (Fla. Dist. Ct. App. 2007).

◆ *A Pennsylvania court upheld a college's decision to sanction a student who was found guilty of plagiarizing a paper for a biology course.*

A student enrolled in an investigative laboratory biology course in which the professor assigned her to work with two classmates on a lab experiment. Parts of the student's paper were identical to a classmate's, and the professor suspected plagiarism. The school investigated, and an honors committee panel found a "reasonable likelihood" that she had violated the honor code. A college judicial board held a hearing and found the student guilty of plagiarism. The board imposed a failing grade for the course and stripped her of an honor she had won in another course. It also ordered her to perform community service and placed her on academic probation for the rest of her time at the school. The student sued the classmates, college and professor in state court for breach of contract, defamation, infliction of emotional distress and negligence.

The court dismissed her complaint. On appeal, the Superior Court of Pennsylvania found the parties had a contractual relationship governed by a student handbook. Although the student claimed the college breached the contract by failing to follow its procedures for misconduct claims, **the record showed she was provided all the procedural protections of the handbook**. The court rejected the breach of contract claim against the professor. The student's vague assertions that he was biased were insufficient. The court rejected the defamation claims against all the defendants, as their statements were opinion, fact, or lacked defamatory intent. As the negligence and emotional distress claims were properly dismissed, the court affirmed the judgment. *Reardon v. Allegheny College*, 926 A.2d 477 (Pa. Super. Ct. 2007).

◆ *Due process requires that an individual with a constitutionally protected interest receive notice and a meaningful opportunity to be heard.*

In a case involving a student accused of repeated violations of a student code of conduct, the Court of Appeals of Michigan **held due process requires that an individual receive notice and a meaningful opportunity to be heard. To prove a constitutional risk of bias, an individual must show the risk or probability of unfairness was too high to be tolerated.** The court held the student in this case did not prove an unacceptable risk of bias. Members of the university honor council and an *ad hoc* committee only submitted recommendations to an executive committee. The court rejected the student's contention that two honor council members who were classmates could not be impartial. As familiarity with a case does not disqualify a decisionmaker, the judgment was affirmed. *Imitiaz v. Board of Regents of Univ. of Michigan*, No. 253107, 2006 WL 510057 (Mich. Ct. App. 3/2/06).

## C. Nonacademic Dismissals

*In Schulman v. Franklin & Marshall College, 538 A.2d 49 (Pa. Super. Ct. 1988), the court held courts should not interfere with internal disciplinary matters unless they are biased, prejudicial or lacking in due process.*

◆ *A New York court upheld a university's disciplinary decision to suspend a student who was accused of rape.*

The student went to a nearby university party, where he met a girl. They had sex. She told friends that he raped her. The woman went to the local police but refused to undergo a rape examination. The prosecutor decided not to press charges. The day after going to the police, the woman sought counseling from her school's health center. She later withdrew from school and was treated for depression and PTSD. Ten months later, the woman contacted the student's university to report the alleged assault. It investigated her claim and notified the student that it was going to conduct a hearing. After hearing testimony from the student, the woman and witnesses, the student council board found him responsible for the assault. It suspended him for two years, and he sued. A state court found the disciplinary decision was proper as it was supported by substantial evidence. Importantly, **the woman promptly reported the incident, went on to leave school and was diagnosed with PTSD**. Though witnesses for both sides contradicted each other, New York courts have held that deciding which witnesses' accounts to believe is the conduct board's call to make. The court confirmed the disciplinary decision was proper – and upheld the suspension. *Lambraia v. State Univ. of New York at Binghamton*, 135 A.D.3d 1144 (N.Y. App. Div. 2016).

◆ *New York's highest court found a law school was within its rights to rescind the admission of a student because he misrepresented and withheld info on his application about a criminal conviction.*

As part of the application process, a prospective law student had to fill out a disclosure form about a prior drug arrest. He said the answer was complete and accurate. After he was admitted, he decided to seek an advanced court ruling regarding the likelihood of his bar admission in light of his criminal past. In connection with that petition, he accidentally sent a copy of a letter to the university. It more fully disclosed the nature and extent of the charges against him. Specifically, he'd been charged with a felony drug offense. That information was not disclosed to the university during his application paperwork. It rescinded his admission. The student sought judicial review. When the court found the decision to rescind the admission was not arbitrary and capricious, the student appealed. New York courts reverse such determinations only if the school was arbitrary, abused its discretion, didn't follow its own rules, or imposed a penalty so excessive it shocks one's sense of fairness. That wasn't true here. **The university said it had an unwritten policy to allow applicants who used drugs but bar those who, like this**

**student, sold drugs. The court found this a rational policy within the school's discretion.** "Given this notice and the school's unquestionable interest in ensuring the integrity of the future attorneys under its tutelage," the court concluded, "the penalty of rescission was not excessive." It upheld the school's decision. *Powers v. St. John's Univ. School of Law*, 25 N.Y.3d 210 (N.Y. App. Div. 2015).

◆ *A Kansas appeals court affirmed a ruling that ordered a university to readmit a student who'd been expelled due to his off-campus conduct.*

The student and his girlfriend had a turbulent relationship. After one incident, they broke up. The girlfriend called the police, and the student faced domestic violence charges. The school investigated and issued a no-contact order, warning that it included electronic contact. While off campus, the student tweeted two comments that referenced his girlfriend – but did not name her specifically. The school found the student violated the no-contact order, and after a hearing, expelled him. He appealed and sought judicial review. The district court held the school's student code did not apply to off-campus conduct – as the code specifically stated misconduct must occur either on campus or at university-sponsored events. Since the student's conduct didn't occur at either, the court ordered the school to readmit him. The state appeals court affirmed, explaining that **the plain language of the code identified where the student conduct must occur in order to be subject to discipline**. The school's student conduct code barred disciplining students for off-campus conduct, so the ruling was affirmed. *Yeasin v. Univ. of Kansas*, 51 Kan.App.2d 939 (Kan. Ct. App. 2015).

◆ *A New York appeals court affirmed a ruling that dismissed a due process claim filed by an expelled student.*

The student had a long history of discipline problems – including a yearlong suspension. After a fifth incident involving violence, the university expelled the student based on repeated violations of the conduct code. He sought to annul the expulsion decision and filed a series of due process claims. The student argued the university violated his due process rights by refusing to provide him with certain documentation before his disciplinary hearing. The court disagreed, noting that the student could have obtained the documents on his own from public records. Next, the student argued the university violated his due process rights by relying on his past conduct when considering the most recent charges. The court rejected that argument as well, explaining that university policy stipulated that a student's past conduct record was to be taken into account when determining sanctions. The claims were dismissed, and the student appealed. The appellate court affirmed the ruling, as **the evidence showed the university followed established policies and the determination was not arbitrary or capricious**. *Budd v. State Univ. of New York at Geneseo*, 133 A.D.3d 1341 (N.Y. App. Div. 2015).

◆ *No due process violation occurred when an Illinois university issued an interim suspension to a student who'd been accused of a violent crime.*

A police officer responded to an off-campus bar fight, where he arrested a student who was charged with aggravated battery for allegedly stabbing a man multiple times. After reading the police reports, the dean issued an interim suspension. He notified the student that he was suspected of committing a stabbing so was banned from campus until further notice. A hearing determined the student violated the conduct code, so he was expelled. He appealed to no avail. He sued, alleging a due process violation. But the court granted the defendants judgment without a trial. **The U.S. Supreme Court has held institutions can remove those who pose a threat to others without prior notice and a hearing if they provide the notice and hearing "as soon as practicable"** – which the university did here. The claim was dismissed. *Hess v. Board of Trustees of Southern Illinois Univ.*, No. 3:14-cv-00727 LJM, 2015 WL 8301461 (S.D. Ill. 12/9/15).

◆    *A Vermont federal judge ordered a university to allow a student to attend classes while he sued to challenge his expulsion.*

The student went on a study abroad program. There, a female program participant from another college accused the student of sexual misconduct. The study abroad school conducted an investigation – and kept both students' colleges informed on the progress. The study abroad school ultimately exonerated the accused student. But when the student returned, his school conducted its own investigation. The student argued the second investigation was unauthorized, as the college's study-abroad policies indicated he'd be subject to the study abroad program's policies during that time. The school expelled the student without a hearing. He sued and asked the court to order the school to allow him to attend classes while the case continued. He said he had a job offer that hinged on his upcoming graduation. The court granted the injunction, as the case presented **the "unique situation" of a student "exonerated by one U.S. institution following an investigation and hearing" and then expelled by another** – after it let him resume his studies but conducted a second investigation of the same charge. The judge pointed out that if the school won the lawsuit, it could revoke his diploma. So the court granted the injunction. *Doe v. Middlebury College*, No. 1:15-cv-192-jgm, 2015 WL 5488109 (D. Vt. 9/16/15).

◆    *An Oregon federal judge dismissed constitutional claims filed by a mentally ill student who was expelled after twice making written threats.*

The student was enrolled in a university and was seeking legal help for a prior felony conviction. Frustrated by the process, he sent an email that stated, "I fear the only way to see justice in this case is to walk into a school and open fire." Police talked to the student and decided he posed a risk. After a conduct hearing, he was suspended for a year and ordered to get counseling as a condition to return. Then the student applied for Social Security benefits, writing, "I am so sorry that I did not walk into a school and open fire, at the very least my punishment would fit the crime. Now I have been suspended for over a year so that I can get on disability and get treatment for my mental illness hopefully before I am forced to enter a school and open fire." The student was expelled. When his appeal was denied, he sued, claiming the school violated his constitutional rights. The court found the university had

Eleventh Amendment immunity to the claims – but even if it didn't, the student didn't state valid causes of action. The university legally suspended a potentially dangerous student. **It gave him notice of the charges, an opportunity to discuss, a hearing and a chance to appeal.** The court dismissed the claims. *Reynolds v. Portland State Univ.*, No. 3:14-cv-01733-MO, 2015 WL 3657288 (D. Or. 6/12/15).

◆   *A Florida federal judge dismissed due process claims filed by a student who was suspended after being accused of sexual assault.*

The student and his girlfriend lived together and were enrolled at the same university. The girlfriend moved out and filed a domestic violence/sexual harassment complaint with the university. As part of the investigation, the school sent an email to the student. The subject line read in part: "No Contact Letter–DO NOT DELETE." The email informed the student that his ex had filed a charge against him, outlined the allegations and asked the student to make an appointment with the dean. It warned a decision would be made – with or without his input. A second email notified the student that the university found he'd committed three code of conduct violations – and he was entitled to a hearing if he disagreed. It warned that if he didn't respond within five days, he'd be suspended indefinitely. The student didn't respond and was suspended. He said he deleted the emails by mistake and asked the university to lift the suspension. It refused, so the student sued alleging a violation of his due process rights. The claims failed because he hadn't exhausted his remedies, the court held. **The student admitted he deleted the emails, and the university followed the procedures outlined in its code of conduct.** The case was dismissed. *Doe v. Univ. of South Florida Board of Trustees*, No. 8:15-cv-682-T-30EAJ, 2015 WL 3453753 (M.D. Fla. 5/29/15).

◆   *A California appeals court affirmed a decision in favor of a university.*

A student hit another so hard the victim lost consciousness and suffered a concussion. The university found the student violated the school code of conduct by fighting and being disorderly while under the influence of alcohol. The student claimed it was self-defense. The matter went before a student conduct board, which recommended putting the student on probation, having him attend an anger-management workshop, making him go to an alcohol risk-reduction seminar and requiring monthly meetings with the student conduct officer assigned to the case. The student conduct officer reviewed the evidence and determined the sanctions weren't enough. As per the conduct officer's recommendation, the council of deans added an eight-month suspension to the sanctions. The student appealed, and the issue ended up in court. The student asked the court to grant an injunction to put a hold on the suspension, alleging the council of deans exceeded its jurisdiction by suspending him. The court granted the injunction but ultimately held the school complied with its policies when it decided to suspend the student. The student appealed. The appellate court affirmed the ruling, noting that the **school's policy specifically says recommended sanctions go straight to the council of deans for a "final review."** *Berman v. Regents of Univ. of California*, 229 Cal.App.4th 1265 (Cal. Ct. App. 2014).

◆    *A Washington state court affirmed a school's decision to ban a student from campus after he was charged with sexual misconduct.*

At a frat party, the student allegedly harassed a female by inappropriately touching her. The victim identified the alleged assailant by viewing the fraternity's Facebook page. The student was arrested, and the charges were later reduced. The university charged the student with sexual misconduct, violation of school policy and violation of law. At the hearing, the student exercised his right to remain silent when it came to the alleged assault. But he testified that he had met with the woman, had paid for a "victim outreach expert" for her and scheduled a risk assessment for himself. When the woman testified, the accused student left the room. No one identified the student as the assailant. The board found all three violations had been committed. The student was banned from campus but was allowed to complete his degree off campus. He appealed the decision, and the court affirmed. The student sought further review with a state appeals court. He insisted that the evidence presented at the hearing was insufficient to show he was the assailant. But the court noted **the proceedings were civil rather than criminal; and that meant the board could infer from the student's refusal to testify about the incident that such testimony might tend to incriminate him**. The court also pointed to other evidence that suggested he was the assailant – he told the board he met with the victim and was doing several things for her as a result of the incident. The decision against the student was affirmed. *Romer v. Washington State Univ.*, 183 Wash.App. 1028 (Wash. Ct. App. 2014).

◆    *A Pennsylvania federal judge refused to order a university to halt discipline against a student who was suspended due to safety concerns.*

After four years in the Marines, the student used G.I. Bill funding to enroll at the university. He told a female professor he often played Russian roulette with a loaded revolver. The professor told him to go to student services and called the police, who used state-law power to commit the student. He was diagnosed with post-traumatic stress disorder and depression. After three weeks, he was released and repeatedly tried to contact the professor, despite her refusal to talk to him. The professor notified the school about the problems. The student was suspended for one semester. When he returned, he sat near the professor's office and refused to leave when the police arrived. He was suspended again, due to safety concerns. A disciplinary hearing was scheduled to determine whether expulsion was appropriate. He sued, claiming a laundry list of allegations. He asked the court for a preliminary injunction to order the school to put disciplinary proceedings on hold until his lawsuit concluded. But the court denied his request because **the student failed to show he would suffer irreparable harm without the injunction**. *B.P.C. v. Temple Univ.*, No. 13-7595, 2014 WL 4632462 (E.D. Pa. 9/16/14).

◆    *A Kansas community college did not violate a student's rights when it dismissed her for repeated disruptive conduct.*

The student was suspended for one year after several employees voiced safety concerns. The student allegedly made false reports, raised her voice and made threatening statements. Before the school issued the suspension, the case was referred to a behavior intervention team. But efforts to reach the student by telephone and email were ignored. The student did not appeal the suspension. But about five months later, she met with the college's HR department and claimed she'd been subjected to racial slurs and discrimination, saying the college's vice president of student services called her "white trash." The college declined to remove the suspension. Then the student sued, alleging she'd been denied due process. The college filed a motion to dismiss the case, saying **the student failed to pursue administrative remedies**. The court granted the motion to dismiss, as the student failed to show violation of a fundamental right or action that shocked the conscience. *Hardman v. Johnson County Community College*, No. 13-2535-JTM, 2014 WL 1400668 (D. Kan. 4/10/14).

◆ *A Kentucky university did not violate a nursing student's rights when it dismissed her for posting comments about patients online.*

The student was assigned to follow a patient through the birthing process. And in spite of signing a confidentiality agreement, she chronicled the experience on her MySpace page. There, she called babies "demons from hell" and referred to a patient's newborn as "the new Creep." The university dismissed the student for violating its honor code and a confidentiality agreement associated with the course. She sued, claiming the university violated her speech rights. Ruling on contract grounds, the court held the post did not violate the confidentiality agreement, as it did not reveal the mother's identity. It ordered the university to reinstate the student. On appeal, the U.S. Court of Appeals, Sixth Circuit, vacated the judgment because the district court had ruled on contract grounds, even though the student had presented only constitutional claims. While the appeal was pending, the student was reinstated, completed her coursework, obtained her degree and left the university. On remand, the court rejected the speech-rights claim, explaining the student didn't have a constitutional right to post information about a childbirth in a public forum. In fact, she had agreed not to do so. Limitations imposed on revealing information about the birth were related to legitimate pedagogical concerns. So on remand, her speech claim failed.

The student appealed again. The Sixth Circuit affirmed the decision in favor of school defendants. The claim for injunctive relief of reinstatement was moot because she'd already graduated. The defendants were entitled to immunity on the First Amendment claim, as the student didn't have a constitutional right to post the blog entry. And **even if she did, it was reasonable for the school to believe she had waived that right by signing the confidentiality agreement and consent form**, the court explained. Finally, her due process claim was dismissed as procedures used in connection with her dismissal were adequate. The lower court's ruling was affirmed. *Yoder v. Univ. of Louisville*, No. 12-5354, 2013 WL 1976515 (6th Cir. 5/15/13).

◆ *No due process violation occurred when a medical school dismissed a student with a history of drug use after she refused to enter a treatment program, the U.S. Court of Appeals for the Fifth Circuit held.*

Because a student admitted she'd used drugs in the past, the university had her sign an agreement to undergo random drug testing. She did. Then questions were raised about the validity of the student's drug test results. So the school had her sign a second agreement. In it, she agreed to follow any directives issued by the school's campus assistance program. The agreement specified that her failure to abide by it would be grounds for immediate dismissal. After she signed the second agreement, the campus assistance sent her to a center that recommended a three-month inpatient program for her. But she refused to enter the program. The dean of the medical school decided to dismiss her from the program. Following his initial decision, the dean met with the student's parents and considered additional information. Ultimately, he dismissed her from the school. The student sued the school and the dean, asserting violation of her due process rights. A district court dismissed the case, and she appealed as to her due process claim against the dean in his official capacity. The Fifth Circuit affirmed. The student argued that the district court wrongfully classified her dismissal as academic. She said her dismissal was disciplinary in nature and that she was therefore entitled to more substantial due process protections. **But even if her dismissal was characterized as disciplinary, it was preceded by a give and take discussion, the court explained.** In addition, the dean met with her parents after the initial decision to consider additional evidence. Also, the student didn't identify what additional process was allegedly due to her. The district court's decision was affirmed. *Mathai v. Board of Supervisors of Louisiana State Univ. and Agricultural and Mechanical College*, No. 13-30829, 2013 WL 6908891 (5th Cir. 12/30/13).

◆   *The University of Minnesota provided all the procedure that was due a male student before expelling him for violating its student conduct code.*

The male had sex with an intoxicated female student at a fraternity party. The university charged him with violating its student conduct code. A hearing panel chair emailed a university attorney to say it was important to spell out the charges. Based on this, the male asked the chair to recuse herself. She declined, and a panel found the male should be expelled. A state court rejected the claim that the chair's email required recusal. The email did not harm the integrity of the proceedings. **The court also rejected the claim that the male was denied a fair hearing because the panel did not have a student majority.** University procedures required only that a reasonable effort be made to have a student majority – not that the panel be composed mostly of students. The court also rejected the contention that the university panel used the wrong standard when determining whether the female had consented. Nor did university procedures fail to provide a chance for a fair review. Finally, the university provost did not abuse his discretion by upholding the panel decision. *Brisbois v. Univ. of Minnesota*, No. A11-1720, 2012 WL 2505826 (Minn. Ct. App. 7/2/12).

◆   *Missouri's court of appeals upheld a lower court decision refraining to order a university to reinstate a student expelled for misappropriating funds.*

The student was class treasurer for the University of Missouri's medical school. He transferred $3,500 to his personal account and spent the money. He then tried to withdraw another $2,000. When the university discovered this, it called the student to a hearing before its honor council. He testified he took the money for "necessary but non-emergent" dental surgery. Although the student repaid the money before the hearing, the council found he violated the honor code. It made nine disciplinary recommendations but did not recommend expulsion. Another hearing was held, this one before a committee on student promotions (CSP). The CSP voted to recommend expulsion, and the student sued the university and some of its officials for due process violations. After a trial, the judge found for the university. On appeal, the Court of Appeals of Missouri found the student's claims boiled down to an allegation that the deans were biased against him. But it held the trial court testimony contradicted this claim. Both university tribunals had found the student violated the honor code, disagreeing only on the penalty to impose. As the student did not show a violation of his rights, the court affirmed the judgment. *Korte v. Curators of Univ. of Missouri*, 316 S.W.3d 481 (Mo. Ct. App. 2010).

## III. STUDENT PRIVACY RIGHTS

### A. The Family Educational Rights and Privacy Act

*The Family Educational Rights and Privacy Act (FERPA), 20 U.S.C. § 1232g, was enacted in 1974 to grant eligible students access to their education records and to protect records from access by unauthorized persons.*

*FERPA applies to any educational institution receiving federal funds. It contains detailed requirements regarding the maintenance and disclosure of student records. These requirements become applicable only upon a student's attendance at an institution. FERPA, at 20 U.S.C. § 1232g(d), requires institutions to allow students to inspect and review their education records.*

*FERPA applies only to "education records," which are records "directly related to a student" that are "maintained by an educational agency or institution or by a party acting for the agency or institution." FERPA regulations state when personally identifiable information may be disclosed without consent by a parent or eligible student. "Personal identifiers" may indirectly identify students without stating names. This includes a student's date and place of birth, mother's maiden name, or "information that, alone or in combination," may allow identification by a person in the community.*

*On December 2, 2011, the U.S. Department of Education revised FERPA regulations to permit a limited directory information policy in which institutions specify the parties or purposes for which information is disclosed.*

*The amended regulations include student email addresses in the term "directory information" and create new sanctions for the improper redisclosure of protected data. Records that originate from a school, or are created by nonschool entities, may become education records if they are "maintained" by an institution. Notes used only as a personal memory aid and kept in the sole possession of the maker are outside FERPA's coverage.*

*FERPA regulations declare that as states develop and refine their information management systems, it is critical to act to protect personally identifiable information on students. A FERPA regulation at 34 C.F.R. Part 99.31(a)(1) requires educational institutions to "use reasonable methods to ensure that school officials obtain access to only those education records in which they have legitimate educational interests." Institutions may disclose education records to another institution without consent, even after a student has enrolled or transferred, for reasons related to enrollment or transfer.*

*FERPA allows educational agencies to enter into agreements with organizations that conduct studies and redisclose personally identifiable information from education records. Parts of the 2011 regulations restrict the redisclosure of personally identifiable information by requiring agreements to include provisions for destroying all personally identifiable information by contractors or other third parties when the information is no longer needed for the purposes for which the study was done. Further disclosures must be in accordance with agreements to other parties and only for specified purposes.*

*To assure that information that is "redisclosed" by an educational agency or institution remains protected by FERPA, the amended regulations declare an intent to enforce the act not only against the educational agency, but against a third-party recipient of the information. A FERPA enforcement tool is the Secretary of Education's declared ability to issue a cease and desist order, and to terminate federal funding eligibility "under any applicable program."*

*If the Secretary finds that a third party outside an educational agency or institution has violated FERPA regulations, the offending educational agency or institution may not allow the third-party violator access to personally identifiable information from education records for at least five years.*

*Under 34 C.F.R. Part 99.36, personally identifiable information from an education record may be disclosed to parents and other appropriate parties in connection with "health and safety emergencies." A student's SSN or student identification number is personally identifiable information that may not be disclosed as directory information under 34 C.F.R. Part 99.3.*

◆ *A Florida court said FERPA permitted a college to withhold the name of a student from an adjunct professor after the student complained about him.*

The adjunct learned a student had emailed his department chair to report him for making humiliating remarks to students and using unorthodox teaching methods. According to the chair, the student's name could not be disclosed under FERPA. When the adjunct's contract was not renewed, he claimed the email was a factor, and he sued the college. A state court dismissed the case.

On appeal, a Florida District Court of Appeal explained that state law tracked FERPA's definition of "education records," which were exempt from disclosure. Although the adjunct was the primary subject of the email in this case, the court found the email also had information directly related to its student author. In ruling for the college, **the court rejected the argument that the email could not "relate directly both to a student and a teacher."** If a record had information directly related to a student, it was irrelevant under FERPA that it might also directly relate to a teacher or other person. Because the plain language of FERPA supported the trial court's decision, the court affirmed the judgment for the college. *Rhea v. District Board of Trustees of Santa Fe College*, 109 So.3d 851 (Fla. Dist. Ct. App. 2013).

◆ *An applicant who was rejected for admission to a Ph.D. program was not entitled to data relating to Ohio State University (OSU) admission practices.*

After being denied admission to OSU's School Psychology Ph.D. program, the applicant filed a disability discrimination lawsuit in a federal court. As the case proceeded, she asked the court to order OSU to divulge documents relating to all program applicants when she applied for admission. This included applications, recommendation letters, curricula vitae and decision forms for a master's program. But **as she never applied to the master's program, the court found these documents irrelevant**. The question of whether the applicant would have been accepted into a master's program shed no light on her claim that she was unlawfully denied admission to the Ph.D. program. The court denied her request for the information. *Sjostrand v. Ohio State Univ.*, No. 2:11-cv-00462, 2012 WL 4442773 (S.D. Ohio 9/25/12).

◆   *A student who claimed that a university violated FERPA could not sue under 42 U.S.C. § 1983 to enforce individual "rights" under the act.*

A student attended a private university in Washington, intending to teach in the state's public school system after his graduation. At the time, the state required new teachers to obtain an affidavit of good moral character from the dean of their college or university. When the university's teacher certification specialist overheard a conversation implicating the student in sexual misconduct with a classmate, she commenced an investigation of the student and reported the allegations against him to the state teacher certification agency. She later informed the student that the university would not provide him with the affidavit of good moral character required for certification as a Washington teacher. The student sued the university and the specialist under state law and under 42 U.S.C. § 1983, alleging a violation of FERPA. A jury awarded the student over $1 million in damages. The case reached the U.S. Supreme Court, which ruled that **FERPA creates no personal rights that can be enforced under Section 1983**. Congress enacted FERPA to force schools to respect students' privacy with respect to educational records. It did not confer upon students enforceable rights. As a result, the Court reversed and remanded the case for further proceedings. *Gonzaga Univ. v. Doe*, 536 U.S. 273, 122 S.Ct. 2268, 153 L.Ed.2d 309 (2002).

◆   *Using students to correct other students' work and call out the grades in a public school classroom did not violate FERPA.*

An Oklahoma parent sued a school district and various administrators under FERPA after learning that students sometimes graded other students' assignments and called out the results in class. A federal court held this practice did not violate FERPA because calling out grades did not involve "education records" within the meaning of the statute. The Tenth Circuit reversed, but the U.S. Supreme Court noted that **student papers are not "maintained" within the meaning of FERPA when students correct them and call out grades**. Moreover, correcting a student's work can be as much a part of the assignment as taking the test itself. The momentary handling of assignments by students was not equivalent to the storing of information in a records room or a school's permanent secure database. *Owasso Independent School Dist. No. I-011 v. Falvo*, 534 U.S. 426, 122 S.Ct. 934, 151 L.Ed.2d 896 (2002).

◆   *FERPA did not prevent an Ohio community college from disclosing prior complaints against an instructor accused of sexually harassing a student.*

In the student's federal district court action against the college, he sought class rosters from classes taught by the instructor for the four years prior to the harassment she claimed. She also sought "every document relevant to any student complaint/concern" about her. The college denied the request, arguing it could not be disclosed under FERPA. The court found some prior student complaints could be relevant to the present claims. Complaints similar in nature to the student's would support charges that the college and supervisor were aware of prior misconduct. However, the court concluded that the request should be limited to prior complaints of alleged sexual harassment. There was insufficient evidence to show that class rosters were relevant to the student's claims. **Any such student complaints were records that related directly to university employees and only indirectly to students**, and they were not "student records" within the meaning of FERPA. FERPA's limitations on disclosure did not apply to the request for student complaints of sexual harassment. *Briggs v. Board of Trustees Columbus State Community College*, No. 2:08-CV-644, 2009 WL 2047899 (S.D. Ohio 7/8/09).

◆  *As FERPA creates no individually enforceable rights, a disabled student could not pursue an action for wrongful disclosure of his condition.*

A Massachusetts university baseball coach told the team that the student had bipolar disorder. The student sued the university in a federal district court for violations of FERPA. The court determined it was unclear as to whether the coach's statement violated the nondisclosure rules of FERPA. **Even if it did, the student had no right of action in court to redress such a violation, because FERPA does not create any individually enforceable rights.** Violations of FERPA are redressed by the Secretary of Education, who may direct in certain circumstances that funds be withheld from the educational institution. Accordingly, the court dismissed the FERPA claim. *Zona v. Clark Univ.*, 436 F.Supp.2d 287 (D. Mass. 2006).

◆  *University disciplinary records were held to be "education records" under FERPA and thus could not be disclosed to the press.*

A student newspaper at an Ohio university sought student disciplinary records from the University Disciplinary Board for an article about crime trends on campus. After a lawsuit, the Ohio Supreme Court held that student disciplinary records were not "education records" under FERPA. As a result, the university had to hand over the records, without name, Social Security number and student identification number. Another newspaper then requested disciplinary records from two Ohio universities. The U.S. Department of Education (DOE) asked a federal court for an order to prevent the universities from disclosing the disciplinary records. The court agreed with the DOE that disciplinary records are "education records" under FERPA] and issued an injunction to prevent the release of the information. The Sixth Circuit Court of Appeals affirmed, noting that **as the disciplinary records related to students and were kept by the universities, they were education records under FERPA**. An order preventing release of the information was appropriate. *U.S. v. Miami Univ.*, 294 F.3d 797 (6th Cir. 2002).

◆  *FERPA does not create a student right to learn how grades are assigned.*

A federal district court held that **neither FERPA nor a Texas school policy provided a means for a student to obtain information on how a** grade was assigned. At most, the student in this case was only entitled to know whether the assigned grade was recorded accurately in the records. *Tarka v. Cunningham*, 741 F.Supp. 1281 (W.D. Tex. 1990).

## B. State Law Privacy Rights

*While there is no private right of action under FERPA for damages under* Gonzaga Univ. v. Doe, *this chapter, state laws modeled on FERPA may create enforceable privacy rights for students. Students may also bring common law claims based on enrollment contracts with educational institutions.*

◆ *A federal court denied a request to seal the record in a sex assault case, finding the public had a right to know about the incident.*

A University of Montana student was subjected to disciplinary proceedings after being accused of sexually assaulting another student at an off-campus residence. He asked a federal court to stop the university proceedings, claiming breach of contract and violations of Title IX and the Equal Protection Clause.

After the court allowed the student to proceed anonymously and sealed the case, the university found he violated the student conduct code and expelled him. The court then agreed to dismiss the case, since the only relief sought was an order to stop those proceedings. It then decided the case should no longer be maintained under seal, as the public had a right to inspect and copy judicial records. Although the student argued the case file should remain sealed because it might influence criminal proceedings, the court explained that the local prosecutor was ethically obligated to ignore the outcome of the disciplinary proceedings. **While there was good reason not to disclose the identities of the students, there was no good reason to keep other information from the public.** As a result, the court ordered that the file be unsealed, but with any identifying information relating to students blocked. *Doe v. Univ. of Montana*, No. CV 12-77-M-DLC, 2012 WL 2416481 (D. Mont. 6/26/12).

◆ *A California university did not violate a state privacy statute by failing to safeguard the privacy of student exams.*

A University of California student accused university officials of failing to safeguard student exams by leaving them unguarded and in plain view in hallways. He sought to inspect and copy his personal records and exams, and to correct information contained in his personal records. The student further claimed the destruction of personal records, including his exams, violated the California's Information Practices Act (CIPA). The CIPA limits the disclosure of personal information about individuals by state agencies and requires them to maintain complete and accurate records.

The case reached the Court of Appeal of California, which held **student exams were not covered by the CIPA because they were not stored or maintained by the university**. The CIPA applied only to "records" containing "personal information." In turn, CIPA defined "records" as "any file or grouping of information about an individual that is maintained by an agency." Student exams were typically returned to students or held by individual instructors, and they did not contain personal information. CIPA defined "personal information" as information that "identifies or describes an individual," such as by physical description, Social Security number or home address. Since exams containing only a name or student number did not constitute "personal information" under the CIPA, the court held for the university. *Moghadam v. Regents of Univ. of California*, 169 Cal.App.4th 466, 86 Cal.Rptr.3d 739 (Cal. Ct. App. 2008).

## C.  Computer Privacy

◆    *A university had to further defend a charge that it violated two federal statutes by accessing a student's Facebook page.*

In 2011, a student at Widener University was summoned to the dean's office. There, he was interrogated by the police, the dean and the campus director of safety. Specifically, he was questioned about emails he sent and things he posted on his Facebook profile. In the emails – sent to 48 other school accounts – the student said he was "trying to maintain his composure" and that was "the only thing keeping me from doing a significant amount of damage." His Facebook page included vague threats and photos of weapons. Due to being a "perceived threat to the community," the student was involuntarily evaluated regarding his mental health. He was committed for testing, during which time a knife and marijuana were found in his backpack. He was suspended for having a weapon and drugs at school. The student sued, raising several claims. Defendants asked for judgment, and most of the claims were dismissed. **But two – alleged violations of the Electronic Communications Protection Act and the Stored Communications Act – survived.** The motion was granted in part and denied in part. *Rodriguez v. Widener Univ.*, No. 13-1336, 2013 WL 3009736 (E.D. Pa. 6/17/13).

◆    *A student who allegedly saved child pornography on university computer-lab computers was not entitled to privacy under the Fourth Amendment.*

A Maine student left an image on a university computer screen that a university employee considered pedophilic. University authorities investigated and discovered similar images on the hard drives of other computers in the lab. The university contacted the police, and the student was indicted for receiving child pornography. The prosecution obtained two hard drives from the university that allegedly contained illegal images, as well as the university's computer usage logs, which indicated when the student used the computers. The student filed a motion to have the hard drives and logs suppressed as the product of searches that violated his Fourth Amendment right against unreasonable searches and seizures. A federal court judge ruled the student had no right to privacy in this matter and denied the motion to suppress. **To assert a right under the Fourth Amendment, a defendant must show that he believes he had a right to privacy and that society would find his expectation objectively reasonable.**

Because the usage logs were maintained for the benefit of the university, they could not be suppressed. The judge cited *Smith v. Maryland*, 442 U.S. 735 (1970), in which the Supreme Court held a telephone customer had no legitimate expectation of privacy in telephone numbers he had dialed. As for the hard drives, the student pointed to no university computer privacy policies, no statements made about the use of the computer lab, no practices concerning access to and retention of hard drive contents. **The student was simply using university computers under circumstances where images on the monitor were visible to others.** *U.S. v. Butler*, 151 F.Supp.2d 82 (D. Me. 2001).

## IV. GRADING AND CURRICULUM

*Courts typically use restraint when considering academic matters. In* Univ. of Pennsylvania v. EEOC, *493 U.S. 182 (1990), the U.S. Supreme Court stated that courts should avoid second-guessing legitimate academic judgments.*

◆ *Columbia University alumni failed to force the elimination of a women's studies program or the addition of a corresponding "men's studies" program.*

In a federal class action lawsuit, two male alumni accused the U.S. Department of Education and Columbia officials of violating the Establishment Clause by "aiding the establishment of the religion of feminism" at the university. They also claimed a violation of their due process rights, their equal protection rights and Title IX of the Education Amendments of 1972. The alumni requested declaratory relief, injunctive relief and nominal damages.

To support their claims, the alumni asserted the women's studies program harmed them by propagating negative information about males. They also said they were harmed by the absence of a men's studies program. According to the court, they did not assert any injury in fact. Neither of the males enrolled in the women's studies program and they had no firsthand exposure to it. At most, the injury they suffered was subjective – not an objective, concrete harm. **Because they did not suffer an injury in fact, the alumni did not have standing to raise their claims relating to the women's studies program.** Similarly, they did not suffer concrete and particularized injury from the absence of a men's studies program at the university. As a result, they could not pursue the case. Later, the U.S. Court of Appeals for the Second Circuit affirmed the dismissal of the action. *Den Hollander v. Institute for Research on Women & Gender at Columbia Univ.*, 372 Fed.Appx. 140 (2d Cir. 2010).

Dissatisfied with the outcome of the case, one of the alumni filed another lawsuit raising essentially the same claims. He again claimed the university could not provide public funding to the Women's Studies Program because it promoted feminism. A federal magistrate judge recommended that judgment be granted to Columbia and the other defendants. Since each of the issues had been decided in the first action, they could not be relitigated. The court rejected the alumnus' other arguments and adopted the recommendation for dismissal. *Den Hollander v. Members of the Board of Regents of the State of New York*, No. 10 Civ. 9277(LTS)(HBP), 2011 WL 5222912 (S.D.N.Y. 10/31/11).

◆ *A New Jersey court rejected a student's claim that a professor conspired with her boyfriend to assign her low grades and waste her financial assistance.*

After the student transferred from another college, she received grades of "C-" in three of four courses for a semester. She filed an appeal within the college. Following review of her academic record, the college placed her on academic probation for a semester. Acting without a lawyer, the student sued the college in the state court system, asserting that one of her professors there "asked a lot of personal questions" and conspired with her boyfriend to assign her low grades, causing her to waste grant and loan money. She also asserted a claim of unlawful discrimination based on national origin. A state trial court dismissed the complaint, and the student appealed.

A New Jersey Appellate Division Court noted that **New Jersey courts typically defer to the academic decisions of higher education institutions**. In this case, the claims involved a challenge to the student's grades, but decisions in that regard were not subject to judicial review. Though she claimed she had a language-based disability, she did not specifically allege that the college discriminated against her based on a disability. There were no facts supporting a disability bias claim. Finally, the court held the student did not state a viable claim of unlawful discrimination based on national origin. As a result, the judgment for the college was affirmed. *Partovi v. Felician College*, No. DC-022681-09, 2011 WL 867275 (N.J. Super. Ct. App. Div. 3/15/11).

◆   *The University of Washington (UW) did not breach a contract with a student when it set conditions on her participation in a foreign studies program.*

Soon after arriving in Cuba to participate in the program, the student began missing required classes and excursions. She complained of medical problems, and Cuban doctors recommended that she return to the U.S. based on the belief that she had a psychiatric condition. She returned to the U.S. but soon asked for permission to continue the program. UW officials insisted upon an updated medical clearance form. When the student failed to submit one, she was not allowed to return to Cuba. Because the student never provided the requested form, she was not allowed to participate in another international studies program. She sued UW and its officials in a state court for discrimination, retaliation, breach of contract, negligence and emotional distress.

Appeal reached the state court of appeals, which found no contractual breach based on sending the student home. The Cuban doctors had recommended that the student be sent home. UW had no contractual obligation to allow her to complete credits for the Cuba program through independent study. Nor did UW breach a contract by declining to assign numerical grades to the Cuba program courses. **As nothing in the UW handbook required it to assign students numerical grades, the court held for UW.** *Ju v. Univ. of Washington*, 156 Wash.App. 1017 (Wash. Ct. App. 2010). The student's petition for review was denied by the Supreme Court of Washington in 2011.

◆   *A federal court refused to dismiss an Arizona student's claim that a university refused to grant him incomplete grades based on his back ailment.*

After being withdrawn from three classes, the student appealed and was allowed to re-enroll in two of them. He emailed a complaint to an administrator about the university's previous refusal to give him incomplete grades, and he later claimed retaliation for sending the email. The student sued the university in a federal district court for disability discrimination, retaliation, breach of contract and infliction of emotional distress.

The court decided a factual issue was present as to whether the student had a disability within the meaning of the law. There was also a factual issue regarding whether the law required the university to accommodate his back condition by granting his request for incomplete grades. While the court refused to dismiss the disability bias claims, the university was entitled to judgment on the retaliation claim. This was because the university provided legitimate reasons for its actions. For example, **the university threatened to dismiss the student because he behaved abusively toward administrators, and it restricted him from taking a course because it was not designed for doctoral students**. The court granted dismissal of a contract claim and the emotional distress claim as nothing indicated extreme and outrageous conduct. *Yount v. Regent Univ.*, No. CV-08-8011-PCT-DGC, 2009 WL 995596 (D. Ariz. 4/14/09).

◆  *New York Law School did not breach an implied contract with a student by assigning him a grade of "C" for a particular course.*

After transferring to New York Law School, the student claimed he was disadvantaged by being placed in a Legal Writing II course instead of Legal Writing I. After being assigned a C grade, he said the law school breached an implied contract with him by arbitrarily assigning the grade. To support his breach of contract claim, the student relied on statements on a law school website. In the student's state court action, the trial court held **New York courts generally do not intervene in grading disputes because doing so would "inappropriately involve the courts in the very core of academic and educational decision making."** Through its student handbook, the law school clearly informed all students that it used a letter grading system, not a pass-fail system. The court granted the law school's motion to dismiss the case.

On appeal, the New York Supreme Court, Appellate Division, held "only specific promises set forth in a school's bulletins, circulars and handbooks which are material to the student's relationship with the school, can establish the existence of an implied contract." While academic judgments are not beyond all judicial review, "that review is limited to the question of whether the challenged determination was arbitrary and capricious, irrational, made in bad faith or contrary to Constitution or statute." As the lower court found no promise to the student that a pass/fail grading system would be used, the court affirmed the judgment for the law school. *Keefe v. New York Law School*, 71 A.D.3d 569, 897 N.Y.S.2d 94 (N.Y. App. Div. 2010).

◆  *A federal appeals court rejected several claims raised by a California university student who was dissatisfied with a grade.*

After expressing dissatisfaction with a grade he received, the student was given an opportunity to appear before a faculty panel. After the panel issued a decision against him, he sued the university in a federal district court for violation of his constitutional rights under 42 U.S.C. § 1983. The student claimed due process and equal protection violations and added a conspiracy claim under 42 U.S.C. § 1985. The court held for the university. On appeal, the U.S. Court of Appeals, Ninth Circuit, held the substantive due process claim failed because **the student did not show the university's academic assessment was arbitrary**. The procedural due process claim failed because he was given the chance to appear before the faculty panel. **The panel considered**

**his concerns and made its decision after careful deliberation.** The equal protection claim also failed, because the student did not claim he was treated differently than similarly situated individuals. The conspiracy claim was based on conclusory allegations without factual support. Accordingly, the court affirmed the judgment for the university. *Negrete v. Trustees of the California State Univ.*, 260 Fed.Appx. 9 (9th Cir. 2007).

◆   *A Vanderbilt University student deserved a chance to convince a jury that his professor was negligent in his method of returning graded papers.*

The student's organic chemistry professor placed graded answer sheets for the class in a stack on a table outside the classroom. Students had to go through the stack to find their answer sheets. The professor allowed students to resubmit their answer sheets for re-grading if they believed he incorrectly marked them. The student found a correct answer marked incorrect and returned the paper for re-grading. The professor believed he changed the answer and reported him to Vanderbilt's honor council. The honor council conducted a hearing and found the student guilty of cheating. He received a failing grade for the class and was suspended. The student sued Vanderbilt in a federal court for negligence.

The case reached the Sixth Circuit, which found **Vanderbilt owed its students a duty not to engage in conduct posing an unreasonable and foreseeable risk of harm**. A jury could conclude the burden on the professor to use another method for returning tests was minimal and find the harm to students was foreseeable. The gravity of harm created by the professor's method was severe. A wrongful conviction by a disciplinary committee could ruin a student's chances of getting into graduate school. The professor breached the university's duty of care by acting in a way that posed an unreasonable and foreseeable risk of harm. A jury would have to decide whether Vanderbilt was liable. *Atria v. Vanderbilt Univ.*, 142 Fed.Appx. 246 (6th Cir 2005).

# CHAPTER TWO

## Discrimination Against Students

## I. DISABILITY DISCRIMINATION

### A. Eligibility for Disability Law Protection

*The Americans with Disabilities Act (ADA), 42 U.S.C. Sections 12101,* et seq., *and Section 504 of the Rehabilitation Act, 29 U.S.C. § 794, are federal laws protecting the rights of disabled individuals. Section 504 states the general rule that "no otherwise qualified individual with a disability" shall, "solely by reason of her or his disability, be excluded from the participation in, be denied the benefits of, or be subjected to discrimination under any program or activity receiving Federal financial assistance."*

*The ADA is based on the anti-discrimination principles of Rehabilitation Act Section 504. While Section 504 applies only to recipients of federal funding, the ADA applies to a broader class of employers, public accommodations and facilities, including institutions of higher education. In 2008, Congress broadened certain ADA provisions to correct Supreme Court decisions that interpreted the Act differently than Section 504 of the Rehabilitation Act. Congress found that the ADA was enacted with the intent to "provide a clear and comprehensive national mandate for the elimination of discrimination against individuals with disabilities," and to provide broad coverage.*

*ADA employment regulations published by the federal government in 2011 noted that the focus of Congress was on whether covered entities have complied with their obligations under the ADA and whether discrimination has occurred, not on whether an individual meets a disability definition. Questions of whether an individual meets this definition should not demand extensive analysis. According to the regulations, Congress wanted an easier, more streamlined analysis that results in more people being covered under the law.*

*While Congress expected the ADA's definition of "disability" would be interpreted consistently with how courts were interpreting the definition of "handicapped individual" under Rehabilitation Act Section 504, it declared "that expectation has not been fulfilled."* Sutton v. United Air Lines, Inc., *527 U.S. 471 (1999) and* Toyota Motor Mfg., Kentucky, Inc. v. Williams, *534 U.S. 184 (2002), were singled out as cases in which the Supreme Court interpreted the term "substantially limits" more restrictively than Congress intended.*

*The 2008 Amendments addressed the term "disability," which is defined as "a physical or mental impairment that substantially limits one or more major life activities" of an individual. At the time of the Amendments, ADA regulations defined "substantially limits" as "significantly restricted." This required "a greater degree of limitation" than Congress intended.*

*"Disability" in the amended ADA is to be construed in favor of broad coverage of individuals, "to the maximum extent permitted by the terms of this Act." Congress specified that "substantially limits" is to be interpreted consistently with its findings and purposes. U.S. Public Laws 110-325 (S. 3406), 110th Congress, Second Session. "ADA Amendments Act of 2008." 29 U.S.C. § 705, 42 U.S.C. §§ 12101-03, 12106-14, 12201, 12205a.*

◆ *A suspended student was not likely to win his disability discrimination lawsuit, so an Ohio federal court refused to grant an injunction in his favor.*

After being accused of sexual assault, a student was investigated and had an accountability hearing. At the hearing, the student submitted a written opening statement and read a closing statement. He testified that he "read her body language" as consenting to have sex, but he failed to give specific examples of what this body language entailed. The board determined the student violated the code of conduct, and he was suspended for one semester. He appealed, arguing that he had a disability that hindered his ability to express himself articulately when he's under pressure. When the appeal was denied, he sued, alleging disability discrimination. He asked the court to order the school not to impose the suspension. The court refused, noting **guidance from the U.S. Department of Education indicates higher ed students are responsible for notifying institutions that they need an accommodation**. The court found the student wasn't entitled to an accommodation during the disciplinary proceedings because he didn't request one until he appealed. The student was not likely to win his claim, so the court refused to grant the court order. *Pierre v. Univ. of Dayton*, 143 F.Supp.3d 703 (S.D. Ohio 2015).

◆ *A Connecticut federal judge refused to dismiss disability discrimination claims against a university filed by a student with dyslexia.*

During a meeting to schedule classes for the upcoming semester, an advisor told the student that he had to take placement tests on a computer. The student told the advisor that he had dyslexia and couldn't take tests on a computer. The advisor didn't respond. The student reported to take the test but was anxious and had to leave. He explained the situation to the test monitor, who allegedly said he could have someone help him on the test. The following day, the student brought his doctor to help him and was accused of cheating. Disciplinary proceedings ended in expulsion. The student sued, alleging the college subjected him "to discrimination in the administration placement examination exam solely by reason of his disability." School defendants asked the court to dismiss the claim. It refused, as **a reasonable jury could find the college discriminated against the student on the basis of his disability**. As a result, the claim had to move forward. *Taylor v. Norwalk Community College*, No. 3:13-CV-1889 (CSH), 2015 WL 5684033 (D. Conn. 9/28/15).

◆ *Finding arbitration was necessary, a Florida federal judge stayed the disability discrimination claims of an expelled student.*

The student was expelled from the college's nursing program after repeatedly falling asleep during clinicals. He filed an ADA claim, saying the incidents were caused by a medical condition – and the college failed to provide reasonable accommodations. The school filed a motion to compel arbitration, as the school's enrollment agreement included a clause requiring it. The student argued the fees associated with arbitration would be more than the costs of going to court. While courts can invalidate arbitration provisions that are "prohibitively expensive," the student did not make this showing. **He threw out a number but failed to provide evidence that arbitration would cost that much in his case or that he would be unable to pay for it.** That wasn't enough to meet his burden, so the court stayed the action pending arbitration. *Sightler v. Remington College*, No. 6:15-cv-273-Orl-37GJK, 2015 WL 4459545 (M.D. Fla. 7/21/15).

◆ *A New York federal court dismissed the claim of a student who alleged a university discriminated against her based on her disability.*

The student contracted E. coli and tonsillitis, and she missed four class meetings. She said her doctors told her the infections were related to thalassemia, which is a group of blood disorders. The instructor wouldn't let the student make up the work, and she failed the course. As a result, she didn't graduate on schedule. She sued, alleging a violation of Section 504 of the Rehabilitation Act. She said the school failed to provide accommodations for her disability: thalassemia. But she didn't provide a medical diagnosis or testimony from a treating physician. Without those things, the court said, a reasonable factfinder could not conclude that she suffered from the impairment. And because thalassemia "is imprecise to the point of being of no utility to a factfinder," the court said there was no evidence that would allow a jury to find the condition substantially limited the student. Moreover, **the student couldn't show she was denied accommodation because of her alleged disability**, the court added. She missed classes due to an E. coli infection and tonsillitis, and those conditions are not disabilities. The claim was dismissed. *Grabin v. Marymount Manhattan College*, No. 12 Civ. 3591(KPF), 2015 WL 4040823 (S.D.N.Y. 7/2/15).

◆ *A federal court in New York rejected a student's claim that a university violated the ADA by dismissing her from a surgical technologist program.*

The woman developed PTSD after her son was murdered. Seven years later, she enrolled in the surgical technologist program. She said other students mocked her by calling her "kook." She confronted one person about it. Afterward, that student was confused and concerned. She relayed the conversation to school officials. The next day, the woman was dismissed from the college. In a follow-up letter, the school told her she was dismissed because it had received "numerous complaints regarding [her] behavior toward students and staff." It added she engaged in "acrimonious behavior" despite being warned by the school not to do so. After administrative appeals failed, the student sued, alleging violations of the ADA. The student's claim failed because **she didn't show a causal connection between her dismissal and her PTSD**. The dismissal letter cited her "acrimonious" behavior toward others, but nothing indicated such behavior was caused by her condition. The claims were dismissed. *Cain v. Mandl College of Allied Health*, No. 14-CV-1729 (ER), 2015 WL 3457143 (S.D.N.Y. 5/29/15).

◆    *A federal court in Pennsylvania rejected a student's claim that a university violated the ADA when it dismissed her from a nursing program.*

The student had trouble in her clinical rotations. She said that during one of them, an instructor grabbed her arm and tried to twist it into what the instructor considered to be a proper position with respect to a particular procedure. At that point, the student explained that she had a history of breast cancer and that her range of motion in her left arm was limited. In another rotation, she made two medication errors in a span of 10 minutes. Specifically, she administered or tried to administer the wrong medication to a patient. School policy called for the dismissal of students who endanger patients, and the student was dismissed. She sued, claiming unlawful discrimination and harassment under the ADA. The school filed a motion for summary judgment. **The court rejected the student's disability discrimination claims because she did not show the school's proffered reason for dismissing her – she endangered patients – was a pretext for unlawful disability discrimination.** The school said it dismissed the student pursuant to its established policy because she engaged in conduct that was dangerous to patients. The motion for summary judgment was granted. *Walsh v. Univ. of Pittsburgh*, No. 13-00189, 2015 WL 128104 (W.D. Pa. 1/8/15).

◆    *The Iowa Supreme Court held that service dog trainers do not have a private right to sue under a state law regarding service animals.*

The student claimed she was denied access to law school classes because she was accompanied by a service dog she was training. She sued the university under a state law that says people with disabilities – and people who are training service animals – have a right to be accompanied by a service dog in specified public places. The statute provides that a violation is a misdemeanor, but it does not say anything about whether individuals can sue under it. The university argued she did not have a private right to sue under the statute. The case reached Iowa's highest court, which framed the issue as whether a right to sue is implicit in the statute. **It determined that the legislature's specific inclusion of a private right of action under other similar statutes was an**

**indication that it did not intend to allow service dog trainers to sue to enforce the rights created under the law.** So the court found the student could not sue. The appeals court's decision was vacated, and the trial court decision was affirmed. *Shumate v. Drake Univ.*, 846 N.W.2d 503 (Iowa 2014).

◆  *A Pennsylvania federal district court dismissed a student's Section 504 claims against individual defendants.*

A student was a member of the school's lacrosse team. She said during her second year, the school discriminated against her based on her dyslexia. The student complained to the athletic director and was removed from the team. She withdrew from school and filed suit against the school, the coach, the athletic director and another school official. She asserted violation of Section 504 and intentional infliction of emotional distress. The defendants filed a motion to dismiss against individual defendants and sought dismissal of the emotional distress claims against all defendants. Addressing the Section 504 claims, the court said under the law of the jurisdiction where the case was filed, Section 504 liability does not extend to individuals. So those claims were dismissed. To state a valid claim of intentional infliction of emotional distress, the student had to "demonstrate intentional, outrageous or extreme conduct by the defendant, which causes severe emotional distress." She also had to allege physical injury. Although the student claimed she was unfairly removed from the team and forced to leave school, she did not sufficiently allege that she suffered physical harm. Though she claimed she was undergoing treatment, she did not adequately describe specific physical symptoms. The court dismissed the emotional distress claims without prejudice. *Borreggine v. Messiah College*, No. 1:13-cv-01423, 2013 WL 6055214 (M.D. Pa. 11/15/13).

In a later motion in the same case, the remaining university defendants asked the court to dismiss the Section 504 claim. It did – as the student's dyslexia wasn't serious enough to be considered a disability. Even if it was, **there was no evidence that she was removed from the team because she had dyslexia.** The motion for summary judgment was granted. *Borreggine v. Messiah College*, No. 1:13-cv-01423, 2015 WL 4950099 (M.D. Pa. 8/19/15).

◆  *A federal court held that having unsteady hands was not a disability under the ADA, defeating a New York student's discrimination and retaliation claims.*

A medical center proctor refused to let the student participate in a required phlebotomy exercise because she observed his hands shaking. The department chair and student met to discuss a number of incomplete reports and the decision to bar him from the phlebotomy exercise. When the student tried to submit missing reports, it was found that he had falsified them, and he was expelled for violating the student code. In a federal court, he accused the university of violating the ADA and retaliating against him by disciplining him after he complained of discrimination. **The court rejected the discrimination claim, finding the student did not have a disability under the ADA.** He also failed to show the university regarded him as having a disability. As for the retaliation claim, the court found the university had a legitimate, nondiscriminatory reason for its decision to discipline the student. He did not present any evidence beyond his personal belief to show a pretext for unlawful retaliation. As a result, the court held for the university. The student appealed, but the Second Circuit affirmed the lower court ruling. *Widomski v. State Univ. of New York*, 748 F.3d 471 (2d Cir. 2014).

◆   *A federal court refused to dismiss a lawsuit filed by a California podiatry student with panic attacks who sought testing accommodations.*

Although the institution granted the student some testing accommodations, she failed part of the American Podiatric Medical Licensing Examination three times. Under the institution's rules, a third failure resulted in dismissal. The student challenged her dismissal by filing a grievance, and she was allowed to take the examination a fourth time. Again, she failed. She sued the institution in a federal court, seeking a preliminary order to grant her inactive student status so she could keep trying to pass the examination. In ruling for the student, the court explained that **Congress had recently amended the ADA to make it clear that the term "disability" should be interpreted broadly**. A 1997 New York case had found test-taking is a major life activity. Since the factors for injunctive relief favored the student, the court issued an order in her favor. In doing so, the court noted that the institution would not be harmed by allowing her to take the examination again. *Doe v. Samuel Merritt Univ.*, No. C-13-00007 JSC, 2013 WL 497903 (N.D. Cal. 2/8/13).

◆   *A federal appeals court rejected a student's claim that he was entitled to sanctions in a discrimination case against a Florida university.*

The student failed four courses in his first two semesters of college and was placed on academic probation. He was then diagnosed with Attention Deficit Hyperactivity Disorder. A university Student Advancement Committee (SAC) allowed the student to retake his examinations, but he failed one of them and was required to repeat his first year of study. After failing two more courses, the university dismissed the student, and he sued the university in a federal district court for disability discrimination. In pretrial activity, the court ordered the university to provide information relating to students who failed courses and appeared before the SAC. It also ordered disclosure of information relating to action taken against these students. In response, the university compiled a chart identifying students by year of enrollment, enrollment status, courses failed, the SAC's recommendation and the action taken.

After a jury found the student did not have a disability, he asked the court to find the university had compiled misleading data. The court denied his request, and he appealed to the U.S. Court of Appeals, Eleventh Circuit. It held the absence of the requested information did not hurt the student's case. **To prevail in a discrimination case, he needed a meaningful comparison between himself and others who had to retake exams.** He did not seek this information, and the university could not be faulted for failing to provide it. Since the lack of more detailed information did not prevent the student from pursuing his case, the court affirmed the judgment for the university. *Hirsch v. Nova Southeastern Univ.*, 289 Fed.Appx. 364 (11th Cir. 2008).

## B. Reasonable Accommodation

*The ADA and Section 504 of the Rehabilitation Act require colleges and universities to provide persons with disabilities "reasonable accommodations" that do not eliminate or substantially modify program requirements.*

*An accommodation is "reasonable" if it is necessary to provide a disabled person the opportunity to obtain program benefits that would be available if not for a disability. If an accommodation would fundamentally alter the nature of an education program, it is not "reasonable," and federal law does not require the institution to offer it. Higher education institutions are not required to provide accommodations that would undercut their academic integrity.*

◆ *The Fifth Circuit affirmed a Texas ruling that dismissed the claims of a student who alleged disability discrimination.*

The student struggled academically and had to retake his first-year classes. Sometime during his second year, he was diagnosed with attention deficit disorder (ADD). He continued to have problems, was placed in remediation and eventually ended up being dismissed. He appealed the dismissal, telling the school for the first time that ADD was the cause of his problems. The school said the explanation was too little, too late. The decision to dismiss was upheld. The student sued, alleging the university failed to accommodate his disability. The court dismissed the claim, explaining that the school didn't know about the disability and the student hadn't asked for accommodations – but only provided late notice about the diagnosis. On appeal, the student argued that he didn't need to ask for accommodations because his limitations were "open, obvious and apparent" to the school. But the evidence didn't back his claim. Moreover, the court noted that **"mental conditions aren't as obvious as physical conditions"** so it would have been very difficult for the university to know the specifics of the student's impairment or need for accommodations. The ruling to dismiss was affirmed. *Choi v. Univ. of Texas Health Science Center at San Antonio*, 633 Fed.Appx. 214 (5th Cir. 2015).

◆ *The Second Circuit revived a medical student's disability discrimination claims against a New York university and remanded the case.*

A student who suffered from depression was enrolled in medical school. As a requisite for entering his third year, he had to pass "Step 1" of the U.S. Medical Licensing Examination. Medical students have one year – and three tries – to pass Step 1. Before his third and final attempt, the student suffered a severe bout of depression. He sought help through the university's counseling services. There, he was put on an antidepressant, and the counselor gave him a note requesting a three-month leave of absence due to his depression. The committee refused to grant the full three-month leave, only allowing a six-week study leave. The student's physician sent a second note requesting a three-month leave. The committee allowed an additional three weeks. The student ultimately missed the deadline – and was dismissed from the program. He sued, alleging the university failed to accommodate his disability. A trial court granted judgment to the university. On appeal the Second Circuit reversed, as schools are required to offer reasonable accommodations so long as it wouldn't impose an undue hardship on the program or fundamentally alter its nature. The appeals court said **a reasonable jury could find the abbreviated time the school allotted for the study leave was not a reasonable accommodation**. The case was remanded. *Dean v. Univ. at Buffalo School of Medicine and Biomedical Sciences*, 804 F.3d 178 (2d Cir. 2015).

◆    *The Sixth Circuit rejected a student's claim that a Tennessee university failed to provide a reasonable accommodation for his disability.*

A student with ADHD and dyslexia submitted medical documentation to the associate dean. The two agreed on accommodations. Then the student took a leave of absence before finishing his first semester. He re-enrolled the following year – but did not mention his disabilities or seek accommodations. After the student failed two classes, a committee decided he should be dismissed. The student asked for an accommodation – a decelerated program that would stretch his four-year program over five years. But he didn't include medical documentation to support the request. After he was dismissed from the program, the student appealed internally, producing for the first time a letter from a professional who recommended a decreased workload. The appeal was denied, and the student sued, alleging violations of the ADA and the Rehabilitation Act. The court ruled for the school, and the Sixth Circuit affirmed, explaining that **the accommodation he belatedly sought – a decelerated program – would have forced the school to significantly modify its curriculum**. Neither the ADA nor Section 504 require schools to substantially modify standards as an accommodation. The ruling was affirmed. *Shaikh v. Lincoln Memorial Univ.*, 608 Fed.Appx. 349 (6th Cir. 2015).

◆    *A federal court in West Virginia rejected a student's claim that a university violated the ADA by dismissing her from a medical program.*

From the first semester, the student had problems meeting the program's standards for professionalism. Issues included coming in late, being disruptive and making improper comments. In her second year, the student was diagnosed with depression and went on medication. During her third-year rotations, she continued to display unprofessional behaviors. After she received a third "critical incident report," she was dismissed. She appealed, saying her inappropriate behavior was due to side effects of her medication. When the appeal was denied, she sued, alleging disability discrimination. The court dismissed the claims – as **the school's professionalism standards were an essential part of its program, and she did not meet those standards**. She did not show she could meet the standards either with or without accommodation, the court said. *Zimmeck v. Marshall Univ. Board of Governors*, 106 F.Supp.3d 776 (S.D. W.Va. 2015).

◆    *A Pennsylvania federal judge allowed a medical expert's testimony that put a dollar amount on the financial damages a student suffered when a university failed to provide reasonable accommodations for her disabilities.*

A student with disabilities was enrolled in a master's degree program. When she couldn't complete the clinical portion, she was dismissed. She sued, alleging the school failed to accommodate her disabilities in violation of Section 504. In the run-up to trial, the university asked the court to bar an expert witness from testifying that, based on the student's work-life expectancy and Bureau of Labor's wage statistics, the loss of the master's degree would cost her an annual salary loss of $21,370 per year for 40.29 years. But the court found the proposed testimony passed scrutiny under Federal Rule of Evidence 702. The parties agreed he was an expert, and the court found **the proposed testimony was sufficiently reliable to help the jury reach accurate results and was also a good-enough fit to the parties' dispute** – here, the student's claim that the alleged failure to accommodate damaged her financially. *Gordon v. LaSalle Univ.*, No. 14-3056, 2015 WL 1736962 (E.D. Pa. 4/16/15).

◆ *Iowa's highest court ruled that a chiropractic college failed to reasonably accommodate a blind student.*

The student successfully completed the school's undergraduate program with accommodations. When it was nearly time to begin his graduate work, the student met with a disability steering committee and suggested accommodations to help him in the graduate program, such as a sighted reader and modifications to exams. The student enrolled in the graduate program, but the school determined that granting his requested accommodations would fundamentally alter its program. The student withdrew and filed a complaint with the state civil rights commission, accusing the school of discriminating against him based on disability. After a long legal battle, Iowa's highest court held the school did not satisfy its obligation to engage in a meaningful dialogue about reasonable accommodations. **It didn't investigate the student's ability to perform with a reader or other accommodations, and it engaged only in minimal interactions with the student.** So the court held for the student, ordering the school to readmit him and provide reasonable accommodations. *Palmer College of Chiropractic v. Davenport Civil Rights Comm'n*, 850 N.W.2d 326 (Iowa 2014).

◆ *The Tenth Circuit rejected a student's claim that a Kansas university failed to provide reasonable accommodations for her disability.*

The student had spinal muscular atrophy, and her impairments limited her arm strength and required her to use a wheelchair. She was admitted to the university's medical program. The school's accreditation required it to set "technical standards" that all students had to meet. Specifically, students had to be able to perform diagnostic procedures, provide general care and provide emergency treatment. The school asked the student what accommodations she needed. Her doctor said the student would need another person to help her lift and position patients, stabilize elderly patients and perform basic life support. After reviewing the physician's accommodation requests, the school rescinded her admission. She sued, alleging violations of the ADA and the Rehabilitation Act. A federal district court dismissed her claims, and the student appealed. The Tenth Circuit affirmed, noting the school met its burden to show the requested accommodations would fundamentally alter the nature of the program. **Having another staffer interact with patients on the student's behalf would**

**fundamentally alter the nature of her medical education**, the court said.The decision of the district court was affirmed. *McCulley v. Univ. of Kansas School of Medicine,* 591 Fed.Appx. 648 (10th Cir. 2014).

◆    *A federal district court in Kansas dismissed a student's claim that a university violated the ADA and the Rehabilitation Act by failing to provide him with adequate testing accommodations.*

A student with Type 1 diabetes and attention deficit disorder was admitted to a physician's assistant program. He disclosed his diagnoses on medical forms during orientation. After he failed an exam, he said it was due to high blood sugar. When he failed the retake, he was dismissed from the program. He appealed, protesting that the professor's office where he took the retest was located in a busy hallway. He said he did not ask for specific accommodations before the retest because he did not know that he would be taking the retest near the hallway. The school upheld the decision to dismiss him from the program. He sued, alleging violations of Title II of the ADA and Section 504 of the Rehabilitation Act based on the alleged denial of a reasonable accommodation for the retest. The court rejected the student's claims. While he presented evidence to show the university had knowledge of his disability, **the student failed to show the university knew he needed an accommodation beyond that which was provided to him**. *Cunningham v. Wichita State Univ.*, No. 6:14-cv-01050-JTM, 2014 WL 4542411 (D. Kan. 9/12/14).

◆    *A Washington federal court issued a preliminary injunction, ordering a university to admit a deaf student to its medical school.*

After the student was admitted, he started discussing accommodations he needed. The school rescinded the admission offer, citing concerns for patient safety. The student sued, alleging a violation of the ADA. He asked the court to order the school to admit him. The university failed to show that using sign-language interpreters would endanger patients, the court explained. **It granted the order, noting the student was likely to win the case and likely to suffer irreparable harm if the relief was denied.** The court also noted the balance of equities tipped in the student's favor and an injunction would serve the public interest. *Featherstone v. Pacific Northwest Univ. of Health Sciences*, No. 1:CV-14-3084-SMJ, 2014 WL 3640803 (E.D. Wash. 7/22/14).

◆    *A Wisconsin federal judge rejected a university's argument that a student's previous lawsuit refuted claims in her current suit – so the claims could proceed.*

The student was dismissed from a vocational rehabilitation graduate program when the university decided her cerebral palsy kept her from communicating effectively. She sued, alleging her dismissal was disability discrimination in violation of the ADA and the Rehabilitation Act. The university argued the doctrine of judicial estoppel applied. Under it, a party who won a prior lawsuit by saying one thing can't try to win a later suit by claiming the opposite is true. The student's prior suit was a negligence claim against the hospital that delivered her. The jury awarded $2 million for future lost earnings. The court weighed in, explaining, "The question in this case is not whether plaintiff's disability prevents her from obtaining a job, but whether it prevents her from completing a master's program." **In her prior suit, the student never claimed she couldn't pursue an education. And the jury didn't award the full lifetime amount for future lost earnings calculated by the expert.** That suggested it may have found the student could work to some extent. Finally, the jury was asked to determine the likelihood she'd be hired, not her ability to work if granted a reasonable accommodation, the court reasoned. Finding the student's claims weren't barred by the doctrine of judicial estoppel, the judge refused to grant the university judgment without a trial. *Busone v. Board of Regents of Univ. of Wisconsin System,* No. 12-cv-671-bbc, 2014 WL 2006717 (W.D.Wis. 5/16/14).

◆ *An Ohio federal judge refused to dismiss a student's disability discrimination claims against a university. The student was dismissed from an accelerated nursing program.*

The student filed a lawsuit claiming the school failed to accommodate her attention deficit hyperactivity disorder, in violation of the ADA and the Rehabilitation Act. The school asked the court to dismiss her claims, arguing she was required to exhaust administrative remedies before suing – but the cases they cited concerned the Individuals with Disabilities Act in Education's (IDEA's) rule that K-12 students must exhaust the IDEA's administrative remedies before suing in federal court. As **the IDEA doesn't apply to higher education students**, the court refused to dismiss the student's disability bias claim on this basis. *Buescher v. Baldwin Wallace Univ.*, No. 1:13 CV 2821, 2014 WL 1910907 (N.D. Ohio 5/12/14).

◆ *A federal appeals court rejected a student's claim that a Texas university failed to provide reasonable accommodations for her disability.*

A student had ADHD that was controlled with medication. She got a C- on her first test and asked for two exam accommodations: extra time and a distraction-free environment. The university granted both. Despite the accommodations, she earned a C for the class. The grades were based on five exams. Claiming a university doctor refused to refill her prescription after she took the first three tests, she asked to retake the exams. The department said no – as her lowest grade was earned while she on medication. The student failed a class the following semester and was expelled from the program. She sued, claiming the university violated the Americans with Disabilities Act by not providing reasonable accommodations. The court granted the university judgment, as the **evidence showed the student was granted accommodations and earned higher grades when she wasn't taking medication. Also, the reason she was expelled had no connection to her disability.** *Maples v. Univ. of Texas Medical Branch at Galveston*, 524 Fed.Appx. 93 (5th Cir. 2013).

◆ *A student who was expelled from a nursing program was not an "employee" under the California Fair Employment and Housing Act (FEHA).*

A student enrolled in a graduate nursing program and requested accommodations for her learning disability. The university's Student Disability Services office suggested accommodations. But one instructor wouldn't allow them, according to the student. She also alleged she was harassed and belittled by the instructor. She failed the course. The following year, she failed another course, and the university expelled her from the program. She sued to challenge the expulsion, claiming the school violated the FEHA, which prohibits employment discrimination. Defendants argued the student wasn't an "employee" so couldn't sue under FEHA. She asked the judge to find she was an employee as a matter of law. The judge refused, saying the murky law doesn't clearly define what constitutes an employee. Instead, the court looked at the Title VII standard to determine whether the student was an employee. **To qualify as an employee under Title VII, the student had to receive remuneration.** That wasn't the case here, as the student's only compensation was training plus credits for her degree. So the claim failed. *Avalos v. Univ. of San Francisco*, No. C 12-5290 RS, 2013 WL 1390406 (N.D. Cal. 4/4/13).

◆ *No legal violation occurred when a Kentucky college dismissed a student with a medical disability who failed to maintain minimum grade requirements for the program.*

A student suffered from a medical disability relating to cirrhosis of the liver. He was frequently absent, and the school accommodated his medical absences by letting him take make-up classes. Still, he couldn't keep up the required grades and course completion requirements, so the school dismissed him from the program. He sued, claiming its decision to expel him amounted to a violation of the Americans with Disabilities Act. **But the evidence showed the school provided reasonable accommodations** and its decision to expel the student was for "legitimate, non-discriminatory reasons." So the claim failed. *Hawkins v. Brown Mackie College/Louisville*, No. 3:11-CV-00679-H, 2013 WL 1703749 (W.D. Ky. 4/19/13).

◆ *A Georgia federal court ruled a university did not break the law when it asked a student with a hernia to provide a medical letter saying he could safely complete the clinical portion of the school's nursing program.*

After a student with a hernia entered the university's nursing program, an associate professor expressed concern about the student's ability to safely lift patients in clinicals. The school asked the student to provide a letter from his doctor saying he could. In response, the student told the school to "back off," saying if the "girls" – meaning his peers – could lift patients, then he could, too. The school repeated its request for medical clearance and set a deadline for the letter. The student missed the deadline. Six days later, the school met with the student. It told him the letter must be submitted immediately and scolded him for his disrespectful behavior toward females. He provided the letter from the doctor and was allowed to return. He continued to refer to the women he worked with as "girls." By that time, he'd already missed a clinical. A committee denied his request to excuse the absence, and he failed the course. The student was later dismissed for failing the course and treating female colleagues disrespectfully. He sued, claiming the school violated Section 504 of the Rehabilitation Act and Title II of the Americans with Disabilities Act by requiring him to produce the letter. The court granted the school judgment, explaining it had a legitimate reason to request the letter. **It pointed out that the student wasn't denied**

**participation in the program. The school merely delayed his participation until he complied with the school's reasonable request.** So the claim could not move forward. *Yancy v. Board of Regents of the Univ. System of Georgia,* No. 4:11-cv-34 (CDL), 2013 WL 3549767 (M.D. Ga. 7/11/13).

◆ *Finding no evidence that a law school refused to grant a former student accommodations or retaliated against him for requesting them, a California federal judge granted school judgment without a trial.*

The Abraham Lincoln University School of Law (ALU) is a private, for-profit school. Students must take and pass the First-Year Law School Students' Examination (FYLSX) at the end of their first year of law school. An ALU law student suffered from attention deficit hyperactivity disorder, narcissistic personality disorder and a physical disability. He often asked for test accommodations, such as extra time, a different test day and/or having tests re-graded. ALU granted the accommodations. In February 2008, he asked for accommodations when taking the FYLSX. The state committee granted his accommodation requests – except one that asked for an extra hour for every three-hour exam. The student took the FYLSX in June and October of 2008 and in June 2009. He received accommodations each time but failed all three attempts. Under the Guidelines for Unaccredited Law School Rules, students who fail the FYLSX three times must be disqualified from the school's Juris Doctor program. In October 2009, the student was notified that he was dismissed. He sued ALU, claiming it violated the Americans with Disabilities Act and retaliated against him for requesting accommodations. **But the opposite was true: The school granted many accommodations the student requested.** Finding no evidence to support his claims, the court dismissed the case. *Shapiro v. Abraham Lincoln Univ. School of Law,* No. CV-10-03177-JGB (FMOx), 2013 WL 4197098 (C.D. Cal. 8/12/13).

◆ *Since a student failed to prove she'd been denied an accommodation, a Maryland federal judge granted the college summary judgment.*

The professor of a public speaking class had a dress code policy that prohibited jeans, hats, tennis shoes, sweats, work uniforms and military fatigues. Students were told they'd have their grades lowered if they violated the dress code. Years earlier, one student suffered an injury that required her ankle to be fused. As a result, she had to wear tennis shoes or diabetic shoes. When she asked for an accommodation to allow her to wear tennis shoes, the professor allegedly denied her request. The student wore tennis shoes anyway. She got a "D" in the class. She filed suit, claiming the school violated the ADA and the Rehabilitation Act by refusing to grant her an accommodation. As part of pretrial discovery, the professor testified 20 points were originally deducted from the student's grades for violating the dress code, but **those points were given back after school administrators said the student had a documented disability. The professor's final, itemized grade sheet showed the student's grade was not lowered due to dress code violations.** Since the school's documentation showed the student was given the grade she earned, the court granted it pretrial judgment. *Benton v. Prince George's Community College,* No. DKC 12-1577, 2013 WL 4501324 (D. Md. 8/21/13).

◆ *The U.S. Court of Appeals for the Eighth Circuit found an Arkansas university was not required to accommodate a student's threatening behavior.*

The student was an undergraduate with Asperger's Syndrome. In October of 2007, the student cursed and ranted in a dormitory. A month later, he had two similar incidents in school treasurer's office and another in the school health center, where he threatened "there could be another Virginia Tech incident." The school put him on interim suspension. As he was escorted off campus, he threatened suicide and made additional threatening remarks about "another Virginia Tech" incident. In 2009, the student was denied re-enrollment after a mental health professional indicated it wasn't safe for him to return to campus. In 2010, the student sent a threatening email to the school chancellor, demanding to be allowed to re-enroll. Then he sued, claiming the school violated Section 504 of the Rehabilitation Act by failing to accommodate his disability. The district court ruled against him. On appeal, the U.S. Court of Appeals for the Eighth Circuit upheld the district's decision. The student was suspended for engaging in violent and threatening behavior. Accommodating him would not have been reasonable, the appeals court explained. Instead, **allowing the behavior to continue would have placed an undue hardship on the school with respect to its efforts to keep its campus safe**. *Stebbins v. Univ. of Arkansas,* 543 Fed.Appx. 616 (8th Cir. 2013).

◆ *A Massachusetts college did not reasonably accommodate a disabled student by offering to reimburse her rental costs for campus housing.*

The student had depression and attention deficit disorder. Due to problems with her roommate, she asked the college to either give her a single room or remove the roommate. The college denied the request and offered the student a new roommate or a room that was a converted study lounge. She declined both options and moved off campus. As requested by the student, the college reimbursed her for the rent she had paid in advance. In a federal lawsuit, she claimed the college violated federal law by denying her requests for accommodation, failing to engage in an interactive process and discriminating against her based on a mental disability. The court refused to dismiss the accommodation claim. Whether the reimbursement was a reasonable accommodation could not be resolved via a pretrial dismissal motion.

But the court found **the college engaged in the interactive process contemplated by federal law by attempting to mediate the student's problems with her roommate**. It also provided her temporary, single housing while it considered her accommodation request. As a result, the court dismissed the claim of failure to engage in an interactive process. As nothing indicated the student's accommodation request would have been handled differently had she been physically disabled, the court dismissed the claim for discrimination based on a mental disability. *Blankmeyer v. Stonehill College*, No. 12-1-378-RWZ, 2012 WL 5378721 (D. Mass. 11/2/12).

◆ *A Florida university did not unlawfully fail to provide disability-related accommodations to a law school student with post-traumatic stress disorder.*

When the student's GPA slipped below 2.0 on a four-point scale, the university placed her on academic probation. She met with an assistant dean to ask for accommodations and informed the university for the first time that she had post-traumatic stress disorder and frequent panic attacks. The dean granted the student's request for some accommodations, but she was denied extended breaks during exams. When the semester ended, her GPA was under 2.0. An academic standing committee decided the student could not remain in the law school, and she sued the university in a federal district court for violating the ADA and Section 504. The court found the law school reasonably accommodated her requests while preserving the integrity of its testing practices. On appeal, the U.S. Court of Appeals, Eleventh Circuit, found that the law school had reasonably accommodated the student's disability.

While the student claimed a right to a private testing room, she did not produce evidence showing her disability made this necessary. Also, she had never previously raised this argument. **In the court's view, there was insufficient evidence to support a claim that her academic unfitness was a pretext for disability discrimination**, and the university was awarded judgment. *Forbes v. St. Thomas Univ.*, 456 Fed.Appx. 809 (11th Cir. 2012).

◆ *A Wisconsin student was unable to convince a federal court that Carroll University violated the law by failing to accommodate her learning disorders.*

After completing one semester in a physical therapy program, the student was diagnosed with ADD. The university allowed her extra time for tests and quizzes and separate testing rooms. But the university denied the student's request for a tutor. She had continuing problems finding classmates to work with her. When an academic advisor intervened, it was learned that classmates believed the student monopolized faculty time, was sarcastic and did not contribute to a group project. After the student had a confrontation with a classmate and her GPA slipped below 3.0, she was dismissed from the program. In a federal court, the student sued the university, claiming it did not reasonably accommodate her and did not stop classmates from harassing her.

**The court held the university was not required to provide a tutor, as this was a service of a personal nature that Section 504 does not require.** There was no failure to accommodate the student by refusing to allow her to reschedule exams and quizzes. No evidence indicated her inability to find a partner was disability-related. A claim regarding failure to provide help with time-management, organizational, communication and study skills was rejected because there was no evidence that the student ever asked for such help. The claim that the university failed to take reasonable steps to stop peer harassment failed because there was no evidence that it was based on her disability. As a result, the court awarded judgment to the university. *Carlson v. Carroll Univ.*, No. 09-C-551, 2011 WL 5921445 (E.D. Wis. 11/28/11).

◆ *A Kansas community college student with multiple sclerosis could not proceed with his claim that the college negligently hired an instructor.*

According to the student, one of his instructors grabbed a computer mouse from him and squeezed his neck "with considerable force." The student filed a federal district court lawsuit against the college and instructor for violating the ADA. He said the college illegally denied his request for accommodations and added claims of negligent hiring, retention and supervision. According to the student, the instructor had been convicted of assault before the college hired him. As for the student's claim that he was denied accommodations for his disability, the court found he did not specify what type of assistance he asked for. He also failed to show he was denied services, programs or activities. Instead, the facts showed that the student was provided access to class and given information about parking for people with disabilities. Since Title II of the ADA applies only to entities, no viable claim existed against the instructor.

No facts suggested how the college failed to accommodate the student's disability. But the court allowed him additional time to amend his complaint in order to state his claim with greater specificity. Therefore, it denied the college's motion to dismiss the ADA Title II claim. It also refused to dismiss a claim of outrage against the instructor. **The college had no duty to uncover the instructor's criminal history**, defeating the claims for negligent hiring, supervision and retention. *Jacobson v. Johnson County Community College*, No. 110cv-2132-JAR-JPO, 2011 WL 4971422 (D. Kan. 10/19/11).

◆    *Indiana University did not violate federal law by dismissing a student from a social work program for failure to complete a practicum requirement.*

The student tried to complete her practicum at four different agencies, but none of them worked out. One of the agencies terminated her placement because she allowed patients and staff members to push her wheelchair. As a result of her inability to complete the practicum requirement, the student was removed from the School of Social Work. She sued the university in federal court, which held for the university. On appeal to the U.S. Court of Appeals, Seventh Circuit, the student argued she could have completed the practicum requirement with a home-based modification she had proposed. The court rejected this argument. **Federal disability laws require educational institutions to reasonably accommodate students with disabilities, but they need not make any modification that would result in a fundamental alteration to the program.** The practicum required students to interact directly with other professionals, and the court found the student would be unable to meet this requirement through her proposed accommodation. There was no merit to the retaliation claim, because the failing grade was assigned before the student filed her initial complaint. As a result, the judgment was affirmed. *Klene v. Trustees of Indiana Univ.*, 413 Fed.Appx. 919 (7th Cir. 2011).

◆    *A Virginia federal court dismissed a disability discrimination lawsuit filed by an unsuccessful medical school applicant.*

The student's undergraduate grades and MCAT test score were far below the median grades and scores for students accepted by Virginia Commonwealth University (VCU) School of Medicine. He unsuccessfully applied to the medical school four times. VCU declined his request for accommodations such as adjustment of his grades and test scores, and he sued VCU in a federal district court for disability discrimination. The court found the student could not show he was "otherwise qualified" as defined by federal law. VCU did not violate its legal duty to grant the student reasonable accommodations. His requests were unreasonable. **VCU was not required to lower its academic standards by adjusting his GPA or disregarding his MCAT scores.** The court held for VCU because there was no disability discrimination and VCU had no duty to grant the accommodations sought. *Manickavasagar v. Virginia Comwlth. Univ. School of Medicine*, 667 F.Supp.2d 635 (E.D. Va. 2010).

◆  *Since a Maryland college had a legitimate reason to dismiss a doctoral candidate, it did not violate the Americans with Disabilities Act.*

Although the student had excellent grades, faculty members were concerned that he lacked "awareness of [his] impact on others" and did not recognize "power differentials." He was accepted for a teaching internship at a Montana university. In his first semester there, he asked out an undergraduate in his class, in violation of a college handbook. The undergraduate later told her professor she was afraid to come to class because of the student. Loyola dismissed the student, and he sued Loyola in a federal court for disability discrimination. **The court held that even if he had a disability, there was no evidence that his ability to learn was substantially limited as compared to the average person.** He performed well academically both before and after he was diagnosed with ADHD. The student had twice denied in writing that he was disabled. The court dismissed the case. *Herzog v. Loyola College in Maryland, Inc.*, No. RDB-07-02416, 2009 WL 3271246 (D. Md. 10/9/09).

◆  *The U.S. Supreme Court held that institutions do not have to make accommodations that fundamentally alter the nature of the programs offered.*

A nursing school applicant with severe hearing impairments claimed she was denied admission in violation of Section 504. The school explained the hearing disability made it unsafe for the applicant to practice as a registered nurse. Even with a hearing aid, she had to rely on her lip-reading skills, and patient safety demanded the ability to understand speech without reliance on lip-reading. Agreeing with the nursing school, **the Supreme Court held the term "otherwise qualified individual with a disability" means an individual who is qualified in spite of his or her disability**. While an institution may need to make minor curricular modifications to accommodate a disability, the applicant was able to take only academic courses. **No accommodations were required since clinical study would be foreclosed due to patient safety concerns.** The Court held Section 504 did not require a major curricular modification such as allowing the applicant to bypass clinical study. The denial of admission was upheld. *Southeastern Community College v. Davis*, 442 U.S. 397, 99 S.Ct. 2361, 60 L.Ed.2d 980 (1979).

## C.  Liability Issues

*Compensatory damages may be awarded in failure-to-accommodate cases if the institution acts knowingly, voluntarily, and deliberately in violation of an individual's rights. A Maryland federal court held that ADA claimants who alleged an unlawful failure to accommodate a disability could recover damages if they showed an institution acted with "deliberate indifference."*

◆  *An Ohio federal court held a housing discrimination case filed by the federal government on behalf of a student with disabilities could proceed.*

The U.S. Department of Justice (DOJ) filed suit against the college after a student filed a complaint that he wasn't allowed to move into campus housing with a service dog trained to alleviate symptoms of his disability. The DOJ's suit alleged the university violated the federal Fair Housing Act (FHA). The suit sought damages. The university asked for immunity, saying there was no controlling authority that placed them on notice that the FHA applies to student housing. The court looked to the language of the statute and noted that the FHA makes it unlawful to discriminate in the sale or rental of a "dwelling" based on disability. The statute defines "dwelling" broadly to include "any building, structure, or portion thereof which is occupied, or designed or intended for occupancy as, a residence by one or more families." In addition, the court said **applicable regulations – issued in 1989 – specifically indicate that dorms are dwelling units under the statute**. The plain language of the FHA makes the statute applicable to student housing, the court said. The defendants weren't entitled to immunity, so the case had to proceed. *United States v. Kent State Univ.*, No. 5:14CV1992, 2015 WL 5522132 (N.D. Ohio 9/16/15).

◆   *A federal appeals court revived a prospective graduate student's claim that her application was rejected because she has Crohn's disease.*

The student had the highest GPA in the applicant pool, and her GRE scores exceeded school requirements. During interviews, two professors asked detailed questions about the student's medical condition. The applicant received a vague rejection letter. She called the school to get more information and was told she "wasn't a good fit." She sued, alleging her application was rejected due to her Crohn's disease, in violation of the Rehabilitation Act and Title II of the Americans with Disabilities Act. The district court granted judgment to the school. On appeal, the Sixth Circuit reversed, saying **a reasonable jury could find the proffered reason was merely a pretext for unlawful bias**. The case was remanded. *Sjostrand v. Ohio State Univ.*, 750 F.3d 596 (6th Cir. 2014).

◆   *Finding a key piece of evidence had been excluded by a lower court, a federal appeals court reinstated a Nebraska medical student's claims.*

After the university denied the student's requests for interpreters, he sought a federal court order that would allow him to use interpreters and require the university to pay for them. The court denied the request, noting that both the ADA and Section 504 only required an institution to do what was "necessary" to avoid discrimination. In this case, the student did not establish the accommodations he requested were necessary. The court cited Supreme Court cases advising courts to "show great respect for the faculty's professional judgment" when an "accommodation involves an academic decision." As the accommodations were unnecessary, the court held for the university. On appeal, the U.S. Court of Appeals, Eighth Circuit, explained that **an individual with a disability is in the best position to decide what accommodations will be effective**. As the student's statement was supported by independent corroborating evidence, the court found the lower court had wrongfully excluded it. As the district court erred by allowing pretrial judgment, the decision was reversed, and the case was returned to the lower court. *Argenyi v. Creighton Univ.*, 703 F.3d 441 (8th Cir. 2013).

◆ *A Louisiana court held a state university violated the ADA by failing to provide adequate restroom access in the student union. An attorneys' fee award for the prevailing students was upheld by the state's highest court.*

A student had difficulty entering a restroom in the student union because the doorway was too narrow for her wheelchair. After a struggle, she was able to enter, but she urinated on herself and was hurt while trying to exit. The student sued the university in a state court for violating the ADA and state law. Rejecting the university's defenses, the court held the student was entitled to ADA protection and found the university had discriminated against her. On appeal, the Court of Appeal of Louisiana found **the university admitted the restroom door was too narrow. It had unlawfully discriminated against the student by not complying with applicable access requirements.** Moreover, providing wheelchair access would not have created an undue financial burden.

In 2007, the student was awarded judgment. After the university agreed to bring itself into compliance with accessibility requirements, more than a year passed without the creation of an accommodation plan. When the plan was finally done, it addressed about 15,000 access problems on campus. The students then sought their attorneys' fees, costs and expenses. The court held in their favor but reduced the requested number of billable hours by 20%, set an hourly rate of $240, and declined to enhance the award as requested. The state court of appeal amended the award by increasing the number of billable hours to the amount requested and setting the hourly rate at $265. It further enhanced the fee award, finding the case was "rare and exceptional" based on the results achieved and the protracted and highly contested shape of the litigation. When the case reached the state supreme court, it found no abuse of discretion by the trial court and reinstated the lower court's judgment. *Covington v. McNeese State Univ.*, 118 So.3d 343 (La. 2013).

◆ *A federal court held an Ohio student could proceed with her claim that a school violated the ADA by failing to provide her effective tutoring services.*

The student had epilepsy, attention deficit hyperactivity disorder, anxiety and depression. She obtained an individual accommodation plan from the university's accessibility office that granted accommodations such as tutoring, drinks in the classroom, use of a tape recorder and extended test time. But when the student took a test, her professor was unaware of the plan. She later claimed a tutoring session was ineffective, and she failed the course. When the university dismissed her from the program, the student filed an ADA complaint in a federal district court, claiming that she was denied effective tutoring. The court issued a temporary restraining order directing the university to reinstate the student. In later proceedings, it considered a request to extend the order. While the court found support for the argument that post-secondary institutions do not have to offer tutoring to accommodate students with disabilities, there was also support for the idea that **institutions must provide tutoring services if they are provided to the general student population**. The university in this case maintained such a policy. Since the student showed she would be irreparably harmed if the extension was not granted, the court extended the temporary order. *Sellers v. Univ. of Rio Grande*, 838 F.Supp.2d 677 (S.D. Ohio 2012).

◆   *A federal court held a Maryland college had to provide accommodations for a disabled student who needed help getting to class when a construction project temporarily blocked access to parking for persons with disabilities.*

According to a student, security staff refused to transport her to her car during the construction project, as promised by the college dean. She fell and hurt herself while leaving campus and later sued the college and its officials in a federal court for ADA violations. The court held that the student alleged facts sufficient to support a claim of unlawful failure to accommodate. **The college had a duty to accommodate students with disabilities, even if the temporary lack of accessible parking was not a separate violation of law.** The court held the student could proceed with her compensatory damage claims. It found claimants who allege an unlawful failure to accommodate a disability can recover damages if they show the institution acted with "deliberate indifference." This required showing the institution acted "knowingly, voluntarily, and deliberately." Since the student met this standard, her damage claims could go forward. *Adams v. Montgomery College (Rockville)*, 834 F.Supp.2d 386 (D. Md. 2011).

◆   *A federal court refused to order an Ohio law school to reinstate an expelled student until his lawsuit over the dismissal was decided.*

In a federal district court action, the student claimed the law school failed to reasonably accommodate him by giving him only half the extra exam time his doctor recommended, denying him another semester to pull up his GPA, and imposing an arbitrary cumulative 2.0 GPA requirement. He asked the court to order the school to reinstate him pending the resolution of his lawsuit. It refused. To receive a preliminary injunction, the student had to show he was likely to win his case. **The court found the expulsion decision was entitled to deference. It appeared the cause behind the student's dismissal was his lack of effort – not any failure to provide him reasonable accommodations.** The court found this conclusion was backed up by the fact that he got higher grades on the exams he took without accommodations. *Oser v. Capital Univ. Law School*, No. 2:09-cv-709, 2009 WL 2913919 (S.D. Ohio 9/8/09).

◆   *The U.S. Supreme Court held a university should receive a final ruling on whether it had to pay the costs of a deaf student's interpreter.*

A deaf graduate student at a Texas university requested a sign-language interpreter. The university refused to pay for an interpreter because he did not meet university financial assistance guidelines. The student sued the university in a federal district court under Section 504. He sought an order requiring the appointment of an interpreter at the university's expense for as long as he remained there. The court granted his request for a preliminary order requiring the university to pay for the interpreter. The university appealed to the U.S. Court of Appeals, Fifth Circuit, which affirmed the preliminary order but vacated the stay pending administrative action. The university complied with the order by paying for the interpreter.

The student completed his graduate program. The U.S. Supreme Court granted review to address the university's argument that the lower courts should make a final ruling on who was to pay for the interpreter. The student argued that the case was now moot in view of his graduation. **The Court vacated the appeals court's decision and remanded the case for a trial to allow the university a full opportunity to argue for recoupment of its payments for the interpreter.** *Univ. of Texas v. Camenisch*, 451 U.S. 390, 101 S.Ct. 1830, 68 L.Ed.2d 175 (1981).

◆ *A student obtained a federal court order requiring a California community college district to improve its campus wheelchair access.*

According to the student, he was encountering multiple barriers to the use of his wheelchair every day on campus. He sought a court order to require the district to comply with ADA Title II access requirements. The court entered a permanent order requiring the community college district to make several improvements, including accessible desks and workstations in all classrooms. It ordered the district to hire an access expert, approved by the student, to oversee placement of accessible desks and workstations. **The district was banned from charging students with disabilities fees for accommodations such as parking spaces or elevator keys.** It was further required to establish a schedule for a wheelchair-accessible shuttle to take students with disabilities to areas of the campus that lacked accessible paths of travel. An access expert was to oversee the removal of physical access barriers and submit status reports on barrier removal every three months. The district was also required to publicize its modified policies relating to access in written materials, and to make those materials available to students with disabilities at student orientations. *Huezo v. Los Angeles Community College Dist.*, No. CV 04-09772 MMM (JWJx), 2008 WL 4184659 (C.D. Cal. 9/9/08).

◆ *A federal court in Nebraska restated the rule that employees and administrators are not individually liable for violations of federal laws protecting disabled individuals, since they do not "operate" an institution.*

The court noted that other federal courts have held **university employees and administrators do not "operate" a university in a way that exposes them to liability under the Americans with Disabilities Act and the Rehabilitation Act.** The student did not allege facts to support his claim for intentional infliction of emotional distress. He did not show intentional or reckless conduct that was so outrageous and extreme as to go beyond all possible bounds of decency. *White v. Creighton Univ.*, No. 8:06 CV 536, 2006 WL 3419782 (D. Neb. 11/27/06).

The court later granted the university's motion for pretrial judgment, finding no evidence to counter the university's explanation that the student was dismissed due to his academic performance. *White v. Creighton Univ.*, No. 06CV536, 2008 WL 64692 (D. Neb. 1/3/08).

◆ *The non-disabled parent of a disabled student could sue a university under Section 504 to vindicate her rights.*

A job applicant sued the University of Missouri in a federal district court, alleging it did not hire her due to her son's disability. The university argued Section 504 did not allow the applicant to claim discrimination on the basis of another person's disability. But the court held Section 504 extends to all persons aggrieved by violations. **Courts have held individuals and entities who are injured by discrimination on the basis of a disability may sue under Section 504, even though they are not themselves disabled.** Congress intended to prohibit discrimination against any disabled individual who would benefit from a federally funded program or activity. *Feurer v. Curators of Univ. of Missouri*, No. 4:06CV750 HEA, 2006 WL 2385260 (E.D. Mo. 9/17/06).

## II.  SEX DISCRIMINATION AND HARASSMENT

*Title IX of the Education Amendments of 1972 prohibits recipients of federal funding from denying program participation or benefits based on gender. States have enacted their own laws prohibiting discrimination on the basis of gender to comply with federal law. If a public institution is involved, students may attach equal protection claims to discrimination complaints.*

### A.  Discrimination

◆   *An Ohio federal judge dismissed the gender discrimination claims of two former students who were accused of sexual assault.*

In the same month, two male students were accused of sexually assaulting female students in separate incidents. The first man was found responsible and suspended for three years. The second was also found responsible. But rather than suspension, he was placed on academic probation and required to write a seven-page research paper. He was allowed to graduate. They filed a Title IX suit against the university, alleging it was biased against men and that the panel was predisposed to find them responsible for sexual assault. The court found the Title IX claims failed because the former students didn't show gender bias was behind the panels' decisions against them. The judge found, "At worst [the university's] actions were biased in favor of alleged victims of sexual assault and against students accused of sexual assault. However, that is **not the same as gender bias because sexual assault victims can be either male or female**." The claims were dismissed. *Doe v. Univ. of Cincinnati*, No. 1:15-CV-681, 2016 WL 1161935 (S.D. Ohio 3/23/16).

◆   *An Indiana federal judge refused to dismiss a student's Title IX claim after the university refused to share evidence against him with his attorneys.*

A student was put on interim suspension and evicted from his dorm after he was accused of sexual misconduct. Early in the investigation, he told the assistant director of student conduct that he'd been sexually assaulted by a female student (not the woman who brought the sexual misconduct charge against him). He said the university investigated a female student's claim against him, but not his claim against a woman student. The university let the student and his attorneys look at the evidence against him but not photograph it or have a copy. It also gave a list of witnesses against him but didn't let the student contact them. After a hearing, the panel found the guilty of personal misconduct. He was expelled. When the student's appeal was denied, he filed a Title IX suit alleging facts that raised an inference that the university discriminated against him because of his sex. He claimed he was harshly investigated and disciplined for an alleged sexual assault, but the university refused to even investigate when he made the same claim against a female student. The university wanted the court to dismiss the claim because the student hadn't alleged "more particularized facts," but **the court noted the defendants were in "sole possession" of those particularized facts – "notably refusing, at all times, to share such information with [the student] or his attorneys."** So the claim had to proceed. *Marshall v. Indiana Univ.*, No. 1:15-cv-00726-TWP-DKL, 2016 WL 1028362 (S.D. Ind. 3/15/16).

◆ *The Sixth Circuit upheld an $850,000 jury award to a former graduate student who claimed a Michigan university discriminated against her based on her pregnancy – and then retaliated against her after she complained.*

The student was enrolled in a social work graduate program, which included class time and field work. She became pregnant before her field placement at a Salvation Army center, which was described as "an all-male rehabilitation center for ex-convicts, drug addicts, etc.," in court records. The field instructor admitted she told the student to stop "rubbing her belly" and to wear looser clothing because men at the facility were "turned on by her pregnancy." The student accused the instructor of pregnancy discrimination. In a meeting, the student said she was scolded for complaining about pregnancy bias and told not to discuss it with the dean. Then the field instructor failed the student, which blocked her from completing the program. She sued, claiming pregnancy discrimination and retaliation. A jury ruled in her favor, awarding $850,000 in damages. The defendants filed an appeal, and the Sixth Circuit affirmed. The award did not shock the conscience. Instead, **the evidence showed that the defendants deprived the student of working in her chosen field and caused her emotional harm**. The ruling was affirmed. *Varlesi v. Wayne State Univ.*, No. 14-1862, 2016 WL 860326 (6th Cir. 3/7/16).

◆ *A Maryland federal court allowed two male students who were disciplined for alleged sexual misconduct to proceed with claims against a university.*

The day after a college house party, a female student who attended accused two male students of sexually assaulting her. She reported it to police, but medical tests didn't provide evidence of a sexual assault. The girl apologized to both men. Nonetheless, the school concluded the two students were responsible for engaging in non-consensual contact with the female. They appealed to no avail. So they sued, asserting several claims. The court dismissed most, but it **allowed the plaintiffs' Title IX claim that the school's decision to discipline them was an erroneous outcome that was motivated by gender bias**. The plaintiffs alleged that the disciplinary proceedings against them were marred by procedural defects, and they might be able to prove that gender was a motivating factor in the school's allegedly flawed procedures and conclusions. The court allowed the Title IX claim to proceed. *Doe v. Salisbury Univ.*, 123 F.Supp.3d 748 (D. Md. 2015).

◆ *A university may have retaliated against a student after he filed a Title IX complaint about the way the school handled a claim against him, so a Maryland federal judge said the case could move forward.*

After the student was suspended for a conduct violation, he filed a Title IX complaint against the university to challenge the way it handled the investigation. Two years later, the student was eligible to reapply if he completed specific prerequisites. He was working on completing them when the university notified him that it had found an earlier sexual assault accusation that had never been investigated. If the university found the accusations were true, it would find the student had violated the sexual misconduct policy. The student informed the school that he would not be returning. He sued, alleging several claims. The court found one – a Title IX retaliation claim – could move forward. The student stated a valid *prima facie* claim by showing he engaged in a protected activity (filing the Title IX complaint against the university), suffered an adverse action (being investigated for an earlier complaint), and **showed a connection between the two (showing the university had been aware of the incident, but didn't act until after the student filed the complaint)**. That was enough to move the case forward, the court held. *Doe v. Salisbury Univ.*, 107 F.Supp.3d 481 (D. Md. 2015).

◆    *An Ohio federal court dismissed Title IX claims filed by a male student who was dismissed after being accused of sexual assault.*

A female student reported that the male student sexually assaulted her. The school conducted disciplinary proceedings and dismissed the accused student. He sued, claiming the university discriminated against him on the basis of gender during the disciplinary proceedings in violation of Title IX. He alleged that the Title IX investigator was also a part-time member of the school police department and served on its task force to prevent sexual assault. The student said the Title IX investigator should have disclosed her positions. The school filed a motion to dismiss. The court dismissed the claim, saying it essentially alleged the Title IX coordinator was biased against the student because she served multiple roles in the school's investigation. **But there was nothing to suggest that the Title IX coordinator would have treated a female suspected of sexual assault any differently**, the court explained. The allegations didn't support an inference of gender bias against the student in connection with the disciplinary proceedings that led to his dismissal, the court concluded. As a result, the defense motion for dismissal was granted. *Sahm v. Miami Univ.*, 110 F.Supp.3d 774 (S.D. Ohio 2015).

◆    *A federal court in Massachusetts rejected a male student's claim that a university's handling of a sexual misconduct investigation violated Title IX.*

The student met a girl at an on-campus party. After drinking, the two left and had sex in the girl's dorm room. The next morning, the female student said she didn't remember what happened. She went to the university health center and filed a report with the dean. The university charged the male with code of conduct violations. After a hearing, the board expelled him. His appeal was denied, and he sought judicial review. He claimed the school violated Title IX by applying disciplinary guidelines and regulations to him in a discriminatory manner on the basis of his sex. But his claim failed as **he did not allege facts showing male and female students accused of sexual harassment were treated differently**. The claim was dismissed. *Doe v. Univ. of Massachusetts-Amherst*, No. 14-30143-MGM, 2015 WL 4306521 (D. Mass. 7/14/15).

◆   *A student who alleged she was sexually harassed by a professor stated a valid* prima facie *Title IX claim, a Mississippi federal court held.*

The student complained to university officials that the professor grabbed her rear end and tried to kiss her. She also filed a complaint with the university police department and the county police. HR investigated and concluded the professor "may have put himself in a compromising position" but determined it could not conclude the professor "severely and pervasively harassed the student based on sex." The student was removed from the professor's class for the remainder of the semester. But she was assigned to the professor's class the following semester – even though she objected. The student filed suit, alleging the university and the professor violated her rights under Title IX. The university filed a motion for pretrial judgment. The U.S. Supreme Court has held that sexual harassment of a student by a teacher is a form of discrimination for purposes of Title IX. The court explained that even one incident may be sufficient to create liability if it is sufficiently severe. The court decided that the touching of an intimate body part can constitute severe sexual harassment and that such conduct is physically threatening and humiliating. In addition, the conduct deprives the victim of educational opportunities. The court also questioned the school's decision to return the student to the professor's class for two reasons. It already determined the professor had placed himself in a "compromising position," and the student strongly objected to taking his class. Finding that genuine issues of material fact existed, the court denied the university's motion for pretrial judgment. *Matthews v. Nwankwo,* 36 F.Supp.3d 718 (N.D. Miss. 2014).

◆   *The Eleventh Circuit held a Georgia medical college did not discriminate against a male applicant who was rejected for enrollment five times.*

After being denied admission to the Medical College of Georgia (MCG) five times, the applicant sued MCG in a federal court for denial of due process, gender discrimination and retaliation. A federal court dismissed the case, and the applicant appealed. Before the Eleventh Circuit Court of Appeals, he asserted a fundamental right to purchase a medical school education. The court held there is no fundamental right to public education, let alone a fundamental right to a public medical school education. The court rejected the argument that MCG discriminated against men in violation of Title IX by applying undergraduate math grades toward the minimum grade average required for admission. Although he claimed MCG retaliated against him for asking it to review his fourth rejection, **the court found a strong and reasonable inference that MCG denied his application because he was unqualified**. The court held the case had been properly dismissed. *Bowers v. Board of Regents of the Univ. System of Georgia,* 509 Fed.Appx. 906 (11th Cir. 2013).

◆   *A New York police academy student was allowed to pursue some of her discrimination claims against a community college.*

Soon after beginning the program, the student complained about unequal treatment based on gender. She said the college responded by dismissing her from the academy. After an internal appeal failed, the student filed two administrative charges with the state human rights division. She asserted gender discrimination and retaliation against the community college for providing negative, false and misleading information to prospective employers.

After the human rights division consolidated the complaints, the college agreed to pay the student $1,000 in settlement of her claims. It also agreed to provide her positive references. The student later claimed the college violated the settlement agreement by continuing to provide prospective employers negative references. She sued the college in a federal district court for gender discrimination, retaliation and constitutional rights violations. The court held the settlement did not bar the action. It rejected the college's argument that her Title IX discrimination and retaliation claims failed because she no longer had a "direct, educational relationship" with it. **The court held the lack of a current relationship with the college did not bar her claims based on negative references.** A valid preliminary claim for retaliation could be based on the negative references. As the college was a state actor, the court refused to dismiss the constitutional claims. *Jordan v. Corning Community College*, No. 11-CV-6182, 2011 WL 4402752 (W.D.N.Y. 9/22/11).

◆   *A Massachusetts appeals court held that state law required the National Board of Medical Examiners (NBME) to provide extra time for a student to pump breast milk during a licensing examination.*

The student was the mother of a four-month-old. The NBME balked when she asked for an extra 60 minutes of break time per test day so she could pump breast milk. It offered alternative accommodations, including permission to pump breast milk in a private room during the allocated break time. The student rejected the alternatives and sued the board in a state court, which denied her request for preliminary relief. On appeal, the state court of appeals recited evidence that a nursing mother of a four-month-old infant should express breast milk at least every three hours and that the failure to do so can lead to medical problems. Nursing mothers required regular trips to the restroom because they consume additional calories and liquids to maintain an adequate milk supply.

Without more time, the student was at a significant disadvantage compared to her peers. **The NBME's test structure unfairly subjected breastfeeding women to greater hardships than other test-takers.** The court vacated the lower court's decision and entered an order requiring the NBME to grant the student an additional 60 minutes of break time per test day. The state's highest court affirmed the judgment without opinion. *Currier v. National Board of Medical Examiners*, 450 Mass. 1102, 875 N.E. 863 (Table) (Mass. 2007).

◆   *The Supreme Court held that a university for women could not justify a policy that denied men the opportunity to enroll for credit.*

The policy of the Mississippi University for Women, a state-supported university, was to limit its enrollment to women. The university denied otherwise qualified males the right to enroll for credit in its School of Nursing. A male who was denied admission sued in federal court claiming that the university violated the Fourteenth Amendment's Equal Protection Clause. The court agreed, and appeal reached the U.S. Supreme Court. The Court held **the university's discriminatory admission policy against men was not substantially and directly related to an important governmental objective**. The school argued that women enrolled in its School of Nursing would be adversely affected by the presence of men. However, the record showed that the nursing school allowed men to attend classes in the school as auditors, thus fatally undermining the school's claim that admission of men would adversely affect women students. The Court held the university's policy, which limited enrollment to women, violated the Equal Protection Clause. *Mississippi Univ. for Women v. Hogan*, 458 U.S. 718, 102 S.Ct. 3331, 73 L.Ed.2d 1090 (1982).

◆   *The U.S. Supreme Court held the categorical exclusion of women from the Virginia Military Institute (VMI) denied equal protection to women.*
        The U.S. Attorney General's office filed a complaint against the state of Virginia and VMI on behalf of a female high school student seeking admission to the state-affiliated, male-only college. A federal court found that because single-gender education conferred substantial benefits on students and preserved the unique military training offered at VMI, the exclusion of women did not violate the Equal Protection Clause. The case eventually reached the U.S. Supreme Court. It stated that parties seeking to defend gender-based government action must demonstrate an exceedingly persuasive justification that is genuine and not invented as a response to litigation.
        Virginia had failed to show an exceedingly persuasive justification for excluding women from VMI. There was evidence that some women would be able to participate at VMI, and the lower courts had improperly found that most women would not gain from the adversative method employed by the college. **The remedy proposed by Virginia left its exclusionary policy intact and afforded women no opportunity to experience the rigorous military training offered at VMI.** *U.S. v. Virginia*, 518 U.S. 515, 116 S.Ct. 2264, 135 L.Ed.2d 735 (1996).

## B. Harassment

### 1. Sexual Harassment by Employees

*Title IX liability standards for sexual harassment were established by the U.S. Supreme Court in* Franklin v. Gwinnett County Public Schools, *503 U.S. 60, 112 S.Ct. 1028, 117 L.Ed.2d 208 (1992),* Gebser v. Lago Vista Independent School Dist., *524 U.S. 274, 118 S.Ct. 1989, 141 L.Ed.2d 277 (1998), and* Davis v. Monroe County Board of Educ., *526 U.S. 629, 119 S.Ct. 1661, 143 L.Ed.2d 839 (1999). Title IX liability based on the conduct of an employee requires proof that an official with authority to take corrective action actually knew of the conduct, but remained deliberately indifferent to it. In addition, the student must show the harassment was so severe, pervasive and objectively offensive that it caused a deprivation of educational benefits. Since Title IX applies only to federal-funding recipients, there is no individual liability under the Act. For this reason, in* Krumlauf v. Benedictine Univ., *No. 09 C 7641, 2010 WL 3075745 (N.D. Ill. 8/4/10), a federal district court dismissed Title IX sexual harassment claims filed against an Illinois university instructor.*

◆   *Southern Illinois University responded to a student's harassment claims against a professor in a manner sufficient to avoid liability under federal law.*
        According to the student, the professor harassed him and improperly

touched him three different times. Upon his first report to the university, he said a supervisor discouraged any report because of the professor's status as a major donor to the university. Later, he said the department chair said the donor could not be held accountable for his actions. After the student changed his major, he lost his job at the university. A supervisor said the decision was motivated by his poor job performance. In a federal court action against the university, the student asserted Title VII and Title IX violations. The court held for the university, and appeal reached the U.S. Court of Appeals for the Seventh Circuit. It found no basis for employer liability, noting that **at every step, the university promptly and adequately responded to reported harassment**.

The university was also credited with quickly moving the student away from the professor to another work area. It immediately investigated when the student filed a formal complaint, reprimanded the professor and banned him from campus after he did not complete required training. Even if officials discouraged a complaint, this did not create liability because the university still promptly investigated. The university was entitled to judgment on the Title VII and Title IX claims, as the student did not show it was deliberately indifferent to his reports. *Milligan v. Board of Trustees of Southern Illinois Univ.*, 686 F.3d 378 (7th Cir. 2012).

◆    *A federal court found no merit to a South Carolina student's harassment lawsuit, as she had consented to a relationship with the alleged harasser.*

The student attended a Halloween party at her instructor's apartment. Over the next three days, she sent him over 100 text messages. Three days after the Halloween party, the two began a sexual relationship that lasted the rest of the semester. Three weeks after the instructor posted the student's course grade, she told the college for the first time that he had been sexually harassing her. She said that up until that time, she had pretended his conduct toward her was welcome because she feared he would otherwise sabotage her course grade.

The college discharged the instructor, and the student sued him and the college in a federal district court for civil rights violations, battery, harassment, stalking, intentional infliction of emotional distress and assault. After the court held for the college, it held **no reasonable jury could return a verdict for the student against the instructor**. It noted she had initiated the relationship and had sent him more than 950 text messages. The student had continued the relationship even after her grade was posted. Under the circumstances, no reasonable jury could find the instructor's conduct was unwelcome. Similarly, the student's claims of assault, battery and intentional infliction of emotional distress were barred because she consented to the conduct. *Ray v. Bowers*, No. 2:08-CV-3512-PMD, 2009 WL 4893209 (D.S.C. 12/17/09).

◆    *An Arizona student lacked evidence to support a sexual harassment claim.*

The student claimed an instructor sexually harassed her and created a hostile environment by telling sexual jokes to students. She said he suggested in front of a class that she should use oral sex for birth control and accused students who were late for class of "fooling around ... with their boyfriends." As the student was married, she interpreted the latter comment as an accusation of adultery. She withdrew from school and filed a federal lawsuit charging the college and instructor with sexual harassment in violation of Title IX and other federal laws. The court held that to prove sexual harassment, the student had to show she was subjected to sexual advances, requests for sexual favors, or other sexual conduct. She also had to show the conduct was unwelcome and was so severe or pervasive that it altered the conditions of her education and created an abusive educational environment. But aside from the student's allegations, no evidence supported these claims. **Even if her claims were true, she did not show misconduct so severe or pervasive that it created a sexually hostile or abusive educational environment.** As the college could not be held liable unless the instructor was acting pursuant to a policy or custom, the claims against the college failed. *Currie v. Maricopa County Community College Dist.*, No. CV-07-2093-PHX-FJM, 2008 WL 4905980 (D. Ariz. 2008).

◆  *A North Carolina court affirmed a decision to award monetary damages to two students who successfully claimed that a professor sexually harassed them.*

A student research assistant claimed a professor sexually harassed her for almost 10 years. She then refused to take a class he taught, but because the class was required, she was forced to discontinue her studies. After the student reported the professor's misconduct to the university sexual harassment officer, she learned that he had harassed other employees and students in the past. The university then conducted an investigation, which revealed that the professor had sexually harassed at least eight other women. There was evidence that the university did not take any corrective action despite being informed of at least one of the cases. The university allowed the professor to resign with a year's pay and a neutral letter of reference. Two students filed separate claims against the university, alleging negligent retention and supervision of the professor. They added claims for negligent infliction of mental and emotional distress.

An administrative commission found for the students and awarded them $150,000 each. The university appealed to the Court of Appeals of North Carolina, arguing that there was no evidence of negligence. The court held the university's failure to properly respond to the earlier harassment incidents caused injury to the students. It rejected the university's argument that it could not investigate one of the past cases because a student did not file a formal complaint. Whether she had filed a formal complaint or not, the university knew about the allegations. **The university should have asked for a written complaint, documented the oral complaint, and investigated the charges.** Doing so might have prevented the later harassment. The decision to award the students monetary damages was affirmed. *Gonzales v. North Carolina State Univ.*, 659 S.E.2d 9 (N.C. Ct. App. 2008); *Wood v. North Carolina State Univ.*, 189 N.C.App. 789, 661 S.E.2d 55 (Table) (N.C. Ct. App. 2008).

◆  *An Oklahoma college did not violate Title IX as it was not deliberately indifferent to a complaint about a professor's sexual behavior.*

A student claimed a professor touched her inappropriately and made sexual comments in front of her peers and while they were alone. She sued the college under Title IX, claiming it knew the professor sexually harassed others before she enrolled there. A federal court found the college did not know about any prior incidents. On appeal, the Tenth Circuit found the courts have differed on whether notice sufficient to trigger liability may consist of prior complaints or must consist of notice regarding current harassment in the recipient's programs. There was evidence that the professor had dated two students close to his age, but the court held this did not provide the college with knowledge that he posed a substantial risk of sexual harassment to students. Other student complaints of inappropriate sexual behavior against the professor occurred almost 10 years earlier. Those complaints involved significantly different behavior, including inappropriate touching and name-calling. **The court rejected the student's contention that the college was deliberately indifferent to her allegations and affirmed the judgment for the college.** *Escue v. Northern Oklahoma College*, 450 F.3d 1146 (10th Cir. 2006).

### 2. Sexual Harassment by Peers

*In* Fitzgerald v. Barnstable School Committee, *555 U.S. 246, 129 S.Ct. 788, 172 L.Ed.2d 582 (2009), the U.S. Supreme Court allowed students who assert Title IX harassment actions to include "parallel and concurrent" gender discrimination claims against their educational institutions under the Equal Protection Clause of the Fourteenth Amendment via 42 U.S.C. Section 1983.*

*Section 1983 is a federal statute that creates no rights itself, but is used to enforce rights created by federal laws and the U.S. Constitution. For additional harassment cases involving student-athletes, please see Chapter Three, Section I.D. of this volume.*

◆ *A New York student failed to state a valid Title IX claim, so a federal judge dismissed his gender-based harassment claim.*

Two students at a university had sex. He said it was consensual, but she turned vengeful after he said no to a relationship. She, on the other hand, called it rape. The female student filed a misconduct charge against the man. After the university found the male was not responsible, the woman conducted a "performing arts" project where she carried her mattress everywhere she went on campus. The man filed a complaint against the woman, but the university refused to investigate. Then he filed a Title IX suit, alleging the university responded with deliberate indifference to the woman's gender-based harassment of him. But the court said he didn't show the harassment was based on gender or deprived him of access to educational opportunities or benefits. "Falsely accusing a male of being a 'rapist' ... is inherently gender based," the student argued. **But the court disagreed, rejecting "the assumption that 'rapist' is a gender-specific term."** The court found the student failed to state a *prima facie* Title IX claim, but if he'd included specific allegations that the harassment deprived him of access to educational opportunities offered by the university, then he might have a valid claim. The court dismissed the suit but gave the student a chance to restate the claim. *Nungesser v. Columbia Univ.*, No. 1:15-cv-3216-GHW, 2016 WL 1049024 (S.D.N.Y. 3/11/16).

◆ *A New Jersey federal judge dismissed a student's Title IX claim as time-barred.*

In 2009, a student reported that he'd been sexually assaulted in his dorm room. The university immediately expelled the assailant. Two years later, the student was arrested for an "explicit and inappropriate" online, off-campus conversation he had with a detective posing as a minor. The university suspended the student over the arrest. In January 2015, the student sued the university, alleging its response to his sexual assault report violated Title IX. The university asked the court to dismiss the suit. The court did. **Under Third Circuit precedent, people asserting Title IX claims have only two years to sue.** The suit was dismissed. *McClelland v. Saint Peter's Univ.*, No. 15-245(JLL), 2016 WL 96145 (D.N.J. 1/7/16).

◆　*A Virginia federal court preserved the Title IX claim of a student who alleged she was sexually assaulted on spring break and the university failed to respond in a timely manner.*

During spring break in Florida, the student was invited to the condo of three fellow students. The student said the men cornered her in a restroom, forcibly removed her bathing suit and groped her. One recorded the incident on his phone. Word of the alleged assault – and the video depicting it – quickly spread. After spring break, the woman said she reported the assault to university officials and notified them about the video, but they discouraged her from filing a report. No investigation was conducted. Several months later, she filed a formal complaint anyway. A hearing found the three men were responsible for sexual assault and sexual harassment. The school imposed the curious punishment of "expulsion after graduation" and barred all three men from having contact with the victim. She sued the school, saying that its failure to adequately respond to her initial report of the alleged assault – as well as its overall handling of her case – violated Title IX. The school moved to dismiss the claim, but the court denied the motion – as **the school didn't investigate the alleged assault or attempt to stop the distribution of the video**. The motion to dismiss was denied. *Butters v. James Madison Univ.*, No. 5:15-cv-000152, 2015 WL 6825420 (W.D. Va. 11/6/15).

◆　*A New York federal court said it lacked jurisdiction to hear Title IX claims filed by a student who said she was raped at a college in Virginia.*

The foreign exchange student was enrolled at a college in Virginia, where she was allegedly raped by a fellow student. The following year, the student moved to New York and filed suit against the university in a New York federal court, alleging Title IX and personal injury claims. The university asked the court to transfer the case to a federal court in Virginia. To support her claim of jurisdiction, the student argued that, although the attack happened in Virginia, she continued to suffer the effects in New York and received treatment there. The court explained that generally, **jurisdiction is improper unless the effect in New York is reasonably foreseeable to the defendant**. It wasn't here, so the court concluded it lacked jurisdiction and transferred the case to a Virginia venue. *Facchetti v. Bridgewater College*, No. 14-CV-10018 (JPO), 2015 WL 3763970 (S.D.N.Y. 6/16/15).

◆　*A California federal judge found parents didn't state a viable Title IX peer-on-peer sexual harassment claim on behalf of their deceased daughter.*

Milanca Lopez was an undergrad student at University of California, Berkeley (UCB). She was in a relationship with graduate student Jose

Lumbreras. The couple lived together in an on-campus apartment. Lumbreras was abusive. Domestic violence incidents were witnessed by students three times between late April and early May 2012. Lopez reached out to the school's student services program, but she never returned calls from the office. On May 7, she sent an email saying she'd "ended up working things out." Two weeks later, Lumbreras was intoxicated. He drove his vehicle straight into a tree. The passengers – Lopez and her child – were killed. Lopez's parents sued UCB under Title IX. But the judge dismissed their claim. In the complaint, **Lopez's parents failed to show UCB had actual notice of the harassment or was deliberately indifferent to it**, a necessary part of a valid Title IX claim. The parents were given an opportunity to amend their claim. *Lopez v. Regents of Univ. of California*, 5 F.Supp.3d 1106 (N.D. Cal. 2013).

◆　*A Delaware university created a hostile environment and violated Title IX by failing to adequately respond to the assault of a student.*

According to the student, a male student at the university assaulted her after she refused to have sex with him. Her injuries required hospitalization, and she reported the incident to campus police. After both parties made statements, the university did not stop the male from attending classes. The student said the university's director of residential life and judicial affairs said she should change her schedule and transfer from any classes she had with the male. She missed a semester due to fear of the male and sued the university in a federal court. According to the student, the university charged her with several violations of the student code, including assault and battery. She said this was done to stop her from complaining about the incident. **The court held the student's complaint adequately alleged a Title IX violation against the university. But she could not proceed with a Title IX claim against any individual, because the statute does not authorize such claims.** Due process claims against the university and its director were blocked by immunity, but a separate due process claim against the director could go forward. The court granted the university's motion to dismiss an abuse of process claim. *Terrell v. Delaware State Univ.*, No. 09-464 (GMS), 2010 WL 2952221 (D. Del. 7/23/10).

## III.  RACE AND NATIONAL ORIGIN DISCRIMINATION

*The Equal Protection Clause of the Fourteenth Amendment, Title VI of the Civil Rights Act of 1964, 42 U.S.C. § 1981 and state anti-discrimination laws all prohibit discrimination against individuals in educational settings. Title VI provides that no person shall on the ground of race or color be excluded from participating in any program receiving federal financial assistance.*

### A.  Affirmative Action

*In 2013, the U.S. Supreme Court held a University of Texas student admission plan was subject to strict judicial scrutiny. "Strict scrutiny" is a searching examination under which a state must show the reasons for any racial classification were "clearly identified and unquestionably legitimate."* **A reviewing court must be satisfied that no workable race-neutral alternative is available.** *The judiciary is charged with ensuring that the means chosen by a university to implement a diversity plan are "narrowly-tailored" to meet its purposes. "Narrow tailoring" involves a careful judicial inquiry into whether a university could achieve sufficient diversity without racial classifications.*

◆ *The U.S. Supreme Court ruled that Michigan voters permissibly banned the use of race-based admission preferences at state universities.*

In 2006, voters adopted an amendment that prohibited state schools from discriminating against – or giving preferential treatment to – any person based on race, color, ethnicity or national origin. The amendment was challenged, and a district court ruled it did not violate the Equal Protection Clause. But the Sixth Circuit reversed, reasoning the amendment targeted a program that benefited minorities. Hearing arguments, the Court explained the issue was whether – and in what manner – voters can choose to ban racial preferences when it comes to school admissions. When voters added the challenged amendment to their state constitution, they were exercising their democratic power, the Court explained, noting that citizens have a right to speak, debate and learn – and then take action via the electoral process. This case wasn't about whether some injury was inflicted, but about whether the people can direct the government to follow a course of action. **The question of whether Michigan should ban the use of race-based preferences with respect to admissions decisions was properly left to the people,** the Court ruled. As a result, the Sixth Circuit's decision was reversed. *Schuette v. Coalition to Defend Affirmative Action*, No. 12-682 (U.S. 4/22/14).

◆ *A student admission plan implemented by the University of Texas was subject to strict judicial scrutiny.*

In *Hopwood v. Texas*, 78 F.3d 932 (5th Cir. 1996), the Fifth Circuit struck down the use of race-based admissions criteria by the University of Texas (UT) law school. UT then started using a "holistic metric" to assess applicants. State legislators passed a law that Texas resident seniors in the top 10% of their high school classes would be automatically admitted to any state university. In 2003, the Supreme Court held colleges could consider race in admissions when this was necessary to promote diversity and to achieve a "critical mass" of minority students. UT then adopted a policy including race as a factor in admissions.

A white applicant sued UT in a federal court, claiming equal protection violations. The court held for UT, and the Fifth Circuit affirmed this result. It held UT admissions decisions were entitled to deference and a presumption of good faith. On appeal, the Supreme Court held diversity in higher education encompasses an array of qualifications and characteristics of which racial or ethnic origin are only a part. **Strict scrutiny requires a university to clearly demonstrate a constitutionally permitted purpose and the necessity of making a racial classification.** Official action that treats a person differently on account of race or ethnic origin is "inherently suspect." If a university establishes a goal of diversity, the university still has to prove it implemented its goals in a narrowly tailored way. "Narrow tailoring" requires a court to verify that the university had to use race to achieve the educational benefits of diversity. A university has to show each applicant was evaluated as an individual, not by race or ethnicity. It is up to the courts to determine whether this was done. Since the lower courts did not apply strict scrutiny, the Court vacated the judgment and returned the case to the Fifth Circuit.

On remand, the student argued that race-conscious admissions decisions were no longer needed because the school had already achieved a "critical mass" of minority students. But the court said **she improperly relied solely on the percentage of minority students enrolled to support her argument, because critical mass is defined by a view of diversity that encompasses more than racial quotas**. So the student's claim was rejected. *Fisher v. Univ. of Texas at Austin*, 758 F.3d 633 (5th Cir. 2014).

◆ *A federal appeals court upheld a California constitutional provision enacted to block public entities from granting race and gender preferences.*

Proposition 209 was a 1996 voter initiative intended to bar the state from granting preferential treatment on the basis of characteristics including race, sex, color, ethnicity or national origin. After it went into effect as a state constitutional amendment, the state's public university system stopped considering race and sex in admissions. Over the next year, the number of minority freshmen at two state universities dropped by more than 50%. A group of high school and college students sued state and university officials in a federal district court for equal protection violations. The case was dismissed, and appeal went to the U.S. Court of Appeals, Ninth Circuit. It held that the equal protection claims were foreclosed by its decision in *Coalition for Economic Equity v. Wilson*, 122 F.3d 692 (9th Cir. 1997). The court held the earlier decision considered the scenario involved in this case and upheld the provision at issue. **There was no merit to the students' theory that the provision created an "unequal political structure" that prevented them from using normal democratic processes.** Nor was the earlier ruling inconsistent with more recent Supreme Court cases regarding affirmative action. As a result, the judgment for state and university officials was affirmed. *Coalition to Defend Affirmative Action v. Brown*, 674 F.3d 1128 (9th Cir. 2012).

◆ *While achieving a diverse student body may be a worthy goal, the means to achieve that goal must comply with the Equal Protection Clause. The U.S. Supreme Court allowed race to be used as a "plus" factor in admissions.*

The University of Michigan had an admissions policy for its law school that used race as a "plus" factor for underrepresented minorities. The policy was flexible, utilized an individualized assessment system, and did not create quotas. The policy was challenged as unconstitutional by white students who were not accepted for enrollment. The case reached the U.S. Supreme Court, which upheld the policy. **The Court first noted that the goal of achieving diversity in the student body was a compelling governmental interest.** As a result, the policy would not violate the Equal Protection Clause if it was narrowly tailored to achieving that goal. Since the law school's policy did not set impermissible quotas, and since **it utilized an individualized assessment system by using race/ethnicity as a "plus" factor when evaluating individual applicants for admission**, it was constitutional. The Court also noted that race-conscious admissions policies should be limited in time so that racial preferences can be ended as soon as practicable. *Grutter v. Bollinger*, 539 U.S. 306, 123 S.Ct. 2325, 156 L.Ed.2d 304 (2003).

◆ *The Supreme Court found unconstitutional the University of Michigan's undergraduate admissions policy, which awarded applicants in underrepresented minority groups 20 points out of 100 needed for admission.*

Applying the same strict scrutiny analysis it used in *Grutter*, above, the Court held the undergraduate policy was not narrowly tailored to achieve the compelling governmental interest in a diverse student body. **The undergraduate admissions policy did not assess points on an individualized basis**, but rather awarded them to all minority applicants. The failure to review each applicant individually doomed the policy under the Equal Protection Clause. *Gratz v. Bollinger*, 539 U.S. 244, 123 S.Ct. 2411, 156 L.Ed.2d 257 (2003). After the decision in *Grutter*, Michigan amended its state constitution to ban the use of race in admissions. The U.S. Supreme Court upheld the ban in *Schuette v. Coalition to Defend Affirmative Action*, 134 S.Ct. 1623 (U.S. 2014).

◆ *In 1978, the Supreme Court held a special admissions program at a California medical school that reserved close to one-sixth of the school's openings each year for minority students violated the Equal Protection Clause.*

The Medical School of the University of California at Davis had two admission programs for its entering class of 100 students. Under the regular procedure, candidates whose overall undergraduate grade point averages fell below 2.5 on a scale of 4.0 were summarily rejected. The special admissions policy, designed to assist minority or other disadvantaged applicants, reserved 16 of the 100 openings each year for medical school admission based upon criteria other than that used in the general admissions program. Special admission applicants did not need to meet the 2.5 or better grade point average of the general admission group, and their Medical College Admission Test scores, measured against general admission candidates.

A white male brought suit to compel his admission to medical school after he was twice rejected for admission, even though candidates with lower grade point averages and lower test score results were being admitted under the special admissions program. The plaintiff alleged that **the special admissions excluded him from medical school on the basis of his race** in violation of the Equal Protection Clause of the Fourteenth Amendment, the California Constitution, and Title VI of the 1964 Civil Rights Act. The California Supreme Court concluded that the special admissions program was not the least intrusive means of achieving the state's goals of integrating the medical profession under a strict scrutiny standard. On appeal, the U.S. Supreme Court held that while the goal of achieving a diverse student body is sufficiently compelling to justify considerations of race in admissions decisions under some circumstances, **the special admissions program, which foreclosed consideration to persons such as the plaintiff, was unnecessary to achieve this compelling goal and was invalid under the Equal Protection Clause**. Since the school could not prove that the plaintiff would not have been admitted even if there had been no special admissions program, the Court ordered that he be admitted to the medical school. *Regents of the Univ. of California v. Bakke*, 438 U.S. 265, 98 S.Ct. 2733, 57 L.Ed.2d 750 (1978).

◆ *The University of Washington (UW) Law School's admission policy did not discriminate against applicants on the basis of race.*

UW's law school had no racial quotas, targets or goals for admission or enrollment, but considered race, ethnicity and other diversity factors as a "plus" in admission decisions. The school also relied on nonracial diversity factors. Several white applicants who were denied admission to the law school sued the university in a federal district court for race discrimination. The court denied summary judgment to the applicants, and they appealed. The Ninth Circuit Court of Appeals relied on *Grutter v. Bollinger*, above. It found the law school acted in good faith to implement its admissions process and satisfied the factors described in *Grutter*. **The school did not establish quotas, targets or goals for admission or enrollment of minorities, nor did it direct the admission of a certain number of minority applicants.** As the law school followed the guidelines in *Grutter* by conducting a "highly-individualized, holistic review of each applicant's file," the court affirmed the judgment. *Smith v. Univ. of Washington Law School*, 392 F.3d 367 (9th Cir. 2004).

◆ *The Supreme Court held that a university could avoid liability for a race-based admission policy if it could show that an applicant would have been denied admission absent the policy.*

An African immigrant of Caucasian descent applied for admission to the Ph.D. program in counseling psychology at a Texas public university. The university considered the race of its applicants at some stage of the review process and denied admission to the applicant. He sued for money damages and injunctive relief, asserting that the race-conscious admission policy violated the Equal Protection Clause. The university moved for summary judgment, arguing that even if it had not used race-based criteria, it would not have admitted the applicant because of his GPA and his GRE score. A federal district court granted summary judgment to the university, but the Fifth Circuit Court of Appeals reversed. The case reached the U.S. Supreme Court, which noted that its decision in *Mt. Healthy City Board of Educ. v. Doyle*, 429 U.S. 274 (1977), made clear that **if the government has considered an impermissible criterion in making an adverse decision to the plaintiff, it can still avoid liability by demonstrating that it would have made the same decision absent the forbidden consideration.** Therefore, if the state could show that it would have made the decision to deny admission to the applicant absent the race-based policy, it would be entitled to summary judgment on the claim for damages. With respect to the claim for injunctive relief, it appeared that the university had stopped using a race-based admissions policy. However, that issue had to be decided on remand. *Texas v. Lesage*, 528 U.S. 18, 120 S.Ct. 467, 145 L.Ed.2d 347 (1999).

## B. Discrimination and Equal Protection

*Title VI of the Civil Rights Act of 1964 prohibits discrimination based on race, color or national origin in any program that receives federal funds. Title*

*VI is based on equal protection principles, and many discrimination complaints allege violations of Title VI, the Equal Protection Clause and analogous state laws. In* Alexander v. Sandoval, *532 U.S. 275 (2001), the Supreme Court noted that the courts require proof of intentional discrimination in Title VI cases.*

◆   *The Sixth Circuit affirmed a decision to dismiss a student's racial discrimination claim against an Ohio university.*

The student was the only black student enrolled in the university's Masters in Health Administration program. She turned in a paper that didn't "sound like the words of a student," according to a professor who reported the suspected plagiarism. After a hearing, the student was suspended for two quarters. She appealed. When it was denied, she filed a complaint with the university, alleging the professor's actions were racially motivated. The university found insufficient evidence to substantiate racial bias. The student filed a lawsuit, but the court dismissed the claim. On appeal, the court explained that even if she'd stated a valid *prima facie* claim of racial bias, **the school provided a legitimate and non-discriminatory reason for the referral: suspected plagiarism**. The student had to provide evidence showing the plagiarism allegation was merely a pretext for unlawful discrimination, the court said. She didn't, so the claim failed. *Thompson v. The Ohio State Univ.*, No. 15-3326, 2016 WL 364795 (6th Cir. 1/26/16).

◆   *An Indiana federal court rejected a racial discrimination claim filed by a student who was dismissed from a university nursing program.*

An African-American student enrolled in the nursing program, which required students to maintain a minimum 2.5 GPA. The student was dismissed when her GPA fell below the required minimum. After an internal appeal failed, the student sued, alleging racial discrimination. She presented evidence relating to three non-African American students who filed successful internal appeals after having similar trouble with their GPAs. The school moved for summary judgment, and the court granted the motion. Only one student was a valid comparator. That student and the plaintiff in the case had their appeals considered by a common decision maker, and their academic records shared similarities. Even with the similarities, the student's claim failed, the court said. The school said it dismissed the student because she did not meet its academic standards and did not submit an adequate corrective plan. It was the student's burden to show the school's proffered reason was merely a pretext for unlawful discrimination, the court explained. She failed to do so. **There was "no weakness, implausibility, inconsistency, or contradiction" in the school's stated reasons for denying the appeal**, the court said. So the claim failed. *Richardson v. Lutheran Univ. Ass'n*, No. 2:14-CV-92-PRC, 2015 WL 6473638 (N.D. Ind. 10/26/15).

◆   *A Pennsylvania federal court rejected the racial discrimination claims of a student who was expelled from a university's medical school.*

The student was born in China and immigrated to Canada as a child. After earning five "unsatisfactory" grades during his first two years, the student was dismissed. He was later reinstated with several conditions – including that another grade below "satisfactory" would be grounds for dismissal. He was assigned two more "unsatisfactory" grades and was dismissed. After an unsuccessful internal appeal, the student sued alleging racial discrimination – but the court found he presented no viable proof of bias. The strongest evidence was his claim that an unpaid affiliate doctor asked if he ate American cuisine or "gook food" and made remarks about not liking "Communist China." That wasn't enough to back the bias claim. **Even if the doctor made the comments, they only constituted "stray remarks" unconnected to the decision to expel the student.** Further, the doctor wasn't a university employee, he didn't weigh in on the decision to expel the student and the actual decision makers relied in no way on the doctor's comments to expel the student. The claim was dismissed. *Ke v. Drexel Univ.*, No. 11-6708, 2015 WL 5316492 (E.D. Pa. 9/4/15).

◆   *A New York federal judge found a dismissed student's Section 1981 claim against a university could proceed.*

A black student was enrolled in a medical program. Under university policy, any student who received two Cs would be dismissed. The student had a history of earning high grades until a preceptor with a reputation for racial discrimination gave the student a poor evaluation. As a result, she had to go to biweekly training sessions, where the director of the program implied the student was a "single mother on welfare" – which wasn't true and showed race-based assumptions, the student said. The director gave the student another C, and she was dismissed. She filed a grievance and was reinstated on the condition that she repeat a semester. On her return, the director assigned her to a clinical rotation under yet another preceptor with a reputation for racial bias. The student received an F and was dismissed. She sued, alleging racial discrimination. The court found the student stated a valid Section 1981 claim, showing among other things, that she was discriminated against in connection to an activity listed in the statute. One activity listed is the right "to make and enforce contracts[.]" Under state law, students enter an implied contract with a school at enrollment. It's implied that the school must award a degree if the student complies with the school's terms and completes the required courses. **Since a student dismissal constitutes a "termination" of this implied contract, a racially motivated dismissal can run afoul of Section 1981.** So the claim moved forward. *Evans v. Columbia Univ. in the City of New York*, No. 14-CV-2658 (NSR), 2015 WL 1730097 (S.D.N.Y. 4/13/15).

◆   *A federal appeals court reinstated a student's claim that she was subjected to a remedial plan based on race and gender discrimination.*

While enrolled in a Ph.D. program in clinical psychology, student Payal Mehta was told she had mismanaged two cases. As a result, faculty members adopted remedial conditions for her. She did not accept the remedial plan. Instead, Mehta resigned from the program and filed suit, making a variety of claims, including race and gender discrimination. After a lower court granted judgment for the school, Mehta appealed. The appellate court vacated the lower court's decision to grant judgment in favor of the school regarding the discrimination claims. Questions remained as to whether she was qualified to study in the program and was meeting the school's expectations. **A question also existed as to whether she was treated differently from other similarly**

**situated students.** The lower court properly dismissed the rest of the claims. The district court's decision was granted in part and denied in part. *Mehta v. Fairleigh Dickinson Univ.*, 530 Fed.Appx. 191 (3d Cir. 2013).

◆ *A federal district court rejected a Missouri student's claim that a community college discriminated against her by assigning her low grades.*

According to the student, she appealed her grades to the academic appeals committee, but the committee denied her appeal for race-related reasons. She said that her instructors' supervisor wrongfully failed to remedy racist acts by instructors. In a federal court action, the student claimed the community college failed to properly discipline staff members, engaged in faulty hiring, and covered up discrimination. **Individual defendants cannot be held personally liable for violating Title VI, the court explained.** As for claims against the community college appeals committee, the court found a committee of this nature could not be sued under Title VI. Finally, the court held the Title VI claim against the community college could not proceed, as the student could not show intentional harassment on the basis of her race or nationality. She made no viable claim that the college had a policy of discrimination or did anything to further discrimination against her. As a result, the case was dismissed. *Tatum v. St. Louis Community College*, No. 4:12CV2218 CDP, 2013 WL 171072 (E.D. Mo. 1/16/13).

◆ *A federal district court in Nebraska rejected an unsuccessful applicant's claim that she was denied admission to law school due to racial discrimination.*

Creighton University law school rejected the applicant in 2010-11 based on her low Law School Admissions Test (LSAT) score and a credential assembly service report used to predict law school grades. No one with an LSAT as low as the applicant's had been admitted to the law school since 2003. Alleging the existence of an unlawful quota system, the applicant sued the university in a federal court for race discrimination. She sought an order requiring her admission, and $10 million in damages. The court found the law school's admissions criteria did not include race, national origin, religion, gender, disability, sexual orientation, marital status or age. The applicant's LSAT score and a related index were far lower than those of anyone who had been admitted for 2010-11. No evidence supported her claim that the law school denied her application based on race. **As the evidence showed the student was denied admission because her academic credentials did not meet objective standards, the court held for the university.** *Goodwin v. Creighton Univ.*, No. 8:10CV423, 2011 WL 2680481 (D. Neb. 7/8/11).

◆ *A former Columbia University student who committed plagiarism did not show the resulting decision to expel him was unlawfully motivated.*

The plagiarism charge was referred to a disciplinary committee, which voted to expel the student. Although he admitted to plagiarism, he claimed he was expelled because of his race and because he had refused to submit to an administrator's sexual advances and filed a complaint about them. In a federal district court lawsuit against the university, the student alleged retaliation under Title IX, race discrimination and breach of contract. After the court held for the university, appeal went before the U.S. Court of Appeals, Second Circuit.

On appeal, the court explained that to prove a retaliation claim, the student had to show he engaged in a protected activity of which the university was aware. Even if he could make this showing, the school could defeat the claim by offering a legitimate, nondiscriminatory reason for its decision. There was no evidence to support the conclusion that the student was really expelled for a reason other than plagiarism. Since he could not show the university gave a pretextual reason for dismissing him, the race discrimination claim failed. **Evidence did not show the university was in breach or that the student performed his contractual duties**, and the judgment was affirmed. *Shelton v. Trustees of Columbia Univ.*, 369 Fed.Appx. 200 (2d Cir. 2010).

◆   *A Kentucky family medicine training program participant was unable to pursue claims against a university after she was released from the program.*

A participant in the University of Louisville's family medicine training program exhibited behavioral problems and was placed on academic probation. A program director referred her to an assistance program, and a psychiatric evaluation was recommended for her. Meanwhile, the participant's pending grievance alleging race discrimination was resolved against her due to lack of evidence of discrimination. When the participant failed to set up a psychiatric appointment, she was released from the family medicine training program.

In a race discrimination case against the university, the participant asserted violations of federal law, breach of contract, defamation, libel, slander, wrongful discharge, breach of the covenant of good faith and fair dealing, and fraud and deceit. The court found several federal claims failed because the program was a private corporation whose actions could not be deemed to have been taken by the state. **There was no indication any action was taken with an intent to discriminate against the participant.** Finally, since she did not show assistance program personnel acted outside their duties or with actual malice, they were entitled by statute to immunity. *Peavey v. Univ. of Louisville*, No. 3:09-CV-00484-R, 2010 WL 2836093 (W.D. Ky. 7/16/10).

◆   *A white student who was beaten by his black roommate failed to prove Tennessee State University (TSU) was responsible for his injuries.*

According to the student, the roommate called him a "cracker" and often used the N-word. While the student and his father met with a university director to discuss the roommate's conduct, they did not raise race as an issue, and they did not request a change in roommate assignments. Soon after one of the meetings, the roommate beat the student with a clothes iron in their dorm room. TSU police arrested the roommate, who promptly moved out of the dorm but finished the semester at TSU. According to the student, TSU did not officially suspend the roommate for several months, and he continued to appear on campus. When the student returned to TSU for his sophomore year, his grades slipped and he lost a scholarship. In the student's federal district court action against the university, he asserted race discrimination in violation of Title VI of the 1964 Civil Rights Act. **The court held TSU did not have knowledge of severe and pervasive harassment because the student did not inform TSU about any racial tensions.** Nor was TSU's conduct unreasonable under the circumstances. After the attack, the roommate was arrested and forced out of his dorm room. TSU's motion for pretrial judgment was granted. *Maislin v. Tennessee State Univ.*, 665 F.Supp.2d 922 (M.D. Tenn. 2009).

◆ *A student of Asian ancestry was unable to prove that a California community college librarian discriminated against her based on her race.*

According to the student, the librarian falsely accused her of using library computers for personal reasons and on some occasions forced her to leave the library. Although the student filed a complaint against the college asserting the librarian bullied and harassed her, she did not allege race discrimination. After an investigation, the community college declined to find bullying by the librarian. The student transferred to another college, but again encountered the librarian, who had also been transferred. In a federal district court, the student sued the community college district and librarian for race discrimination. The court found insufficient evidence of discrimination based on race. **Undisputed evidence showed the librarian treated all students poorly.** The student did not counter this evidence, and one of her own witnesses stated that the librarian's behavior was not based on race. As a result, the court held for the librarian and community college district. *Santos v. Peralta Community College Dist.*, No. C-07-5227 EMC, 2009 WL 3809797 (N.D. Cal. 11/13/09).

◆ *A Florida university did not unlawfully discriminate against an unqualified intern by declining to hire him for a paid position.*

As a non-student and a volunteer, the intern received no pay or benefits, although he tried to secure paid positions. His applications were denied, since one was open only to students and the other was filled before he applied for it. In a federal district court action, the intern accused the university of race discrimination. The court agreed with the university, noting he was ineligible for the first position as a non-student. As for the other position, he did not show he was as well qualified for the job as the person chosen for it. **The university said the intern performed poorly, and this was a legitimate, nondiscriminatory reason for the decision not to hire him.** Because he did not show this reason was a pretext for unlawful discrimination, his claim of race discrimination failed, and the case was dismissed. *Cummings v. Univ. of Florida*, No. 1:04cv430-SPM/AK, 2008 WL 4534262 (N.D. Fla. 9/30/08).

◆ *A Georgia university properly suspended an African-American nursing student for selling stolen textbooks to the university's bookstore.*

A nursing student was accused of violating the university code of conduct by re-selling four stolen textbooks to a university bookstore. A disciplinary hearing was held, and she was suspended for two years. The student claimed race discrimination, as five white students who were accused of theft were not penalized as harshly as she was. The student sued the university in a federal district court, asserting due process and equal protection violations. She added discrimination and breach of contract claims. The court held for the university, and the student appealed. The U.S. Court of Appeals, Eleventh Circuit, upheld the dismissal of the due process and equal protection claims and rejected a Title VI race discrimination claim. As the court explained, **Title VI bars recipients of federal funding from discriminating on the basis of race in any federally**

**funded program**. Applying an equal protection analysis, the Eleventh Circuit rejected the claim that the suspension was motivated by intentional race discrimination. As white students disciplined by the university were not similarly situated to the student, the different punishment did not prove racial discrimination. According to the court, differences in individual circumstances justified imposing less severe punishment on the white students. *Carr v. Board of Regents of the Univ. System of Georgia*, 249 Fed.Appx. 146 (11th Cir. 2007).

## C.  National Origin

*Because Title VI covers only entities that receive federal funding, there is potential Title VI liability for entities that discriminate on the basis of race, color or national original, but no liability is possible for individuals.*

◆  *A Ph.D. candidate did not present factual allegations sufficient to support his claim of unlawful discrimination based on national origin, the U.S. Court of Appeals for the Fifth Circuit decided.*

A Ph.D. student asserted a chairperson used the fact that the student is from India to coerce him into doing more lab work and also threatened to give him an unsatisfactory grade that would result in the loss of his visa. The student sued the university, raising claims under Titles VI and VII. The district court dismissed the claims. On appeal, the Fifth Circuit looked at whether the student had raised a viable claim under Title VI. To win his Title VI claim, the student had to show the university intentionally discriminated against him on the basis of his race, color or national origin and that the university received federal financial assistance. The court said the student's allegations – at best – could support an inference of discrimination based on immigration status or citizenship and visa vulnerability – not national origin. Citizenship and nation origin "should not be conflated," the court explained. **Citizenship is not a protected category under Title VI.** The district court's ruling was affirmed. *Pathria v. Univ. of Texas Health Science Center at San Antonio*, 531 Fed.Appx. 454 (5th Cir. 2013).

◆  *An Indiana student of Korean descent stated a valid equal protection claim based on intensive scrutiny for plagiarism due to his race and orientation.*

A final paper submitted by the student was reviewed for plagiarism by three professors. One of them veered from usual practices by running it through a plagiarism-checking program. After the check showed part of the paper had been plagiarized, the student was expelled. He claimed two students in the program – non-Asians, one a woman – turned in papers with more plagiarism than his paper. A program director refused to reconsider the expulsion, and the other students were not disciplined. In a federal district court action, the student claimed professors subjected his paper to increased scrutiny because of race and sexual orientation. The professors and director sought dismissal of the due process and equal protection claims. As they were sued in their individual capacities, the court held the Eleventh Amendment did not bar the due process and equal protection claims. Nor did they have qualified immunity on the equal protection claim, because **the student alleged a violation of a clearly established equal protection right not to be arbitrarily subjected to different standards of plagiarism review than other students based on**

**race, national origin, sex or orientation**. The due process claims failed because he was not deprived of a protected interest and was given a fair chance to respond to the charges. *Park v. Trustees of Purdue Univ.*, No. 4:09-CV-87 JVB, 2011 WL 1361409 (N.D. Ind. 4/11/11).

◆ *Columbia University's decision to deny admission to a woman who failed to demonstrate English language proficiency was not based on her ancestry.*

At age 50, the woman sought admission to the special education program offered at the Teachers College of Columbia University. The college required an English language proficiency examination for non-native speakers. After the woman scored 190 on a test that had a minimum passing grade of 500, the college told her she could take a different exam at the university, or take an exam that was administered only in Australia. After she took and failed the in-house exam, the woman filed an administrative complaint with the U.S. Department of Education's Office for Civil Rights (OCR), claiming age discrimination. The OCR rejected her claim as untimely but she sued Columbia in a federal district court for "civil conspiracy to commit humiliation," tortious interference with her rights, age and race discrimination and other claims.

A federal magistrate judge recommended dismissal of the federal claims. He also said it would be appropriate not to consider the remaining state claims. A federal district court agreed with the magistrate that the age discrimination claims were barred because the woman did not file a timely administrative complaint. **It also agreed to reject her national origin discrimination claim because none of the allegations in her complaint related to her Romanian ancestry.** As the remaining claims lacked merit, the court adopted the magistrate's report and recommendation. *Strujan v. Teachers College Columbia Univ.*, No. 08 Civ. 9589(WHP)(HBP), 2010 WL 3466251 (S.D.N.Y. 9/3/10).

◆ *A federal court held a Texas university expelled a foreign student for nondiscriminatory reasons and dismissed the student's claims.*

Two professors used a plagiarism detection service and determined the student had plagiarized his papers. He received a failing grade for both courses. A week after meeting with the dean, another student reported to the police that the student had talked about his plagiarism charge and then said, "I understand why people shoot up or bomb schools in America." The dean of students suspended the student from campus, and the college then decided to expel him for plagiarism. The same day, students from a study group in the library went to university police and said the student had talked about a bomb threat.

A university judicial appeals board found the student should be suspended from campus for a year. Separately, the university charged him with academic dishonesty for plagiarism and lying, and held two hearings – one for each paper. Both ended with the board finding plagiarism, and the student was expelled. In a federal court, the student alleged due process and discrimination violations. The court held the expulsion was an academic decision and that the student could not show it was made arbitrarily. Instead, the court found it was properly made by faculty exercising professional judgment. **A national origin discrimination claim failed as the university had valid, nondiscriminatory reasons for suspending and expelling him.** There was no evidence of pretext, as the student had made a threatening statement and plagiarized two term papers. *Mawle v. Texas A&M Univ.-Kingsville*, No. CC-08-64, 2010 WL 1782214 (S.D. Tex. 4/30/10).

◆   *A student who was dismissed from Howard University for poor academic performance was unable to proceed with a federal case against the university.*

University rules specified that students who received more than nine credit hours of grade C or below should be dropped from their courses. University rules allowed graduate faculty to recommend the dismissal of any student who was not performing satisfactorily. In four semesters, the student did not achieve any grade higher than C, and his advisor did not approve his thesis proposal. After he was dismissed for poor academic performance and unwillingness to listen to his academic advisor, he sued the university and several faculty members in a federal court for national origin and disability discrimination. **Claims asserted against the individual defendants could not proceed because none of the laws under which they were brought permitted claims against individuals.** The student did not show the reason the school provided for the dismissal – poor academic performance – was really a pretext for unlawful discrimination. *Mwabira-Simera v. Howard Univ.*, 692 F.Supp.2d 65 (D.D.C. 2010).

◆   *A federal district court denied a trial for a student who did not provide enough information to support his race and national origin claims.*

According to the student, two architecture professors complained about his accent, criticized his proposal based on preconceived racial beliefs, and created a hostile learning environment. They eventually dropped him from the class. But when the student took the same class from a different professor, he again failed. After the university expelled the student, he sued the university and architecture professors in a federal district court. **It found the student "utterly fail[ed] to make the minimal showing necessary to avoid dismissal."** Under the rules for filing federal cases, legal papers are supposed to provide plain, short statements that give notice of the claims and grounds for asserting them. Since the student merely made "labels and conclusions" and not a factual basis sufficient to avoid dismissal, he was unable to proceed with the case. The court dismissed the action, saying it refused to "second-guess an educational institution's application of its own academic standards and procedures" without a valid allegation it had acted with an illegal motive. *Wanko v. Catholic Univ. of America*, No. 08-2115 (RJL), 2009 WL 3052477 (D.D.C. 9/22/09).

◆   *A Texas federal district court dismissed a Cameroon native's race and national origin discrimination claims against an associate professor.*

The student sought a doctoral degree in English. She claimed an associate professor questioned her about her country of origin and academic profile. The professor allegedly threatened to ruin the student's transcript and delay her graduation. She brought grading and discrimination complaints against the professor under a university policy. The English department dismissed the accusations as unfounded. Another professor in the English department accused the student of plagiarism. The university honesty panel, which included the associate professor, concluded the student had plagiarized, and she received an F for that class. The student was later expelled after another charge of plagiarism by the same professor. The student sued the university, professor and others in a federal district court for discrimination and retaliation under Title VI. The court held **Title VI claims may only be brought against entities that receive federal funding, not individuals. It dismissed the Title VI claim against the associate professor.** *Bisong v. Univ. of Houston*, Civil Action No. H-06-1815, 2006 WL 2414410 (S.D. Tex. 8/18/06).

## IV. AGE DISCRIMINATION

*In addition to state laws, the Age Discrimination Act of 1975 (42 U.S.C. § 6101, et seq.) provides the basis for claims of age discrimination by students. Similar to Title IX claims, however, the Age Discrimination Act applies only to programs or activities receiving federal funding. The Age Discrimination in Employment Act (ADEA) has broad coverage in employment cases.*

◆ *Calling a 20-year-old student's age discrimination case "patently absurd," a federal court dismissed his action against a New Hampshire law school.*

After falling two points short of the required score for early admission, the student was invited to apply for admission the next year. Instead, he sued the law school, claiming he was denied admission based on age and that the law school violated his equal protection rights. A federal court held the student did not comply with Age Discrimination Act notice and exhaustion requirements, requiring the dismissal of that claim. As for the equal protection claim, the court noted the law school was a private, non-governmental entity. It held **the receipt of federal financial assistance did not make the law school a public actor for Equal Protection purposes**. There was no showing that the government had influenced the decision being challenged in the lawsuit. As a result, the court dismissed the action. *Prete v. Roger Williams Univ. School*, No. 12-cv-474-JL, 2012 WL 6203083 (D.N.H. 12/12/12).

◆ *A New York student could not proceed with her discrimination claim due to her untimely filing and other procedural errors.*

During her time at the university, the student wanted to live with her son in on-campus housing. After her requests were denied, she sued the university, accusing it of unlawfully discriminating against her based on her familial status. A federal court found a claim relating to study abroad was untimely. As for the rest of the time that she was enrolled at the university, **she was not eligible for housing because she was a part-time student**. The university made its housing available only to students who were enrolled on a full-time basis. After the court held for the university, the student sought to overturn the judgment. But the court held she did not meet the standard applicable to motions for relief from judgment, and her motion was denied. *Whitaker v. New York Univ.*, No. 09 Civ. 8410(LTS), 2012 WL 2369510 (S.D.N.Y. 6/20/12).

◆ *A New York student did not convince a federal court that a community college gave preferential treatment to younger, minority students.*

The community college's student handbook specified nursing students must earn at least a C in required classes and repeat any failed required class. Three failed classes meant dismissal unless a student obtained a waiver. The student failed three classes, but obtained a waiver based on recent deaths in her family. She then used a paper towel instead of sterile gauze while giving an injection and was promptly expelled. The student claimed the college gave younger, minority students preferential treatment by bending rules for them, but not for her. She sued the community college and several of its officials under Title VI, asserting discrimination based on her Caucasian race and "advanced years." But the court rejected her claims, based on the absence of admissible evidence to support them. **Even if the inadmissible hearsay she relied on was true, it did not prove to the court that the community college did not follow its handbook.** *Maya v. Bronx Community College*, No. 09 Civ. 3605(CM)(DCF), 2011 WL 2732519 (S.D.N.Y. 7/6/11).

◆  *A Washington student's lawsuit against a university failed because state law prohibited age discrimination in employment but not education.*

Faculty members grew concerned about the student's lack of progress after six semesters of a graduate psychology program. She received two extensions but refused to sign a contract intended to help her prepare for her exams. After a "not negotiable" deadline was set, the student filed an age discrimination complaint. Meanwhile, a deadline passed without her taking required exams, and faculty members assigned her an F for the course. Her grade average dropped below the program minimum, and she was disenrolled.

In a state court, the student accused the university of breach of contract, age discrimination and retaliation. After the case was dismissed, the state court of appeals found no merit to a contract claim based on breach of a duty to provide clear guidelines for academic expectations. These requirements were set out in a graduate school program description and were otherwise made clear to the student. The court held Washington law allows employee claims for age discrimination but not student claims. **Work as a teaching assistant did not make the student an employee**, as she argued. There was no merit to a retaliation claim based on the filing of an age discrimination complaint. As the university had a legitimate, nondiscriminatory reason to disenroll the student, the judgment was affirmed. *Becker v. Washington State Univ.*, 164 Wash.App. 1016 (Wash. Ct. App. 2011).

◆  *A federal court rejected a claim that Alabama State University violated the federal Age Discrimination Act by removing him from campus housing.*

When the student was 41 years old, the university removed him from campus housing for unspecified reasons. He sued the university in a federal district court for violating the Age Discrimination Act, a federal law that bars discrimination on the basis of age in programs and activities that receive any form of federal financial assistance. **The court dismissed the case for failing to comply with an Age Discrimination Act requirement that he first file an administrative complaint.** An Age Discrimination Act provision requires claimants to provide written notice to the Secretary of Health and Human Services, the Attorney General of the United States and the person against whom the action is directed before filing suit. As the student admitted that he did not file an administrative complaint, the court granted the university's motion to dismiss the case. *McGhee v. Alabama State Univ.*, No. 2:09-cv-0092-MEF, 2009 WL 1684604 (M.D. Ala. 6/12/09).

◆  *The claim that a California college librarian subjected a student to harassing and discriminatory conduct was ordered to proceed.*

A Merritt College student claimed a college librarian harassed her at least five times. She said the librarian falsely accused her of using a library computer for personal use. After complaining to the dean of the library and other college employees, the student sued the college in a federal district court for violating the state's Fair Employment and Housing Act (FEHA). She added federal age and race discrimination claims against the college and librarian under 42 U.S.C. § 1981, along with state law claims of intentional infliction of emotional distress, breach of contract and negligent misrepresentation. The court first dismissed the FEHA claim against the college, as the statute covers only discrimination in employment. The Section 1981 claims were also dismissed, because they were based on age discrimination, which Section 1981 does not address. However, **the court refused to dismiss the Section 1981 claim of race discrimination against the librarian in her individual capacity**. The court dismissed the remaining state law claims so the student could re-file them in a state court. *Santos v. Merritt College*, No. C-07-5227 EMC, 2008 WL 131696 (N.D. Cal. 1/11/08).

◆  *The Second Circuit held Cornell University had a valid reason to expel a student that was not based on her age or gender.*

The female student attended Cornell's veterinary program. She twice failed required exams, and the university expelled her. The student sued the university in a federal district court, alleging discrimination based on her gender and because of her age in violation of the Age Discrimination Act. The court held the student did not prove the motivation to expel her was based on gender or age discrimination and dismissed the claims. The student appealed to the Second Circuit. The court found she had failed to exhaust her administrative remedies before she filed suit. **The court agreed with the district court's finding that the student failed to prove the university had expelled male students who twice failed required exams. It affirmed the judgment.** *Curto v. Edmundson*, 392 F.3d 502 (2d Cir. 2004).

# CHAPTER THREE

## Athletics and Student Activities

## I. ATHLETIC PROGRAMS

### A. Eligibility of Participants

*There is no recognized constitutional right to participate in interscholastic athletics or other extracurricular activities. The possibility of obtaining a college athletic scholarship is also not protected. The National Collegiate Athletic Association (NCAA) has broad powers to enforce its rules.*

◆ *An Ohio federal judge refused to order the school not to enforce a student-athlete's suspension during his final year of eligibility.*

The student-athlete was on the university football team. A female classmate filed a Title IX complaint, accusing him of sexual assault. After a hearing, the university determined the football player violated the code of student conduct. He was suspended for a year – his final one of academic eligibility. His appeal was denied. He filed a due process and Title IX lawsuit. He asked the court to grant a temporary restraining order prohibiting the school from suspending him. The court refused. While the student showed that losing his final year of eligibility could constitute irreparable harm, **he didn't show he was likely to win his case**. That finding was "fatal" to his request for the restraining order, the judge explained. The student claimed the school violated his due process rights by using biased decision makers. But under Sixth Circuit precedent, courts presume higher ed disciplinary committees acted with honesty and integrity unless there is evidence of actual bias. There was no such evidence in this case. Likewise, the Title IX claim was doomed to fail – as no evidence that showed bias against him as a man played a role in the proceedings. He wasn't likely to win, so the court refused to grant the order. *Doe v. Univ. of Cincinnati*, No. 1:15-cv-600, 2015 WL 5729328 (S.D. Ohio 9/30/15).

◆ *A Michigan student-athlete was unable to pursue due process claims against a university based on the loss of eligibility for four football games.*

The student's father, who served as varsity football coach at the university, arranged for a below-market-rate lease on an apartment located near campus and also paid for the rental. In a separate action, the university accused the coach of violating NCAA rules. But a jury held for the father/coach, and the case against him was dismissed. Meanwhile, university officials informed the student that he had violated NCAA rules by obtaining the below-market rental rate. Although the university informed him he was ineligible to play football, the NCAA reinstated his eligibility and he transferred. In a federal district court action against the university, the student asserted due process violations.

The court considered the university's dismissal motion and noted that the student had missed four games and less than one month of the season. His scholarship status was not affected, nor was he deprived of a right to continue his education. There was no merit to the student's claim to a due process "right" to play football. **The Sixth Circuit does not recognize a constitutionally protected property interest in athletic participation.** While the student asserted a liberty interest in his good name and reputation, he lost this claim by failing to ask the university for a name-clearing hearing. Moreover, university officials were entitled to qualified immunity. As a result, the court dismissed the student's case. *Awrey v. Gilbertson*, 833 F.Supp.2d 738 (E.D. Mich. 2011).

◆ *A federal court rejected a student-athlete's request for reinstatement of his admission to a Connecticut university after he was arrested on felony charges.*

As a Florida high school senior, the student was arrested and charged with aggravated stalking of a minor. At the time, he had accepted a partial lacrosse scholarship from Quinnipiac University in Connecticut. He said the arrest was based on a "horseplay" incident in which he "fake raped" a younger male. But the high school suspended him, and he did not graduate with his class. After receiving a diploma through an online program, the student pleaded guilty to misdemeanor battery. He was sentenced to probation, community service and counseling, and was also required to report to a probation officer in person.

Florida officials granted him a temporary travel permit, and he enrolled at Quinnipiac. But the Florida Department of Corrections (DOC) sent Quinnipiac a letter saying the student was a "sexual predator or sexual offender." Quinnipiac rescinded his admission pending an investigation. The DOC sent another letter explaining that the first letter had been sent in error, and the student sued Quinnipiac in a federal court for breach of contract. The court denied his request for a preliminary order requiring his reinstatement, finding claims that he would otherwise fall behind his peers and lose his lacrosse scholarship purely speculative. Inability to play lacrosse during the current semester resulted from the student's own actions. He was still unable to travel with the team in several states. As the student could reapply to the university for the next semester and might miss just one semester, the court denied the request for an injunction. It held **Quinnipiac made a reasonable decision to rescind his admission pending an investigation**. *Stockstill v. Quinnipiac Univ.*, No. 3:10-cv-265 (VLB), 2010 WL 2011152 (D. Conn. 5/19/10).

◆ *No contract was breached when a Duke University golf coach dismissed a student from the golf team and revoked his access to university golf facilities.*

According to the student, Duke University head golf coach Rod Myers promised him lifetime access to Duke's state-of-the-art training facilities when he recruited him as a high school golfer. While the student accepted an offer to attend Duke and play on the golf team, he was not awarded a scholarship. After Myers died, his successor dismissed the student from the team and revoked his access to Duke's golf facilities. The student sued the successor coach and Duke in a federal district court for breach of contract and related claims. A federal magistrate judge rejected the contract claim, explaining that **student policy manuals are not binding contracts**. The manuals upon which the student relied to support his breach of contract claim could be unilaterally altered at any time. The magistrate judge rejected a claim that the university and the coach breached a covenant of good faith and fair dealing. **Without a contract, a covenant of good faith and fair dealing does not exist, and the student could not claim tortious interference with any contract.** *Giuliani v. Duke Univ.*, No. 1:08CV502, 2009 WL 1408869 (M.D.N.C. 5/19/09).

◆ *A soccer player who was subject to an athletic conference transfer rule failed to demonstrate that the rule violated federal antitrust laws.*

After the player learned that other University of Southern California (USC) student-athletes received fraudulent academic credits, she transferred to the University of California, Los Angeles (UCLA). Both USC and UCLA were members of the Pacific 10 Athletic Association (PAC 10). USC opposed the transfer and sought sanctions against the player under a PAC 10 transfer rule, which would bar her from competing for UCLA during her first year there. In a federal district court, the player sued USC, USC officials and the PAC 10, asserting that USC enforced PAC 10 sanctions against her, but not others. She alleged retaliation and claimed the transfer rule conflicted with the Sherman Act, which prohibits contracts or conspiracies that restrain trade or commerce.

After the court dismissed the case, the player appealed to the U.S. Court of Appeals, Ninth Circuit. It held her antitrust claim required proof that the transfer rule produced significant anticompetitive effects in relevant geographic and product markets. The player claimed the relevant geographic market in this case was the Los Angeles area, and the relevant product market was the UCLA women's soccer program. The Ninth Circuit rejected this interpretation, noting that the player was recruited by similar soccer programs outside the area. In any event, the claim failed because the PAC 10 transfer rule only applied to member schools. **As the player admitted she was the only USC athlete** to suffer sanctions under the transfer rule, she conceded that the rule did not affect all relevant consumers, foiling her antitrust claim. *Tanaka v. Univ. of Southern California*, 252 F.3d 1059 (9th Cir. 2001).

◆   *The California Supreme Court held student-athletes have lower privacy expectations than the general student population.*

In 1986, the NCAA instituted a drug testing program for six categories of banned drugs including steroids and street drugs. In order to participate, all students had to sign a consent form at the start of each school year allowing the drug tests. Two Stanford athletes instituted an action in a California trial court, alleging that the drug testing program violated their right to privacy. The case reached the Supreme Court of California, which held that student-athletes have lower expectations of privacy than the general student population. Competitive events involved close regulation and scrutiny of student-athletes. **Required physical examinations (including urinalysis) and the special regulation of sleep habits, diet, fitness and other activities that intrude significantly on privacy interests are routine aspects of a college athlete's life not shared by other students or the population at large.** Further, the court noted that drug testing programs involving student-athletes have routinely survived Fourth Amendment privacy challenges. The court held the NCAA had an interest in protecting the health and safety of student-athletes involved in NCAA-regulated competition. *Hill v. NCAA*, 26 Cal.Rptr.2d 834 (Cal. 1994).

◆   *A drug testing program was struck down where it was not voluntary, and where the college athletes did not have a diminished expectation of privacy.*

The Supreme Court of Colorado held the university did not articulate an important governmental interest for the program. **Unlike cases involving high school athletes, college students did not have a diminished expectation of privacy under the Fourth Amendment that justified government searches in the absence of an important governmental interest.** Random, suspicionless urinalysis was unconstitutional. Student-athletes did not consent to participation in the program because there could be no voluntary consent where the failure to consent resulted in denial of a governmental benefit. As the program did not ensure confidentiality and was mandatory, the court held for the athletes. *Univ. of Colorado v. Derdeyn*, 863 P.2d 929 (Colo. 1993).

## B.  NCAA Rules

*The National Collegiate Athletic Association (NCAA) is a voluntary, nonprofit association which regulates college athletics, defines eligibility for players and imposes sanctions for violating its rules. NCAA rules limit student eligibility for interscholastic competition to a five-year period and prevent athletic participation for one year after a transfer between member institutions. The NCAA's core course requirement excludes from consideration for initial eligibility all courses taught below regular high school instructional levels.*

◆   *Two student-athletes, who lost their scholarships to play football at NCAA Division I institutions due to career-ending injuries, made an unsuccessful challenge to two NCAA rules. One rule prohibited multiyear scholarships, and the other capped the number of scholarships available to a member institution.*

Two NCAA Division I football players suffered career-ending injuries while they were in college. Their injuries prevented them from playing football, and their institutions refused to renew their scholarships. The students claimed NCAA rules prevented them from obtaining scholarships that would have covered the full costs of their college education. One of the rules limited the number of scholarships available to a team. The other rule concerned the NCAA's prohibition on multi-year scholarships.

In an Indiana federal court, the students asserted the NCAA regulations had an anti-competitive effect on the market for student-athletes that violated the Sherman Antitrust Act. The court dismissed the case, and the players appealed to the U.S. Court of Appeals, Seventh Circuit. It held the proposed "market" between universities and student-athletes for bachelor's degrees was not legally recognized. Moreover, **the students did not identify a labor market for collegiate student-athletes**. Since the lower court did not abuse its discretion in dismissing the case, the court affirmed the judgment for the NCAA. *Agnew v. NCAA*, 683 F.3d 328 (7th Cir. 2012).

In February 2012, the NCAA announced a majority of NCAA institutions had voted to allow Division I schools the option of offering multi-year scholarships. The rule change did not affect the students in the *Agnew v. NCAA* case, summarized above.

◆ *The U.S. Supreme Court has held that the NCAA is not a recipient of federal funds and is therefore not subject to suit under Title IX.*

The case was filed by a college graduate who had played two years of intercollegiate volleyball at a private college before enrolling in postgraduate programs at two other colleges. Because she had exhausted only two years of her athletic eligibility, she sought a waiver from the NCAA's Postbaccalaureate Bylaw, which allows postgraduate student-athletes to compete in intercollegiate sports only at the institution where they received an undergraduate degree. The student sued the NCAA in a Pennsylvania federal court after it denied her requests for a waiver. She claimed that the NCAA discriminated against her on the basis of gender in violation of Title IX. The complaint asserted that the NCAA granted more waivers to male postgraduate students than it did to females. The case reached the U.S. Supreme Court, which noted that Title IX covers entities that receive federal financial assistance – whether direct or indirect – whereas those entities that only benefit economically from federal financial assistance are not covered. **Because the NCAA only benefited economically from institutions that received federal financial assistance, it could not be sued under Title IX.** *NCAA v. Smith*, 525 U.S. 459, 119 S.Ct. 924, 142 L.Ed.2d 929 (1999).

◆ *An assistant football coach who was forced to give up his job due to rules violations was unable to advance various claims against the NCAA.*

Officials at the University of Kentucky (UK) confronted the coach with evidence of NCAA rules violations. He agreed to step down and later claimed that he did so based on assurances that no further action would be taken against him. However, UK conducted an internal investigation and turned over its findings to the NCAA. In turn, the NCAA held a hearing to consider charges of improper recruiting practices, such as improperly inducing prospective athletes and high school coaches, and fraudulently assisting student-athletes in the form of preparation of their work. The NCAA sanctioned UK for the rules violations. It also imposed an eight-year restriction on the coach and any NCAA member seeking to hire him for an athletic-related position. He sued the NCAA, UK and the Southeastern Conference in a federal district court.

The court dismissed the action, and the coach appealed. The U.S. Court of Appeals, Sixth Circuit, held his antitrust claim was properly dismissed. Since the coach did not advance a commercial claim, he failed to allege an antitrust injury. **NCAA rules were not commercial and were designed to promote and ensure competitiveness among its members.** The coach admitted his own misconduct had caused any injury he suffered, defeating his fraud claim. A breach of contract claim was disallowed as against public policy. The court noted that if not for the coach's own misconduct, he would still have his job, and affirmed the judgment. *Bassett v. NCAA*, 528 F.3d 426 (6th Cir. 2008).

◆ *A federal district court denied a Kansas student-athlete's request for an order to prevent the enforcement of an NCAA athletic eligibility rule.*

The student transferred to the University of Kansas (KU) in 2004 after beginning college at another school. He eventually made the KU football team. The NCAA denied a request for a waiver of the NCAA's five-year eligibility rule. After an unsuccessful appeal, the student sued KU and the NCAA in a federal district court for civil rights violations. He petitioned a court for an order preventing the university from enforcing the NCAA's eligibility ruling.

The court found the five-year eligibility period begins to run when a student-athlete initially registers and attends the first day of classes in a regular term of an academic year for a full-time program of studies. The NCAA may waive the eligibility rule for reasons beyond the control of the student or institution which deprive the student of the opportunity to participate for more than one season within the five-year period. **An NCAA member school may grant a one-year extension of the five-year period for a female student-athlete for reasons of pregnancy.** The student contended that he missed the chance to participate in football when his girlfriend became pregnant some time before he enrolled at KU. He said he decided not to attend college so he could work and care for his daughter. The court rejected the student's gender discrimination claim. It also found no merit to his claim that he would be unable to complete his education and lose any chance to be recruited by a professional football team. The student's financial aid package was not an athletic grant, and the threat of losing a professional career was speculative. The court denied the student's request for relief, finding it was in the public interest to allow the NCAA to enforce its own rules without court intervention. *Butler v. NCAA*, Civ. Act. No. 06-2319 KHV, 2006 WL 2398683 (D. Kan. 8/15/06).

◆ *A federal court held a student's religious courses and computer classes were not "core courses" under the NCAA academic eligibility requirements.*

The NCAA sets eligibility requirements for Division I competition, which mandate that students take at least 13 high school "core courses" and that students achieve a specified minimum grade point average in those courses as well as a specified minimum score on either the SAT or ACT. The higher a student's test score, the lower the required GPA needed. An 18-year-old black student, who excelled at basketball, graduated from a private, Catholic high school. He was heavily recruited by colleges and universities, and selected a private Illinois university. The NCAA ruled the student was not qualified to compete in Division I play during his freshman season, and he sued the NCAA.

A federal district court held the high school religion courses **were taught from a particular religious point of view – based on a Christian ideology**. The court also determined that, based on the syllabi **for the computer classes, at least 50% of the course instruction included keyboarding or word processing**, which took the classes outside core status. As a result, the student did not have even a negligible chance of success on the merits of his claim, and he was not entitled to injunctive relief. The court refused to overrule the NCAA's eligibility determination, and the student was not allowed to play basketball as a freshman. *Hall v. NCAA*, 985 F.Supp. 782 (N.D. Ill. 1997).

◆  *A wrestler who transferred from a Rhode Island university had to sit out for one year because he was not in good academic standing.*

The student, a talented wrestler, failed a course during his first semester at Nebraska and did not repeat the course before transferring to Brown. The NCAA notified him he would be prohibited from wrestling the next academic year because he had not successfully repeated the course. The student sued the NCAA in a federal district court, seeking an injunction to restrain the NCAA from preventing him from wrestling. The court denied the injunction. **NCAA regulations prevent athletic participation for one year after transfer.** There is an exception to this rule for students in good academic standing who would have been eligible to participate had they remained at their previous institution. As the student had failed the course, he would have been ineligible at both Nebraska and Brown. He could not bring constitutional claims against the NCAA, as it is private entity. *Collier v. NCAA*, 783 F.Supp. 1576 (D.R.I. 1992).

## C. Individuals with Disabilities

*In* PGA Tour v. Martin, *532 U.S. 661 (U.S. 2001), the U.S. Supreme Court recited a general rule that the Americans with Disabilities Act (ADA) requires an individualized inquiry to determine whether a requested modification is reasonable and necessary for a disabled individual, and whether the modification would fundamentally alter the nature of the competition.*

◆  *A Maryland federal court refused to dismiss dueling motions from both parties in a pending disability access case.*

Individuals with disabilities sued the school, alleging violations of the ADA and the Rehabilitation Act because aural content was not captioned at stadium sporting events or on the school's sports website. At the district court, the plaintiffs filed a motion for partial summary judgment and the school filed a motion for summary judgment. In this case, **a factual dispute existed as to whether meeting the request for the "line of sight" captioning the plaintiffs**

**sought would have created an undue burden**. A university official said it would cost about $3.75 million to do what the plaintiffs asked, and it was too soon in the case to decide whether the request was one that would result in an undue burden. Similarly, **a factual issue existed as to whether captioning live and pre-produced website content would be unduly burdensome**, the court said. The school said the site "operates on a shoestring" and that a captioning requirement would hurt its ability to produce content in a timely manner. But the court said it was too soon to tell whether that burden is beyond one that the school is legally required to bear. Both motions were denied. *Innes v. Board of Regents of the Univ. System of Maryland*, No. DKC 13-2800, 2015 WL 1210484 (D. Md. 3/16/15).

The university went on to spend $3.75 million to install ribbon boards in both venues. At the cost of $325 per basketball game and $565 per football game, a specialist typed real-time captions that were displayed on the boards. Post-game press conferences were also captioned – at additional cost. The university asked the court to reconsider dismissing the claim, arguing it provided the accommodation the fans requested, so the suit was moot. **The judge disagreed, as the university did not show the matter was completely resolved.** First, it could stop providing the captioning at any time. And moreover, the fans disagreed that the new system provided effective communication. The court held the case had to proceed. *Innes v. Board of Regents of the Univ. System of Maryland*, 121 F.Supp.3d 504 (D. Md. 2015).

In a related ruling in the same case, the plaintiffs sought to depose the president of the university. He filed a motion for a protective order that asked the court to bar the taking of his deposition. He said his deposition would be fruitless because he had no knowledge of the subjects relating to the complaint. He also claimed that even if he did, his testimony would duplicate the testimony of the athletic director, the multimedia production team and the assistant athletic director of facilities and events. **He submitted an affidavit saying he had no personal knowledge of the access issues raised by the plaintiffs in the suit. He also pointed to the burden he faced if deposed, noting his busy travel schedule and the need to meet with potential donors.** In light of the president's lack of knowledge relating to the issues in the case and the burden a forced deposition would create for him, the court decided it wasn't necessary. *Innes v. Board of Regents of the Univ. System of Maryland*, No. DKC 13-2800, 2014 WL 2436088 (D. Md. 5/29/14).

◆ *A deceased student-athlete's claims against several colleges that stopped recruiting him survived his death.*

The student had learning disabilities but was recruited for football by several NCAA Division I schools. The NCAA ruled that a number of his high school special education classes did not satisfy its core course requirement and declared him ineligible during his freshman season. He filed a federal district court action against the NCAA, the ACT/Clearinghouse and several universities. After the student died, his estate continued the litigation. After years of court activity, the student's mother revealed that he had been in and out of drug treatment and mental health programs and that his death resulted from an apparent drug overdose. The court sanctioned the mother and her attorneys, finding that the failure to disclose this information was willful and in bad faith.

On appeal, the U.S. Court of Appeals, Third Circuit, held the alleged discrimination took place during the 1995-96 school year, when the student was declared ineligible by the NCAA. Evidence of substance abuse in 1995-96 was minimal and was irrelevant for liability purposes. **A determination of whether a person is a "qualified individual with a disability" under the ADA is made "from the time at which the alleged discriminatory decision was made."** The district court's contrary ruling was reversed. The mother could not use posthumously revealed information to her own advantage, but an order sanctioning the mother's attorneys for failing to disclose the student's full medical history was reversed. The case was returned to the district court for a determination of whether the NCAA and universities had violated the ADA and Rehabilitation Act. *Bowers v. NCAA*, 475 F.3d 524 (3d Cir. 2007).

◆  *A college football player with a disability could be prohibited from continuing to play.*

A University of Kansas physician discovered that a student had a congenital condition that put him at an extremely high risk for suffering severe and potentially permanent injuries, including quadriplegia. The university disqualified the student from participating in intercollegiate football. Although the student obtained opinions from three other doctors stating that his risk of injury was no greater than any other player's, the university denied his request to rejoin the football team. He filed a lawsuit against the university in a federal court, claiming it had violated Section 504 of the Rehabilitation Act.

The court denied the university's motion to dismiss the lawsuit, and the student sought an order to require his reinstatement to the football team. Because Section 504's definition of a person with a disability involves a consideration of whether the individual is impaired in some major life activity, the court considered whether intercollegiate athletic participation was a major life activity. **The court agreed that playing football was related to the major life activity of learning, but it held that his disqualification did not substantially limit his ability to learn.** The university had not revoked the student's athletic scholarship, and he retained the opportunity to participate in the football program in a role other than player. The court accepted the conclusion of the university's physicians that there was a reasonable basis for his exclusion from the team. The court denied the student's motion. *Pahulu v. Univ. of Kansas*, 897 F.Supp. 1387 (D. Kan. 1995).

## D.  Discrimination and Harassment

### 1.  Gender Equity in Athletics

*Title IX of the Education Amendments of 1972 (20 U.S.C. § 1681, et seq.) prohibits sex discrimination in education programs, including interscholastic, intercollegiate, club and intramural athletics. It applies only to programs that receive federal financial assistance. One of the most important Title IX implementing regulations is 34 C.F.R. § 106.41(c). It states that:*

A [federal funding] recipient which operates or sponsors interscholastic, intercollegiate, club or intramural athletics shall provide equal athletic opportunity for members of both sexes. In determining whether equal opportunities are available the Director will consider, among other factors:

1) Whether the selection of sports and levels of competition effectively accommodate the interests and abilities of members of both sexes; 2) The provision of equipment and supplies; 3) Scheduling of games and practice time; 4) Travel and per diem allowance; 5) Opportunity to receive coaching and academic tutoring; 6) Assignment and compensation of coaches and tutors; 7) Provision of locker rooms, practice and competitive facilities; 8) Provision of medical and training facilities and services; 9) Provision of housing and dining facilities and services; 10) Publicity.

Unequal aggregate expenditures for members of each sex or unequal expenditures for male and female teams if a recipient operates or sponsors separate teams will not constitute noncompliance with this section, but the Assistant Secretary [for Civil Rights of the U.S. Department of Education] may consider the failure to provide necessary funds for teams for one sex in assessing equality of opportunity for members of each sex.

A "three-part test" approved by the Office for Civil Rights (OCR) affords educational institutions three ways to demonstrate Title IX compliance. Compliance with Title IX may be shown by demonstrating: 1) **substantial proportionality** (the number of men and women in intercollegiate athletics is proportionate to their enrollment at the institution); or 2) **the institution has a "history and continuing practice of program expansion" for the underrepresented sex. If a university cannot satisfy the first two options, a third method allows it to show it "fully and effectively accommodates" the interests of women.** See 44 Fed.Reg. 71,413 (1979).

◆   *A Delaware federal judge dismissed the Title IX claims of a student-athlete who had her athletic scholarship reduced.*

When a female field hockey player was still in high school, she made an official visit to the university. At that time, the current field hockey coach offered the player a 35% scholarship in year one and 75% in year two. In an email clarification, the coach wrote the student was "guaranteed" to get at least as much in years three and four as she would get in year two. Then the coach sent the student a letter saying she had been selected to receive a 35% scholarship for only one year. **She signed a letter of intent that expressly nullified any prior oral agreements.** During the student's first semester, the coach resigned. The new coach told the student her scholarship would be reduced in her second year. The student left the team and sued the school and the new coach, claiming a Title IX violation. The defendants filed a motion for summary judgment. The student's claim was based on the theory that her scholarship was reduced while the scholarships of some male athletes were not. She relied on statements from four football players who allegedly told her they were promised scholarships spanning more than a year. But she said **she did not know whether those players received what they were promised or whether the scholarships were adjusted annually**. As a result, her evidence did not support her claim under Title IX. *Eppley v. Univ. of Delaware*, No. 12-cv-99 (GMS), 2015 WL 156754 (D. Del. 1/12/15).

◆ *A federal court held cheerleading is not a sport, so Quinnipiac University could not count cheerleaders toward the total it needed to establish it provided female students equitable opportunities to participate in varsity athletics.*

Quinnipiac University eliminated varsity women's volleyball, men's golf, and men's track and field teams. At the same time, it announced a new women's cheerleading squad. Women's volleyball players and their coach sued the university, claiming the changes would violate Title IX. After a hearing, the district court issued a preliminary injunction that stopped the university from cutting women's volleyball. **It found Quinnipiac had artificially increased women's team rosters and decreased men's rosters to make it look like it was complying with Title IX.** After a trial, the court found Quinnipiac violated Title IX. Appeal reached the U.S. Court of Appeals, Second Circuit. First, the court agreed with the district court's decision to exclude cheerleaders from the total number of student-athletes for Title IX compliance purposes.

**Neither the NCAA nor the federal Department of Education has recognized cheerleading as a varsity sport.** Cheerleaders did not have team locker rooms, and Quinnipiac did not hold off-campus recruiting for the team. There was no uniform set of rules for cheerleading competitions. Finally, a 3.62% disparity between female athletic participation and the percentage of females in the entire student body was not too small to show females were denied equitable opportunities to participate in varsity athletics. *Biediger v. Quinnipiac Univ.*, 691 F.3d 85 (2d Cir. 2012).

◆ *An Indiana university tennis coach may proceed with her claim that she was fired while another coach was only reprimanded for similar misconduct.*

Over an 18-year period, the coach often complained about lack of equity in the school's athletic programs. Her contract was renewed via a letter describing her performance as "exemplary." The coach then told her associate athletic director she might have violated NCAA rules. When he asked for her practice log, she texted three student-athletes, asking them to misrepresent when the practices were held. Later, the coach sent players another text asking them to run a practice. When the university learned of the texts, it released her from employment. In a federal court, the coach sued the university for violating Title IX and her First and Fourteenth Amendment rights. In the court's view, the coach produced enough evidence to avoid pretrial judgment on her Title IX claim. **She showed another coach had violated the same NCAA rule and was reprimanded but not discharged.** The court also refused to dismiss the First Amendment claim. There was no Fourteenth Amendment due process violation because the coach received a hearing. Her defamation claims failed because of a state immunity law. *Bull v. Board of Trustees of Ball State Univ.*, No. 1:10-cv-00878-JMS-TAB, 2012 WL 1564061 (S.D. Ind. 5/2/12).

◆ *The Fourth Circuit held a Virginia university did not violate Title IX or other laws when it cut a number of athletic programs.*

To remedy a 10% disparity between its undergraduate student population against its population of varsity athletes, James Madison University planned to cut seven men's teams and three women's teams. Opponents of the cuts, including athletes, coaches, alumni and fans, formed an organization to oppose the action. The group sued the U.S. Department of Education (DOE) and others, claiming DOE guidelines violated Title IX, the Constitution and the Administrative Procedure Act (APA). When the university rejected the group's request to hold off on the cuts, the group added claims against it and university officials. After a federal district court dismissed the lawsuit, appeal reached the Fourth Circuit. It upheld the three-part federal test for Title IX compliance first published in 1979 (above). **According to the court, Title IX permitted consideration of proportionality between participation and enrollment.** It found nothing in the test mandated statistical balancing. Instead, it creates a presumption that compliance is achieved when statistical balance is reached.

The court held that eliminating gender bias in collegiate athletics served an important government objective. It did not violate the Constitution to consider gender when decreasing athletic offerings to create a better balance. Neither the initial policy interpretation nor subsequent clarifications were subject to APA notice and comment requirements, as they were interpretive guidelines that did not create new law. For the same reason, the test did not require presidential approval. State law claims against the university were barred by the Eleventh Amendment, and an equal protection claim failed because the group did not show it was subject to disparate treatment or discrimination. Rejecting the group's additional arguments, the court upheld the judgment and found the university was motivated by the desire to achieve proportionality. *Equity in Athletics, Inc. v. Dep't of Educ.*, 639 F.3d 91 (4th Cir. 2011).

◆   *Central Michigan University (CMU) was entitled to immunity on a breach-of-contract claim filed by a student who lost her athletic scholarship.*

CMU offered a student an athletic scholarship to play basketball. She declined other scholarship offers and enrolled at CMU. She later claimed CMU's first-year coach harassed her, said she was not her "type" of person and repeatedly tried to force her to transfer. After missing practices, the student was dismissed from the team and lost her scholarship. The student sued CMU, the coach and other CMU officials for breach of contract and violations of her due process and equal protection rights. She added claims of defamation, interference with contract, intentional infliction of emotional distress, negligent hiring and negligent supervision. **The court dismissed the breach of contract claims against CMU and individual officials on the basis of sovereign immunity.** However, the court granted the student an opportunity to further develop her negligent hiring and supervision claims. *Heike v. Guevera*, 654 F.Supp.2d 658 (E.D. Mich. 2009).

A year later, the student and a teammate filed a second action in the same court, alleging violations of Title VI of the 1964 Civil Rights Act, the Equal Protection Clause of the Fourteenth Amendment and other laws. They claimed the defendants discriminated against them based on their races (Caucasian/Native American and Caucasian) and their sexual preference by not renewing their scholarships. The court agreed with the university that **nothing prevented the women from bringing these claims in the first case.** Since the dismissal of the first lawsuit constituted a final decision on the merits of a dispute involving the same parties, and both cases were based on the same facts, **the second action had to be dismissed on the basis on claim preclusion**. The appeals court held the lower court correctly found all of the requirements for the doctrine of claim preclusion were met. As a result, it affirmed the district court's decision for the university. *Heike v. Cent. Michigan Univ. Board of Trustees*, 573 Fed.Appx. 476 (6th Cir. 2014).

◆ *A federal district court agreed to let female student-athletes at Delaware State University proceed with their Title IX case as a class action.*

Delaware State University (DSU) decided to eliminate its women's equestrian team at the end of the 2009-10 academic year. In response, 15 of the team's 21 members filed a lawsuit against the university, accusing it of violating Title IX by failing to provide female student-athletes with equal opportunities to participate in varsity intercollegiate athletics. Team members sought court orders that would block DSU from eliminating the team. DSU agreed not to eliminate the team until the end of the 2010-11 year. A new group of eight student-athletes sought permission to have the case proceed as a class action. **Applying the test used by federal courts for class certification, the court held the team members could adequately represent a class of persons with an interest in the lawsuit.** They could represent other student-athletes regarding whether DSU was meeting its Title IX obligations. If it was held that DSU was out of compliance with Title IX, the class could represent others regarding whether proposed corrective actions would bring DSU into compliance. As a result, the motion for class certification was granted. *Foltz v. Delaware State Univ.*, 269 F.R.D. 419 (D. Del. 2010).

## 2. Sex Discrimination and Harassment

*As explained in Chapter Two, Title IX of the 1972 Education Amendments prohibits all federal-funding recipients from denying program participation or benefits based on gender. The courts have interpreted Title IX as barring sexual harassment, and most student harassment claims arise under Title IX.*

◆ *A California federal judge refused to dismiss the Title IX claims filed by basketball players who alleged they were discriminated against based on their sexual orientation.*

Two students were members of the university's women's basketball team. After they started dating, the students claimed that the coach and athletic coordinator repeatedly harassed them and discriminated against them to get them to quit the team. In one instance, the coach said lesbianism is a reason that teams lose, so it would not be tolerated. The students sued, alleging sex discrimination. The university asked the court to dismiss the claim. It refused, noting that Title IX bans discrimination on the basis of sex in education programs or activities that receive federal financial assistance. The court said the line between discrimination based on gender stereotyping and discrimination based on sexual orientation is "blurry, at best." Moreover, the court said, the actual sexual orientation of the alleged victim is not relevant. Instead, it concluded, **the focus of the analysis should be on "the biased**

**mind of the alleged discriminator."** The students stated a valid claim, so the case could move forward. *Videckis v. Pepperdine Univ.*, 150 F.Supp.3d 1151 (C.D. Cal. 2015).

◆ *A Pennsylvania federal court rejected the Title IX retaliation claim of a female athlete who alleged she was removed from the team for reporting a male athlete's harassment.*

A female student who was on a full volleyball scholarship dated a male athlete. After they broke up, the ex-boyfriend went to her dorm. Visibly drunk, he punched a wall, broke a window and threatened to kill her. The girl called campus police. The ex-boyfriend was detained and later suspended. The following school year, the girl was removed from the volleyball team and lost her scholarship. Her scholarship was partly reinstated after she filed a grievance, but she was kept off the team. She sued, alleging the school violated Title IX by retaliating against her by taking her off the team and revoking her scholarship. **Given the time lag between these events and her failure to present any antagonistic conduct from the school, she couldn't show one was caused by the other.** The court dismissed her suit. *Frazer v. Temple Univ.*, 25 F.Supp.3d 598 (E.D. Pa. 2014).

◆ *Finding no Title IX violation, a Kentucky federal judge dismissed a student's federal claims and sent her state-law claims back to state court.*

A sexually assaulted student-athlete sued, claiming her coach's failure to report the assault caused the student to lose her place on the team, her scholarship and her full-time-student status. The student was sexually assaulted by a male classmate in 2011. Six weeks later, the victim emailed her coach to report the attack and explain why she missed mandatory team activities. She also asked for resources to help her handle the aftermath of the attack. The coach responded by referring the student to the university's women's center. Allegedly, the coach never reported the incident to police or followed up with the student. Three months after the attack, the student reported the incident to police and sued the university in state court, claiming negligence. She also added Title IX claim – a federal issue. The university removed the case to federal court and asked the judge to dismiss the complaint. It did, as **the student could not show the university knew about – and was indifferent to – the sexual harassment**. So the federal claim failed. The court sent the state claims back to the court where they were originally filed. *Moore v. Murray State Univ.*, No. 5:12-CV_00178, 2013 WL 960320 (W.D. Ky. 3/12/13).

◆ *Finding the former student manager of a university's football team could state a valid claim that she lost her job for complaining about sexual harassment by student-athletes, the Second Circuit reversed a decision to dismiss the suit.*

A graduate student at Hofstra University was hired as the football team's manager. An email explained that she would be paid $700 for the fall season and $300 for the spring season. Several football players made inappropriate comments and created an inappropriate Facebook page featuring the student. Upset, she went to the coach, who ordered the players to delete the page. They did. After the last game of the season, the assistant coach played an R-rated movie on the team bus. Players made lewd remarks and sounds during the sex scenes. One turned to the student and made a vulgar remark. She complained to the assistant coach, and he turned the movie off. Players began chanting, "We want boobies." When they arrived at the school, the student reported the incident to the head coach. He asked her to let it go, as the football program would suffer from such attention. She reported the incident. An investigation took place, and training was provided. The student emailed the coach before "spring ball" started to ask about her schedule. He told her they'd hired someone else. The student filed suit, claiming retaliation for reporting sexual harassment. Hofstra asked the court to dismiss the claim. It did. The student appealed, and the Second Circuit reversed, saying **the university's email stated her salary for both seasons, so it was reasonable for her to expect she'd have the job for both semesters**. And that meant a reasonable juror could conclude she was replaced as team manager in retaliation for reporting the harassment. *Summa v. Hofstra Univ.*, 708 F.3d 115 (2d Cir. 2013).

◆   *A federal court rejected Title IX claims by a California student who said she was sexually assaulted by three members of the men's basketball team.*

The student said the team members sexually assaulted her in an on-campus apartment. She did not immediately report the incident, and her friends relayed her story to an assistant coach of the women's team. Within a day, the information was provided to the university athletic director and a vice president of student affairs. Two days after the friends' report, the university issued a campus-wide safety alert and forwarded the charge to local police. University officials also offered the student counseling and a victim advocacy program.

The student sued the university in a federal court for violating Title IX. The court rejected a claim that the university failed to investigate a prior assault involving the same men. There was evidence that the university investigated the incident promptly, provided counseling services, encouraged the student to file criminal charges and punished the men. The court rejected a claim that the university retaliated against the student for reporting the incident by temporarily barring social interaction between the men's and women's teams. On appeal, the U.S. Court of Appeals, Ninth Circuit, held the student did not show university officials acted with "deliberate indifference" or that their response was "clearly unreasonable in light of the known circumstances." Officials had no knowledge that any of the individuals who assaulted the student were involved in the prior attack. The court rejected the claim that the university acted unreasonably by declining to expel the assailants. **The student was not entitled to the precise remedy she preferred.** As the steps taken by the university in response to the assault were not clearly unreasonable, her Title IX claim failed. Nothing suggested the university acted with a retaliatory motive, defeating the retaliation claim. As a result, the judgment was affirmed. *Doe v. Univ. of the Pacific*, 467 Fed.Appx. 685 (9th Cir. 2012).

◆   *A federal district court in Massachusetts declined to dismiss most of the sexual harassment claims filed against a college by a student.*

The student joined the college's all-female equestrian team, which was coached by a 67-year-old male who the student soon accused of frequent and ongoing sexual harassment. A sexual harassment complaint was filed against the coach by another student, and the college issued him a "final warning." But the student said she then accepted offers to sleep at his house because she was having problems with a roommate. She said the coach touched her and forced her to stay in his hotel room on an overnight team trip. The student withdrew from college and sued both the college and coach in a federal district court for violations of Title IX and state law. She added claims against the coach for assault and battery and false imprisonment, and negligence and breach of contract claims against the college. **The court held the college could be held liable under Title IX if it had knowledge of a risk of abuse to students based on prior complaints about the coach.** There was evidence of a valid complaint against him, and this was held sufficient to support a Title IX claim.

The court refused to dismiss state-law sexual harassment claims, but dismissed the assault and battery claims. It held such acts went far beyond the scope of the coach's employment. False imprisonment claims based on the charge that he trapped the student in his home and hotel room were allowed to go forward because it was conceivable that he was acting in the interest of the college when he did so. The court refused to dismiss the negligent retention and supervision claims, noting the college had been put on notice of the coach's sexual misconduct, yet failed to limit or even monitor his activities. Finally, the court granted dismissal of the breach of contract claim. *Bloomer v. Becker College*, No. 09-11342-FDS, 2010 WL 3221969 (D. Mass. 8/13/10).

◆   *An Alabama community college was not liable for the rape of a student athlete by one of her basketball coaches.*

In her state court lawsuit, the student claimed the community college hired her assailant to act as an assistant, even though he had been jailed "relating to the death of a child." A teammate claimed he touched her inappropriately on two occasions. The player stated she initially viewed the assistant as a father figure and spent time at his home. He also gave her rides. But the assistant later raped the student in a motel room after an away basketball game. She sued the college in a state court for violating Title IX and other federal laws. The court held for the college and officials, and the student appealed to the state supreme court. The court rejected claims that the college did not properly investigate the touching incidents or the inappropriate relationship between the student and assistant. Evidence showed the touching incident was promptly investigated. **While the head basketball coach's failure to strictly follow investigation procedures might have been negligent, it did not prove deliberate indifference.** The court also rejected the student's argument that the head coach should have seen the assistant was sexually harassing her and should have unilaterally initiated procedures under the college's sexual harassment policy. This argument failed because she admitted she did not consider her relationship with him to be sexual. The judgment against the student was affirmed. *J.B. v. Lawson State Community College*, 29 So.3d 164 (Ala. 2009).

◆   *The Supreme Court recognized a retaliation claim under Title IX, finding coaches are often in the best position to vindicate the rights of student-athletes.*

An Alabama high school teacher discovered the girls' basketball team did not receive the same funding or access to equipment and facilities as did boys' teams. He began complaining to supervisors, but said the school district did not respond. The teacher said he was given negative evaluations and was removed as girls' coach. He sued the school board in a federal court, claiming the loss of his coaching contract constituted unlawful retaliation in violation of Title IX.

Appeal reached the U.S. Supreme Court, which held Title IX covers retaliation against a person for complaining about sex discrimination. "Retaliation is, by definition an intentional act," and it is a form of discrimination, since the person who complains is treated differently than others. A program that retaliates against a person based on a sex discrimination complaint intentionally discriminates in violation of Title IX. Without finding that actual discrimination had occurred, the Court held the teacher was entitled to bring his case before the district court and attempt to show the board was liable. A private right of action for retaliation was within the statute's prohibition of intentional sex discrimination. Title IX did not require the victim of retaliation to also be the victim of discrimination. **The text of Title IX gave the board sufficient notice that it could not retaliate against the teacher after he complained of discrimination.** The Court found a reasonable school board would realize it could not cover up violations of Title IX by retaliating against teachers. It returned the case to the district court, where the teacher would be allowed to try to prove retaliation by the school board. *Jackson v. Birmingham Board of Educ.*, 544 U.S. 167, 125 S.Ct. 1497, 161 L.Ed.2d 361 (2005).

◆   *A federal appeals court reinstated claims that the University of Colorado (CU) violated Title IX by encouraging student-athletes to commit rape.*

Two female students claimed that a football player and a female tutor for the athletic department planned a football recruiting event to provide recruits an opportunity to have sex with intoxicated female students. They further claimed recruits and players sexually assaulted them, and they sued CU for violating Title IX. The students contended the university had control over recruits and players, but failed to control or eliminate the risk. The court held the university could not be deliberately indifferent to acts it knew nothing about. The students could not prove CU was liable without showing it had actual knowledge and was deliberately indifferent to the misconduct.

On appeal, the Tenth Circuit explained that CU could not be liable under Title IX unless it showed the assaults resulted from its deliberate indifference. **Deliberate indifference could be established by proving a failure to train regarding obvious risks.** In this case, there was evidence that CU and its head football coach were deliberately indifferent to the need to provide training and undermined efforts to prevent harassment. Evidence showed that player-hosts received little or no direction regarding proper behavior or level of responsibility. In addition, the coach prevented a female player from remaining on the team after she complained of harassment, and hired an assistant coach who had been accused of assaulting a woman. As a jury could find the coach knew of a serious risk of sexual harassment, the judgment was reversed. *Simpson v. Univ. of Colorado*, 500 F.3d 1170 (10th Cir. 2007). CU reportedly agreed to pay one of the students $2.5 million to settle the case. A settlement called for a payment of $385,000 to the other student.

◆   *The informal atmosphere of collegiate athletics includes profanity, slang, and sarcasm that does not always create a hostile educational environment.*

A University of North Carolina women's varsity soccer team member claimed a coach asked players about their sexual activities, commented about their legs and breasts and called one player a "slut." The coach met with the student in his hotel room and asked her about her social life and who she was sleeping with. She told him it was not his business, and he soon kicked her off the team. After the university investigated the student's complaint, the coach apologized to her and promised to refrain from further discussing sexual matters with players. However, the student sued the university in a federal district court, alleging he had created a hostile sexual environment. The court held for the university. A three-judge panel of the U.S. Court of Appeals, Fourth Circuit, found no jury could find the coach's remarks created a hostile environment. *Jennings v. Univ. of North Carolina*, 444 F.3d 255 (4th Cir. 2006).

All the judges of the Fourth Circuit agreed to reconsider the appeal, and decided the student had stated a valid discrimination claim under Title IX based on a hostile environment. She made a sufficient showing that she was subjected to severe or pervasive sexual harassment. **The evidence indicated the coach's comments were not "of a joking and teasing nature," but were degrading and humiliating.** The student also showed the coach's conduct negatively affected her ability to participate in soccer. The fact that she was disappointed at being cut did not defeat her Title IX claim. There was enough evidence to show the university had actual notice of a hostile environment. *Jennings v. Univ. of North Carolina*, 482 F.3d 686 (4th Cir. 2007).

### 3. Race Discrimination

*Higher education institutions may be subject to liability for intentional discrimination based on race, color or national origin under Title VI of the Civil Rights Act of 1964, and the Equal Protection Clause. Some claims have also been filed against universities under 42 U.S.C. Section 1981, which prohibits race discrimination in the making and enforcement of contracts.*

*In* Cureton v. NCAA, *198 F.3d 107 (3d Cir. 1999), the U.S. Court of Appeals, Third Circuit, held the National Collegiate Athletic Association (NCAA) was not subject to a Title VI claim. It held the NCAA was not a direct recipient of federal funds and did not exert sufficient authority over its member institutions to make it liable for Title VI violations.*

◆   *A federal appeals court rejected a female basketball player's claim of racial discrimination.*

The student received an athletic scholarship and played on the basketball team during her freshman and sophomore years. In her freshman year, she had the lowest shooting percentage on the team and the least on-court-time average. During her sophomore year, the student had the second-lowest scoring total and playing time on the team. She said the coach reduced her playing time because she was white and "too girly." She also claimed black teammates got more playing time because the coach "wanted a tough looking, thug-looking team." At the end of her sophomore season, the coach didn't renew the student's scholarship. She sued, claiming a breach of her constitutional right to equal protection based on race and sexual orientation bias. The court dismissed her claim. She appealed, but the Sixth Circuit affirmed, saying **she didn't produce evidence showing a valid racial discrimination claim, and the student's "proof" – that the coach preferred "thugs" – was itself racially biased**. So the claim failed. *Heike v. Guevara*, 519 Fed.Appx. 911 (6th Cir. 2013).

◆ *An NCAA eligibility rule survived a challenge by California student-athletes who claimed the rule unfairly excluded financially disadvantaged minority students from obtaining Division I athletic scholarships.*

NCAA Division I Bylaw 14.5.4.2 disqualified student-athletes from athletic scholarships and sports participation if they transferred from two-year colleges to four-year Division I colleges under certain circumstances. A group of seven students sued the NCAA and the University of California system's president in a federal court, claiming the bylaw violated their right to equal protection. In reviewing the case, the court found that the NCAA classifies college applicants as "qualifiers" or "non-qualifiers" – meaning they do or do not qualify for athletic scholarships or participation under NCAA rules.

Nonqualifiers from four-year and two-year institutions alike were eligible to compete and receive athletic scholarships after a transfer to a Division I institution if they completed one year in residence, earned a minimum number of credits, and attained a minimum GPA. Eligibility requirements were stricter for non-qualifiers transferring from a two-year school to a Division I school. After August 2009, the NCAA required students transferring under these circumstances to pass the equivalent of one math class and two English classes. According to the student-athletes, the bylaw put an unfair barrier between them and a Division I athletic scholarship. But the court held **the rule supported the legitimate purpose of assuring nonqualifiers had the academic tools to succeed at a Division I institution**. The rule's different transfer requirements were rationally related to that purpose. As hardship alone did not state an equal protection claim, the court dismissed the case. *Davis v. NCAA*, No. C 11-01207 WHA, 2011 WL 2531394 (N.D. Cal. 6/24/11).

◆ *Two African-American student-athletes could pursue their race discrimination lawsuit against the NCAA under Proposition 16.*

The NCAA used Proposition 16 to determine which first-year college students could play Division I and II sports. The rule used a combination of high school grades in NCAA-approved "core courses" and scores on such standardized tests as the SAT and the ACT to determine eligibility. Two African-American students who signed national letters of intent to play sports at Division I schools failed to meet the NCAA's test score requirements. They were not allowed to play intercollegiate athletics their freshman year.

The students sued the NCAA in a federal district court, alleging the NCAA intentionally discriminated against them on the basis of race in violation of Title VI of the Civil Rights Act of 1964 and 42 U.S.C. § 1981, and violated the Americans with Disabilities Act (ADA) and Section 504 regarding one of the athletes. One athlete proved causation by claiming the design of Proposition 16 discriminated against her because of a disability. But the claims failed because an NCAA rule change allows student-athletes who do not qualify for their initial year of eligibility to recoup that lost year with good grades. As a result, the athlete was not denied a year of eligibility by failing to meet the qualifying requirements, and lacked standing to bring ADA and Section 504 claims. The court dismissed the race discrimination claims, but on appeal, the Third Circuit held **the students sufficiently alleged race discrimination** to survive pretrial dismissal. Their claim that the NCAA considered race when it adopted Proposition 16 could proceed. However, the Title VI, ADA, and Section 504 claims were properly dismissed. *Pryor v. NCAA*, 288 F.3d 548 (3d Cir. 2002).

### E.  Injuries

*Collegiate athletes assume the risks inherent in sports competition. The Supreme Judicial Court of Massachusetts explained that to hold a university liable for injuries to a student-athlete during a competitive athletic event, there must be a showing of willful, wanton or reckless conduct by participants. In* Gauvin v. Clark, *404 Mass. 450, 537 N.E.2d 94 (Mass. 1989), the court said players engaging in sports agree to undergo some physical contacts which could amount to assault and battery without their consent. For that reason, college hockey participants only had a duty to refrain from reckless misconduct. This standard applies to non-contact sports, but may not apply to cheerleading injuries.*

◆   *A cheerleader could not proceed with negligence claims against a university after being injured at a mandatory training camp run by a cheerleading organization, a Pennsylvania appeals court affirmed.*

The student was chosen for the cheerleading squad. She attended a mandatory camp run by a national cheerleading organization, where she was injured. After hitting her head on the floor, she wound up with a concussion, a closed head injury and impaired vision. She sued the university for personal injury, alleging the coach should've known the stunt was too dangerous. The trial court determined **the university didn't owe the student a duty of care as she was injured at the national cheerleading organization's camp** and it had total control over hiring and certifying instructors and evaluating and teaching the cheerleaders. She appealed, but the appeals court affirmed. *Kennedy v. Robert Morris Univ.*, 133 A.3d 38 (Pa. Super. Ct. 2016).

◆   *The Fourth Circuit vacated a Maryland court order that would have allowed an injured football player to return to the gridiron.*

The student-athlete collapsed during football practice. He was rushed to a hospital, where he was diagnosed with heatstroke, suffered organ failure and spent nine days in a coma. A year later, a private doctor cleared the student to play football with specific recommendations. But the team doctor refused to allow the student to return to the team, saying it would present an "unacceptable risk of serious injury or death." The university's policy gave the team doctor the final say-so on whether injured students could return. The student sued, alleging disability bias. The trial court decided the accommodation requests were reasonable. It issued an injunction ordering the university to let the student play football. The university appealed, saying the student wasn't "disabled" under the ADA. The Fourth Circuit overturned the ruling, saying it didn't need to rule on whether the student has a disability under the definition of the law. When it comes to determining whether eligibility requirements are essential, courts generally give "a measure of deference to the school's professional judgment," the court explained. In this case, **the university's policy was clear that the team doctor had the authority to make the call and "a student-athlete's private physician DOES NOT have any jurisdiction as to the participation status of the student-athlete."** So the ruling was overturned, and the injunction was vacated. *Class v. Towson Univ.*, 806 F.3d 236 (4th Cir. 2015).

◆ *A jury's award to the parents of a football player who died at practice had to be reduced from $10 million to $200,000, Florida's highest court held.*

After the student died during football practice, his parents sued the university and the state's athletic association, which administers the school's athletic department. A jury awarded the family $10 million. On appeal, the court found the athletic association was entitled to limited sovereign immunity – which meant **plaintiffs, under Florida law, could not recover more than $200,000 for tort claims against state agencies or subdivisions**. As a result, the award was reduced.

The parents appealed to the Florida Supreme Court, which upheld the ruling that the athletic association was entitled to immunity, as it was not an autonomous entity – instead, it was subject to the school's control. *Plancher v. UCF Athletics Ass'n*, 175 So.3d 724 (Fla. 2015).

◆ *A Georgia football player who was injured during spring training could not sue the university to recover damages for the injury.*

The student was recruited to play football at Georgia Southern University (GSU). During spring training, the team was working out in full pads when the head football coach had players form two lines. Wanting to see "who was tough enough to be on the team," the coach walked down the line, randomly ordering two players to fight with no holds barred and continue fighting until he blew the whistle. The student in this action suffered permanent and severe injuries to his knee and leg when his opponent jumped on him. The student sued the coach and athletic director for negligence and sought punitive damages. Those claims were settled. He also sued the board of regents of the University System of Georgia, as GSU is one of its state schools. The court dismissed the claim, finding **the board was immune to the suit based on sovereign immunity**. The student appealed, and the appellate court affirmed. Expressing sympathy, the court said, "[We] certainly do not condone the alleged misconduct ... of the coaching staff in this case." But it found the case could not continue. *Pelham v. Board of Regents of the Univ. System of Georgia*, 743 S.E.2d 469 (Ga. Ct. App. 2013).

◆ *Finding there was adequate evidence to support the award, a Louisiana appeals court upheld a large judgment favoring a former basketball player.*

A student-athlete arrived on campus three days after a mandated reporting date. He and other players who were late were told there would be an "unorganized" practice for them two days later. During that practice, players lifted weights and went on 4.5-mile run. The players were told they could be suspended from the team if they didn't complete the run within 45 minutes. At the time, the temperature was 91 degrees, and the heat index was near 100. After the student finished the run, he lost consciousness. An athletic trainer was summoned, and she called 911. The student's core temperature had reached 104.2 by the time he arrived at the hospital. He later died. In a suit filed by his mother, the school was accused of causing his death. A jury ruled in his favor, and the trial court entered a judgment of nearly $1.6 million. The school appealed, raising only evidentiary and procedural issues regarding wrongfully excluded evidence. It said the jury should've heard about the student's positive THC screen when he was admitted to the hospital as well as the student's prior arrest and drug use. The court disagreed, finding it was not an abuse of discretion for the trial court to exclude the evidence. It explained **the probative value of evidence relating to the arrest, which was for drugs, was far outweighed by the prejudicial effect it would produce**. Evidence relating to what the student may have earned as a professional player was properly admitted, as was the testimony of a junior college coach regarding the student's work ethic and the testimony of the school's strength and conditioning coach – who said he would not have had players running outside that day. The trial court's judgment was affirmed. *Williams v. Board of Supervisors of the Univ. of Louisiana System*, 135 So.3d 804 (La. Ct. App. 2014).

◆  *The New York Court of Appeals held a college baseball pitcher assumed the risk of being hit by a line drive when he participated in an indoor practice.*

Coaches told the pitcher he would pitch from an artificial mound inside a nylon cage. He observed other pitchers throwing to batters inside the cage without an L-screen, which protects pitchers from balls batted back at them. After about six pitches, the pitcher was hit in the jaw by a batted ball. He sued the university and a coach in the state court system. After a trial court held for the university, the case reached the state's highest court. It explained that a legal doctrine called **assumption of the risk bars recovery for injuries to participants in sporting and amusement activities, if the participant is aware of the risks, appreciates their nature, and voluntarily assumes them**.

An educational institution can be liable for injuries to a student-athlete if it does not take reasonable care to protect him from risks that are "unassumed, concealed, or enhanced." In this case, the student was aware of the risk of getting hurt playing baseball. He had played for more than 13 years in varying conditions. He knew it was dangerous to pitch without an L-screen and had observed the conditions before the incident. Since the university met its duty to make conditions as safe as they appeared to be, the court held for the university. *Bukowski v. Clarkson Univ.*, 19 N.Y.3d 353, 971 N.E.2d 849 (N.Y. 2012).

◆  *A Florida court reinstated a negligence claim filed by an injured wrestler against the president of a university wrestling club.*

The student was hurt while participating in a wrestling club practice at Florida Atlantic University (FAU). After the accident, he sued FAU and the president of the wrestling club. The student said the president did not inspect wrestling equipment, failed to correct a dangerous condition in the gym where the accident happened, and did not adequately fasten wrestling mats together. Applying Florida law, **a state trial court held the claim against the president was barred because he was acting as an agent of FAU at the time of the accident**. On appeal, a state district court of appeal found genuine issues of fact relating to whether the president was acting as FAU's agent at the time of the accident. As a result, the court of appeal held the trial court should not have granted pretrial judgment against the student on his negligence claim. The trial court judgment was reversed, and the case was returned to that court for further proceedings. *Florida Atlantic Univ. Board of Trustees v. Lindsey*, 50 So.3d 1205 (Fla. Dist. Ct. App. 2010).

◆  *A spectator assumed the risk of injury at a Syracuse University hockey game and could not recover damages from the university for his injuries.*

Near the end of the game, the spectator was in an area of the rink where the players would exit the ice. Some players stopped to talk to him, and one of them got into a fight with another fan. The spectator tried to pull them apart, but fell over a barricade and broke his ankle. He later sued both universities and the individuals involved in the fight in a New York supreme court. He claimed Syracuse failed to provide enough supervision at the game. The court found the spectator had voluntarily involved himself in the fight. In so doing, he assumed the risk of getting hurt. He appealed to a state appellate court. It held the university owed spectators a duty of reasonable care to maintain safety.

**There was no duty to protect spectators from unexpected and unforeseeable assaults.** There had never been a fight between a spectator and a hockey player at the facility before, and the fight was not preceded by escalating hostilities. The confrontation was not reasonably foreseeable, and it was quickly stopped by university staff. As the university acted reasonably, the judgment was affirmed. The court held **the spectator could not recover damages from them because he assumed the risk of injury by intervening**. Under a rule called the "danger invites rescue" doctrine, a person is not barred from recovery for attempting a rescue based on a reasonable belief that the party in need of rescue was about to suffer a serious injury. A jury would have to decide whether the spectator acted reasonably and could rely on the "danger invites rescue" doctrine. *O'Connor v. Syracuse Univ.*, 66 A.D.3d 1187, 887 N.Y.S.2d 353 (N.Y. App. Div. 2009).

The Court of Appeals of New York denied a motion for appeal. *O'Connor v. Syracuse Univ.*, 14 N.Y.3d 766, 898 N.Y.S.2d 92 (N.Y. 2010).

◆  *A New York Appellate Division court preserved negligence claims raised by a student who injured her back while swimming for a university team.*

The student said her injury was caused by the training methods used by her coach, and that he continued to use the same methods even after she complained of back pain. She sued the university and the coach in a state court for negligent hiring and supervision. The university and coach argued that the student was an experienced swimmer who assumed the risk of hurting her back. The court denied them pretrial judgment, and appeal went to the state appellate division. On appeal, the appellate court held the lower court should have awarded pretrial judgment to the university on the negligent hiring and supervision claims. It explained that **when an injured plaintiff seeks to recover damages based on actions taken by an employee within the scope of employment, the doctrines of negligent hiring and negligent supervision do not apply**. However, the court upheld the ruling in favor of the student on her claim that the coach negligently continued to employ particular training methods even after she complained of back pain. A question of fact was also present as to whether she had assumed the risk of injury. *Segal v. St. John's Univ.*, 69 A.D.3d 702, 893 N.Y.S.2d 221 (N.Y. App. Div. 2010).

◆   *A New York court allowed a student-athlete to proceed with a claim that Iona College failed to keep MRSA bacteria out of its athletic facilities.*

The student-athlete claimed he contracted an MRSA infection at Iona's athletic facilities. He filed a state court action against Iona asserting the college had a duty to keep its facilities free of MRSA bacteria and to routinely screen for the presence of MRSA bacteria. The student asserted Iona had a duty to provide medical care and to instruct him regarding precautionary measures to help him avoid infection, and that the college had actual or constructive notice of MRSA bacteria in its facilities but negligently failed to remove it.

After the court dismissed the claims, the student appealed to the New York Supreme Court, Appellate Division. **The court held the trial court properly dismissed the claim that Iona had a duty to maintain MRSA-free facilities.** Such an obligation exceeded any recognized duty under law. However, the court held the lower court should not have dismissed the claim that Iona knew that its athletic facilities were not MRSA-free but failed to properly address the situation. The claim could proceed in further court activity. *Zaffarese v. Iona College*, 879 N.Y.S.2d 348 (N.Y. App. Div. 2009).

◆   *A Georgia court held an insurer was required to provide a defense to an athletic association sued by a college athlete for failing to provide disability insurance.*

An assistant athletic director (AAD) at the University of Georgia coordinated a disability insurance program for student-athletes. He obtained a coverage quote for a student from an insurance broker, but he failed to send the broker a coverage request form with the student's signature. The student was seriously hurt while playing for the football team and became disabled for life from playing any contact sports. The insurer refused to backdate coverage, and the student was denied $500,000 that would have been payable under the policy. He sued the university athletic association and AAD in a state court for breach of fiduciary duties, breach of contract, and negligence. The association notified its liability carrier of the lawsuit and asked for defense and indemnity.

The carrier refused to provide a defense, claiming that two policy exceptions relieved it of any duty to defend the action. The association then sued the carrier in the state court system. The court ruled for the association, and the carrier appealed. The Court of Appeals of Georgia affirmed the determination that the policy required the carrier to provide a defense to the suit. Moreover, **the connection between the student's injury and his claims was too attenuated to apply a bodily injury exclusion**. The conduct of the insured parties was not causally related to the injury, and the conduct that gave rise to the student's claims occurred before he was injured. Therefore, the exception did not apply. The court affirmed the judgment for the university association, noting a question remained as to whether the carrier was required to cover the loss. *Fireman's Fund Insurance Co. v. Univ. of Georgia Athletic Ass'n*, 288 Ga.App. 355, 654 S.E.2d 207 (Ga. Ct. App. 2007).

◆ *The Supreme Court of California held a community college was not liable for injuries to a student who was hit by a pitch during a baseball game.*

During a preseason road game against another community college, the host team's pitcher hit the student in the head with a pitch, cracking his batting helmet. The student said he was intentionally hit in retaliation for an earlier pitch thrown by a pitcher for his team that hit an opposing batter. The student staggered, felt dizzy, and was in pain, but his manager and first base coach told him to stay in the game. He was later told to sit on the bench, but his injuries were not immediately treated. The student sued the host community college in a state superior court. The case was dismissed, but the Court of Appeal of California reversed the judgment, finding the college owed the student a duty of supervision. The Supreme Court of California agreed to review the case.

The court held the college players were co-participants, and its coaches and managers had supervisory authority over the game. **Co-participants had a duty not to act recklessly, outside the bounds of the sport. Coaches and instructors had a duty not to increase the risks inherent in sports participation.** Colleges derive economic and marketing benefits from a major sports program. These benefits justified finding that a host school owed a duty to home and visiting players to not increase the risk inherent in the sport. The court found the host college did not fail in its duty to supervise and control the pitcher. **Being hit by a pitch was an inherent risk of baseball. The failure to provide umpires did not increase the inherent risk.** The host college had no duty to provide medical care, as the student did not submit evidence of injury. Colleges are not vicariously liable for the actions of their student-athletes during competition. The court reversed the judgment. *Avila v. Citrus Community College Dist.*, 38 Cal.4th 148, 131 P.3d 383 (Cal. 2006).

◆ *A Massachusetts cheerleader was allowed to proceed with a negligence action against her university after being severely injured at practice.*

The cheerleader fell during a maneuver that required two cheerleaders to stand on the shoulders of two others, who launched her about 10 feet up to the shoulders of cheerleaders on the upper tier. Although she was experienced, the cheerleader had never tried this maneuver before. The coach talked her through the exercise and placed spotters at the front and sides of the pyramid – but none in the rear. He spent about five minutes instructing the spotters. The squad attempted the stunt when the coach was not there. The cheerleader fell from the top of the pyramid, suffering serious neck fractures that caused her to become disabled. She sued the university in a Massachusetts superior court, alleging negligence by the coach. The university argued it could not be held liable for negligence under *Gauvin v. Clark*, 404 Mass. 450, 537 N.E.2d 94 (Mass. 1989), unless there was evidence of willful or reckless conduct. **The court disagreed and held the university owed the student a duty to exercise reasonable**

**care.** The failure to do so in this case caused her injuries. *Torres v. Univ. of Massachusetts*, 20 Mass.L.Rptr. 310 (Mass. Super. Ct. 2005).

### F. Player Compensation

*The issue of whether college athletes should be compensated has become a hot topic in recent years.*

◆   *An Indiana federal judge rejected a claim that participating on a university's track-and-field team rendered the students employees who were entitled to compensation under the Fair Labor Standards Act (FLSA).*

The plaintiffs alleged that by virtue of their participation on sports teams they were employees within the meaning of the FLSA and were thus entitled to be paid at least minimum wage for their time. The defendants filed a motion to dismiss. The court explained that the plaintiffs made "essentially a fairness argument." They alleged the school wrongfully took the position that they were less deserving of employee status and pay than students who participated in work-study programs. Those students, the plaintiffs pointed out, were designated as employees by the U.S. Department of Labor. But the question was not whether the plaintiffs were "deserving" of employee status, the court explained. Instead, it was whether Congress intended for the FLSA and its pay requirements to apply to student-athletes. Courts must look to the "economic reality" of the situation to determine whether an employment relationship exists, the court said. Citing the "revered tradition of amateurism in college sports," the court called that tradition "an essential part of the 'economic reality' of the relationship" between the plaintiffs and the university. The court also leaned on the fact that **the DOL has not taken action to apply the FLSA to student-athletes, even though it knows there are thousands of unpaid student-athletes on college campuses every year**. The court determined the athletes were not employees of the university for purposes of the FLSA. The motion to dismiss was granted. *Berger v. National Collegiate Athletic Ass'n*, No. 1:14-cv-1710-WTL-MJD, 2016 WL 614365 (S.D. Ind. 2/16/16).

◆   *A Tennessee federal judge dismissed a putative class action that sought to recover money for student-athletes for use of their likenesses.*

To participate in NCAA sports, the athletes were required to sign a form authorizing the NCAA to use their names and pictures to promote events. The athletes claimed they were illegally excluded from the marketplace of their own likenesses. They filed suit. Claims included, among other things, violations of the federal Sherman Act and the federal Lanham Act. The Sherman Act claim failed because the athletes didn't have a right to publicity in sports broadcasts. **They couldn't have been injured by an alleged conspiracy to deprive them of rights they didn't have**, the court explained. The Lanham Act claim also failed, as that act only regulates commercial speech, and moreover, the athletes failed to adequately allege that the challenged broadcasts created a likelihood of confusion – as required. There was no confusion about what the players were doing when the broadcasts were shown, the court held. The claims were dismissed. *Marshall v. ESPN Inc.*, 111 F.Supp.3d 815 (M.D. Tenn. 2015).

◆   *The Ninth Circuit reversed part of a California ruling that held Division I schools could pay basketball and football players up to $5,000 per year in deferred compensation.*

In a class action suit, players argued the NCAA's amateurism rules illegally barred student-athletes from being compensated for use of their name, likeness and image in products such as video games. The district court agreed that the ban violated federal antitrust laws and barred the NCAA from prohibiting member schools from providing student-athletes scholarships up to the full cost of attendance and up to $5,000 a year in deferred compensation. On appeal, the Ninth Circuit upheld in part and reversed in part. First, it affirmed the ruling to require the NCAA to allow schools to provide compensation up to the full cost of attendance. But, noting **the U.S Supreme Court has held the NCAA's amateurism rules are valid as a matter of law**, it overturned the part of the ruling that held student-athletes could be paid up to $5,000 a year in deferred compensation because there was no justification for paying compensation "untethered to educational expenses." *O'Bannon v. National Collegiate Athletic Ass'n*, 802 F.3d 1049 (9th Cir. 2015).

◆   *The National Labor Relations Board declined to assert jurisdiction in a dispute between a university and its scholarship football players.*

The unanimous decision overturned a 2014 ruling that held the players were employees – and were eligible for collective bargaining. Importantly, **the ruling repeatedly stated the board did not consider whether football players were "statutory employees."** Instead, the NLRB held that asserting jurisdiction over just one team in the NCAA's Division I Football Bowl Subdivision "would … likely have ramifications for other teams" in the division, as the very nature of competitive sports requires teams to abide by the same set of rules. Because of the control the NCAA holds over the teams, the NLRB held that asserting jurisdiction would not promote stability in labor relations. *Northwestern Univ. and College Athletes Players Ass'n*, No. 13-RC-121359 (NLRB 8/14/15).

◆   *A video game company had to defend its use of likenesses of college football players without compensation, the U.S. Court of Appeals for the Ninth Circuit ruled.*

In 2005, Samuel Keller was the starting quarterback for Arizona State University. Video game developer Electronic Arts (EA) sold a game called NCAA Football. In its 2005 version, it included a virtual Arizona State quarterback that looked and played like Keller. The virtual Keller had the same weight, height, hair color, hair style, play style and home state as the real one. Along with eight other players, Keller sued to challenge EA's use of his likeness. He claimed that EA violated his right of publicity under a California statute as well as the state's common law. A district court denied EA's motion to strike the complaint, and EA appealed. EA relied on what's known as the "transformative use defense," which asserts that the user of the likeness has added creative elements that transform the work in question "into something more than a mere celebrity likeness or imitation." When the defense applies, the user's First Amendment right is deemed to trump the right of publicity held by the subject of the likeness. After considering the earlier cases in which the test was applied, the Ninth Circuit concluded that EA was not entitled to use the defense. **Quite simply, the court found, Keller and the other players were represented as what they were in real life: football players on a field.** The district court's decision to deny EA's motion was affirmed. *Keller v. Electronic Arts Inc.*, 724 F.3d 1268 (9th Cir. 2013).

## II.  STUDENT ACTIVITIES

*In* Beach v. Univ. of Utah, *726 P.2d 413 (Utah 1986), the Supreme Court of Utah explained that "colleges and universities are educational institutions, not custodial." It held imposing liability on higher educational institutions for injuries arising from illegally drinking alcohol would require them to "baby-sit" each student. Colleges and universities may limit official recognition of particular organizations and impose restrictions on them.*

### A.  Operation and School Supervision

◆ *A state court in New York rejected a former student's claim that a university negligently failed to supervise the activities of a fraternity.*

A student pledged for membership in the Kappa Sigma Fraternity Omicron-Beta Chapter. The court ruling does not provide details, but the student suffered personal injuries during the pledging for membership. The student sued the university, claiming it was negligent because it failed to supervise and control the frat's activities. The trial court dismissed the claim, and the student appealed. To prove negligence, the student had to show the existence of a legal duty, a breach of that duty, proximate causation and damages. **The student did not adequately claim the university was so involved in the initiation activities that a duty to control and/or supervise was created.** The appellate court affirmed the decision. *Pasquaretto v. Long Island Univ.*, 964 N.Y.S.2d 599 (N.Y. App. Div. 2013).

◆ *Neither a fraternity nor its local chapter could be held liable for negligence in an action by a student who said she was raped at a fraternity party.*

In a federal district court, the student claimed she was raped by a fraternity member. She claimed the fraternity negligently failed to supervise the party. In pretrial activity, the court observed that the fraternity did not own or control the premises where the party took place. Only two of the three tenants that leased the property were associated with the fraternity. There was also a dispute as to whether the student was even invited. Under state law, owners or possessors of premises had no duty to protect visitors from criminal acts of third parties – unless criminal activity was foreseeable. In this case, **the fraternity did not have any knowledge of prior violent crimes or sexual assaults occurring on the premises**. Nothing suggested that the individual who was charged with the rape had any history of violence, aggressive behavior or history of sexual assault. As the fraternity did not have a duty to protect the student and she was a social guest, her negligence claims against the fraternity could not proceed. *Roe v. Saint Louis Univ.*, No. 4:08CV1474 HEA, 2012 WL 5377895 (E.D. Mo. 10/31/12).

◆ *Immunity shielded a Kentucky state university from claims that campus police did not respond properly to a student's assault report.*

An African-American student claimed he was assaulted and called racial epithets by fraternity brothers at a fraternity party. He asserted that campus police took no action against the fraternity or its members. Claiming that university-related groups sanctioned the party, the student sued the university and its president in a federal district court. He asserted interference with a right to contract in violation of 42 U.S.C. § 1981, violation of his due process rights, conspiracy to interfere with civil rights, and state-law claims including assault and battery. But the court held **much of the lawsuit was barred by the Eleventh Amendment to the Constitution**. This amendment generally bars suits brought in federal courts against a state, state agencies, and state officials in their official capacities. As Kentucky public universities and directors are protected by Eleventh Amendment immunity, the federal claims could not go forward. Constitutional claims against the president in his individual capacity failed, as no personal involvement was alleged. The state-law claims against the president were equally flawed, and the court dismissed them. *Jackson v. Murray State Univ.*, 834 F.Supp.2d 609 (W.D. Ky. 2011).

◆ *Washington State University (WSU) was allowed to revoke official recognition of a fraternity for five years for drug and alcohol violations.*

WSU said fraternity members used, possessed, manufactured and/or distributed illegal drugs on fraternity property and at a rental house occupied by fraternity members. WSU cited the fraternity for a number of violations, including supplying alcohol to minors at fraternity-sponsored events. A student conduct board held a hearing, where the fraternity's national executive director admitted underage drinking issues. The board found the fraternity responsible for each charge and withdrew official recognition for five years. In a state court action, the fraternity alleged that WSU failed to follow proper procedures and violated the fraternity's constitutional rights to freedom of association.

Appeal reached the Court of Appeals of Washington. It found **the evidence showed illegal activity was "actively condoned" by fraternity officers**. The fraternity's risk manager, live-in advisor and social chair had all bought illegal drugs, and the fraternity failed to take reasonable steps to stop illegal activity. Fraternities at WSU were expected to follow the law and university policies and to respond promptly if officers, members or guests engaged in illegal behavior. As the evidence supported WSU's decision, and the sanction imposed was not arbitrary and capricious, the court affirmed the discipline. *Alpha Kappa Lambda Fraternity v. Washington State Univ.*, 152 Wash.App. 401, 216 P.3d 451 (Wash. Ct. App. 2009).

◆ *A court rejected a fraternity's claim that a New York university violated federal antitrust law by requiring all students to live in university housing.*

Four people died in a car crash on the campus of Colgate University in 2000. One was an underage member of Delta Kappa Epsilon (DKE). Colgate responded by announcing it would require all its students to live in university-owned housing. Colgate took steps to buy and operate all fraternity and sorority housing and residential services on its campus. Many chapters negotiated for purchase prices in excess of their market values. Colgate offered DKE $725,000 for its fraternity house, but DKE chose not to sell. In response, Colgate withdrew its recognition of the local DKE chapter. DKE sued Colgate in a federal district court for violating the federal Sherman Antitrust Act.

The court held that to prevail, DKE needed to show Colgate had engaged in improper conduct that had the effect of controlling prices or excluding competition, resulting in a high degree of market power. The court determined that the relevant market for purposes of an antitrust claim was the student housing market for all selective colleges nationwide. **Once a student decided to enroll at a particular college, the student agreed to submit to college policies to protect the welfare of its students.** In this case, Colgate created a residential policy that was part of the education it provided. The court held that Colgate's residential policy, which required all students to live in housing it owned, was an exercise of its lawful rights. *Delta Kappa Epsilon (DKE) Alumni Corp. v. Colgate Univ.*, 492 F.Supp.2d 106 (N.D.N.Y. 2007).

◆ *A college could use money from a fund-raising campaign to eliminate single-sex fraternities and sororities.*

A New Hampshire college initiated a five-year fund-raising campaign that raised about $568 million from alumni. Several years later, the board of trustees announced that it was going to use some of the money raised to eliminate single-sex fraternities and sororities. A group of alumni who had contributed to the campaign sued the college to prevent it from using the funds for that purpose. They asserted the college had engaged in misrepresentation in violation of the state Consumer Protection Act, and that the board of trustees had withheld information about its intent to eliminate traditional fraternities and sororities. They also alleged that the board was in a fiduciary relationship to the alumni because there were alums on the board. A state court dismissed the case, and the Supreme Court of New Hampshire affirmed the judgment. First, the board of trustees did not owe a fiduciary duty to the alumni despite the existence of alums on the board. Second, **the alumni failed to show that the board engaged in intentional, fraudulent nondisclosure**. And third, since the fund-raising campaign was not commerce (the transactions were in the nature of a gift), there was no violation of the Consumer Protection Act. *Brzica v. Trustees of Dartmouth College*, 791 A.2d 990 (N.H. 2002).

## B. Organizational Liability

◆ *Indiana's highest court affirmed a ruling that found a national fraternity could not be held liable for the alcohol-related death of a fraternity pledge.*

The Beta Psi Chapter of the Delta Tau Delta fraternity hosted a party. Alcohol was served. A freshman pledge began drinking around 9 p.m. Upperclassmen encouraged him to continue drinking. Around midnight, the student was limp and his breathing was shallow. Eight hours later, the student was found dead, lying in his own vomit. Delta Tau Delta – the national fraternity – implemented a program that taught members to recognize the signs of alcohol poisoning and handle alcohol-related emergencies. It also used "chapter advisors," who were assigned to local chapters and charged with the duty of keeping the national fraternity "fully and accurately informed of the affairs of the chapter." One such chapter advisor was present at the party when the student died. Representatives of the student's estate filed suit against the national fraternity, the local chapter, the college and the risk manager, claiming negligence and other legal violations. The trial court granted the national fraternity's motion for pretrial judgment. The estate appealed, and the legal battle went all the way to the state supreme court. It held the national fraternity assumed a duty to provide guidance, **but the duty did not go so far as to require it to ensure the safety of pledges at local chapters. Though it could discipline local fraternities and members, no evidence showed it assumed a direct duty to supervise and control the conduct of local chapter members.** The duty undertaken by the national fraternity with respect to the local chapter was only an educational one, and it was not nearly as expansive as the parents suggested. So the national fraternity couldn't be held liable. *Smith v. Delta Tau Delta, Inc.*, 9 N.E.3d 154 (Ind. 2014).

◆ *Nevada's highest court refused to impose liability on a fraternity in a lawsuit filed by a spectator who had part of his nose bitten off during a fight.*

According to the spectator, an alumnus of another college bit off a piece of his nose during a fight in a tailgating area prior to a college football game. The spectator sued the alumnus, local chapters of a fraternity, its national affiliate and several others in a state court. The court held the case could not proceed due to the family's failure to try to ascertain the identities of certain alumni entities. It also held the fraternities were entitled to judgment. On appeal, the Supreme Court of Nevada agreed with the lower court that the spectator did not exercise reasonable diligence in ascertaining the identity of the alumni entities. In addition, the trial court had properly held that neither the national fraternity nor its local chapters were liable for his injuries. **The spectator did not provide any rationale for making the national fraternity responsible for the safety of a tailgate party, even if it was being hosted by one of its local chapters.** There was no special relationship between the national fraternity and the spectator, and the national fraternity did not owe him a duty to protect him from injuries inflicted by a third party. Similarly, the local fraternity chapters were not liable. The alumnus was not a fraternity member and was not under the control of the fraternity. Moreover, the fight began unexpectedly and ended quickly. The lower court judgment was affirmed. *Sparks v. The Alpha Tau Omega Fraternity*, 255 P.3d 238 (Nev. 2011).

◆ *The Phi Kappa Tau fraternity chapter at the University of Mississippi was not liable in negligence for a woman's injuries.*

A fraternity brother provided beer to an underage fraternity member at the fraternity house when school was not in session. The woman was riding on the back of a four-wheeler on the grounds of the house. The fraternity member confronted the driver and threw a bottle that struck the woman in the face. She sued the local and national chapters of the fraternity for negligence in a federal court. The court held the fraternity chapters did not owe the woman any legal duty under state law. She appealed to the U.S. Court of Appeals, Fifth Circuit. The court affirmed the judgment. **As unincorporated associations, the chapters were not liable for the wrongful acts of their members unless they "encouraged, promoted, or subsequently ratified them." There was no evidence that the chapters encouraged or ratified the member's behavior.** There was no duty on the part of the national chapter to supervise the local chapter more closely, as no special relationship existed in this case. *Lewis v. Univ. of Southern Mississippi*, 227 Fed.Appx. 340 (5th Cir. 2007).

◆ *A Texas fraternity and its members were not liable to a student for statements resulting in the withdrawal of his pledge invitation.*

A student who had pledged to join the Phi Gamma Delta Fraternity was accused of sexual misconduct. He denied the allegations, claiming they were part of an extortion scheme to gain money. Phi Gamma withdrew its pledge invitation. A year later, the student pledged to join a chapter of the same fraternity at a different Texas university campus. He was denied admittance based on information communicated between fraternity members at different chapters. The student sued the fraternity and various fraternity members in the state court system for damaging his reputation and subjecting him to increased hazing based on the allegations of sexual misconduct. The court held for the fraternities and their members. The student appealed, arguing that Phi Gamma owed him a duty of care because its members made statements in the course and scope of their fraternity membership. The Court of Appeals of Texas found no evidence indicating the fraternity was incorporated in the state.

**As an unincorporated entity, the fraternity did not owe the student any duty of care.** Moreover, he was unable to show a member's remarks were made in the course of his official duties as a fraternity historian. **There was no evidence that these comments were communicated to other fraternities at the University of Texas.** The court agreed with the trial court that the hazing claim was untimely filed under a two-year state statute of limitation. The judgment was affirmed. *Waddill v. Phi Gamma Delta Fraternity Lambda Tau Chapter, Texas Tech Univ.*, 114 S.W.3d 136 (Tex. Ct. App. 2003).

◆ *A Kansas fraternity pledge could not sue the fraternity or its members when he passed out after drinking too much.*

A student attended a Pledge Dad night at a fraternity at the University of Kansas. While there, he consumed a large amount of alcoholic beverages. At 2:00 a.m., his pledge dad found him passed out in the living room of the fraternity house and took him to a local hospital emergency room, where his blood alcohol level was measured at .294. The student later sued the national fraternity, the local chapter and five individual members for negligence, and the company that owned the property for premises liability. The court ruled in favor of all the defendants, and the state supreme court agreed. The local chapter was not a legal entity and therefore could not be sued. Individual members could not be liable because **they did not breach any duty they owed him; he**

**voluntarily drank alcohol**. As far as the national fraternity was concerned, there was no special relationship between the student and the fraternity so as to give rise to liability. Finally, the company that owned the property could not be held liable for conditions on the premises at a fraternity party. *Prime v. Beta Gamma Chapter of Pi Kappa Alpha*, 47 P.3d 402 (Kan. 2002).

## C. Injuries

◆   *The injuries suffered by a fraternity pledge were not the fault of the college he attended, Indiana's highest court decided.*

A pledge was injured after four upperclassmen fraternity brothers decided to carry him to a shower and run water on him. On the way to the shower, another upperclassman joined in and placed the student in a chokehold. The student suffered injuries severe enough to force him to withdraw from school. He filed a negligence claim. In it, he alleged the school breached a duty to protect students by failing to implement a policy that banned hazing. **To establish a duty to protect, the student had to show more than a policy evincing a general intent to elicit good behavior by members of the student body.** Because the student didn't show the college assumed a duty to protect him, his claim failed. *Yost v. Wabash College*, 3 N.E.3d 509 (Ind. 2014).

◆   *A North Carolina university was not liable for injuries suffered by a 21-year-old student at an off-campus party.*

During a confrontation with a fraternity member, the student was pushed down and became permanently paralyzed. Although the fraternity chapter rented the house where the incident took place, it was off campus. In a state court, the student sued the university, fraternity and others, alleging negligence. The court rejected his claims, and the case reached the North Carolina Court of Appeals. It held neither the university nor the fraternity owed the student a duty of care that might create liability. **University regulations regarding fraternities did not create an obligation to keep students safe.** There was no special relationship between the student and the university. He voluntarily attended a party he was not invited to attend. In addition, the university did not know about the party. Finally, the court disagreed with the student's claim that the individual who caused his injuries was acting as an agent of the university or fraternity. *Mynhardt v. Elon Univ.*, 725 S.E.2d 632 (N.C. Ct. App. 2012).

◆   *A Vermont student was not relieved of a university sexual harassment reporting requirement that was mandated by state law.*

The student reported being drugged and raped at a fraternity party. A university advocate understood she was reporting rape, not harassment. Acting on the advocate's advice, the student reported the incident to the University Center for Student Ethics and Standards, and she and a male student soon agreed in writing not to have any contact with each other. At a disciplinary hearing, the university found the student did not prove her rape charge. She sued the university for failing to promptly investigate harassment. A state court held for the university, finding the student should have used the university's harassment policy. The student appealed to the Supreme Court of Vermont, which held state law required institutions to conduct prompt investigations when they received actual notice of conduct that may constitute harassment. **The law specifies that complainants cannot sue before exhausting an available harassment policy.** Rejecting the student's claim that she gave notice of conduct that could be construed as harassment, the court held the university was not required to automatically treat the complaint as one for sexual harassment. *Allen v. Univ. of Vermont*, 973 A.2d 1183 (Vt. 2009).

◆   *A New Jersey court held a university was not liable for the death of a student who died when he fell from his fourth-floor dorm window after a party.*

A county prosecutor investigated and found that the student had leaned out the window and accidentally fallen. The student's family filed a negligence action against the university in a state court, asserting its alcohol policy was not appropriate and was negligently enforced. A jury found the death was caused by negligence, and it assessed damages of $520,000. As the parties were equally negligent, the court entered a judgment against the university in the amount of $260,000. The university appealed to a state appellate court, where it argued any negligence claim was barred by a state charitable immunity act.

Under the act, the university was immune from negligence claims raised by a person injured while benefiting from the university. But no immunity was available if injury resulted from "willful, wanton or grossly negligent" conduct. The court said providing student housing "falls within the broad range of reasonable educational goals" the university sought to achieve. Students living in dormitories received the benefit of the university's educational works. The student's violation of a university alcohol policy did not alter his status as a beneficiary of the university's works while he lived in the dormitory. **As he was a beneficiary of the university's works, the immunity statute was applicable**, and the judgment for the family was reversed. *Orzech v. Fairleigh Dickinson Univ.*, 985 A.2d 189 (N.J. Super. App. Div. 2009).

## D.  Hazing

◆   *A North Carolina state appeals court affirmed a decision to dismiss negligence claims in connection with a student's hazing death.*

The student died while participating in off-campus fraternity hazing activities. Two years later, his estate sued the university and its director of security. The defendants filed a motion to dismiss, which the court granted. The estate appealed. To establish a preliminary case of negligence, the estate had to show, among other things, that the defendants owed the student a duty of care. It didn't make that showing. Next, the estate argued that the university undertook a duty to protect frat pledges. The court rejected the argument, as **prior relevant case law established the mere adoption of general safety rules doesn't create a duty to a class of individuals**. The ruling was affirmed. *Estate of Tipton v. High Point Univ.*, 775 S.E.2d (N.C. Ct. App. 2015).

◆   *A Virginia federal court refused to dismiss hazing and other claims filed by a former swimmer.*

After being recruited by many schools, a swimmer chose to attend the university, in part, because it had an anti-hazing policy. When he arrived at school, an email ordered the new students to attend a "team bonding" meeting and warned that they'd be sodomized if they told anyone about the meeting. It was later determined that five upperclass team members wrote the email. At the meeting, the older teammates allegedly poured buckets of water over the new swimmers' heads and locked them in a dark restroom. The student was ordered to drink a gallon of milk and four glasses of prune juice. He was also forced to eat live goldfish, causing him to vomit. The ordeal lasted five hours. He left the team and the school. He sued the five upperclass teammates, alleging hazing, assault, battery, false imprisonment and other claims. **To state a valid hazing claim, the student had to show "bodily injury" – he did, as he said he vomited.** So the court allowed the hazing claim. It also allowed the assault claim to proceed, as allegations of throwing buckets of water and threatening sodomy were sufficient. It also green-lighted the battery claims, rejecting the argument that the student voluntarily participated in the alleged activities. The allegation that the student was trapped in a bathroom was enough to support the false imprisonment claim, the court also determined. So the claims could proceed. *Marcantonio v. Dudzinski,* No. 3:15-cv-00029, 2015 WL 9239009 (W.D. Va. 12/17/15).

◆  *A New York appeals court upheld the suspension of a student who hosted a party at his off-campus apartment.*

The student was a fraternity member, and the party was held during the peak of the pledging period. Police responded to noise complaints and found dozens of underage people were drinking. They also found alcohol and a 15-gallon plastic tub of vomit. Three pledges needed medical attention. The student was arrested and referred to the school's disciplinary process for violating the code of conduct with regard to hazing and alcohol. He was suspended for more than a year. He sought judicial review, saying there wasn't enough evidence to show he violated the code of conduct's provisions on hazing and alcohol. He said the penalty was too harsh. The court noted the students who needed medical attention were pledges, which permitted a reasonable inference that the hazing and alcohol provisions of the code of conduct were violated. The court also rejected his argument that the penalty assessed against him was too harsh. **It didn't shock one's sense of fairness, the court explained.** The suspension was upheld. *Lampert v. State Univ. of New York at Albany*, 116 A.D.3d 1292 (N.Y. App. Div. 2014).

◆  *Indiana's highest court decided to consider whether a freshman could sue a college and fraternity for injuries suffered in a hazing incident.*

While the student was pledging a fraternity, members tried to place him in a shower. When he resisted, one member placed him in a chokehold. The student passed out and suffered physical and mental injuries. He filed a state court personal injury action against the fraternity, local fraternity chapter, and the student who placed him in the chokehold. A trial court held for the college and fraternity. It found the student was not the victim of hazing, finding he instigated the events that led to his injury. On appeal, the student argued the college and fraternity had a duty to protect him from injury. According to the Court of Appeals of Indiana, there was no breach of the applicable standard of care. While landowners must take reasonable precautions to protect visitors from foreseeable criminal attacks, the court found no indication that harm was foreseeable in this case. And though hazing is a crime in Indiana, the court found the incident was not the result of hazing. **Appeal reached the Supreme Court of Indiana, which agreed to transfer the case to its docket.** *Yost v. Wabash College*, 984 N.E.2d 221 (Ind. 2013).

◆   *Although a fraternity had a duty to a Pennsylvania student, it did not breach that duty when local chapter members hazed him.*

A University of Pittsburgh student applied to the Beta Epsilon chapter of the Kappa Alpha Psi fraternity after Kappa lifted a restriction on inducting new members that had been imposed when a Kappa pledge died in Missouri. The student attended a fraternity gathering and was paddled more than 200 times by four fraternity brothers. He went to the hospital the next day and remained there for three weeks with renal failure, seizures and hypertension. He sued Kappa, the local chapter, the chapter advisor and a number of others for negligence. A Pennsylvania trial court held for the defendants, and an appellate court largely affirmed. Here, even though Kappa owed a duty of care to the student, the student failed to show that it breached that duty. For example, he failed to show that the two-year moratorium on new members was merely a symbolic gesture and not a sincere attempt to curb hazing. However, **he was allowed to proceed with his lawsuit against the chapter advisor**. The evidence indicated that the chapter advisor failed to discuss hazing with local chapter members and did not advise them to read the executive orders that imposed sanctions for hazing. *Kenner v. Kappa Alpha Psi Fraternity,* 808 A.2d 178 (Pa. Super. Ct. 2002).

# CHAPTER FOUR

## Freedom of Speech and Religion

## I.  EMPLOYEES

### A.  Protected Speech

#### 1. Retaliation

*To prove a First Amendment retaliation claim, public employees must show their speech resulted in adverse employment action. In any speech rights claim against a public employer, the employee must show (1) the statements at issue were not made pursuant to professional job duties, (2) that the speech involved a matter of public concern, and (3) that the exercise of protected speech outweighed the employer's interest in efficient workplace operations.*

◆   *A Connecticut federal judge rejected a professor's claim that a university's decision not to renew his contract amounted to speech retaliation.*

The professor worked at the university in a director's position. In his fourth year, he spoke up about several things, including his concern that the dean's decision to appoint his wife as director of the business school might violate state ethics rules against nepotism. The following year, his contract wasn't renewed. He sued, alleging the university retaliated against him for exercising his speech rights. The professor showed his nepotism statement was protected speech, the court held, as it was a matter of public concern. But under the U.S. Supreme Court's decision in *Pickering v. Board of Educ.*, **courts must weigh a governmental employer's needs against an employee's speech rights. Here, the court found the university's needs outweighed the professor's rights.** He alleged one instance of possible nepotism that affected only a limited number of people and a small amount of public money. By contrast, his high-level position meant his criticism of the dean "had the potential to undermine his authority as a dean and his capacity to continue to set policies for the Business school." The court dismissed the claim and closed the case. *Weinstein v. Univ. of Connecticut*, 136 F.Supp.3d 221 (D. Conn. 2016).

◆   *The Eleventh Circuit affirmed the dismissal of speech retaliation claims against a Georgia university filed by terminated employees.*

Five psychologists began having problems when a new supervisor started in the department. The psychologists submitted a formal memorandum to university officials. In it, they criticized the supervisor's management style and accused her of creating a hostile work environment. The school investigated and determined no evidence backed the concerns raised. A few months later, all five were terminated, purportedly as part of a cost-cutting reduction in force. They sued, claiming they were fired for exercising their speech rights. The district court ruled against them. The psychologists appealed, arguing the terminations amounted to retaliation. The Eleventh Circuit affirmed, as the speech wasn't a matter of public concern so it wasn't protected from retaliation by the First Amendment. The psychologists argued that they were speaking as citizens on a matter of public concern in the memo. But **the argument failed because the concerns they raised all related to the ability to do their jobs**, the court said. So the ruling for the university was affirmed. *Alves v. Board of Regents of the Univ. System of Georgia*, 804 F.3d 1149 (11th Cir. 2015).

◆   *The Fifth Circuit affirmed a ruling that held a Louisiana university did not retaliate against a professor for exercising his speech rights.*

The professor was open and vocal about his views on several controversial issues. He frequently spoke about them in class and often used his own textbook as a supplementary teaching text. After he was put on a different track, he sued, alleging the university violated his speech rights. A federal court granted judgment to school defendants, and the professor appealed. The Fifth Circuit affirmed, as **the professor failed to show any adverse employment action**. He was allowed to use his own textbook, and he failed to show how the reclassification affected his pay, benefits or other privileges of employment. So the ruling was affirmed. *Oller v. Roussel*, 609 Fed.Appx. 770 (5th Cir. 2015).

◆ *A District of Columbia federal judge refused to dismiss the First Amendment retaliation claim of an employee who was fired after reporting concerns about potential violations of privacy laws.*

The employee had a 38-year career at a university. In 2010, he was moved to the position of records officer for the recruitment and admissions office. The job entailed scanning more than 22,000 student files. Two years later, the employee discovered student interns had access to other students' records as part of their work. He let the director know he thought this violated D.C.'s privacy laws. When she ignored his reports, he emailed a records official outside of the university to report that student interns were "handling confidential student records." Within three months, the employee was let go. He sued, alleging First Amendment retaliation. The university asked the court to dismiss the claim. It refused, noting that a public university's mismanagement of student records and possible disregard for illegal behavior that compromises student privacy qualifies as a matter of public concern. Moreover, **the fact that he was relieved of duties within weeks of his speech was enough to infer it could have been a substantial or motivating factor in his termination**. A trial was needed, so the court refused to dismiss the suit. *Hill v. Board of Trustees of the Univ. of the District of Columbia*, 146 F.Supp.3d 178 (D.C. 2015).

◆ *The U.S. Supreme Court held a community college retaliated against a public employee for speech that was protected under the First Amendment.*

The employee was hired to direct an underprivileged youth program that was struggling financially. He conducted an audit and found an Alabama state representative was on the program's payroll but didn't show up for work. The director reported this to the college president and was warned that firing the representative would make waves politically. Nonetheless, he fired the representative and told a grand jury why. He also testified – under subpoena – at her criminal trial. She was convicted of mail fraud and theft. She was sentenced to 30 months in prison and ordered to repay more than $177,000. The financial problems continued, so the director suggested that the program president consider layoffs. Following that suggestion – and less than a year after he testified before the grand jury – the president fired the director. The director sued, alleging his termination was in retaliation for his testimony against the state representative. A federal district court ruled against him, and the Eleventh Circuit affirmed.

The U.S. Supreme Court heard the case and decided his sworn testimony, which was provided outside the scope of his ordinary job duties, was entitled to First Amendment protection. The Court held that the testimony was speech engaged in as a citizen on a matter of public concern. The fact that he learned of the subject matter of his testimony while he was at work did not mean it was delivered as part of his job. **He testified as a citizen – not as an employee – because the testimony was not ordinarily within the scope of his job duties. It involved a matter of public concern because it related to corruption and misuse of state funds.** Though the speech was protected, the program president was entitled to qualified immunity as to the claim raised against him in his individual capacity, the Court added. This was because at the time of the termination, it was unclear whether the testimony was protected speech. A claim against the program president's successor in her official capacity was remanded for further proceedings. *Lane v. Franks*, 134 S.Ct. 2369 (U.S. 2014).

◆   *The Sixth Circuit affirmed a ruling that a university did not retaliate against a professor for exercising his speech rights.*

The employee was a tenure-track assistant professor. He was on probation for six years, and student reviews of his teaching remained "consistently abysmal." The university ultimately denied him tenure. The professor believed he lost his job because the school didn't approve of his "idiosyncratic teaching methods" – and offered an example of one instance where he displayed his middle finger to a class during a lesson on symbols for "sexual sin." He filed suit, alleging the school fired him in violation of his First Amendment rights. A Kentucky judge dismissed the claim, and the professor appealed. He claimed his termination amounted to retaliation for First-Amendment protected expression. But the Sixth Circuit affirmed that **"teaching methods" don't fit that bill**. The court wrote that even if it assumed "that the Constitution protects [the professor's] one-fingered salute ..., a free speech retaliation claim still requires retaliation – a showing that his gesture motivated the university's tenure decision." No evidence showed it did. The professor wasn't disciplined for the incident or even, the court commented, "told not to flip off students in the future." So the court affirmed the judgment in favor of the school defendants. *Frieder v. Morehead State Univ.*, 770 F.3d 428 (6th Cir. 2014).

◆   *A Texas federal judge refused to dismiss the retaliation claims of an administrative assistant who testified in a sexual harassment investigation.*

The employee was listed as a witness when a co-worker filed a sexual harassment complaint against the dean of the department. She was interviewed by the college's office of diversity. Afterward, the employee said the dean moved her to a less desirable work space and excluded her from meetings. He also stripped her of her duties – which resulted in a pay cut. When the co-worker who initiated the investigation filed suit, the dean issued the employee a disciplinary letter for "slander," which accused her of making a comment she denied. The employee filed suit, alleging First Amendment retaliation. The community college asked the court to dismiss the claim. It refused, saying the employee stated a valid claim. So a trial was needed. *Slaughter v. College of the Mainland*, No. G-12-018, 2014 WL 1917981 (S.D. Tex. 5/13/14).

◆   *A University of Colorado professor did not show the university violated his speech rights by firing him after he published a controversial essay.*

In the essay, the professor compared those killed in the World Trade Center on 9/11 to a Nazi officer and convicted war criminal. In response to public outcry, the board of regents voted to investigate his work. A formal investigation yielded findings that his work fell below the relevant academic standards of professional integrity, including two acts of plagiarism and an act of falsification. As a result, the university discharged the professor.

In a state court, the professor accused the university and its board of speech rights violations and retaliation for writing his controversial essay. A trial court held for the university on all claims except the retaliatory termination claim, which went to a jury. The jury found for the professor but awarded him only one dollar in damages. On appeal, the Supreme Court of Colorado held the regents were entitled to absolute immunity because their decision was quasi-judicial. It held the professor was not entitled to reinstatement or front pay regarding his retaliatory termination claim. The bad relationship of the parties made reinstatement inappropriate, and front pay was not warranted because the professor made no attempt to mitigate the salary he lost. **The court found it proper to reject the claim that the university investigated his academic record in bad faith**, as this activity was shielded by qualified immunity. *Churchill v. Univ. of Colorado at Boulder*, 285 P.3d 986 (Colo. 2012).

◆ *A Georgia university defeated an employee's speech rights case by showing she was fired for insubordination and not for retaliatory reasons.*

University officials fired the employee shortly after she yelled at her supervisor. A university committee upheld the discharge, and she sued the university's board of regents in a Georgia trial court under the state whistleblower statute. According to the employee, she was fired in retaliation for reporting the supervisor's wrongdoing, and not for yelling at him. She said that in the two years before her firing, she had spoken out three times to report that he was breaking rules. The court held for the university, and the employee appealed. The state court of appeals held **the whistleblowers' law prohibited public employers from retaliating against employees** for objecting to or refusing to participate in any practice the employee reasonably believed was in violation of a law, rule, or regulation. But the court of appeals found direct evidence that the employee had been discharged for insubordination, not her speech. As the evidence supported the board's valid, nonretaliatory reason for firing her, the court affirmed the judgment. *Caldon v. Board of Regents of Univ. System of Georgia*, 311 Ga.App. 155, 715 S.E.2d 487 (Ga. Ct. App. 2011).

◆ *An Idaho State University (ISU) professor was unable to convince the state's supreme court that officials retaliated against him based on his speech.*

The professor began working for ISU in 1991. He later began to criticize ISU administrators in a newspaper on a range of topics, declaring his dislike for a former university president and administrators. In a paid advertisement, the professor speculated that ISU was conspiring with another institution to move an engineering program and create a medical school. He said that as a result of his criticisms, ISU retaliated against him by not evaluating his job performance for five years, declining to hire him as a department chair and increasing his salary by the lowest possible increments, among other things. In a state court, the professor sued ISU for retaliation, defamation and breach of contract. The case reached the Supreme Court of Idaho, which held the professor's speech was made as a private citizen. **His speech on the issue of creating a medical school at ISU was a matter of public concern.** But the professor's claim that ISU retaliated against him for exercising his speech rights failed because he did not show he suffered any adverse employment action. ISU was not required to conduct evaluations annually, and he never applied for the department chair he claimed to have been wrongfully denied. The contract claim had been correctly rejected, and the professor was liable for attorneys' fees related to the claim. *Sadid v. Idaho State Univ.*, 151 Idaho 932, 265 P.3d 1144 (Idaho 2011).

◆   *The University of Connecticut's decision to take a deanship away from a professor who railed against official policies did not violate his speech rights.*

In his second term as dean of the engineering school, the professor became an outspoken critic of university policies, including the university's plan to establish a campus in Dubai. He opposed plans to close three schools at the university and was charged with verbally attacking a provost. The professor accused the university of mismanaging construction funds, opposed university supported-funding, criticized the university's handling of a federal audit related to billing practices, and complained about support for faculty researchers.

The university president, provost and faculty grew unhappy with the professor's leadership, and he was asked to resign. He refused to resign and was removed from the deanship. The professor sued the university, its president and its provost in a federal district court, asserting a First Amendment violation. After the court denied a request for pretrial judgment by university officials, the Second Circuit held the university's interest in efficient administration justified its decision to remove the professor as dean. The deanship of the engineering school was an executive, policymaking position. For this reason, **the university could expect the person who held the position to refrain from voicing opposition to university policies**. As it was entitled to remove the professor for expressing opposition to several university policies, the court reversed the judgment. *Faghri v. Univ. of Connecticut*, 621 F.3d 92 (2d Cir. 2010).

◆   *A tenured Mississippi business professor was unable to show he was removed from his teaching duties in retaliation for his behavior.*

According to the dean of the college of business, the professor's behavior created an environment where students and faculty members felt unsafe. In a letter to the university president, the dean described the professor's "negative and disruptive behavior" and charged him with failing to engage in scholarly or professional activities. The president removed the professor from teaching duties but directed him to continue research activities. The professor stopped doing his research and sued the university and several officials in a federal court for speech rights and due process violations. He claimed the discipline came in retaliation for creating a website critical of the university and for filing a complaint with an accrediting agency. The case reached the Fifth Circuit, which held **he could not show retaliation since he did not suffer "adverse employment action."** All the "tangible accoutrements of his position – except his teaching duties – remained stable." *DePree v. Saunders*, 588 F.3d 282 (5th Cir. 2009).

## 2. Speech Pursuant to Official Duties

In Garcetti v. Ceballos, *547 U.S. 410, 126 S.Ct. 1951, 164 L.Ed.2d 689 (2006), the Supreme Court restated the general rule that public employees have limited First Amendment rights to speak as private citizens on matters of public concern.* Garcetti *clarified that **a public employee's speech made pursuant to official duties is not protected by the First Amendment**. The Court held "when public employees make statements pursuant to their official duties, the employees are not speaking as citizens for First Amendment purposes."*

◆ *A Massachusetts appeals court affirmed a decision to dismiss a professor's free speech lawsuit.*

After the professor made questionable comments about the credentials of a graduate student from the People's Republic of China to a graduate registrar, the vice provost revoked the professor's Graduate Faculty status. As a result, the professor could no longer teach graduate-level courses and would not be allowed to sit on or chair thesis and doctoral dissertation committees. The change did not affect the professor's salary. He sued, alleging the university violated his speech rights. In *Garcetti v. Ceballos*, the U.S. Supreme Court held the First Amendment protects employees from retaliation at work for statements made as a private citizen on a matter of public concern. The court dismissed the claim, and the appellate court affirmed the ruling, explaining that **the professor's comments were made about his official duties – not a matter of public concern – so the speech wasn't protected**. *Levin v. Univ. of Massachusetts*, 88 Mass. App. Ct. 1115 (Mass. App. Ct. 2015).

◆ *A University of Oregon instructor enjoyed no First Amendment protection to threaten his students.*

The instructor had a "voices off" policy for certain parts of his classes so he could teach American Sign Language. A group of students violated the policy and disrupted class. The instructor told the class that while he was in Pakistan, he encountered tribesmen with rifles. He said he treated them with respect to avoid being shot. According to the instructor, the point of the story was that his students needed to respect his "voices off" policy, just as he needed to respect the tribesmen. But when students kept talking, the instructor asked "do you want me to take out a gun and shoot you in the head?" The remark was recorded and later, the instructor's contract was not renewed. He sued the university, its dean and other officials, asserting First Amendment violations.

A federal court found no speech rights violation. The instructor was not speaking as a private citizen and was not speaking about the public concern. The statements were made in his capacity as a public employee. While the instructor tried to link his statement about shooting students to his talk about respect for different cultures, the court held he "simply crossed the line." **There is no First Amendment right to make threats.** A disability rights claim failed, as no evidence showed students violated his policy because of his deafness. *Quint v. Univ. of Oregon*, No. 6:11-CV-6371-TC, 2013 WL 363782 (D. Or. 1/30/13).

◆ *A federal court rejected a former faculty member's claim that she was fired for expressing concerns about a Michigan university's treatment of animals.*

For 27 of her 37 years at the university, the employee sat on a committee that attempted to assure humane treatment of lab animals. She publicly sided with another committee member's charges of non-compliant conditions at the facility, and she spoke out at meetings. After the university discharged her, the employee filed a federal court action for First Amendment violations. The court held she did not show she was speaking as a citizen on a matter of public concern because **the statements at issue were pursuant to her professional responsibilities**. This meant her statements were not protected by the First Amendment. It did not matter to the court that there were members of the public present when the employee was speaking. Nor was the court impressed by the fact that some of her statements were made outside the workplace. As a result, the court held for the university. *Hrapkiewicz v. Board of Governors of Wayne State Univ.*, No. 11-13418, 2012 WL 393133 (E.D. Mich. 2/6/12).

◆   *A Louisiana professor may pursue a claim that he was discharged because he criticized the U.S. Army Corps of Engineers after Hurricane Katrina.*

The professor had worked at the state geological survey since 1992 and co-founded the Louisiana State University (LSU) Hurricane Center in 2000. Soon after Hurricane Katrina hit in 2005, the professor was chosen by a state agency to lead a research group to find the cause of the catastrophic flooding in New Orleans. Later, he made public statements suggesting the flooding was caused by the Army Corps of Engineers' failure to properly engineer and maintain the city's levees. After LSU officials ordered the professor not to make public statements or provide testimony about causes of the levee failures, he continued to make public statements about the case and testified before the Louisiana Legislature and Congress. In 2006, he published a book discussing the case and LSU's efforts to keep him quiet. After LSU demoted the professor, he sued LSU in a federal court. The court refused to dismiss the professor's retaliation claim, rejecting LSU's argument that his comments were made pursuant to his official duties and thus were not protected. Instead, **the court found he was not performing official job duties when he criticized the Army Corps of Engineers**. There was enough evidence of retaliation for the claim to proceed. *Van Heerden v. Board of Supervisors of Louisiana State Univ.*, No. 3:10-CV-155-JJB-CN, 2011 WL 5008410 (M.D. La. 10/20/11).

### 3. Speech About the Public Concern

*In* Pickering v. Board of Educ., *391 U.S. 563 (1968), the Supreme Court held a public employee may not be disciplined for speaking on matters of public concern unless the communication was made in reckless disregard for the truth. In* Connick v. Myers, *461 U.S. 138 (1983), the Court held **a public employee's speech upon matters of purely personal interest has no constitutional protection**. In* Rankin v. McPherson, *483 U.S. 378 (1987), the Court held that "the public concern" is determined by the content, form, and context of speech.*

◆   *The Seventh Circuit revived a former adjunct professor's claim that she was illegally fired from her job because she complained about how her employer treated adjuncts.*

The adjunct wrote a letter accusing the school of treating adjuncts as "a disposable resource" and "a separate, lower class of people." It said adjuncts were underpaid, wrongfully denied access to health care and denied certain classes without explanation. She also criticized the college's decision to ban adjuncts from working on an hourly basis. Two days later, she was fired. The college explicitly cited the letter as the reason for the termination. The college told her that she would be charged with trespass if she set foot on campus. She sued, claiming the college illegally retaliated against her for exercising her speech rights. A district court dismissed the suit, and the adjunct professor appealed. The Seventh Circuit reversed, explaining **the letter discussed several matters of public concern and listed multiple references to difficulties faced by all adjuncts. The letter was not merely an expression of a personal grievance.** Instead, its content "placed it squarely among matters of public concern," the appeals court said. The case was remanded for further proceedings. *Meade v. Moraine Valley Community College*, 770 F.3d 680 (7th Cir. 2014).

◆   *A Texas federal judge refused to dismiss a terminated professor's third free speech suit against a college.*

The professor filed the first suit after the board of trustees refused to allow him to speak at a meeting. After he won an injunction, the school settled the claim. Two years later, he filed a second lawsuit after he was reprimanded for voicing displeasure when the school chose to end its longstanding practice of deducting union dues directly from employees' paychecks. After the court denied a defense motion for summary judgment, the parties settled that case. Four months later, the school terminated the professor, saying he was insubordinate and "fostered a climate of fear amongst his fellow faculty." He filed a third suit, claiming was terminated because he exercised his First Amendment rights in the immediately preceding suit. The school filed a motion for pretrial judgment, claiming entitlement to qualified immunity. The court denied the motion. Whether the decision to terminate the professor was motivated by the speech was a question for a jury, the court explained. **Evidence suggested that the professor's prior suits played a role in the decision to fire him.** The college president said in her deposition that the professor's habit of going "directly to the press" played a role in "detract[ing] from the environment" of the college. *Smith v. The College of the Mainland,* 63 F.Supp.3d 712 (S.D. Tex. 2014).

◆   *The Eighth Circuit Court of Appeals affirmed a Minnesota judge's decision to dismiss a fired law professor's speech claim.*

A tenured law professor taught classes on policing, discussing issues like police misconduct and race problems. In April 2007, a local paper ran a commentary by the professor in which she criticized a state judge's decision not to investigate racism allegations in a murder trial where the victim was a police officer. The paper ran responses by the police chief and an officer who was the president of a private group representing police officers. The group questioned her "fitness to teach" and declared a boycott against the school. Two years later, the professor was charged with violating state tax law. She was suspended from teaching. After she was convicted of four gross misdemeanors, the dean initiated disciplinary proceedings against her. She was terminated following a faculty vote. She sued, alleging the school, the dean and the police conspired to deny her constitutional right to free speech. She claimed her termination was "to prevent her from teaching about police misconduct, and retaliation for past speech criticizing [the] government." A Minnesota federal judge dismissed her suit for failure to state a claim. She appealed, but the Eighth Circuit Court of Appeals affirmed. The professor sued under 42 U.S.C. § 1983. To be liable under Section 1983, the U.S. Supreme Court has held a private actor must be "a willful participant in joint activity with the State" in breaching the plaintiff's rights. To show this was the case, the professor **had to show the school and the dean had an understanding with the police defendants and they were all working together to get her fired**. She didn't, so the Eighth Circuit affirmed the decision to dismiss. *Magee v. Trustees of Hamline Univ.*, 747 F.3d 532 (8th Cir. 2014).

◆   *An Oklahoma federal judge ruled a professor's speech claim could move forward. But the court dismissed his Title VII claim, as he didn't first file a claim with the EEOC.*

Alfred Duckett is African-American. During the 2011-12 school year, Duckett was a tenured associate music professor at Cameron University (CU). He was also a member of the hiring committee. Duckett had a long history of advocating for a more racially diverse faculty at CU. In the summer of 2012, Duckett reportedly accused the chair of the hiring committee of being a racist. Duckett claimed CU put him on paid leave shortly afterward and barred him from campus. Duckett sued the state, the board of regents and other defendants. His suit accused the defendants of violating Title VII by subjecting him to racial discrimination and retaliation by complaining about racial bias. It also alleged a violation of his right to free speech. The university asked the court to dismiss the claims. It dismissed the Title VII claim but allowed the speech claim to move forward. Under U.S. Supreme Court precedent, a public employee has a right to speak as a citizen if the speech wasn't made pursuant to the employee's official duties and involved a matter of public concern. **As a general rule, speech that reveals official impropriety involves a matter of public concern while speech that simply airs a personal grievance does not.** As such, the court found Duckett stated a plausible free speech claim. So the motion was granted in part and denied in part. *Duckett v. Oklahoma ex rel. Board of Regents of Univ. of Oklahoma*, 986 F. Supp.2d 1249 (W.D. Okla. 2013).

◆   *A University of Toledo interim Associate Vice President (VP) for human resources did not show her speech rights outweighed those of the university.*

The VP objected to an editorial that compared the civil rights movement with the gay rights movement. She wrote a column stating that gay people should not have the same protections as African-Americans. At a university hearing, the VP insisted she had expressed her own views as a private citizen in the column. But the university terminated her employment because she took a public position that directly contradicted university policies and procedures.

In the VP's lawsuit against the university and its officials, she claimed speech and equal protection violations. Appeal reached the U.S. Court of Appeals, Sixth Circuit. After finding the column involved a matter of public concern, the court sought to resolve whether her speech interests outweighed the university's interests. It found that **if a policymaking public employee is discharged due to speech that relates to political or policy views, a presumption exists that the government employer's interest in efficiency outweighs the employee's free speech interests**. That presumption applied in this case. The column implied that LGBT individuals should not be compared with African-Americans when it comes to affording civil rights protections, and this sentiment contravened relevant university policies. A lower court had correctly ruled against the VP on her First Amendment and equal protection claims. *Dixon v. Univ. of Toledo*, 702 F.3d 269 (6th Cir. 2012).

◆   *A University of Arkansas public safety officer was unable to show the denial of a promotion was based upon his speech.*

The officer reported to university officials that the chief of the university's department of public safety was misusing resources. Three years later, state police investigated the chief for misappropriating university resources, resulting in the chief's resignation. Although the officer sought to replace the chief, another candidate was selected for the position, and the officer sued the university board in a federal district court for First Amendment violations.

The court held for the board, and the officer appealed. The U.S. Court of Appeals, Eighth Circuit, explained that **public employee speech is protected only if the employee speaks as a citizen on a matter of public concern**. The speech must also outweigh the government interest in efficient services. While the officer's internal complaints about the chief were protected by the First Amendment, his statement to state police investigators was made pursuant to his job duties and was unprotected. To prevail on his First Amendment claim, the officer needed to show a connection between his internal complaints and the decision not to promote him. **The court found no evidence showing his internal complaints about the chief were a substantial or motivating factor in the decision to deny him the job as chief many years later.** As a result, the district court had proper grounds to deny the First Amendment claim. The district court correctly rejected a claim that the university violated the officer's due process rights, since he presented no evidence of any legitimate claim to a promotion. The judgment against the officer was affirmed. *Davenport v. Univ. of Arkansas Board of Trustees*, 553 F.3d 1110 (8th Cir. 2009).

◆   *A California university did not violate employee speech rights by using a form with a confidentiality provision for reporting violations.*

A nurse reported unsafe and unsanitary practices at a university hospital. She then claimed the university retaliated and discriminated against her, and she sued university regents in a state superior court. But the nurse did not first file an administrative complaint. She claimed she was excused from this requirement because the form the university used for filing complaints violated her First Amendment rights by requiring employees to keep subject matter confidential. The court denied relief, and the nurse appealed. **The Court of Appeal of California explained that the form required confidentiality only until a matter was resolved and did not prevent any additional reporting.** Because the nurse was not required to submit to the confidentiality provision in order to file a retaliation complaint, she did not prove a speech violation. The court affirmed the judgment. *Jones v. Regents of the Univ. of California*, 164 Cal.App.4th 1072, 79 Cal.Rptr.3d 817 (Cal. Ct. App. 2008).

◆ *When employees are disciplined or discharged for legitimate reasons, the First Amendment will not protect them from the adverse action.*

An untenured Ohio teacher was not rehired after a number of incidents that led the school board to conclude he lacked tactfulness in handling professional matters. His federal case reached the U.S. Supreme Court. It held that apart from the actions for which the teacher might claim First Amendment protection, the board could have chosen not to rehire him on the basis of several other incidents and could have reached the same decision had he not engaged in constitutionally protected conduct. **A marginal employee should not be able to prevent dismissal by engaging in constitutionally protected activity and then hiding under a constitutional shield as protection from all other actions that were not constitutionally protected.** *Mt. Healthy City School Dist. v. Doyle*, 429 U.S. 274, 97 S.Ct. 568, 50 L.Ed.2d 471 (1977).

◆ *The U.S. Supreme Court held a reasonable belief of workplace disruption can be enough to outweigh a speaker's rights under the First Amendment.*

In *Waters v. Churchill,* the Supreme Court held public employee termination is permitted where only a likelihood of disruption existed. **It was unnecessary to demonstrate an actual disruption if termination was based on the employer's reasonable belief that a disruption could occur.** *Waters v. Churchill*, 511 U.S. 661, 114 S.Ct. 1878, 128 L.Ed.2d 686 (1994).

## B. Religion and Free Speech

*The First Amendment's Establishment Clause prohibits Congress from making any law respecting the establishment of a religion. The Free Exercise Clause of the First Amendment bars Congress from making any law that prohibits the free exercise of religion. Since the First Amendment applies only to governmental action, it does not bind private institutions and their employees.*

◆ *An Ohio federal judge refused to dismiss an employee's claim that a ban on religious talk was unconstitutionally broad.*

An IT professional gave a talk to colleagues. He illustrated his points by referring to the Bible – but made a point of stressing the Christian viewpoint he was expressing was his, not the university's. Someone complained, and the school investigated. It told the employee to "refrain from using biblical quotations during presentations and work related interactions" and to attend a diversity training session. The employee sued, alleging a violation of his speech rights. The court found the employee's talk to the academy was not protected by the First Amendment. But the school's ban on "using biblical quotations during presentations and work related interactions" may have been too broad. The court compared this case to the 1996 decision *Tucker v. California Dep't of Educ*. In that case, the Ninth Circuit found a public employer's complete ban on religious speech and advocacy at work violated a computer analyst's speech rights. Similarly, **the ban on this employee's speech could infringe his rights by applying to private conversations with colleagues and all kinds of other "interactions."** The court needed more information, so it refused to dismiss the claim that the ban violated the employee's rights. *Faulkner v. Univ. of Cincinnati,* No. 1:14-cv-758, 2015 WL 1299283 (S.D. Ohio 3/23/15).

◆ *The Supreme Court held the act of certifying a union by the National Labor Relations Board (NLRB) infringed on a Catholic school's rights.*

The right of employees of a Catholic school system to join together and be recognized as a bargaining unit was successfully challenged in a case decided by the U.S. Supreme Court. In this case, the unions were certified by the NLRB as bargaining units, but the diocese refused to bargain. The Court said that the religion clauses of the U.S. Constitution, which require religious organizations to finance their educational systems without governmental aid, also free the religious organizations of the obviously inhibiting effect and impact of unionization of their teachers. The court agreed with the employer's contention that **the very threshold act of certification of the union by the NLRB would necessarily alter and infringe upon the religious character of parochial schools**, since this would mean that the bishop would no longer be the sole repository of authority as required by church law. Instead, he would have to share some decision-making with the union. This, said the Court, violated the religion clauses of the U.S. Constitution. *NLRB v. Catholic Bishop of Chicago*, 440 U.S. 490, 99 S.Ct. 1313, 59 L.Ed.2d 533 (1979).

## C. Electronic Communications

*In* Faculty Rights Coalition v. Shahrokhi, *204 Fed.Appx. 416 (5th Cir. 2006), the Fifth Circuit Court of Appeals held Texas university officials did not violate an adjunct professor's speech rights by limiting his email access. It noted that in* Perry Educ. Ass'n v. Perry Local Educators' Ass'n, *460 U.S. 37 (1983), the Supreme Court held a public school system's internal mail system is not a "state-created forum" for unlimited expression. State agencies may reserve such forums for their intended purposes, as long as their regulations are reasonable and not intended to suppress expression. In* Shahrokhi, *the court found no speech rights violation, as restrictions created by a spam filter and an email access policy were uniformly applied and not content-based.*

◆ *An Illinois federal judge refused to dismiss a suit that challenged the constitutionality of a university's computer-related policies.*

Two professors contributed to a blog that often censured the school's administration. They claimed the school tried to shut down the blog by adopting a cyberbullying policy that limits electronic speech. The policy said speech would violate it even if the speaker didn't use a university computer. The professors received three official letters objecting to the blog. One alleged the blog was misusing the school's legally protected marks and demanded that the professors shut it down. The suit alleged violations of the professors' speech rights, as the school tried to shut down the blog, adopted the cyberbullying policy and claimed without basis that the blog's use of the school's name and marks "caused confusion, diminished the University's brand, and implied [the school's] endorsement of the blog's commentary." The university asked the judge to dismiss the case, but the court refused to do so. When someone's First Amendment rights are "chilled," it means he's been intimidated from exercising them. **The professors showed an actual controversy existed by alleging that a letter that was ostensibly about trademark violations was actually an attempt to chill their First Amendment rights to free speech by suggesting they could be sued under trademark law or disciplined under the school's policy.** So the proceedings could continue. *Beverley v. Watson*, 78 F.Supp.3d 717 (N.D. Ill. 2015).

◆ *An Idaho faculty association was denied a temporary order it sought in order to force a university to allow faculty members to use a university listserv.*

Idaho State University (ISU) used an email service to create email lists. Users could easily send emails to the entire faculty through the service. Members of ISU's provisional faculty senate wanted to use the service to circulate and vote on a draft constitution. When permission was denied, a faculty association sued ISU and several university officials in a state court for First Amendment violations. The court denied the association's request for a temporary restraining order and preliminary injunction. Using a test applied to decide First Amendment cases, the court considered whether there was speech on a matter of public concern. It had to be found that the speech was a substantial or motivating factor in adverse action. In the court's view, ISU had good reason to prevent the faculty senate from using the service, as it opposed the association's message. The court explained that **when faculty members speak about job-related matters, they speak as public employees**. Because their messages could be seen as reflecting ISU's position, the university could take steps to make sure its own message was not distorted. For this reason, the association was not entitled to a preliminary order. *Idaho State Univ. Faculty Ass'n for the Preservation of the First Amendment v. Idaho State Univ.*, 857 F.Supp.2d 1055 (D. Idaho 2012).

◆ *A California community college district did not violate a professor's rights by ordering him to stop sending incendiary electronic communications.*

The professor sent racially charged emails to a distribution list maintained by the community college district. He questioned the district's endorsement of what he called the "racist event" of "Dia de la raza," and said it was "time to acknowledge and celebrate the superiority of Western Civilization." Another email by the professor stated "[o]ur survival depends on discrimination," and another said "if we don't pull ourselves out of the multicultural stupor, another culture with some pretty unsavory characteristics ... will dominate." The final email linked to his website on the district's server that urged the "preservation of White majority" and said the "persistent inflow of Hispanic immigrants" was a threat to the U.S. The community college did not discipline him, even after some employees complained. Hispanic employees sued the community college district. A federal court denied judgment to the community college president and chancellor, and they appealed, seeking qualified immunity.

On appeal, the U.S. Court of Appeals, Ninth Circuit, explained that the employees were entitled to be free from harassment on the basis of protected status. **Employers who are made aware of unlawful harassment must "take reasonable and appropriate steps to investigate and make it stop."** But in this case, the court held the professor's speech was not unlawful harassment. Hispanic employees objected to the speech based on his viewpoint. **According to the court, the government cannot silence speech because it promotes ideas that are considered offensive.** The court held substantial deference was due for an official decision not to take disciplinary action. As the court expressed doubt that a college professor's expression on a matter of public concern could ever be unlawful harassment, it reversed the district court's decision to deny the officials qualified immunity and returned the case to the lower court. *Rodriguez v. Maricopa County Community College Dist.*, 605 F.3d 703 (9th Cir. 2010).

◆    *A University of Virginia employee's email to a member of a local NAACP chapter regarding the university pay scale was not protected speech.*

The employee used her university email account to send university payroll data to the NAACP. University officials investigated the action. The employee refused to answer questions involving her NAACP membership. Supervisors notified her "she was facing termination." According to the employee, she was not informed of the nature of the claims and a "hearing" amounted to being handed pink slips. She sued the university in a federal district court for First Amendment, due process and state law violations. After issuing a favorable initial ruling to the employee, the court awarded judgment to the university.

On appeal, **the U.S. Court of Appeals, Fourth Circuit, rejected the claim that the email and attachments from the employee's work computer were protected speech**. Instead, the university's interest in providing effective and efficient services to the public strongly outweighed her interest in expression. The employee violated a state policy limiting personal emails from state computers and accounts. This policy supported the university's efforts to disseminate its own message. Even though the employee had an interest in her own communication, it did not outweigh that of the university. Questions by the university regarding her NAACP affiliation did not violate her association rights, as there was a legitimate interest in ascertaining the source of potentially false data about the university pay structure. As a result, the judgment for the university was affirmed. *Bowers v. Scurry*, 276 Fed.Appx. 278 (4th Cir. 2008).

### D.  Academic Freedom

*In* Rodriguez v. Maricopa County Community College Dist., *this chapter, the Ninth Circuit held academic speech requires "breathing room." Courts must defer to university decisions that err on the side of free speech and academic freedom. Another court has held that universities have the right to decide "who may teach, what may be taught, how it may be taught, and who may be admitted to study."* **The right to academic freedom belongs to the** *institution, not to any individual. Thus, courts have held that public university professors lack First Amendment rights to determine what will be taught.*

◆   *Finding an Iowa law school employee made out a claim of political discrimination based on her conservative views, a federal appeals court allowed her to pursue First Amendment claims against the law school dean.*

After being hired as a part-time associate director in a law school writing center, the employee applied for a full-time job teaching writing. Although there were 50 applicants, and she was one of only three candidates to reach a final interview, she believed her conservative political beliefs would preclude her hiring. The employee raised this concern to an associate dean, who then relayed her comments to the law school dean. The dean acted on a committee recommendation to hire another candidate with less teaching experience, who presented himself as a liberal. After being denied four adjunct positions, the employee sued the law school dean for violating her First Amendment rights.

The court held the dean had qualified immunity, and the employee appealed to the U.S. Court of Appeals, Eighth Circuit. It held **the employee had a First Amendment right to be free from political discrimination**. This right was clearly established by *Rutan v. Republican Party of Illinois*, 497 U.S. 62 (1990). Since the employee offered enough evidence for a reasonable jury to find her political affiliation was a motivating factor in the decision not to hire her, the court held the claim against the dean in her individual capacity could go forward. To prevail, the dean had to prove it was more likely than not that she would have made the same hiring decision regardless of the employee's political beliefs. *Wagner v. Jones*, 664 F.3d 259 (8th Cir. 2011).

◆   *Because he was not speaking as a citizen on a matter of public concern, a New York community college professor lost his speech rights case.*

The professor said that when his department chair stepped down, an election was held to choose her successor. The professor supported a candidate who eventually lost. After the election, he claimed the winning candidate retaliated against him for supporting his opponent. Among the professor's claims was that the new chair fabricated student complaints, changed his work assignments and gave him a poor performance review. After the professor lost his job, he filed a federal lawsuit against the community college for First Amendment speech and association violations. The college sought dismissal, arguing he could not proceed because his speech and employment associations were made pursuant to his job duties and did not involve the public concern.

The court explained that although the First Amendment may protect the right of public employees to speak as citizens on matters of public concern, **public employees must accept some limitations on their free speech rights**. To decide whether public employee speech is protected from retaliation, courts ask whether the employee spoke as a citizen on a matter of public concern, and if so, whether the government entity had a good reason to treat him differently than a member of the general public. In this case, the professor did not show that his support of a particular candidate addressed a matter of public concern. He did not show his participation in the election "reflected anything more than a personal interest." The motion to dismiss was granted. *Flyr v. City Univ. of New York*, No. 09 Civ. 9159(JGK), 2011 WL 1675997 (S.D.N.Y. 4/25/11).

### 1. Classroom Speech

◆ *Virginia State University (VSU) administrators did not violate a professor's rights by changing a student's grade.*

For a physics course, the professor calculated each student's final grade by averaging the three highest scores on five quizzes. This calculation resulted in an average of 59 for one student. He said the student achieved quiz scores of 16, 66, 89, 21 and 22. Although the score of 59 merited a grade of F, the professor assigned the student a D. The student protested, believing he had earned higher scores on two quizzes, which would have entitled him to an A.

The student handed in faxed copies of the quizzes showing scores of 95, but the professor believed they were doctored and refused to change the grade. The department chairman sided with the student and changed the grade to an A. The professor sued VSU in a federal district court for violating an asserted right to academic freedom. He also said administrators changed the grade to retaliate against him for testifying on behalf of a colleague who had filed a lawsuit against VSU. The professor asked the court to order VSU to change the grade to a D. He also sought monetary damages. The court explained that the U.S. Supreme Court has recognized that the Constitution gives "some measure of academic freedom to academic institutions." Universities have the right to determine "who may teach, what may be taught, how it may be taught, and who may be admitted to study." **The right to academic freedom belongs to universities and not to individual professors.** VSU officials exercised their authority to change the grade without requiring the professor to do so personally. He lacked a constitutional right to academic freedom that would prevent VSU officials from changing the grade. The court granted VSU's motion to dismiss the claim. *Stronach v. Virginia State Univ.*, No. 3:07CV646-HEH, 2008 WL 161304 (E.D. Va. 1/15/08).

◆ *Institutions are entitled to direct their instructors to keep personal discussions about sexual orientation or religion out of their classes.*

An Illinois college instructor gave a gay student religious pamphlets on the sinfulness of homosexuality. One was entitled "Sin City" and told the story of a man who was beaten when he tried to stop a gay pride parade and was arrested by police. It also said a demon urged on a minister who preached that "God loves even gay people." The student complained to college officials and urged them to fire the instructor. In a follow-up letter, the student reported that the instructor had accused him of trying to get her fired.

The college investigated the report and concluded that the instructor had sexually harassed the student based on sexual orientation. It did not offer the instructor a job the following semester, and she sued the college in a federal district court for speech rights violations. The court held for the college, and the instructor appealed to the U.S. Court of Appeals, Seventh Circuit. The court relied on *Garcetti v. Ceballos*, this chapter, noting the case signalled the Court's concern that the courts give appropriate weight to a public employer's interests in First Amendment cases. In this case, **the college had an interest in ensuring that instructors stayed on the subject matter of their clinics and classrooms**. The court affirmed the judgment for the college, as it could lawfully direct instructors to keep personal discussions about sexual orientation or religion out of a class or clinic. *Piggee v. Carl Sandburg College*, 464 F.3d 667 (7th Cir. 2006).

◆   *An Ohio university did not violate a lecturer's First Amendment rights by telling her to communicate grading requirements more clearly to her students.*

The lecturer gave incomplete grades to 13 of 17 students in a writing class for improper formatting, improper citations, and/or textual changes to their work. She left it up to each student to determine which reason applied in his or her own case. The lecturer's listserv postings did not specify particular reasons for which students received incomplete grades, and at least one student complained. A supervisor told the lecturer her listserv postings were not sufficiently clear to inform students how to complete the course. She asked her to send each student in the class a letter with individualized instructions for earning a final grade. Five weeks later, several students complained that the lecturer did not provide this information. The supervisor again asked the lecturer to draft letters to each student and emphasized that incomplete grades were a serious problem affecting student academic and financial aid status. The lecturer never responded and did not prepare the letters. She later sued the director of the English department and the supervisor for violating her rights to speech and academic freedom. A federal district court dismissed the case.

On appeal, the U.S. Court of Appeals, Sixth Circuit, rejected the lecturer's claim that an instruction by a supervisor to communicate with students violated the First Amendment. **Any right to academic freedom recognized by the First Amendment applied to the university, not the lecturer. A university is entitled to determine who may teach, what may be taught, how it is taught, and who may be admitted.** Professors have certain protections under the First Amendment, like making decisions about instruction and grading that differ from those of the university. In this case, the university simply asked the lecturer to explain to students exactly what was required to obtain a final grade. As the university did not violate her rights, the court affirmed the judgment. *Johnson-Kurek v. Abu-Absi*, 423 F.3d 590 (6th Cir. 2005).

## 2. Loyalty Oaths

*In* Sweezy v. New Hampshire, *354 U.S. 234 (1957), the U.S. Supreme Court declared unconstitutional a university policy aimed at prohibiting the employment of Communist Party members.*

◆   *An Arizona statute that prohibited even associating with the Communist Party was struck down by the U.S. Supreme Court.*

An Arizona teacher who was a Quaker refused to take an oath required of all public employees under Arizona law. The oath swore that the employees would support both the Arizona and the U.S. Constitutions as well as state laws. The legislation also stated that anyone who took the oath and supported the Communist Party or the violent overthrow of government would be discharged from employment and charged with perjury. The teacher sued for declaratory relief in the Arizona courts, having decided she could not take the oath in good conscience because she did not know what it meant.

The U.S. Supreme Court held that political groups may have both legal and illegal aims and that there should not be a blanket prohibition on all groups that might have both legal and illegal goals. Such a prohibition would threaten legitimate political expression and association. The Court held that mere association with a group cannot be prohibited without a showing of "specific intent" to carry out the group's illegal purpose. It went on to say that **the Arizona statute was constitutionally deficient because it was not confined to those employees with a "specific intent" to do something illegal**. The statute infringed upon employee rights to free association by not punishing specific behavior that yielded a clear and present danger to government. The statute was struck down as unconstitutional. *Elfbrandt v. Russell*, 384 U.S. 11, 86 S.Ct. 1238, 16 L.Ed.2d 321 (1965).

◆ *A state could not require teachers to file annual affidavits listing every organization they belonged to in the past five years.*

The Arkansas Legislature established **a statute that required every teacher employed by a state-supported school or college to file an annual affidavit listing every organization to which he or she had belonged in the past five years**. A teacher who had worked for an Arkansas school system for 25 years and who was a member of the NAACP was told he would have to file such an affidavit before the start of the next school year. After he failed to do so, his contract for the next year was not renewed. He filed a class action lawsuit against the school district in a federal district court. The court found that the teacher was not a member of the Communist Party or any organization advocating the violent overthrow of the government. It upheld the statute, finding that the information requested by the school district was relevant. The Supreme Court of Arkansas had upheld the statute's constitutionality in a case brought by other teachers. The U.S. Supreme Court noted that the state had a right to investigate teachers, since education of youth was a vital public interest. It stated that the requirement of the affidavit was reasonably related to the state's interest. However, **requiring teachers to name all their associations interfered with teacher free speech and association rights**. Because fundamental rights were involved, governmental screening of teachers was required to be narrowly tailored to the state's ends. Because the statute went beyond what was necessary to meet the state's inquiry into the fitness of its teachers, the Court ruled it unconstitutional. *Shelton v. Tucker*, 364 U.S. 479, 81 S.Ct. 247, 5 L.Ed.2d 231 (1960).

◆ *A Washington statute aimed at prohibiting subversives from becoming teachers was too vague to be constitutional.*

Faculty members sued to declare two state statutes unconstitutional. One statute required all state employees to take loyalty oaths, and the other required all teachers to take an oath as a condition of employment. Both oaths dealt with employee loyalty to the U.S. Constitution and to the government. The public employee statute applied to all public employees and defined a "subversive person" as one who conspired to overthrow the government. The Communist Party also was named as a subversive organization. Persons designated as subversives or Communist Party members were ineligible for public employment. The U.S. Supreme Court held that the statutes were vague and overbroad, and violated the Fourteenth Amendment's Due Process Clause. The statutes did not provide sufficient notice of what conduct was prohibited. This constituted a denial of the teachers' due process rights. **The university could not require its teachers to take an oath that applied to some vague behavior in the future**, especially since there were First Amendment freedom of speech and association claims at stake. *Baggett v. Bullitt,* 377 U.S. 360, 84 S.Ct. 1316, 12 L.Ed.2d 377 (1963).

◆   *A loyalty oath could not be administered to two applicants who objected to it on religious grounds.*

As part of state-mandated pre-employment procedures, a California community college district required applicants to sign an oath swearing "true faith and allegiance" and to "support and defend" the United States and California Constitutions. Two Jehovah's Witnesses applied for positions but refused to take the oath due to their religious beliefs. They sued the district under the Religious Freedom Restoration Act of 1993 (RFRA), challenging the validity of the loyalty oath as a condition precedent for employment. A federal court held that **requiring the applicants to take an oath that violated their religious tenets placed an undue burden on their right to free exercise of religion**. The district failed to assert that the loyalty oath furthered a compelling government interest or was the least restrictive means of achieving that interest. Although employee loyalty was a compelling interest, the evidence failed to establish that a loyalty oath effectively achieved this goal. An alternative oath directed to an applicant's actions rather than his or her beliefs would be equally effective and less restrictive. Because the loyalty oath could not be justified under the compelling interest test articulated in the RFRA, the court enjoined the district from administering the loyalty oath to the applicants. *Bessard v. California Community Colleges,* 867 F.Supp. 1454 (E.D. Cal. 1994).

[*Editor's Note*: The U.S. Supreme Court held that the RFRA was unconstitutional as applied to state actions in *City of Boerne, Texas v. Flores,* 521 U.S. 507, 117 S.Ct. 2157, 138 L.Ed.2d 624 (1997).]

## II.  DEFAMATION

*To pursue a defamation claim, a defamed party must allege that false material was "published" to a third party who understands it refers to the defamed party. The defamed party must suffer a loss of reputation and a "tangible injury," which is usually some harm to an economic interest.*

*Defenses to defamation include truth, privilege, consent and opinion. The defense of privilege defeats many otherwise actionable defamation claims in employment cases. In* Fink v. California State Univ. Northridge, *No. B183977, 2006 WL 465947 (Cal. Ct. App. 2/28/06), the Court of Appeal of California held that statements reporting suspected criminal activity to law enforcement officers are privileged and cannot form the basis of a defamation claim.*

*A judicial privilege applies to proceedings before government bodies and pursuant to a statute or administrative regulation. The U.S. Court of Appeals,*

*Third Circuit, has limited an absolute privilege to judicial proceedings. Applying Pennsylvania law, the court held internal grievance proceedings are not entitled to the same absolute immunity as regular judicial proceedings.* Overall v. Univ. of Pennsylvania, *412 F.3d 492 (3d Cir. 2005).*

◆ *A Connecticut appeals court upheld a ruling that rejected the defamation claim of a tenured professor who was arrested after submitting a falsified expense report.*

The professor was given permission to attend and present at a conference. When he returned, he submitted an expense report to a dean. The $175 conference registration receipt was not an original copy. The dean asked the professor to provide better documentation. He didn't. The dean contacted the conference host, who sent documentation indicating the professor had neither attended nor presented at the conference. The dean sent a memorandum to the university president, including supporting documentation that suggested the expense report was not legitimate. The professor was arrested, and the charges were later dropped. He sued, alleging defamation. The trial court dismissed the claim, and the professor appealed. On appeal, the professor's evidence consisted of his own assertions that the defendants made false statements about him. **But he admitted falsifying the expense report, and he offered no evidence to counter the defendants' evidence that all the statements they made about him were true.** The ruling was affirmed. *Nodoushani v. Southern Connecticut State Univ.*, 95 A.3d 1248 (Conn. App. Ct. 2014).

◆ *A North Carolina appeals court rejected a student's defamation claims. The student was a recipient of merit scholarships.*

At the end of his second year at school, the student's benefits were reduced because he was ranked in the bottom third of his class. The student took a number of steps to challenge the reduction and pursue his claim that the class rank requirement did not apply to some scholarships. Ultimately, he took his argument to the dean and was unsuccessful in his attempts to change the school's position. The dean ended up writing a letter to the student, reiterating the school's position regarding his scholarship and "remind[ing him] of the code of conduct expected of students." In the letter, the dean said, "From my experience with you on this issue, if people disagree with you, you appear to assume that those persons are acting in bad faith and you accuse them of fraud and deceit." The student sued, raising claims of defamation. A trial court granted a defense motion for dismissal, and he filed an appeal. **The student's libel per se claim failed because the statement in the letter he relied on was an opinion statement**, the appellate court explained. His libel per quod claim failed because he did not allege facts supporting the damages he claimed. So the decision to dismiss was affirmed. *Skinner v. Reynolds,* 764 S.E.2d 652 (N.C. Ct. App. 2014).

◆ *A federal district court in Colorado refused to dismiss the First Amendment claim of a student who was disciplined for writing an explicit letter to a female classmate.*

Both students were freshmen. The male was a teaching assistant, and the female was a student in the class. Fans of the "Fifty Shades of Grey" novels, the couple started a sexual relationship that included bondage and sadomasochism. They also exchanged poetry that reflected the role-playing in their relationship. At one point, the male wrote a letter outlining the sadomasochistic acts he wanted to perform on the girl. After the relationship ended, the girl's mother learned the sexual details of the relationship and complained to the school. She provided a copy of the letter about sadomasochism. The school emailed the student, informing him that he would not be allowed to continue as a teaching assistant in the upcoming semester. The school told the student it was investigating whether his conduct toward the female violated Title IX. A disciplinary board found in the student's favor. He filed suit, alleging several claims. Most were dismissed, but the court allowed a speech claim to move forward. The student produced enough evidence at this stage of the case to show the disciplinary proceeding was motivated by his protected speech. The school said the letter was not protected because it was a threat, but the court said **a reasonable juror could find the letter was not threatening**. Although First Amendment claims for most forms of relief were barred by Eleventh Amendment immunity, the student could seek to have the record of the disciplinary proceedings against him expunged. *Johnson v. Western State Colorado Univ.*, 71 F.Supp.3d 1217 (D. Colo. 2014).

◆   *A Pennsylvania student was allowed to proceed with a defamation claim against a university.*

The student was accused of sexually assaulting a female student at the school. After a hearing, the school concluded that the student was responsible for sexual assault. The student filed a lawsuit, alleging a multitude of claims. The court granted a motion to dismiss most of the claims, but it refused to dismiss the defamation claim. **The student sufficiently alleged publication of defamatory matter when he claimed that the defendants referred to him as the perpetrator of a sexual assault**, the court explained. So that claim could proceed. *Harris v. Saint Joseph's Univ.*, No. 13-3937, 2014 WL 1910242 (E.D. Pa. 5/13/14).

◆   *A Minnesota student who was disciplined for an in-class incident did not show the university's investigation of the case supported a defamation claim.*

Due to multiple sclerosis, the student needed help for many daily activities. She brought a note-taker to class without permission, and the university charged her with violating its conduct code. A letter documenting the incident described her as agitated, threatening and apparently under the influence of alcohol. After an appeal, the university revoked its finding that the student violated student conduct code provisions on alcohol. But other conduct code violations were found, and she was banned from classes taught by the teachers involved in the incident. The student sued the university for defamation. Her case reached the state court of appeals, which held the publication requirement of the defamation claim could be satisfied if the student was compelled to make the publication. But the court found she was not obligated to disclose any information about the incident. Although the university had published statements internally during its investigation, it had a qualified privilege to do so. **The university had good reason to share the information among**

**internal parties involved with the investigation.** A privilege is lost when statements are made with actual malice, which was not shown in this case. The decision for the university was affirmed. *De Jong v. Metropolitan State Univ.*, No. A12-0829, 2012 WL 5990306 (Minn. Ct. App. 12/3/12).

◆   *Ill will among employees was not enough to establish "actual malice," defeating a Michigan employee's defamation lawsuit.*

A University of Michigan (UM) researcher had a personality conflict with two supervisors and was fired during her probationary term. She claimed one of them told her she would never work at UM again and threatened to ruin her reputation. When the researcher applied for another UM job, she said a professor told her he initially planned to hire her but could not because her discharge during a probationary period resulted in automatic "do not hire status." The researcher sued UM and the supervisors in a state court for defamation. In pretrial activity, the court found UM had valid cause to fire her for not following lab protocols. But it issued a protective order requiring UM to provide a neutral reference and not to discuss her termination with any outside parties. On appeal, the state court of appeals held the statements were only communicated to the UM human resources department and were privileged communications.

**To state a valid defamation claim, the researcher had to show that statements were made with actual malice** – defined as making a statement despite knowing it is false or with a reckless disregard for the truth. Ill will or hatred alone is not enough to establish actual malice. The researcher's own testimony suggested that a supervisor believed she had falsified data. The court held the supervisor's dislike for her was not enough to establish actual malice. For this reason, the court affirmed the judgment for UM. *Osak v. Univ. of Michigan Regents*, No. 306239, 2012 WL 5061640 (Mich. Ct. App. 10/18/12).

◆   *A New York court rejected claims that graduate psychology administrators defamed a student by making misleading statements about her dismissal.*

Administrators became concerned with the student's professionalism, ethics and conduct, and they developed a remediation plan for her. She was to write a paper addressing the concerns raised about her performance. Administrators reviewed the paper, ultimately finding it was unsatisfactory. In the process, they shared documents evaluating the student's fitness to continue. After being dismissed from the program, she sued the university and some administrators in a state court for defamation. She claimed statements in the remediation paper evaluation were materially and knowingly false, made in bad faith, with actual malice and in reckless disregard of the truth. The court explained that to show defamation, a person has to prove a false statement was published to a third party without authorization. There must be evidence of fault and special harm.

**"Privileged statements" do not support a defamation claim. These include good-faith communications between parties having an interest in the subject matter.** In this case, the student did not show that the statements made about her were published to anyone other than individuals involved in evaluating her academic conduct. The statements were protected by privilege, as they were made among faculty members who were evaluating her fitness as a doctoral degree candidate. In addition, she admitted she acted unprofessionally and sometimes lied to her professors. The court dismissed the case. *Lipsky v. Gonzalez*, 39 Misc.3d 1202(A) (N.Y. Sup. Ct. 2013).

◆ *A Michigan court held state law protected educators who criticized student performance from libel claims, defeating a student's claim for defamation.*

American University of Antigua College of Medicine (AUA) put a student on nonacademic probation for unprofessional conduct. He also had a 1.5 grade point average. Later, the student was placed in a clinical experience rotation at a Michigan hospital. There, he said the program was a waste of time, and he was disrespectful and disruptive in class. Among other things, the student used inappropriate language and passwords. AUA eventually initiated proceedings before its grievance and disciplinary committee, but he skipped his hearing.

After being dismissed from medical school, the student sued AUA and the hospital owner in a Michigan court for defamation. A judge found no trial necessary and dismissed the case. On appeal, the Court of Appeals of Michigan held the student could not show any statements about him by AUA or the hospital were false. He also failed to show the statements were not entitled to a "qualified privilege." Instead, **the lower court correctly found the statements were made in good faith, motivated by an interest in the program's integrity, and communicated to proper parties only**. It was important to the court that internal records established AUA was concerned about the student's poor grades and unprofessional conduct. Statements about him were protected, and the court affirmed the judgment. *Woodward v. Trinity Health-Michigan*, No. 292172, 2011 WL 118812 (Mich. Ct. App. 1/13/11).

◆ *A California dental student was unable to show a conspiracy to keep her from earning a degree by misreporting her academic performance.*

Near her expected graduation date, the student had a problem with a patient at a school clinic. After the patient left, the chair of her department made disparaging remarks about the student in front of other faculty members. Four days before graduation, the student was notified that she had failed part of an exam and would not graduate based on a vote by a student academic committee. Believing the department chair had influenced the vote against her, the student sued the university and several instructors and administrators for defamation. She also asserted her official transcript had been altered. A federal district court held the student offered no facts to show any oral or written defamatory statements resulting in errors on her official transcript. Another problem was that defamation claims cannot be based on opinions. **California courts have found "statements regarding a student's academic competence" to be "non-actionable statements of opinion."** Finding the student's defamation claim was based on speculation, the court dismissed it. *Rashdan v. Geissberger*, No. C 10-00634 SBA, Docket No. 10, 2011 WL 197957 (N.D. Cal. 1/14/11).

◆ *As opinions cannot form the basis for a defamation claim, a first-year Texas residency program student could not pursue his case.*

Within a few weeks of entering the program, faculty members advised the director that the student was not performing at the level expected of first-year residents. The faculty terminated his rotation 10 days early, and he was placed in a remediation rotation. Despite the extra feedback and attention he received, the student continued to struggle and was discharged. He sued the medical program officials in a federal district court for defamation, claiming the program director asked him disparaging questions in front of other residents. He said she then wrote in a dismissal letter that he was "unable to complete the simplest task independently" and provided it to the Accreditation Council for Graduate Medical Education. But the court granted the director's request for pretrial judgment. **Generally speaking, a statement is defamatory when it is both false and damaging to the person's reputation.** In this case, the student could not prove the director published the statements. And the statements he attributed to her were expressions of opinion, not assertions of fact needed to support a defamation claim. Noting that only assertions of fact – not expressions of opinion – can qualify as defamatory, the court held for the program director. *Sayibu v. Univ. of Texas Southwestern Medical Center at Dallas*, No. 3:09-CV-1244-B, 2010 WL 5139494 (N.D. Tex. 12/17/10).

◆  *A tenured Illinois professor was allowed to proceed with a defamation case against a university and its vice president in the federal court system.*

At a faculty council meeting, the professor complained that the arrest of student demonstrators on campus was part of a pattern of harassment against students who opposed the war in Iraq. A vice president who oversaw the campus police and student affairs said the professor and students were responsible for the incident. He also claimed the professor had been charged with stalking a student. Although she had been elected to be the chair by members of her department, the university declined to appoint her, and it did not give her a faculty excellence award for which she claimed to be eligible.

In a federal district court action against the vice president and university for defamation and retaliation, the court explained that **as a government official, the vice president had immunity if the defamatory statement was reasonably related to his public duties**. In making this determination, the relevant factors included whether the statements were made in his role as a supervisor, as part of an official duty to speak on behalf of his department, and to defend against allegations of wrongdoing. Based on the papers filed so far, there was little information regarding the vice president's duties. The court refused to dismiss the defamation and law retaliation claims. *Capeheart v. Northern Illinois Univ.*, No. 08 CV 1423, 2010 WL 894052 (N.D. Ill. 3/9/10).

◆  *A Louisiana university coach who submitted a false resume could not claim defamation or breach of contract based on his subsequent discharge.*

The coach was hired as head basketball coach after he submitted a resume indicating he had earned a degree from the University of Texas at San Antonio (UTSA). In fact, he had attended UTSA but did not graduate. After being hired, the coach filled out forms correctly indicating he had graduated from another university that was not accredited by the Southern Association of Colleges and Schools. After the hiring, a newspaper article mentioned his failure to graduate from UTSA, and the university fired him for lying on his resume. The coach sued the university for defamation and breach of contract, claiming the resume was sent by mistake and that he later submitted correct information. The case reached the Supreme Court of Louisiana. It held the defamation claim failed because the statements indicating the coach had misrepresented his qualifications on his resume were true. **A party cannot recover for defamation based on a true statement.** The breach of contract claim failed, because the university had a valid reason to rescind the contract. Evidence showed the coach would not have been hired if the university had known he did not have a degree from an accredited institution. *Cyprien v. Board of Supervisors for the Univ. of Louisiana System*, 5 So.3d 862 (La. 2009).

◆   *The Supreme Court of Indiana rejected a professor's defamation claims against two students who filed complaints of sexual harassment against him.*

Two female students filed formal complaints of sexual harassment against an Indiana education professor. Pursuant to its anti-harassment policy, the university affirmative action office investigated. After a series of interviews, the investigator found the professor had created a hostile educational environment. The investigator specifically found harassment in one of the complaints, but the second complaint was not timely reported. A three-person panel and a senior executive officer accepted the investigator's recommendation that the professor should not have teaching responsibilities or student contact. He was assigned to a research position for the remainder of his contract. The professor sued the university in a state court for defamation and malicious interference with his employment contract. The case reached the Supreme Court of Indiana.

According to the state supreme court, **there is an absolute privilege for statements made during judicial proceedings, regardless of their truth or the motive behind them**. The rule is intended to allow people to participate in judicial proceedings without fear of being sued for defamation. At least three other states – Maryland, California and New York – have extended the privilege to complaints to school authorities against educators. It was appropriate to extend the privilege in this way so students could raise complaints without fear of retaliatory litigation. *Hartman v. Keri*, 883 N.E.2d 774 (Ind. 2008).

◆   *A Rhode Island university did not defame a student when its security office posted a "crime alert" to inform the campus community about him.*

The student became involved in a late-night fight with another student. He punched the other student and knocked him to the ground, where he hit his head. A witness told the police that the student had a knife during the fight. Police filed criminal charges against the student, and the incident was reported to a university safety and security office. The office investigated and filed an incident report stating that the student was the likely aggressor in the fight. The security office then posted a crime alert at various campus locations, naming the student as the party responsible for the crime. After being dismissed from the university, the student filed a federal court action against the university for defamation and breach of contract. The court held the university had a qualified privilege to publish the alert. On appeal, the U.S. Court of Appeals, First Circuit, held the university enjoyed a qualified privilege with respect to the defamation claim. **The university reasonably believed it had a duty to**

**report the crime to the campus community under the federal Clery Act.**
The student did not show the university published the alert with spite, ill will
or malice. The court also rejected the breach of contract claim, as the university
complied with student handbook terms relating to the appeal process. *Havlik v.
Johnson & Wales Univ.*, 509 F.3d 25 (1st Cir. 2007).

## III. STUDENTS

### A. Protected Speech

*The Establishment Clause of the First Amendment to the U.S. Constitution
requires government neutrality with respect to religion and non-religion. The
Free Exercise Clause of the First Amendment prohibits government
interference with the reasonable exercise of religious rights. Public institutions
must refrain from content-based restrictions on speech.*

### 1. Religious Speech

◆ *A Michigan federal court rejected a student's claim that she was dismissed
from an occupational therapy program due to her religion.*

The student was an Orthodox Jew, and during her placement in the
program she asked to leave before sundown on Fridays for the Sabbath. In
addition, she sought more time off for Jewish holidays. All of her requests were
granted. Later, she received negative feedback regarding her work
performance. The meeting became heated, and she got emotional. The school
said her conduct was so unprofessional that it warranted a decision to terminate
her placement and dismiss her from the program. She appealed, claiming she
was viewed unfavorably because she took time off to observe Jewish holidays.
A series of appeals were denied, and the decision to terminate her from the
program was finalized. She sued, alleging violations of her religious rights. The
court said there was no evidence supporting her First Amendment claim. **The
defendants did not prevent her from freely exercising her religious beliefs**,
the court said. The claim was dismissed. *Goldman v. Wayne State Univ.*, No.
13-14395, 2015 WL 4940108 (E.D. Mich. 8/18/15).

◆ *A Maryland federal judge refused to dismiss a lawsuit filed by
a prospective student who claimed he was not admitted based on his religion.*

The student applied to the college's radiation therapy program. His GPA
exceeded the requirements, and he was invited to an interview with the
program director. During the interview, the student brought up his religion
many times, including by saying that "God was the most important thing" to
him and "God led him to pursue" a career in radiation therapy. The student was
not selected for admission. When he asked why, the program director sent him
an email that read, "this field is not the place for religion." The email also said
the student should "leave [his] thoughts and beliefs out of the process" if he
interviewed again in the future. He sued. Most claims were dismissed, but the
court allowed claims against the program director, in her individual and official

capacities. **If proven, the allegations could show a violation of the Establishment Clause.** So a trial was needed. *Jenkins v. Kurtinitis*, No. ELH-14-01346, 2015 WL 1285355 (D. Md. 3/20/15).

◆ *Since the First Amendment binds only governmental institutions and employees, a federal action against Duke University was dismissed.*

Duke University Press owns and operates a lesbian and gay studies journal. When an author submitted "The Crucible of a Gay Jew: A Resolution to an Orthodox Duress" for publication as a paid advertisement, the university rejected it. In a federal court, the author asserted First Amendment violations. A federal magistrate found the claims to be so insufficient as to make the case a clearly frivolous action. **A First Amendment violation claim can be brought only against a government agency or employee.** Because Duke University is a private institution, the case had to be dismissed. *Kanli v. Duke Univ.*, No. 1:12CV63, 2012 WL 2366449 (M.D.N.C. 6/21/12).

◆ *A federal court refused to dismiss a lawsuit by a Michigan graduate counseling student who refused to counsel a homosexual client.*

Near the end of her graduate counseling program, the student took a course where she would counsel persons who paid a small fee. Before meeting a client, she read his file and saw he wanted help with a homosexual relationship. The student refused to counsel him, stating religious reasons. She was expelled after a hearing where it was found that she violated a student handbook and a counseling code of ethics by imposing values inconsistent with counseling goals and discriminating on the basis of sexual orientation. The student filed a federal district court action for speech rights violations. The court held for the officials, and appeal reached the U.S. Court of Appeals, Sixth Circuit. It held that public institutions cannot selectively enforce curricular requirements or single out students based on their speech. The court found the student had made the request to avoid imposing her values on homosexual clients and declared that she was willing to counsel them about other issues. She said the university discriminated against her because it let other students limit their counseling roles. For instance, a grieving student had been allowed to avoid counseling a grieving client. **Because it was possible that a jury could find the student was expelled for her speech, the judgment for the university officials was reversed.** *Ward v. Polite*, 667 F.3d 727 (6th Cir. 2012).

◆ *A federal appeals court rejected claims that a University of California (UC) policy for evaluating high school religion courses was unconstitutional.*

UC's policy for recognizing high school religion and ethics courses required that they "treat the study of religion or ethics from the standpoint of scholarly inquiry, rather than in a manner limited to one denomination or viewpoint." UC justified the policy to assure a multidisciplinary study of religion. An association representing Christian schools and students sued UC officials in a federal district court, asserting speech, free exercise, Establishment Clause and equal protection violations. After the court held for UC, appeal reached the U.S. Court of Appeals, Ninth Circuit, which said the association showed no risk that the policy would suppress protected speech.

**The court held the policy did not stop high schools from teaching what they wanted, or prevent high school students from taking the courses they wanted.** UC did not punish high schools or students, and the court found no unlawful viewpoint discrimination. Evidence indicated UC approved courses with religious content and viewpoints, even those using religious textbooks as primary texts. UC's refusal to accept four courses offered by a Christian school was reasonable because the courses were not college preparatory, lacked necessary course information or materials, or had other procedural defects. The court rejected an equal protection challenge and affirmed the judgment for UC. *Ass'n of Christian Schools Int'l v. Stearns*, 362 Fed.Appx. 640 (9th Cir. 2010).

◆ *Temple University's sexual harassment policy was worded so broadly that it violated a student's First Amendment rights.*

A Temple policy prohibited "expressive, visual, or physical conduct of a sexual or gender-motivated nature," if the conduct had the "purpose or effect" of unreasonably interfering with another person's "work, educational performance, or status." The policy also barred "sexual or gender-motivated" conduct intended to create "an intimidating, hostile or offensive environment" for others. A graduate student who served in the National Guard claimed the policy inhibited him from expressing his views about women in the military. He sued Temple, its president and two professors in a federal district court for First Amendment violations. While the case was pending, Temple modified the policy. The court considered the old policy and held it was unconstitutional.

On appeal, the U.S. Court of Appeals, Third Circuit, rejected Temple's claim that the case was moot since the old policy had been revised. It then found there is no "harassment exception" to the First Amendment. The policy violated a general rule that **student speech cannot be barred unless it creates a real threat of disruption**. Under the policy, students could be punished even if their actions had no effect on others. Terms such as "hostile," "offensive," and "gender-motivated" were broad enough to ban some protected speech. The policy lacked a requirement that conduct or speech actually create a hostile environment or interfere with the work of others. The phrase "gender-motivated" required inquiry into the motivation of a speaker. It was also unclear whether it was the speaker's gender or the listener's that served as the motivation. A policy prohibition of conduct that "unreasonably interfere[d] with an individual's work" was suspect as well. The court affirmed the judgment. *DeJohn v. Temple Univ.*, 537 F.3d 301 (3d Cir. 2008).

◆ *A federal district court dismissed claims that an assignment to read a religious-related book violated student free exercise rights.*

An orientation program held by the University of North Carolina, Chapel Hill (UNC) required incoming freshmen to read a book that explored Islam. Although the program had an exception for students with religious objections, several students sued UNC in a federal district court for Free Exercise Clause violations. **The court considered UNC's motion for dismissal and noted the book was not a religious reading.** It found the orientation program was an academic exercise. The court said UNC had attempted to engage students in a scholarly debate about a religious subject and encouraged them to express their opinions. Students who objected to reading the book could refrain from doing so. **UNC did not compel the affirmation of any particular religious belief, favor any religious dogma, or punish the expression of any particular religion**. As UNC did not ask students to compromise or give up their religious beliefs, the court dismissed the action. It gave permission for the students to add new allegations. *Yacovelli v. Moeser*, 324 F.Supp.2d 760 (M.D.N.C. 2004).

◆   *A Seventh Circuit panel allowed a theater student to continue with his production of a play that was alleged to be anti-Christian.*

The dispute arose after a theater student at an Indiana university chose to produce a play depicting a homosexual Christ-like character who engaged in sex with his apostles. A group of taxpayers, members of the state General Assembly, and Purdue University board members alleged that the publicly funded university would be violating the Establishment Clause by allowing the performance. A federal district court denied a request to stop the production. **Because the theater was a limited public forum, the university could not discriminate against the viewpoint of performers.** On appeal, the U.S. Court of Appeals, Seventh Circuit, upheld the decision. It found "absurd" the assertion that the First Amendment prevents state universities from providing venues for un-Christian ideas. There was no evidence that the university was hostile to Christianity because it did not tell the student to produce the play. *Linnemeir v. Board of Trustees of Purdue Univ.*, 260 F.3d 757 (7th Cir. 2001).

## 2. Academic Practices

◆   *The Ninth Circuit rejected First Amendment claims filed against a Hawaii university that denied a student admission to its teaching program.*

After completing undergraduate work and obtaining a master's degree, the student applied to the university's secondary education certification program. But some faculty members were concerned about his suitability for the teaching profession. For example, the applicant said he "thought it would be fine" for a 12-year-old student to have a "consensual" relationship with a teacher. The school denied admission, telling the student that the views he expressed were inconsistent with standards set by the Hawaii Department of Education, the National Council for the Accreditation of Teachers and the Hawaii Teacher Standards Board. He sued, alleging a violation of his speech rights. After a lower court issued a ruling for the defendants, the student appealed. The Ninth Circuit affirmed, saying its decision was more properly guided by cases involving free speech claims that were made in the context of certification. **Here, the decision was directly related to defined and established professional standards, was narrowly tailored to serve the school's mission of evaluating the applicant's suitability to teach and reflected the exercise of reasonable professional judgment**, the court explained. No First Amendment violation occurred, so the ruling was affirmed. *Oyama v. Univ. of Hawaii*, 813 F.3d 850 (9th Cir. 2015).

◆   *A Louisiana student charged with harassing his girlfriend was denied a preliminary order in his First Amendment challenge to a code of conduct rule.*

After the student and his girlfriend broke up, she told campus police he was threatening her. University officials investigated and found the student had violated its conduct code. He declined an offer of disciplinary probation for a year with an anger management class requirement. A hearing panel found the student had violated a code provision prohibiting "extreme, outrageous or persistent acts, or communications that are intended or reasonably likely to harass, intimidate, harm, or humiliate another." He sued the university's board and chancellor for First Amendment violations in a federal district court.

After the court denied the student's request for preliminary relief, he appealed to the U.S. Court of Appeals, Fifth Circuit. Like the district court, the court rejected the claim that the code of conduct violated the First Amendment by restricting more protected speech than necessary to achieve a legitimate goal. While state institutions cannot limit protected speech with which they disagree, the court held **state institutions can legally limit speech that intrudes on other students' rights**. And a code provision requiring expression to be "extreme," "persistent" and "reasonably likely" to cause a violation prevented application of the code to speech or conduct that was only offensive. *Esfeller v. O'Keefe*, 391 Fed.Appx. 337 (5th Cir. 2010).

◆   *The U.S. Court of Appeals, Third Circuit, found three challenged university rules were constitutionally overbroad.*

A student at the University of the Virgin Islands (UVI) was charged with violating a student code paragraph that banned "any act which causes or is likely to cause serious physical or mental harm or which tends to injure or actually injures, frightens, demeans, degrades or disgraces any person. This includes but is not limited to violation of the University policies on hazing, sexual harassment or sexual assault." The student sued UVI in a federal court, arguing four student code provisions were unconstitutionally overbroad. The case reached the Third Circuit, which found three of the rules overbroad. **An overbroad rule is assumed to violate First Amendment rights by "chilling" expression.** State universities cannot prohibit offensive or unpopular opinions. UVI did not specify what steps students could take to obtain authorization for signs. The second rule banned conduct "which causes emotional distress" – which the court found was not based on conduct but the reaction to it. All three rules were held unconstitutional as precluding more protected activity than the university could legally prohibit. *McCauley v. Univ. of the Virgin Islands*, 618 F.3d 232 (3d Cir. 2010).

◆   *The University of Tennessee (UT) did not violate the Constitution by suspending a student for displaying anti-war banners in violation of its policy.*

The student hung anti-war banners from UT buildings and painted the words "NO WAR" on them. He was arrested for vandalism, public intoxication and evading arrest. UT's student handbook barred vandalism and acts violating any law. A UT facilities guide allowed notices only on designated bulletin boards and barred political signs. Relying in part on the fact that other graffiti was present on campus, the student insisted he did not know that painting on university buildings or hanging banners on them violated UT policy or state law. He sued UT officials in a federal district court for violating the First Amendment. He also claimed that he was arrested in violation of the Fourth Amendment. Appeal reached the U.S. Court of Appeals, Sixth Circuit, which explained that campus grounds were not public forums. So the university could reasonably restrict speech. **The evidence showed the messages were removed as they were "unusually noticeable and intrusive," not because they expressed a particular viewpoint.** The court rejected the student's Fourth Amendment claim, as well as his claim that UT's policy on vandalism was unconstitutionally vague. The term "vandalism" was readily understood, and UT was not required to make sure all students had specific notice of its policies. *Wilson v. Johnson*, 247 Fed.Appx. 620 (6th Cir. 2007).

◆   *A federal district court upheld the U.S. government's decision to tighten restrictions on American higher education programs offered in Cuba.*

In 1999, federal Cuban Assets Control Regulations (CACR) allowed American colleges and universities to participate in structured educational programs in Cuba. These regulations had no minimum durational requirements, and students could enroll in Cuban educational institutions even if they were not enrolled in an undergraduate or degree program. In 2004, the government added a requirement that educational programs conducted by American schools in Cuba last at least 10 weeks. It also required any student using an institution's license for educational travel to Cuba to be enrolled at that school, and required teachers to be full-time, permanent faculty members. Students, professors and others challenged the regulations.

A federal court held **the regulations did not violate the First Amendment, as they were neutral with respect to content** and supported by the government interest in denying hard currency to Cuba. The court held the amendments did not violate an asserted Fifth Amendment right to international travel. Denying U.S. currency to the Castro government was an important government interest, and courts defer to the political branches of government with respect to foreign affairs. *Emergency Coalition to Defend Educational Travel v. U.S. Dep't of Treasury*, 498 F.Supp.2d 150 (D.D.C. 2007).

### 3. Retaliation

◆   *A federal New York judge rejected a student's claim that he was illegally suspended in retaliation for exercising his speech rights.*

The student got into an altercation with a classmate. As a result, he was called to the dean of students. In the meeting, for an unknown reason, the student shared a CD he had made with the dean. It had an obscene name, and the dean was offended by it. The dean called security and had the student escorted from her office. Based on the altercation and his conduct at the meeting, the student was suspended for two semesters. He never returned to school. Five years later, he sued, alleging the university wrongfully suspended him. He claimed his First Amendment rights were violated when he was kicked out of the dean's office because of his CD. The court decided the

First Amendment claim was filed too late. The complaint was filed in 2014, and the challenged conduct occurred in 2006. Thus, **the complaint was filed well beyond the applicable three-year limitations period**. The claim was dismissed. *Durham v. SUNY Rockland Community College*, No. 14-cv-607 (TPG), 2016 WL 128214 (S.D.N.Y. 1/12/16).

◆ *A student was unable to show Central Michigan University (CMU) dismissed her in retaliation for exercising her constitutional rights.*

During her master's program in speech-language pathology, the student abruptly cancelled client appointments without obtaining a substitute and without providing adequate notice to supervisors. She was assigned an F grade for patient abandonment, and she was recommended for dismissal from the program. Instead of complying with CMU grievance procedures, she sued the university in a federal court, asserting retaliation for constitutionally protected speech. In pretrial activity, the student claimed she had reported "unethical misconduct" and lack of professionalism by faculty members in emails to her supervisors. The court disagreed, finding **any message she may have intended was "vague and cryptic."** CMU instructors acted according to CMU policy when preparing to dismiss the student. She abandoned her clients. Her instructors lowered her grade because of it, as specified in the relevant handbook provision. As the student failed to make a valid speech claim and instructors properly followed the handbook in lowering her grade, the case was dismissed. *Stephenson v. Cent. Michigan Univ.*, 897 F.Supp.2d 556 (E.D. Mich. 2012).

CMU then sought $141,428 in attorneys' fees and $11,577.82 in costs as sanctions from the student for a baseless filing. **The court held it was not in a position to second-guess good-faith academic decisions by university staff.** Exercising its broad discretion to determine a sanction, the court awarded only fees and costs incurred after the motion for sanctions. This resulted in an award to CMU of $11,582 in attorneys' fees and $59.25 in costs. *Stephenson v. Cent. Michigan Univ.*, No. 11-12681, 2013 WL 306514 (E.D. Mich. 1/25/13).

◆ *Georgia technical college administrators had qualified immunity against a nursing student's due process and speech rights retaliation claims.*

After the college suspended the student from her licensed practical nursing program, she filed a federal district court action for retaliation. She claimed she was suspended for reporting instructors for falsifying attendance records. A federal district court held a jury trial, after which a jury returned a $450,000 verdict for the student. The court overturned the verdict and held college instructors had qualified immunity. On appeal, the Eleventh Circuit held the law at the time of the alleged offenses was unclear as to whether the student was entitled to an immediate appeal of her discipline. For this reason, college administrators were entitled to qualified immunity as to the due process claims. As for the student's speech rights claim, the record showed she often disrupted class and was warned that her behavior had to improve or she would face expulsion. Despite being warned, the student was twice reported for misconduct by her instructors, and there was evidence that she pressured a student to sign a petition. Another student said she had threatened him. After the student reported teachers were leaving class early, one of the instructors filed a grievance against her, stating she had bullied her, spread lies about her, called her names and disrupted class. As the court found a lawful motive for suspending the student, it agreed with the lower court that **the administrators were entitled to immunity. They could have reasonably believed the suspension would not violate her First Amendment speech rights.** *Castle v. Appalachian Technical College*, 631 F.3d 1194 (11th Cir. 2011).

## B. Electronic Communications

*Use of electronic media does not enhance or detract from speech rights. The same principles apply to cyberspace speech as for other media.*

◆ *An Indiana university had the authority to discipline two students who violated its honor code by harassing their roommate on Facebook.*

Two students didn't get along with their roommate. At their off-campus apartment, the pair played a series of "pranks" on their roommate, including creating a fake Facebook profile of an underage girl and using it to pursue a "relationship." The prank escalated when the culprits revealed the hoax, videotaped the victim's shock and posted it online to embarrass him. The school suspended both students for one year, saying their actions violated the school's honor code. They sued, claiming the university overstepped its bounds by disciplining them for off-campus speech. But state law said **state universities could govern students' conduct to prevent "unlawful or objectionable acts" that threaten the school, violate its reasonable rules, or present a serious threat – regardless of where the conduct takes place.** So the claim was dismissed. *Zimmerman v. Board of Trustees of Ball State Univ.*, 940 F.Supp.2d 875 (S.D. Ind. 2013).

◆ *University of Minnesota officials were entitled to assign a failing grade to a mortuary school student who made Facebook posts about a lab cadaver.*

On a Facebook page, the student referred to the lab cadaver as "Bernie" from the film "Weekend at Bernie's." She also posted a "Death List" and a post about stabbing "a certain someone in the throat." After the posts were reported, the university's office for student conduct and academic integrity filed a formal complaint. It found the student violated the conduct code based on threatening, harassing or assaultive conduct and breaking university rules. As a result, she was assigned a failing grade in her anatomy laboratory class, required to enroll in an ethics course and ordered to write a letter about professional respect.

The student was instructed to undergo a psychiatric evaluation and placed on academic probation. In a state court lawsuit, she challenged the discipline. Her case reached the Supreme Court of Minnesota, where she argued the discipline violated her speech rights. In ruling for the university, the court based its decision on the relevant professional standards at issue. It held **a university did not violate student speech rights in a professional program by imposing sanctions for Facebook posts that violated academic program rules**. This ruling assumed university rules were narrowly tailored and directly related to established professional conduct standards. State law concerning professional conduct for mortuary science licensees and interns made it unprofessional conduct not to treat the body of the deceased with dignity and respect. The court also found the lab rules were narrowly tailored because they allowed "respectful and discreet" speech. In this case, the student was sanctioned for posts that might be viewed by thousands – and for taking those posts to the media. *Tatro v. Univ. of Minnesota*, 816 N.W.2d 509 (Minn. 2012).

◆   *A Michigan student who was discharged before completing his degree and then filed a losing defamation case also lost a court challenge to his dismissal.*

After being dismissed from medical school, the student launched a website with a domain name nearly identical to that of the college. The college sued him in a federal district court, seeking to shut down the site and asserting claims for trademark infringement, unlawful publication of student records and defamation. At a hearing, the student agreed to prevent the public from viewing the website and to mark videos he had posted on YouTube as private. Based on these assurances, the court declined to issue an injunction. The college later said the student reactivated his site without court approval, and it renewed its motion for an order to stop him from publishing information and from using his website domain. It also sought to stop him from publishing student records.

The court explained that preliminary injunctive relief is not typically granted in defamation cases, because courts may not impose prior restraints on speech. Instead, **the typical remedy for defamation is monetary damages**. Since there had been no final finding that information on the student's site was false and defamatory, the court found it would be inappropriate to grant injunctive relief. But the court denied the student's request to dismiss the case. *American Univ. of Antigua College of Medicine v. Woodward*, No. 10-10978, 2010 WL 5185075 (E.D. Mich. 12/16/10).

◆   *Like a traditional classroom, an online university discussion board is not a public forum where students have an absolute right to say what they want.*

A Southern Oregon University (SOU) online class was delivered entirely over the Internet. A student was disrespectful to classmates and the instructor in an online forum. After being warned about his conduct, the student enrolled in another online class and was charged with classroom defiance and disrespect. After a disciplinary hearing, SOU placed the student on probation. He sued SOU in a federal district court for civil rights violations. The court said a university conduct policy which prohibited the display of defiance or disrespect of others was not unconstitutionally vague or overbroad. Some regulation of speech is permissible. In the educational context, it is reasonable to limit speech rights to maintain order and discipline on university property.

**The student was not barred from expressing his views. He was only barred from insulting others.** As the SOU policy furthered the important government interest in maintaining decorum and order in an online classroom environment, and students were put on notice of what conduct was prohibited, the policy was upheld as constitutional. **A classroom is not a public forum where students have an absolute right to say whatever they want.** The court denied the student's request for an order and held SOU could limit speech that might lead to disruption of its activities. *Harrell v. Southern Oregon Univ.*, No. 08-3037-CL, 2009 WL 3562732 (D. Or. 10/30/09).

◆   *A California community college policy violated student speech rights by improperly restricting use of its library Internet service.*

A student viewed MySpace member profiles on a computer in the college library. A campus police officer accused him of viewing pornography and told him he could not access the site at the library. Although the student was not disciplined, he sued the community college district in a state superior court for violating a state law that gives students the same speech rights on campus they have when not on campus. The court held that the district's policy, which limited library Internet use to "appropriate academic, professional or institutional purposes," violated the state law because it was overbroad. The court ordered the district to revise its Internet use policy. The district revised the policy, and the court entered judgment in the case. Both sides appealed.

The Court of Appeal of California held that the revised policy complied with state law. While the student claimed the law gave students the same speech rights on campus that they enjoyed in their homes, the court held the law guaranteed only the speech rights they enjoyed "off campus." **Speech rights varied, depending on where the speech took place. In this case, the activities took place in a college library, which was like a public library.** For that reason, whether the revised policy met free speech requirements depended on whether it would be permissible if applied to public library users. Relying on a U.S. Supreme Court decision addressing Internet access in public libraries, the court held the revised policy was reasonable and not an effort to suppress expression based on viewpoint. As a result, the trial court had properly limited relief to declaring the old policy invalid and requiring the district to adopt a new one. *Crosby v. South Orange County Community College Dist.*, 172 Cal.App.4th 433, 91 Cal.Rptr.3d 161 (Cal. Ct. App. 2009).

## C.  Newspapers and Yearbooks

◆   *The Seventh Circuit held a university dean was entitled to immunity for prior restraint of the content of a student newspaper.*

The university became interested in the school newspaper, the *Innovator*, after it printed articles attacking the integrity of the dean of the college of arts and sciences. The dean and university president issued statements accusing the *Innovator* of irresponsible and defamatory journalism. The newspaper refused to retract comments that officials insisted were false, or even to print their responses. When the dean of student affairs notified the newspaper's printing company that a university official had to review and approve the newspaper's content before each issue was printed, the students sued the university for speech rights violations. A federal district court refused to dismiss the claims against the dean. The Seventh Circuit held in 2003 that she was not entitled to qualified immunity because the prohibition against censorship within the university setting was clearly established at the time she acted.

In *Hazelwood School Dist. v. Kuhlmeier*, 484 U.S. 260 (1988), the U.S.

**Supreme Court held that high school officials have broad powers to censor school-sponsored newspapers, if their actions are supported by valid educational purposes.** The Court had allowed prior restraint in *Hazelwood* because the student newspaper was prepared as part of a high school journalism curriculum. In this case, the Seventh Circuit found the greater maturity of college students made censorship of college newspapers untenable, and it held in their favor. *Hosty v. Carter*, 325 F.3d 945 (7th Cir. 2003).

The dean then petitioned the Seventh Circuit for reconsideration. The petition was granted, and the court reversed its 2003 decision. The court held the *Hazelwood* standard could apply to a public university. Since public officials need not predict constitutional uncertainties, the dean was entitled to qualified immunity. *Hosty v. Carter*, 412 F.3d 731 (7th Cir. 2005).

◆  *The U.S. Supreme Court has held that, at the collegiate level, the conduct of students and the dissemination of ideas – no matter how offensive – could not be curtailed based solely on the "conventions of decency."*

A graduate student at the University of Missouri was expelled for distributing on campus a newspaper that violated university bylaws since it contained forms of "indecent speech." The newspaper was found objectionable for two reasons. First, on the front cover was a political cartoon of policemen raping the Statue of Liberty and the Goddess of Justice with a caption that read "… with Liberty and Justice for All." Secondly, the issue contained an article entitled "Mother Fucker Acquitted," which discussed the trial and acquittal on an assault charge of a New York youth. The student sued the university in a federal district court, for First Amendment violations. The court denied relief, but the U.S. Supreme Court held the student should be reinstated. It stated that **while a university has an undoubted prerogative to enforce reasonable rules governing student conduct, it is not immune from the sweep of the First Amendment**. *Healy v. James*, 408 U.S. 169 (1972), made it clear that the mere dissemination of ideas – no matter how offensive to good taste – may not be shut off in the name of "conventions of decency" alone. *Papish v. Univ. of Missouri*, 410 U.S. 667, 93 S.Ct. 1197, 35 L.Ed.2d 618 (1973).

◆  *A university violated the First and Fourteenth Amendment rights of a yearbook editor when it confiscated yearbooks for being "inappropriate."*

The editor of Kentucky State University's (KSU's) yearbook during the 1993–1994 school year decided to be innovative and, for the first time, gave the yearbook a theme: "Destination Unknown." The theme reflected the students' uncertainty about life after college and the pending question of whether the university was to become a community college. The yearbook included pictures from KSU events as well as current national and world events. KSU's vice president for student affairs objected to the final product. She opposed the yearbook's cover, theme, the lack of captions under many photos and the inclusion of current events unrelated to KSU. **The vice president and other university officials prohibited the yearbooks from being distributed and confiscated them.** The editor and another student sued the school on behalf of all KSU students in federal court, claiming their First and Fourteenth Amendment rights were violated. The court dismissed the suit, finding that the yearbook was a nonpublic forum because it was not intended to be a journal of expression, but rather a record of the events at KSU for its students.

The students appealed to the U.S. Court of Appeals, Sixth Circuit, which held a high school yearbook is not a public forum and is subject to strict control by school officials. **A college yearbook is a limited public forum.** KSU's policy toward the yearbook gave the student editors control over the publication because it did not allow a faculty/staff advisor to change the yearbook in order to alter the content. In addition, **the language of the university's student publication policy indicated that such publications were intended to be limited public forums.** The policy begins by saying, "The Board of Regents respects the integrity of student publications and the press, and the rights to exist in an atmosphere of free and responsible discussion and of intellectual exploration." The Sixth Circuit remanded the matter to the district court for further proceedings. *Kincaid v. Gibson*, 236 F.3d 342 (6th Cir. 2000).

### D.  Student Activity Fees

*A "facial challenge" to a government law or policy proceeds on the premise that the law or policy always violates the Constitution. On the other hand, an "as-applied challenge" relies on the argument that a policy violated the Constitution as it was applied to a particular party in a certain situation.*

◆   *A Wisconsin university was required to grant religious groups equal access to a public forum and did not violate the Establishment Clause by doing so.*

The University of Wisconsin-Madison collected about $400 per semester from each student for non-instructional student services, programs and facilities. About $33 of this went into a General Student Services Fund (GSSF), which funded student organizations. The stated purpose of the GSSF was to give students a way to "engage in dynamic discussions" relating to a number of enumerated topics – including religion – in extracurricular activities.

The Roman Catholic Foundation (RCF) received funding from segregated fees, but the university denied reimbursement for expenditures that supported worship, proselytizing, or religious instruction. The RCF and student members sued the university in a federal court for viewpoint discrimination. The court issued a preliminary order barring the university from enforcing any policy that prevented RCF from being reimbursed for activities on the basis of prayer, worship or proselytizing. Later, the court issued an order denying the group's request for permanent relief, limiting its relief to a declaration and denying damages. It declined to characterize the university's conduct as "content based discrimination." *Roman Catholic Foundation, UW-Madison v. Regents of the Univ. of Wisconsin System*, 590 F.Supp.2d 1083 (W.D. Wis. 2008).

On appeal, the Seventh Circuit held the district court had correctly interpreted Supreme Court cases in finding the university would not violate the Establishment Clause by funding the RCF programs. *Widmar v. Vincent*, 454 U.S. 263 (1981), and *Rosenberger v. Rector and Visitors of Univ. of Virginia*, 515 U.S. 819 (1995), supported the lower court's conclusion. These and other cases led the court to declare that "**underwriting a religious speaker's costs, as part**

**of a neutral program justified by the program's secular benefits, does not violate the Establishment Clause** even if the religious speaker uses some of the money for prayer or sectarian instruction." *Badger Catholic, Inc. v. Walsh*, 620 F.3d 775 (7th Cir. 2010).

◆ *A federal appeals court refused to hear a case involving the constitutionality of a university policy that was no longer in effect.*

College Standard Magazine (CSM) published a conservative newspaper on the campus of a New York state university. The university student association denied funding to CSM from revenues made up of mandatory student activity fees. A federal district court agreed with CSM's claim that a university policy was facially unconstitutional because it gave the student association "unbridled discretion" when it came to distributing funding. The student association appealed to the U.S. Court of Appeals, Second Circuit, which found nothing in the record to show the university's former policy would be reinstated. The association was asking for a ruling on the constitutionality of a policy that was no longer in effect. **Court powers are limited to deciding actual controversies, and the court held it could not issue an order that could have any effect on the relationship between the parties.** Any ruling on the constitutionality of the old policy would be "strictly advisory." The challenged policy had been repealed, and CSM had conceded an "as-applied" challenge to it. Thus, the court denied the appeal. *College Standard Magazine v. Student Ass'n of the State Univ. of New York at Albany*, 610 F.3d 33 (2d Cir. 2010).

◆ *The Supreme Court held a university could not withhold authorization for payments to a printer on behalf of a Christian student organization.*

The University of Virginia collected a mandatory $14 student activity fee from full-time students each semester. The fees supported extracurricular activities that were related to the educational purposes of the university. University-recognized student groups could apply for funding by the activities fund, although not all groups requested funds. University guidelines excluded religious groups from student funding as well as activities that could jeopardize the university's tax-exempt status. A university-recognized student group published a Christian newspaper for which it sought $5,862 from the activities fund for printing costs. The student council denied funding because the group's activities were deemed religious under university guidelines. After exhausting appeals within the university, group members filed suit in a federal district court, claiming constitutional violations. The court held for the university.

Appeal reached the U.S. Supreme Court. The Court observed that **government entities must abstain from regulating speech on the basis of the speaker's opinion.** Upon establishing a limited public forum, state entities must respect the forum by refraining from the exclusion of speech based upon content. **Because the university had opened a limited public forum by paying other third-party contractors on behalf of student groups, it could not deny the religious group's claim for funds on the basis of its viewpoint.** Allowing the payment of the group's printing costs amounted to a policy of government neutrality for different viewpoints. The Court distinguished the student fee from a general tax and placed emphasis on the indirect nature of the benefit. The Court reversed the lower court decisions, ruling that access to public university facilities on a neutral basis does not violate the Establishment Clause of the First Amendment. *Rosenberger v. Rector and Visitors of Univ. of Virginia*, 515 U.S. 819, 115 S.Ct. 2510, 132 L.Ed.2d 700 (1995).

## E. Student Elections

◆   *A Washington college violated the speech rights of students when it turned them away from an on-campus political rally because of the shirts they wore.*

Although the college announced the rally was open to all college students, faculty and staff members, five students were told they could not attend the event because they were wearing T-shirts with the name of an opposing candidate. The students later sued the college and officials for speech rights violations. A federal district court held it was clear that the college had violated their speech rights. As the law regarding expression in an open forum such as a political rally was clearly established at the time of the violation, the officials did not have immunity. Although the college argued it rented the space to one candidate's campaign, it had encouraged all students, faculty and staff to attend. As a result, **the students could not be excluded from the rally just because they showed support for the other candidate**. *Yates v. Fithian*, No. CV09-01289-RSM, 2010 WL 3788272 (W.D. Wash. 9/23/10).

◆   *A Montana student's constitutional challenge to a university rule limiting campaign spending in student elections failed.*

The student was elected president of the Associated Students of the University of Montana (ASUM). However, he violated an ASUM bylaw that limited candidates from spending more than $100 on their campaigns by spending about $300 on the campaign with his running mate. Although the two were censured, they were allowed to retain their offices. The student exceeded the limit again when he ran for the student senate the next year. This time, he was denied permission to assume office. The student sued university officials in a federal district court, claiming the spending cap violated the Speech Clause of the First Amendment. The district court upheld the cap and ruled against him, finding the spending limitation was reasonable. The student appealed. The Ninth Circuit noted that the student had graduated, but sought an order requiring the university to clear all records of disciplinary sanctions based on the spending limit. Therefore, his graduation did not moot the case. **The court held the election was a limited public forum, created by the university to allow students to gain the educational experience of campaigning for a student government position.** Because the election was a limited public forum, the spending limitation was constitutional as long as it was viewpoint neutral and reasonable. The limitation met these requirements, because it did not favor one speaker's message over another's. It was reasonable, as it served the goal of teaching students responsible leadership and behavior. The ruling in favor of university officials was affirmed. *Flint v. Dennison*, 488 F.3d 816 (9th Cir. 2007). In 2008, the U.S. Supreme Court denied a petition to review.

## IV.  USE OF CAMPUS FACILITIES

### A.  Students and Student Groups

*In* Christian Legal Society Chapter of the Univ. of California, Hastings College of Law v. Martinez, *this chapter, the Supreme Court stated the general rule that public university speech regulations are allowed if they are narrowly drawn and serve a compelling state interest. Under the "forum analysis" used by the courts, public institutions may designate particular forums for expression and limit their use, so long as there is no viewpoint discrimination.*

◆  *An Iowa federal judge granted a permanent injunction that barred a university from using a trademark policy to prevent student groups from printing T-shirts featuring a marijuana leaf.*

A student group promoted the reform of marijuana legislation. It submitted a shirt design that displayed the name of the organization, the university mascot and a picture of a cannabis leaf. The university's trademark office approved the T-shirt for production and sale. But due to the political backlash, the university put a hold on the group's T-shirt order, updated its trademark policy so it restricted the use of university trademarks for certain classes of student groups, required the group to obtain preapproval before submitting designs and rejected four additional T-shirt designs. The group sued, citing students' speech rights. Courts have "repeatedly affirmed that student groups may not be denied benefits on the basis of their espoused views," the court pointed out. In this case, the "defendants' politically motivated reaction to [state congressmen] made it more difficult for Plaintiffs to receive trademark licenses," the court said. Moreover, the group was subjected to more scrutiny than other student groups when administrators required special preapproval before submitting designs to the trademark office, the court found. It held the conduct amounted to discrimination based on the student group's viewpoint. Arguing this was the first case to address whether students have a right to access public university trademarks, the defendants said they were entitled to qualified immunity. The court disagreed, finding the case wasn't about trademarks – but about the familiar issue of whether schools can discriminate against student groups based on their views. **"Any reasonable person in [the defendants'] positions would understand that their conduct, aimed at silencing political controversy associated with the group's political views, was unlawful,"** the court held. It granted a permanent injunction ordering the university to allow student groups to produce licensed apparel with a cannabis leaf. *Gerlich v. Leath*, 152 F.Supp.3d 1152 (S.D. Iowa 2016).

◆  *A protest group stated valid First Amendment claims against a university chancellor, a college and city police officers, a California federal court held.*

A coalition of students, staff and faculty formed the group to protest changes that led to cuts in programs, staffing and pay as well as a tuition hike. The group held an on-campus protest rally. As the protesters marched to a university hall to demand a meeting with the chancellor, he ordered the hall closed to the protesters. When the group tried to enter, police allegedly responded with "unnecessary and excessive force, shoving and hitting numerous students." The protest group alleged constitutional violations – including violations of their speech rights. The defendants asked the court to dismiss the First Amendment claims. To state a valid claim, the protest group had to show, among other things, that **the protest was a substantial or motivating factor in the defendants' acts**. It did. The college was entitled to Eleventh Amendment immunity. But the court found the claims against the chancellor, the chief of police, one city officer and four university officers could move forward. *Save CCSF Coalition v. Lim*, Nos. 14-CV-05286-SI & 3:14-cv-05286, 2015 WL 3409260 (N.D. Cal. 5/27/2015).

◆ *An Alabama federal court refused to dismiss viewpoint discrimination claims against university administrators on the basis of qualified immunity.*

A student organization at the university wanted to promote its pro-life message on campus using flyers, signs and peaceful demonstrations. Administrators restricted the group's display to have "a cemetery of innocents" only in an area around the student center. That area was the only place on campus clearly allowed for student speech under the policy at that time. The group had wanted to have its display at other campus locations, including an area between an academic building and two public roads. The school denied that request via email. The group filed suit, alleging the school's policies violated several constitutional laws. Many claims were dismissed, but First Amendment claims of viewpoint discrimination had to proceed against the assistant vice president for student affairs and the dean. They asked the court to dismiss the viewpoint discrimination claims on the basis that they were entitled to qualified immunity – but the judge found they weren't. The judge agreed with the group that **the reason stated in the email for denying their request "constitute[d] evidence" that the officials "denied permission due to the plaintiff's viewpoint on abortion."** So the court refused to dismiss their viewpoint discrimination claims against the administrators on the basis of qualified immunity. *Students for Life USA v. Waldrop*, 90 F.Supp.3d 1265 (S.D. Ala. 2015).

◆ *A New York University may have violated a leafleting student's speech rights, a federal district court ruled.*

A vegetarian student decided to hand out fliers at school touting the benefits of a plant-based diet. A campus security officer told the student he needed permission from administration before he could distribute materials. In the administrative office, the student was told he needed to file a written request to hand out the fliers on campus, but he could distribute them on the sidewalk outside the campus gates. The student did – and was told to move by another security officer. When the student refused to comply, he was arrested. He sued, claiming violations of his speech rights. The university asked the court to dismiss the claim, saying the college was a limited public forum. But the court refused, explaining that even though the college was a limited public forum, **there's a different standard for a public sidewalk – a traditional public forum which must "leave open ample alternative channels of communication."** So the claim moved forward. *Hershey v. Goldstein*, 938 F.Supp.2d 491 (S.D.N.Y. 2013).

◆ *Ohio students obtained a temporary order preventing the University of Cincinnati (UC) from enforcing a policy placing prior restraints on speech.*

Students who wanted to solicit signatures for a political cause sought a federal court order against UC for policies confining such activities to a "free speech area" on campus. The court granted their request for a preliminary injunction, finding the policies imposed an unconstitutional prior restraint on expressive activity. UC policies had restricted all demonstrations, picketing, and rallies to an area comprising less than 0.1% of the campus. UC also required students to provide UC officials with five to 15 days of notice in advance of all expressive activities on campus and to obtain a permit first. **A restriction on protected speech in a designated public forum must be narrowly tailored and justified by a compelling government interest.** In the court's view, the restrictions here were not narrowly tailored. *Univ. of Cincinnati Chapter of Young Americans for Liberty v. Williams*, No. 1:11-cv-155, 2012 WL 2160969 (S.D. Ohio 6/12/12).

◆ *The U.S. Supreme Court held a California law college could deny official recognition to a Christian student organization that only accepted members who shared the organization's beliefs about religion and sexual orientation.*

Hastings College of Law allowed officially recognized Registered Student Organizations (RSOs) to use college communications channels, office space and email accounts. RSO events were subsidized by student fees. To gain RSO status, groups had to comply with a school nondiscrimination policy. The Christian Legal Society (CLS) did not accept students whose religious convictions differed from its Statement of Faith. The CLS sought an exemption from the nondiscrimination policy, but Hastings denied the request due to noncompliance with the nondiscrimination policy. In a federal district court action, the CLS asserted speech, religious free exercise and due process violations. The court upheld Hastings' policy, and the case eventually reached the U.S. Supreme Court. The Court held regulations on speech are allowed if they serve a compelling state interest. According to the Court, the CLS faced only indirect pressure to modify its policies. The group could still exclude any person for any reason if it decided to forego the benefits of RSO recognition.

**Hastings' policy applied to "all comers," which ensured a student was not forced to fund any group that might exclude her.** An all-comers requirement helped Hastings "police" its policy without inquiring into the reasons for restricting RSO membership. Social networking sites reduced the importance of RSO channels. As for the CLS's argument that Hastings had no legitimate interest in regulating its membership, the Court held Hastings could "reasonably draw a line in the sand permitting all organizations to express what they wish but no group to discriminate in membership." The policy did not distinguish among groups based on viewpoint and was "textbook viewpoint neutral." *Christian Legal Society Chapter of the Univ. of California, Hastings College of Law v. Martinez*, 130 S.Ct. 2971, 177 L.Ed.2d 838 (U.S. 2010).

◆ *San Diego State University (SDSU) could deny official recognition to groups that did not comply with a viewpoint-neutral nondiscrimination policy.*

SDSU denied official recognition to a Christian fraternity and sorority, stating their membership rules were in conflict with SDSU's nondiscrimination policy. The policy barred recognizing student groups that discriminated based on race, religion, ethnicity, age, gender, or sexual orientation. The fraternity and sorority sued SDSU officials in a federal court for violation of their speech and association rights. The case reached the U.S. Court of Appeals, Ninth Circuit. It held the SDSU student organization program was a limited public forum. This meant exclusion of the fraternity and the sorority was permissible if it was viewpoint neutral and reasonable in view of the forum's purposes. In the court's view, the SDSU policy was reasonable in light of its purpose to promote diversity and nondiscrimination. **The policy was viewpoint neutral because it did not target specific speech or discriminate based on content.**

There was no evidence before the court that SDSU purposely suppressed any viewpoint or that it even restricted expression at all. The court held SDSU merely withheld benefits. But the fraternity and sorority presented evidence that the policy had not been applied evenly. SDSU had officially recognized other religious groups with similar membership restrictions. As SDSU did not explain why some student groups had been recognized despite violating the nondiscrimination policy, further consideration by a lower court was needed. *Alpha Delta Chi-Delta Chapter v. Reed*, 648 F.3d 790 (9th Cir. 2011).

◆  *A federal appeals court rejected claims by a pro-life student rights group that accused university officials of violating its right to free expression.*

A Maryland student organization sought permission to display posters on campus to show "what abortion actually does to unborn children." A university official said the posters would block access to a building, and a lawyer said the university had a right to prevent the "emotional harassment" of students. The university let the group set up the display in a different area of campus. After being told it would have to use this less-preferred area for a second demonstration, the group sued university officials in a federal district court for speech rights violations. The court held for the university officials, finding the group lacked standing to pursue claims based on code of conduct and sexual harassment policies. On appeal, the U.S. Court of Appeals, Fourth Circuit, held **the group lacked standing to challenge the sexual harassment policy. It did not show a true threat that the policy would be enforced against it.** The group had no standing to challenge the conduct code. University officials were entitled to qualified immunity, and the judgment was affirmed. *Rock for Life-UMBC v. Hrabowski*, 411 Fed.Appx. 541 (4th Cir. 2010).

◆  *A Texas college could not halt students from participating in a demonstration staged by "Students for Concealed Carry on Campus" (SCCC).*

The SCCC promoted "empty-holster protests" to prompt changes in laws and college rules to allow concealed handguns on campuses. Tarrant County College District (TCC) limited student protests to a "free speech zone." To hold a protest there, students had to ask for permission at least 24 hours in advance. Two SCCC student leaders sued TCC in a federal district court for speech rights violations. The court held TCC interfered with their rights to speak in public by requiring a permit and limiting protests to the free speech zone. TCC could not enforce those rules. TCC removed the permit requirement from its manual and eliminated the free speech zone. It added new rules banning disruptive activities and on-campus speech that was "co-sponsored" by off-campus organizations. The court struck down these rules and held TCC must let students wear empty holsters in classrooms. **Student speech – which includes wearing something to symbolically communicate a message – can be restricted in classrooms only if the restriction is viewpoint neutral, furthers a substantial governmental interest, is unrelated to suppressing student speech, and does not overly restrict protective activities.**

While TCC could ban speech-making and leafleting in classes and halls, it could not show that the wearing of empty holsters was "inherently" disruptive. The court struck TCC's co-sponsorship rule, finding it could not prohibit speech for being affiliated with an off-campus group. *Smith v. Tarrant County College Dist.*, 694 F.Supp.2d 610 (N.D. Tex. 2010).

◆ *A New York university did not violate a fraternity's association rights by declining to recognize it as a student group because it refused to admit females.*

The university denied the fraternity's application for official recognition due to a conflict with the university's nondiscrimination policy. The fraternity sued the university in a federal district court for First Amendment violations. The court held the fraternity qualified as an "intimate association." Forcing it to admit females would burden its associational rights. The university appealed to the U.S. Court of Appeals, Second Circuit, which held the fraternity's interest in intimacy did not merit strict scrutiny. It placed no limit on membership size, and many Jewish men who expressed an interest in the fraternity were invited to join. The fraternity's purposes were inclusive, and it allowed non-members into some functions. **The college had a strong interest in assuring its resources were available to all students.** As the district court applied the wrong standard, its order was vacated. *Chi Iota Colony of Alpha Epsilon Pi Fraternity v. City Univ. of New York*, 502 F.3d 136 (2d Cir. 2007).

◆ *A student Christian organization obtained a preliminary order preventing a law school from revoking its official status.*

The dean of an Illinois law school revoked the official student organization status of the Christian Legal Society (CLS) because the organization excluded those who engaged in or affirmed homosexual conduct. This violated the university's affirmative action/equal opportunity (EEO) policy. The CLS sued the university in a federal district court for First Amendment violations. The court denied its request for an order requiring the university to restore its official status. The CLS appealed to the Seventh Circuit. The court found it unclear whether the CLS had violated any university policy. **It was likely that the university impermissibly infringed on the CLS's right of expressive association, and its speech rights.** The university failed to identify which federal or state law it believed the CLS had violated. CLS membership requirements did not exclude members on the basis of sexual orientation. Rather, the organization required members to adhere to certain standards of sexual conduct. **The university's affirmative action/EEO policy did not apply to CLS because the organization did not employ anyone.** The court reversed the judgment and granted the CLS its requested order. *Christian Legal Society v. Walker*, 453 F.3d 853 (7th Cir. 2006).

◆   *Student rights to association may not be disregarded or limited.*

A group of students desired to form a local chapter of Students for a Democratic Society (SDS) at a state-supported college. They were, however, denied recognition as a campus organization. The students sued for declaratory and injunctive relief. A federal district court held the college's refusal to recognize the group, in light of the disruptive and violent nature of the national organization, was justifiable. The U.S. Court of Appeals for the Second Circuit affirmed, stating that the students had failed to avail themselves of the due process of law accorded to them and had failed to meet their burden of complying with the prevailing standards for recognition.

The U.S. Supreme Court held that **the lower courts erred in disregarding the First Amendment interest in freedom of association that the students had in furthering their personal beliefs**. It also held that putting the burden on the students (to show entitlement to recognition) rather than on the president (to justify nonrecognition) was also in error. The Court stated that the denial of recognition was based on the group's affiliation with the national SDS, or as a result of disagreement with the group's philosophy, the president's decision violated the students' First Amendment rights. A proper basis for nonrecognition might have been that the group refused to comply with a rule requiring them to abide by reasonable campus regulations. Since it was not clear that the college had such a rule, and whether the students intended to observe it, the case was remanded to the district court for resolution. *Healy v. James*, 408 U.S. 169, 92 S.Ct. 2338, 33 L.Ed.2d 266 (1972).

◆   *A Texas state university policy that was used to prohibit students from distributing pro-life leaflets was held unconstitutional.*

The university policy required the name of each organization handing out leaflets to be stated on leaflets. After a student anti-abortion group distributed leaflets on campus without doing so, the university acted to stop them. They sued the university in a federal district court for speech rights violations. The court held the policy was unconstitutional, and appeal reached the U.S. Court of Appeals, Fifth Circuit. It found the Supreme Court has held anonymous pamphleteering is a form of advocacy that exemplifies the purpose behind the First Amendment. But public universities can and typically do restrict access to campus facilities. Students often must identify themselves before they can use campus facilities. The Fifth Circuit held that on-campus speech is almost never totally anonymous. **The court held the policy was too far-reaching, as it required each speaker to identify him or herself to every person receiving literature.** *Justice for All v. Faulkner*, 410 F.3d 760 (5th Cir. 2005).

◆   *Where a Washington college allowed secular demonstrations, it could not place restrictions on a demonstration based on religion.*

The dean of a community college allowed an anti-abortion demonstration on campus. His office received a number of complaints, leading him to ask campus security to remove the demonstrators. When they refused to leave, police were called, and a demonstrator was arrested. He later sued the dean and the head of campus security under 42 U.S.C. § 1983 for violating his First Amendment rights. A federal court granted pretrial judgment to the defendants, but the Ninth Circuit Court of Appeals reversed the judgment. The court held **a "no religious instruction or worship" condition imposed by the college dean violated the First Amendment as a content-based restriction on speech**. Only if that restriction was necessary to achieve a compelling state interest, and was narrowly designed to accomplish that interest, would it be constitutional. The court also held that the dean was not entitled to immunity under Section 1983 because he should have known that placing the "no religion" restriction on the demonstration violated the First Amendment. There also was a question of fact, requiring a trial, as to whether the security head was entitled to immunity. *Orin v. Barclay*, 272 F.3d 1207 (9th Cir. 2001).

◆ *The Establishment Clause does not prevent private citizens from using public facilities for religious purposes.*

The University of Missouri at Kansas City, a state university, made its facilities available for the general use of registered student groups. A registered student religious group that had previously received permission to conduct its meetings in university facilities was informed that it could no longer do so because of a university regulation that prohibited use of its facilities for the purposes of religious worship or teaching. Members of the group sued in federal court, alleging that the regulation violated their First Amendment rights to free exercise of religion and freedom of speech. The court upheld the school's regulation, but the U.S. Court of Appeals, Eighth Circuit, reversed, stating that the regulation was discriminatory against religious speech and that the Establishment Clause does not bar a policy of equal access.

The Supreme Court agreed with the court of appeals' assessment, stating **that the university policy violated the fundamental principle that state regulation of speech must be content neutral**. It is obligatory upon the state to show that the regulation is necessary to serve a compelling state interest and that it is narrowly drawn to achieve that end. The state was unable to do that here. The state's interest in achieving greater separation of church and state than is already ensured under the Establishment Clause was not sufficiently "compelling" to justify content-based discrimination against religious speech of the student group in question. *Widmar v. Vincent*, 454 U.S. 263, 102 S.Ct. 269, 70 L.Ed.2d 400 (1981).

## B.  Commercial Speech

◆ *A Virginia regulation banning alcohol advertisements in college newspapers violated the First Amendment as applied to two publishers, a federal appeals court ruled.*

To combat underage drinking, a provision of the Virginia Administrative Code generally bans advertisements for alcoholic beverages in college student publications. Advertisements for alcohol are permissible only if they are made in connection with a reference to a dining establishment. Two publishers that owned student newspapers sued to challenge the regulation, claiming it violated the First Amendment. A district court ruled for the publishers, but a panel of the U.S. Court of Appeals for the Fourth Circuit reversed, finding the regulation did not violate the First Amendment on its face. On remand, the district court ruled in favor of the state and held the regulation did not violate the First Amendment as it applied to the publishers. They appealed. The Fourth Circuit again considered the case, this time to determine whether the regulation violated the First Amendment as applied. Ultimately, the court determined the regulation was constitutionally overbroad as applied to the publishers because it kept ads away from many adults who were at least 21 years old. **A majority of the publishers' readers were 21 or older.** The lower court's ruling was reversed. *Educ. Media Co. at Virginia Tech, Inc. v. Insley,* 731 F.3d 291 (4th Cir. 2013).

◆   *A university did not have to allow the KKK to underwrite a radio program.*

A not-for-profit public broadcast radio station operated by the University of Missouri (and a member of National Public Radio) received a request from the state coordinator for the Ku Klux Klan to underwrite a number of 15-second spots on the station's "All Things Considered" program. This would require the station to acknowledge the gift by reading a message from the Klan stating that it was a white Christian organization standing up for the rights and values of white Christians and leaving contact information. The university's chancellor decided that allowing the underwriting would result in a loss of revenue to the station of at least $5 million, and rejected the offer.

The state coordinator and the Klan sued the station manager, asserting that the station could not reject the offer because it was a public forum and could not discriminate by viewpoint. A federal court held **the station did not have to accept the Klan's offer. Station employees had the discretion to choose which offers to accept, and the underwriting program could not be deemed a public forum.** Further, the decision to reject the offer was not based on viewpoint but on business considerations. The court granted pretrial judgment to the station manager. The Eighth Circuit Court of Appeals affirmed. It noted that the underwriting spots constituted governmental speech and that the government could exercise discretion over what it chose to say. Since the station had the right to reject the proposed spots, the Klan's lawsuit could not succeed. *KKK v. Bennett,* 203 F.3d 1085 (8th Cir. 2000).

◆   *The Supreme Court has held that restrictions on commercial free speech need not be subjected to as rigorous an analysis to determine the restrictions' reasonableness. As long as the restriction is reasonable, it will be upheld.*

The State University of New York (SUNY) prohibited private commercial enterprises from operating in SUNY facilities. Campus police prevented a housewares manufacturer from demonstrating and selling its products at a party hosted in a student dormitory. The manufacturer and a group of students sued SUNY in a federal district court, stating that the policy violated the First Amendment. The court held for SUNY, stating that the student dormitories did not constitute a public forum for purposes of commercial activity, and the restrictions were reasonable in light of the dormitories' purpose. The Second Circuit Court of Appeals reversed, stating that it was unclear whether the policy directly advanced SUNY's interest and whether it was the least restrictive means of achieving that interest. The U.S. Supreme Court granted review and stated that the court of appeals erred in requiring the district court to apply a least restrictive means test. The Court stated that **regulations on commercial speech require only a reasonable "fit" between the government's ends and the means chosen to accomplish those ends**. The Court reversed and remanded the case. *Board of Trustees of the State Univ. of New York v. Fox*, 492 U.S. 469, 109 S.Ct. 3028, 106 L.Ed.2d 388 (1989).

◆ *A student newspaper lost its First Amendment challenge to a Pennsylvania statute sanctioning businesses that advertise alcohol in any school publication.*

*The Pitt News* filed suit seeking to prevent the enforcement of "Act 199," a 1996 amendment to the state's liquor code that sanctioned advertisers of alcohol products in school newspapers. The U.S. Court of Appeals, Third Circuit, ruled that the newspaper could not sue because it could not demonstrate that its constitutional rights were being violated, and it could not sue on behalf of third parties. **The paper's loss of advertising revenue and subsequent decrease in the length of the publication did not demonstrate that its First Amendment rights were violated.** *The Pitt News v. Fisher*, 215 F.3d 354 (3d Cir. 2000), *cert. denied*, 121 S.Ct. 857 (U.S. 2001).

## C.  Non-Students

◆ *A Wisconsin appeals court upheld the conviction of a local man who alleged he had a constitutional right to watch pornography on a public university library computer.*

When two female students noticed that a man at the next computer was watching porn, they complained to university police. The students showed the officer a photo they'd taken of the images the man had been watching. The officer told the man he'd caused a disturbance by watching pornography at the library and issued a citation for breaching a state law that prohibited disorderly conduct on university property. After a trial, the man was convicted. He appealed, arguing his First Amendment rights had been violated because he had a right to watch porn at a public university. The appeals court upheld the conviction. **Evidence showed the man's viewing of porn at the library "was indecent or otherwise disorderly and that it tended to provoke a disturbance."** *State v. Reidinger*, 367 Wis.2d 350 (Wis. Ct. App. 2016).

◆ *A Nevada federal judge rejected the First Amendment claim of a Ph.D. candidate who was polling students at a nearby university.*

A man was working on his Ph.D. via an online university. To collect data for his dissertation, he surveyed students in the free-speech zone at a nearby brick-and-mortar university. That school and the online university had a policy requiring a memorandum of understanding in order for the man to have site authorization to do so. The chair of the online school's review board emailed the man to tell him to stop conducting the surveys because there was a problem with the paperwork for his site approval. In response, the man contacted a director at the brick-and-mortar college and went to her office to complain. The director contacted the online school and informed it that she'd found the

Ph.D. candidate "disruptive and disrespectful." The online school conducted a hearing but did not issue discipline. The student went on to earn his Ph.D. – and then he sued the brick-and-mortar school, alleging free speech violations. The court dismissed the claim, as **it was actually the online school – not the defendant – who halted his research**. *Hoot v. Univ. of Nevada*, Las Vegas, No. 15-cv-00175-APG-PAL, 2016 WL 320115 (D. Nev. 1/25/16).

◆  *An Illinois federal judge granted an injunction ordering a public college to allow anti-gay leafletting by a non-student group on campus.*

The founder of Heterosexuals Organized for a Moral Environment (H.O.M.E.) contacted the university about distributing flyers on campus. After looking at the proposed flyers – "The Uncensored Truth About Homosexuality" and "'Gay' Activism and Freedom of Speech and Religion" – the university denied the request, saying it "is not a public forum" and "consistently limits campus activities to events that are not disruptive of the college's educational mission." Two individuals from H.O.M.E. sued to allege First Amendment violations. They asked for a preliminary injunction to order the school to let them hand out flyers on campus. The court granted it. The school argued its campus is not an open public forum and it validly banned H.O.M.E.'s speech based on its solicitation, facilities and anti-discrimination policies. The court disagreed. **Since the school lets other outside groups engage in speech activities on its campus, it can't discriminate based on the content of a group's speech,** the court explained. The school also argued it was justified in denying the request as letting H.O.M.E. leaflet on campus in 2005 had led students to protest the group's presence – and campus police had to escort the leafletters to their cars for their own protection. The court said accepting that argument would mean enforcing an illegal "heckler's veto." It explained, "First Amendment rights cannot be vetoed by listeners who, in disapproving of the message, create a disturbance, thereby silencing the speaker." The school raised concerns about violence on campus, but the court saw no evidence that would be an issue here. The court granted the injunction, finding the school discriminated based on the content of speech, so the H.O.M.E. plaintiffs were highly likely to win. It ordered the college defendants to "submit to the court a written proposal for reasonable time, place, and manner for such leafletting, consistent with this opinion." *Lela v. Board of Trustees of Community College Dist.* No. 14 CV 5417, 2015 WL 351243 (N.D. Ill. 1/27/15).

◆  *Because they were hostile and disruptive, two disability rights activists were permissibly banned from the campus of a New Jersey university.*

The activists took pictures and videos on campus to document the university's noncompliance with accessible parking requirements. After people complained that the couple harassed, frightened and threatened them, the university issued a trespass notice banning the couple from campus. The activists sued the university in a federal court under the Americans with Disabilities Act (ADA), state laws and federal constitutional provisions. The court held they lacked standing to bring the ADA and state law discrimination claims because they were not disabled. Their retaliation claims failed because they engaged in hostile, harassing, disruptive and aggressive behavior. There was no due process violation because **the activists had no constitutional right**

**to enter the campus**. An equal protection claim failed because they did not show activists who engaged in similar behavior were not barred from campus. There was no evidence that the activists were barred from campus based on protected speech. *Cottrell v. Rowan Univ.*, 786 F.Supp.2d 851 (D.N.J. 2011).

◆ *Tufts College did not violate a private veterinarian's speech rights by excluding her from a lecture because she had failed to pay a bill.*

A veterinarian refused to pay Tufts College for a surgical procedure for a horse. Eight years later, she went to a lecture at the college. A college official recognized her and said she would be arrested if she entered the lecture hall. In a state court action against Tufts, the veterinarian claimed a constitutional right to attend the lecture and asserted defamation, breach of contract, infliction of emotional distress, negligence and other claims. The court held for the college, and the case reached the Supreme Judicial Court of Massachusetts. First, the court found no interference with the veterinarian's constitutional rights by way of threats, intimidation or coercion. The lecture did not take place on public property. At most, the veterinarian had the rights accorded those seeking access to a limited public forum. **Restrictions on speech in a limited public forum need only be reasonable and neutral as to content and viewpoint.** It was reasonable for the college to deny to the veterinarian access until she paid her bill. In addition, the decision to exclude her was content neutral and viewpoint neutral. It did not reflect any judgment on the part of the college about the substance of the veterinarian's speech. The court also upheld the lower court's decision to reject the remaining claims, and the judgment was affirmed. *Roman v. Trustees of Tufts College*, 461 Mass. 707 (Mass. 2012).

◆ *A traveling preacher could not stop Georgia Southern University from enforcing reasonable policies regulating non-students.*

The preacher refused to seek a permit to speak on campus, claiming a constitutional right to speak. After being arrested for trespass, he sued several university officials for constitutional rights violations. A federal district court denied the preacher's request for a preliminary order that would stop the university from enforcing its speech policies. On appeal, the U.S. Court of Appeals, Eleventh Circuit, explained **"the First Amendment does not guarantee access to property just because it is owned by the government."** Instead, the degree of access that must be provided depends on the nature of the property involved. A public university has the purpose of education and can place content-neutral time, place and manner restrictions on speech. The court also upheld university speech policies relating to its sidewalks, pedestrian mall and rotunda. Each of these sites was a limited public forum, and any time, place and manner restrictions regulating them were upheld as viewpoint neutral and reasonable. *Bloedorn v. Grube*, 631 F.3d 1218 (11th Cir. 2011).

◆ *The U.S. Supreme Court held a federal law requiring higher education institutions to provide equal access to military recruiters or forfeit certain federal funding did not violate university speech or association rights.*

Congress enacted the Solomon Amendment to address restrictions put on military recruiting by law schools that disagreed with the U.S. government's policy on homosexuals in the military. The amendment disqualified institutions of higher learning from receiving certain federal funds, if any part of an institution denied access to military recruiters that was equal to that provided other recruiters. An association of law schools and faculties sued the U.S. government in a federal district court, asserting the Solomon Amendment violated the schools' First Amendment speech and association rights. The court denied the association's request for an order preventing enforcement of the Amendment. Congress took note of the court's finding that the law could be interpreted as allowing promotion of nondiscrimination policies by limiting military recruiting to undergraduate campuses. It amended the law to require equal access for military recruiters. The U.S. Court of Appeals, Third Circuit, then held the Amendment regulated speech, and reversed the decision.

**On appeal, the U.S. Supreme Court explained that the First Amendment protects rights of association, as well as free speech. The law schools "associated" with military recruiters only in the sense of their interactions with them.** The Solomon Amendment forbade higher education institutions from applying their general nondiscrimination policies to military recruiters. Law schools had to provide the military the same access they provided to all other employment recruiters. The Solomon Amendment did not force the schools to associate with the military. Students and faculty remained free to associate and voice their disapproval of the military's message, and the Court reversed the judgment. *Rumsfeld v. Forum for Academic and Institutional Rights*, 547 U.S. 47, 126 S.Ct. 1297, 164 L.Ed.2d 156 (2006).

◆   *The University of North Dakota (UND) did not violate speech rights by placing restrictions on how individuals can solicit petition signatures.*

UND's code of student life required completing a "special events form" for on-campus events and before soliciting petition signatures in student housing. Petitioners had to sit at designated tables and wait for students to come to them. UND policy prohibited signature collectors from harassing, embarrassing or intimidating people. A group of solicitors obtained UND's permission to collect signatures on campus sidewalks and lawns and inside campus buildings. But a student manager told the group that it could not seek signatures in the building unless the solicitors agreed to stay behind designated tables. One of the solicitors sued UND in a state court for First Amendment violations.

The court held for UND, and the solicitor appealed to the Supreme Court of North Dakota. It rejected the solicitor's claim that he should not have been required to gain UND permission before seeking signatures on UND property. **The First Amendment did not guarantee the solicitor an unrestricted right to use campus property to gather signatures.** Expressive activity on government property is subject to time, place and manner restrictions. UND's policy was content neutral and narrowly tailored to serve the goals of aiding in event planning, protecting the safety of UND property and people on campus, and making sure facilities were used appropriately. UND's ban on harassing, embarrassing or intimidating people asked to sign a petition did not violate the First Amendment. *Riemers v. State*, 767 N.W.2d 832 (N.D. 2009).

◆   *An Indiana university did not violate the First Amendment when it prohibited a traveling evangelist from preaching on its campus.*

Traveling preacher James Gilles appeared in public places and preached for many years. His confrontational style led to disturbances, and he was arrested many times. In 2001, Gilles began preaching at Vincennes University without an invitation to be on the campus. His preaching led to a disturbance, and campus police asked him to leave. Following that incident, the university adopted a new policy requiring prior approval by the dean of students for all sales and solicitations on campus. Approved solicitors could solicit only on a walkway in front of the student union. Gilles sued university officials in a federal district court, claiming the policy violated his right to free speech.

The case reached the U.S. Court of Appeals, Seventh Circuit. It held **public universities are not required to make all their facilities equally available to students and non-students. As owners of public property, public universities have the right to ensure the property is used only for lawfully dedicated purposes.** The university had the right to bar access to any outsider, as long as the exclusion was not based on the content of the speaker's message. In this case, the university had placed the area where Gilles sought to speak completely off limits to those who were not invited by a faculty member or student group. Because the university could lawfully bar uninvited guests from using a particular area to speak, the district court's ruling was affirmed. *Gilles v. Blanchard*, 477 F.3d 466 (7th Cir. 2007).

◆ *A federal appeals court reinstated a traveling preacher's claim that a university violated his due process and speech rights.*

James Gilles, the evangelist described in the case above, spoke on the campus of Miami University for about 45 minutes before being interrupted by a security guard who threatened to arrest him if he did not obtain permission to speak on campus. A university policy stated that anyone with "legitimate business" had "the privilege of free access" to public areas of the university's buildings and grounds during times when they were open. The university informed Gilles his speech was not "legitimate business" and that its policy was to permit formal speeches only when the speaker was invited by the school or a recognized student organization. After trying without success to get an invitation to speak, Gilles sued the university in a federal district court for speech and due process violations. The court dismissed his complaint. On appeal, the Sixth Circuit noted the university did not maintain a written policy requiring an invitation to speak. Nor was the policy well understood by the university officials who had the duty to enforce it. **In addition, the policy had no standards by which requests for permission to speak were to be evaluated.** The policy was vulnerable to a due process claim. Because the policy was so ill-defined, the court held it was improper to dismiss the speech claim at this stage. Although the speech claim was "improbable" and recovery was unlikely, the court found dismissal of the claim was premature. The case was remanded. *Gilles v. Garland*, 281 Fed.Appx. 501 (6th Cir. 2008).

◆ *Faculty members at Yale Law School failed to show their rights were violated by the Solomon Amendment.*

Yale Law School faculty members claimed the Solomon Amendment conflicted with Yale's nondiscrimination policy. Accordingly, the school prohibited military interview programs. When the military warned Yale that it could lose federal funding by denying access, Yale exempted military recruiters from its nondiscrimination policy. Members of the law school faculty then sued the Secretary of Defense, claiming the Solomon Amendment violated their First Amendment rights of freedom of speech and freedom of association. After the district court agreed, the U.S. Supreme Court held the Solomon Amendment does not violate the First Amendment in *Rumsfeld v. Forum for Academic and Institutional Rights*, above. With the benefit of that ruling, the Second Circuit Court of Appeals then considered an appeal in the Yale case.

The court held the Supreme Court most likely intended its ruling to include rejection of an academic freedom claim. Even if it did not, **the Solomon Amendment did not restrict the content of teaching or membership of teachers in organizations**. The claim that the amendment violated a right to academic freedom was indirect and speculative. The Second Circuit rejected the claim that the Solomon Amendment violated First Amendment rights to boycott recruiters, noting that the faculty members remained free to disassociate themselves from the recruiters in other ways. A judgment for the Secretary of Defense was issued. *Burt v. Gates*, 502 F.3d 183 (2d Cir. 2007).

# CHAPTER FIVE

## Employment

## I. BREACH OF CONTRACT

*Breach of contract claims arise from written contracts, academic custom and usage, faculty handbooks and reliance on written and oral statements implying or modifying an employment contract.*

### A. Written Contracts

◆ *A Wisconsin appellate court rejected the claims of a coach who alleged his termination amounted to a breach of contract.*

When the school began work on a new sports complex, the coach offered to head fundraising to expand and renovate the baseball stadium. The school accepted his offer but said the coach didn't follow through with agreed-on fundraising efforts. The school claimed the coach's inadequate fundraising left it $285,000 in debt for the work on the baseball stadium. When the time came, his contract wasn't renewed. The school said the reason was the coach's inadequate performance in fundraising and other areas. The coach disputed the problems, but after a hearing the decision was upheld. The coach sought judicial review, and the court affirmed the termination. He appealed, and the

195

appellate court agreed that **the school's decision not to renew the contract was supported by substantial evidence**. It affirmed the order granting the school judgment. *Lechnir v. Univ. of Wisconsin-Oshkosh*, No. 2014AP1114, 2015 WL 1186272 (Wis. Ct. App. 3/11/15).

◆   *A state appeals court in North Carolina rejected a basketball coach's claim that he was illegally forced to resign.*

The veteran coach was employed for 16 years and never received a subpar performance review. Then charges surfaced about him using inappropriate language when speaking to the team. There were also allegations that he assaulted a team member and improperly threatened to terminate the athletic scholarships of some team members. The university police department investigated, and the university's chancellor decided there were grounds for termination. The school informed the coach that it would begin the termination process if he did not resign. He retired, even though his contract did not expire for another year. He sued for breach of contract, alleging the university did not have cause to terminate his employment and forced him to resign. The trial court granted a defense motion to dismiss, but an appeals court reversed. The case was remanded, and the coach voluntarily dismissed his complaint. He refiled, claiming the defendants breached his employment contract by forcing him to resign. The trial court dismissed the coach's complaint and granted a defense motion for summary judgment. The coach appealed. The appeals court explained that an action should be dismissed for lack of jurisdiction when the plaintiff has not exhausted his administrative remedies. The coach was subject to the university's employment policies, which included internal administrative grievance procedures. **The procedures specifically included the filing of a written grievance, a hearing before a grievance committee and review of the grievance by a university board of governors.** The coach did not pursue these procedures. The trial court properly ruled for the defendants on the basis that the coach did not exhaust the administrative remedies that were available to him, the appeals court decided. The trial court's ruling was affirmed. *Tucker v. Fayetteville State Univ.*, 767 S.E.2d 60 (N.C. Ct. App. 2014).

◆   *A Georgia appeals court dismissed a professor's claim that a university breached its contract with him.*

In 2007, a 21-year veteran marketing professor and the dean negotiated an early retirement. They agreed the professor's annual salary would be increased and she would start working 12 months a year – as opposed to having summers off. They also agreed unused leave would not be paid at the date of her retirement, meaning she'd lose it if she didn't take the time off. In 2010, the professor met with the HR department, who didn't know about the leave-time provision in her contract. She was told the university would pay for any leave time that was unused. She requested that her accrued leave be "paid out in cash with her final check." The university didn't pay, so the professor sued, claiming a breach of contract. The trial court granted the university judgment without a trial. The professor appealed, and the appellate court affirmed. Under state law, **if contract terms are ambiguous, a judge will apply the rules of contract**

**construction to determine what the parties intended**. The court found no breach of contract. The professor agreed not to be paid for unused leave time. The ruling was affirmed. *Carroll v. Board of Regents of Univ. System of Georgia,* 751 S.E.2d 421 (Ga. Ct. App. 2013).

◆ *A former Grambling State University head football coach received a fraction of the amount a jury awarded him in his breach of contract action.*

A state governing board accused the coach of wrongdoing. This included charges that he gave drug tests to players, caused an NCAA investigation by letting a player use his vehicle, ran up the score in a game, and made insensitive remarks about a team affected by Hurricane Katrina. When advised of these charges, the coach was defiant and uncooperative, and he was given two weeks' notice of contract termination. The contract required a 60-day notice of termination, and he sued the university for breach of contract and defamation.

A jury rejected the defamation claim but found the university had breached its contract. It awarded the coach $642,500 in salary, penalty wages, and attorneys' fees. On appeal, the Court of Appeal of Louisiana held the trial court should have allowed into evidence newspaper articles to show the coach had generated bad publicity for the university. The court found evidence that he had been insubordinate, impugned the university's reputation and prompted an investigation. This led the court to find the jury had impermissibly found a lack of just cause for discharge. **Failure to provide the full 60-day notice of contract termination did not justify an award of the entire remaining salary under the contract.** Instead, the court found the coach was entitled to 47 days of pay – about $20,000. It reduced the penalty wages from $54,000 to $38,000. Finally, the court reduced the attorneys' fees to $34,500, leaving a total award of $93,053.80. *Spears v. Grambling State Univ.,* 111 So.3d 392 (La. Ct. App. 2012).

◆ *Howard University did not breach a contract with a probationary professor when it denied his application for tenure.*

In 2003 and again in 2005, the professor received two-year appointments but never received a performance evaluation. In 2006, a tenure committee supported his application. However, his department chair, a college dean and the university president accepted a provost's recommendation to deny it. In an action filed in the District of Columbia court system, the professor said the university breached its contractual obligations to evaluate him and to provide him with specific tenure criteria. In addition, he claimed the university officials breached an implied covenant of good faith and fair dealing by making inconsistent and inaccurate assertions regarding his application. After the trial court held for the university, appeal reached the District of Columbia Court of Appeals. It agreed with the lower court that the breach of contract claim was untimely, because it was not filed within the allotted three years.

A claim regarding the lack of more specific tenure criteria was also rejected as untimely. Although the professor said he could not correct any deficiencies because he was not advised of them, the court disagreed and upheld the trial court's decision to reject the claim for breach of the implied covenant of good faith and fair dealing. **While there were inaccuracies and inconsistencies in the tenure review process, they did not show bad faith or**

**unfair conduct sufficient to support the claim.** As a result, the court affirmed the judgment for the university. *Wright v. Howard Univ.*, 60 A.3d 749 (D.C. 2013).

◆   *Factual issues about the scope of a release signed by a former employee prevented the dismissal of his bias suit against a New York university.*

The employee sued the university for discrimination based on his sexual orientation. The university argued he had waived all his claims by signing a waiver and accepting a $4,651.94 payment at the time of his separation. The employee said that at the time of his separation, he was unaware of potential discrimination claims and did not understand he was giving up any such claims. Instead, he asserted that the payment he received represented compensation for unused vacation and sick time. A state court held for the university, finding the release was "a straightforward, uncomplicated document." A state appellate division court reviewed the case and explained that under state law, **a waiver or release of employment discrimination claims must have been "fairly and knowingly made."** The university had the burden of showing the document was unambiguous with respect to what it covered. According to the court, the university did not meet this burden. It held the employee raised a factual issue on the question of whether a release of discrimination claims was fairly and knowingly made. The relatively small amount of the payment supported the view that the scope of the release was narrower than the university suggested. As a result, the judgment was reversed. *Johnson v. Lebanese American Univ.*, 84 A.D.3d 427, 922 N.Y.S.2d 57 (N.Y. App. Div. 2011).

◆   *A New Hampshire community college did not violate the constitutional rights of an adjunct professor when it declined to hire him on a full-time basis.*

According to the professor, the community college retaliated against him for accusing it of not providing sufficient services to students with disabilities. He said the college violated his due process and equal protection rights by failing to renew his contract and wrongly refusing to hire him on a full-time basis. The professor added state law fraud and whistleblowers' protection act claims. A federal magistrate recommended dismissal of the complaint. **The due process claims failed because the professor did not show he had any property interest in the renewal of his contract.** There was no "promise, policy, rule or practice" entitling him to contract renewal. The equal protection claim failed, as the professor did not claim he was treated differently than others. His retaliation claim failed because he did not show any link between his complaints and the non-renewal of his contract or the refusal to hire him for a full-time job. Having rejected the federal claims, the court declined to rule on the remaining state law claims. *Coleman v. Great Bay Community College*, No. 09-cv-161-SM, 2009 WL 3698398 (D.N.H. 10/30/09).

◆   *A librarian failed to show a Texas university breached its employment contract with her or constructively discharged her from employment.*

The university hired the librarian in 1972 and granted her tenure on the faculty of the library in 1981. Things went smoothly until the university hired a new library director in 1987. The director was not satisfied with the librarian's work performance, and he reassigned some of her duties. In 1993, the director and another official documented the librarian's alleged history of "low quality and quantity of work," rude behavior toward staff and the public, and excessive absenteeism. The director changed the librarian's title, and she complained that he had demoted her. The librarian requested retirement, then sued the university, director and another official in the state court system for breaching her employment contract and constructive discharge. The court held a trial. It refused to instruct the jury to consider the question of breach. Instead, it focused the jury on constructive discharge. The jury found for the university.

On appeal, the state court of appeals found the jury had received improper instructions and reversed the judgment. The university appealed to the Supreme Court of Texas, which reinstated the verdict. Although the librarian claimed she was demoted in breach of her contract, there was no evidence that she ever held any job other than as a tenured librarian. Her contract with the university did not specify any particular job functions. Nor did the librarian show she was constructively discharged from employment. **Constructive discharge does not take place merely because job assignments have changed. Instead, an employee must show she was subjected to unendurable working conditions.** As the librarian did not show this, the court reversed the judgment. *Baylor Univ. v. Coley*, 221 S.W.3d 599 (Tex. 2007).

◆  *Ohio State University (OSU) failed to negate a multi-million dollar verdict for a former basketball coach who was fired for loaning money to a recruit.*

The coach was a former national coach of the year. He began recruiting a seven-foot, three-inch player from the Republic of Serbia who was playing at a community college. The coach learned the recruit had played professionally in Europe. Although the coach knew this made the recruit ineligible to play for OSU, he continued to recruit him in hopes that the NCAA would allow him a waiver. The coach had an assistant deliver $6,000 to the recruit's family.

The recruit never enrolled at OSU, but when the coach disclosed the loan, he was fired for violating NCAA rules and a contract term requiring him to "run a clean and compliant program." The coach sued OSU in a state court for breach of contract. At the time of trial, the NCAA had opened an investigation but had not yet reached any conclusion. The court held the coach breached his contract by making the loan but found the breach was not "material" and did not justify discharge. It rendered a verdict for the coach and entered a judgment for nearly $2.5 million. On appeal, **the Court of Appeals of Ohio held the contract could be terminated only under specific conditions, none of which had occurred at the time OSU acted**. Although the loan could have constituted a material breach of contract if the NCAA determined it was a major infraction of its rules, OSU reached its own conclusion before the NCAA had finished its investigation. The trial court's finding that the loan did not substantially harm OSU was supported by the evidence, and the court affirmed the judgment. *O'Brien v. Ohio State Univ.*, No. 06AP-946, 2007 WL 2729077 (Ohio Ct. App. 9/20/07). In 2008, the state supreme court denied review.

◆  *The Third Circuit held a Pennsylvania college did not breach a professor's employment contract by discharging her.*

The college hired the professor to be its Director of Athletics and Professor and Head of Physical Education and Athletics. She continued to work after her initial 2.5 year term and received salary letters advising her of annual increases. The college faculty handbook provided further guidance as to the terms and conditions of employment for faculty members. The college later discharged the professor, stating it believed the athletic department needed new leadership. It notified her a year and a half before the termination was to be effective. Assuming she was tenured, the professor tried to appeal the decision. The college president refused to accept the professor's claim she was tenured. He explained that she had never been tenured, but instead the professor served at the pleasure of the president as stated in her appointment letter.

The professor wrote to the president again and requested a hearing before a faculty tenure review appeals committee. The president denied the request, and the professor sued the college in a federal district court for breach of contract. **The court noted the professor's appointment letter clearly provided that the term of her position is "at the pleasure of the President of the College." This language expressly negated any possibility of tenured status as a faculty member.** As the language was unambiguous, the case was dismissed. *Atkinson v. Lafayette College*, 460 F.3d 447 (3d Cir. 2006).

◆   *A South Carolina faculty member could not sue a university for missing office items after he signed a release agreeing not to file further claims.*

The university suspended the faculty member after a student filed a sexual harassment complaint against him. The faculty member was instructed to leave the campus immediately and was not allowed to return pending a criminal investigation. He left behind several volumes of his private library in his locked office, along with teaching materials, maps, and personal mementos. After the faculty member was acquitted of the criminal charge, he sued the university, alleging it wrongfully suspended him. The parties settled the case through mediation. Under the terms of the agreement, the faculty member released the university of any claims arising out of his employment and retained tenure.

The faculty member returned to the university and discovered his property was gone. The university never located the missing items, and he sued it in a state court for negligence. The court determined the release was comprehensive and dismissed the action. The faculty member appealed to the state court of appeals. It held **a valid release barred subsequent claims arising from the same circumstances, even if the parties may not have intended to release a specific claim**. The court held the release in this case clearly precluded future claims arising out of the faculty member's employment. *Abu-Shawareb v. South Carolina State Univ.*, 613 S.E.2d 757 (S.C. Ct. App. 2004).

## B. Handbooks

◆   *Washington's highest court upheld a university's decision to suspend a professor after holding the kind of hearing specified in a faculty handbook.*

Soon after receiving tenure, the professor was accused of widespread and repeated verbal abuse of students, staff members and faculty members. He was repeatedly admonished for making demeaning, inappropriate comments about women, gay students and minorities, and for misconduct including carrying a knife in class. After tolerating this conduct for years, the university suspended the professor. Although he sought a hearing that was open to the public, the university stated the faculty handbook required a closed one. After the hearing, the professor was suspended for two semesters. A state trial court denied his request for relief. On appeal, the Supreme Court of Washington held the state Administrative Procedure Act (APA) generally required open hearings.

An APA exception allowed the presiding officer to close a meeting under a provision of law authorizing closure. In this case, the university based its decision to close the hearing on a faculty handbook provision that said disciplinary hearings were generally closed. **The court held the university did not improperly close the hearing because the handbook provision was a "provision of law" under the APA.** It was reasonable to conclude that the state law provision authorizing the establishment of rules relating to peer review proceedings contemplated a faculty handbook rule calling for closure of the hearing. Closing the hearing did not violate the state APA. *Mills v. Western Washington Univ.*, 170 Wash.2d 903, 246 P.3d 1254 (Wash. 2011).

◆  *Two California professors were entitled to a trial to consider if a Christian college discharged them based on marital status.*

The professors taught in the marriage and family counseling department of the college, which was affiliated with the Church of Christ. The church looked to the Bible as its ultimate constitution and required professors to accept the Bible as the word of God. The professors' teaching contracts indicated they were to comply with the faculty handbook. The handbook also stated that faculty members should conduct their on- and off-campus activities and relationships in a Christ-like manner. One of the professors filed for divorce, and a rumor circulated that he was having an affair with the other professor.

The dean asked the divorcing professor to step down from his chair position but allowed him to keep teaching. When the professors announced their wedding, the college refused to renew their teaching contracts. Both professors sued the college in a state court, alleging discrimination on the basis of marital status and breach of contract. The court denied the college pretrial judgment. **The college appealed to the California Court of Appeal, arguing it was entitled to the "ministerial exception," which allows religious institutions to enjoy immunity from examination into religious doctrine.** The court found no evidence that the college cared about marital status. It showed concern only for whether the professors were perceived to be committing adultery. The court said the claim was based on a contract, not marital status discrimination. It held the trial court had to further consider whether the professors fell within the ministerial exception. *Hope Univ. v. Superior Court*, 119 Cal.App.4th 719, 14 Cal.Rptr.3d 643 (Cal. Ct. App. 2004).

### C.  AAUP Guidelines

*Language from the American Association of University Professors (AAUP) "1940 Statement of Principles on Academic Freedom and Tenure with 1970 Interpretive Comments" has been included in the conditions of employment in some contracts for college faculty members. The AAUP Statement on Tenure provides: "[I]f the decision [on tenure] is negative, the appointment for the* *following year becomes a terminal one." Accordingly, a federal court held **the general rule in academia is that if a faculty member is denied tenure, he or she completes a terminal year of employment and then leaves the institution**.* See McMahon v. Carroll College, *2007 WL 804149 (E.D. Wis. 3/9/07).*

*A 1925 AAUP Conference Statement on Academic Freedom and Tenure provides that the termination of a permanent or long-term appointment due to financial exigencies "should be sought only as a last resort, after every effort has been made to meet the need in other ways and to find for the teacher other employment in the institution. Situations which make drastic retrenchment of this sort necessary should preclude expansions of the staff at other points at the same time, except in extraordinary circumstances."* Saxe v. Board of Trustees of Metropolitan State College of Denver, *179 P.3d 67 (Colo. Ct. App. 2007).*

◆　*A university followed the proper procedures when it fired a professor for sexual harassment.*

A tenured anthropology professor at Baylor University took several students on a university-sponsored academic field trip to Guatemala. While there, he engaged in inappropriate sexual contact with female students and made crude sexual remarks to them. A student reported his conduct to university officials upon returning, and an investigation found the student's accusations to be true. When the professor refused to accept a demotion and mandated counseling, a hearing was conducted, after which the tenure committee recommended the professor's termination.

The president fired the professor, who sued for breach of contract and defamation. A jury found the university breached its contract with the professor, but the Texas Court of Appeals reversed. The inclusion of an American Association of University Professors (AAUP) statement in the employment manual did not mean that the manual incorporated the AAUP's termination procedures. **The university had clearly set forth its termination procedures and followed them in this case.** The professor received written notice of the charges against him and had an opportunity to challenge the evidence and confront witnesses at the hearing. The termination was upheld. *Fox v. Parker*, 98 S.W.3d 713 (Tex. Ct. App. 2003).

◆　*A professor could not use the American Association of University Professors (AAUP) guidelines, which had been incorporated into his contract, to modify the intent of the contract.*

A professor and a New Jersey private university entered into five separate employment contracts, each of which incorporated the terms of the university's collective bargaining agreement with the AAUP guidelines. However, the professor's applications for tenure were denied due to his lack of a doctorate degree and his failure to publish. His contract for a sixth academic year stated that his associate professor position was a "non-tenured position." In the following year, he was appointed as an associate dean but continued to teach three credits per semester without additional compensation. He was fired several years later because his overall performance was found to be "significantly below expectations." The professor filed a lawsuit in a New

Jersey superior court, alleging that he had acquired *de facto* tenure under the provisions of the AAUP contract. The AAUP contract required that faculty members who had taught for 14 continuous academic semesters be granted tenure. The superior court held for the university, and the professor appealed.

A state appellate division court noted that **the provision requiring tenure for faculty members teaching 14 continuous semesters was a subsidiary provision that should not be interpreted so as to conflict with the principal purpose of the contract**. The court rejected the professor's disproportionate emphasis on the provision to support his tenure claim. The interpretation of the probationary appointments provision urged by the professor unlawfully conflicted with the principal purpose of the university's formal tenure policy, which placed substantive and procedural prerequisites on the acquisition of tenure. The superior court ruling was affirmed. *Healy v. Fairleigh Dickinson Univ.*, 671 A.2d 182 (N.J. Super. Ct. App. Div. 1996).

◆ *Where a part of the AAUP guidelines was excluded from an employment contract, the university did not have to follow the procedures listed in that part.*

A private Louisiana university dismissed a tenured professor for alleged professional incompetence. She sued the university for reinstatement of tenure and employment. She argued that the university, after agreeing to modify her existing employment contract, failed to apply Paragraph Seven of the AAUP guidelines, which provide procedures for the termination of a tenured professor. The trial court held that the college had no obligation to comply with Paragraph Seven, and the professor appealed, arguing Paragraph Seven was implied in her employment contract. The court held **the faculty handbook and contract clearly excluded Paragraph Seven of the AAUP guidelines. As a result, the paragraph did not apply to any procedures established by the university for the termination of tenured professors.** The court further stated that there was no merit to the professor's argument that the college agreed to modify her original employment contract. The court affirmed the trial court's decision. *Olivier v. Xavier Univ.*, 553 So.2d 1004 (La. Ct. App. 1989).

## D.  Implied Contracts

◆ *A Texas coach did not show Baylor University breached his contract by failing to rehire him. The Supreme Court of Texas also rejected his fraud claim.*

Baylor hired the coach to lead its women's volleyball team in 1989 without a written contract, as was its practice. In 1995, Baylor told its coaches that it planned to begin the practice of entering into written contracts. The volleyball coach said Baylor's general counsel announced it would enter into two-year contracts with its head coaches beginning in 1995-96. However, he never received a written contract. The coach sued Baylor in a state court, claiming it breached an oral promise to enter into a two-year written contract. He added a fraud claim based on a promise. The court held for Baylor, but the state court of appeals reversed the judgment. On appeal, the state supreme court noted the coach had admitted a written contract was never delivered. **Any contract for a period of more than one year must be evidenced by writing.** The court rejected the fraud claim, which was based on benefits the coach would have gained if a contract had been enforced. The court reversed the judgment and held for Baylor. *Baylor Univ. v. Sonnichsen*, 221 S.W.3d 632 (Tex. 2007).

◆ *The Court of Appeals of Wisconsin held Ripon College did not misrepresent information to an applicant for an assistant professor position.*

A college vice president interviewed the applicant, who asked him about the college's financial condition. The vice president described the college's endowment, and discussed past and present student enrollment numbers. He told the applicant that the college intended to raise faculty salaries so it could better compete with comparable institutions. The applicant turned down a higher-paying offer from another institution to work at the college. But the position was ended at the end of an academic year, and she sued the college in a state court for misrepresentation. Appeal reached the state court of appeals, which found the information disclosed during the applicant's interview was true. **The court found she was asking the court to impose a duty on the college to provide her with predictions, not facts.** As the college had no duty to predict future economic events, the court held for the college. *Bellon v. Ripon College*, 278 Wis.2d 790, 693 N.W.2d 330 (Wis. Ct. App. 2005).

◆ *The Ninth Circuit held against an instructor who sued an Oregon community college for misrepresentation.*

The instructor was offered a contract and was assured his position was "as official as it gets." Based on these assurances, he resigned from a prior tenured teaching position. Because of budget shortfalls, the college president refused to recommend the approval of his contract, and the board declined to do so. The college then claimed the contract was not binding without board approval and denied the instructor the secure position he originally had been offered.

The instructor sued the college in a federal district court. **The case reached the Ninth Circuit, which held he could not show the type of justifiable reliance required to establish a claim for misrepresentation.** It then granted a petition for a rehearing. After the rehearing, the Ninth Circuit found the instructor again did not show he justifiably relied on representations. Without the board's approval, no offer was within the community college's powers. *Oja v. Blue Mountain Community College*, 184 Fed.Appx. 597 (9th Cir. 2006).

◆ *A private New Jersey college did not breach its employment contract with an employee by firing her without a hearing for not revealing a criminal embezzlement matter.*

The college hired the employee as its director of graduate programs. She did not reveal that she and her husband were defending federal criminal charges of embezzling over $1 million in employee pension and profit-sharing funds from a previous venture. The college learned of the employee's indictment and guilty plea and suggested she resign. The employee agreed to resign but then changed her mind. The college stated it could discharge her without a hearing or other due process protections because she was an at-will employee. The employee sued the university in a federal district court. The court dismissed the case, finding the employee was not a full-time faculty member and that there was no employment contract. The professor appealed to the U.S. Court of Appeals, Third Circuit. **Under New Jersey law, the professor was an employee at-will unless she presented evidence to show the parties intended to renew a fixed term contract.** As she did not submit such evidence, the court held she was an employee at-will. The college was not obligated to offer the professor due process when it terminated her employment. Since there was no employment contract at the time of the alleged breach, the court affirmed the judgment. *Fanelli v. Centenary College*, 112 Fed.Appx. 210 (3d Cir. 2004).

◆ *The Supreme Court of New Hampshire upheld a jury verdict that found reappointment letters created an employment contract.*

A New Hampshire college audio-visual director worked for 11 years under annual reappointment letters describing terms such as his salary, employment period and duties. The college discharged the director prior to the end of the term of a reappointment letter. He sued the college for breach of contract in the state court system, alleging termination without good cause. The case went to trial, which resulted in a verdict for the director. The court denied the college's motion for a directed verdict. The college appealed to the state supreme court. It reviewed the terms of the reappointment letters and held a reasonable jury could find they constituted an employment contract. The fact that they stated 12-month terms was persuasive evidence that the director was not an "at-will" employee. **The reappointment rights section of the college handbook stated employees could be disciplined for just cause.** As there was sufficient evidence for a jury to find an employment contract existed, the court upheld the verdict. *Dillman v. New Hampshire College*, 838 A.2d 1274 (N.H. 2003).

## II. EMPLOYEE MISCONDUCT

*Employee misconduct includes a variety of actions such as inappropriate, unethical, or criminal behavior. In addressing such actions, educational institutions may be bound by faculty handbooks or requirements for hearings.*

◆ *An Oregon appeals court affirmed a decision to deny legal defense for an employee who was criminally charged for allegedly raping a co-worker.*

Two university employees attended an out-of-town work conference. One night, they went out drinking and dancing. They had sex. The man said it was consensual; the woman said she was raped. She sued the man, the university and the state Board of Higher Education. All of her claims against the man were related to his conduct in committing the alleged rape. He asked to be provided with a legal defense by the state attorney general pursuant to a state law that provides for such a defense when suits are based on "an alleged act or omission in the performance of duty." The attorney general denied the request. The employee appealed, and the appellate court affirmed. The man argued he was covered because he was accused of creating a hostile work environment and holding a position of control over the woman. But the court said **all the claims against him were based on the sexual encounter and that whether** the encounter was consensual or not, it could not be considered an act that was performed in the course and scope of employment or in the performance of a duty. *Johnson v. Oregon State Board of Higher Educ.*, 272 Or.App. 710 (Or. Ct. App. 2015).

◆ *A Tennessee appeals court held a university's decision to terminate an employee was justified.*

The male employee made inappropriate comments to a young female employee who was working alone. The female reported the incident to a manager a few days later. On the day that she made the report, a co-worker told the supervisor that the male employee said he wanted to "have his way with" the female and "have sex with her" during a recent phone conversation. The supervisor met with the male employee, who did not deny the statements. The employee was terminated, and a hearing upheld the decision. The employee sought judicial review, and a court found sufficient evidence to support the termination decision. He appealed.

The appellate court said the sole issue for consideration was whether there was enough evidence to support the decision to terminate the employee for gross misconduct under the university's code of conduct. The code of conduct specifically barred sexual harassment of other employees. **The school's policy defined gross misconduct to include acts of moral turpitude and "intolerable behavior." In cases of gross misconduct, it said, employees could be discharged immediately.** The court concluded it was clear that the employee's harassment did not have to be tolerated. It qualified as sexual harassment of another university employee, and it was made on university property. Because the employee's undisputed conduct qualified as an act of gross misconduct under the school's code of conduct, the decision to terminate his employment was justified, the court said. *Fralix v. Univ. of Tennessee*, No. M2014-003420COA-R3CV, 2014 WL 6851611 (Tenn. Ct. App. 12/2/14).

◆ *A tenured professor failed to state a valid due process claim, so an Arkansas federal judge dismissed her suit against a university.*

The professor was a Ph.D. advisor. When a student's dissertation proposal wasn't accepted by the committee, the student blamed the professor and confronted her as she was walking into a classroom. In front of the class, the professor made inappropriate comments about the student's national origin. The next day, the student said the professor "made a gun gesture with her hand" and pointed it at her. The student also claimed the professor said, "I'll kill you." Two months later, the professor advised the student to apply for an Incomplete. The student filed an academic integrity report accusing the professor of academic fraud. **The university launched an investigation, and other students' statements corroborated the student's account of the professor's actions.** HR told the professor about the investigation. The professor was ultimately fired. After a formal review upheld the termination, she sued, alleging a violation of her due process rights. The court dismissed the claim, explaining that **tenured employees receive sufficient due process if they receive notice, an opportunity to respond to the charge and a post-termination review**. The professor had all three, so no due process violation occurred. *Tarasenko v. Univ. of Arkansas*, 63 F.Supp.3d 910 (E.D. Ark. 2014).

◆   *A Mississippi University did not violate the due process rights of a non-tenured professor when it decided not to renew his contract.*

In an online course that included a chat component, the professor was logged out of the discussion but could still see the students' conversation. During this time, one student referred to the professor as a "joke" who did not prepare for the class. The next day, the professor allegedly told another student that although he'd never shot a student, that student's comment bothered him and he thought about it "a lot." The student reported the comment, and school security removed the professor from campus. An investigation determined the professor's comments were made "in jest." Still, the following year, the school decided not to renew his contract. The professor filed a grievance, asserting a right to hear the charges against him. The school held a grievance conference, but the professor refused to attend. The decision stood, and the professor sued, claiming a violation of his due process rights. School defendants asked for pretrial judgment. The court noted that **the professor didn't have a constitutionally protected right in reemployment**. He was not entitled to a hearing when the school decided not to renew his contract. Nor was he entitled to a name-clearing hearing, the court decided. The defense motion for judgment was granted. *Klinger v. Univ. of Southern Mississippi*, No. 2:12cv150-KS-MTP, 2013 WL 6328852 (S.D. Miss. 12/5/13).

◆   *An Indiana professor was unable to recast his discharge for sexual harassment as a breach of contract matter.*

The professor, who had been on the faculty for 25 years, was charged with several incidents of improper conduct with female students. Students complained that he made derogatory comments about women, used "crude and scary" language, and touched them inappropriately. When confronted with the complaints, the professor insisted he had done nothing wrong. A student then filed a formal internal complaint against him. The university placed the professor on paid leave and conducted an investigation that found he had violated its sexual harassment policy. He declined an option to retire early and was dismissed from the university. In a state court, the professor claimed the university discharged him in breach of his contract. The case reached the state supreme court, which found the professor failed to prove breach of contract. He also failed to show he had a contractual right of entry onto university property.

**There was sufficient evidence to show the professor violated the terms of his employment contract, which barred him from engaging in harassing behavior.** In the court's view, his conduct met the employment contract's definitions of harassment. Moreover, the court held the professor received all the process he was due. The decision for the university was affirmed. *Haegert v. Univ. of Evansville*, 977 N.E.2d 924 (Ind. 2012).

◆   *A federal court held a Pennsylvania campus police officer did not have a due process right "to refuse to violate the constitutional rights of others."*

An anti-gay group demonstration on campus prompted some objections by students. A university police chief arrived and found the crowd was acting disorderly. He ordered the officer to "push" away anti-gay demonstrators, but the officer did not believe they were being disorderly, and he told the chief that arresting them might violate their civil rights. He also feared he might be held personally liable if he arrested them without good cause. After a disciplinary hearing, the officer was suspended without pay for five days and warned in writing that he could be discharged if he disobeyed another order. The officer said he was then assigned menial tasks, given poor evaluations, and denied training opportunities. He sued the chief and other university officials in a federal district court, claiming a right to refuse to obey unconstitutional orders.

The court dismissed the officer's speech rights claim, as he had spoken in his capacity as a public employee and not as a private citizen. It also declined to accept the theory that a substantive due process claim can be premised on the refusal to violate the constitutional rights of others. On appeal to the U.S. Court of Appeals, Third Circuit, the officer dropped his First Amendment claim. But like the lower court, **the Third Circuit declined to recognize a fundamental substantive due process right to refuse to violate the constitutional rights of others**. It held paramilitary organizations like university police would not be able to function effectively if the relief he sought was granted. *Armbruster v. Cavanaugh*, 410 Fed.Appx. 564 (3d Cir. 2011).

◆   *A New York university did not commit constitutional violations when it discharged an ethics professor who pleaded guilty to embezzlement charges.*

The professor had taught at the university for more than 25 years when he pleaded guilty to third-degree robbery charges based on the embezzlement of almost $80,000 from a church where he served as an accountant. After the plea, he took a leave of absence from the university, but he later sought reinstatement with a full course load. The university instead informed the professor he would be discharged, and an arbitrator upheld the decision. After an unsuccessful state court lawsuit, he sued the university in a federal court for constitutional violations. The court held that the state court had decided all relevant issues, including the professor's claim that he was not provided adequate due process.

On appeal, the U.S. Court of Appeals, Second Circuit, held the applicable collective bargaining agreement provided disciplinary procedures for faculty members who were convicted of felonies. The professor identified no fundamental right with which this provision interfered. He also identified no suspect class under which he could claim any discrimination. **While a hearing is normally provided for tenured faculty, there was no need for one where the professor was suspended without pay after having been convicted of a felony.** A conviction "demonstrates that the deprivation is not arbitrary and serves to assure that the employer's decision is not baseless or unwarranted." As none of the professor's arguments had any merit, the court affirmed the judgment. *Rosa v. City Univ. of New York*, 306 Fed.Appx. 655 (2d Cir. 2007).

◆   *The University of Minnesota could suspend a tenured professor who was found to have submitted false student evaluations for a class.*

Student evaluations were used to determine whether merit-based salary increases should be granted. A department chairperson who reviewed the professor's evaluations became suspicious because of abnormally high ratings. The chairperson was also suspicious because the forms were turned in after the semester was over and because in a prior semester, the professor had asked a secretary to make changes to forms that were already submitted. An investigation showed students in the course did not submit the evaluations. A university committee found the professor had engaged in serious misconduct, and the president suspended him for one year without salary or benefits. A state trial court affirmed the university's decision, and the professor appealed. The Court of Appeals of Minnesota found the evidence sufficient to support the suspension. **The professor was the only person who would benefit from the false evaluations, and he had been in the office on the day the secretary found them.** He was not a credible witness and had engaged in questionable behavior in the past regarding evaluations. As a result, the court upheld the judgment for the university. *Tennyson v. Univ. of Minnesota*, No. A07-1095, 2008 WL 2344257 (Minn. Ct. App. 6/10/08).

## III. TENURE AND PROMOTION DENIALS

### A. Tenure and Promotion Cases

*Tenured employees are entitled to any employment protections promised by their institutions. A public institution must comply with constitutional requirements for due process. At minimum, this amounts to notice and an opportunity to respond to any charges. Private institutions are not bound by the Constitution, but must afford employees any procedures that they have been promised. If an institution's policy (or a state law or regulation) requires it, an employee may also be entitled to a hearing with the right to confront and cross-examine witnesses, and the right to be represented by counsel.*

◆  *A Pennsylvania court upheld a decision that ordered a university to reinstate a professor who was denied tenure and reimburse him for lost wages.*

The processor's tenure application was denied due to "a lack of scholarly growth," and he was terminated. He filed a grievance under the collective bargaining agreement (CBA), and he was reinstated two years later. The following year, the professor was again denied tenure for the same reason. He filed a second grievance. The arbitrator found the university president violated the CBA by failing to follow the tenure review process. The president admitted she didn't review the recommendations of the department chair as part of her decision-making process – which was required under the CBA. The arbitrator determined the professor should be reinstated with an opportunity to reapply for tenure. In addition, the arbitrator said the professor was entitled to lost wages, benefits and seniority. The university appealed, but the court affirmed the ruling. **The president admitted she didn't follow the requirements outlined in the CBA.** So the ruling was proper. *East Stroudsburg Univ. of Pennsylvania v. Ass'n of Pennsylvania State College and Univ. Faculties,* 125 A.3d 870 (Pa. Commw. Ct. 2015).

◆  *The Sixth Circuit rejected an Ohio professor's claim that the judge in his tenure-denial suit should have recused herself.*

The university denied the professor's tenure application because it wasn't confident in the professor's ability to produce scholarly articles on a consistent basis. He sued, alleging violations of Title IX and the Equal Protection Clause. When the district court ruled against him, the professor appealed, saying the judge should have been disqualified because she was in a relationship with a tenured faculty member of the university. The appeals court explained that recusal is proper "if a reasonable, objective person, knowing all of the circumstances, would have questioned the judge's impartiality." But the court said **a relationship between a judge and tenured faculty member, without more, is not enough to call the judge's impartiality into question**. Recusal was not required, the appeals court concluded. The ruling was affirmed. *Ragozzine v. Youngstown State Univ.*, No. 4:13-cv-00750 (6th Cir. 4/22/15).

◆   *Overturning a jury verdict for a coach who challenged his former university's decision not to renew his contract, an Indiana appeals court held the university should've been granted judgment without a trial.*

The coach had given up tenure in lieu of being fired immediately for his role in a recruit's fraudulent application – so he had no right to continued employment. The coach gave up tenure in 2003. A year later the coach was told his contract would not be renewed for the 2005-06 school year. He agreed to retire. Then in 2007, the coach sued the university for breach of contract. The jury found for the coach, but the appellate court reversed, saying **the agreement meant he had reverted to being employed under year-to-year contracts**. As the coach had no right to continuing employment without tenure, the appeals court found the university should've been granted judgment without a trial. *Vincennes Univ. ex rel. Board of Trustees Vincennes v. Sparks*, 988 N.E.2d 1160 (Ind. Ct. App. 2013).

◆   *Massachusetts' highest court affirmed a decision to reverse a confirmation of an arbitration award.*

Roxbury Community College (RCC) is part of Massachusetts' Public Higher Education System. In 2001, RCC hired Virgilio Acevedo as a tenure-track assistant professor in the sociology department. The terms of his employment were covered by the collective bargaining agreement (CBA) between his union – Massachusetts Community College Council – and the Massachusetts Board of Higher Education/RCC. The CBA specified: "The granting or failure to grant tenure shall be arbitrable but any award is not binding." In other words, an employee could ask for and receive arbitration concerning a tenure decision, but the college or university wasn't required to put into effect any award decided on by an arbitrator. In 2004, RCC promoted Acevedo to associate professor. Then it followed the procedure outlined in the CBA by notifying Acevedo two years later that he was eligible to apply for tenure, having its tenure review committee consider his application, and offering him a final one-year contract after the committee denied his tenure application. He filed a grievance, claiming the decision was arbitrary. Unable to resolve the issue with the grievance process outlined in the CBA, the union demanded arbitration. The arbitrator determined the procedure determining Acevedo's tenure request was "seriously flawed" and violated the CBA. She ordered RCC to reinstate Acevedo and form a new tenure review committee to evaluate him based on the criteria outlined in the CBA. The union asked the court to confirm the award. It did. RCC appealed, and the appellate court reversed. The union appealed to the state's highest court – but it found the arbitrator's award wasn't binding on RCC, noting that **the provision about arbitration set limits on what is binding**. It sent the case back to the trial court with instructions to dismiss it. *Massachusetts Community College Council v. Massachusetts Board of Higher Educ.*, 465 Mass. 791 (Mass. 2013).

◆ *A college successfully pared two claims from a lawsuit filed by an assistant professor who was denied tenure.*

In 2005, North Central College hired Paloma Martinez-Cruz as an assistant tenure-track professor of Spanish. In 2011, she was denied tenure due to negative student evaluations. The professor filed an internal grievance to challenge the denial, alleging a variety of discrimination claims. The tenure committee affirmed the decision. Martinez-Cruz sued, alleging she was denied tenure due to racial, national origin and gender bias. She also added claims of retaliation, breach of contract and fraudulent misrepresentation. The defendants asked the court to dismiss two of the claims: breach of contract and fraudulent misrepresentation. The court dismissed the breach of contract claim, explaining the faculty handbook included a disclaimer specifically saying it did not create a contractual relationship. And to state a valid misrepresentation claim, the professor had to show the alleged false statement was part of a scheme to defraud. In essence, **she had to show that the school had no intention of fulfilling its promise at the time the promise was made**. She didn't. The motion to dismiss that claim was also granted. *Martinez-Cruz v. North Cent. College*, No. 13-cv-4328, 2013 WL 6498761 (N.D. Ill. 12/11/13).

◆ *New Jersey county college lecturers who did not hold positions conferring academic rank were unable to gain tenure under state law.*

New Jersey law permitted county college faculty members to gain tenure if they completed five years of satisfactory service in tenure-eligible positions and were in academic rank at the time they completed the service requirement. Burlington County College denied a group of lecturers tenure rights, because they were not appointed to positions that conferred academic rank.

The lecturers and a county college faculty association sued the college in a state court, arguing the college had transformed their temporary positions into tenure-eligible ones. They also claimed their duties were the same as those of instructors and other faculty members. The court found the decision of the college trustees was entitled to great deference. Under state law, tenure was available to faculty members "in academic rank" after five years. **The law defined "academic rank" to include an instructor, assistant professor, associate professor and professor.** A faculty member was "any full-time member of the teaching staff appointed with academic rank." The court rejected the lecturers' theory that they held positions that were functionally equivalent to the tenure-eligible position of instructor, and it held they did not qualify for tenure under state law. *Burlington County College Faculty Ass'n v. Burlington County College*, 2010 WL 1427253 (N.J. Super. Ct. App. Div. 4/7/10).

◆ *Board of Regents v. Roth,* 408 U.S. 564 (1972) and *Perry v. Sindermann,* 408 U.S. 593 (1972), help define employee due process rights. *Roth* and *Sindermann* emphasize, first, that there must be an independent source for a liberty or property interest to exist. Such interests are not created by the Constitution, but arise by employment contract or by operation of state tenure laws. Second, if a liberty or property interest is not established, no requirement of due process exists under the Fourteenth Amendment. Third, **if a teacher possesses a liberty or property interest in employment, then due process is required and the teacher may not be dismissed without a hearing**.

A tenured teacher, or an untenured teacher during the term of his or her contract, possesses a property interest in continued employment. An untenured teacher who is not rehired after expiration of his or her contract is entitled to a due process hearing if the decision not to rehire is accompanied by a finding of incompetence or immorality, because the teacher's liberty of employment would be impaired by such a finding. However, probationary employees or at-will employees generally do not enjoy due process protections.

The teacher in *Roth* was hired at a Wisconsin university for a fixed contract term of one year. At the end of the year, he was informed that he would not be rehired. No hearing was provided and no reason was given for the decision. In dismissing the teacher's due process claims, the Supreme Court stated that no liberty interest was implicated. In declining to rehire the teacher, the university made no charge against him such as incompetence or immorality. Such a charge would have made it difficult for the teacher to gain employment elsewhere and thus would have deprived him of liberty. As no reason was given for the non-renewal of his contract, his liberty interest in future employment was not impaired, and he was not entitled to a hearing on these grounds.

The Court declared that because the teacher had not acquired tenure he possessed no property interest in continued employment at the university. To be sure, the teacher had a property interest in employment during the term of his one-year contract, but upon its expiration the teacher's property interest ceased to exist. The Court stated: **"To have a property interest in a benefit, a person clearly must have more than an abstract need or desire for it. He must have more than a unilateral expectation of it. He must, instead, have a legitimate claim of entitlement to it."** *Board of Regents v. Roth*, 408 U.S. 564, 92 S.Ct. 2701, 33 L.Ed.2d 548 (1972).

◆  The *Sindermann* case involved a teacher employed at a Texas university for four years under a series of one-year contracts. When he was not rehired for a fifth year, he brought suit contending that due process required a dismissal hearing. The Supreme Court held that "a person's interest in a benefit is a 'property' interest for due process purposes if there are such rules and mutually explicit understandings that support his claim of entitlement to the benefit that he may invoke at a hearing." Because the teacher had been employed at the university for four years, the Court felt that he may have acquired a protectable property interest in continued employment. The case was remanded to the trial court to determine whether there was an unwritten "common law" of tenure at the university. If so, the teacher would be entitled to a dismissal hearing. *Perry v. Sindermann*, 408 U.S. 593, 92 S.Ct. 2694, 33 L.Ed.2d 570 (1972).

◆  *A federal court upheld a decision to revoke the tenure of a faculty member based on charges that he neglected his professional responsibilities.*

University administrators filed a complaint seeking the revocation of the professor's tenure. The complaint referenced a suspension eight years earlier and a letter allegedly written by a university vice president on October 30, 1997. The complaint was supplemented by a statement of misconduct, which did not mention a letter of October 30, 1997. A faculty panel agreed with the charge of neglect for professional responsibilities and noted its decision was based on the professor's conduct after April 1999. During the revocation proceedings, the university did not release any letter dated October 30, 1997, to him. The professor sued the university in a federal court for breach of contract. After dismissing most of his claims, the court held that even if a letter dated October 30, 1997 did exist, it was not relevant to the tenure revocation.

The letter was not mentioned in the statement of misconduct that supported the complaint. **In addition, the panel clearly indicated its decision was based on actions after April 1999.** Therefore, whether or not the letter existed was immaterial, and the university was entitled to judgment. On appeal, the U.S. Court of Appeals, District of Columbia Circuit, affirmed the judgment. It found no binding contract, as the professor did not identify a relevant faculty code provision that was violated. Despite 28 alleged contractual breaches, there was no plausible claim for relief. The judgment was affirmed. *Saha v. George Washington Univ.*, 358 Fed.Appx. 205 (D.C. Cir. 2009).

◆   *A North Carolina university employee was not entitled to priority consideration for a vacant position based on her 10 years of work there.*

The employee worked in the university's Animal Science Department. She left for three years and returned as an administrative billing assistant in the Communication Technologies Department. The university promoted the employee to the position of Telecom Project Manager/Telecom Analyst II. A few months later, she was laid off, but a Telecom Analyst I position soon became vacant. The employee applied for the job, but the university hired a less experienced former employee who had also been let go. The employee filed a complaint with the state office of administrative hearings, alleging she was entitled to priority consideration for the job under North Carolina General Statutes Section 126-7.1. This law provides state employees with more than 10 years of service priority consideration over state employees with less than 10 years of service in the same or a related job classification. A state trial court held the employee was entitled to priority consideration for the job.

The university appealed. The Court of Appeals of North Carolina held the trial court misinterpreted the law. Under the trial court's reading, a state employee with over 10 years of service, regardless of the position, should receive priority consideration over another person with less than 10 years of service in the same or a related position classification. **As the employee did not have more than 10 years in the same or a related classification as the position for which she applied, she was not entitled to priority consideration** for the job. The court reversed the judgment. *Wilkins v. North Carolina State Univ.*, 178 N.C.App. 377, 631 S.E.2d 221 (N.C. Ct. App. 2006).

◆   *A District of Columbia professor did not prove a university interfered with her bid for tenure in a way that breached its duty of good faith and fair dealing.*

The professor worked in a tenure track position for five years, then applied for a tenured associate professor position. The tenure committee voted against tenure because it considered her research weak. A scholarly journal notified the professor that it had rejected a paper she authored due to serious criticism by reviewers. The university again denied the professor's request for tenure based on lack of progress in publishing. The professor sued the university in a District of Columbia court for breach of contract and breach of the covenant of good faith and fair dealing. The court held for the university, and she appealed.

On appeal to the District of Columbia Court of Appeals, the professor stated that she was denied sufficient lab space and that her research grant was arbitrarily cancelled. This made her unable to perform contractual publishing obligations, breaching both her contract and the covenant of good faith and fair dealing. **The court noted all contracts contain an implied duty of good faith and fair dealing. This means neither party may do anything which has the effect of destroying or injuring the rights of the other party under the contract.** The university took steps to make lab space available to the professor, but she failed to progress in her scholarly productivity. The court agreed with the university that courts are reluctant to interfere with tenure decisions. As the professor failed to satisfy the tenure requirements of the faculty handbook, the judgment was affirmed. *Allworth v. Howard Univ.*, 890 A.2d 194 (D.C. 2006).

◆   *A professor's position as associate dean was not a protected property interest preserved by her tenured faculty position.*

A University of North Dakota (UND) professor had administrative duties as director of the School of Communication and associate dean of the College of Fine Arts and Communication. After being dismissed from administrative duties, she sued UND, alleging the action violated her protected property interests under tenure law. A federal court dismissed her claim that she had a protected property interest in her administrative positions. Citing the North Dakota State Board of Higher Education Policy Manual, which was included in her employment contract, the district court noted that tenure does not extend to administrative positions. The Eighth Circuit agreed, noting that the professor's administrative position was at will and thus did not evoke a protected property interest. A letter of understanding supplementing her employment contract stated, "Associate Deans have no specific term, but rather serve at the pleasure of the Dean." The court found the professor's position as director of the School of Communication included a three-year contract, but her protected property interest had been satisfied. **UND had fully compensated her for the salary associated with the position even though she did not serve out the full term.** *Rakow v. State of North Dakota*, 208 F.3d 218 (8th Cir. 2000).

## B.  Claims of Discrimination

◆   *A Mississippi federal judge OK'd a trial for unequal-pay and failure-to-accommodate claims.*

The University of Southern Mississippi (USM) hired Bonnie Gerald in 2007 as a tenure-track associate professor. But in the fall of Gerald's third year at USM, she was in an accident and suffered serious injuries. Gerald was on leave for the rest of the academic year. When she returned to the classroom, the department chair saw her using a cane or a walker and urged Gerald to get a "handicapped" tag so she could park closer to the building. In her pre-tenure review, the committee recommended against renewing her contract. It found Gerald hadn't met minimum requirements for research, her student evaluation scores were below the department average, and she hadn't been responsive to students. The department chair agreed, saying Gerald hadn't met "important expectations," and her teaching performance was "a particular issue of chronic concern." So Gerald's tenure was denied. She resigned and sued, alleging discrimination based on her disability and gender.

The court granted USM judgment on virtually all of Gerald's Title VII and ADA claims as they were based on allegedly discriminatory acts that happened more than 180 days before she filed her charge with the EEOC. But the court decided two claims – a failure-to-accommodate claim under the Rehabilitation Act and a discriminatory-pay claim under the Lilly Ledbetter Fair Pay Act – required a trial. **The statute of limitations didn't bar Gerald's wage discrimination claim because Ledbetter makes each discriminatory paycheck a discriminatory act.** Gerald claimed USM paid her, a non-tenured female professor, $55,000 a year, but paid a non-tenured male professor $64,000. That was enough to state a *prima facie* case of wage bias. And as Gerald received a paycheck from USM within 180 days before filing her EEOC charge, her claim required a trial. Gerald's failure-to-accommodate claim under the Rehabilitation Act could also move forward. USM asked the court to dismiss this claim, arguing Gerald didn't submit accommodation requests in writing. The court refused, as a request in writing isn't a requirement. So the professor's pay and accommodation claims would have to be decided by a trial. *Gerald v. Univ. of Southern Mississippi*, No. 2:12cv147-KS-MTP, 2014 WL 172113 (S.D. Miss. 1/15/14).

◆ *Northwestern University (NU) medical school successfully defended a gender discrimination claim with evidence of increasing female tenure rates.*

NU denied a female professor's tenure application, finding her scholarship was below average, and her teaching and service contributions were minimal. She also did not prove an ability to gain renewal of research awards. In a federal court action against NU, the professor claimed the stated reasons were a pretext for unlawful discrimination. After a federal district court issued a decision favoring NU, the professor proceeded to file an appeal with the U.S. Court of Appeals for the Seventh Circuit. The Seventh Circuit appeals court found the professor had relied on stray remarks to support an inference of discrimination. The professor said someone described her as "a woman scientist who reproduces" with an "emotional need to be heard." In the appeals court's opinion, these remarks were ambiguous and did not support her claim. The fact that a male earned tenure at approximately the same time when her application was denied did not support the professor's claim. The male had been a lead author on six articles, while the professor was the lead author on just one. Also, the male obtained six funding grants while the professor obtained only two. There was evidence that the percentage of tenure-track female faculty members at the NU medical school was increasing and that females were in fact earning tenure at a higher rate than males were. **As no evidence indicated any** decisionmaker was biased against women with regard to tenure decisions, the court affirmed the ruling for the university. *Blasdel v. Northwestern Univ.*, 687 F.3d 813 (7th Cir. 2012).

◆ *A federal district court in Mississippi rejected a Mississippi professor's claim that he was denied tenure based on his race and national origin rather than his performance.*

After completing his probationary period of employment with a state university, the professor filed an application to be granted tenured status. But the department of electrical and computer engineering tenure review committee unanimously voted to deny his application. Following the department's decision to deny the application, the professor proceeded to seek internal review of the review committee's decision against him. However, the professor's attempt to reverse the review committee's decision by way of an internal review was unsuccessful. The professor then chose to file an administrative charge of unlawful discrimination. In the administrative charge, the professor alleged that he was denied tenure based on his race and Cypriot origin. At a later point in time, the professor sued the university in a federal district court for race and national origin discrimination. The university asked the court to grant pretrial judgment in its favor. In support of the request, the university insisted that it had nondiscriminatory reasons for its decision to deny the professor's request for tenure. The university noted that the professor had published only two referenced journal articles. In addition, the university pointed out that the professor had received no grants based on research as a principal investigator. The professor countered the university's evidence by asserting that a similarly situated faculty member was granted tenure. When the court compared the qualifications of the professor and the faculty member who was granted tenure, it discovered that the faculty member had better evaluations, a better publishing record, and strong research projects and grant work. By contrast, the professor misrepresented some of his research projects in applying for tenure. **The court held he did not produce enough evidence to show he was denied tenure based on unlawful discrimination.** As a result, it held for the university. *Lazarou v. Mississippi State Univ.*, 923 F.Supp.2d 882 (N.D. Miss. 2013).

◆ *A court rejected a University of North Carolina professor's claim that she was denied a promotion and tenure based on her race.*

A professor at a university claimed she was denied tenure and a promotion based on her race, in violation of Title VII of the 1964 Civil Rights Act. A federal district court held for the university, and appeal went to the U.S. Court of Appeals, Fourth Circuit. It held that the professor did not meet a filing deadline for the position she sought. She did not support her allegation it would have been futile for her to submit a timely application package. **Her discrimination claim failed because she did not show she had the necessary qualifications for promotion and tenure.** Moreover, the professor would have failed to prove her case because she did not identify a faculty member outside her protected class with a similar academic record who gained tenure and a promotion. *Weathers v. Univ. of North Carolina at Chapel Hill*, 447 Fed.Appx. 508 (4th Cir. 2011).

◆ *A professor who was denied tenure and discharged earned a chance to show that a Michigan university breached his employment contract.*

A university terminated a professor's faculty appointment after an investigating committee found the professor had misrepresented grant information, falsely stated he was the primary author of an article and keynote speaker at a conference from which he wrongfully withheld money, failed to accurately list dates on his employment application and made other misrepresentations. He sued the university in a federal court for breach of contract, retaliation and national origin discrimination. The court found none of the comments he relied on to support his national origin discrimination claim mentioned his Iranian descent. The professor did not show the stated reasons for discharge were a pretext. The Sixth Circuit agreed with the university that its stated reasons for terminating the professor's employment were not a pretext for unlawful retaliation. But the court held **there were genuine issues of material fact regarding whether the termination was in violation of the "just cause" provisions of the employment contract**. Since the professor raised some doubt as to whether just cause existed to discharge him, the contract claim was remanded. *Sanders v. Kettering Univ.*, 411 Fed.Appx. 771 (6th Cir. 2010).

◆ *A Tennessee professor who was a Hindu and a native of India failed to prove he was denied a promotion based on his religion or national origin.*

The professor joined Tennessee State University as an assistant professor in 1990. He was granted tenure and promoted to associate professor in 1997. But the university denied the professor's application for full professor, telling him he needed more substantial achievements in research and public service to be promoted. After he was again denied a promotion, the professor sued the university in a state court, claiming he was denied the promotions based on his national origin and religion. He accused the university of violating its faculty handbook policies by allowing a professor to serve on two committees that considered his application and failing to provide timely access to committee recommendations. The court granted a pretrial order for the university. On appeal, the state appeals court noted that the university faculty handbook confirmed its claim that research and public service activities were important considerations in the promotions process. **The university had consistently maintained that the professor was denied promotion due to his deficiencies in these areas.** He failed to submit evidence of public service or research activities, and the record showed he was not qualified for promotion. As a result, the judgment was affirmed. *Marpaka v. Hefner*, 289 S.W.3d 308 (Tenn. Ct. App. 2008). The Supreme Court of Tennessee denied an appeal in 2009.

◆ *A Missouri professor's due process claim against a private college failed because she did not show the college engaged in state action.*

The professor claimed male professors with similar responsibilities in her department were paid about $13,000 more annually than females. The college initially renewed her appointment for the 2006-07 term, but the college president then informed her that she would be placed on leave with pay and that she would not be reappointed for 2007-08. The college denied her grievance without a hearing. She then filed bias charges with state and federal agencies before suing the college's board of trustees for due process violations, retaliation, sex and age discrimination, breach of contract, tortious interference with her contract of employment and violation of the Equal Pay Act.

**The court rejected the due process claim because the professor failed to show the private college had engaged in any state action.** Next, the court granted the motion to dismiss the retaliation claim. The professor had admitted the college took no action relating to her employment after she filed the grievance. The claim of tortious interference with a contractual relationship was also dismissed, as such claims can be filed only against a third party. However, the court retained the discrimination claims. Both Title VII and the state's human rights act allowed punitive damage awards in cases of discrimination with malice or reckless indifference to federally protected rights. *Reed v. Board of Trustees of Columbia College*, No. 07-04155-CV-W-NKL, 2007 WL 4365749 (W.D. Mo. 2007).

◆ *The Supreme Court of Rhode Island refused to overturn a $455,000 jury verdict for a professor who was denied tenure for unlawful reasons.*

After serving in the engineering division for three years, the professor had a falling out with the division's director of undergraduate programs over a grading controversy. The professor eventually changed the grades under protest, but his relationship with the director remained sour. The director asked the professor to interview a minority candidate for a vacant position. The professor claimed the director's secretary told him the interview was being conducted for "affirmative action considerations." The professor refused to conduct the interview, saying he was concerned it might be illegal to interview a candidate for a job that had been set aside. He was denied tenure, and his internal grievance was then denied. In a state court action against the university, the professor claimed the director retaliated against him for opposing discriminatory practices, and he asserted national origin discrimination. A jury sided with the professor with respect to his retaliation claim and awarded him $675,000 in damages. On appeal, the state supreme court upheld the verdict for the retaliation claim. **While a rational jury could have reached a contrary verdict, the court found enough evidence to support the conclusion that the professor was denied tenure because he opposed the university's hiring practices.** *Shoucair v. Brown Univ.*, 917 A.2d 418 (R.I. 2007).

## C. Collegiality and Animosity

◆ *A federal court held the University of Washington (UW) denied tenure to an assistant professor based on her lack of collegiality, not discrimination.*

All three of the tenured professors in the assistant professor's department were male. She personalized workplace problems and was humiliated when a student chose to work with another professor on a project. Assessments of the professor noted she felt threatened when her colleagues began projects in her perceived areas of expertise. She reacted angrily when she was not given credit she thought she was due, and she suspected unfairness when she was denied grants. Student evaluations of her teaching were mostly neutral or negative.

Twice, the department director decided not to support the professor's requests for tenure. Although the university provost considered the application, a decision was postponed due to concerns about her teaching effectiveness, concerns about collegiality, and a need for clarification relating to her scholarly achievements. Evidence indicated the professor believed collegiality should not be a factor in the tenure analysis. After her application for tenure was rejected a third time, she sued UW in a federal court for discrimination and retaliation. **The court held gender was not a motivating factor in the tenure decisions.** Even if the director disliked the professor, his recommendations did not cause the denial of tenure. As the professor could not prove unlawful retaliation, the court ordered the entry of judgment for UW. *Bichindaritz v. Univ. of Washington*, No. C10-1371RSL, 2012 WL 1378699 (W.D. Wash. 4/20/12).

◆  *Lack of collegiality was a valid basis upon which to discharge a tenured North Carolina State engineering professor.*

After gaining tenure at North Carolina State University, the professor was given unsatisfactory performance reviews for three straight years. A faculty hearing committee found he was not incompetent, but university trustees discharged him for incompetence of service. Among the university's findings was a lack of collegiality with colleagues that had become so disruptive that the professor's department was unable to operate efficiently. A state court upheld the discharge, and he appealed to the Court of Appeals of North Carolina.

On appeal, the professor claimed that tenured professors cannot be discharged on grounds other than incompetence, misconduct or neglect of duty under the state university code. The court rejected this argument, as the discharge was for incompetence – one of the permissible reasons for discharge under the code. **A university regulation authorized discharge for incompetence when a tenured professor had unsatisfactory reviews for two straight years. Moreover, disruptive behavior may also constitute incompetence.** The professor's due process claim failed because the university followed the relevant code provisions. Since there was "ample evidence" that he disrupted his department to the point that its functions and operations were impaired, the discharge was affirmed. *Bernold v. Board of Governors of the Univ. of North Carolina*, 683 S.E.2d 428 (N.C. Ct. App. 2009).

◆  *A tenured Arkansas professor did not show any causal connection between his dismissal and his filing of a lawsuit four years earlier.*

The professor claimed he was removed as department chair in violation of his constitutional rights. To settle his lawsuit, the university paid him a nominal sum. After the settlement, friction developed between the professor and the new chair. Following a series of insubordinate acts by the professor, the chair told him he could not teach during a summer session. When the professor went to a class he would have taught and started filming it, he was removed by university security and warned that further disruptions would result in his dismissal. A short time later, he filmed students as they registered for classes and was again removed by security. The professor did not appear at a meeting called by the university chancellor, and he was soon dismissed. In a federal district court action against university officials, the professor accused the chair and university of retaliating against him for filing a lawsuit. He also claimed race discrimination and due process violations.

The court ruled for the university. On appeal to the U.S. Court of Appeals,

Eighth Circuit, the university asserted Eleventh Amendment immunity. The professor provided no authority to support his argument that the university could not claim immunity because it did not timely raise this defense. The retaliation claim failed because he did not show a causal connection between a protected activity and his dismissal. In any event, the university had legitimate reasons for its decision. **There was evidence that the professor was insubordinate, refused to attend meetings and acted unprofessionally.** No due process violation occurred, since he did not show university officials acted arbitrarily, and he did not comply with university procedures. As a result, the judgment was affirmed. *Satcher v. Univ. of Arkansas at Pine Bluff Board of Trustees*, 558 F.3d 731 (8th Cir. 2009).

◆   *A federal district court dismissed an Illinois professor's constitutional rights violation claims.*

The professor was disciplined after having confrontations with other faculty members. After a no-confidence vote by the faculty, he lost his position as a member and chair of a college personnel committee. He was also removed from the University Council Personnel Committee position. The professor sued university officials in a federal district court for denial of due process and equal protection rights. The court dismissed the claims against the board and officials on Eleventh Amendment grounds, finding they were not subject to constitutional claims for damages. The claims of deprivation of property and liberty without due process lacked merit. Although the professor had a property interest in his employment as a tenured faculty member, he did not have any interest in membership on committees. As he did not show damage to his good name, reputation, honor or integrity, the court dismissed his claim based on deprivation of a liberty interest. Since the university did not take adverse employment action against the professor, such as termination, demotion, or a loss of pay and benefits, he failed to allege any significant legally cognizable injury, and the case was dismissed. *Ganesan v. NIU Board of Trustees*, No. 02 C 50498, 2003 WL 22872139 (N.D. Ill. 2003).

## D.  Handbooks and Procedures

◆   *Finding a professor couldn't appeal a claim he didn't bring in earlier proceedings, a Kansas appeals court upheld a tenure decision.*

In 2005, the University of Kansas (KU) hired Albert Romkes as a tenure-track assistant professor of mechanical engineering. In November 2009, the faculty in the department approved a requirement that called for tenure candidates to demonstrate they could successfully obtain outside research grants. The requirement was discussed with Romkes during his third-year tenure-track review in 2008. He submitted his tenure application in 2010. Reviewers found him an excellent teacher and advisor plus a "valued member of the department[,]" but his poor track record in funding was raised as a black mark against him at every level of review. The chancellor decided not to grant him tenure. Romkes sued, alleging the decision to deny him tenure wasn't supported by the evidence, but the trial court found it was – and an appeals court affirmed. To uphold KU's decision, the Kansas Judicial Review Act required the courts to find it was supported by "substantial evidence" –

meaning a reasonable person could accept it as sufficient to support the decision. Romkes didn't suggest his tenure evaluations were based on false info, only that KU put too much weight on a factor that weighed against him. The appeals court found this was a "straightforward business decision" and deferred to KU's judgment. On appeal, **Romkes also argued KU introduced the requirement when it was "too late for him to do anything about it."** But the appellate court found Romkes couldn't "appeal" this claim as he never brought it against KU in his earlier proceedings against it. It also pointed out he didn't object to the new requirement when it was raised at his third-year tenure-track review. The appeals court upheld the tenure decision, finding it was supported by substantial evidence. *Romkes v. Univ. of Kansas*, 317 P.3d 124 (Kan. Ct. App. 2014).

◆ *A trial court was ordered to reexamine claims that changes to an employment handbook wrongfully deprived professors of vested tenure rights.*

Until 2002, the Metropolitan State College of Denver was a part of the Colorado State Colleges System. At that time, the state removed the college from the system and created a board of trustees to govern it. In 2003, the board issued a new handbook describing the rights of professional personnel at the college. The new handbook superseded one that had been in place since 1994, and it included some changes that did not sit well with tenured professors. For example, it did not afford tenured faculty priority over nontenured faculty in the event of a layoff. In addition, it removed the requirement that the college try to relocate dismissed faculty and eliminated a hearing committee procedure that was used when tenured faculty members sought to challenge their dismissal.

Five tenured professors filed a state court action against the board of trustees, claiming the new handbook breached their employment contracts and violated their due process rights. The court held the new handbook did not breach employment contracts. It also rejected the due process claim, because none of the professors had been subjected to dismissal or layoff under the new handbook. **On appeal, the Court of Appeals of Colorado held the board lacked authority to unilaterally modify handbook provisions that afforded the professors substantive and vested rights.** Provisions in the new handbook relating to priority and relocation in the event of layoffs affected the professors' substantive rights. It was up to the trial court to determine whether those rights were vested. The new handbook violated due process because it allowed the college president to institute and resolve dismissals. *Saxe v. Board of Trustees of Metropolitan State College of Denver*, 179 P.3d 67 (Colo. Ct. App. 2007).

In 2008, the Supreme Court of Colorado rejected further appeal of the action. *Saxe v. Board of Trustees of Metropolitan State College of Denver,* No. 07SC301, 2008 WL 698945 (Colo. 2008).

◆ *A private Minnesota university did not breach a professor's contract when it decided not to grant her application for tenure.*

A university faculty handbook called for evaluation of tenure cases by an academic council, which then made tenure recommendations to the university president. The president had final authority regarding all tenure decisions. The academic council recommended denying the professor's application for tenure, and the university president accepted the recommendation. After a hearing, the council reversed itself and recommended tenure. But the president again denied the application, and the professor sued the university and its president in a state court for breach of contract and breach of the covenant of good faith in employment. All the claims were dismissed, and the professor appealed.

Before the Court of Appeals of Minnesota, the professor claimed the faculty handbook created a contract and required it to grant her tenure. She argued that the president was obligated to grant tenure to candidates who met applicable criteria for tenure and were recommended for tenure by the academic council. **The court affirmed the judgment, finding that the handbook set out procedures for candidates seeking tenure but explicitly reserved final tenure decisions for the president.** *Nash-Marshall v. Univ. of Saint Thomas*, No. A07-2028, 2008 WL 3290383 (Minn. Ct. App. 8/12/08).

## IV.  INVESTIGATIONS, HEARINGS AND PROCEDURES

### A.  Investigations

*Public institutions and administrative agencies are bound to respect the due process rights of public employees during investigations.*

◆ *A Minnesota community college did not violate a part-time English instructor's right to due process by declining to renew his contract.*

The instructor's contracts ran from semester to semester. Near the end of his sixth consecutive semester, the college legal affairs director advised him that a student had filed a sexual harassment complaint against him. The director told the instructor to stay away from the bookstore where the student worked, but she did not give him a written notice or a copy of applicable college policies and procedures, or tell him he could submit a written response to the charge. At a later interview, the director failed to give the instructor notices required by state law. After interviewing the instructor, the student and three witnesses, she wrote up a report concluding he had violated the college's sexual harassment policy. After she completed her report, she threw away her notes.

The instructor was informed of the non-renewal of his contract, and he sued the college and various officials in a state court. The case reached the Court of Appeals of Minnesota. It found the instructor **could not show any property interest in continued employment because the terms of his contract called only for part-time, temporary employment that ended each semester**. The court was not persuaded by his argument that ordering textbooks for the classes he expected to teach showed he had a protected interest in continued employment. No liberty interest in reputation was implicated, as the college did not publicize either the letter informing the instructor he would not be rehired or the investigator's sexual harassment report. The college was entitled to judgment. *Phillips v. State*, 725 N.W.2d 778 (Minn. Ct. App. 2007).

◆ *A Colorado university improperly released an audit report to the media without providing a name-clearing hearing.*

The University of Colorado at Denver (UCD) investigated a managing director for fiscal misconduct. An auditors' report found evidence that he had granted employees paid time off without required approval. The director also gave a subordinate paid time off to prepare for a foreign teaching assignment and falsified an employee's termination date. The director's supervisor told him he would be assigned other duties for 30 days and then discharged. However, the director did not receive a copy of the audit report until two weeks later.

Meanwhile, the UCD newspaper ran an article detailing the report. Another article appeared in a local paper. After the director was discharged, he said the release of the report created a stigma on his reputation and prevented him from applying for jobs he otherwise would have sought. In his federal lawsuit against UCD, the director claimed his due process rights were violated. A federal district court ruled against him, and he appealed. The U.S. Court of Appeals, Tenth Circuit, found enough evidence to create a factual issue as to whether the damaging statements in the audit report were false. The director said he believed he had the authority to grant administrative leave without the approval of his supervisor, and insisted he had made no misrepresentation in allowing an employee to take time off to teach. As to the third incident, the director said the employee worked a full day on each day of her last week of employment. The court found this evidence was important, because **UCD could not prove fiscal misconduct unless it showed the director acted intentionally**. The case was returned to the district court for further proceedings. *Evers v. Regents of the Univ. of Colorado*, 509 F.3d 1304 (10th Cir. 2007).

◆    *An Ohio university football coach was allowed to discover and present information to a trial court before it resolved his breach of contract claim.*

The coach became aware that some of his players were conducting voluntary throwing sessions. He knew players could get hurt unless there was some organization to these workouts. An NFL scout arrived at the university looking for game films and information about a senior quarterback. During the visit, the coach allegedly directed the quarterback while the scout watched. The coach's supervisor reprimanded the coach in writing, stating that such contact with players outside NCAA-approved dates was unacceptable. The university investigated and found the coach violated NCAA rules at a pre-season camp.

After the investigation, the university held a hearing before a five-person faculty committee, then voted to dismiss the coach. He appealed through a grievance process, but the grievance committee rejected the appeal as untimely. The coach sued the university in a state court for breach of contract. The court held for the university, and the coach appealed to the Court of Appeals of Ohio. There, he alleged the trial court should have provided him an opportunity to conduct the pretrial fact-finding process called "discovery." The court agreed, finding **the evidence was not developed in a way necessary to properly determine a motion for summary judgment**. It vacated the judgment and returned the case to the trial court to allow discovery. *Kaczkowski v. Ohio Northern Univ.*, No. 6-05-08, 2006 WL 1312401 (Ohio Ct. App. 5/15/06).

◆    *A private college had to disclose certain records to the EEOC.*

A professor, who had been employed at a Pennsylvania private college for three years, was denied tenure after he was reviewed by the school's Professional Standards Committee. The committee, composed of the dean and five faculty members, recommended that tenure not be granted to the professor. The committee's recommendation was also reaffirmed by the college's grievance committee. The professor then filed a complaint with the EEOC alleging discrimination based on his French national origin. The EEOC issued a subpoena for the committee's records. Although the EEOC offered to accept the records with names deleted, the school refused to disclose them.

The EEOC then filed suit in federal district court to compel the college to comply with the subpoena. The district court ordered disclosure of the records, and the college appealed. The court of appeals affirmed, holding that **although the disclosure might burden the tenure process or invade the privacy of other professors, the records had to be disclosed because they were "relevant" to the EEOC's case**. The college appealed to the U.S. Supreme Court, but its petition for review was denied. *Franklin & Marshall College v. EEOC*, 476 U.S. 1163, 106 S.Ct. 2288, 90 L.Ed.2d 729 (1986).

◆  *The U.S. Supreme Court required a university to comply with an EEOC subpoena seeking peer review information.*

After the University of Pennsylvania, a private institution, denied tenure to an associate professor, she filed a charge with the EEOC alleging discrimination based on race, sex and national origin in violation of Title VII. During its investigation, the EEOC issued a subpoena seeking disclosure of the professor's tenure-review file and the tenure files of five male faculty members identified as having received more favorable treatment. The university refused to produce a number of the tenure-file documents and asked the EEOC to modify the subpoena to exclude "confidential peer review information."

The EEOC successfully sought enforcement of its subpoena through a federal district court. The U.S. Court of Appeals, Third Circuit, rejected a claim that academic freedom required recognition of a qualified privilege or the adoption of a balancing approach that would require the EEOC to demonstrate a showing of need to obtain peer review materials. The U.S. Supreme Court then held **a university does not enjoy a special privilege requiring a judicial finding of necessity prior to access of peer review materials**. It was reluctant to add such a privilege to protect "academic autonomy" when Congress had failed to do so in Title VII. The Court also held "academic freedom" could not be used as the basis for such a privilege. *Univ. of Pennsylvania v. EEOC*, 493 U.S. 182, 110 S.Ct. 577, 107 L.Ed.2d 571 (1990).

## B.  Hearings and Procedures

◆  *A Pennsylvania federal court upheld a university's decision to dismiss a professor who was accused of grooming a student for a sexual relationship.*

A student filed a sexual harassment complaint against a professor. After a hearing, he was terminated for "grave misconduct." He sued, asserting a violation of his due process rights and other claims. The university filed a motion to dismiss. The court rejected the professor's procedural due process claim that he was deprived of his liberty interest in his reputation, as he did not adequately allege the defendants made a public statement that was false and stigmatizing. It also dismissed his procedural due process claim that he was deprived of his property interest in tenured employment, as he didn't show he was denied safeguards to which he was entitled. The court also rejected his substantive due process rights to a property interest in tenured, continued employment and a liberty interest in his reputation. **Tenured public employment is not a fundamental property interest entitled to substantive due process protection**, the court explained. *Winter v. The Pennsylvania State Univ.,* No. 3:15-CV-01166, 2016 WL 1110215 (M.D. Pa. 3/22/16).

◆  *A Kansas federal judge rejected a due process claim filed by an assistant professor based on his employer's response to a race-related incident.*

The professor and his wife worked in different departments of a university. The professor's wife told him someone had written "NIGGAZ" on a notepad in her office. He and his wife, who are African-American, said they reported the incident but the school did not adequately respond. The professor had a handwriting expert look at the note. After comparing handwriting samples, the expert identified another school employee as the probable author of the slur. The school disagreed with the assessment, and it issued a statement exonerating the accused employee. After the professor and his wife led a protest march, the school's interim president sent the professor a letter detailing conditions for his continued employment. These conditions required him to either provide "credible, substantive" evidence supporting the accusation or retract it, participate in mediation with faculty and staff, acknowledge certain behavior that wasn't acceptable at work, and follow the school's grievance procedures going forward. He sued, alleging the university violated his right to due process. The defendants filed a motion to dismiss. The court focused its analysis on whether the professor stated a claim under 42 U.S.C. § 1983 for denial of procedural due process. It concluded he did not, explaining that **a threat of discharge is not enough to qualify as a liberty interest. Instead, termination, demotion or foreclosure of employment opportunity is required.** The court gave the professor 21 days to amend his complaint. If he didn't, the court said, it would dismiss the matter. *Hale v. Emporia State Univ.,* No. 15-4947-SAC-KGS, 2016 WL 141655 (D. Kan. 1/12/16).

◆  *An Alabama federal judge allowed some due process claims of a Chinese-born employee to move forward.*

Xingzhong Shi was born in China. He came to the U.S., where he earned a Ph.D. in applied math with a minor in computer science from the University of Alabama, Huntsville. Shi's job experience included five years developing and maintaining software. He was hired as an assistant professor in the computer science department at Alabama A&M University and was later promoted to associate professor. There, he and other colleagues expected to be able to vote on the appointment of an interim chair. They weren't. Shi alleged the person appointed had fewer qualifications for the position than he and other colleagues had. He emailed to complain, but said he was ignored. Then Shi questioned the administrator about the decision at a college-wide meeting in August of 2011. Afterward, the administrator put him on leave without pay through the rest of 2011. Another administrator fired him in December 2011 "without stating any reason," Shi claimed. He filed suit under Section 1983, alleging his due process rights had been breached. The court dismissed the claims against the university's grievance committee, its board of trustees and administrators in their official capacities, as they had Eleventh Amendment immunity. **But Shi's claims against administrators in their individual capacities could proceed.** *Xingzhong Shi v. Alabama A&M Univ.*, No. CV-13-S-327-NE, 2013 WL 3746066 (N.D. Ala. 7/15/13).

◆ *University of North Carolina (UNC) employees must follow UNC employment dispute resolution procedures before filing a lawsuit.*

An associate professor completed a probationary year and earned a two-year employment contract. The agreement specified it was "subject to and governed by" UNC's code. A month before his contract was up, the university notified the professor that he would not be rehired. Instead of pursuing an appeal, he sued UNC for wrongful termination. A court dismissed the case, finding it lacked jurisdiction (authority) to hear it. The professor had not exhausted his administrative remedies by completing university appeals before suing. On appeal, the Court of Appeals of North Carolina affirmed the judgment. **North Carolina law required UNC employees to complete university procedures intended to resolve employment disputes before going to court.** As a result, the judgment for UNC was affirmed. *Johnson v. Univ. of North Carolina*, 688 S.E.2d 546 (N.C. Ct. App. 2010).

◆ *When a property right to employment exists, due process requires that the employee receive notice and an opportunity to be heard before discipline.*

In two consolidated cases, the U.S. Supreme Court considered what pretermination process must be afforded a public employee who can be discharged only for cause. In the first case, a security guard hired by a school board stated on his job application that he had never been convicted of a felony. Upon discovering that he had in fact been convicted of grand larceny, the school board summarily dismissed him for dishonesty in filling out the job application. He was not afforded an opportunity to respond to the dishonesty charge or to challenge the dismissal until nine months later. In the second case, a school bus mechanic was fired because he had failed an eye examination.

The mechanic appealed his dismissal after the fact because he had not been afforded a pretermination hearing. The Supreme Court held that **because the employees possessed a property right in their employment, they were entitled to a pretermination opportunity to at least respond to the charges against them**. The pretermination hearing need not fully resolve the propriety of the discharge, but should be a check against mistaken decisions. The Court held that in this case, the employees were entitled to a pretermination opportunity to respond, coupled with a full-blown administrative hearing at a later time. *Cleveland Board of Educ. v. Loudermill*, 470 U.S. 532, 105 S.Ct. 1487, 84 L.Ed.2d 494 (1985).

◆ *When the disciplinary action is something less than termination, the protections afforded by due process are not the same as required in* Loudermill.

A police officer employed by a Pennsylvania state university was arrested in a drug raid and charged with several felony counts related to marijuana possession and distribution. State police notified the university of the arrest and charges, and the university's human resources director immediately suspended the officer without pay pursuant to a state executive order requiring such action where a state employee is formally charged with a felony. Although the criminal charges were dismissed, university officials demoted the officer because of the felony charges. The university did not inform the officer that it had obtained his confession from police records, and he was thus unable to fully respond to damaging statements in the police reports. He filed a federal district court action against university officials for failing to provide him with notice and an opportunity to be heard before his suspension without pay.

The court granted pretrial judgment to the officials, but the U.S. Court of Appeals, Third Circuit, reversed and remanded the case. The U.S. Supreme Court stated that the court of appeals had improperly held that a suspended public employee must always receive a paid suspension under *Cleveland Board of Educ. v. Loudermill*, above. The Court held that **the university did not violate due process by refusing to pay a suspended employee charged with a felony pending a hearing**. It accepted the officials' argument that the Pennsylvania executive order made any pre-suspension hearing useless, since the filing of charges established an independent basis for believing that the officer had committed a felony. The Court noted that the officer here faced only a temporary suspension without pay, and not employment termination as in *Loudermill*. The Court reversed and remanded the case. *Gilbert v. Homar*, 520 U.S. 924, 117 S.Ct. 1807, 138 L.Ed.2d 120 (1997).

◆    *A Kentucky community and technical college professor was afforded due process before being demoted for poor job performance.*

The professor received three consecutive negative performance evaluations. After the third, she appealed, but the college president agreed with the evaluations and the college notified her she would be demoted to a temporary, part-time adjunct position. A letter informing the professor of the decision cited her violations of administrative policies and procedures, and her poor job performance. The letter notified her she was on leave without pay and told her she had a right to a pre-demotion hearing. The professor received an administrative hearing where she was represented by counsel and was given the opportunity to show why she should not be demoted. The college allowed her to submit additional information after the hearing, but the college president informed her in writing that she would be demoted. The college then sent the professor a letter advising her of her appeal rights, but later informed her that the demotion was final. This letter outlined reasons for the decision, including job carelessness, poor behavior toward students and staff, and failure to follow security procedures. The letter advised the professor that she had not been discharged and indicated she remained eligible for substitute duties.

The professor sued the college in a state court, claiming it violated her due process rights. The court dismissed her complaint, and she appealed to the Court of Appeals of Kentucky. **The court affirmed the decision, noting that procedural due process is a flexible concept.** Its key components are notice and an opportunity to be heard. In this case, the professor acknowledged that she was given adequate written notice of the charges against her. She also acknowledged that she received a chance to be heard and to present her evidence. As the professor received all the process she was due, the trial court's decision was affirmed. *Bassett v. Board of Regents*, No. 2006-CA-002131-MR,

2007 WL 2687399 (Ky. Ct. App. 9/14/07). In 2008, the Supreme Court of Kentucky denied further consideration of the case.

◆  *An employee on probationary status could not show a California university violated his due process rights.*

The University of California hired the employee under a union contract providing for an initial six-month probationary period. During this time, the university had discretion to fire probationary employees without following collective bargaining grievance procedures. While the employee was still on probation, he was fired for sexual harassment of a co-worker. He sued the university in a federal district court for due process violations. He also argued the university violated his Fourteenth Amendment liberty rights by publicly disclosing the sexual harassment allegation that had been made against him.

The court held for the university, and the employee appealed. The U.S. Court of Appeals, Ninth Circuit, **explained that to be entitled to a notice and a hearing, an employee must have a property interest in employment**. There was no due process violation in this case, as the employee knew he was still in his probationary term and had no property interest in continuing employment. While public employers can violate employee liberty interests by publicly disclosing sexual harassment allegations, the university committed no violation here. The employee could not prove that any co-workers had learned about the sexual harassment charges from the university. As the university had been properly granted pretrial judgment, the court affirmed the judgment. *Whitworth v. Regents of Univ. of California*, 274 Fed.Appx. 559 (9th Cir. 2008).

◆  *The Supreme Court of Nevada was liable to a tenured professor for breach of contract because it discharged him based on outdated evaluations.*

The university gave the professor consecutive unsatisfactory evaluations, which was cause for termination. It filed a complaint against the professor with its administrative code officer and scheduled a hearing. The parties reached a settlement under which the professor agreed to resign at the end of the academic year. The university agreed to cancel the hearing and offer him a non-tenured teaching contract. The professor refused to sign an employment contract without guaranteed language and sued the university for breach of contract in a Nevada trial court. The court prohibited the university from using the unsatisfactory evaluations as a basis for firing the professor. It ordered the university to continue the professor's employment unless it revoked his tenure.

The university filed another administrative complaint against the professor based on the unsatisfactory evaluations, which were now six years old. It decided its own six-month deadline for hearings did not apply to the time of the settlement and its present administrative complaint. After a hearing, the university fired the professor. He sued the university a second time, alleging the prior court order prohibited the university from using the old evaluations as a basis for termination. **The court held for the professor, and the university appealed. The Supreme Court of Nevada held the university breached the settlement by holding the hearing based on an outdated complaint that included the prior evaluations.** The court found the hearing violated the terms of the settlement agreement and held the university breached the agreement when it unilaterally determined it could proceed with a new hearing. *State of Nevada, Univ. and Community System v. Sutton*, 103 P.3d 8 (Nev. 2004).

◆ *The Court of Appeals of North Carolina held state law precluded administrative review of layoff actions involving state university employees.*

Permanent state funding reductions forced the University of North Carolina at Chapel Hill to eliminate staff positions in various departments. Three employees who were included in the reduction of force pursued grievances that were upheld under university procedures. All three employees filed petitions with the state office of administrative hearings (OAH), alleging they were improperly laid off. A state trial court denied the university's dismissal motions and held the OAH had jurisdiction to determine if just cause supported the layoffs. **The state court of appeals held the OAH only had jurisdiction to hear state employee cases involving demotion, retaliation for opposition to discrimination and disputes relating to veterans preferences.** The state legislature enacted a law that intentionally excluded reductions in force based on procedural violations from OAH jurisdiction. The court directed the trial court to grant the university's dismissal motions. *Univ. of North Carolina v. Feinstein*, 590 S.E.2d 401 (N.C. Ct. App. 2003).

◆ *A New York university was not liable for firing a professor for harassment prior to a hearing.*

Although no grievance or complaint was filed under the university's grievance procedures, the university took the student's information, gathered other information, and decided to fire the professor. When the student failed to appear at the arbitration hearings mandated by the collective bargaining agreement, the termination was rescinded, and the charges against the professor were dismissed. He nevertheless sued the university for failing to follow its own rules when disciplining him. A jury awarded him $25,000 in damages, but the Second Circuit Court of Appeals reversed. Here, **the professor failed to show that the university was required to follow the grievance procedures exclusively when making a finding that an employee had engaged in illegal discrimination**. Because the university's grievance procedures gave it the flexibility to discipline the professor without formal hearings, there was no breach of duty by the university. *Garcia v. State Univ. of New York at Albany*, 320 F.3d 148 (2d Cir. 2003).

◆ *College officials were not entitled to immunity in a lawsuit brought by a teacher accused of misconduct and barred from campus.*

A music instructor at a Nebraska public college taught for 29 years before retiring. He directed a performance group called "Chorale" in addition to teaching, and continued to work in a part-time capacity after he retired until the college eliminated his position. At that time, the college informed him it was banning him from campus, pending an investigation into alleged embezzlement. The college's letter also accused him of permitting Chorale to have inappropriate sexual overtones in their performances. He sued the college and its officials under 42 U.S.C. § 1983, alleging violations of his substantive and procedural due process rights as well as his free speech and freedom of association rights under the First Amendment. The college and officials asserted qualified immunity and sought a dismissal. A federal court dismissed the substantive due process claims, but refused to dismiss the others.

On appeal, the Eighth Circuit Court of Appeals affirmed. **The instructor was entitled to a name-clearing hearing because the accusations of dishonesty and immorality were stigmatizing and were known by faculty members at several campuses.** He had a liberty interest in his name and reputation, and the college officials were not entitled to qualified immunity after refusing to provide the hearing. Finally, since the college was a public forum, its officials should have determined whether banning the instructor from campus was the least restrictive way to serve a compelling interest. They were not entitled to qualified immunity on the First Amendment claims either. *Putnam v. Keller*, 332 F.3d 541 (8th Cir. 2003).

◆ *A Kentucky university police officer whose contract was not renewed could not sue for due process violations.*

A Kentucky university hired a police officer under an annual contract. It later suspended him with pay for his involvement in the dubious arrest of several students. He did not challenge the suspension. When the university refused to renew his contract the following year, he sued it under 42 U.S.C. § 1983, asserting due process and equal protection violations. A federal court ruled in favor of the university, and the Sixth Circuit affirmed. It noted that he could not succeed because **he could not show that he had a legitimate expectation of continued employment with the university**. The university's personnel manual did not create a property interest in employment, nor did it require the university to reappoint him. *Baker v. Kentucky State Univ.*, 45 Fed. Appx. 328 (6th Cir. 2002).

◆ *A North Dakota professor was properly fired where he was able to confront witnesses and challenge evidence in two hearings before his termination.*

A university professor served as chairman of the physics department until his relationships with other faculty members deteriorated and he was removed as chairman. He criticized the department in a number of letters that he sent to university officials and local newspapers. Subsequently, the university received numerous complaints from students about his poor teaching performance. More than 90% of his introductory students transferred out of his class in one semester. The university then sent him a letter of termination that listed six grounds for his firing, including his libelous conduct, his disciplinary record, and his lack of cooperation with faculty members. He obtained a hearing before a special review committee, which ruled in his favor, but the president of the university rejected the committee's findings.

The committee on faculty rights then upheld the dismissal. The professor sued the university in a federal court under 42 U.S.C. § 1983 for violating his First and Fourteenth Amendment rights. The case reached the Eighth Circuit. It noted that while two of the professor's letters addressed matters of public concern, most of them did not. The professor could not claim First Amendment protection for all the letters, and allegedly libelous material in the unprotected letters could be used as a reason for termination. Also, **the professor received**

**due process in that he was given notice of the charges against him and an opportunity to respond**. Thus, his Fourteenth Amendment claim could not succeed. *de Llano v. Berglund*, 282 F.3d 1031 (8th Cir. 2002).

## V.  WRONGFUL DISCHARGE

*"Employment at-will" exists in the absence of an oral or written contract of employment. When an employee works "at will," the law presumes the employment relationship may be terminated by either party at any time and for any reason. But an employer may not discharge an employee for an unlawful reason, such as reporting illegal or fraudulent conduct or agreeing to give testimony that may be adverse to the employer's interests.*

◆   *A university's former chief of police could proceed with his claim that his public and condemnatory termination deprived him of his liberty interest in future employment in law enforcement, an Illinois federal court held.*

After an officer was accused of rape, the police department mishandled evidence that may have exonerated him. The state's attorney's office issued a press release demanding an investigation and accusing the university police of jeopardizing the accused officer's defense "and the police department's credibility." The chief was put on paid administrative leave, and university police issued a press release announcing he had been suspended "pending finalization of charges and disciplinary actions." After pursuing an unsuccessful grievance, the chief sued, claiming he was deprived of a liberty interest in future employment in law enforcement. The court found the chief stated a valid claim, as the school "pursued a highly public termination process in which [the chief] was accused of serious personal and supervisory misconduct." Both the press release and the letters sent to the chief received wide and negative media coverage. As a result, he could not find work as a law enforcement officer "at any level." The school argued it was the attorney's office that made the matter public. But the court pointed out, **the school "alone took the further step of naming [the chief] specifically, and it was the university's decision to publicize his termination that likely inflicted the most damage on his ability to find future employment."** So the court refused to dismiss the claim. *Grady v. Board of Trustees of Northern Illinois Univ.*, No. 14 C 12451:14-cv-01245, 2015 WL 232192 (N.D. Ill. 1/16/2015).

◆   *A New Jersey appeals court overturned a trial judge's evidence call during discovery.*

In the 2009-10 school year, Glenn Hedden was Kean University's (KU) athletic director and Michele Sharp was its head women's basketball coach. Sharp organized a team trip to Spain where they would develop their basketball skills and also earn three credits in a Spanish history course. She drafted a letter to potential donors and attached the letter to an email to KU's general counsel.

The trip took place in August. Hedden didn't find out about the course until the following November, when a math professor told him a member of the women's basketball team wasn't taking enough credits to maintain her athletic eligibility. Hedden checked the student's academic record and saw her schedule contained "History of Spain" as an "added course." Investigating further, he found the class only had nine students — all past or present members of the women's basketball team. Hedden was sure the course violated KU regulations and National Collegiate Athletic Association (NCAA) guidelines. He reported the incident. The NCAA investigated and filed a complaint. In the meantime, Hedden received word about another problem associated with the women's basketball team. Grades had been changed to help students keep their eligibility. He filed a second report with NCAA. The NCAA investigated Hedden's reports and sanctioned KU for violating NCAA rules.

The following May, KU fired Hedden, claiming he failed to properly supervise subordinates and caused the NCAA to issue sanctions. Hedden sued KU for defamation and wrongful termination under New Jersey's Conscientious Employee Protection Act. In discovery, Hedden asked KU to share Sharp's email to the general counsel. KU refused, claiming the email was protected by attorney-client privilege. Hedden asked the judge to order KU to produce the email. After looking at the email privately, the judge decided the privilege didn't apply and KU had to share it. KU appealed, and the appellate court reversed. **Under New Jersey law, attorney-client privilege generally applies, meaning the other party has no right to discover as trial evidence any confidential communications in which legal counsel is sought from an attorney acting as a legal advisor.** *Hedden v. Kean Univ.*, 82 A.3d 238 (N.J. Super. Ct. App. Div. 2013).

◆   *A Maryland university police officer's reporting of misconduct could be protected by a state whistleblower act, even if it was personally motivated.*

The officer became concerned that the arrest of a student by other campus officers violated the Fourth Amendment. He wrote a letter but instead of sending it to his supervisor, he sent it to a university vice president. He was suspended and, after a hearing, he was discharged for failing to follow the proper chain of command. The officer filed an administrative whistleblower complaint. An ALJ found the letter to the vice president was not protected because it was motivated by a "crusade to make changes to the department," rather than to report government abuses. Appeal reached the state's highest court, which explained that **an objective test is used to determine whether a whistleblower has a reasonable belief that he is identifying a legal violation and thus is making a protected disclosure**. The whistleblower does not have to show his disclosure exposes an actual violation. In this case, the court held the ALJ was improperly preoccupied with the officer's motive. The law required only that he had a reasonable belief that he was reporting a violation. As a personal motive was not a reason to deny whistleblower protection, the court ordered the ALJ to reconsider the whistleblower claim under an objective standard. *Lawson v. Bowie State Univ.*, 421 Md. 245, 26 A.3d 866 (Md. 2011).

◆   *A University of Washington (UW) employee's state-law claim of retaliation was rejected by a federal district court.*

The employee worked in UW's Computing and Communications (C&C) Department. He used his UW email account to send a vulgar email to the

United Way. UW issued the employee a letter of counsel, but a month later he received a favorable performance review and a raise. The employee filed a complaint with the UW department of human resources, claiming a co-worker had distributed a harsh critique of his work and that his supervisor failed to address it. He also claimed he was perceived differently by others who learned about the United Way email, and that he was denied an interview for a job based on the critique and email. The employee then resigned to accept another job at UW. He was placed on home assignment for the duration of his two-week notice period. The employee complained that the C&C Department had discriminated and retaliated against him, but the UW complaint resolution office found the complaint unfounded. He then sent harassing emails to several UW officials, leading to the termination of his employment.

The employee sued UW in a federal district court for retaliation. However, the claim was filed under a state law that makes it unlawful to discharge an employee who has opposed unlawful employment practices. **The court granted UW's motion for pretrial judgment, because the employee did not show he opposed any practice forbidden by the state law against discrimination.** He did not show how a critique of his work, or his supervisor's alleged failure to intervene regarding criticism, constituted behavior prohibited by the statute. Even if the employee could show he engaged in protected conduct, his claim would fail because he was fired for sending harassing emails. The court awarded pretrial judgment to UW. *Cooper v. Univ. of Washington*, No. C06-1365RSL, 2007 WL 3356809 (W.D. Wash. 11/8/07).

◆   *The Court of Appeals of Michigan interpreted the term "public body" broadly to allow an employee to pursue a whistleblower action.*

The U.S. Department of Education (DOE) investigated student financial assistance programs at a Michigan college. An administrator who cooperated with the DOE was later discharged. She sued the college in a state court, claiming she was fired for participating in the DOE investigation. The court held for the college, finding the DOE was not a "public body" under a state whistleblower law. The administrator appealed to the Court of Appeals of Michigan, which noted the power to arrest was not the only factor to consider when determining whether an agency was a "law enforcement agency" under the whistleblower law. Instead, it was appropriate to consider the extent of the DOE's overall power to detect and punish legal violations. The DOE has broad investigatory powers, including the power to gain access to people and documents and to issue subpoenas. DOE officials are authorized to execute warrants and make arrests. **In light of the broad powers granted to the DOE, the appeals court concluded the DOE was a "law enforcement agency" within the meaning of the state whistleblower law.** It reversed and remanded the case for further proceedings. *Ernsting v. Ave Maria College*, 274 Mich. App. 506, 736 N.W.2d 574 (Mich. Ct. App. 2007).

◆   *A federal district court held Connecticut College did not cause a director of development emotional distress during termination proceedings.*

After the director of development had worked for the college about two years, a newly hired vice president stated at a meeting that he perceived her position to be a "senior major gift officer" and not director of development. A month later, the acting vice president of development and alumni relations gave the director a negative performance evaluation. The college soon demoted her to a position designated "senior development officer of major gifts." The director's next performance evaluation was critical of her performance and a month later, the college discharged her. The director sued the college in a federal district court for negligently inflicting emotional distress, among other claims. The college moved for dismissal of the emotional distress claim.

The court stated that the time period identified by the director as the basis for her emotional distress claim involved routine employment matters such as job performance evaluations, work assignments, job transfers and title transfers. While these actions may have played a part in the employment action, they did not occur during a "termination process." **A claim for negligent infliction of emotional distress must be based on conduct during the termination itself, not during the time leading up to it.** Since the employee offered insufficient evidence of negligent conduct by the university at a relevant time, the court dismissed the case. *Stitt v. Connecticut College*, No. Civ. A. 3:04 CV577 (CFD), 2005 WL 646218 (D. Conn. 2005).

◆   *The Supreme Court of Iowa held that opposition to a co-worker's discharge was not "protected activity."*

Drake University investigated a security officer for an arrest he made during the annual Drake Relays. The officer was placed on desk duty for three months, then discharged. A university shift sergeant defended the officer's actions and offered to testify on his behalf. The university asked the sergeant to stop discussing the incident with the press, but he continued to talk openly about it. The university then demoted him one rank, resulting in a pay cut. The sergeant resigned and sued the university in an Iowa court, asserting he was constructively discharged for engaging in protected activity. The court awarded the university summary judgment. The state appeals court affirmed.

The state supreme court held that to succeed in a wrongful discharge claim, the sergeant had to establish that his advocacy established a clearly defined public policy that would be undermined by his termination. He would also have to show his termination resulted from his participation in a protected activity and for no other reason. **The court found that opposing a co-worker's wrongful termination was not a "protected activity" under state law.** While public policy protected employees offering truthful testimony at legal proceedings, there was no indication the discharged officer had intended to sue the university. The court affirmed the judgment for the university. *Shoop v. Drake Univ.*, 672 N.W.2d 335 (Iowa 2003).

◆   *An Illinois court denied a professor's claims against a university for defamation, breach of contract and invasion of privacy.*

A divinity school was considering an associate professor for tenure when the administration received complaints about the way he ran his classes. A tenure committee conducted an investigation and learned that students considered him rude and abrasive. They reported he deviated from class topics and was unprofessional. School administrators spoke with the professor several times about these concerns and warned him that failure to change his conduct would result in termination. The professor denied the charges, and the school suspended him. He sued the school for defamation and breach of contract. The court dismissed the defamation claim and characterized the termination of his contract as a "buy-out," since it paid the professor in full. The professor appealed. The Appellate Court of Illinois rejected contract claims relating to the university handbook, which allowed the interviewing of students about classroom decorum. **The university did not breach his contract by failing to renew it after extending the tenure review process.** Under the faculty constitution, notice of termination was to be given by March 1 of the year, except in cases of moral turpitude. Since the professor did not receive notice by this deadline, he argued colleagues and students would infer he was fired on grounds of moral turpitude. The court rejected his claim and affirmed the judgment. The invasion of privacy claim failed because the professor did not show the university put him in a false light. *Green v. Trinity Int'l Univ.*, 801 N.E.2d 1208 (Ill. App. Ct. 2003).

◆ *A Florida District Court of Appeal held a whistleblower complaint was properly dismissed by the state human relations commission.*

After being discharged, a community college provost filed a complaint with the Florida Commission on Human Relations, accusing college trustees of violating the state whistleblower act. The commission dismissed her complaint because the college was not a "state agency" under state law. The provost appealed to a state district court of appeal. The court found the list of statutory terms for the definition of "state agency" included any official, officer, commission, board or department of the executive branch of state government. For the provost to establish the commission's jurisdiction to investigate her claim, she would have to show the board of trustees was part of the executive branch. However, state law described community colleges as state political subdivisions and emphasized the difference between political subdivisions and state agencies. **As the board of trustees was not a board of the executive branch of state government, the commission lacked jurisdiction to investigate the complaint.** *Caldwell v. Board of Trustees Broward Community College,* 858 So.2d 1199 (Fla. Dist. Ct. App. 2003).

◆ *A university employee could not show that he was fired because of complaints he made about co-workers stealing.*

A receiving clerk in the maintenance department at a Florida university complained to university security officers that his supervisor and co-workers were stealing university property. He was then allegedly subjected to certain retaliatory actions, including a glued office lock, a smoke-filled office, and interference with his radio transmissions. He later asked to take a leave, but his request was rejected when the university determined that he had already exhausted his leave time. He took the time off anyway and was fired. **He sued the university for retaliation under the state whistleblower act**, and a state court ruled against him. The Florida District Court of Appeal affirmed. Here, even if the employee's complaint about stealing was protected speech, he failed to show a causal connection between his complaint and his firing. For being absent without leave, he would have been fired regardless of the complaint. Also, as for the retaliatory actions, he was unable to prove that management was either implicated in the attacks or that it condoned them. *Amador v. Florida Board of Regents*, 830 So.2d 120 (Fla. Dist. Ct. App. 2002).

# CHAPTER SIX

## Employment Practices and Labor Relations

## I. PRIVACY RIGHTS

*The Fourth Amendment standard of reasonableness applies to searches of public employees as well as their workspaces, offices and computers. Courts reviewing public employee privacy cases typically balance the employee's reasonable expectations of privacy against the government employer's interest in supervision, control and workplace efficiency.*

*In O'Connor v. Ortega, 480 U.S. 709 (1987), the U.S. Supreme Court held public employees have a reasonable expectation of privacy in their personal workspaces, desks and file cabinets. Acceptable use policies and other workplace rules place limits on reasonable privacy expectations.*

*In* City of Ontario, California v. Quon, *this chapter, the U.S. Supreme Court cautioned courts against departing from established law when interpreting privacy rights in electronic forums such as texting. It said "the judiciary risks error by elaborating too fully on the Fourth Amendment implications of emerging technology before its role in society has become clear."* **A person's constitutional right to privacy is violated only if an alleged invasion occurs where the person has a reasonable expectation of privacy.**

## A.  Electronic Data and Communications

◆   *A California city did not violate a police officer's rights by reviewing text messages on his department-owned pager to find the cause of excess charges.*

A California police department informed employees that they had "no expectation of privacy or confidentiality when using" department-owned pagers capable of sending and receiving text messages. An officer's monthly pager usage soon exceeded his text message character allotment under the department's contract with the pager service. To find out why, a supervisor investigated. He found many messages on the officer's pager were not work-related and some were sexually explicit. The officer sued the department for Fourth Amendment violations. The U.S. Supreme Court agreed to review the case and noted that a public employer's search was reasonable if justified at its inception and not excessively intrusive in light of the reasons for the search.

The Court determined that the search in this case was justified at its inception, as there were reasonable grounds for investigating pager use. The supervisor had ordered the search to see if the character limit on pagers was sufficient for department needs. As this was a legitimate, work-related reason, the Court found no Fourth Amendment violation. Review of the text messages was not excessively intrusive. Supervisors took care to investigate only pager usage that took place during work hours. **The officer and others had received no assurances of privacy and had limited privacy expectations.** The text-message search did not violate the officer's rights or the rights of those with whom he communicated. The Court noted "the judiciary risks error by elaborating too fully on the Fourth Amendment implications of emerging technology before its role in society has become clear." *City of Ontario, California v. Quon*, 130 S.Ct. 2619, 177 L.Ed.2d 216 (U.S. 2010).

◆   *Officials properly seized an Oklahoma university department head's personal laptop computer as part of a child pornography investigation.*

The case involved a department head at Oklahoma State University (OSU). Another OSU employee reported finding child pornography in a box belonging to the department head. A university dean and associate dean seized the box and turned it over to university police. After legal counsel was consulted, a decision was made to seize the desktop computer in the department head's office. Two members of the university's computer information services security office went to the office and saw a laptop computer on a table near his desk.

The security specialists took the hard drive from the desktop computer and also seized the laptop. The contents were retained by the university's police department. The department head sued university officials, including one of the security specialists, in a federal district court. He claimed the seizure violated the Fourth Amendment. The court relied heavily on the U.S. Supreme Court's ruling in *O'Connor v. Ortega*, this chapter. **It found the search was reasonable, as the purpose was to investigate suspected misconduct involving the possibility that child pornography was being stored on computers located in an on-campus office.** The personal laptop computer was open and running when the security specialists entered the department head's office. The laptop was showing an email program that was supported by the university as well as spreadsheets that looked like they contained university records. Under these circumstances, the search was justified at its inception, and as its scope was reasonable, there was no Fourth Amendment violation. *Soderstrand v. State of Oklahoma*, 463 F.Supp.2d 1308 (W.D. Okla. 2006).

◆ *The Tennessee Court of Appeals applied Florida decisions in finding public school Internet records and emails were not open to public inspection.*

A Tennessee citizen made a written request to a county education board to view and inspect digital records of Internet activity, including emails sent and received, websites visited, and the identity of Internet service providers used during school hours or stored on school-owned computers. A trial court judge reviewed the requested records privately and found they were not accessible under the state Public Records Act (PRA). The citizen appealed to the Court of Appeals of Tennessee, asserting the digital records or documents were open to public inspection because they had been made during business hours or were stored on the school's computers. **The court found the PRA's clear purpose favored the disclosure of public records.** The PRA defined "public record" to include documents, papers, electronic data processing files and other material "made or received pursuant to law or ordinance or in connection with the transaction of official business by any governmental agency." The PRA did not limit access to records based on the time a record was created or the place the record was produced or stored. The trial court judge had properly inspected documents in private to decide if they were "made or received pursuant to law or ordinance or in connection with the transaction of official business."

**The Supreme Court of Florida has rejected arguments that placement of a document in a public employee's file made the document a "public record."** The Tennessee PRA definition of "public records" nearly matches the definition used in Florida Law. The court held that while it was not bound by Florida public records cases, it found them well-reasoned and applicable. The trial court did not commit error in privately reviewing the records, and the judgment was affirmed. *Brennan v. Giles County Board of Educ.*, No. M2004-00998-COA-R3-CV, 2005 WL 1996625 (Tenn. Ct. App. 2005).

◆ *A Florida District Court of Appeal held personal email fell outside the current definition of public records.*

The case involved a newspaper's request for emails sent from or received by municipal employees on government-owned computers. The court of appeal held personal email was not "made or received pursuant to law or ordinance." **Although digital in nature, "there was little to distinguish a personal email from personal letters delivered to public employees through a government**

**post office box and stored in a government-owned desk.**" The court noted the state supreme court has held "only materials prepared 'with the intent of perpetuating and formalizing knowledge' fit the definition of a public record." The court denied a publisher's request to compel a municipality to release all email sent from or received by two employees on their government-owned computers. *Times Publishing Co. v. City of Clearwater*, 830 So.2d 844 (Fla. Dist. Ct. App. 2002).

◆ *The Second Circuit upheld discipline against a New York state employee for downloading personal tax programs on the state-owned computer he used.*

The state had a policy prohibiting use of state equipment for personal business. The employee came under suspicion of neglecting his duties, and the state authorized an investigation of his computer usage. A list of file names revealed non-standard software was loaded on the computer, and additional searches determined the employee loaded a personal tax preparation program on it. The employee challenged the search of his computer in a federal district court. The court awarded pretrial judgment to the state. On appeal, the U.S. Court of Appeals, Second Circuit, found no Fourth Amendment violation. **Although the employee had a reasonable expectation of privacy in his office computer, the investigatory searches by the state were upheld as reasonable. The searches of his computer were reasonably related to the objectives of the search and not excessively intrusive** in light of the nature of his suspected misconduct. *Leventhal v. Knapek*, 266 F.3d 64 (2d Cir. 2001).

## B. Employee Search and Seizure

*Searches and seizures conducted by government employers implicate the Fourth Amendment. Because these searches are not carried out to enforce criminal laws, the courts consider them "administrative searches," which may be justified by the need to protect campus safety and ensure order.*

◆ *After being criminally prosecuted for stalking a colleague, a professor filed an unsuccessful civil action against the University of New Hampshire.*

The professor was arrested for disorderly conduct and stalking of a colleague who accused him of kicking a garbage can and repeatedly screaming at her. He was also accused of threatening another professor three times and was suspended and banned from campus after having a tantrum about a parking ticket. After the criminal charges were dismissed, the university reinstated the professor, but he filed a federal lawsuit against the university for violating his First, Fourth, Fifth, Ninth and Fourteenth Amendment rights. The court rejected the Fourth Amendment claim, as people can be arrested based on "violations" of a state criminal code. Moreover, the arrest was based on a valid warrant. A warrant is valid if it is supported by probable cause, which was satisfied in this case by a law enforcement officer's belief that the professor had threatened a colleague three times. According to the court, the standard of probable cause is not difficult to meet, requiring only a reasonable belief that a crime has been committed. Since the arrest warrant for stalking was supported by probable cause, there was no violation of the Fourth Amendment, and the university was entitled to judgment on the claims of false arrest and stalking.

On appeal, **the U.S. Court of Appeals, First Circuit, rejected the professor's claim that the arrest was an unreasonable seizure and found probable cause for the disorderly conduct and stalking charges**. The university did not violate his due process rights when it suspended him with pay, limited his campus access and removed him from his post as a department chair. Because the suspension was with pay, the professor was not deprived of a property interest that would require pre-suspension process. No defamation was found, as the university had good reason to warn faculty and staff to avoid the professor and tell police if they saw him on campus. As a result, the judgment for the university was affirmed in its entirety. *Collins v. Univ. of New Hampshire*, 664 F.3d 8 (1st Cir. 2011).

◆   *A court upheld a jury's decision to award $1.65 million to a professor whose laboratory contents were cleared out while he was at a conference.*

Upon accepting adjunct work at the University of the District of Columbia (UDC), the professor brought course materials, research data and lab equipment from another institution, where he had created materials and notes for 20 different courses. UDC had renewed his contract annually for several years when he accused it of reneging on a promise to grant him tenure. The professor filed a lawsuit against UDC. During settlement negotiations, UDC's provost told him to vacate his lab because the space was needed for other programs. After several delays, UDC hired a contractor to clear out the lab while the professor was at a conference. No inventory was made and the movers may have "thrown stuff out." The professor found that 90% of his belongings were gone and that some of his property had been thrown into trash dumpsters.

In a lawsuit against UDC, the professor sought compensation for course materials, research data, scientific instruments and other items. Since most of the property was unique or had no fair market value, he offered testimony from a collaborating biomedical engineering researcher and engineering professor to establish its value. He claimed that class materials he developed for 21 different courses had been taken, and that he lost at least 10 ongoing research projects. A jury found UDC liable for trespass, conversion and negligence and set the damages at $1.65 million. UDC sought a new trial, but the District of Columbia Court of Appeals held the valuation testimony was admissible, rejecting UDC's argument that the experts lacked subject-matter knowledge. **The experts had extensive research experience, were familiar with the professor's work, and articulated their methodologies for estimating damages.** As the jury had reasonably found UDC destroyed much of the professor's life work and ruined his career, the damage award was affirmed. *Trustees of the Univ. of the District of Columbia v. Vossoughi*, 963 A.2d 1162 (D.C. Ct. App. 2009).

◆   *The special needs of public employers justify allowing them to avoid the warrant and probable cause requirements of the Fourth Amendment.*

The U.S. Supreme Court held that the search of a public employee's office was reasonable when the measures adopted were reasonably related to the objectives of the search and not excessively intrusive in light of its purpose. The

Court held that workplace searches by government employers "should be judged by the standard of reasonableness under all the circumstances."

**The Court announced a case-by-case standard for evaluating employee privacy expectations, stating that a public employee's expectation of privacy in the workplace may be reduced by actual office practices, work procedures or rules.** Acceptable-use policies governing employee usage of computers and email are examples of such workplace procedures or rules. *O'Connor v. Ortega*, 480 U.S. 709, 107 S.Ct. 1492, 94 L.Ed.2d 714 (1987).

### C.  Video Surveillance

*A Texas federal district court recently held that video surveillance of areas in which an employee has a reasonable expectation of privacy constitutes a Fourth Amendment "search." Moreover, the court found that video monitoring of employees may be a particularly intrusive form of search that is "a very serious, some say Orwellian, invasion of privacy."*

◆   *Texas community college security officers made out a valid challenge to the placement of a hidden camera that recorded them changing clothes.*

Security officers learned that a contractor had put surveillance cameras in hidden areas such as in air vents, behind clocks, and in smoke detectors. They said some cameras could record audio, and that anyone who knew a camera's IP address could access it. The officers sued college officials for Fourth Amendment violations. College officials sought to dismiss the action, arguing the officers had no reasonable expectation of privacy in a room where they changed their clothes. The court rejected this argument. It found employees may have a reasonable expectation of privacy in an office, especially one that is routinely used as a locker room. Federal cases have established that **public employees have a reasonable expectation of privacy in an office against unexpected intrusions by their employers**. Video surveillance of areas in which one has a reasonable expectation of privacy constitutes a Fourth Amendment search, and video monitoring is a particularly intrusive form of search – one which the court called "a very serious, some say Orwellian, invasion of privacy." As case law provided college officials with fair warning that their conduct violated the law, they could not claim immunity, and the case would not be dismissed. *Jones v. Houston Community College System*, 816 F.Supp.2d 418 (S.D. Tex. 2011).

◆   *California officials were immune to invasion of privacy claims based on the videotaping of an employee's wedding and part of her honeymoon.*

A California teacher was married while she was on a disability leave. The School Insurance Program for Employees (SIPE) and her school district hired an investigator to surreptitiously attend her wedding and obtain videotape of her. The investigator went to the wedding and represented himself as a guest. He videotaped the ceremony, reception and the teacher with her husband on their honeymoon sunbathing. The teacher sued the district, SIPE and others in a state court for invasion of privacy and negligence. The court dismissed the case, and the teacher appealed. The state court of appeal held that **state law immunized public employees for injuries caused by instituting or prosecuting any judicial or administrative proceeding within the scope of their employment**, even if an employee acted maliciously. The court rejected the teacher's claim that SIPE and her district "intended to harass her." The investigation was an essential step to a judicial or administrative proceeding and was "cloaked in immunity." The investigation was within the scope of the investigator's employment. For this reason, the district and SIPE were entitled to immunity. *Richardson-Tunnell v. School Insurance Program for Employees (SIPE)*, 157 Cal.App.4th 1065, 69 Cal.Rptr.3d 176 (Cal. Ct. App. 2007).

◆    *A Massachusetts state college did not violate an employee's privacy rights by videotaping her without her knowledge.*

The college learned a former client had entered a building without permission after hours. Without informing the employee, the college installed a hidden security camera in the office in an attempt to record the former client. For three weeks, the employee went to a rear work area, unbuttoned her blouse and applied ointment to a severe sunburn. The area was under video surveillance, but no images of her were recorded. The employee learned about the videotaping and sued the college in a state court for violating her Fourth Amendment privacy rights.The court held the college had qualified immunity.

On appeal, **the Supreme Judicial Court of Massachusetts stated a person's constitutional right to privacy is violated only if an invasion of privacy occurs where a person has a reasonable expectation of privacy**. While the law recognizes some privacy interests in business premises, people cannot have a reasonable expectation of privacy in open places. The office was open to the public, and volunteers and employees could enter at any time. There was no absolute guarantee of privacy, even when the employee locked the front door. Despite her efforts to discreetly conduct personal and private acts in the office, the court held she had no objectively reasonable expectation of privacy there. Accordingly, the court affirmed the judgment for the college. *Nelson v. Salem State College*, 446 Mass. 525, 845 N.E.2d 338 (Mass. 2006).

### D.  Personnel Records

*State data privacy acts protect the confidentiality of public employee personnel files. Common law rules of defamation may also provide a basis for legal action against a school district or its officers for wrongful disclosure of private facts or erroneous factual statements.*

### 1.  Media Access

◆    *A Pennsylvania newspaper and reporter had a right to see current and past salary information for certain employees of a state university.*

The reporter asked the State Employees' Retirement System (SERS) for salary information on state university employees. The state right-to-know act provides that "public records" kept by a government agency are accessible for inspection. A "public record" is "any account, voucher or contract dealing with the receipt or disbursement of funds by an agency." But any record or document, which would prejudice or impair a person's reputation or personal security, is not considered a public record. Before SERS responded to the request, it notified the university. The university and employees claimed the salary information was private and protected from release by the Constitution. The State Employees' Retirement Board granted the request, finding the information was a public record. The case reached the Supreme Court of Pennsylvania, which held it was proper to disclose the requested information under the state's right-to-know act. The SERS' fiduciary duties extended to investment matters but were not applicable to requests for salary information.

The court rejected the argument that disclosure was barred by the federal Gramm-Leach-Bliley Act, which protects the privacy of consumer information held by financial services industry institutions. Finally, the court rejected the employees' argument that disclosure would violate their right to privacy. **Although a privacy exception in the right-to-know law excused disclosure that would "prejudice or [impair] a person's reputation or personal security," the exception did not apply because the employees' privacy rights did not outweigh the public interest** in information about the disbursement of state funds. *Pennsylvania State Univ. v. State Employees' Retirement Board*, 594 Pa. 244, 935 A.2d 530 (Pa. 2007).

◆ *The private consideration of applicants for a university president violated the Minnesota Open Meetings Law and Government Data Practices Act.*

The University of Minnesota Board of Regents searched for a new president. Some applicants requested anonymity, and the board voted to screen them privately. The board denied information requests by media organizations about unsuccessful candidates. The organizations sued the board in the state court system for an order forcing disclosure of the information and enjoining the university from holding closed meetings. The court held for the media, and the board appealed. The state court of appeals noted that **the government data privacy act made public all personnel data on current and former applicants for employment by a statewide agency**. The names of applicants were considered "private data," except for finalists. Since the university was a statewide agency, and because the candidates were deemed "finalists," the court held the data practices act applied to procedures for selecting a university president. The only exception to the open meetings law applied to disciplinary proceedings and did not apply in this case. Accordingly, the court affirmed the decision to grant the media organizations' motion. *Star Tribune Co. v. Univ. of Minnesota*, 667 N.W.2d 447 (Minn. Ct. App. 2003).

### 2. Disclosure to Third Parties

◆ *California State University (CSU) trustees did not violate the state open meetings act by discussing a former chancellor's status in a closed session.*

A former CSU chancellor wanted to return to CSU as a trustee professor. Anticipating his return would result in publicity, he scheduled a closed session of the board of trustees. At the meeting, the board approved his return as a trustee professor. The president of the union representing faculty members sued the board under the state open meetings act, claiming the subject matter required a public session, and seeking an order to disclose what happened in the session. A state superior court rejected the action, and the union appealed.

The Court of Appeal of California held **an open meetings act exception applied to meetings held to consider the appointment, employment, evaluation of performance, or dismissal of a public employee**. The court held that disclosure in this case would run counter to the policy of shielding employees from unwarranted embarrassment and publicity. The board simply wanted to discuss the former chancellor's vested right to return as a professor and to address any questions. As the superior court did not commit error, the judgment was affirmed. *Travis v. Board of Trustees of California State Univ.*, 161 Cal.App.4th 335, 73 Cal.Rptr.3d 854 (Cal. Ct. App. 2008).

◆ *The Family Educational Rights and Privacy Act (FERPA) did not prevent an Ohio community college from disclosing prior complaints against an instructor accused of sexually harassing a student.*

In a federal district court action against the college, it was claimed that an instructor's supervisor knew of past misconduct and that the college and supervisor failed to take adequate steps to eliminate the risk he posed. During pretrial activity, the student sought rosters from classes taught by the instructor for the four years prior to the harassment she claimed. She also sought "every document relevant to any student complaint/concern" about the instructor. The college denied the requested information, arguing it could not be disclosed under FERPA. The court disagreed, finding some prior student complaints could be relevant. Complaints that were similar to the student's would support charges that the college and supervisor were aware of prior misconduct. The court concluded that the request should be limited to prior complaints of alleged sexual harassment. **There was insufficient evidence to show that class rosters were relevant to the student's claims**, and FERPA did not bar the request for prior student complaints relating to alleged sexual harassment. *Briggs v. Board of Trustees Columbus State Community College*, No. 2:08-CV-644, 2009 WL 2047899 (S.D. Ohio 7/8/09).

◆ *Michigan law permitted a public university to decline disclosing a record containing personal information, if disclosure would be a privacy invasion.*

The Michigan Federation of Teachers submitted a Freedom of Information Act (FOIA) request to the University of Michigan (UM) for employee names, home addresses, home phone numbers, job titles, pay rates, and work contact information. UM provided most of the information, including home addresses and phone numbers for about 21,000 employees who had given permission to publish this information in a staff and faculty directory. As to the remaining 16,406 employees, UM denied the request on privacy grounds. The Michigan Federation of Teachers and School Related Personnel sued UM in a state court, seeking the remaining addresses and phone numbers. The court held employee home addresses and phone numbers were personal information and not likely to contribute to the public's understanding of how the government works.

The case reached the Supreme Court of Michigan, which explained that **public entities may refuse to disclose a public record, if the record includes**

**information of a personal nature and disclosure "would constitute a clearly unwarranted invasion of an individual's privacy."** The court expanded the definition of "information of a personal nature" to include private or confidential information. Employee home addresses and phone numbers were clearly of a private and confidential nature. Disclosure of this information could subject employees to potential abuses, such as having it used for marketing purposes. Disclosure could also place employees in physical danger if their information fell into the wrong hands. The court held disclosure was unwarranted because it would reveal little or nothing about the conduct of the university and would do nothing to advance the public policy behind the FOIA. *Michigan Federation of Teachers and School Related Personnel v. Univ. of Michigan*, 481 Mich. 657, 753 N.W.2d 28 (Mich. 2008).

## II.  LABOR RELATIONS

*The National Labor Relations Act (NLRA), as amended by the Labor Management Relations Act (LMRA), 29 U.S.C. § 141, et seq., governs unionization and collective bargaining matters in the private sector, including private education. States are also subject to the dictates of the act. The NLRA was passed to protect the rights of employees to organize, or to choose not to organize, and to ensure that commerce is not interrupted by labor disputes. Managerial employees are unprotected by the NLRA.*

### A.  Appropriate Bargaining Units

◆ *The Supreme Court held a public university could require faculty to emphasize undergraduate instruction without bargaining over the new rule.*

The Ohio legislature passed a statute requiring state universities to adopt faculty workload policies and made them an inappropriate subject for collective bargaining. The law was enacted to address the decline in the amount of time faculty spent teaching, as opposed to time spent on research. Any university policy prevailed over the contrary provisions of collective bargaining agreements. One university adopted a workload policy pursuant to the law and notified the collective bargaining agent that it would not bargain over the policy. As a result, the professors' union filed a state court action, seeking an order that the statute violated public employee equal protection rights.

The Supreme Court of Ohio struck down the statute, finding the collective bargaining exemption was not rationally related to the state's interest of encouraging public university professors to spend less time researching at the expense of undergraduate teaching. The U.S. Supreme Court accepted the university's appeal and held that the state supreme court had not applied the correct standard of review under the Equal Protection Clause. In Equal Protection Clause cases that do not involve fundamental rights or suspect classifications, there need only be a rational relationship between disparity of treatment and some legitimate government purpose. In this case, the disputed statute met the rational relationship standard. Ohio could reasonably conclude that the policy would be undercut if it were subjected to collective bargaining. **The state legislature could properly determine that collective bargaining**

**would interfere with the legitimate goal of achieving uniformity in faculty workloads.** The Ohio Supreme Court decision was reversed and remanded. *Cent. State Univ. v. American Ass'n of Univ. Professors, Cent. State Univ. Chapter,* 526 U.S. 124, 119 S.Ct. 1162, 143 L.Ed.2d 227 (1999).

◆ *An exclusive bargaining representative should have the sole voice in discussing employment-related matters with the employer.*

Minnesota Community College faculty members brought suit against the State Board for Community Colleges, claiming a state statute requiring public employers to engage in official exchanges of views only with their professional employees' exclusive representatives on certain policy questions violated their speech rights. Under the statute, public employers were required to bargain only with the employees' exclusive bargaining representative. The statute gave professional employees, such as college faculty members, the right to "meet and confer" with the employer on matters outside the scope of the collective bargaining agreement. The faculty members objected to the "meet and confer" provision, saying that rights of professional employees within the bargaining unit who were not members of the exclusive representative were violated.

The Supreme Court upheld the "meet and confer" provision. **There was no constitutional right to force public employers to listen to member views.** The fact that an academic setting was involved did not give them special constitutional rights to a voice in employer policymaking decisions. Further, the state had a legitimate interest in ensuring that a public employer heard one voice presenting the majority view of professional employees on employment-related policy questions. *Minnesota Community College Ass'n v. Knight,* 465 U.S. 271, 104 S.Ct. 1058, 79 L.Ed.2d 299 (1984).

◆ *In the following unique circumstances, faculty members at a private educational institution could be considered managerial employees.*

Yeshiva University's faculty association petitioned the National Labor Relations Board (NLRB) for certification as their bargaining agent. The NLRB granted certification, but Yeshiva refused to bargain, claiming faculty members were "managerial" and exempt from NLRA coverage. The case reached the Supreme Court, which noted the high degree of control over academic practices exercised by Yeshiva's faculty. Faculty members exercised authority which in any other context would be managerial. They determined teaching methods, grading policies, and the university's admission, graduation and matriculation standards. The Court held schools where faculty do not exercise binding managerial discretion do not fall within the scope of the managerial employee exclusion. **The Court noted that its decision applied only to schools that were "like Yeshiva," not to those where the faculty exercised less control.** *NLRB v. Yeshiva Univ.,* 444 U.S. 672, 100 S.Ct. 856, 63 L.Ed.2d 115 (1980).

◆ *A Michigan court upheld a determination by the State Employment Relations Commission to deny a petition to merge two bargaining units.*

Kendall College of Art and Design is a sub-unit of Ferris State University that retains its academic governance and operates autonomously. The Ferris Faculty Association, which represented full-time faculty members at the university, petitioned to add the Kendall bargaining unit to its bargaining unit.

The Kendall unit was composed of full-time and part-time faculty members.

The Michigan Employment Relations Commission denied the petition, and the association appealed. The Court of Appeals of Michigan explained a commission's determination of appropriate bargaining units was factual and could not be disturbed unless there was a lack of competent, material, and substantial evidence. In reaching its decision, the commission focused on Kendall's academic autonomy from the university and the differences between the two educational institutions. The court rejected the association's argument that the commission erred in considering the bargaining history of the Kendall union. **Bargaining history is a relevant factor in considering whether a bargaining unit is appropriate.** The commission acknowledged the need "to avoid fractionalization or multiplicity of bargaining units." As the Kendall bargaining unit served its members well, it was an appropriate bargaining unit. The commission's decision was affirmed. *Ferris Faculty Ass'n v. Ferris State Univ.*, No. 243885, 2004 WL 144671 (Mich. Ct. App. 2004).

◆ *A District of Columbia court returned an NLRB decision recognizing a bargaining unit for college faculty members to the NLRB.*

Approximately 60 full-time faculty members at LeMoyne-Owen College attempted to form a collective bargaining unit. The college denied the request because it considered them managerial employees who were exempt from NLRA coverage. The faculty petitioned the NLRB for recognition as a bargaining unit. The college opposed the petition, citing the Supreme Court's decision in *NLRB v. Yeshiva Univ.*, above, as controlling precedent. The NLRB regional director found the college's faculty were not managerial employees and certified the bargaining unit. The college sought review, arguing the regional director deviated from *Yeshiva* and other precedents. The NLRB found the college committed an unfair labor practice when it refused to bargain with the new bargaining unit. The college petitioned for review of the NLRB's order. The District of Columbia Circuit Court returned the case to the NLRB. While deference is generally afforded to the NLRB's authority to certify bargaining units, **the decision in this case departed from precedent without explanation**. The college made a reasoned argument based on the *Yeshiva* case, and the regional director did not explain why the college's argument should be rejected. *LeMoyne-Owen College v. NLRB*, 357 F.3d 55 (D.C. Cir. 2004).

◆ *The Second Circuit refused to enforce an NLRB order requiring a New York college to bargain with a union because supervisors belonged to the union.*

The Security Department Membership (SDM) is the organization certified by the NLRB to represent Quinnipiac College's security personnel in collective bargaining. Quinnipiac refused to bargain with SDM, maintaining the organization was improperly certified because it included supervisors, who are excluded from collective bargaining under the NLRA. The NLRB conducted a hearing, but held the shift supervisors were not "supervisors" under the act and ordered Quinnipiac to bargain with SDM. The college refused. The NLRB petitioned the U.S. Court of Appeals, Second Circuit to enforce the order.

**The NLRA defines "supervisor" as an employee who has the authority to hire, transfer, suspend, lay off, recall, promote, discharge, assign, reward, discipline or responsibly direct other employees, or address**

**grievances.** According to the Second Circuit, Quinnipiac's shift supervisors made assignment decisions based on their own expertise and experience, despite the existence of college procedures. Shift supervisors also disciplined employees. Although security directors had to review any disciplinary procedures taken by the shift supervisors, they still amounted to a supervisor's duty. Lastly, the shift supervisors responsibly directed other security employees. In declining to enforce the NLRB's order, the Second Circuit remanded the matter, with the suggestion that the board review the membership of SDM and consider eliminating the shift supervisors from the bargaining unit. *NLRB v. Quinnipiac College*, 256 F.3d 68 (2d Cir. 2001).

◆  *A state labor relations board used incorrect tests to determine whether two employees were "confidential employees" who were ineligible for the union.*

A union sought to represent all classified and specialist employees at an Illinois college. In the representation election, the union won by a single vote. The college challenged the result, asserting that two of the employees should not have been allowed to vote because they were "confidential employees" under the state labor relations act. One was a secretary; the other was a research associate – both reported to an assistant vice president for administrative affairs. An administrative law judge determined that the employees were confidential employees, and the state labor relations board upheld that decision.

The Appellate Court of Illinois reversed and remanded the case, finding that the board used the wrong tests to determine whether the employees were "confidential." Here, **although the college asserted that the employees were going to be performing duties related to the collective bargaining process, they had not yet done so**. Thus, the board should have determined whether there was a reasonable expectation that future job duties would satisfy the definition of a confidential position. *One Equal Voice v. Illinois Educ. Labor Relations Board*, 777 N.E.2d 648 (Ill. App. Ct. 2002).

## B.  Agency Fees

*"Agency-shop agreements" entitle unions to charge "agency fees" to employees who are not union members, but who enjoy the representation of unions.*

◆  *The U.S. Supreme Court upheld a Washington law requiring public employee unions to obtain affirmative authorization from nonmember employees before using agency fees for election-related purposes.*

Washington law permits public employee unions to charge nonmembers who are in the collective bargaining unit an "agency fee" that is equivalent to full union membership dues. State voters approved an initiative that prohibited unions from spending the agency fees collected from union nonmembers unless the expenditure was "affirmatively authorized by the individual" nonmember. The initiative became Section 760 of the Fair Campaign Practices Act.

The Washington Education Association (WEA) faced separate state court actions claiming it used nonmember agency fees for election-related purposes without the affirmative authorization of union nonmembers. The state supreme court held this authorization requirement violated the First Amendment. On appeal, the U.S. Supreme Court held *Abood* **and later decisions did not require public sector unions to obtain affirmative consent before spending nonmember agency fees for purposes unrelated to collective bargaining**. Section 760 was a "modest limitation" on the extraordinary power of a private union over public employees to prohibit the use of agency fees for election-related purposes. This did not violate the First Amendment, and it would be constitutional for the state to eliminate agency fees. The Court vacated the state court decision, finding Section 760 was a constitutional condition that presented no realistic threat of official suppression of ideas. *Davenport v. Washington Educ. Ass'n*, 551 U.S. 177, 127 S.Ct. 2372, 168 L.Ed.2d 71 (2007).

◆ *In order to justify agency fees, the activities for which the fees are collected must be germane to collective bargaining activity, be justified by the government's interest in labor peace (and the avoidance of free riders), and present only an insignificant burden on employee speech.*

The exclusive bargaining representative of the faculty at a state college in Michigan entered into an agency-shop arrangement with the college requiring nonunion bargaining unit employees to pay a service or agency fee equivalent to a union member's dues. Employees who objected to particular uses by the unions of their service fee brought suit under 42 U.S.C. § 1983, claiming that using the fees for purposes other than negotiating and administering the collective bargaining agreement violated their First and Fourteenth Amendment rights. A federal district court held that certain collective bargaining expenses were chargeable to the dissenting employees. The U.S. Court of Appeals affirmed, and the U.S. Supreme Court granted certiorari.

The Court first noted that chargeable activities must be "germane" to collective bargaining activity and be justified by the policy interest of avoiding "free riders" who benefit from union efforts without paying for union services. It then stated that **the local union could charge the objecting employees for their *pro rata* share of costs associated with chargeable activities of its state and national affiliates, even if those activities did not directly benefit the local bargaining unit**. The local could even charge the dissenters for expenses incident to preparation for a strike, which would be illegal under Michigan law. However, lobbying activities and public relations efforts were not chargeable to the objecting employees. The Court affirmed in part and reversed in part the lower courts' decisions and remanded the case. *Lehnert v. Ferris Faculty Ass'n*, 500 U.S. 507, 111 S.Ct. 1950, 114 L.Ed.2d 572 (1991).

◆ *A union's objection procedures for challenging nonmembers' dues were constitutional.*

Two University of Alaska professors challenged their union's procedures for calculating nonmember dues. Under the collective bargaining agreement, if they declined union membership, they had a choice of either objecting to the use of their dues for unrelated union activities (and paying a reduced agency fee) or requesting arbitration to determine if the nonmember fee was accurate. Under the second option, the arbitrator had the option of raising the amount. A federal court ruled that the union's procedure was constitutional, and the Ninth Circuit Court of Appeals affirmed. Here, the procedures complied with the requirements set forth by the U.S. Supreme Court in *Chicago Teachers Union v. Hudson*, 475 U.S. 292 (1986). **The professors received an adequate explanation of the basis for calculating the agency fee, and they were provided with a reasonably prompt opportunity to challenge the amount of the fee before an impartial decisionmaker.** *Carlson v. United Academics-AAUP/AFT/APEA AFL-CIO*, 265 F.3d 778 (9th Cir. 2001).

◆ *An Illinois local failed to provide adequate procedural protections to non-bargaining unit members who objected to its nonrepresentational activities.*

In federal court, a group of non-bargaining unit members, employed by a university as clerical employees, filed a class action suit against the union. The nonmembers asserted that the union's fair share fee collection procedure failed to provide sufficient safeguards, thereby violating the First and Fourteenth Amendments. The court interpreted the union's response as a pretrial judgment motion and ruled in favor of the union. The employees appealed.

The Seventh Circuit reversed the judgment. Pursuant to the Illinois Educational Labor Relations Act (IELRA), the amount of fair share fees "can neither exceed union dues nor include any costs related to supporting candidates for political office." In *Chicago Teachers Union v. Hudson*, 475 U.S. 292 (1986), the U.S. Supreme Court required a union to satisfy the following three prongs in collecting these fees: 1) provide "an adequate explanation of the basis for the fee"; 2) provide the nonmember with a reasonable opportunity to protest the fee amount; and 3) establish "an escrow account for the amounts in dispute." Here, the union had the university collect 100% of union dues from both members and nonmembers, even though the fair share fee calculated for two of the disputed years amounted to about 85% of full dues. When an objection was filed, the nonmember fees were then held in an escrow account, which could not be accessed by the union. **The collection of fees, based on an advance reduction approach, was not as problematic as the dispute resolution procedure.** Under the IELRA, objectors were deprived of 15% of their funds for a year, a portion of which was not even being disputed. In addition, the fee objections had to be renewed annually. These burdens violated the *Hudson* test. *Tavernor v. Illinois Federation of Teachers*, 226 F.3d 842 (7th Cir. 2000).

◆ *Massachusetts' highest court held expenses related to a two-day strike by university faculty were not germane to collective bargaining.*

Public school teachers and state university instructors sued the Massachusetts Teachers Association (MTA) for charging them agency fees for activities the teachers claimed were not part of doing business as a bargaining representative. The state Labor Relations Commission found the MTA had demanded $26.77 in excess fees from each nonunion member. The Supreme Judicial Court of Massachusetts found most of the MTA's accounting expenses were chargeable. **The union president and vice president's salaries were overhead and therefore chargeable in proportion to the union's overall chargeable activities.** Discussions the union had about a statewide strike to publicize the condition of public education funding were not chargeable.

Expenses related to days when faculty at the University of Massachusetts at Amherst withheld services to protest the lack of funding for their collective bargaining agreement were also not chargeable, even though the university administration approved of and participated in the protest. Because the faculty had withheld services, the two-day action was a strike, and the expenses incidental to it were not chargeable. Nor were the costs of flyers distributed during commencement exercises at the University of Massachusetts at Boston chargeable to nonunion members. However, expenses related to an article that appeared in a union magazine providing pointers on how to communicate during a strike or some other unusual event were chargeable. *Belhumeur v. Labor Relations Comm'n*, 432 Mass. 458, 735 N.E.2d 860 (Mass. 2000).

## C.  Collective Bargaining

*In* NLRB v. Catholic Bishop of Chicago, *this chapter, the U.S. Supreme Court held the First Amendment prevents inquiry by the National Labor Relations Board (NLRB) into a school's religious mission.*

◆   *A collective bargaining agreement didn't give an arbitrator the authority to grant a professor tenure, so a Pennsylvania court reversed the decision.*
Under a CBA, the professor could apply for tenure during her fifth year. When she submitted her application, a department tenure committee and a university tenure committee recommended that tenure be granted. But the university president denied the professor's application, citing a lack of scholarly growth. The professor appealed. An arbitrator concluded the president violated the CBA by denying the tenure application. As a remedy, the arbitrator granted tenure retroactively and ordered the university to reimburse the professor for any losses she sustained. The university sought review, challenging arbitrator's authority to award tenure as a remedy. It said the CBA did not permit the arbitrator to award tenure and that the arbitrator impermissibly substituted her judgment for that of the university president. The court agreed because **the CBA vested the authority to award tenure solely with the university president**. The arbitrator could restore the professor's probationary status and allow her to reapply but couldn't grant tenure, the court concluded. The arbitrator exceeded her authority, so the court reversed the decision. *Edinboro Univ. of Pennsylvania v. Ass'n of Pennsylvania State College and Univ. Faculties*, 128 A.3d 322 (Pa. Commw. Ct. 2015).

◆   *As the NLRB had no jurisdiction over a church-affiliated Wisconsin college, it could not order the college to bargain with a faculty union.*
The NLRB ordered Carroll College to recognize and bargain with the collective bargaining agent of its faculty. The college appealed to the federal court system, asserting its religious environment and affiliation with the United Presbyterian Church placed it beyond NLRB jurisdiction under *NLRB v. Catholic Bishop of Chicago* and *Univ. of Great Falls v. NLRB*, this chapter. It also said faculty members were managerial employees who were not covered by the National Labor Relations Act. The case reached the U.S. Court of Appeals, District of Columbia Circuit, which stated that the First Amendment religion clauses preclude NLRB review of church-affiliated schools.
The court applied the three-part *Great Falls* analysis to determine whether

the college had a "substantial religious character" that exempted it from NLRB review. It found **the college held itself out to students, faculty and the community as providing a religious educational environment**. Second, the college was a nonprofit, and third, it was affiliated with the Presbyterian Church. The court found the college easily satisfied the *Great Falls* test. In assessing religious affiliation, it was unnecessary to show the college was sponsored or controlled by a church. Since the NLRB had no jurisdiction over the college, the NLRB could not order it to recognize and bargain with the union. *Carroll College v. NLRB*, 558 F.3d 568 (D.C. Cir. 2009).

◆ *A Kansas professor's refusal to hold office hours at a particular community college campus justified her discharge for insubordination.*

The college denied the professor's request for mileage reimbursement for her trips between a satellite campus in Leavenworth and its main campus in Kansas City. The disagreement escalated, and she filed a grievance over the college's decision to assign her to the main campus. College trustees denied the grievance but failed to issue a timely decision. The professor believed she was entitled to the relief requested in her grievance and insisted on having her office in Leavenworth, even though she was not assigned to teach any courses there.

A college provost ordered the professor to hold office hours on the Kansas City campus. Although her caseload included online instruction, the provost noted that a relevant master contract required her to hold five office hours per week on campus. When the professor resisted, she was suspended without pay. College trustees discharged the professor for insubordination. A hearing officer found the provost had the sole authority to set class schedules and assign office locations, and held the professor had been insubordinate. She appealed to the state court system, where the Court of Appeals of Kansas rejected her argument that the hearing officer's decision was unsupported. **The college provost had the authority to assign faculty to specific work locations.** The professor failed to show that work locations could be changed only with her consent. The master contract required faculty members who taught online courses to hold at least five office hours per week on campus. There was substantial evidence that the professor refused to comply with the provost's order and was insubordinate. As the record showed she acted in an antagonistic and unprofessional manner, the judgment was affirmed. *Heflin v. Kansas City Kansas Community College*, 43 Kan.App.2d 371, 224 P.3d 1201 (Kan. Ct. App. 2010).

◆ *A union's waiver of employee rights to negotiate an intellectual property policy survived the expiration of a collective bargaining agreement. For that reason, refusal to negotiate the policy was not an improper labor practice.*

A City University of New York (CUNY) policy addressed intellectual property developed by its employees. The policy was not the subject of bargaining between CUNY and the Professional Staff Congress (PSC), which represented CUNY employees. The parties' 1996-2000 collective bargaining agreement expired, and PSC demanded that the intellectual property policy be negotiated. CUNY asserted Article 2 of the expired agreement constituted a waiver by the union to negotiate particular items, including the policy. Article 2 authorized CUNY's board of trustees to alter existing bylaws or policies "respecting a term or condition of employment" after giving PSC notice and an opportunity to consult. PSC filed an improper practice charge with the state public employment relations board (PERB). The parties reached a new agreement covering 2000-2002, which carried forward Article 2 unchanged.

Just before expiration of the 2000-2002 agreement, PSC again sought to negotiate the intellectual property policy. An administrative law judge held CUNY committed an improper practice by refusing to negotiate the policy. The PERB held PSC waived its right to negotiate the intellectual property policy in Article 2. The case reached the Court of Appeals of New York, which held the resolution of improper practice charges was generally within the PERB's discretion. Article 2 granted CUNY the right to unilaterally alter bylaws and policies respecting terms or conditions of employment that did not conflict with the agreement. Article 2 explicitly referred to "terms and conditions of employment," and it was not confined to "management prerogatives." **The court held the intellectual property policy was squarely within the coverage of Article 2, since it was never a part of a collective bargaining agreement and did not conflict with any terms of the current agreement.** Civil Service Law Section 209-a(1)(e) required employers to continue all terms of an expired agreement while a new one was being negotiated. This enhanced the negotiating process by preserving the status quo pending a new agreement. As the PERB had correctly determined the status quo and found the Article 2 waiver remained in effect, the court reinstated its decision. *Professional Staff Congress-City Univ. of New York v. New York State Public Employment Relations Board*, 7 N.Y.3d 458, 857 N.E.2d 1108 (N.Y. 2006).

◆ *The D.C. Circuit adopted a test for determining whether a religious institution can exempt itself from NLRB jurisdiction for collective bargaining.*

The University of Great Falls is operated by a Roman Catholic religious order. It refused to recognize or bargain with the Montana Federation of Teachers. The university maintained that the NLRB lacked jurisdiction because it was a religiously run institution, and the Religious Freedom Restoration Act barred the NLRB from ordering it to engage in collective bargaining. The union petitioned the NLRB for relief, and a regional director held the NLRB had jurisdiction. The NLRB upheld that determination, and the university appealed.

The U.S. Court of Appeals, D.C. Circuit, stated that the NLRB had improperly examined the university's religious character. It adopted **a three-part test for determining whether an institution can avail itself of the exemption in *NLRB v. Catholic Bishop of Chicago***, see Chapter Four, Section I.B., where the Supreme Court held the NLRB did not have jurisdiction over religious institutions. Under this test, an institution must: 1) provide a religious educational environment and hold itself out as such, 2) be organized by a nonprofit, and 3) be "affiliated with, or owned, operated or controlled directly or indirectly, by either a recognized religious organization or with an entity, membership of which is determined, at least in part, with reference to religion." Here, the university easily passed that test. As a result, the NLRB did not have jurisdiction, and the university did not have to bargain with the union. *Univ. of Great Falls v. NLRB*, 278 F.3d 1335 (D.C. Cir. 2002).

◆ *A union could use a university's email system to contact members where the collective bargaining agreement did not prohibit it.*

The union representing Oregon University System employees negotiated a collective bargaining agreement that allowed union officers and stewards to "have access to electronic bulletin boards under specified conditions." The union then began using email to transmit information to its members' work computers. The university objected to this practice, claiming that the bargaining agreement did not allow the union to use email in that way. After two arbitrators determined that the university could prohibit union officials from using the email system, the Oregon Court of Appeals determined that the union's use of email neither violated the terms of the bargaining agreement nor breached its duty of good faith and fair dealing. **The bargaining agreement was silent with respect to the union's use of email.** Thus, there was no breach of contract and no bad faith. *Oregon Univ. System v. Oregon Public Employees Union, Local 503*, 60 P.3d 567 (Or. Ct. App. 2002).

◆ *Adjunct faculty members were allowed to join a union in New Hampshire.*

A labor association seeking to represent 147 adjunct faculty members at a New Hampshire state college petitioned for certification by the Public Employees Labor Relations Board (PELRB). The university system opposed the petition, arguing that adjunct faculty are temporary employees who are excluded from bargaining because of their temporary status. A hearing officer granted the petition, allowing instructors who were currently teaching, and those who had taught two of the last three semesters, to join the union. The PELRB upheld that decision, and the adjunct faculty voted for the union.

The case reached the Supreme Court of New Hampshire, which found that there is some expectation that adjunct faculty members will return annually – they are compensated for longevity. The court affirmed the PELRB's decision that **adjunct faculty members are not temporary employees**. Even though their contracts did not include an expectation of continued employment, that did not diminish the adjunct faculty members' **reasonable expectation of continued employment**. The fact that adjunct instructors taught one-third of the college's courses indicated that they were not just "last-minute" hires. The court remanded the case to consider who was eligible for union membership. The PELRB did not provide an explanation for why only adjuncts who were currently teaching or who had taught two of the last three semesters were eligible. *In re Univ. System of New Hampshire*, 795 A.2d 840 (N.H. 2002).

## D. Arbitration

◆ *A Michigan court held it was an arbitrator's job to interpret conflicting interpretations of a university faculty collective bargaining agreement (CBA).*

Central Michigan University (CMU) denied a faculty member tenure for two consecutive years. She filed grievances that were referred to arbitration. An arbitrator denied both grievances, finding the faculty member's submissions for publication did not satisfy CBA requirements. A state court judge agreed with the faculty member that the arbitrator had added to the CBA and changed its terms by reading in a quality requirement where none existed. The Court of

Appeals of Michigan held that courts reviewing arbitration decisions had authority only to determine if the arbitrator stayed within the boundaries of the CBA. The CBA in this case granted the arbitrator authority to decide promotion disputes and alleged breaches of the CBA. **The lower court was wrong to conclude the arbitrator acted outside his authority by considering the quality of the faculty member's work.** It was the arbitrator's job to decide between conflicting interpretations of the CBA and CMU's department bylaws, and as the arbitrator did not exceed his authority, the court upheld the denial of the tenure grievance. *Cent. Michigan Univ. Faculty Ass'n v. Cent. Michigan Univ.*, No. 293003, 2011 WL 475461 (Mich. Ct. App. 2/10/11).

◆   *Because a settlement voided an earlier pact to arbitrate any employment dispute, a coach could sue Duke University for defamation.*

In 2006, three Duke men's lacrosse team members were accused of rape. The head lacrosse coach resigned, and the parties executed a release to resolve any matters regarding his separation. The release declared an intent to cancel all earlier agreements between the parties but said nothing about arbitrating any future claims that might arise. Two years later, the coach sued Duke and a senior vice president in the state court system for defamation. Duke sought to force him to arbitrate the claims, asserting they were subject to an arbitration agreement in the university's employment policy. The court denied the request, and Duke appealed. The Court of Appeals of North Carolina found the release clearly rescinded all earlier agreements to arbitrate. **There was no doubt that the release stated the intent of both parties to cancel all earlier agreements, and it discharged their duties under previously existing contracts.** The coach was not bound to arbitrate his libel and slander claims and could proceed with his action. *Pressler v. Duke Univ.*, 685 S.E.2d 6 (N.C. Ct. App. 2009).

◆   *The Vermont State Colleges Federation did not unlawfully retaliate against a faculty member by declining to accommodate her scheduling request.*

The faculty member worked part time at a state college. The applicable collective bargaining agreement required the college to give priority to full-time faculty and administrators in scheduling matters. The faculty member filed a grievance when she was not assigned a schedule that accommodated her childcare and commuting needs. She later complained about a new schedule. The department decided not to change the new schedule, and she filed another grievance, this time for retaliation for her earlier grievance. A grievance board found the college was unlawfully motivated by the prior grievance. On appeal, the Supreme Court of Vermont found the faculty member did not present any direct evidence of a discriminatory motive. The court disagreed with the board's findings that the timing of the new schedule was suspicious, and that the college treated her less favorably than others. **The court said the faculty member presented no other evidence to infer the college retaliated because of her earlier grievance.** As the court found no basis to find the college had an unlawful motivation, the judgment was reversed. *Grievance of Rosenberg v. Vermont State Colleges*, 852 A.2d 599 (Vt. 2004).

## III. OVERTIME AND WAGE DISPUTES

*While wages are typically covered by contract, they may also be subject to the requirements of the Fair Labor Standards Act (FLSA) and state wage laws. Instructors are typically exempt from FLSA overtime coverage, as they are considered professional employees. The FLSA requires employers to pay covered workers the prevailing minimum wage and any earned overtime.*

◆ *A Pennsylvania professor who signed a Memorandum of Agreement after mediation to resolve his discrimination case could not later evade its terms.*

After suffering a stroke that limited his daily activities, the professor sought to teach online courses only. This request was rejected, and he sued the university in a federal court for disability discrimination. The parties agreed to mediation, which led to a Memorandum of Agreement (MOA) describing a settlement. The MOA set a formula for an estimated $35,000 in back pay, and the university agreed to cooperate with the professor's disability retirement application. The MOA called for a formal agreement and the professor's employment termination. When the formula was applied, it yielded less than $35,000. Although the university offered to pay the professor $35,000, he balked. The university sought a court order enforcing the MOA.

A federal court held the MOA was an enforceable contract. On appeal, the U.S. Court of Appeals, Third Circuit, explained that contract law applied to the question of whether the MOA was enforceable. The professor argued the MOA was not enforceable because it did not set forth the precise amount of back pay. But **the parties agreed to a formula to calculate back pay, and this was sufficient to create enforceability**. Rejecting the professor's argument that he was forced to sign the agreement, the court affirmed the judgment. *DeHainaut v. California Univ. of Pennsylvania*, 490 Fed.Appx. 420 (3d Cir. 2012).

◆ *An African-American professor and program director did not show that Ohio State University used discriminatory evaluation criteria when it denied him substantial wage increases over a three-year period.*

After being replaced as a program director of social work and enjoying no substantial pay raises for three consecutive years, the professor sued the university in a federal district court. He added a claim for retaliation based on his request for salary-related information, the fact that he had filed an administrative charge of discrimination and his opposition to a pledge declaring that social workers should not discriminate on the basis of sexual orientation. A federal court held for the university and its officials, and the case reached the U.S. Court of Appeals, Sixth Circuit. The court rejected the race discrimination claims, since the professor's replacement as program director was also African-American. With respect to the pay raises, he did not show he was treated differently than similarly situated faculty. **There was no evidence that the university used evaluation criteria that were different than criteria for similarly situated professors.** There was no merit to the professor's retaliation claims, as evidence showed he was removed because he did not develop an undergraduate honors program, a social justice minor or any new courses. The court affirmed the judgment for the university and officials. *Alexander v. Ohio State Univ. College of Social Work*, 429 Fed.Appx. 481 (6th Cir. 2011).

◆   *An Illinois court has found that using state financing to fund construction projects triggers the state's Prevailing Wage Act (PWA).*

A nonprofit corporation operated a Presbyterian ministry at the University of Illinois, Urbana-Champaign. It built a student housing unit at the university that was located on foundation property. The foundation partly financed the project with tax-free bonds issued through the Illinois Finance Authority. The Illinois Department of Labor determined the project was subject to the PWA, which imposes minimum wage requirements on "public work" construction projects. The department ordered the foundation to pay workers certain wages and a fine. The foundation responded by suing the labor department in a state court, asserting the PWA did not apply to the project. The court agreed with the foundation, and the case reached the Appellate Court of Illinois. **The court held "public works" included all projects financed with bonds issued under the Illinois Finance Authority Act.** The act's legislative history made it clear that lawmakers wanted the PWA to apply to entities that benefitted from public financing – even if the entity would not have otherwise been considered a "public body." As the PWA applied to the foundation's construction project, the court reversed the judgment and returned the case to the trial court for further proceedings. *McKinley Foundation at Univ. of Illinois v. Illinois Dep't of Labor*, 936 N.E.2d 708 (Ill. App. Ct. 2010).

◆   *West Virginia's Wage Payment and Collection Act (WPCA) does not protect public institutions through government immunity and does not require employees to exhaust administrative procedures before filing a lawsuit.*

An assistant physics professor became a tenure-track associate at West Virginia University at Parkersburg (WVU-P). He was denied tenure after six years of work because of falling enrollment in physics classes. The professor sued WVU-P in the state court system, asserting he was not paid under faculty overload contracts for performing extra work. In addition to seeking unpaid wages and attorneys' fees, he requested triple the amount of claimed wages under a WPCA liquidated damages provision. A state court held the case was barred by sovereign immunity and the failure to exhaust administrative remedies.

On appeal, the state supreme court of appeals held WPCA remedies were optional and permitted employees or the state labor commissioner to bring "any legal action necessary" to recover unpaid wages. Sovereign immunity did not bar the action. **The legislature intended the WPCA to protect wage claims by both private and public employees.** As the action was not barred, the court returned it to the trial court for further proceedings. *Beichler v. West Virginia Univ. at Parkersburg*, 700 S.E.2d 532 (W.Va. 2010).

◆   *A federal district court approved a class action lawsuit to address wage claims against the University of Phoenix (UP) by enrollment counselors.*

Two UP enrollment counselors brought state and federal claims in a federal district court in California, alleging UP required employees to work off the clock, miscalculated overtime, failed to itemize wage statements and did not provide them meal breaks. Their federal claims under the Fair Labor Standards Act were transferred to a nationwide class action lawsuit in Pennsylvania. The counselors then asked the California court to certify their state law claims as a class action suit for a potential class of more than 1,000 members. **The court agreed to do so as the action involved citizens of different states and there was more than $5 million at stake.** The court found common issues of law in all the claims, and it held the size of the class made individual lawsuits impractical. Three classes of current or former enrollment counselors were certified, including counselors bringing claims for overtime and meal breaks, incorrect pay records, and willful failure to pay overtime. *Adoma v. Univ. of Phoenix, Inc.*, 270 F.R.D. 543 (E.D. Cal. 2010).

◆ *A federal court dismissed a foreign national's claim that increasing his workload without a salary increase was akin to human trafficking.*

A Florida university paid a foreign national $95,000 to serve as an interim program director. When the university director of recruitment and admissions resigned, extra duties were assigned to the foreign national. His request for a salary increase was rejected, in part because the university claimed it was paying attorneys' fees and costs associated with obtaining permanent labor certification in order to retain him. The foreign national sued the university in a federal district court for breach of contract and violation of 18 U.S.C. Section 1589, a law intended to stop forced labor and human trafficking. Section 1589 is part of the Trafficking Victims Protection Act of 2000, which calls trafficking a form of slavery that mainly victimizes women and children.

Section 1589(a)(3) prohibited employers from obtaining labor by abuse of the law or legal process. **The court rejected the foreign national's argument that the university abused any law by expecting him to work for "free" in return for certification.** The real prohibition in Section 1589 is against using a law as a tool of coercion. Given the foreign national's "healthy salary," the court rejected his claims based on financial harm. His contract had an option allowing him to resign. As the foreign national "was not trafficked" to the U.S. and was in the same shoes as others who assumed responsibilities not explicitly mentioned in a job description, the court dismissed the case. *Alvarado v. Univ. Carlos Albizu*, No. 10-22072-CIV, 2010 WL 3385345 (S.D. Fla. 8/25/10).

◆ *A New York university was forced to face a collective FLSA action based on a student's preliminary showing that she was not paid for overtime work.*

A Hofstra University undergraduate assistant was paid a $700 stipend to be a football team manager. Since she held other on-campus jobs, she claimed she was entitled to overtime compensation for all hours worked beyond 40 hours a week. Hofstra's student employment handbook forbade students from working more than 25 hours per week when school was in session and 35 when classes were in recess. No student was to work on campus more than 40 hours a week, and extra care was to be taken to make sure the 40-hour limit was not exceeded when a student worked in more than one department. **The student said Hofstra routinely disregarded these policies and that she worked at least 40 hours per week as the football team manager.** In her federal lawsuit, she accused Hofstra of violating the Fair Labor Standards Act (FLSA), since she regularly worked more than 40 hours a week but was not paid overtime.

The student moved the court to certify a collective FLSA action. She also sought an order requiring Hofstra to provide her with names, addresses, email addresses, Social Security numbers and dates of employment of all students who had worked as undergraduate or graduate assistants in the previous six years. The court held the student was similarly situated to the other undergraduate and graduate assistants, and it conditionally certified a collective action of students who were not paid minimum wage or did not receive overtime pay. The class was limited to students who had worked for Hofstra in the previous three years. *Summa v. Hofstra Univ.*, No. CV 07-3307(DRH)(ARL), 2008 WL 3852160 (E.D.N.Y. 8/14/08).

◆ *A Georgia university did not breach a professor's employment contract when it recalculated his salary following a demotion.*

When the professor acquired tenure, the university paid him an annual salary of $49,537. It then appointed him to an associate vice president position at a salary of $70,000. Over the next three years, the professor entered into a series of one-year contracts, each providing for a pay increase. The university then decided to eliminate the associate vice president position. It notified the professor in writing of its decision and gave him the option of returning to the classroom at an annual salary of $54,341. The professor argued his salary computation was wrong, but his appeal failed. He sued the university in a state court for breach of contract. The court awarded summary judgment to the university, and the professor appealed to the Court of Appeals of Georgia.

The court found the university had compared the professor's salary to those of others in his department. The head of the department earned $59,472 for the same academic year, and the salaries of three associate professors who worked for the university for similar or longer time periods than the professor were less than his. The court found the terms of the professor's contract were unambiguous. **As the contract was clear, the trial court had the discretion to determine its terms.** The court affirmed the judgment. *Homer v. Board of Regents of the Univ. System of Georgia,* 613 S.E.2d 205 (Ga. Ct. App. 2005).

◆ *A California trade school qualified as an institution of higher learning, and its instructors were professionals who did not qualify for overtime pay.*

The school received state accreditation and became a degree-granting institution in 2002. Its instructors held certificates of authorization for service under the Education Code. The state division of labor standards enforcement notified the school its instructors were not exempt from overtime pay under an administrative wage order. The school sought a declaration that its instructors were exempt from overtime pay as professional employees. A state trial court agreed and held the instructors were exempt from the overtime wage order.

The state court of appeal held the school qualified as a "college." It complied with statutory requirements to obtain accreditation. **The "teaching exception" was not limited to institutions granting bachelor's or higher degrees.** The division relied on outdated records and evidence in arguing trade schools did not meet the definition of "higher learning." Instead, the boundaries of California's education system had expanded to include a much broader category of institutions. **Since the professional exemption was not limited to instructors at institutions granting baccalaureate degrees or higher, the school's instructors were entitled to the professional exception**, and the court affirmed the judgment. *California School of Culinary Arts v. Lujan*, 112 Cal.App.4th 16, 4 Cal.Rptr.3d 785 (Cal. Ct. App. 2003).

◆ *A New York court held that a fee required by medical schools from physicians as a condition of employment violated state education law.*

Ophthalmologists who worked as full-time assistant professors at Columbia University wanted to continue practicing ophthalmology and remain on the faculty. In exchange for allowing them to change their appointments to part time, Columbia requested that they pay a 10% "Dean's Tax" on all their practice income. When they refused, their appointments were terminated. The doctors sued Columbia in a state trial court, which held in their favor. A state appellate division court held that the **payment of the "Dean's Tax" as a condition of employment constituted illegal fee-splitting**. Because the doctors were no longer employees, and because Columbia was no longer providing them with benefits, facilities or malpractice insurance, the request was a violation of law. The court directed Columbia to review the applications for part-time appointments and affirmed the judgment. *Odrich v. Trustees of Columbia Univ.*, 764 N.Y.S.2d 448 (N.Y. App. Div. 2003).

◆ *Two part-time Washington community college instructors were not entitled to overtime wages.*

Part-time instructors from five community colleges in Washington brought a lawsuit alleging that the colleges violated the state's Minimum Wage Act by failing to compensate them for overtime work. Their wages were determined by multiplying their classroom hours by a negotiated hourly rate that included payment for time spent on course preparation, grading and office hours. However, they asserted that they were not exempt professional employees paid on a salary basis because the colleges docked their pay for time missed after all their accrued sick and annual leave was exhausted. The case reached the Washington Supreme Court, which ruled against them. It noted that as long as **their predetermined wages were not subject to reduction because of variations in the quality or quantity of work performed**, they still could be considered salary-basis employees. Under U.S. Department of Labor regulations adopted by the court, deductions for missed time after accrued sick and annual leave expire do not alter an employee's professional status. *Clawson v. Grays Harbor College Dist. No. 2*, 61 P.3d 1130 (Wash. 2003).

◆ *Probationary campus police officers were not entitled to overtime for attending EMT classes.*

A Massachusetts university hired four probationary campus police officers. As a condition of employment, they had to be certified as emergency medical technicians within one year of their hire date. The officers took the EMT course at the university and completed the course. Although they were not paid for attending EMT classes after work, they were compensated when EMT classes occurred during their regular working hours. They sued the university under the FLSA, seeking overtime pay for time spent working toward their EMT certification. The case reached the U.S. Court of Appeals, First Circuit, which held **the Portal-to-Portal Act permits an employer to avoid paying an employee for activities that are "preliminary or postliminary" to the principal activities the employee is engaged to perform**.

Here, that condition was satisfied because the officers were attending the EMT classes during their probationary period, and they did not perform any EMT-related work until after obtaining certification. Thus, they could be characterized as students during their probationary period for purposes of avoiding overtime compensation. *Bienkowski v. Northeastern Univ.*, 285 F.3d 138 (1st Cir. 2002).

## IV. EMPLOYEE LEAVE

### A. Generally

*The Family and Medical Leave Act of 1993 (FMLA), 29 U.S.C. §§ 2601–2654, makes available to eligible employees up to 12 weeks of unpaid leave per year: 1) because of the birth of a son or daughter of the employee and in order to care for such son or daughter; 2) because of the placement of a son or daughter with the employee for adoption or foster care; 3) in order to care for the spouse, or a son, daughter, or parent, of the employee, if such spouse, son, daughter or parent has a serious health condition; or 4) because of a serious health condition that makes the employee unable to perform the functions of the position of such employee. 29 U.S.C. § 2612.*

*To be eligible for leave, an employee must have been employed by the covered employer for at least 12 months, and must have worked at least 1,250 hours during the 12-month period preceding the start of the leave. 29 U.S.C. § 2611. If the employer provides paid leave for which the employee is eligible, the employee may elect, or the employer may require the employee, to substitute the paid leave for any part of the 12 weeks of leave to which the employee is entitled under the act. When the need for leave is foreseeable, the employee must provide reasonable prior notice.*

*An employer may require medical certification to support a claim for leave, and may require, at its own expense, a second opinion. An employer is under no obligation to allow the employee to accrue seniority or other employment benefits during a leave.*

◆ *The Third Circuit reversed a ruling that dismissed the claims of an instructor who alleged a university interfered with her FMLA rights and retaliated against her for taking FMLA leave.*

The instructor requested time off for depression. Her doctor filled out a "Certification of Health Provider" form – a standard U.S. Department of Labor form used to certify a mental health condition. The HR department determined the instructor was eligible for FMLA leave, but it didn't share that information with the employee. When the instructor's return to work was delayed by the school's request for a different release from her doctor, she was fired for failing to return to work within 12 weeks. HR said it sent the instructor a letter that explained the leave was designated as FMLA leave and explained her FMLA rights. She said she never got the letter. The instructor sued, alleging violations of FMLA. The school asked the court to dismiss the claims, saying the state's "mailbox rule" applied. Under it, courts deem a letter received if it has been properly addressed and mailed – and the school provided evidence from its mailroom supervisor and the HR staffer who prepared the letter and put it in the outgoing mail bin. **But the Third Circuit said the "mailbox rule" is a rebuttable presumption, and a weak one if the letter has been sent by regular mail rather than by registered or certified mail.** The ruling was reversed, and the case was remanded. *Lupyan v. Corinthian Colleges Inc.*, 761 F.3d 314 (3d Cir. 2014).

◆ *A fired employee couldn't state a valid claim of retaliation for taking FMLA leave, so a Missouri federal judge granted the university judgment without a trial.*

Wanting more of a challenge, an employee who worked as a Grants Assistant III applied for a promotion in the university's business office. She got it. Within two years, the employee felt "overwhelmed by the workload." During her performance review, the employee was told her attitude needed to improve. Three months later, there was a problem with the employee's performance. The university had to create a position because of the employee's increasingly bad reputation. Two faculty members refused to work with her. Thinking the new position would be a promotion, the employee applied for the job. When a co-worker was chosen for the new position, the employee became surly. She received a written warning to behave in a professional manner. Five days later, she submitted an FMLA leave request.

While the employee was on leave, more **financial problems came to light, including a $17,000 discrepancy in a grant application**. Ultimately, the employee was let go. She sued, alleging her termination was retaliation for taking FMLA leave. The court found no evidence to suggest the claim was valid, so the case was dismissed. *Tomlin v. Washington Univ.*, No. 4:11CV1871 HEA, 2013 WL 5406484 (E.D. Mo. 9/25/13).

◆ *Florida university officials had to justify their refusal to rehire or offer an equivalent job to an employee upon her return from FMLA leave.*

After the employee worked for more than 10 years as an administrative assistant in a university hospital, her supervisor started eliminating her duties without discussing the reasons. The employee claimed the prospect of losing her job caused her to take medication for anxiety, panic attacks and contagious dermatitis. After the university granted her FMLA leave for dermatitis, she was transferred to a temporary position with a drastic reduction in duties upon her return. She then left under circumstances that were later disputed.

In a federal court action against the university, the employee claimed FMLA violations. The court dismissed the case, and appeal reached the U.S. Court of Appeals, Eleventh Circuit. It found no merit to the university's claim that the employee was not entitled to be restored to the same job or given an equivalent position. While the university claimed she could not perform the job and had performance issues, **the court found it suspicious that performance**

**issues were not discussed until after she took FMLA leave**. A reasonable jury could believe the employee's story, making further proceedings regarding reinstatement necessary. But the court held for the university on the claim regarding employment termination. If her separation was deemed a discharge, there were legitimate performance-based reasons for it. *Rodriguez v. Univ. of Miami Hospital*, 499 Fed.Appx. 920 (11th Cir. 2012).

◆   *An Ohio instructor did not have a valid claim based on his request for a special schedule five years after he first requested FMLA leave.*

Wilberforce University (WU) approved the instructor's request for intermittent FMLA leave for treatment of asthma symptoms. But it denied the special schedule he asked for because it differed considerably from his physician's certification. In a federal court, the instructor claimed interference with his FMLA rights because WU had required him to file a new medical certification and denied his request for a special schedule. In reviewing the case, the court found WU had granted FMLA requests according to the instructor's medical certification. It also held the request for recertification was reasonable.

**The FMLA allows employers to require employees to obtain subsequent recertifications on a reasonable basis.** FMLA regulations provide that when an employee's medical certification indicates the employee will need intermittent leave for more than six months, the employer can request recertification every six months in connection with an absence. The regulations also say an employer can request a recertification because circumstances have changed – which was the case here. Because the instructor's leave request was inconsistent with the medical certification from his doctor, the leave was not medically necessary for FMLA purposes. As a result, the case could not go forward. *Grisby v. Wilberforce Univ.*, No. 3:10-CV-184, 2012 WL 4957544 (S.D. Ohio 10/16/12).

◆   *A Utah university did not violate the FMLA by eliminating the position of a program manager who disregarded instructions from his supervisor.*

An internal audit indicated "systematic problems, resulting in mistakes on grants" in the manager's department. His supervisor pressed him to prepare a response, but he failed to do so. The supervisor then decided to eliminate the manager's position due to reduced grants. The manager told the supervisor he wanted to take FMLA leave for childcare. But when his leave began, the supervisor went to his office and found he had emptied his drawers and had left no information about the audit. The manager was discharged for his conduct regarding the audit response, and he sued the university for FMLA violations. A federal court held for the university. On appeal, the U.S. Court of Appeals, Tenth Circuit, held the reduction in force did not violate the law. **Evidence showed that the supervisor made that decision before she learned that the manager might take leave.** Nor did the decision to convert the reduction in force to a termination for cause violate the FMLA.

According to the court, the university had produced extensive and undisputed evidence that the manager impeded and obstructed its efforts to respond to the audit report and otherwise do his job while he was on leave. *Sabourin v. Univ. of Utah*, 676 F.3d 950 (10th Cir. 2012).

◆ *A Texas university employee with a record of excessive absences could not show she was fired for requesting and taking FMLA leave.*

A biology lab research assistant received a poor job evaluation, largely due to her unscheduled absences. She requested FMLA leave after being diagnosed with a goiter and hyperthyroidism. A doctor certified the employee to miss up to three days of work a month for four months. The day after he released her to return to work, she called in sick. The employee attended work sporadically over the next six months, and the university fired her for not following directions about reporting absences. She sued university officials in a federal court for FMLA violations. The court noted the employee had ignored multiple instructions to inform supervisors about her absences. It held the FMLA allows intermittent leave. But FMLA regulations required employees to tell their employers the dates they required for leave as soon as practicable.

It was significant to the court that the employee had signed an FMLA acknowledgement stating that she was required to remain in contact with her work area as required by a university policy. The court held **the FMLA "does not allow an employee to violate company job requirements or work rules."** As the employee could not show she was fired for requesting and taking FMLA leave, the court held for the university and its officials. *Harville v. Texas A&M Univ.*, 833 F.Supp.2d 645 (S.D. Tex. 2011).

◆ *A Michigan university employee who did not have medical documentation of a "serious health condition" was unable to claim FMLA protection.*

The employee's duties included data entry. She had carpal tunnel repair surgery and took time off for pain. After a performance review cited the employee's attendance issues, the university eliminated her position, citing budget cuts. The employee sued the university in a federal court for retaliating against her for taking leave protected by the FMLA. The court held that to prevail, she had to show she took FMLA-protected leave and was fired because she took the leave. But the court found that **to invoke FMLA protections, an employee must provide notice and a qualifying reason for requesting the leave**. The employee did not present documentation from her doctor specifying why she was missing work. For this reason, she could not claim to have a "serious health condition" protected by the FMLA. Since her leave requests were unprotected by the FMLA, the court dismissed the case. *Davis v. Wayne State Univ.*, No. 11-10324, 2011 WL 2786186 (E.D. Mich. 7/15/11).

## B.  Disability Cases

*Many employee leave cases combine claims under the Family and Medical Leave Act (FMLA) with disability discrimination claims arising under the Americans with Disabilities Act (ADA), Section 504 of the Rehabilitation Act and state laws protecting individuals with disabilities. For additional disability discrimination cases in employment, see Chapter Seven, Section V.*

◆ *A Maryland university employee who was not cleared by her physician to return to work was not "qualified" to perform her duties under state law.*

After being injured in two car accidents, the employee took four days off work for knee surgery. She suffered complications that made her return date indefinite. As the employee's paid leave was almost exhausted, a supervisor suggested she apply for FMLA leave. A doctor's note to the university stated she might not be able to return to work and would be reevaluated in six weeks.

Although the employee was instructed to return to work at the end of her leave, she did not and was soon fired for job abandonment. In a federal court, she asserted violations of the FMLA, ADA and state disability law. In pretrial activity, the court held the university had Eleventh Amendment immunity as to her federal claims for monetary damages. To prove her state law disability claims, the employee had to show she was qualified to perform her job at the time of her discharge. But the U.S. Court of Appeals, Fourth Circuit, has held attendance is an essential function of a job, and the court agreed. **As the employee had not been cleared to return to work by her doctor, she was not qualified to perform her job under state law.** Even if she had been qualified, her accommodation claim failed as it was based on a failure to extend her leave – which she had not requested. *Lewis v. Univ. of Maryland, Baltimore*, No. SAG-12-298, 2012 WL 5193820 (D. Md. 10/18/12).

◆   *A federal court dismissed a University of Illinois employee's ADA and FMLA claims based on discrimination for requesting FMLA leave.*

Two years after the employee started work as a university customer service representative, she was diagnosed with kidney cancer. She took FMLA leave, then returned to work part time. After a brief disability leave, the employee returned to work full time. She asked the university to provide her with a part-time schedule and an ergonomic chair, and she claimed the university responded with harassing and retaliatory acts. The employee claimed the university constructively discharged her by manipulating time records, denying her pay and suspending her. She sued the university in a federal court under the ADA and FMLA. However, the court held the ADA claim was untimely filed. It dismissed the FMLA retaliation claim because the employee did not claim she was harassed because she took leave. According to the court, **she did not link any mistreatment to the taking of FMLA leave**. But as the employee might be able to show she was constructively discharged, the court allowed her to amend her complaint to pursue that claim. *Baldwin v. Board of Trustees of the Univ. of Illinois*, No. 10 C 5569, 2012 WL 3292831 (N.D. Ill. 8/8/12).

◆   *A federal court held for an Illinois community college in a discrimination and FMLA case filed by an employee with many performance problems.*

Although the employee said she had mononucleosis, she did not provide evidence of this to her employer. She also said she had chronic fatigue syndrome, but she did not have any medical documentation to support the diagnosis. After several performance-related incidents, including incorrectly changing a student's grade, the community college offered the employee a "Final Job Warning and Employee Action Plan." She rejected its terms and was fired. In a federal court lawsuit, the employee asserted ADA and FMLA violations. After reviewing the evidence, the court noted the employee had many performance problems and had refused to accept the Employee Action Plan Agreement. It held no reasonable jury could find the reasons for discharge were a pretext for disability discrimination. As a result, the community college was entitled to judgment on the ADA claim. The court also rejected the FMLA claim, as **the employee did not provide adequate notice to the college regarding an intent to take FMLA leave**. *Wirey v. Richland Community College*, No. 10-CV-02216, 2012 WL 6681214 (C.D. Ill. 12/21/12).

◆ *A Florida community college did not violate the Americans with Disabilities Act (ADA), the Family and Medical Leave Act (FMLA) or state law by refusing to renew an instructor's contract and denying him tenure.*

The instructor worked under renewable full-time annual contracts. After three years of service, he would become eligible for tenure. At one point, the instructor was told he should become more involved in the college community to improve his chances of a continuing contract. An evaluation noted he had some deficiencies, and his supervisor determined the annual goals he set were unsatisfactory. A short time later, the instructor requested FMLA leave for surgery. The community college did not offer him tenure or a new contract.

The instructor sued the college in a federal district court, asserting violation of the ADA, the FMLA and a Florida civil rights act. The court held his disability discrimination claims under the ADA and state law failed because he did not show he had a disability. He did not prove his cervical spondylosis and headaches substantially limited a major life activity. Instead, the court found the ailments were temporary. Temporary conditions were not disabilities under either the ADA or state law. **The court rejected the instructor's FMLA claim because he did not show a causal connection between his taking of FMLA leave and the decisions to non-renew his contract and deny him tenure.** The court held the temporal proximity between his request for FMLA leave and the college's decision was not enough to prove an FMLA violation – especially since he had been placed on notice of performance issues well before he sought FMLA leave. *Trabulsky v. Polk Community College*, No. 8:08-cv-02271-T-33AEP, 2010 WL 1837909 (M.D. Fla. 5/3/10).

◆ *A Texas career services director could not pursue FMLA claims, as she did not prove she requested leave and was discharged for unprofessional conduct.*

The director injured herself at work and took a few days off to have back surgery. When she returned to work, she used a cane to walk. The director maintained that she advised her supervisor that her doctor suggested she take a medical leave, but the supervisor later denied any such conversation. A short time later, a staff member notified the supervisor that the director had engaged in unprofessional conduct with students and staff. This included counseling students to file complaints against the supervisor and seek tuition refunds because of his alleged management deficiencies. After the misconduct was corroborated by other employees, the supervisor discharged the director.

In a federal district court lawsuit against the supervisor and others, the director claimed interference with her FMLA rights, retaliation and various state law violations. The case reached the U.S. Court of Appeals, Fifth Circuit, which found her FMLA claims failed. **In order to succeed with a case for interference with FMLA rights, it must be shown that an employee took a leave that was protected by the FMLA.** There was no proof in this case that the supervisor even knew that the director had requested leave. The director's retaliation claim failed because she could not counter evidence of her unprofessional conduct. A lower court judgment against her was affirmed. *Burris v. Brazell*, 351 Fed.Appx. 961 (5th Cir. 2009).

◆  *A maintenance worker at a Seattle community college failed to show an FMLA violation or discrimination against him based on disability.*

After the worker compiled a record of chronic tardiness and absenteeism, he asked to change schedules. The college did not want to let him work the shift he sought because doing so would leave him unsupervised for three hours. However, the worker was permitted to work his desired shift on a trial basis. Even with the later start time, he continued to be late or absent and missed safety meetings. After the college reclassified the worker to a lower-paying position, he filed a federal district court action under the FMLA and the Americans with Disabilities Act (ADA). The court held he did not show he had a disability under the ADA. Even if he was disabled, he did not show the college failed to accommodate him, since he was offered a position with a later start time. The court rejected the worker's claim that the college violated the FMLA by ending a period of FMLA leave without justification. **He never commenced an FMLA leave.** Although the worker said the college retaliated against him for filing a complaint under the state industrial safety and health act, he did not show the college was aware that he had filed the complaint or that it took action against him because of it. *Elkins v. North Seattle Community College*, No. C08-1466RSL, 2009 WL 3698516 (W.D. Wash. 11/3/09).

◆  *A college did not violate the FMLA or Americans with Disabilities Act (ADA) by denying a professor's request to work on campus three days a week.*

The professor typically worked only three days per week on campus. When his department changed its policy to require full-time staff members to be on campus for at least four hours a day for at least four days a week, the professor did not comply. He then took leave under the FMLA due to stress-related problems. He told the college that his department chair was "the source of his physical problems." When the professor returned to work, the college granted him a temporary transfer away from the department chair. He was also offered a transfer to a non-teaching position under a different supervisor. After the professor failed to report for this job, the college considered him to have resigned. He sued the college in a federal district court for violations of the ADA and FMLA. The court held for the college, and the professor appealed.

On appeal, the U.S. Court of Appeals, Third Circuit, held the professor did not show he had a disability under the ADA. Despite being treated for panic attacks and agoraphobia, he did not show he had a substantial limitation of a major life activity. The court also rejected the professor's claim that the college wrongly discharged him instead of granting him additional leave. **He was not eligible for FMLA leave because he did not have a "serious health condition"** as defined by the act. Even if he was FMLA-eligible, he took more leave than he was entitled to receive. As a result, the judgment was affirmed. *Lloyd v. Washington & Jefferson College*, 288 Fed.Appx. 786 (3d Cir. 2008).

◆    *A federal appeals court held FMLA posting requirements are met when the employer posts notices on its intranet site.*

A Massachusetts employee was involved in an accident and took a leave of absence from his supervisory job. The employer sent him a letter that provided information about the FMLA and told him the leave was being counted as FMLA leave. The employer also asked the employee to provide a medical certification regarding his condition. He provided a disability claim form signed by a physician and was given 15 weeks of leave. The employer later discharged the employee after he failed to return to work. He filed a federal district court action claiming the employer failed to post FMLA notices.

The court held for the employer, and the employee appealed. The U.S. Court of Appeals, First Circuit, noted the employer posted an adequate FMLA notice on its intranet website. This defeated the claim that employees did not receive notice of their FMLA rights. The site was accessible to all employees while they were at work, and the employee admitted he had used it at work. The court rejected the claim that the employer violated the FMLA because the site could not be accessed from home. **FMLA regulations only required that notice be posted at the workplace.** The district court's decision was affirmed. *Dube v. J.P. Morgan Investor Services*, 201 Fed.Appx. 786 (1st Cir. 2006).

◆    *An Illinois college did not retaliate against an employee who violated an employee dress code by discharging her after she sought time off.*

The employee was suspended for wearing maternity shorts in violation of the college dress code. The college president said her conduct was the grossest form of insubordination he had seen in 34 years at the college. The college board voted to approve the president's recommendation to fire the employee. She sued the college in a federal district court, which held that to prevail on her FMLA claim, she had to show the college fired her to prevent her from taking leave to which she was entitled. **Under the FMLA, an employee must provide sufficient notice to qualify for leave. Employees are not required to mention the FMLA by name.** They only need to put the employer on notice that FMLA leave would be necessary. For leave that is foreseeable, such as for the birth of a child, at least 30 days advance notice is required. The employee said she told the college months in advance that she was pregnant and intended to take leave. The court held she gave sufficient notice, but did not show she would not have been fired for other reasons. As there was evidence of other reasons for firing, the court dismissed the case. *Sample v. Rend Lake College*, No. 04-CV-4161-JPG, 2005 WL 2465905 (S.D. Ill. 10/5/05).

◆    *An Iowa university did not violate the Equal Protection Clause by allowing mothers, but not fathers, the benefit of paid leave after childbirth.*

The university's parental leave policy allowed biological mothers to take sick leave for any pregnancy-related temporary disability. A male employee alleged the policy violated the Equal Protection Clause. He filed a class action to represent biological fathers at the university. The case reached the U.S. Court of Appeals, Eighth Circuit. It found the policy did not allow mothers to use accrued sick leave after their disability ended. The time off was disability leave even though mothers often cared for a newborn during that time. The court held the university reasonably established a period of presumptive disability. **A distinction between biological mothers and fathers was rationally related to legitimate concerns**, and the policy did not violate the Equal Protection Clause. *Johnson v. Univ. of Iowa*, 431 F.3d 325 (8th Cir. 2005).

## V.  EMPLOYEE BENEFITS

*Like their counterparts in the public sector, many private schools offer a broad range of employment benefits to employees. These benefit programs are subject to federal civil rights laws such as Title VII and the Equal Pay Act as well as income tax laws. Employer-employee disputes concerning benefits will generally be resolved according to contract law rules (see Section I).*

### A.  Retirement Benefits

◆  *A Pennsylvania court reversed the state retirement board's decision to revoke the pension of a former employee who was convicted of child sex abuse.*
   The former professor and football coach retired in 1999. In 2012, he was convicted of sex crimes against children. The assaults happened between 2005 and 2008. Under the state's pension forfeiture law, pension rights of public employees are forfeited upon the conviction of "any crime related to the public office or public employment." The crimes the professor was convicted of were included in the list of specific crimes in the act. So the state retirement board stopped paying the professor's pension. Appeal reached a Pennsylvania state court, which reversed the decision. Under the law, the appellate court noted, **the professor had to be a "school employee" when he committed the crimes**. He'd already retired, so he wasn't an employee at the time. The state had to reinstate his pension and provide missed payments – plus interest. *Sandusky v. Pennsylvania State Employees' Retirement Board*, 127 A.3d 34 (Pa. Commw. Ct. 2015).

◆  *An Ohio university did not have to establish an early retirement incentive plan under state law based on the size of an employee's "state employing unit."*
   A student affairs department employee who had worked for 26 years at the University of Toledo was one of 85 employees who lost their jobs due to layoff. She claimed the university had to establish an early retirement incentive plan under Ohio law. The case reached the Court of Appeals of Ohio, which held **the layoff was not large enough to trigger the legal obligation to establish an early retirement incentive plan** under Ohio R.C. Section 145.298 and state regulations. The law required a state entity to establish a plan based on the number of layoffs in an "employing unit." The number was the lesser of 350 or 40% of the employees in the employing unit. While the employee claimed this requirement was triggered by counting all 85 employees who lost their jobs, the court disagreed. It found the university correctly argued that the student affairs department was the relevant "employing unit" in this case. Only four employees in the department lost their jobs. As a result, the university did not have to establish an early retirement incentive plan. *State ex rel. Edgeworth v. Univ. of Toledo,* 185 Ohio App.3d 48, 923 N.E.2d 175 (Ohio Ct. App. 2009).

◆   *A professor could not enroll in an early retirement program because he waited too long to submit his application.*

An Ohio state university instituted an early retirement incentive program, which Ohio law authorized as long as enrollment did not exceed 5% of eligible employees. A professor/associate dean applied for the program but then withdrew his application. He later attempted to resubmit his application, but the university denied his request. After resigning, the professor sued, seeking an order that he be enrolled in the early retirement program. A state court ruled in his favor, but the Court of Appeals of Ohio reversed. Here, the university had improperly expanded the program to allow more than 5% of eligible employees to participate. As a result, even though the professor's initial application would have placed him in the eligible 5%, his resubmitted application came after the 5% threshold had already been met. He was ineligible for the program. *Bee v. Univ. of Akron*, No. 21081, 2002 WL 31387127 (Ohio Ct. App. 2002).

◆   *A New York professor could pursue a lawsuit for unpaid pension benefits.*

After 10 years teaching, a tenured assistant professor was notified that he would be reassigned to an administrative position. While trying to agree on a position, the professor performed no services for the university, which then stopped paying his salary and began dismissal proceedings against him. The university did not complete the proceedings because it determined that he had abandoned his job. When he sued for reinstatement and back pay, a New York court dismissed the case on the grounds that he should have filed an Article 78 proceeding. An appellate division court reversed the judgment, but the lawsuit was dismissed when he failed to appear. He later sued for unpaid salary and pension contributions, asserting the university had never formally fired him. A federal district court dismissed the case, but the U.S. Court of Appeals, Second Circuit, reversed the judgment in part, finding that **if his employment status claim was valid, he might be able to succeed on his pension claim**. However, his claim for unpaid salary had been properly dismissed. *Yoon v. Fordham Univ. Faculty and Administrative Retirement Plan*, 263 F.3d 196 (2d Cir. 2001).

◆   *Where a university reasonably modified a retirement plan, it was not liable for violating the Employee Retirement Income Security Act (ERISA).*

A professor employed by a New York private university retired in 1977 and began receiving benefits under the school's contributory retirement plan. The board of trustees amended the plan periodically to provide cost of living adjustments (COLAs) to plan members or their beneficiaries. Subsequently, the retirement committee amended the COLA, and the board of trustees amended the plan again to provide that "the retirement committee shall have exclusive authority and discretion to construe any disputed term." After the retirement committee denied the professor's claim for additional benefits, he filed suit against the retirement plan and the university under ERISA in a state trial court.

The case was ultimately transferred to a U.S. magistrate judge. The magistrate judge granted the university's motion for pretrial judgment, and the professor appealed to the U.S. Court of Appeals, Second Circuit. The retirement committee claimed it had properly modified the earlier increases by calculating what each retiree's monthly benefit would have been under the amended COLA, subtracting the value of increases actually given, and adding the difference to each retiree's monthly benefits. The professor contended that the base figure to which the above formula would be applied should include all prior COLAs. The court ruled that **the retirement committee had discretion to construe any uncertain or disputed term**. Consequently, the court applied the arbitrary and capricious standard of review. Because the retirement committee's interpretation of the statute was reasonable, the court affirmed the magistrate judge's ruling in favor of the university. *Jordan v. Retirement Committee of Rensselaer Polytechnic Institute,* 46 F.3d 1264 (2d Cir. 1995).

## B. Other Benefits

◆ *A police instructor was not entitled to disability benefits because his injuries predated his membership in the state retirement system.*

The instructor was involved in two automobile accidents during his employment by a state university. He had been involved in an accident prior to his employment by the university that caused severe injuries to his spine, for which he underwent spinal fusion surgery and received psychiatric treatment for post-traumatic stress disorder. After going to work for the university, the instructor was involved in another motor vehicle crash and was diagnosed as having a sprain. His third accident occurred when he was going to work. After this accident, the instructor underwent a second cervical fusion operation. He applied for disability benefits based on his cervical injury and mental illness. A medical board denied his request, and a hearing officer upheld the denial.

The state retirement system adopted the hearing officer's findings, and the instructor appealed to the Court of Appeals of Kentucky. The court found medical testimony supported the hearing officer's finding that the instructor's physical and mental disabilities resulted from the first automobile accident and predated his university employment. The court rejected his argument that his injuries from the third accident occurred during the course of his employment because he changed his route to obtain water for use in his police training class. The record showed the instructor traveled just a mile out of his way and was not on campus when the accident occurred. **The university did not file an accident report or a workers' compensation claim, which would have indicated the accident was in the course of his employment.** The court affirmed the denial of benefits. *Morris v. Kentucky Retirement Systems,* No. 2002-CA-001570-MR, 2003 WL 21834980 (Ky. Ct. App. 2003).

◆ *A New Hampshire college could provide less insurance benefits for mental illnesses than for physical illnesses.*

A college professor was treated for depression through medication and outpatient medical care. The college funded its own health care plan, which contained an annual limit of $3,000 for outpatient mental health benefits and a lifetime cap of $10,000. After the professor reached the lifetime cap, he filed a grievance, arguing that the cap violated a state statute and the collective bargaining agreement by providing less benefits for mental illnesses than physical illnesses. An arbitrator ruled that neither the state statute nor the bargaining agreement had been violated, and the Supreme Court of New

Hampshire upheld that decision. **Because the college was not an insurer, the court held it was not subject to the statute requiring equal health insurance coverage for mental and physical illnesses.** *Marshall v. Keene State College*, 785 A.2d 418 (N.H. 2001).

## C. Discrimination

◆ *A Michigan nonprofit corporation lacked standing to challenge a policy of providing benefits to same-sex domestic partners of state university employees.*

The corporation sued state entities to challenge the benefits policy, claiming it violated a state constitutional provision that required a marriage to be between a man and a woman. The corporation claimed the policy resulted in an illegal expenditure of state funds and violated state laws relating to marriage and divorce. Appeal reached the Court of Appeals of Michigan. It held that **to establish a right to bring a lawsuit, a party must have an injury that can be redressed by a favorable court decision**. The corporation did not show it suffered an injury that was different from any "injury" to the public at large. The only injury claimed was that the policy was "at odds with that which [it] seeks to promote." As this vague assertion was not enough to confer standing on the corporation, the court held for the state officials. *American Family Ass'n of Michigan v. Michigan State Univ. Board of Trustees,* 276 Mich.App. 42, 739 N.W.2d 908 (Mich. Ct. App. 2007).

◆ *An Ohio university employee lacked standing to challenge a university policy granting health insurance benefits to same-sex partners of employees.*

Miami University (MU) made health insurance benefits available to same-sex domestic partners of university employees. To receive benefits for a domestic partner, employees were required to submit an affidavit attesting to the existence of a same-sex domestic partnership. For the 2004-05 academic year, the university paid about $100,000 in premiums for domestic partner insurance coverage, which was about .5% of its total budget for faculty and staff compensation. Five months after the university adopted the policy, Ohio voters approved a state constitutional amendment recognizing only marriages between men and women. It also barred the state from creating or recognizing a legal status for unmarried couples that "approximate[d] the design, qualities, significance or effect of marriage." An MU employee sued the university and its board of trustees to challenge the same-sex benefits policy. A state court entered judgment for MU. On appeal, **the Court of Appeals of Ohio held the insurance premiums were funded by private party donations and not tax money**. Therefore, the employee could not claim a right to challenge the policy based on his status as a taxpayer. *Brinkman v. Miami Univ.*, No. CA2006-12-313, 2007 WL 2410390 (Ohio Ct. App. 7/27/07).

◆ *A California institute could not discontinue disability benefits to an employee who turned 65 because he was not receiving pension benefits.*

A research scientist at a California research and education institute was diagnosed with Parkinson's disease and took a medical leave. He became eligible for long-term disability benefits through the institute's insurance plan, but he retained his employee status and his right to return to work if his health improved. While still receiving his disability benefits, he turned 65 and became eligible for retirement. **Although he did not retire (and thus did not receive pension benefits), the institute offset his disability benefits with the amount of pension benefits he would have received by retiring, thereby reducing his income to zero.** The scientist filed suit against the institute, alleging violations of the Age Discrimination in Employment Act (ADEA) and a state statute. The institute cross-claimed for the amount of disability benefits it had inadvertently paid him after he turned 65 and filed a motion to dismiss.

The case reached the U.S. Court of Appeals, Ninth Circuit. In order to preclude an employee from receiving both long-term disability benefits and pension benefits for which he is eligible, the ADEA allows employers to offset the amount of disability benefits by the amount of pension benefits. As the employee had not retired, he was not receiving any pension benefits. The ADEA prohibits employee benefit plans from requiring or permitting involuntary retirement. The primary effect of the institute's policy was to leave an employee without an income unless he or she retired, and a reasonable person in the employee's position would believe he had no choice but to retire. Finding that **the offsetting of long-term disability benefits is allowed only when pension benefits are being paid concurrently,** the court held the institute's disability plan violated the ADEA. *Kalvinskas v. California Institute of Technology*, 96 F.3d 1305 (9th Cir. 1996).

## VI.  UNEMPLOYMENT AND WORKERS' COMPENSATION

### A.  Unemployment Benefits

*The Federal Unemployment Tax Act (FUTA), 26 U.S.C. § 3301, et seq., establishes a federal program to compensate temporarily unemployed workers. Although the federal Department of Labor oversees the program, states meeting specific criteria administer it. A major exemption from coverage, in Section 3309(b)(1) of the act, states: "This section shall not apply to service performed ... in the employ of (A) a church or convention or association of churches, or (B) an organization which is operated primarily for religious purposes and which is operated, supervised, controlled, or principally supported by a church or convention or association of churches."*

◆  *A part-time instructor was not entitled to $2,928 in unemployment benefits she received during a summer vacation, so she had to return the money, a New Jersey state court held.*

The instructor was a part-time adjunct professor whose duties ended after a spring semester. She was told she'd be asked to teach again in the fall. She applied for and started receiving unemployment benefits. The state's division of unemployment insurance notified the adjunct that she wasn't eligible for benefits – and would have to return the money she'd already received. She appealed, but the appeal tribunal affirmed. She sought judicial review, but it also affirmed. Under New Jersey law, employees of educational institutions are not eligible to receive unemployment compensation "for any week of unemployment commencing during the period between two successive academic years, or ... regular terms ... if there is a contract or a reasonable assurance" the person will be back for the next year or term. **The adjunct argued this provision didn't apply to her because the nature of adjunct work is that there is no guarantee of being offered the same amount of work – or any work – in the future. The court disagreed.** She had a reasonable assurance her employment would continue – and it did – so she wasn't entitled to unemployment compensation for the institution's summer vacation months. *Massaro-Johnson v. Board of Review,* Dep't of Labor, No. A-2695-13T3, 2015 WL 1208644 (N.J. Super. Ct. App. Div. 3/18/15).

◆  *A New Jersey appellate court held an adjunct faculty member was not entitled to unemployment benefits over the summer if a community college couldn't definitely promise him work for the coming fall.*

The chair of his department told the adjunct he would be rehired for the fall semester if there was sufficient enrollment – which he wouldn't know until late summer. He filed for unemployment benefits in June. Under New Jersey law, a person isn't entitled to unemployment benefits for the time between two school years if the person has "a contract or reasonable assurance" of work in the coming school year. The New Jersey Department of Labor and Workforce Development denied the claim. Based on his work history with the university, the department found "it was implied" he'd be reemployed based on enrollment. That fall, the university rehired the adjunct. But he appealed the decision to deny him benefits. When the board of review upheld it, he sought judicial review. The court affirmed the ruling. **One semester wasn't a long work history, but it was enough for the university to decide it would offer him work for the fall if enough students enrolled, the court said.** State law requires the agency to deny unemployment benefits if an educator has "reasonable assurance" of work the following semester – and a court can reverse an agency decision only if it's arbitrary, capricious, unreasonable or inconsistent with its statutory mission or another state policy. That wasn't the case here, so the court affirmed the decision. *Lombardi v. Board of Review,* No. A-0229-12T3, 2014 WL 4055822 (N.J. Super. Ct. App. Div. 8/18/14).

◆  *A tenured Idaho State University (ISU) professor who said he was fired for exercising his speech rights was instead found to have engaged in misconduct.*

After obtaining tenure in ISU's civil engineering department, the professor openly criticized the university and its administrators. He claimed unethical and criminal conduct by ISU administrators. Warnings did not stop the professor's comments, and ISU discharged him following a disciplinary proceeding. His application for unemployment benefits was denied by an appeals examiner who found he was discharged for employment-related misconduct. Appeal reached Idaho's highest court. It found misconduct was adequately shown in this case. Under state law, **disqualifying misconduct included "a disregard of the employer's expected standard of behavior."** In addition to misconduct, the court found the professor failed to be collegial and acted in an insubordinate manner. His conduct was not protected by the First

Amendment. The decision to deny benefits was affirmed. *Sadid v. Idaho State Univ.*, 154 Idaho 88, 294 P.3d 1100 (Idaho 2013).

◆ *An adjunct professor was not justified in quitting work after a college paid her wages in an untimely manner four times.*

After four late paychecks, the adjunct quit working for the college and applied for unemployment compensation benefits. A state unemployment law judge found that the fourth late paycheck was caused by a miscommunication regarding the correct pay rate and held the adjunct did not have good reason to quit. On appeal, the state court of appeals explained that an employee who quits is eligible for unemployment benefits only if he or she had good reason to do so. A good reason is one that is directly related to employment and for which the employer is totally responsible – and would compel an average, reasonable worker to quit. An employee is not eligible for unemployment benefits unless he or she first gives the employer a reasonable opportunity to correct the adverse working conditions. **Evidence showed the adjunct had submitted her resignation after the college took steps to correct the problem that led to the fourth late paycheck.** The court upheld the finding that she did not provide the college a reasonable opportunity to correct adverse working conditions, and it affirmed the decision against her. *Jones-Schroyer v. Lake Superior College*, No. A11-1256, 2012 WL 1658893 (Minn. Ct. App. 5/14/12).

◆ *A New York university adjunct professor could keep his benefits despite improperly stating he had no reasonable assurance of continued employment.*

The professor filed for and received unemployment insurance benefits after the end of the spring semester of 2004. On his application for benefits, he denied that he was filing the claim between academic terms or years. The university rehired the professor for two courses in the fall 2004 semester. An administrative hearing law judge (ALJ) then found the professor received a reasonable assurance of continued employment and willfully misrepresented this on his application for benefits. The ALJ held he was ineligible to receive benefits, charged him with a recoverable overpayment and assessed a penalty.

The case reached the New York Supreme Court, Appellate Division. **The court held New York Labor Law Section 590(10) precludes an employee from receiving unemployment insurance benefits during the time period between two successive academic years, or terms, where he or she had received a reasonable assurance that he would perform services in the same capacity for those academic years or terms.** Because the professor taught three courses during the spring 2004 term and only two courses during the fall 2004 semester, the appellate court agreed with the board. The professor could not meet the economic standard of earning in the fall 2004 semester of at least 90% of what he earned during the spring 2004 semester. He therefore could keep the benefits he had already received. *In re Kendall*, 30 A.D.3d 863, 817 N.Y.S.2d 715 (N.Y. App. Div. 2006).

◆ *The Supreme Court of Hawaii held that a student, who was also a university employee, was not entitled to receive unemployment benefits.*

The student attended the University of Hawaii for five consecutive academic years. He was hired as a university peer counselor full time during a summer when he did not attend school. The student resumed his studies at the university that fall, then filed an unemployment insurance claim. The state Department of Labor and Industrial Relations determined the wages from his summer job could be considered for the purpose of unemployment benefits, since he was not enrolled or regularly attending classes during the summer session. A state trial court noted state law made students ineligible for unemployment benefits if they were enrolled or regularly attended classes while working for a university. It held the student's services were excluded from the unemployment statute's definition of "services." The Supreme Court of Hawaii held that **because the student attended classes full time for five consecutive academic years, his primary relationship was that of a student**. He would have been ineligible for summer work with the school without his status as a student. As the summer job was excluded from the term "employment," the court affirmed the judgment. *Univ. of Hawaii v. Befitel*, 100 P.3d 55 (Haw. 2004).

## B.  Workers' Compensation

*An award of workers' compensation benefits is typically an employee's exclusive remedy for an injury in the course and scope of employment. This precludes personal injury suits by employees in most cases. A large group of cases in this area involves determining whether a student at a university may be deemed an "employee" based on performing on-campus jobs.*

◆   *A Florida court held a college bookstore student-employee who was hit by a van while on campus could not file a negligence claim against the college.*

The student collided with a van on the college campus as she rode back to work on her bicycle. The college submitted a workers' compensation claim on her behalf. She filed a personal injury claim against the college, claiming it was responsible for the van driver's conduct. The case reached a Florida district court of appeals, which recited the general rule that **workers' compensation benefits generally are the exclusive remedy for employees who are injured during the course and scope of their employment**. The court found the student was an employee of the college. She had entered into a written contract with the college under which she agreed to work for affiliates of the college, such as the bookstore. Second, the court held the student was injured during the course and scope of her employment. The case was returned to a lower court with instructions to enter judgment for the college. *Pensacola Christian College v. Bruhn*, 80 So.3d 1046 (Fla. Dist. Ct. App. 2011).

◆   *A Pennsylvania State University employee who made insufficient efforts to regain employment lost his workers' compensation benefits.*

The employee received workers' compensation benefits for almost two years after injuring his shoulder. He then applied for a disability pension. The university petitioned for modification of the employee's compensation benefits, asserting work was available for him. A workers' compensation judge agreed with the university and substantially reduced the employee's benefits. Two years later, the university petitioned to suspend his benefits entirely based on voluntarily retirement and withdrawal from the work force. It presented the testimony of a vocational rehabilitation specialist, who identified several jobs the employee could perform. In response, the employee said he had registered with a career services organization and had checked websites and newspapers for job openings. Although there was no documentation to confirm these claims, the judge denied the university's suspension petition, finding he sought employment and did not voluntarily remove himself from the work force.

A workers' compensation board affirmed the ruling, and the university appealed. The Commonwealth Court of Pennsylvania held that a claimant who accepts a pension is presumed to have left the work force and the former employer is generally entitled to have benefits suspended. In this situation, the employee could avoid suspension by showing he was seeking employment or that his work-related injury forced his retirement. According to the court, **searching the Internet and newspaper ads was not enough** to show a good-faith effort to find employment. **The employee had to show he actually applied for work or did something to try to land a job.** Since he did not show good faith, he was not entitled to benefits. *Pennsylvania State Univ. v. Workers' Compensation Appeal Board*, 948 A.2d 907 (Pa. Commw. Ct. 2008).

◆   *A Michigan court reversed a grant of workers' compensation benefits to a university employee that was based on alleged harassment by her supervisor.*

The employee claimed psychological injury based on her supervisor's repeated harassment at work. A workers' compensation magistrate granted her application for benefits, finding she suffered a work-related psychiatric condition "that was significantly contributed to by actual events of her employment." The magistrate also found the employee showed she was disabled. The Court of Appeals of Michigan reviewed the case. It explained that to prove an entitlement to benefits based on a mental disability, the employee had to show a mental disability caused by an event that occurred in connection with her employment. Moreover, she had to show her perception of the event was "grounded in fact or reality," when viewed objectively. In awarding benefits, the magistrate had failed to address a crucial question of whether the employee reasonably perceived her supervisor's actions as racist, vindictive or discriminatory. So the court returned the case to the magistrate.

**Any disability in this case ended when the employee's psychologist released her to return to work.** Although the university refused to allow her to return to work because its own doctor had not cleared her, she nonetheless had the capacity to return to a job of a comparable salary as of the date of her release by her own psychologist. In the event that a magistrate found the employee was entitled to benefits, the award could not extend beyond the date on which her psychologist released her to return to work. *Swinton v. Michigan State Univ.*, No. 280135, 2008 WL 4604096 (Mich. Ct. App. 10/7/08). The state Supreme Court denied the employee's appeal. *Swinton v. Michigan State Univ.*, 763 N.W.2d 280 (2009).

◆   *A resident assistant at a North Carolina university was limited to workers' compensation benefits for contracting asthma in a dormitory.*

A North Carolina State University student enlisted as a naval reserve and entered the Navy's Nuclear Propulsion Officer Candidate Program. A Navy physical did not reveal any significant abnormalities, and he was declared "fit for full service." The university hired the student as a resident advisor for a residence hall. Near the start of his second year of work, he resigned due to mold and mildew in living spaces of the hall. A month after resigning, the student was diagnosed with a permanent asthmatic and respiratory condition.

The student sought to recover $150,000 from the university under the state Tort Claims Act for exposing him to a substandard and unhealthy environment when he was a resident advisor. An administrative commission agreed with the university that the exclusive remedy was a claim for workers' compensation benefits. On review, the Court of Appeals of North Carolina held **the state workers' compensation act is the exclusive remedy for any employee who is injured in the course and scope of employment**. Since the student was an employee of the university while he attended classes there, his injuries arose out of the course of his employment. For this reason, the commission had correctly found the workers' compensation act was his exclusive remedy. *Christopher v. North Carolina State Univ.*, 661 S.E.2d 36 (N.C. Ct. App. 2008).

◆   *Columbia University could not avoid a worker's negligence claim on the basis that workers' compensation was his exclusive remedy.*

A temporary employment agency assigned the employee to kitchen work at Columbia. While working there, he was injured when he slipped and fell on a wet, greasy floor. The worker sued Columbia for negligence. Under state law, he would be unable to sue Columbia for negligence if it was his employer because negligence claims against employers are generally barred by the exclusive remedy provisions of the state's workers' compensation law.

The temporary agency was the worker's employer. It paid his salary and benefits, and it set his assignments. **A special employment relationship does not exist unless an entity has completely transferred control over the employee to another entity.** Columbia argued that it met this test, and it asked the court for judgment. The court denied the motion, and Columbia appealed. A state appellate division court held the evidence did not conclusively establish the existence of a special employment relation between the worker and Columbia. Uncontradicted evidence showed that no one at Columbia told him how to do his job or supervised him. There was a factual question as to whether the agency transferred control to Columbia to an extent that would justify the conclusion that Columbia became a special employer. Columbia was properly denied judgment. *Bellamy v. Columbia Univ.*, 50 A.D.3d 160, 851 N.Y.S.2d 406 (N.Y. App. Div. 2008).

◆   *A Minnesota appeals court upheld a decision for a college and a chemistry professor who were blamed for a student accident in a chemistry lab.*

The student was hurt while participating in a summer research program. He was paid a stipend and permitted to live in a campus dormitory at no charge. The student was seriously hurt when a chemistry flask exploded and chemical debris ignited his clothes. He sued the college, chemistry professor and several college officials for personal injury in a state court. The court noted that Minnesota law generally makes workers' compensation the exclusive remedy for employees injured on the job. It denied a motion for pretrial judgment.

The state appeals court said the facts related to the student's activities were not developed enough to support a determination regarding whether he was acting as an employee when hurt. The state workers' compensation act treated medical residents as employees but said nothing about how to treat other student workers. **The determination of whether an individual should be treated as an employee or a student depends on the context.** Deciding whether a student is an "employee" for purposes of the workers' compensation act required an analysis of purposes and character of the work performed. Because neither side offered detailed information about the nature of the work the student performed, the court upheld the trial court's decision. *Lindsay v. St. Olaf College*, No. A06-2137, 2008 WL 223119 (Minn. Ct. App. 1/29/08).

◆   *A Florida District Court of Appeal held a student who was injured while interning was not an "employee" under state workers' compensation law.*

A student at the University of Central Florida was injured when she was pushed into a wall. After the university advised her it was not responsible for her injuries, she sought workers' compensation benefits. A workers' compensation judge determined the student was entitled to benefits. Even though the student did not receive pay from the school board, the judge reasoned she was an employee because the internship was required for her to earn a degree. The board appealed to a state district court of appeal, which noted the workers' compensation statute defined "employee" as a person who received remuneration from an employer for performing work or a service.

**Although the student received a benefit as a result of the internship, she was merely a participant in an internship course.** This participation did not make her an "employee" under the state's workers' compensation law. Nor did a separate state law provision, which gave students in teacher preparation programs the "same protection of law" as certified educators, entitle the student to benefits. That provision did not supersede state workers' compensation law, which defined "employee" in a way that excluded the student from its coverage. The student was not covered under a workers' compensation law provision applicable to volunteers. She was at the school to complete a required course. The decision of the workers' compensation judge was reversed. *Orange County School Board v. Powers*, 959 So.2d 370 (Fla. Dist. Ct. App. 2007).

◆   *Missouri's labor and industrial relations commission erred in finding a sexual harassment incident could not trigger workers' compensation eligibility.*

The employee worked as a licensed practical nurse for about 21 years. Most of that time, she worked in the outpatient dialysis department. The employee was sexually harassed while administering dialysis treatment to a male patient. She notified the nurse in charge about the incident. After the employee left work that day, she broke down emotionally. She then took vacation time and began psychiatric treatment. The employee was diagnosed with depression and post-traumatic stress disorder. She took medication and received counseling. She resigned from her job because of the incident. A vocational expert found the employee permanently disabled due to emotional problems. The employee filed a claim for workers' compensation benefits.

The case reached the Missouri Court of Appeals, which explained that the employee's mental injury claim was based on a physical assault. Accordingly, it resulted from a traumatic incident, not work-related stress. The employee was not required to prove the stress was extraordinary or unusual. The Missouri Workers' Compensation Act requires compensation of employees for personal injury arising out of and in the course of employment. The court reversed the decision and returned the case to administrative levels to determine if the employee deserved compensation. *Jones v. Washington Univ.*, 199 S.W.3d 793 (Mo. Ct. App. 2006).

◆   *The Court of Appeals of South Carolina held an administrative assistant who was hurt on the job could collect lifetime workers' compensation benefits.*

In 2000, the administrative assistant hurt herself when she fell at work. She had a previous history of injury, including a 1973 spinal injury from a car accident. As a result of the 2000 work accident, the assistant began using a walker and lost her ability to control her bowels. Because of these problems, the assistant became able to carry out only menial tasks and was unable to pursue additional vocational training. She sought lifetime medical care and weekly compensation benefits for life. The workers' compensation commission determined the assistant was entitled to lifetime benefits. The decision was largely based on the testimony of a treating physician.

A state court affirmed the commission's decision, and the university appealed to the Court of Appeals of South Carolina. The court held **S.C. Code Section 42-9-10 provides that any person who is found totally and permanently disabled and is paraplegic from an injury is to receive workers' compensation benefits for life**. The university argued the circuit court was wrong in determining the assistant was paraplegic because the statute did not differentiate between complete and incomplete paraplegia. The court of appeals found the circuit court had reasonably relied on the physician's testimony. The university offered no evidence to refute the court's interpretation that the term "paraplegic" included incomplete paraplegia. *Reed-Richards v. Clemson Univ.*, 638 S.E.2d 77 (S.C. Ct. App. 2006).

# CHAPTER SEVEN

## Employment Discrimination

## I. RACE AND NATIONAL ORIGIN DISCRIMINATION

*Title VII of the Civil Rights Act of 1964, 42 U.S.C. § 2000e, et seq., prohibits discrimination in employment based upon race, color, sex, religion or national origin by any institution with 15 or more employees that effects commerce. Title VII exempts employment decisions based on religion, sex or national origin where these characteristics are bona fide occupational qualifications that are reasonably necessary to the operation of a particular business or enterprise.*

*Race discrimination lawsuits often include claims under 42 U.S.C. § 1981, which makes it unlawful for any person or entity to discriminate on the basis of race in the making and enforcement of contracts. Recently, the U.S. Supreme Court explained that a "ministerial exception" exempts religious employees from the coverage of anti-discrimination laws. See* Hosanna-Tabor Evangelical Lutheran Church and School v. EEOC, *Section V.B. of this chapter.*

## A.  Race Discrimination

◆   *The Third Circuit affirmed a Pennsylvania federal court's decision to dismiss a racial discrimination claim against a university.*

When an African-American applied for a radiology position at the university, she specifically asked for a part-time position. It hired her – and two years later offered her a salaried position at another site. Because she expressed a strong preference to work part time, she was classified as an "8/10ths employee" – meaning she was eligible for benefits without working full time. Shortly after her transfer, the university's head of radiology hired a head of radiology for the other site. The full-time position was never advertised and only the candidate who was interviewed was hired. The candidate was highly recommended by faculty members. But the woman objected, saying she would've been interested in the position. The following year, a budget shortfall required elimination of one position in the radiology department. The woman's position was chosen for the cut because she wasn't a faculty member and so could be dismissed with only 90 days' notice. She sued, alleging racial discrimination. The court granted the university judgment. She appealed, but the Third Circuit affirmed, as **she failed to submit evidence that suggested her race was the reason she wasn't chosen for the position and later terminated**. The ruling was affirmed. *Jones v. Temple Univ.*, 622 Fed.Appx. 131 (3d Cir. 2015).

◆   *The Seventh Circuit affirmed an Illinois ruling that held an author who submitted an article to a university's journal wasn't an employee, so he couldn't sue for race discrimination under Title VII.*

The author in this suit is a black man who never worked on staff at the university. In the late 1960s, he co-authored an article with a white professor that was published in a university journal. Then in 2014, the man submitted another article he'd written alone, but it was rejected for publication. The man filed a suit alleging a violation of Title VII. He claimed the rejection of his second submission reflected a longstanding practice of discriminating against black scholars. An Illinois judge dismissed the suit. On appeal, the Seventh Circuit affirmed, explaining that **Title VII didn't apply because there was no employment relationship between the author and the university**. So the suit was properly dismissed. *Douglas v. Univ. of Chicago*, 619 Fed.Appx. 556 (7th Cir. 2015).

◆   *The Tenth Circuit affirmed the dismissal of racial bias claims filed against a New Mexico university by a married couple whose teaching contracts weren't renewed.*

A Hispanic man and his African-American wife were both employed as non-tenure-track professors during their Ph.D. programs. They spent part of a year doing research in Seattle. When they returned to the university, they submitted expense reports. An audit revealed duplicate requests, and the auditor determined they looked more like fraudulent than honest mistakes. Their teaching contracts weren't renewed. The couple went on to apply to the school of social work. Their applications were accepted – but admission was later rescinded because they failed to provide medical records as required. They sued, alleging racial discrimination. The court dismissed the claim, and the Tenth Circuit affirmed. **The university showed it had valid reasons – the couple's recordkeeping failures – for terminating their contracts and rescinding their admissions.** The couple didn't provide evidence showing this was a pretext for bias, so the court correctly dismissed the claim. *Bird v. Regents of New Mexico State Univ.*, 619 Fed.Appx. 733 (10th Cir. 2015).

◆ *A Colorado federal judge dismissed the claim of an employee who resigned and then sued, alleging a racially hostile work environment.*

After an African-American woman was hired to be an assistant director of communications, she said her new supervisor told her that the university wanted to increase its Latino enrollment. The employee said she got the impression that what the supervisor really meant what that she'd wanted to hire a Latino, not a black person. Over the next year, the supervisor had several complaints with the employee's work. Her responsibilities were reduced, and she'd been written up twice. She resigned and sued, alleging a racially hostile work environment. She claimed her first conversation with the supervisor made her feel "[un]welcome because of her race." But the supervisor never said that; that was only what the employee read into the remark. While a single incident, if serious enough, can establish a hostile work environment, the court agreed with the university that this single incident couldn't. **The employee failed to cite evidence that race was connected to the harassment she said she suffered at work.** The case was dismissed. *McGowan v. Board of Trustees for Metropolitan State Univ. of Denver*, 114 F.Supp.3d 1129 (D. Colo. 2015).

◆ *A Pennsylvania federal judge rejected a discrimination claim filed by a black academic advisor who alleged he wasn't promoted due to his race.*

A university decided to restructure its academic advisor positions in 2010. Its new system had four tiers: a principal advisor at the top, a senior advisor in the No. 2 spot, then two "advisor II" positions; the rest were classified as "advisor I." The employee applied for the principal and senior advisor spots. He was not selected. He didn't apply for an "advisor II" position, so he wasn't considered. When the restructuring was complete, he had an "advisor I" title. He filed internal grievances that failed. In 2013, the employee was promoted to "advisor II." He sued, alleging the university refused to promote him to the top positions due to his race. Explaining the reasons it hired the successful candidates, the university asked the court to dismiss the claim. It did. **The advisor failed to provide believable evidence to show the university's reasons were only a pretext for bias.** So the claim failed. *Ruff v. Temple Univ.*, 122 F.Supp.3d 212 (E.D. Pa. 2015).

◆ *A New York federal judge refused to dismiss a race discrimination claim filed by a black employee who was terminated in a layoff – and quickly replaced with a white applicant.*

The black employee worked as an audio-visual services manager. His duties centered around the audio-visual equipment: managing the schedule to use it, keeping the inventory up to date, overseeing repair and replacement and helping set the budget. In 2012, the university fired him, citing a need to downsize. **He was the only employee listed in the university's record of the 2012 layoff.** A few weeks before the employee was let go, the school posted a position for an assistant director of technology. The job duties were basically the same – but the salary was about $10,000 more than the employee's salary had been. He applied for the position but was not hired. Instead, the university hired a white applicant to fill the position. The former employee sued, alleging a handful of claims including racial discrimination. The court dismissed most of the claims, but held the race-based claim had to proceed because more info was needed to determine whether racial bias had occurred. *Boyd v. Broome Community College*, No. 3:14-CV-0397 (GTS/DEP), 2015 WL 6962498 (N.D.N.Y 11/10/15).

◆ *An Illinois federal judge rejected a racial discrimination claim filed by a black employee who alleged he was paid less than white co-workers.*

The employee had a bachelor's degree in chemical engineering and worked as a manufacturing-process engineer in the university's waste management resource center. When the department downsized, the employee was laid off. He sued, alleging discriminatory wages due to racial bias. To state a valid *prima facie* claim of discrimination under Title VII, he had to show, among other things, that the employer treated similarly situated white employees better. He alleged he was paid less than "non-black chemical engineers." Problem was, he wasn't a chemical engineer. He was a manufacturing-process engineer. The court explained, "The comparison to the pay rate of chemical engineers – an entirely different type of engineer with a different job description – cannot serve as a similarly situated comparator to support the discrimination claim." **Employees with the same degree can have different job titles with different job descriptions and different pay grades**, which was the case here, and that "doomed his similarly situated argument," the court held. The claim was dismissed. *Brown v. Univ. of Illinois*, No. 10 C 06104, 2015 WL 6756266 (N.D. Ill. 11/5/15).

◆ *A North Carolina federal judge dismissed the racial discrimination claim of a black police officer who was not promoted to a managerial role.*

The officer had four years of experience when he applied for an internal promotion to a Captain/Emergency Manager Coordinator position. He had no management experience and was not invited for interviews. A white officer was hired. He had worked at the university for eight years – three of which were in a managerial role. The black officer sued, alleging the university failed to promote him due to racial bias. To state a valid claim, he had to show, among other things, that he was qualified for the position. He didn't make that showing as **he lacked supervisory experience when he applied for the promotion**. Even if the officer had stated a valid *prima facie* case, the court explained, he couldn't have shown the reason the candidate was hired – management experience, a valid and nondiscriminatory business reason – was a pretext for racial bias. So the claim failed. *Cherry v. Elizabeth City State Univ.*, No. 2:13-CV-71-D, 2015 WL 6690070 (E.D.N.C. 11/2/15).

◆ *An Alaska federal judge rejected a racial bias claim filed by a black employee who was not promoted to a new position created by a university.*

When the university created a new position in the student affairs office, a search committee assessed seven of 15 applicants who were qualified for the position. Two were invited to formal interviews – the plaintiff in this case and another applicant, who was Hispanic and a woman. She ultimately got the job. The man sued, accusing the university of racial bias. He said, "[D]espite being the most qualified and the most experienced applicant for the job," it chose "a less qualified applicant." But there was no evidence to suggest this was due to anyone's race. **"Title VII does not ensure the best will be selected – only that the selection process will be free from impermissible discrimination,"** the court noted. The case was dismissed. *Patterson v. Univ. of Alaska, Anchorage*, No. 3:14-cv-00111 RRB, 2015 WL 4757677 (D. Alaska 8/11/15).

◆ *A Maryland federal judge rejected racial bias claims filed by an employee who resigned rather than attend anger-management counseling.*

An African-American employee didn't get along with an Asian co-worker. In two incidents two years apart, the Asian man played movie clips with racial slurs. The black employee reported both incidents to HR. About a year after the second movie incident, the two men got into a fight. Both claimed the other "started it." The college investigated and found the Asian worker had instigated two racial incidents that contributed to the men's poor working relationship. He had to go to counseling. The college also determined the black employee had a history of hostile interactions with co-workers. He had to go to anger-management counseling. He refused and was suspended. He resigned and sued, alleging the college subjected him to a racially hostile workplace. The court **dismissed the claim. It failed because "two isolated racially charged incidents occurring years apart" wasn't enough to show the college looked the other way concerning racial harassment**, the court held. It noted, "Title VII does not protect employees from a bad relationship with a co-worker that is unrelated to race." *Palmer v. Prince George Community College*, No. RWT 14-0897, 2015 WL 4744845 (D. Md. 8/7/15).

◆ *A Maryland federal judge found a student's internship may have qualified him as an "employee" entitled to sue for employment bias under Title VII – but he failed to state a* prima facie *claim of racial bias, so the case was dismissed.*

A black student was enrolled in three classes in an Urban Leadership Program that had a minimum grade requirement. A student who received two Cs would be dismissed. The student also had an internship at the school. A white professor oversaw the internship program. Over the semester, the student changed his internship research plans several times. The professor found the finished project unacceptable, and the student received an incomplete. He also received two Cs on papers and was placed on academic probation. The professor offered to work with the student. But the student appealed the grades instead. An independent committee upheld the Cs – and changed the incomplete to an F. The student was dismissed. He sued, claiming race discrimination in violation of Title VII, which prohibits discrimination in employment. The school asked the court to dismiss the claim, saying the student's position as an intern didn't give him status as an employee. The court refused, as **the Fourth Circuit has held a person can be an "employee" under Title VII by receiving compensation – which doesn't have to mean money – in exchange for service to the employer that it has the right to control. But it granted the university judgment because the student failed to make a *prima facie* case of bias or show that the school's reason for dismissing him was only a pretext for racial bias.** The evidence supported the school's assertion that the decision was based on the student's academic work. *Stewart v. Morgan State Univ.*, 46 F.Supp.3d 590 (D. Md. 2014).

◆   *An Illinois federal judge rejected the Title VII claims of an Italian-American employee who was not rehired after he resigned.*

The employee was the director of labor relations at the university. He conducted a training program for university managers. During a portion of the program, someone asked him "if he was going to do the 'Guido' thing." A month later, in a one-on-one meeting, a different supervisor referred to Caucasians as "crackers." The employee complained to the director of employee relations. He also met with the school's associate provost, who investigated and concluded the comments were not intended to be derogatory and did not constitute racial discrimination. The employee resigned. Six months later, he asked to come back. The school refused his request. He unsuccessfully applied for another job at the school about 10 months later. The employee filed discrimination charges with the EEOC, asserting that he resigned because the two comments created a hostile work environment. He later sued the school, alleging retaliation under Title VII. The school filed a motion to dismiss. In this case, **the two isolated comments on which the employee relied did not violate Title VII**, the court held. They were made a month apart by two different people in two different settings, and they did not create a racially hostile employment environment. The motion to dismiss was granted. *Panico v. Univ. of Chicago*, No. 13 C 1987, 2014 WL 1097883 (N.D. Ill. 3/20/14).

◆   *This U.S. Supreme Court ruling narrows the definition of a "supervisor" under Title VII.*

An African-American employee complained a co-worker used the N-word and boasted of family ties to the Ku Klux Klan. A supervisor investigated and substantially confirmed the report, and the university issued the co-worker a written warning and required her to meet with a compliance supervisor. An investigation of another incident involving the two produced conflicting accounts, so the university provided counseling for both. The employee filed suit against the university for creating a racially hostile work environment. The court held for the university, and she appealed to the Seventh Circuit. It found complaints were investigated promptly, and necessary discipline was imposed. No retaliation was shown, and there was no evidence of "adverse action" by the university. The court upheld the ruling.

The employee sought a review by the U.S. Supreme Court. The employee specifically alleged the supervisor was the harasser. Under Title VII, an employer can be liable for harassment by employees in different ways. If the harasser is a supervisor and the harassment culminates in a tangible negative employment action, the employer is liable. If the supervisor's harassment doesn't involve a tangible negative employment action, the employer can still win by showing it took reasonable steps to prevent and correct the harassment – and the victim did not use available preventative or corrective opportunities. Here, the Court made the question of whether an employee is a supervisor under Title VII "relatively straightforward" by holding that a supervisor is someone who can take tangible employment actions against the victim. In this case, the **evidence did not show the harasser directed the day-to-day activities of the victim or had the authority to take a tangible employment action against the victim**. As a result, the lower court's ruling for the school was affirmed. *Vance v. Ball State Univ.*, 133 S.Ct. 2434 (U.S. 2013).

◆   *A New Jersey's appellate court found the termination of an employee was nondiscriminatory.*

In July 2013, the New Jersey Medical and Health Sciences Education Restructuring Act went into effect. Under the legislation, most of what used to be the University of Medicine and Dentistry of New Jersey (UMDNJ) was incorporated into Rutgers University. In 2005, the U.S. Attorney for New Jersey (USA-NJ) investigated two UMDNJ institutions for double-billing Medicaid. When the investigation launched, Vivian Sanks-King, a black woman, was the institution's general counsel. Four years earlier, Sanks-King had been notified that there was a problem with Medicaid billing. She claimed her efforts to investigate were blocked. She also insisted that she form a task force to find solutions. After the feds investigated, the U.S. Attorney's Office for the District of New Jersey filed a criminal complaint against UMDNJ, alleging it knowingly and willfully submitted many fraudulent claims to Medicaid. The USA-NJ gave an ultimatum: UMDNJ could enter into a deferred prosecution agreement (PDA), or the feds would criminally prosecute for double-billing Medicaid. It chose to enter into a PDA. At a meeting to negotiate the PDA, the USA-NJ told UMDNJ that firing four employees was a condition of the PDA. All four employees were women, and three were black. Sanks-King was one of the employees. She resigned – but later sued, claiming her termination amounted to racial- and gender-based discrimination. The trial court granted UMDNJ pretrial judgment. Sanks-King appealed, and the appellate court affirmed, ruling that **the USA-NJ's demand to terminate Sanks-King was a legitimate, nondiscriminatory reason to fire her**. So the claim failed. *Sanks-King v. Univ. of Medicine and Dentistry of New Jersey*, No. L-10130-07, 2013 WL 3744098 (N.J. Super. Ct. App. Div. 7/18/13).

◆   *A New Jersey federal judge dismissed a former faculty member's racial bias claims.*

Mercer County Community College (MCCC) hired Renee Walker in 1999 to work on a federally funded program to provide educational services to incarcerated students. In 2006, she received tenure. Afterward, Walker submitted a proposal to reorganize the federally funded program she worked on. The changes she suggested included releasing her from her teaching responsibilities and increasing her salary. MCCC rejected her proposal. In 2009, Walker's supervisor recommended that she be moved from her position to a 10-month faculty job, as the federally funded program had been cut back, and she'd arranged for other staff to teach courses she'd been paid to teach. MCCC accepted the recommendations. She contacted EEOC and filed a race and gender discrimination claim. In it, she said MCCC reassigned her to a faculty position because she was a "black alpha female with a bad attitude." The supervisor denied the comment. A year later – after a hearing – MCCC stripped Walker of tenure and fired her for taking an unauthorized leave and not teaching her scheduled classes. She sued, claiming racial and gender bias. **But she'd had a 14 year career at MCCC with only one disputed racial remark as evidence of discrimination.** And because MCCC showed a legitimate business reason to terminate Walker, the court dismissed her claim. *Walker v. Mercer County Community College,* No. 11-4973, 2013 WL 5739149 (D.N.J. 10/22/13).

◆   *Claims against administrators in a fired coach's race and sex bias suit were dismissed by a Louisiana federal judge, but his claims against the university could proceed.*

When he was hired by Louisiana State University (LSU), Anthony Minnis was a black tennis coach with more than 21 years under his belt and an impressive resume. Minnis suspected he was being paid less than other coaches. He asked administrators to tell him the salaries of all head coaches and assistant coaches in his conference. They did, saying Minnis' salary was "in proportion" with his peer coaches. But he learned he was the lowest-paid head coach as LSU. When he complained, he said LSU administrators gave him two "needs improvements" ratings and threatened his employment. Then he complained that LSU wasn't providing women's athletics equitable treatment. Four months later, LSU fired him without explanation. Minnis claimed LSU told potential employers calling for references that Minnis "had issues." Minnis sued LSU and the administrators, alleging they breached his federal liberty and equal protection rights, discriminated against him based on race and breached Title IX by not giving women's athletics equal treatment. The court dismissed the claims against the administrators. But **the coach's claims against LSU could continue**. *Minnis v. Board of Supervisors of Louisiana State Univ. and Agricultural and Mechanical College*, 972 F.Supp.2d 878 (M.D. La. 2013).

◆   *Dismissing a fired employee's bias claim, a South Carolina federal judge gave the woman 15 days to refile it.*

A black woman worked at Webster University (WU) on a campus in South Carolina. She took FMLA leave for severe depression. Two weeks later, she was demoted. She claims her supervisor demoted her because she refused his sexual advances. Five days later, she was fired for allegedly kicking another woman. Proceeding without an attorney, the employee sued WU for racial bias and gender-based retaliation, as well as retaliation under FMLA. **To make a valid claim, the woman had to show "similarly situated employees received**

**more favorable treatment."** She didn't do so, so the court dismissed the claim. But the judge gave the woman 15 days to rewrite and refile the claim. *Erby v. Webster Univ.*, No. C/A No. 3:13-518-JFA-SVH, 2013 WL 5495586 (D.S.C. 10/1/13).

◆  *A Pennsylvania federal court dismissed a professor's Title VII claim because he failed to first file a timely charge of discrimination with the EEOC.*

In 2003, Kwame Botwe-Asamoah began a three-year probationary period as a tenure-track professor at the University of Pittsburgh (Pitt). He claims his mentor warned that tenure at Pitt "is like a boys club" and only those who are "in" get tenure. Botwe-Asamoah applied for tenure in 2009. At a meeting with members of the review committee, Botwe-Asamoah claimed the department chair told him the university would turn him down, even if they recommended him, because it "tenured only two black professors in the past 10 years." Four months later, his tenure request was denied. He asked the dean to reconsider. The dean refused. In July 2011, Botwe-Asamoah filed a charge of discrimination based on race, color and national origin with the Pennsylvania Human Relations Commission (PHRC), but it refused to act on his charge because it was filed outside the 180-day time limit. Botwe-Asamoah filed suit against Pitt, alleging it refused him tenure because of his race – a violation of Title VII and the Pennsylvania Human Rights Act (PHRA). Pitt asked the court to dismiss the case. It did. **Finding Botwe-Asamoah didn't file a charge with the EEOC before bringing this claim in court, the judge dismissed the Title VII claim.** And since he'd failed to file a charge with the PHRC within the 180-day statute of limitations, the court dismissed the PHRA claim, too. *Bowte-Asamoah v. Univ. of Pittsburgh*, No. 13-cv-817, 2013 WL 5806464 (W.D. Pa. 10/29/13).

◆  *The U.S. Sixth Circuit Court of Appeals affirmed an Ohio federal judge's decision to dismiss a former professor's bias claims.*

Sam Han – an Asian-American – was hired as a tenure-track professor at a private university in Ohio. In his third year, Han received a poor evaluation from the tenure committee. Based on that, the school didn't renew his contract. Han contested the evaluation and eventually sued the university, alleging his termination was motivated by racial and gender bias. An Ohio federal judge dismissed his claim, and Han appealed to the Sixth Circuit. It affirmed. To state a valid Title VII claim, Han had to file a charge of discrimination with the EEOC within 300 days of the day he was notified his contract wouldn't be renewed. **But he missed that deadline, so the judge was correct to dismiss the Title VII claim.** To state valid racial bias claims under Section 1981, Han had to provide evidence that he was fired due to racial bias. He didn't. So the Sixth Circuit affirmed the decision. *Han v. Univ. of Dayton*, 541 Fed.Appx. 622 (6th Cir. 2013).

◆  *A federal appeals court held a white woman could not show an Alabama community college denied her a full-time teaching job based on her race.*

After working for the community college as a full-time instructor and clinical coordinator, the employee was assigned to part-time work. Near this time, the college hired a black woman on a full-time basis. The employee sued the community college in a federal court, claiming she was more qualified for the full-time job. The court held for the community college, and appeal reached the U.S. Court of Appeals, Eleventh Circuit. Like the lower court, the appeals court held the employee could not show the reasons given for the decision were a pretext for unlawful discrimination. Evidence showed the community college faced serious financial problems. It was reasonable to believe the employee could successfully teach part time. **The only evidence presented to support the race discrimination claim was that the college concurrently hired an African-American on a full-time basis.** But an accrediting agency had required the college to take this action, and it was not enough to permit the claim to proceed. The decision for the college was affirmed. *Patrick v. Bishop State Community College*, 470 Fed.Appx. 797 (11th Cir. 2012).

◆   *An African-American campus police officer could proceed with federal race discrimination claims against a District of Columbia university.*

After an ankle injury limited the police officer's mobility, the university restructured his duties to include sedentary work, such as manning dispatch or the front desk. He claimed a supervisor assigned him tasks outside his physical limits, told him he was insubordinate and lazy, and threatened to discipline him when he objected to walking or lifting. He said co-workers also made offensive remarks about his size and race almost daily. Claiming severe stress and anxiety, he took leave under the Family and Medical Leave Act and began to see a therapist. When his leave was up, the university discharged him, and he filed a race discrimination lawsuit. A federal court denied pretrial judgment to the university, finding the officer presented sufficient evidence to proceed to a trial. **He alleged discriminatory conduct that occurred on a nearly daily basis for almost three years.** In the court's opinion, a reasonable person could find this was enough to change the terms and conditions of his employment. *Leftwich v. Gallaudet Univ.*, 875 F.Supp.2d 81 (D.D.C. 2012).

◆   *A Tennessee career college did not convince a federal court that it had legitimate reasons to discharge African-American admission representatives.*

Three African-American admission representatives at the college said their supervisor repeatedly made racially offensive remarks. They said she referred to African-Americans as "you people" and described their conduct as "ghetto." The representatives said the supervisor overwhelmingly assigned leads to white representatives, and that when they complained, they were fired. They sued the college in a federal court, asserting claims under Title VII, the state Human Rights Act and related laws. **The court held a reasonable jury could find that the college gave false reasons for firing the representatives.** The reason stated for firing two of the representatives was poor performance, but they countered this with evidence that leads had been distributed in a discriminatory way. They also presented evidence that white employees were not fired for not meeting quotas. Since the representatives were entitled to present their claims to a jury, the court denied a request for pretrial judgment. *Smith v. Draughons Junior College*, No. 3:10-00873, 2012 WL 86935 (M.D. Tenn. 1/11/12).

◆  *An Alabama federal court noted the Eleventh Circuit has held that claims under 42 U.S.C. § 1981 are analyzed the same way as Title VII claims.*

A white community college instructor repeatedly asked to be appointed chair of his division. He was not appointed as division chair, and two African-American women were appointed to replace departing chairs in other divisions. Noting that only one of the college's division chairs was white, the instructor sued the college in a federal court under Title VII and 42 U.S.C. § 1981. The court found the college was not seeking anyone to chair his division. **It held the appointment of two African-Americans as division chairs was not relevant to the instructor's case and was not evidence of racial bias.** As there was no inference of race discrimination, the university was entitled to judgment. *Thompson v. Bishop State Community College*, No. 1:10-246-KD-B, 2011 WL 1464846 (S.D. Ala. 4/15/11).

◆  *Discourteous and rude treatment of African-American campus safety officers did not support a claim of hostile work environment based on race.*

The officers said white supervisors gave them the "cold shoulder," used racial epithets, ignored them, and falsely accused them of sleeping on the job. They said the supervisors interfered with their radio transmissions, gave them unnecessary reprimands, assigned them difficult tasks and denied them backup in dangerous situations. After a college human resources officer investigated the complaints, she suggested brief suspensions and letters of discipline for the supervisors. She further recommended anti-discrimination training for the entire department and special training for the supervisors. The African-American officers said the supervisors continued ignoring them, and they sued the college and supervisors in a state court. They claimed they were subjected to a hostile work environment in violation of the state Law Against Discrimination (LAD). The court found the evidence did not establish a claim and dismissed the case. On appeal, **a state appellate court noted that the test for liability under the LAD is virtually the same as the test under Title VII**. The officers not only failed to show a hostile work environment; they did not show any adverse employment action. The college promptly and thoroughly investigated their complaints and was shielded from any liability. As a result, the case had been properly dismissed. *Shockley v. College of New Jersey*, 2012 WL 996621 (N.J. Super. Ct. App. Div. 3/27/12).

◆  *Oklahoma university administrators were denied qualified immunity in a federal discrimination lawsuit by a business professor of Indian ancestry.*

According to the professor, the chair of his department said he was considered too "expensive" for an Asian Indian and that another Indian professor in their department was accepting less pay than the official salary schedule. At the end of the academic year, the university did not renew his contract. He sued the university and the four administrators who recommended his nonrenewal in a federal district court. His claim arose under 42 U.S.C. Section 1981, which prohibits race discrimination in the making of contracts.

According to the administrators, race had no part in the decision not to renew the contract and their decision was based on the professor's behavior problems. They said he started sleeping overnight in his office, left late night voice mails for a supervisor and sent her an inappropriate letter. The court denied the administrators' request for qualified immunity, and they appealed to the Tenth Circuit. It found the university president was entitled to pretrial judgment. His acceptance of a recommendation not to renew the professor's contract did not create an inference of intentional racial discrimination. But the court held the case against the other administrators should go forward. **Tenth Circuit decisions made it clear well before the time of their actions that employment discrimination on the basis of race violates Section 1981.** *Dasgupta v. Harris*, 407 Fed.Appx. 325 (10th Cir. 2011).

◆ *Finding the former department head of an Indiana religious university was a "ministerial employee," a federal court refused to hear her Title VII action.*

The department head said she was repeatedly exposed to discriminatory acts and harassed on account of her African-American race. She quit because of a dispute concerning a co-worker. The department head sued the university in a federal district court for racial bias under Title VII. But the court held she was a ministerial employee. Application of the ministerial exception to Title VII resulted in dismissal of certain federal claims by ministerial employees against religious employers. **The ministerial exception is based on a religious institution's First Amendment right to be free of government interference with employees who authoritatively interpret and preach its doctrine.**

According to the department head, her position did not make her the virtual equivalent of a minister. She argued the social work department was not designed to spread the faith, but instead had secular purposes. But the court noted that the Social Work Student Handbook declared one of the program's objectives was to "provide opportunities for the integration of Christian principles within the context of professional social work values and ethics." Finding the nature and character of her duties were ministerial, the court applied the ministerial exception and dismissed the case. *Adams v. Indiana Wesleyan Univ.*, No. 3:09-CV-468, 2010 WL 2803077 (N.D. Ind. 7/15/10).

◆ *A single incident of racial discrimination was not enough to support a Title VII claim of hostile work environment.*

Appalachian State University (ASU) hired an African-American clerical worker. A Caldwell Community College (CCC) employee who was at ASU to pick up mail used a racial epithet in a conversation with an ASU secretary. The clerical worker said the secretary expressed agreement with the comment, and he claimed that ASU failed to take action to address the incident despite his complaints. The clerical worker later sued ASU and CCC in a federal district court for race discrimination under Title VII. He alleged no other incidents of discrimination. The court stated that to prove a hostile work environment exists, an employee must show harassment that is so severe or pervasive that it alters his or her working conditions and creates an abusive environment.

**Hostile work environments generally result from repeated instances of harassment rather than single, isolated occurrences.** Factors to consider in determining whether a hostile environment exists include the frequency of the conduct, whether the conduct is physically threatening or humiliating, and whether it unreasonably interferes with an employee's work performance. As the clerical worker was unable to show the hostility in his work environment was so severe that it altered his employment conditions or created an abusive atmosphere, the claims against both institutions failed. *Blue v. Appalachian State Univ.*, No. 5:07cv108, 2009 WL 703851 (W.D.N.C. 3/16/09).

◆   *A white assistant coach was allowed to go forward with a Title VII claim that he was discharged because he was married to an African-American woman.*

The coach claimed college athletic directors made numerous racially biased remarks, including disparaging comments about his African-American wife. The team was investigated for possible rules infractions. An athletic director's report criticized the coaching staff but proposed retaining the coaches under improvement plans. The college president and two other officials decided to fire the white assistant coach and an assistant of African-American heritage. The assistant coach claimed an athletic director referred to an African-American employee as a "jungle bunny" and to his wife as an "Aunt Jemima." The assistant coach sued the college in a federal court, which held for the college. On appeal, **the U.S. Court of Appeals, Second Circuit, held Title VII's prohibition of race discrimination applied to claims based on a relationship with another person**. The court reasoned that an employee is subjected to discrimination based on race when an adverse job action is taken because an employer disapproves of interracial association. As the assistant coach was a member of a protected class, he could proceed with his Title VII claim. *Holcomb v. Iona College*, 521 F.3d 130 (2d Cir. 2008).

◆   *Auburn University did not discriminate against an African-American employee by declining to reclassify her job.*

According to the employee, Auburn classified her position lower than for the same jobs performed by white employees. She said the university failed to promote her and retaliated against her for complaining about racial disparities in employee salaries and classifications. The employee sued Auburn in an Alabama federal district court, alleging it violated Title VII. In an attempt to support her claims, she compared herself to several other employees. The court found the other employees were not relevant for comparison as they had different job duties. **The court found no evidence to show any different treatment was based on race, and held the employee did not show a causal connection between her complaints about disparities and the failure to reclassify her position.** As the university offered legitimate nondiscriminatory reasons for its failure to reclassify the employee, the court held for Auburn. On appeal to the U.S. Court of Appeals, Eleventh Circuit, the court determined the decision by the district court was proper and affirmed the judgment for Auburn. *Johnson v. Auburn Univ.*, 193 Fed.Appx. 955 (11th Cir. 2006).

### B.  National Origin Discrimination

*National origin discrimination cases are usually filed under Title VII. State anti-discrimination laws also include national origin as a protected class. In*

Delaware State College v. Ricks, *449 U.S. 250 (1980), the Supreme Court held the limitations period for a Title VII national origin discrimination case began to run on the date a teacher was denied tenure, not his final employment date.*

*In* St. Francis College v. Al-Khazraji, *481 U.S. 604 (1987), the Supreme Court held that ethnic groups are not to be considered a single race under 42 U.S.C. § 1981. For that reason, an Arab professor was entitled to prove that he was subjected to intentional discrimination because he was an Arab, rather than solely because of his place of origin or his religion. Persons of Arab descent were protected from discrimination under Section 1981.*

◆ *A Connecticut federal judge refused to dismiss the claim of a professor who alleged that he was denied a promotion because of national origin bias.*

The professor was born in India and hired by the college in 1976. In early 2012, the employee complained to the dean that he was being treated differently than colleagues – and he felt it was due to his ethnic background. That summer, a full-time employee left, and the professor expressed interest in the position. The dean told him that he wouldn't be considered – instead, when a new faculty member was hired, that person would become the program director. But a colleague – not a new faculty member – was promoted to the position. The professor sued, alleging the school violated Title VII by failing to promote him because of his national origin. The court refused to dismiss the claim. To state a *prima facie* case of discriminatory failure to promote, the professor had to show he's of Indian national origin, and applied for and was qualified for the job, but was rejected under circumstances that suggest unlawful discrimination. The school argued that the professor never applied for the position. But the court said **his expression of interest in the position was enough to let the case proceed**. *Shah v. Tunxis Community College*, No. 3:14-cv-00712 (MPS), 2015 WL 4254909 (D. Conn. 7/14/15).

◆ *A Florida federal court rejected the claims of a professor who alleged he was denied a sabbatical, suspended and fired on the basis of race and national origin discrimination.*

A tenured professor of African ancestry was born in Haiti. When the 2010 earthquake hit his homeland, he wanted to travel to Haiti, conduct research there and help in the recovery effort. In 2012, his performance evaluations were "below expectation" in every area he was evaluated in. The sabbatical committee recommended him for a sabbatical, but the provost refused to grant it because the dean and department chair wouldn't recommend him due to his poor performance. Under a provision added to the faculty's union contract in 2009, the professor had to submit to a performance improvement plan (PIP) due to seven years of performance problems. He missed three deadlines on the PIP and was suspended. The professor submitted a draft of the PIP, but the chair rejected it. Despite being given specific guidance over the course of multiple drafts, the professor missed the deadline and was fired. He sued, alleging race and national origin discrimination. But the court granted pretrial judgment because **the school had valid reasons to deny him a sabbatical, suspend him and fire him – and the professor didn't show those reasons weren't true**. It found the school had legitimate business reasons – so granted it summary judgment. *Jolibois v. Florida Int'l Univ. Board of Trustees,* 92 F.Supp.3d 1239 (S.D. Fla. 2015).

◆    *An Italian-American employee failed to show the change in his job title was due to bias and retaliation based on his national origin.*

An Italian-American started working at the John D. Calandra Italian American Institute of the City of New York (CUNY) in 1987. In 1994, the institute was made part of CUNY's Queens College. The following year, the employee became the institute's "Director for Research and Education." Part of his job duties included overseeing research related to CUNY'S Italian-American affirmative action programs. In March 2006, the incoming dean – also an Italian-American – made plans to change the focus from affirmative action to promoting higher education for Italian-Americans. As part of the shift, the dean wanted to change the employee's job title to "Director of Demographic Studies." When the employee's new title went into effect, his salary and benefits didn't change. But he considered it a demotion because he lost staff and had to abandon his affirmative-action research. He gave two speeches criticizing CUNY's affirmative-action efforts. Then he was told he needed the new dean's prior approval before he gave presentations about his research. He sued CUNY, alleging bias and retaliation on the basis of his national origin. The judge dismissed both claims. **The bias claim failed because he didn't prove the changes to his job title and duties occurred because he is an Italian-American.** And the retaliation claim failed because CUNY defendants showed the changes to his job title and duties were in the works in March – before the presentations he claims were the reason he was retaliated against. *Milione v. City Univ. of New York*, 950 F.Supp.2d 704 (S.D.N.Y. 2013).

◆    *The Fifth Circuit affirmed a ruling that a former employee failed to show she was let go because of discrimination against her as an Asian.*

A Vietnamese employee transfered to a different department. At the time, the assistant dean and associate director exchanged emails about the employee. In the exchange, the dean commented: "Impressive – NOTE her email name 'shedragon' at GMAIL." They hired the employee and gave her a personalized job description. In it, the dean wrote employees were expected to treat everyone "politely and with a friendly, interested, helpful, cheerful demeanor." He specified the importance "in American/Texas business culture to look at people when speaking to them and being spoken to – looking down, looking away or facial expressions of disinterest, eye-rolling, boredom or contempt are completely unacceptable." From the start, the dean was not happy with the employee's performance. When her one-year contract was up, she was told that her work and level of communication weren't acceptable. Her contract was renewed for six months. When that contract ended, she was let go. She sued, claiming she was discriminated against based on her Asian heritage. She pointed to the comment about her email address and instructions on how to behave in "American/Texas business culture." The judge dismissed the claim without a trial. She appealed to the Fifth Circuit, and it affirmed, saying **the comments were "stray remarks – too vague and indirect to demonstrate**

**racial animus."** So the ruling was affirmed. *Nguyen v. Univ. of Texas School of Law*, 542 Fed.Appx. 320 (5th Cir. 2013).

◆   *A Texas college instructor's failure to prove he had the required credentials for his job was a valid reason to fire him.*

When the college audited its faculty qualifications, the instructor came under scrutiny. He held degrees from Addis Ababa University in Ethiopia and Odessa Civil Engineering Institute in Russia. To be qualified for his position, the instructor needed the equivalent of an advanced degree from a U.S. institution. The audit evaluated his degrees as only equivalent to an A.S. in Drafting Technology and a B.S. in Architecture. As a result, the instructor was let go as not properly credentialed. In a federal court, he asserted the real reason for dismissal was his race and national origin. **But the court found the college had a valid, nondiscriminatory reason for dismissing the instructor.** He lacked the credentials to be qualified for the job. Without evidence of an appropriate degree, the court found no reasonable jury would find the college dismissed the instructor for an unlawful purpose. *Tesso v. Westwood College*, No. 3:11-CV-0246-D, 2012 WL 3204916 (N.D. Tex. 8/8/12).

◆   *A Hispanic candidate for an associate professor job failed to show his application was rejected based on his race, color or national origin.*

The candidate sought an associate professor position in the anthropology department at Montclair State University (MSU). Job announcements generated about 52 applications for the job, which were reviewed by a six-member hiring committee. A hiring committee narrowed the field to three. A Caucasian applicant was eventually chosen, and the Hispanic candidate filed a federal district court lawsuit against MSU for race, color and national origin discrimination under Title VII. The court held for MSU, and the candidate appealed to the U.S. Court of Appeals, Third Circuit.

Although the court found the candidate satisfied the preliminary elements of his case by showing he was qualified for the job and it was awarded to a non-Hispanic candidate, he failed to prove the reasons given by MSU for not hiring him were a pretext for discrimination. MSU said it chose another candidate because he did not have the qualifications it sought for the job. Specifically, the candidate's research focused on great apes, whereas the department was looking for someone who was an expert in the study of the social and cultural aspects of disease or health patterns. In addition, the candidate did not provide much evidence of past successful teaching performance. **Since MSU had legitimate and nondiscriminatory reasons for its decision, and there was not enough evidence to show a pretext, he did not prove MSU's decision was discriminatory**, and the judgment was affirmed. *Sarmiento v. Montclair State Univ.*, 285 Fed.Appx. 905 (3d Cir. 2008).

◆   *A Virginia university was not motivated by discrimination when it chose not to renew a temporary professor's contract.*

The professor was a Nigerian national who was hired under a nine-month contract for a non-tenure track position in the agriculture department. He was relocating from Australia, and he said the department chair emailed him about the possibility of reimbursement for moving expenses. But the written contract did not mention reimbursement. During his first semester of work, a colleague and students made repeated complaints about him. Despite the complaints, the department chair gave the professor a favorable evaluation. The next semester, another colleague began complaining about the professor. Students continued to complain about him, but the university again renewed his contract. However, it did not offer him a tenure-track position. Similar problems recurred the next year, and other faculty members complained about his condescending attitude.

After learning that his contract would not be renewed, the professor sued the university and officials in a federal district court, claiming his contract was not renewed based on his national origin and age. He also said the university breached a contract by disregarding a promise to pay his moving expenses. The court held for the university, and the professor appealed to the U.S. Court of Appeals, Fourth Circuit. It found **a reasonable jury could not find that the decision not to renew his contract was based on national origin or age discrimination**. Instead, the decision was based on the many problems the professor had at work. He did not dispute that colleagues who co-taught classes with him complained about him and said they would not work with him again. There was simply no evidence of national origin discrimination. The court also rejected the breach of contract claim and affirmed the judgment. *Ilozor v. Hampton Univ.*, 286 Fed.Appx. 834 (4th Cir. 2008).

◆   *A university that provided a research associate with an office, phone and business cards was not her employer under Title VII of the Civil Rights Act.*

The University of Utah granted the research associate a one-year appointment in its civil and environmental engineering department. She shared an office, phone and mailbox with other workers. However, the university did not pay her a salary or contribute Social Security or other taxes on her behalf. The associate used her own computer. The university did not monitor her day-to-day activities, but retained an ownership interest in the work she produced. After the university declined to renew the associate's contract, she claimed discrimination based on national origin and gender, and she sued the university in a federal district court. The court dismissed the case, finding the associate could not sue under Title VII because she was not a university employee. On appeal, the Tenth Circuit found **the key inquiry was whether the university controlled "the means and manner by which the work [was] accomplished."** In affirming the conclusion that the associate was not an employee, the court relied heavily on the fact that the university exercised very little control over her daily activities. The associate was free to pursue any research activities she chose, and her research was not supervised. The university did not pay her a salary, and it provided only minimal supplies to her. The associate was different from faculty members because she had no teaching or administrative obligations. As the university exercised little control over her activities, she was not an employee and her Title VII claim failed. *Xie v. Univ. of Utah*, 243 Fed.Appx. 367 (10th Cir. 2007).

◆   *A Muslim job applicant failed to show an Ohio college based its decision not to hire him upon his race.*

The applicant was denied a full-time tenure-track position as an assistant professor of mathematics despite over 10 years of teaching experience and an extensive record of publishing. A hiring committee eliminated him from consideration because he had recently been denied tenure by another university and submitted outdated reference letters. One of the letters indicated concern about the applicant's performance. The college selected a white person for the position who had formerly studied under the department chair as a student. The applicant sued the college in a federal district court, alleging it violated Title VII of the Civil Rights Act and Section 1981. The court dismissed the case.

The applicant appealed to the Sixth Circuit, which held that **to prevail in a Section 1981 race discrimination case, there must be proof of intentional discrimination**. The applicant argued the district court did not properly consider preferential treatment for the white applicant as proof of intent to discriminate. The court disagreed, finding the department chair's preference for the white applicant, whom he knew personally, did not prove discrimination. The court accepted the college's position – that the applicant was not one of the most qualified candidates and that the former student was the most likely to succeed – as legitimate, nondiscriminatory reasons for its actions. The judgment was affirmed. *Amini v. Oberlin College*, 440 F.3d 350 (6th Cir. 2006).

## II.  SEX DISCRIMINATION

*Sex discrimination is prohibited by Title VII, the Equal Pay Act, and state laws. These laws apply to public and private institutions of higher education. Colleges and universities may not engage in discriminatory employment practices. The First Amendment "ministerial exception" precludes discrimination claims by ministerial employees against religious institutions.*

### A.  Different Treatment

◆ *A woman who alleged she was treated differently than male colleagues failed to state a valid discriminatory termination claim because she didn't show she was qualified for the job. A Florida federal judge dismissed her case.*

An applicant was two classes shy of the required degree for the job. The university hired the woman, warning her that she had to finish the courses and obtain her degree by a specified time. Failing to do so would be grounds for termination. She tried to enroll in a nearby university but missed the enrollment deadline for the upcoming semester. When the woman told her male supervisor that she'd have to wait until the following semester to complete the classes, he said that would be fine. Later, she complained to HR that the manager micromanaged her but not her male colleagues. The woman was transferred to another department. Her new supervisor fired the woman when she didn't complete the degree in the required time frame. She sued for sex discrimination under Title VII. But the judge dismissed the claim, as she failed to show that she was qualified for the position. **She didn't obtain the degree within the specified time frame, so she wasn't qualified for the position**, the court held. The claim was dismissed. *Lima v. Univ. of Miami*, No. 14-cv-22712-SEITZ/TURNOFF, 2015 WL 4480341 (S.D. Fla. 7/21/15).

◆ *A federal district court in Illinois dismissed Title IX claims that were filed by a professor who was the subject of two sexual harassment investigations.*

After receiving a complaint alleging the professor made improper sexual advances toward a female student, the school conducted an investigation. The school concluded the professor had violated the school's sexual harassment policy. The professor was not terminated or barred from teaching. However, he was given undisclosed discipline. The professor asked for a formal investigation but the request was denied. The student who filed the complaint sued the school. The suit received media coverage. The school and the professor agreed he would not teach any classes during that semester. He asked the school to be discreet about his absence. But he claimed the school made a series of false statements to students and the media about his leave. Another student filed a complaint against the professor. It was investigated by a third party who concluded that there was insufficient evidence to support the charge of non-consensual sex. However, the third party also found the professor violated the school's sexual harassment policy "because he had unequal power in the relationship." The professor sued, claiming the school violated Title IX by discriminating against him on the basis of his gender "when it issued a discriminatory and baseless investigative report." **The court determined the professor's claim failed because he did not show circumstances legitimately suggested that gender played a role in the investigation.** His claim that the investigation was flawed was not connected to his gender. So the claim was dismissed. *Ludlow v. Northwestern Univ.*, 79 F.Supp.3d 824 (N.D. Ill. 2015).

◆ *An Arkansas federal judge rejected the claim of a terminated professor who alleged she was treated more harshly than male professors.*

While at home, a professor threatened her neighbors with a weapon. The neighbors called the police. She was arrested on a felony charge. The next day, a newspaper reported the arrest. The college put the professor on administrative leave and investigated the matter, looking at the situation as a campus safety matter. The professor was fired and later banned from campus due to the assault charge. She sued the college, alleging gender bias. She claimed two male professors had been arrested, and their charges were published in the paper but they weren't fired. Her argument didn't sway the judge, who explained one man was arrested for nonviolent misdemeanors: possession of marijuana and contempt of court – much less serious charges than felonious aggravated assault. The other man's charge was similar to hers, but his discipline was decided by different decision-makers. A different decision-maker suggests a reason other than bias is behind the different treatment, the court explained. **The court found the men weren't valid "comparators" as one was charged with less serious offenses and the other's case was decided by a different supervisor**, so the judge granted the college judgment without a trial. *Moore v. Philander Smith College*, 25 F.Supp.3d 1095 (E.D. Ark. 2014).

◆ *A Pennsylvania federal judge refused to dismiss the sex-bias claim of a professor who was allegedly fired for creating a "hostile and threatening academic environment" for a female student.*

The student accused the tenured associate professor of impropriety. The president fired him, finding his "written and verbal communications to [the student] created a hostile and threatening academic environment" and interfered with her academic performance. The professor filed a grievance that went to arbitration. But it was denied at a hearing. The professor sued, claiming the school and 12 individuals discriminated against him on the basis of race, gender, age and religion. The court dismissed most of the claims without a trial. **But the sex discrimination claim had to go forward because the president, dean, chair of his former department and the person hired to replace him were all women.** That was enough to keep the claim alive in the early stages of the proceedings. *Obotetukudo v. Clarion Univ.*, No. 13-0639, 2014 WL 3870003 (W.D. Pa. 8/6/14).

◆   *The Tenth Circuit affirmed a Colorado federal court's decision to grant a university judgment on an associate professor's gender bias claim.*

In 1987, an employee was hired as a tenure-track associate professor, and she was granted tenure in 1992. In 2004, a new interim dean was named. He and the associate professor didn't get along. In 2006, the interim dean became the permanent dean. Later than year, the employee applied for a promotion to professor. To apply for the promotion, she had to submit a comprehensive dossier of materials for seven levels of reviewers to evaluate her performance in teaching, advising, professional development and service. The first two levels – the tenured faculty in her department and the department chair – recommended promoting her. At level three, a six-member school committee pointed to a gap in her published work from 1984-2006 and did not recommend her promotion. She reapplied the following year. This time, only the first level recommended her. At the second level, the department chair noted problems with her professional development. She sued, alleging gender bias. Her suit claimed the dean was biased against her because she's a woman, and he used the president as his "cat's paw" to deny her the promotion. The judge rejected her argument. She appealed, but the appellate court affirmed. **To merit a trial on a "cat's paw" theory, she had to provide evidence of the dean's bias and also show that he caused her to lose the promotion.** She couldn't meet the second requirement, so the Tenth Circuit affirmed the decision to grant judgment. *Frederick v. Metropolitan State Univ. of Denver Board of Trustees*, 535 Fed.Appx. 713 (10th Cir. 2013).

◆   *The Third Circuit affirmed a Pennsylvania federal judge's refusal to order a new trial and upheld a jury's verdict that a tenure denial wasn't based on gender bias.*

The employee went to work as a tenure-track assistant professor. Tenure decisions were made by the university's tenure committee. Faculty members, are rated "excellent," "good," "fair" or "unsatisfactory." During the employee's first three years, the committee rated him "good." In his fourth year, the 11-member committee gave a split decision, with only four members rating him "good." Five others rated him "fair," and one rated him "unsatisfactory." In his fifth year, he received only one "good" rating. Five rated him "fair," and five rated him "unsatisfactory." He applied for tenure, which was denied by a 9-2 vote. He sued, claiming the university violated Title VII by denying him tenure based on his gender. At trial, he argued the university's bias against men was demonstrated by the fact that it granted tenure to three women who he claimed were less qualified. Before the jury retired, the judge gave it a "pretext instruction," telling members he had to prove "his gender was a determinative factor" in being denied tenure. The jury found for the school. The employee appealed to the Third Circuit, claiming the judge gave the wrong jury instruction and the verdict went against the weight of the evidence. But the Third Circuit wasn't swayed, explaining that **a new trial is appropriate only when the jury's verdict is so flawed that it "cries out to be overturned or shocks the conscience."** That wasn't the case here. The Third Circuit affirmed the judgment for the university. *Kull v. Kutztown Univ. of Pennsylvania*, 543 Fed.Appx. 244 (3d Cir. 2013).

◆  *A female law professor did not prove she was subjected to unlawful gender discrimination or retaliation by the University of Puerto Rico School of Law.*

During her five-year probationary period, the professor worked with a male professor who became romantically involved with a female student. At the time, there was no rule banning such relationships or requiring faculty to report them. While the professor's request for tenure was pending, the law school dean chastised her for failing to report the male professor's relationship. Later, the law school denied her request to extend her probationary period. The professor sued the university for gender discrimination and retaliation. A federal court held for the university, and she appealed. The U.S. Court of Appeals, First Circuit, held the professor was unable to show an adverse employment action based on failure to conform to gender stereotypes. **Nothing indicated she was held to a different standard based on her gender.** Descriptions of the professor made during the tenure process were found to be gender neutral. Since these comments did not support a claim of unlawful gender discrimination under Title VII, the court affirmed the judgment. *Morales-Cruz v. Univ. of Puerto Rico*, 676 F.3d 220 (1st Cir. 2012).

◆  *Gender discrimination claims brought by a male professor will go forward against a dean but not against a Pennsylvania community college.*

A male theater professor claimed a female faculty member was openly hostile to men and tried to get rid of him. After he received tenure, the female reported he had sexually harassed a student and given beer to others who were underage. His tenure was revoked, and he was fired. The male sued the college and dean in a federal district court, alleging he was fired and deprived of tenure because of his sex. The court held **the male could not show the college had a policy or custom that deprived him of his constitutional rights, acted deliberately and was the moving force behind the violation**. Nor could he show the college caused him injury via policy or custom. The court dismissed the claims against the college, but not the claims against the dean. The male alleged that the dean was the supervisor of the female faculty member who he charged with discrimination. *Heneghan v. Northampton Community College*, No. 09-04979, 2010 WL 2730638 (E.D. Pa. 7/8/10).

◆  *A Michigan defeated a gender bias claim by a male faculty candidate despite evidence that female candidates were preferred.*

After twice being denied tenured positions, the candidate filed an internal complaint for gender discrimination. A few months later, he claimed his work laboratory was substantially reduced in size. The candidate sued the university in a state court for gender bias and retaliation. It conceded that a dean involved in the hiring process had shown a preference for female candidates, but argued this was irrelevant because the candidate was not qualified for either job. He did not hold a relevant doctoral degree, and was not an otherwise competitive applicant. The university asserted that the candidate was also subject to discipline for assaulting a student. After the trial court held for the university, the case came before the Court of Appeals of Michigan. **Despite the dean's bias toward females, the candidate was considered equally with other applicants in the early screening process.** The university would have rejected him even if bias did not play a role in the hiring process. *Dybas v. Michigan State Univ.*, No. 281547, 2009 WL 2195110 (Mich. Ct. App. 7/23/09).

◆   *An Ohio community college did not commit age or gender discrimination by refusing to hire an overqualified candidate as an academic advisor.*

Sinclair Community College created and advertised two entry-level academic advisor positions. Nearly 200 women and more than 80 men applied for the jobs. Of nine finalists, the search committee chose to interview only one man, who was 59 years old at the time and had over 20 years of experience as a university director of academic advising. The new positions at Sinclair were entry level and paid much less than the director's current job. After Sinclair chose two women for the vacancies who were younger and less experienced than the director, he sued the community college in an Ohio court for sex and age discrimination. While the director stated a case of age discrimination, he could not pursue the claim because the college gave valid, nondiscriminatory reasons for not hiring him. The court found the gender disparity was not caused by favoritism, but because women dominate the field of academic advising.

The case reached the Court of Appeals of Ohio, which agreed with the director that he had a more impressive resume than the women who were hired. But his resume was not so impressive that an employer would have been compelled to hire him. **The college considered him overqualified for an entry-level job.** It had a good reason to hire the women, who had experience with Ohio community colleges. The court held the trial court had properly granted judgment to the college. *Silberstein v. Montgomery County Community College Dist.*, No. 23439, 2009 WL 3977080 (Ohio Ct. App. 11/20/09).

◆   *An Arizona community college could lawfully prohibit a transgender instructor from using a women's restroom.*

The college received complaints about the instructor's use of a women's restroom and banned her from it until she completed sex reassignment surgery. Later, the college declined to renew her employment contract. The instructor sued the college in a federal district court for gender discrimination under Title VII. She also alleged a violation of Title IX and constitutional violations. After the court held for the college, appeal reached the Ninth Circuit. According to the court, gender stereotyping is direct evidence of sex discrimination. Transgender individuals can sue for sex discrimination based on the theory that they were subjected to discrimination because they did not conform to "socially constructed gender norms." As a result, the court held **employers cannot discriminate against a transgender employee solely because the employee does not behave in a way that the employer believes is gender-appropriate**. But the college produced evidence that it barred her from using the women's restroom for safety-related concerns. Since the instructor could not show this was pretextual and that its real reason for the ban was illegal gender discrimination, her Title VII claim failed. The court also affirmed the judgment on related Title IX and equal protection claims. *Kastl v. Maricopa County Community College Dist.*, 325 Fed.Appx. 492 (9th Cir. 2009).

◆  *The discharge of a North Carolina campus police officer for various insubordinate acts did not violate Title VII.*

The officer refused to comply with an instruction to wear a tie, which led to a written warning for unacceptable personal conduct. She filed a grievance but was told that she was not eligible to do so because she was not a permanent employee. The officer later struck a guard rail while driving her patrol car on campus. A report indicated she did not contact her superior until she realized he had learned about the accident. A week later, the officer met with a fellow officer at the university's cafeteria for breakfast during her shift, even though officers were prohibited from eating with other officers while on duty. A university police captain ordered the officer not to charge a student for a misconduct incident as this would violate university policy. Because the officer refused his order, she was placed on administrative leave. After an investigation, the officer was discharged for unacceptable personal conduct and insubordination. She sued the university in a federal district court for sex discrimination. **The court held the officer did not show she was performing her job in a satisfactory manner at the time of discharge.** She failed to follow instructions, violated a rule against eating with other officers while on duty, and issued two criminal citations to a university student even though she knew it was against university policy. On appeal, the Fourth Circuit, affirmed the decision for the reasons stated by the district court. *Hooper v. State of North Carolina*, 222 Fed.Appx. 271 (4th Cir. 2007).

◆  *A 13-year veteran Indiana university tennis coach was allowed to pursue a claim that she was fired from her job based on her gender.*

In the coach's final year as head coach of the women's tennis team at Indiana University-Purdue (Indianapolis), the team had its best season ever and qualified for the National Collegiate Athletic Association tournament for the first time. It also had the highest grade point average of all athletic teams at the school. Despite her performance, the university discharged the 53-year-old coach for violating rules requiring coaches "to treat others with dignity and respect" and to "exhibit a higher standard of behavior." About a month later, the university hired the 23-year-old sister of the men's tennis coach to replace her.

The coach sued the university in a federal district court for gender and age discrimination. The court held for the university, and she appealed to the U.S. Court of Appeals, Seventh Circuit. **The court found evidence that the university treated similarly situated male employees more favorably than the coach.** Specifically, there was evidence that the men's soccer coach and the men's tennis coach committed the same rules violations as the coach. The male coaches were provided with progressive discipline, while the female was not. The university never warned her she was in danger of losing her job and simply told her they were looking to move in a "new, different direction." Under these circumstances, it was improper to dismiss the gender discrimination claim. But the dismissal of her age discrimination claim was affirmed. *Peirick v. Indiana Univ.-Purdue Univ. Indianapolis Athletic's Dep't*, 510 F.3d 681 (7th Cir. 2007).

◆   *A professor who was turned down for a tenure-track position did not show the denial was based on her gender or ethnicity.*

The professor applied for a tenure-track professorship at the University of Texas-El Paso (UTEP). UTEP instead offered her a visiting professor position, which she accepted. The professor soon reapplied for the tenure-track position but was not offered the job. She appealed unsuccessfully within the university, then sued UTEP in a federal district court. The professor claimed UTEP denied her a promotion on the basis of her Hispanic origin and gender.

The district court noted UTEP had stated nondiscriminatory reasons for its decision that were not shown to be false. Specifically, UTEP said it rejected the professor for the job due to her lack of experience in strategic management, level of potential for publishing, and level of collegiality with UTEP faculty during her employment as a visiting professor. As she did not convince the court that any of these reasons were false, the court held for UTEP. On appeal, the U.S. Court of Appeals, Fifth Circuit, noted that **UTEP set forth legitimate, nondiscriminatory reasons for declining to hire the professor for a tenure-track position. She could prevail only by showing these reasons were pretextual.** As the professor's own testimony was not enough to show UTEP's stated reasons were false, the court affirmed the judgment. *Alvarez-Diemer v. Univ. of Texas-El Paso*, 258 Fed.Appx. 689 (5th Cir. 2007).

◆   *A Maryland university discharged a professor for professional misconduct and neglect of duty, not for discriminatory reasons.*

The head of the department considered the assistant professor to be a top-notch researcher. The university sometimes paid overload compensation, which must be recommended and approved by the dean's office and approved by the provost. It is paid when teaching or research exceeds the normal workload. The assistant professor asked the chair for overload compensation for overtime hours she claimed to have logged and for additional childcare expenses. The chair strongly endorsed her request and noted her extraordinary efforts in attracting research grants and contracts. The university rejected the request.

The assistant professor's relationships with university staff and faculty began to deteriorate. She accused the department head and other faculty members of sex discrimination. The university received allegations that the assistant professor had engaged in scientific misconduct in connection with the grant for which she sought overload compensation. After an investigation, the university discharged her for professional misconduct and willful neglect of duty. The assistant professor sued the university and others in a federal court for sex discrimination. The court found no evidence of discrimination. **The university had a legitimate, nondiscriminatory reason for every action it took.** The Fourth Circuit affirmed the judgment. *Britton v. Univ. of Maryland at Baltimore*, 206 Fed.Appx. 282 (4th Cir. 2006).

◆   *The U.S. Supreme Court held that a Title VII "charge" did not have to be verified by oath or affirmation at the time it was filed with the Equal Employment Opportunity Commission (EEOC).*

Five months after a Virginia college denied tenure to a professor, he faxed a letter to an EEOC field office claiming he had been subjected to gender, national origin and religious discrimination. He then filed charges with the state and, 313 days after the denial of tenure, he filed a verified "Form 5 Charge of Discrimination." When he sued the college under Title VII, the college sought to dismiss the case on the grounds that he had failed to comply with the 300-day statute of limitations. A federal court found that the faxed letter was not a "charge" of discrimination within the meaning of Title VII and that the verification could not relate back to the letter. The Fourth Circuit agreed, but the U.S. Supreme Court reversed, finding that **the faxed letter to the EEOC could qualify as a "charge" under Title VII** and that the verification could relate back to the letter. Nothing in Title VII required the charge to be verified at the time it was made. The Court remanded the case. *Edelman v. Lynchburg College*, 535 U.S. 106, 122 S.Ct. 1145, 152 L.Ed.2d 188 (2002).

◆   *In an employment discrimination lawsuit filed under Title VII, the aggrieved party bears the burden of proving employer pretext.*

A federal district court ruled that a college had discriminated against a professor on the basis of sex. The U.S. Court of Appeals, First Circuit, affirmed the decision, ruling that Title VII of the 1964 Civil Rights Act, 42 U.S.C. § 2000e, *et seq.*, required the college to prove absence of discriminatory motive. The U.S. Supreme Court held that this burden was too great. It ruled that **in an employment discrimination case, the employer need only "articulate some legitimate, nondiscriminatory reason for the employee's rejection."** In other words, the employee has the burden of proving that the reason for the employee's rejection was a mere pretext. The Court vacated the court of appeals' decision and remanded the case for reconsideration under the lesser standard. *Trustees of Keene State College v. Sweeney*, 439 U.S. 24, 99 S.Ct. 295, 58 L.Ed.2d 216 (1978).

## B. Harassment

*Sexual harassment is a form of sex discrimination, which violates Title VII of the Civil Rights Act of 1964, Title IX of the Education Amendments of 1972 and state anti-discrimination laws. To pursue a harassment claim under Title VII, there must be "adverse employment action," which alters the terms and conditions of employment. In order to prove a harassment case under federal law, there must be severe or pervasive harassment based on gender, such as unwelcome sexual advances or requests for sexual favors.*

*Title IX of the Education Amendments of 1972 prohibits sex discrimination by all recipients of federal funding. In* Davis v. Monroe County Board of Educ., *526 U.S. 629 (1999), the U.S. Supreme Court first held federal-funding recipients could be liable under Title IX for student-on-student harassment. The Court established a three-part test for institutional liability in* Davis *for peer-sexual harassment: (1) sexual harassment by peers; (2) deliberate indifference by officials who have actual knowledge of the harassment; and (3) harassment so severe, pervasive and objectively offensive it deprives the student of access to educational opportunities. A teacher's knowledge of peer harassment is sufficient to create "actual knowledge" that may trigger liability.*

*In* Fitzgerald v. Barnstable School Committee, *129 S.Ct. 788 (U.S. 2009), the Court held Title IX does not bar students from advancing parallel gender discrimination claims under 42 U.S.C. § 1983. Section 1983 is a federal statute that creates no rights, but enforces rights created by federal laws and the Constitution. Sexual comments may be harassment if they affect a person's employment, or create an intimidating, hostile or offensive work environment.*

◆ *A Pennsylvania federal judge rejected the claims of a tenure-track assistant professor who alleged sexual harassment and racial bias.*

A Mexican-American was hired as an assistant professor. The position required teaching both English and Hispanic literature. The professor worked more than 40 hours per week, and her commute was more than an hour. A female colleague offered to let the assistant professor sleep over if she was too tired to drive. The employee found the invitation offensive, as the female colleague lived with her same-sex partner. The school decided not to renew the professor's contract a fourth year because she hadn't resolved ongoing performance issues. She sued, alleging sexual harassment and racial bias. Her sexual harassment claim was based on the lesbian colleague's invitation to stay over. The racial claim was based on the chair's objection that she devoted a survey class on American literature to Hispanic literature. **The evidence didn't support the claims, so the court granted the school judgment without a trial.** *Jiron-King v. Indiana Univ. of Pennsylvania*, No. 13-176, 2015 WL 540008 (W.D. Pa. 2/10/15).

◆ *A New York federal judge found a professor could not base a retaliation claim on having reported another professor for sexually harassing students.*

A former assistant professor claimed she was fired for making complaints "regarding rampant corruption in the administration" at the school concerning faculty harassing students. She sued, claiming the school violated Title VII by firing her in retaliation for protesting sexual harassment. The school asked the court to dismiss the claim. It did. To state a valid retaliation claim, she had to show she participated in an activity protected by Title VII, the school fired her, and the protected activity was the cause of her termination. Title VII outlaws workplace discrimination and protects employees' complaints of illegal discrimination from retaliation by the employee. The school pointed out that Title VII doesn't protect an employee's reports of co-workers' sexual harassment of non-employees. The court agreed, citing a 2013 New York federal court decision that states, **"Courts have repeatedly held … that a teacher's complaints about alleged discrimination directed against a student do not constitute opposition to an illegal employment practice"** under Title VII. So the claim failed, but the court explained she can refile her claims in state court. *Saliba v. Five Towns College*, 991 F.Supp.2d 449 (E.D.N.Y. 2014).

◆   *A Maryland federal court has found a public university was immune to a campus police officer's sexual bias and harassment charges brought under the Equal Protection Clause – but its police chief and a police captain were not.*

A female police officer claimed she was sexually harassed at work by her supervisor – then a lieutenant, now a captain. Parks sued the university, the captain and the chief of police for sexual discrimination not only under Title VII but also under the Equal Protection Clause. The defendants asked the court to dismiss her constitutional claim on the basis of sovereign immunity. As a state university, the school is an arm of the state and entitled to sovereign immunity – so that claim was dismissed. But the court refused to dismiss claims against the chief and captain. Intentional sexual harassment of an employee by persons acting under color of state law can be a breach of the Fourteenth Amendment's Equal Protection Clause, and the employee can sue them on that basis under Section 1983. The employee alleged the captain sexually harassed and otherwise discriminated against her on the basis of sex. While she didn't accuse the chief of the same wrongdoing, the court found **the evidence suggested the chief's "actions or lack thereof caused [... the female officer] to be harassed." So the Section 1983 claim could go forward against both the chief and the captain who was accused of sexually harassing her on the chief's watch.** *Parks v. Bowie State Univ.*, No. RWT-12-2462, 2014 WL 992789 (D. Md. 3/13/14).

◆   *A lesbian University of Washington (UW) program coordinator's sexual orientation discrimination claim could proceed in the state court system.*

The program coordinator accused her supervisor of maintaining a hostile work environment. She said he told her not to flaunt her sexuality around him. In addition, the coordinator claimed the supervisor often discussed his hatred of others and told her he kept a gun in his vehicle. After the supervisor learned of the coordinator's sexual orientation, she said he revoked her flexible work schedule, denied her overtime work, denied her advancement opportunities and tried to intimidate her. At a staff meeting before he was deployed for a military assignment, he announced that he was "going to come back a very angry man."

In a state court, the coordinator sued UW and the supervisor for creating a hostile work environment based on her sexual orientation in violation of state law. Washington did not amend its law against discrimination to include sexual orientation until after most of the relevant incidents in this case had taken place. The court held the coordinator could only rely on the "angry man" comment to support her claims because the amendment to the law was not retroactive. It held the comment was insufficient to prove sexual orientation discrimination. Appeal reached the Supreme Court of Washington, which held that conduct occurring before the effective date of the amendment was not actionable. But it found pre-amendment conduct was admissible as background evidence. And the "angry man" comment was sufficient to establish a preliminary claim of hostile work environment. **Since the coordinator established a preliminary claim for hostile work environment, she could pursue the lawsuit.** *Loeffelholz v. Univ. of Washington*, 175 Wash.2d 264, 285 P.3d 854 (Wash. 2012).

◆   *A federal court refused to dismiss a hostile environment case based on an employee's claim that a university did not protect her from sexual harassment.*

A university communications assistant said a business school finance director said, "I cannot control my feelings for you," made "moaning sounds" and told her he was obsessed with sex. She said he grabbed her arm so hard it left a bruise, told her he had been watching her, and implied that she should keep her guard up or he might assault her. When the assistant complained to her supervisor, he doubted the report. She filed an administrative complaint, but she said the supervisor then ignored instructions to minimize her contact with the director. After being fired for unexcused absences, the assistant sued the university in a District of Columbia federal court for allowing a hostile environment based on sexual harassment. The court denied the university's request for judgment, finding the claims met the required standard for showing a hostile work environment. The assistant alleged that **sexual harassment had interfered with her work performance and created an intimidating, hostile, or offensive working environment**. There was evidence suggesting that the university knew about the harassment but did not promptly address it. As the assistant's factual assertions met the requirements for a hostile work environment claim, the court denied the university's motion for pretrial judgment. *Hoskins v. Howard Univ.*, 839 F.Supp.2d 268 (D.D.C. 2012).

◆   *A New York court rejected a graduate student's claim that she was improperly disciplined after she sexually propositioned one of her professors.*

When the graduate student suggested a sexual affair, the professor asked her to stop contacting him. But the student did not, even after he said he would take formal action against her if she did not. Following that warning, the student did not contact the professor for two years, when she copied him on an email to the university president claiming the faculty of a college department violated her "institutional rights." The professor filed a sexual harassment complaint against the student, and she responded with her own complaint for sexual harassment and retaliation. The university rejected the student's complaint and determined she had harassed the professor. It issued a written reprimand and a no-contact order. A state supreme court upheld the university's decision, and later a state appellate division court reached the same result. **There was no indication that the university deviated from its disciplinary procedures with respect to the complaint against the student, and the decision was supported by the evidence.** There was clear and convincing evidence that she violated the university's conduct code. Nor did the university violate any procedural rules with respect to the discipline. *Hyman v. Cornell Univ.*, 82 A.D.3d 1309 (N.Y. App. Div. 2011).

◆   *Virginia's highest court upheld the firing of a university business manager after his second violation of a sexual harassment and discrimination policy.*

The business manager volunteered at a local youth boxing club that was seeking to raise funds by selling calendars with attractive young women posing in boxing settings. A supervisor who worked for the business manager at the university asked female students if they would be interested in posing. The two interviewed a student and asked her if she would be interested in posing in a bathing suit or short shorts. During the meeting, the manager told the student she should not eat a piece of candy she was reaching for because "you will look like a little refrigerator with your head on top." The comment upset the student, and she reported it. A formal investigation of the manager was begun for violating the university's sexual harassment and discrimination policy. He filed a grievance, but a hearing officer upheld the discharge on grounds that this was the manager's second harassment policy violation in three years.

A state court reversed the decision, and the case reached the Supreme Court of Virginia. It found that while the lower court found federal decisions persuasive, the hearing officer had rejected sexual harassment as a basis for the decision. **The hearing officer noted this was the business manager's second relevant offense in three years.** He had previously violated the policy when he used a university computer to access pornography. Since the business manager did not identify any applicable law that the hearing officer's decision contradicted, the lower courts lacked any basis for reviewing the decision. The court reinstated the hearing officer's decision. *Virginia Polytechnic Institute and State Univ. v. Quesenberry*, 277 Va. 420, 674 S.E.2d 854 (Va. 2009).

◆ *A federal district court held a sexual harassment claim cannot be based on conduct that is merely "bizarre."*

A New York college administrator was appointed to a regular, tenure-track position in 2003. A married, heterosexual female faculty member told others in her department that they "meant a lot to her" and were "very important to her." The administrator made several vague complaints to superiors about the faculty member, saying the two "did not always see eye to eye" and were involved in an "unhealthy relationship." She then told the faculty member of her intent to resign and seek a position elsewhere within the college. The faculty member stated she was unhappy as she was concerned about covering her teaching load.

The administrator moved to another department, but continued to collaborate with the faculty member on a grant. She later resigned as co-administrator of the grant, asserting her relationship with the faculty member affected her psychologically. The administrator sued the college in a federal district court, alleging a hostile work environment based on sex. The court found the incidents of allegedly harassing conduct were all facially neutral. The faculty member never made any sexual remarks to the administrator and did not touch her. **The administrator admitted that the faculty member's conduct toward her was not romantic in nature.** Instead, she characterized it as "bizarre." As there was not enough evidence to establish sexual harassment, the court dismissed the case. On appeal, the U.S. Court of Appeals, Second Circuit, found that while the faculty member's conduct was unwelcome or inappropriate, no reasonable jury could find that it took place because of gender. There was no evidence that her conduct was based on sex, and thus no hostile work environment under Title VII. No "adverse employment action" supported a retaliation claim, and the judgment was affirmed. *Guarino v. St. John Fisher College*, 321 Fed.Appx. 55 (2d Cir. 2008).

◆ *A court rejected a police officer's claim that a Pennsylvania university discriminated against her based on her need to produce breast milk at work.*

The university granted the officer's request for permission to express milk during breaks after she returned from maternity leave. However, supervisors refused to provide her a courtesy transport from her foot patrol to headquarters, where she expressed the milk. The officer claimed she was treated differently from colleagues in other ways and was assigned to menial tasks. She quit and sued the university in federal district court for race and pregnancy discrimination. The court held for the university, and the officer appealed.

The U.S. Court of Appeals, Third Circuit, explained that **to prove she was subjected to a hostile work environment, the officer had to show harassment that was so "severe or pervasive" that it changed the terms and conditions of her employment and created an abusive environment**. In addition, she needed to show she was subjected to conduct that was offensive both subjectively and objectively. It was clear that the conduct in this case was subjectively offensive. However, the officer did not show she was subjected to conduct that a reasonable person in her position would have found to be hostile or abusive. Other officers who were placed on light duty were also assigned menial tasks. The university provided breaks to express breast milk and switched the officer to a patrol route that was closer to headquarters. As no reasonable jury could conclude the university created a hostile work environment in violation of Title VII, the court upheld the judgment. *Page v. Trustees of the Univ. of Pennsylvania*, 222 Fed.Appx. 144 (3d Cir. 2007).

◆   *An Illinois university did not subject an employee to a sexually hostile environment or treat her differently from her male counterparts.*

The employee worked for the university as a building services worker. She claimed male supervisors called her degrading and obscene names, although not to her face. The employee also asserted that a male employee asked her to join him on his boat for "a weekend of drinking and other things." School officials suspended her for insubordination and failure to follow departmental guidelines and practices. The employee sued the university in a federal district court, alleging it violated Title VII for allowing a sexually hostile environment.

The court found the employee did not present any evidence that the university treated her less favorably than the males. While there had been offensive conduct, there was no showing this was frequent, severe, threatening or humiliating. On appeal, the U.S. Court of Appeals, Seventh Circuit, held that **to establish a claim for Title VII sex discrimination, there had to be "adverse employment action."** Adverse employment action typically involves an economic injury, like suspension without pay. Because the employee voluntarily left her job, she was not subjected to economic injury. **An employment action is "adverse" only if it alters the terms and conditions of employment.** As the university did not change the terms or conditions of the employee's job, she could not prevail in a Title VII case, and the judgment was affirmed. *Whittaker v. Northern Illinois Univ.*, 424 F.3d 640 (7th Cir. 2005).

◆   *An Alabama university did not violate Title VII when it declined to renew the contract of a former dean of students.*

The dean claimed her supervisor made indirect sexual advances and comments toward her. The supervisor told the dean he wanted to come visit her at home sometime, and that women sleep with their bosses to keep their jobs and get promotions. The supervisor denied he made sexual advances or comments toward the dean. After a poor performance evaluation, the supervisor told the dean the university was not renewing her contract.

The dean sued the college in a federal district court for violating Title VII. The court held sexual harassment is a form of sex discrimination which violates Title VII. **Unwelcome sexual advances, requests for sexual favors, and comments of a sexual nature may constitute sexual harassment if they affect an individual's employment, or create an intimidating, hostile or offensive work environment.** The court found the dean did not present evidence that the supervisor threatened to fire her if she refused to comply. She never let the supervisor know she was uncomfortable about his sexual remarks. No evidence supported the dean's contention that the decision not to renew her contract was connected to sexual advances. Even after the dean turned down her supervisor's advances, he appointed her dean of students. The court granted the university's motion for summary judgment. On appeal, the U.S. Court of Appeals, Eleventh Circuit, found the lower court had correctly held the dean did not satisfy the burden of proof framework established by *McDonnell Douglas Corp. v. Green*. It affirmed the judgment for the college. *Hammons v. George C. Wallace State Community College*, 174 Fed.Appx. 459 (11th Cir. 2005).

### C. Equal Pay Issues

*The Equal Pay Act (EPA) requires that employers pay males and females the same wages for equal work. Employees are protected by the EPA as long as the employer is engaged in an enterprise affecting interstate commerce. The EPA has been interpreted by the courts to require only that the jobs under comparison be "substantially" equal. Strict equality of the jobs under comparison is not required.*

*The EPA requires equal pay for jobs involving "equal skill, effort, and responsibility, and which are performed under similar working conditions, except where such payment is made pursuant to (i) a seniority system; (ii) a merit system; (iii) a system which measures earnings by quantity or quality of production; or (iv) a differential based on any other factor other than sex." Many cases alleging disparate pay rates based on sex include claims under Title VII and analogous state laws. If employers can prove that the difference in pay is for a reason other than the difference in sex, they do not have to provide the same pay and benefits. It is for the employer to show that such a factor exists and that it is the real reason for the difference.*

◆  *The Fifth Circuit affirmed a Texas ruling that dismissed the claims of two black women who said they were underpaid due to their gender and race.*

The women drove campus shuttle buses on fixed routes during normal business hours during the week. When they complained they were paid less than white and male employees, the supervisor allegedly responded that if they weren't happy with their pay, they should "just quit." They sued, alleging wage discrimination based on the gender and race, violations of the Equal Pay Act and Title VII, respectively. The district court dismissed the claims, and the women appealed. The Fifth Circuit affirmed, as the higher-paid employees were not similarly situated to the women. They had different responsibilities that required them to work weekends, evening hours and overnight shifts. **The additional job requirements warranted different levels of pay**, so the dismissal was affirmed. *Fields v. Stephen F. Austin State Univ.*, 611 Fed.Appx. 830 (5th Cir. 2015).

◆ *A Nebraska federal judge dismissed discrimination claims filed by a female professor who alleged she was paid less than male counterparts.*

The woman worked half-time as a non-tenured professor. When her contract came up for renewal, she complained that the salary offered was too low. But she accepted the contract anyway. A short time later, a male professor was hired for a tenure-track position. His salary was about $20,000 higher than hers. She brought sexual discrimination claims under Title VII and the Equal Pay Act. To prove her Title VII claim, she alleged the university had a practice of hiring men over women for tenure-track positions. The argument failed because she had never applied for a tenure-track position. Next, she claimed the university violated the Equal Pay Act by paying male professors more than female professors. The court rejected the argument as the male professors weren't similarly situated. They were in tenured positions – which had different job duties, including research and community service. Her job only required instruction time. **The difference in the tenured employees' duties justified the extra pay**, so the claims were dismissed. *Knapp v. Ruser*, 145 F.Supp.3d 846 (D. Neb. 2015).

◆ *An Indiana federal court refused to dismiss the gender bias claims of a female math professor.*

The professor was denied tenure due to poor student evaluations, according to the school. The professor claimed she was not being treated the same as her male colleagues. She broke the numbers down to prove it. For example, she was assigned many more introductory courses than male counterparts – which resulted in lower student evaluations. The school accepted her data and granted her tenure. She sued, claiming sex discrimination. The school asked for pretrial judgment, saying the professor couldn't show an adverse employment action because she was granted tenure. **The court disagreed, explaining that the tenure denial was an adverse action because it caused material suffering in the form of lost wages. "This loss of earnings is more than *de minimis* and constitutes a materially adverse effect of the initial denial."** The professor stated a valid *prima facie* claim, so the court refused to grant the university pretrial judgment. *Barron v. Univ. of Notre Dame du Lac*, 93 F.Supp.3d 906 (N.D. Ind. 2015).

◆ *A Wisconsin university lecturer earned a trial to determine if a university violated the Equal Pay Act by paying males more than she received.*

The lecturer was an untenured senior lecturer in the university's business school who was not on a tenure track. She taught business statistics, a required course for all business school students. Three of her male colleagues earned more money per course than she did. Two taught management courses, and one taught a marketing course. The lecturer asked the department chair to perform a gender equity review of her salary. The dean concluded her pay was appropriate. The lecturer sued the university in a federal district court, alleging it violated the EPA by paying more money to the male lecturers. **The court**

**explained that to determine whether the university violated the EPA, it must compare job requirements, not individuals.** Under the EPA, the university could lawfully pay the male lecturers more than the female lecturer based on seniority, a merit system, a system which measured earnings by production, or another reason besides sex. The university argued that the difference between the lecturer's salary and the salaries of the other three lecturers was valid because she did not teach in the core area of the business school. According to the lecturer, the university failed to prove her skill, effort and responsibility were different from those of the male lecturers. The court found a genuine issue of fact concerning whether the lecturer and the male lecturers had the same skill and responsibility and put forth the same effort. For that reason, it denied the university's motion for dismissal and ordered that the case proceed to trial. *Mullins v. Board of Regents of the Univ. of Wisconsin System*, No. 05-C-581-S, 2006 WL 641079 (W.D. Wis. 3/10/06).

◆  *A Minnesota assistant women's hockey coach lost his EPA and Title VII action because he did not prove he suffered any adverse employment action.*

The assistant coach learned the university paid him $13,000 per year less than a female assistant coach. He complained to the director of women's athletics, and then asserted the head coach retaliated against him and gave him a poor performance evaluation. The male assistant coach resigned and sued the university in a federal district court for EPA and Title VII violations. **The court noted the female assistant coach performed many job duties that the male assistant coach did not perform, such as recruiting and public relations. Their positions were not "substantially equal" under the EPA.**

The male assistant coach appealed to the Eighth Circuit, which upheld the EPA ruling. **It also rejected his Title VII retaliation claim because the performance evaluation was not an "adverse employment action."** The assistant's discomfort with the situation was not enough to create an adverse employment action under Title VII. As his working conditions were not so intolerable as to force his resignation, the court affirmed the judgment for the university. *Horn v. Univ. of Minnesota*, 362 F.3d 1042 (8th Cir. 2004).

◆  *An Ohio university did not discriminate or retaliate against a female professor who was paid less than a male counterpart.*

The university hired the professor at $2,000 less per year than a newly hired male professor in the same department. When she learned of the salary difference two years later, the university honored her request to begin to adjust her salary so it would eventually equal his pay. Three years later, the professor was promoted to full professor. She took sabbatical leave, and over the next three and a half years, she taught at the university only one semester. The professor then sued the university in a federal court, stating her salary was lower than eight other full-time professors in her department and $13,314 less than the male professor who was hired at the time of her hire. The court held for the university, and the professor appealed. The Sixth Circuit held that **to prevail under a Title VII sex discrimination claim, the professor had to prove she was treated differently from similarly situated members of a non-protected class**. The court found the university offered legitimate, nondiscriminatory reasons for paying her less than the male professor. The disparity was based on merit differences awarded during her absences and budgetary constraints. Because the professor had no evidence to counter the university's nondiscriminatory reasons, the court affirmed the judgment. *Harrison-Pepper v. Miami Univ.*, 103 Fed.Appx. 596 (6th Cir. 2004).

◆   *A Louisiana professor failed to show an EPA violation because she did not show her job was "substantially equal" to a male professor's.*

The professor worked as an adjunct for nine years before becoming a tenured associate. The university turned her down twice for a full professorship before doing so after 11 years. She claimed the university violated the EPA by paying her less than a male professor doing the same work she did and that she was more experienced than anyone else in her department. The professor sued the university in a state court for EPA violations. The case went before a jury, which rejected the university's evidence that the pay disparity reflected the different starting dates and annual performance reports of the two professors. The university appealed to the Court of Appeal of Louisiana, which held the **professor did not show her job was substantially equal to that of the male professor or involved the same skills**. Because of this, she failed to show an EPA violation, and the court reversed the judgment. *Ramelow v. Board of Trustees of Univ. of Louisiana*, 870 So.2d 415 (La. Ct. App. 2004).

## D.  Pregnancy Discrimination

*Pregnancy discrimination is prohibited by the Pregnancy Discrimination Act (42 U.S.C. § 2000e(k)), which amended Title VII. The act specifies that discrimination "on the basis of sex" includes discrimination on the basis of pregnancy. It also requires employees to treat pregnant women the same as other employees for "all employment-related purposes" – including benefits.*

◆   *A North Carolina federal judge dismissed the claim of a former instructor who alleged she was discriminated against on the basis of her pregnancy.*

The employee was working on a doctorate from another school when the University of North Carolina-Pembroke (NCP) hired her as a full-time instructor. In the fall of her seventh year as an instructor, the employee told the chair she was pregnant and requested paid maternity leave. The chair said he'd approve the leave if she completed her Ph.D. by the following August. At her next performance review, the chair downgraded her performance from "very good" to "adequate" – as her failure to wrap up her Ph.D. created staffing uncertainties. She filed a complaint with the EEOC, claiming the less favorable performance review was retaliation for requesting paid maternity leave. She also notified NCP she wouldn't meet the Ph.D. deadline. NCP hired her on a one-year contract as a lecturer. She applied for paid maternity leave a second time, but the request was denied. NCP said maternity leave was designed to allow parents to care for newborns, but her child was already several months old. She sued NCP for gender discrimination, claiming she received a bad performance review after asking for paid maternity leave. NCP asked the court to dismiss her claim. It did, noting **the performance review had no "adverse employment action" required to prove the claim**. So pre-trial judgment was appropriate. *McBroom v. Univ. of North Carolina-Pembroke*, No. 7:11-cv-00217-FL, 2013 WL 3177202 (E.D.N.C. 6/24/13).

◆ *A New York federal judge granted university defendants judgment without a trial on an employee's claim of pregnancy discrimination.*

The employee was pregnant when she started in her position as an accounts receivable specialist for the university. She'd been on the job for three weeks when she was unable to come to work due to a pregnancy-related illness. Her supervisor suggested she apply for short-term disability benefits. She did. The school's HR department notified her that only employees who'd spent at least four weeks on the job were eligible for short-term disability benefits. But the letter also notified her, to accommodate her disability, the university would refrain from immediately filling her position. It told her to come back to work on a specific date, with a doctor's release that cleared her to work. Deciding this amounted to discrimination based on her pregnancy, the employee filed a charge with the EEOC. The employee and the school disagreed on her return-to-work deadline. When the school eventually filled her position, the woman sued, claiming a violation of Title VII for pregnancy bias. The court dismissed her claim. **To state a valid claim of pregnancy bias, the employee had to show the school treated nonpregnant employees in her circumstances better than it treated her.** She couldn't. Since the employee couldn't state a valid claim, the judge granted the university judgment without a trial. *Wilcox v. Cornell Univ.*, 986 F.Supp.2d 281 (S.D.N.Y. 2013).

◆ *A federal district court refused to grant summary judgment to a university accused of retaliating against an adjunct professor for filing an earlier lawsuit.*

In a federal district court action filed in 1998, the adjunct professor claimed the university did not reappoint her because of her pregnancy. Her Title VII suit was settled in 2000, with the university agreeing to appoint the adjunct to teaching jobs for spring and fall in 2001. But as a result of a clerical error, she was not offered the fall assignment, and she threatened to sue to enforce the settlement agreement. Three years later, the adjunct did so, this time claiming the university declined to reappoint her in retaliation for the first action. The court found there was a possible causal connection between the first lawsuit and the decision not to reappoint her some time later. In addition, there was evidence that the professor who decided not to reappoint the adjunct played a role in evaluating her and had objected to the terms of the settlement.

There was enough evidence for a jury to infer retaliation in this case. Also, although the college claimed the decision not to reappoint the adjunct was based on student complaints, it did not produce any written records of complaints. **There was evidence that professors with equal or lower student evaluation scores were reappointed.** Thus, pretrial judgment was improper. *Rumain v. Baruch College of City Univ. of New York*, No. 06 Civ. 8256 (PKC) (MHD), 2008 WL 4866019 (S.D.N.Y. 11/6/08).

◆ *Columbia University did not subject an employee to "adverse employment action" by changing her supervisor.*

The employee worked as an associate director for the university until the associate dean decided to restructure her department. She suspected the restructuring was based on her pregnancy. She told the associate director she was having a high-risk pregnancy and took disability leave. Meanwhile, the associate dean criticized her performance. The employee sued the university in a federal district court for pregnancy discrimination under Title VII, the Pregnancy Discrimination Act, and state law. The court found the employee did not prove the university subjected her to adverse employment action. It said **the assignment to report to a different supervisor was not a demotion or an "adverse employment action."** The executive director was senior to the employee in title and grade, and the change did not affect her title, grade, salary or benefits. The court explained that criticizing an employee was not an adverse employment action. **"Adverse employment actions" include demotion, termination, or a change that results in significantly diminished material responsibilities.** As the employee did not establish any of these, the court awarded summary judgment in favor of Columbia. *Palomo v. Trustees of Columbia Univ. in City of New York*, No. 03 Civ. 7853 (DLC), 2005 WL 1683586 (S.D.N.Y. 7/20/05).

### E. Sexual Orientation

*You probably know federal law only protects federal government employees from discrimination based on sexual orientation – but nearly half the states plus the District of Columbia provide this protection for employees in their states. And with the U.S. Supreme Court's recent decisions regarding same-sex marriages, this area of law will likely face many changes in the coming years.*

◆   *A Florida federal judge rejected the claim of a former administrator who alleged the university underpaid her on the basis of her sexual orientation.*

The employee had been in an administrative role for about a year when she married her same-sex partner. Two years later, her contract wasn't renewed due to performance issues, and she agreed to resign. She was given a teaching position in the math department. As a result, her salary dropped. She filed grievances alleging she wasn't paid as much as similarly situated colleagues in traditional marriages. When the grievances were denied, she sued alleging gender stereotype bias under Title VII. In *Price Waterhouse v. Hopkins*, the U.S. Supreme Court held that Title VII applies to adverse employment actions based on bias against behavior that doesn't conform to gender stereotypes. The judge said **the employee didn't state a gender stereotyping claim – which concerns characteristics on display in the workplace, such as "mannerisms, and appearances."** Instead, she'd stated a sexual orientation discrimination claim, "which is not cognizable under Title VII." The court dismissed the claim. *Burrows v. College of Cent. Florida*, No. 5:14-cv-197-Oc-30PRL, 2015 WL 4250427 (M.D. Fla. 7/13/15).

◆   *A California state law prohibits employers from discriminating against employees based on their sexual orientation.*

John Gliha worked as the executive director of development at a community college for seven years. In June 2011, his supervisor put Gliha on a performance improvement plan. Gliha scheduled a meeting with the president, where he confided he was gay and claimed his supervisor discriminated against him because of his sexual orientation. After an investigation, Gliha's claim was determined meritless. Then the president said Gliha "did not fit in with the culture" and issued an ultimatum: Resign or be fired. Gliha sent the president a letter, trying to continue the conversation without making a choice. The president responded, saying Gliha's employment would be officially terminated the following month. Gliha filed suit, making several claims, including sexual orientation discrimination and retaliation under California's Fair Employment and Housing Act. School defendants asked the court for pretrial judgment, but **the judge refused to dismiss the retaliation claim, as Gliha made a *prima facie* case by showing a connection between unlawful bias and getting fired**. The judge dismissed the orientation-bias claim, saying he didn't support the claim. But he could rewrite and refile it. To state a valid claim, he would have to show: He's gay, he was performing competently in his job, the college fired him, and other evidence suggested he was fired because of anti-gay bias. In the meantime, the retaliation claim could move forward. *Gliha v. Butte-Glenn Community College Dist.*, No. 2:12-cv-02781-KJM-CMK, 2013 WL 3013660 (E.D. Cal. 6/14/13).

◆  *A Michigan appeals court affirmed a decision that rejected a professor's claim that he was denied tenure based on his sexual orientation.*

In 1995, a dean of the University of Michigan Law School (UMLS) hired an assistant professor, knowing he is gay. UMLS provided health benefits for the new employee and his domestic partner. In 2000, the employee applied for tenure. To grant tenure, two-thirds of the faculty had to vote in his favor. They didn't, so the request was denied. The committee invited him to reapply in two years. He did, but tenure was denied, as only 18 of the 32 members voted to grant tenure. The employee sued, alleging he was denied tenure because other professors were biased against homosexuals.

To get around the problem that neither federal nor Michigan law protected employees from sexual preference discrimination, he argued UMLS had "held itself out as an employer" that would "honor" diversity, such as by providing medical coverage to his same-sex partner. Based on the university's nondiscrimination policy, he said UMLS had "assured" him "he would not be the victim of discrimination based on his sexual preference" on the job. UMLS acknowledged its policy could provide a basis for a discrimination suit based on sexual orientation – **but the court found "no reason to believe" the decision to deny tenure was based on anything other than his qualifications as a scholar**. The appeals court affirmed the decision for the university. *Hammer v. Univ. of Michigan Board of Regents*, No. 305568, 2013 WL 6244703 (Mich. Ct. App. 12/3/13).

## III. RELIGIOUS DISCRIMINATION

*Title VII generally prohibits religious discrimination. However, religious hiring preferences are permitted if the institution is substantially "owned, supported, controlled, or managed" by a religious organization or if the curriculum "is directed toward the propagation of a particular religion."*

◆   *A federal district court in North Carolina refused to dismiss the claim of a Jehovah's Witness who alleged a university failed to accommodate his religious beliefs.*

The employee was hired on a temporary basis as a vehicle operator. When he was moved to a permanent position, he was assigned to the school's Department of Police and Public Safety, where he worked as a parking services officer. Ten years after the employee's transfer, a new interim police chief arrived. The new chief began to enforce a rule that required parking services officers to be trained in and carry weapons. The employee objected on religious grounds, and sought help from HR to find a transfer accommodation. Before a replacement position was found, the employee was fired. He sued, alleging several claims. Most were dismissed, but the court allowed one claim – failure to accommodate his religious beliefs – to move forward. The court said **factual issues existed as to whether the university could have provided a reasonable accommodation that wasn't an undue hardship**. So the claim had to proceed. *Westbrook v. North Carolina AT&T Univ.*, 51 F.Supp.3d 612 (M.D.N.C. 2014).

◆   *A Seventh-Day Adventist who worked as a University of Tennessee (UT) coordinator could have a trial concerning her religious accommodation request.*

Soon after she started working for UT, the coordinator told her supervisor her religion prevented her from working from sundown on Fridays to sundown on Saturdays. This created a problem because an emergency cell phone had to be monitored on weekends. The coordinator suggested that others cover the emergency cell phone on weekends while she worked more days during the week. But the proposal was rejected, and she refused other options. UT finally determined the coordinator could not fulfill her job duties, and her employment was terminated. She sued UT in a federal district court for Title VII violations. When the case reached the U.S. Court of Appeals, Sixth Circuit, it explained that **Title VII requires employers to accommodate employee religious practices unless doing so would create an undue hardship**. Whether a religious accommodation poses an undue hardship to the employer is generally a question for a jury. In this case, a fact question was present as to whether UT met its duty to attempt to provide reasonable accommodations for the coordinator. No evidence showed the requested accommodation would be so disruptive as to create an undue hardship for UT. As a result, the case was returned to the lower court for further proceedings. *Crider v. Univ. of Tennessee, Knoxville*, 492 Fed.Appx. 609 (6th Cir. 2012).

◆   *A federal court refused to grant an Ohio college pretrial judgment on a Muslim professor's abusive work environment claim.*

The professor became Imam and religious advisor for the college's Muslim student association. He accused his department head of excluding him from meetings and other events and calling him a terrorist. The two yelled at each other in a department meeting, and the professor emailed the dean, asking him to "resolve what has become a long and sustained pattern of workplace harassment." An investigative panel found no professional misconduct, but reported **years of miscommunication, staffing changes, and conflict had caused the department to become dysfunctional**. The panel recommended that the dean create a solution. The professor claimed the dean failed to do so and filed a federal district court action against the college, alleging it subjected him to a hostile work environment. The court held that if the claims were true, a jury would have to decide whether the behavior was sufficiently severe and pervasive to create an abusive working environment. For this reason, the court refused to dismiss the case. *Yedes v. Oberlin College*, No. 1-11 CV 465, 2012 WL 1004726 (N.D. Ohio 3/23/12).

◆ *A Texas community college groundskeeping employee could not convince the state court of appeals that he was fired because of his religion.*

The employee was a Catholic who had worked as a groundskeeper and foreman for 24 years at the community college. He said that when he applied for a promotion to be grounds manager, the department director asked if he was Catholic, then denounced Catholics as "a bunch of liars." Another employee received the promotion, and the employee said the director kept making anti-Catholic remarks to him. After repeated conflicts with the director and another groundskeeping foreman, the employee called the director a vulgar word and was promptly fired for insubordination. The employee sued the college in the state court system for discrimination, harassment and retaliation based on his religion. The case reached the Court of Appeals of Texas, which found the college had a valid nondiscriminatory reason for firing him. **The college had justified the insubordination charge because the employee had called his supervisor a vulgar word.** This was not a pretext for anti-Catholic discrimination. In addition, the employee acknowledged that calling his boss "pendejo" was a terminable offense. A lower court judgment for the community college was affirmed. *Leija v. Laredo Community College*, No. 04-10-00410-CV, 2011 WL 1499440 (Tex. Ct. App. 4/20/11).

◆ *A federal court held a trial was needed to decide if a Texas university violated Title VII by firing staff members who chanted at a colleague's cubicle.*

Three administrative support staff workers decided to stay after work one night to discuss a problem colleague. They rubbed olive oil on the metal doorway to the colleague's cubicle and chanted for demons to leave the area. They then said "I command you demons to leave [the colleague], you vicious evil dogs get the hell out of here in the name of Jesus, get the hell out of [the colleague]." They also said "amen" and "yes, Lord." One of the workers reported the incident to a supervisor, and the matter was investigated. The two workers who did not report the incident were discharged for harassment of a co-worker and for "blatant disregard for university property." They sued the university in a federal district court for religious discrimination under Title VII.

According to the university, there were valid, nondiscriminatory reasons to fire the workers. But the court found no disregard for university property, as the oil did not damage the cubicle. Any harassment claim was undercut by the fact that the colleague was unaware of the incident at the time and for two months afterward. **According to the court, praying for someone who did not know she was being prayed for was unlikely to constitute harassment.** And the university's nondiscrimination policy permitted religious expression, even if it might be offensive to others. There was evidence that the university only talked to employees for yelling at the colleague, but fired them for praying about her after hours. As a result, the court held a trial was necessary. *Shatkin v. Univ. of Texas at Arlington*, No. 4:06-CV-882-Y, 2010 WL 2730585 (N.D. Tex. 7/9/10).

◆  *A physical altercation, not improper discrimination, motivated the discharge of a New York university employee.*

A supervisor accused the employee of punching the time card of a co-worker who was not at work. Their argument culminated in physical contact. The employee's union filed a grievance on her behalf but later declined to arbitrate it. The university determined the employee started the fight, but she denied this and sued the university, alleging discrimination based on her race, age, religion and color. The court held the employee did not state a claim of age discrimination. Because the university concluded she had struck the supervisor and that the supervisor had not struck her back, the two were not subject to the same disciplinary standards. There was no evidence to support the employee's claim that the person who investigated the incident was biased against her for any reason. The employee admitted that she struck the supervisor, and that act justified her termination. The employee asserted she was discriminated against based on her Christian faith, and claimed that religious materials she left on a break room table were thrown to the floor. **The court found these incidents did not prove religious bias by the university. It rejected the employee's remaining claims and dismissed the case.** On appeal, the Second Circuit held the employee raised an inference of discrimination because she claimed the supervisor had struck her first. However, even if this were true, she did not show the reasons given for her discharge were false. There was also no evidence of age discrimination, or any showing that an investigation of the incident had been biased. As the employee did not show the explanation for her discharge was a pretext for discrimination, the judgment for the university was affirmed. *Mincey v. Univ. of Rochester*, 262 Fed.Appx. 319 (2d Cir. 2008).

◆  *A Texas court reinstated a former university librarian's claim that she was discharged based on her Christian faith.*

The librarian claimed she was subjected to a hostile work environment based on her religion. She stated she was asked to view a computer image of "Jesus in a satan costume," and was subjected to anti-Christian comments such as "Christianity is a 'cop out'" and "Catholics are paying for forgiveness." According to the librarian, her supervisor instructed her to turn off her Christian radio programs when others were present in the library. She complained to a school dean about the supervisor's conduct, but about five months later, the university discharged her. In a state court lawsuit against the university, the librarian claimed she was fired based on her religion and in retaliation for complaining about a hostile work environment. She also asserted a claim for hostile work environment. The court held for the university.

On appeal, the Court of Appeals of Texas reversed the judgment on the religious discrimination claim. Although the lower court had found it was untimely filed, the court of appeals found this was error. On the other hand, the hostile work environment claim failed because the administrative complaint did not identify any acts of harassment occurring within 180 days from the date of the complaint. **The court affirmed the judgment on the retaliation claim,**

**based on the delay of over five months between the time the librarian filed a complaint with the dean and the date of her discharge.** Without more evidence that her complaint caused her discharge, the retaliation claim failed. *Bartosh v. Sam Houston State Univ.*, 259 S.W.3d 317 (Tex. Ct. App. 2008).

◆ *A Missouri university did not discriminate against a doctor by refusing to rehire him because of license suspensions and criminal conduct.*

The doctor sued the university in a federal district court, alleging it violated Title VII when it did not hire him because the Catholic Church did not approve of his divorce. The university stated it did not rehire him because of medical license suspensions in Missouri and Illinois, criminal conduct, failure to provide a complete residency application, and past unprofessional conduct. **The court found the university had legitimate nondiscriminatory reasons for not rehiring the doctor.** He presented no evidence to show the decision was motivated by discrimination instead of the reasons it offered, and the case was dismissed. In a brief memorandum opinion, the U.S. Court of Appeals, Eighth Circuit, held that even if the doctor had shown discrimination, the university produced sufficient nondiscriminatory evidence to deserve pretrial judgment. The district court judgment was affirmed. *Kaminsky v. St. Louis Univ. School of Medicine*, 226 Fed.Appx. 646 (8th Cir. 2007).

◆ *A Georgia state university did not violate a Christian cheerleading coordinator's constitutional right to the free exercise of her religion.*

Two Jewish cheerleaders complained to the athletic department that the coordinator discriminated against them because of their religion. They said the coordinator treated them unfavorably and used her position to encourage students to pray, study the Bible and engage in other religious practices. The university placed the coordinator on probation, and it informed her she would be discharged if she continued to violate the university's policy on religious discrimination. She read a statement to the cheerleading squad, stating a Jewish cheerleader had accused her of religious discrimination and that the claim was without merit. The university fired the coordinator, who filed a federal lawsuit.

A federal district court held the university was entitled to Eleventh Amendment immunity. The terms of the coordinator's probation letter simply mandated that she keep her religious activities separate from the cheerleading program. **As the university did not compromise her religious beliefs or prevent her from doing anything essential to exercising her religion, the court dismissed the case.** *Braswell v. Board of Regents of the Univ. System of Georgia*, 369 F. Supp. 2d 1371 (N.D. Ga. 2005).

## IV. AGE DISCRIMINATION

### A. ADEA

*The Age Discrimination in Employment Act (ADEA), 29 U.S.C. § 621, et seq., prohibits age discrimination against individuals who are at least 40 years old. As part of the Fair Labor Standards Act, it applies to institutions with 20 or more employees and which affect interstate commerce. State human rights acts may offer additional protection against discrimination on the basis of age.*

◆ *Finding no evidence of age discrimination, an Illinois federal judge rejected a fired professor's ADEA claim against a university.*

A tenured professor created a customized textbook with a publisher. He wrote an introductory chapter, but the rest of the content came from previously published books. After his book was published, the professor found it was riddled with errors. Among other things, it lacked citations to the other published works. He and his colleague decided not to use the book. Three years later, the department got a new chair. The 56-year-old professor said the new chair was confrontational and made ageist remarks about how he and the other older professors didn't have the "right image" to "create a young and hip look for the program." In the meantime, someone brought a copy of the professor's book to the chair. Finding it appeared to include plagiarized material, the chair recorded specifics in a memo and sent it to the dean, who passed it on to the provost. In a letter, the provost notified the professor that he was being terminated for violating the "academic dishonesty" provision of his tenure agreement. He sued, alleging the proffered reason was a pretext for firing him because of his age. The court dismissed the claim because – even if he showed the chair was biased against him due to his age – **the chair didn't make the decision to fire him; the provost made that call**. The chair "played no direct role" in the decision to fire the professor, so statements the chair may have made elsewhere couldn't be used to show the decision to fire the professor was because of his age. The claim was dismissed. *Roberts v. Columbia College Chicago*, 102 F.Supp.3d 994 (N.D. Ill. 2015).

◆ *An applicant failed to show that his age was the reason he wasn't hired, so an Oregon federal judge dismissed his ADEA claim.*

A 60-year-old candidate applied for a tenure-track assistant professor position. The job was advertised as 50% teaching and curriculum development, 40% research and publishing, and 10% service. The university also required the successful candidate to have the potential to publish in highly ranked accounting journals and be able to demonstrate excellence in teaching students. The hiring committee decided the man didn't meet the job requirements because he hadn't taught for 20 years, hadn't provided any evaluations of his teaching, and his only recent publications were opinion pieces in a new and C-rated accounting journal. The candidate who was hired met all the job requirements, and she had a working paper under review for an A-rated journal. The rejected candidate sued, alleging age discrimination. The court dismissed his claim, as the university had a valid, nondiscriminatory reason to go with another candidate: **The man didn't meet the minimum requirements for the position.** While the man argued he was the better candidate, the court found his "unsupported opinion that he was better qualified" than her was "insufficient to show [the university] had a discriminatory motive when it chose not to hire him." *Committe v. Oregon State Univ.*, No. 3:13-cv-01341-ST, 2015 WL 2170122 (D. Or. 5/8/15).

◆   *A university's failure to comply exactly with the Older Workers Benefit Protection Act (OWBPA) was inadvertent, but a New York federal judge still found it invalidated an employee's waiver of his right to sue for age bias.*

Salmen Loksen worked as a director and safety officer at the Columbia University (CU) Medical Center's radiation safety office. For budgetary reasons, CU merged that office with another department. Loksen was one of the employees chosen for layoff. He was 61 at the time. CU offered Loksen a severance agreement of six months' salary in return for a waiver releasing CU from all legal claims. As required by the OWBPA amendments to the ADEA, a disclosure was attached to the proposed agreements. It was supposed to list the age and position of every employee in the office and indicate those who had been selected for layoff. The disclosure marked only Loksen and a 57-year-old office administrator as selected for layoff. Due to a computer glitch, a 41-year-old radiation safety officer was left off the list. The error was corrected in the system soon after, but an updated copy of the disclosure wasn't attached to the final agreement. Claiming the waiver he signed was ineffective because it violated the OWPBA, Loksen sued, claiming age bias. CU asked for judgment, but the court found **the OWBPA noncompliance meant his age bias claim can go forward**. Though the spirit of the OWBPA wasn't violated, the technical noncompliance was enough to invalidate the waiver of his right to bring an age bias claim. *Loksen v. Columbia Univ.*, No. 12 Civ. 7701 (CM), 2013 WL 5549780 (S.D.N.Y. 10/4/13).

◆   *Finding no evidence of age discrimination, a federal district court rejected an applicant's ADEA claim against a university.*

After retiring from a corporate position, a lawyer sought an academic career. He uploaded his credentials into an online database that was available to several schools, including the Georgetown University Law Center. During the 2010-11 hiring cycle, Georgetown looked at 800 applicants' credentials and chose 25 for initial phone interviews. Then it narrowed the pool to 10 for call-back interviews before extending job offers to four candidates. Three accepted. They were all 35 years old. The retired attorney was not chosen for an initial interview. He sued, claiming age discrimination under the ADEA. The school asked for pretrial judgment, saying it declined to interview the retired attorney because he lacked a scholarship-related background. **Citing a legitimate business reason for its decision, Georgetown shifted the responsibility back to the attorney, requiring him to show that the school's asserted decision was not its real reason but instead a pretextual reason offered to avoid liability for age discrimination.** He couldn't, so the court dismissed his claim. *Spaeth v. Georgetown Univ.*, 943 F.Supp.2d 198 (D.D.C. 2013).

◆   *A veteran Texas college executive assistant who lost her job to a much younger employee made out a valid age discrimination claim.*

After 31 years as an executive assistant to five college presidents, the college reassigned the employee to an administrative associate position and cut her annual pay by more than $15,000. Her replacement was 15 years younger and had worked for the college for only two years. The employee sued the college in a federal court for age discrimination. The college said its action was needed because of her strong links to the previous administration. It said the current president distrusted the employee based on reports that she had complained about his policies and proposed changes. The court agreed with the employee that her service to five prior administrations undercut the college's defense. She also claimed she was more qualified than her replacement as she had a bachelor's degree, while her replacement did not. For these reasons, **the court found enough evidence for a jury to conclude that the college's stated reasons for the reassignment were a pretext for age discrimination**. The court denied the college's motion for judgment. *Robinson v. Jarvis Christian College*, No. 6:11-cv-073, 2011 WL 5080167 (E.D. Tex. 10/25/11).

◆    *A university administrative assistant failed to prove that the non-renewal of her contract was motivated by race or national origin discrimination.*

The administrative assistant began working for the university in 1995 when she was already over 40. She received good performance evaluations until a new dean arrived at her department in 2000. The dean later recommended that the university not rehire the assistant. She was replaced by a person of Hispanic origin. The administrative assistant sued the university in a federal district court for race, national origin and age discrimination. She also claimed officials retaliated against her and engaged in a conspiracy to discriminate against her.

The court held for the university, and the assistant appealed to the U.S. Court of Appeals, Third Circuit. The court held the allegations did not prove race discrimination. An assertion that the university wanted to diversify its staff was purely speculative, and the fact that the assistant dean and president were not Caucasian failed to prove racial discrimination. **There was no evidence that the university's affirmative action guidelines had been improperly applied or that the timing of the opening for the administrative assistant's old job was suspicious.** The age discrimination claim failed because the university produced evidence of unsatisfactory job performance. Despite the positive job evaluations from some supervisors, the court found the administrative assistant did not prove the negative ones from the other supervisor were a pretext for discrimination. The court affirmed the judgment for the university. *Hunter v. Rowan Univ.*, 299 Fed.Appx. 190 (3d Cir. 2008).

◆    *The Eighth Circuit held that replacement by a substantially younger person is necessary to prove age discrimination.*

A Minnesota university promoted an employee to serve as a dean at the age of 62. He had a heart attack three years later, and learned of rumors indicating he wanted to retire and that a plan had been developed to replace him. The dean denied the rumors in a formal letter to the university president. He stated he was profoundly disturbed by the rumors and accused the president of trying to force his resignation. The next year, the university reorganized, and a newly hired provost/vice president soon recommended replacing the dean. The reasons stated were the dean's creation of a divisive environment, ineffective handling of conflicts, and favoritism and bias in personnel evaluations. The dean's permanent replacement was 64 years old at the time of his appointment. The dean sued the university in a federal district court for ADEA violations. The court held for the university, and the dean appealed. The Eighth Circuit explained that the ADEA bars employers from taking age-based adverse employment actions against employees who are 40 or older. **The U.S. Supreme Court held in a 1996 case that the replacement of a 68-year-old by a 65-year-old was "very thin evidence" of discrimination.** The Eighth Circuit held the dean did not prove age discrimination based on his replacement by an employee who was only two-and-a-half years younger than he was. **The university had legitimate nondiscriminatory reasons for demoting him, and the court did not "sit as a super-personnel department and second guess" its decisions.** The dean's other discrimination and retaliation claims failed for the same reasons. The court affirmed the judgment for the university. *Lewis v. St. Cloud State Univ.*, 467 F.3d 1133 (8th Cir. 2006).

◆ *The U.S. Supreme Court held employees may bring "disparate impact" actions under the ADEA. Disparate impact actions do not require proof of intentional age discrimination. Instead, they require an employee to show an employment policy has the effect of discriminating on the basis of age.*

The city of Jackson, Mississippi increased the salaries of all employees in 1999. Those with under five years of experience received comparatively higher raises than more experienced employees. The city justified the action as a way to remain competitive and "ensure equitable compensation to all employees."

A group of veteran police officers, most over 40 years old, claimed the city's action constituted discrimination on the basis of age. The officers sued the city in a federal district court for ADEA violations, alleging both disparate treatment and disparate impact. The court held for the city, and the U.S. Court of Appeals, Fifth Circuit, affirmed the judgment. The Supreme Court agreed to review the disparate impact claim. It compared the ADEA with Title VII of the Civil Rights Act of 1964. **Except for substitution of the word "age" for "race, color, religion, sex, or national origin," the language of the ADEA and Title VII was identical.** Title VII disparate impact claims have long been recognized by the Court. The Court stated the ADEA authorizes potential recovery for disparate impact cases, in a manner comparable to Title VII disparate impact claims for race, religion or sex discrimination. **Employees alleging an employer practice has a disparate impact on a class of employees need not show the practice is intentional.** While the Court held the officers were entitled to bring a disparate impact claim under the ADEA, they could not show the city violated the ADEA in this case. The Court noted the ADEA's coverage for disparate impact is narrower than that of Title VII. Under the ADEA, an employer can treat workers differently if the employer is motivated by reasonable factors other than age. Congress narrowed the ADEA's scope because there is often a connection between age and ability to perform a job. The city's decision to make itself competitive in the job market was based on a reasonable factor other than age. As the employees could not prove disparate impact, the Court affirmed the judgment. *Smith v. City of Jackson*, 544 U.S. 228, 125 S.Ct. 1536, 161 L.Ed.2d 410 (2005).

◆ *The Supreme Court held state employees could not sue their employers under the ADEA.*

Two associate professors at the University of Montevallo sued the university in an Alabama federal court under the ADEA. They alleged that the university had discriminated against them on the basis of their age, that it had retaliated against them for filing charges with the Equal Employment Opportunity Commission, and that its College of Business, where they were employed, used an evaluation system that had a disparate impact on older faculty members. The university sought to dismiss the action on the grounds of Eleventh Amendment immunity, and the district court agreed, finding that the ADEA did not eliminate the state's immunity. A group of current and former faculty and librarians of Florida State University and Florida International University filed suit against the Florida Board of Regents under the ADEA, alleging that the board refused to require the two state universities to allocate funds to provide previously agreed-upon market adjustments to the salaries of eligible university employees. They maintained that this failure had a disparate impact on the base pay of older employees with a longer record of service.

The court refused to dismiss the action. On appeal, the Eleventh Circuit consolidated the cases and held the ADEA did not abrogate (do away with) state Eleventh Amendment immunity. The U.S. Supreme Court noted that **although the ADEA contains a clear statement of Congress' intent to eliminate the states' immunity under the Eleventh Amendment, such action exceeded Congress' authority under Section 5 of the Fourteenth Amendment** (which grants Congress the power to enact laws under the Equal Protection Clause). Although state employees cannot sue their employers for discrimination under the ADEA, they are not without remedies. Every state has age discrimination statutes, and almost all of them allow the recovery of money damages from state employers. *Kimel v. Florida Board of Regents*, 528 U.S. 62, 120 S.Ct. 631, 145 L.Ed.2d 522 (2000).

## 1. Applicability to Religious Schools

◆  *The ADEA did not apply to a pervasively religious Missouri seminary.*

A Missouri seminary allegedly dismissed an employee because of his age. He sued the seminary in a federal district court under the ADEA. The seminary brought a motion for pretrial judgment, stating that the ADEA was inapplicable because the institution was pervasively religious. The court agreed. It considered the U.S. Supreme Court's decision in *NLRB v. Catholic Bishop of Chicago*, 440 U.S. 490 (1979), in which the Court held the National Labor Relations Act (NLRA) inapplicable to church-operated schools. Although the ADEA was a remedial statute rather than a regulatory statute such as the NLRA, the ruling in *Catholic Bishop* applied here. Because application of the ADEA could implicate enforcement by the EEOC, government regulatory powers were involved. **As the potential existed for impinging the seminary's religious freedoms, the court ruled that the ADEA was inapplicable.** It held for the seminary. *Cochran v. St. Louis Preparatory Seminary*, 717 F.Supp. 1413 (E.D. Mo. 1989).

◆  *An Ohio federal court held that the ADEA could be applied to a religious institution.*

An employee at Xavier University, an institution operated by the Order of Jesuits, sued the university under the ADEA in an Ohio federal court. The university asserted that the court had no authority to rule on the case because the university, as a religious institution, was exempt from the ADEA's provisions. The court observed that because the ADEA gave no indication that religious institutions were exempt from its provisions, the issue became whether application of the ADEA to the university would violate the Free Exercise and Establishment Clauses of the First Amendment.

The court held for the employee, noting that the Fourth Circuit held in *Ritter v. Mount St. Mary's College*, 814 F.2d 986 (4th Cir. 1987), that **application of the ADEA to a religious institution did not present a significant risk of infringement on the institution's First Amendment rights.** Here, the facts gave no indication that enforcement of the ADEA would violate the religion clauses of the First Amendment. Accordingly, the university was not entitled to have the case dismissed. *Soriano v. Xavier Univ.*, 687 F.Supp. 1188 (S.D. Ohio 1988).

## 2. Defenses

*The Eleventh Amendment protects state entities from private lawsuits but not from suits filed by the federal government. Thus, the U.S. Equal Employment Opportunity Commission (EEOC) may sue state entities for violating the Age Discrimination in Employment Act.* EEOC v. Board of Supervisors for the Univ. of Louisiana System, *559 F.3d 270 (5th Cir. 2009).*

◆  *A federal court dismissed age discrimination claims against the University of Missouri because a lower court did not rule on a qualified immunity issue.*

A University of Missouri professor filed a lawsuit in federal court against the university, his department chair and department administrator, claiming age discrimination and hostile work environment. He added claims for federal due process and equal protection violations, and state law tortious interference with his employment contract. The defendants filed a motion to dismiss the case, arguing the professor did not state valid claims for due process or equal protection violations. They also argued they had qualified immunity from the due process and equal protection claims. Without addressing the issue of qualified immunity, the district court granted the defense motion to dismiss the equal protection claim. The chair and administrator appealed to the U.S. Court of Appeals, Eighth Circuit, arguing that the district court improperly rejected their qualified immunity defense. The court explained that it could not grant the requested review because the lower court did not rule on qualified immunity. The district court did not even mention qualified immunity in its decision. **Since the district court did not make a finding with respect to the qualified immunity issue, there was nothing to review.** The appeal was dismissed. *Mitra v. Curators of the Univ. of Missouri*, 322 Fed.Appx. 467 (8th Cir. 2009).

◆  *A former women's basketball coach failed to show the decision to buy out the last year of her contract was motivated by age or gender discrimination.*

After the University of Miami exercised its contractual right to buy out the last year of the coach's contract, she filed a state court action for discrimination based on age and gender. A trial court held for the university, finding at least three legitimate business reasons for its decision. In addition, the court ordered the coach to pay the university's attorneys' fees. A Florida District Court of Appeal explained that once the university offered legitimate, nondiscriminatory reasons for its action, the burden shifted to the coach to show the claimed reasons for its actions were a pretext for discrimination. She tried to meet this burden with evidence about the university's treatment of other coaches, but the court found this evidence was insufficient. **Since the university provided a legitimate reason for its decision, the trial court had properly ruled for the university on the discrimination claims.** However, the court held the trial court should not have awarded attorneys' fees to the university, since the coach's claims were not "frivolous, unreasonable, or without foundation." *Labati v. Univ. of Miami*, 16 So.3d 886 (Fla. Dist. Ct. App. 2009).

◆   *Texas Tech University's decision to eliminate a college director's position was based on budgetary reasons, not age discrimination.*

The director had worked for Texas Tech since 1990, and earned outstanding job evaluations for several years. But some time later, several of her former and then-current subordinates filed written complaints stating she was an inflexible authoritarian who created an unpleasant work environment. When the director took a medical leave, her supervisor reassigned some of her job duties to others. The director claimed the changes constituted a demotion, and she filed an age, sex and disability discrimination claim with the EEOC. After being reassigned to a different job that she also considered a demotion, the university informed her the job was being eliminated. The director filed another EEOC charge, then sued the university for age and sex discrimination as well as retaliation. The court awarded the university pretrial judgment. On appeal, the court agreed with the lower court that the university had a legitimate reason for eliminating the director's position. She did not show this was a pretext for discrimination. **The university provided detailed information showing the decision to eliminate the position was made as part of an effort to reduce operating expenses.** The retaliation claim failed because the person who eliminated the position was unaware of the EEOC complaint. As a result, the judgment was affirmed. *Ptomey v. Texas Tech Univ.*, 277 S.W.3d 487 (Tex. Ct. App. 2009).

◆   *A federal court rejected a 57-year-old Illinois applicant's claim that she was not hired as a university enrollment counselor based on her age.*

The university sought applicants who had a general knowledge of the higher education market to contact and enroll prospective students. The applicant was invited to participate in a group assessment with about 10 other applicants, even though the university had already chosen two younger candidates, contingent on background checks. The university then filled other jobs by hiring people ages 31 or younger. The applicant sued the university in a federal district court for violating the ADEA. The university sought pretrial judgment, arguing she failed to show she applied for the four positions that opened after she initially submitted her resume. **The court found no age discrimination, because the university showed the individuals chosen for employment were better qualified than the applicant.** Each of the selected applicants held a bachelor's degree, which the candidate lacked. She also had no background in higher education. Because she did not present enough evidence to support her age discrimination claim, the court granted the university's motion for pretrial judgment. *Czubernat v. Univ. of Phoenix*, No. 07 C 2821, 2008 WL 2339570 (N.D. Ill. 6/4/08).

### 3. Evidence of Discrimination

◆   *The First Circuit affirmed a Massachusetts judge's ruling to dismiss an IT worker's age-bias lawsuit.*

During a restructuring, a 47-year-old IT worker's job title and duties were changed. His title was changed to "manager of desktop services – field support." A 30-year-old female co-worker was made "manager of desktop services – central support." Then the department adopted a ticketing system that the female manager helped develop. As a result, desktop services only needed one manager. It chose the female manager and the older male employee was laid off. He sued under the ADEA. The federal district court found the employee didn't show the circumstances suggested age bias. On appeal, the First Circuit agreed. The employee argued the age difference was enough to suggest age bias. **But First Circuit precedent has established that merely showing the employer "consolidated positions ... of discharged employees to other existing employees" in a layoff isn't enough to prove age bias.** The university presented a solid business reason to award the position to the younger female worker. So the ruling for the university was affirmed. *Dunn v. Trustees of Boston Univ.*, 761 F.3d 63 (1st Cir. 2014).

◆   *An employee who lasted only three days at a Pennsylvania university failed to show discrimination based on her race or age.*

The employee claimed she was assigned to a small office with child-sized furniture and no phone or computer. The people she was supposed to supervise shared a larger office that had adult-sized furniture, a phone and a computer. The employee became sick and dizzy in her office because it was too hot. She told a supervisor about the problem, but when she reported for her third day of work, she was told she was being fired because she had complained about her office. The university later filled the post with a black female over age 40. In a federal district court action against the university and supervisor, the employee alleged race-based claims of wrongful termination, disparate treatment and hostile work environment under Title VII. She also claimed age discrimination under the ADEA. The court explained that the employee did not show other employees were treated more favorably than she was. She did not identify circumstances indicating race played a role in the decision to discharge her. The court also rejected the age discrimination claim, as **the employee did not show she was replaced by someone who was younger than her by a margin that allowed an inference of discrimination**. She was either 43 or 44 at the time of her discharge, and she was replaced by someone over 40. This was not enough of an age difference to permit a finding of age discrimination. None of the evidence showed the employee was subjected to severe, extreme or pervasive discrimination, and the university was entitled to judgment. *Beaubrun v. Thomas Jefferson Univ.*, 578 F.Supp.2d 777 (E.D. Pa. 2008).

◆   *A candidate for a college instructor job failed to prove age discrimination.*
    The college hired the candidate, who was in his 50s, as a sociology
instructor under a temporary teaching appointment that was renewed on a
semester-by-semester basis. A full-time, tenure-track appointment to teach
sociology became available the next academic year. The position attracted 29
applicants, including the candidate. Applicants ranged in age from 27 to 55.
The candidate performed poorly on a teaching demonstration and was not
selected as a finalist. The position was awarded to a candidate in his early 30s
who had teaching experience, a doctorate degree, and had presented an
interactive technology-based teaching demonstration that impressed the college
hiring committee. The candidate sued the college in a federal district court for
violating the ADEA. The court held the college offered a legitimate,
nondiscriminatory reason for its decision. Specifically, the college said it
decided not to hire the candidate because he performed poorly during his
teaching demonstration. The hiring committee believed he did not demonstrate
the ability to engage students and interact effectively with them. The candidate
did not show these reasons were false. There was no other evidence showing
the college decided not to hire him based on his age. Therefore, the college's
motion for summary judgment was granted. *Salerno v. Ridgewater College*, No.
06-1717, 2008 WL 509001 (D. Minn. 2/8/08).

◆   *A Tennessee university did not violate the ADEA by changing a 69-year-*
*old professor's position and decreasing his lab space.*
    The professor had worked for the university for nearly 30 years
when a newly hired pathology department chairman asked whether he would
consider early retirement. The professor told him he had no intention of retiring
any time soon, and claimed the chairman then began a series of retaliatory
actions, including orders to vacate his lab and office space. The chairman
offered him several employment options, but they all meant a lower salary
and several included early retirement. The professor sued the university
in a federal district court for age discrimination. The court dismissed the
case, and he appealed to the Sixth Circuit. The court found no adverse
employment action under the ADEA. The reduction in lab space did not affect
salary or job status. **Any proposal to reduce the professor's salary was never**
**carried out, and threats alone are not an adverse action.** The professor
presented no evidence the job changes significantly decreased his
responsibilities. As he could not prevail on his claim without evidence of an
adverse employment action, the court affirmed the judgment for the university.
*Mitchell v. Vanderbilt Univ.*, 389 F.3d 177 (6th Cir. 2004).

## B.  Retirement

◆   *An Illinois federal judge rejected the age discrimination suit of an*
*employee who was not given a raise the year before she retired.*
    An IT employee notified the college that she'd be retiring on a specific
date. A month later, she asked for a different job title and raise. Her supervisor
never turned in the request to HR. Six months after the request, the IT worker

filed an internal complaint, explaining she'd asked her supervisor about the raise three times – and all three times he'd mentioned her upcoming retirement. The matter was not resolved before her final day of work. She sued, alleging age bias. But the court dismissed her complaint, explaining that **courts have long held that "retirement" is not a synonym for old age**. Furthermore, it was appropriate for the supervisor to consider an employee's upcoming retirement as a factor in a business decision about raises and job transfers, the court noted. The claim failed. *David v. Board of Trustees of Community College Dist. No. 508*, No. 13 C 2508, 2015 WL 1887752 (N.D. Ill. 4/24/15).

◆ *The Alabama Legislature had the authority to set a mandatory retirement age of 70 for Alabama State University board members.*
An Alabama State University board member reached the age of 70 before his second 12-year term expired. The terms of an amended state law barred him from serving on the board for his full term. In an attempt to block his removal, the board member sued state and university officials in the federal court system for Equal Protection violations. He claimed the law discriminated on the basis of age without a rational basis and treated trustees at Alabama State University differently than trustees at other Alabama public universities. A district court held for the university, and the board member appealed. On appeal, the Eleventh Circuit applied a deferential rational basis review. It found the law did not involve a fundamental right or suspect classification. The court referenced *Gregory v. Ashcroft*, 501 U.S. 452 (1991), in which the Supreme Court upheld what the Eleventh Circuit said was "a remarkably similar retirement provision." **The court said that the age limit for trustees in this case satisfied rational basis review.** As for the claim that the law set an age limit for the trustees of some state universities but not others, the court held the legislature had leeway to do so. The court also upheld the finding that nothing prevented application of the mandatory retirement age rule. The lower court's ruling was affirmed. *Clark v. Riley*, 595 F.3d 1258 (11th Cir. 2010).

### C. State Statutes

◆ *Two tenured business professors could proceed with their age discrimination case against St. John's University (SJU) under New York law.*
According to the professors, SJU practices led to systematic discrimination against older employees. They complained to SJU but claimed this led to retaliation. In a state court, the professors sued SJU for age discrimination in violation of the State Human Rights Law and the New York City Human Rights Law. SJU sought dismissal, claiming the action brought its academic judgment into question and was properly resolved as an administrative matter with only limited possibilities for court review. A state appellate division court agreed with SJU that decisions by educational institutions involve the exercise of highly specialized professional judgment. While the court agreed that higher education institutions are better suited to make final decisions concerning their internal matters, this case concerned age discrimination, not SJU policies. It held **the fact that the employer was an educational institution did not permit it to discriminate on the basis of age** or otherwise insulate it from

liability for violations of state or city human rights laws. As these were not academic matters, a lower court properly refused to dismiss the case. *Wander v. St. John's Univ.*, 99 A.D.3d 891, 953 N.Y.S.2d 68 (N.Y. App. Div. 2012).

◆   *New Jersey's highest court held a community college dean could pursue a claim that her contract was not renewed because of age discrimination.*

In 2001, when the dean was 69 years old, she was informed by the college's acting president by letter that her contract might not be renewed for job performance. She had over 26 years of experience working for the community college at that time. The dean obtained a reprieve, but three years later she was informed that her contract would not be renewed when it expired for performance reasons. At the time, the dean was over 70 years old. She filed a state-law claim of age discrimination. The trial court ruled against her, and she filed an appeal. On appeal, the New Jersey Superior Court, Appellate Division, held the state Law Against Discrimination (LAD) does not allow employers to discriminate against employees who are age 70 or older.

Appeal then reached the Supreme Court of New Jersey, which held the LAD permits employers to refuse to accept for employment any person who is over the age of 70. **The court held the protection extended by the LAD applied to the non-renewal of an existing employee's contract.** It found that the refusal to renew the contract of an employee over 70, on the basis of age, was a prohibited discriminatory act under the LAD. For this reason, the appellate division's decision for the dean was affirmed. Although the parties advised the court that the case had been settled, the case was found not moot because it involved an important matter of public interest. *Nini v. Mercer County Community College*, 202 N.J. 98, 995 A.2d 1094 (N.J. 2010).

◆   *The Court of Appeals of Missouri upheld an award of more than $1.2 million to a baseball coach for age discrimination.*

The coach was over the age of 40 at the time of his hiring. His team had a winning record every year, and 80% of his players graduated. After he pursued an administrative charge of age discrimination in 1998, the university reduced his job to a half-time position, cut his pay in half and eliminated his benefits. It also moved his office to a basement near a swimming pool. During the same time his position was cut to part time, the university classified a younger compliance officer who worked 5.5 hours per day as a full-time employee. An assistant basketball coach who was under 40 and had far less experience than the baseball coach received a higher salary. The baseball coach sued the university in the state court system for violating the Missouri Human Rights Act. A jury awarded him $1,275,000 in damages.

On appeal, the court upheld the punitive damage award, finding that state law specifically authorized it. The court found the evidence was sufficient to support the punitive damages award. **Evidence showed younger employees were treated better with respect to pay, hours and benefits.** The baseball field did not comply with National Collegiate Athletic Association requirements, and coaches who were hired after the baseball coach were given nicer offices in an athletic complex. The amount of scholarship money allotted for baseball was low compared with the amount allotted for other sports.

**The university discontinued the coach's medical insurance with knowledge that he was a cancer survivor.** The court rejected the university's argument that the amount awarded exceeded reasonable compensation for any injury he suffered. The verdict against the university was upheld. *Brady v. Curators of the Univ. of Missouri*, 213 S.W.3d 101 (Mo. Ct. App. 2006).

◆ *A Pennsylvania law school did not violate a state anti-discrimination act when it discharged an employee who was over 40 years old.*

The law school asked the employee to resign shortly before it merged with a Pennsylvania university. The law school and employee entered into a separation agreement and general release placing him on administrative leave at full salary with full benefits. In return for signing the agreement and giving up his right to unemployment benefits, the employee agreed not to make any claims under the Pennsylvania Human Relations Act (PHRA). However, he filed age discrimination charges against the university with state and federal civil rights agencies. Later, the employee sued the university and law school in a state court, alleging they violated the PHRA. He argued the agreement was invalid because it did not meet the requirements of the Older Workers Benefit Protection Act. The court held for the university and law school. The employee appealed to the Superior Court of Pennsylvania. **The court held the agreement was binding unless the employee proved fraud, duress or other circumstances to invalidate it.** Contracts are interpreted according to their plain language, and the court found this contract was clear. It affirmed the judgment for the university and law school. *Griest v. Pennsylvania State Univ. & Dickinson School of Law*, 897 A.2d 1186 (Pa. Super. 2006).

◆ *A graduate student could not sue for discrimination under Kentucky's employment laws because she was not an employee of the university.*

A 44-year-old graduate psychology student received a Regent's Fellowship that provided her with full tuition and a yearly stipend. She lost her fellowship after her third year of study due to her failure to have her thesis proposal approved by a department committee. She remained in the graduate program for another year, but was subsequently dismissed. The student filed an unsuccessful grievance, then sued for sex and age discrimination in violation of Kentucky law and the university handbook. A state court held the student had no claim under state discrimination law, because she was not a university employee. The Kentucky Court of Appeals found it clear that **nearly all of her duties and activities were in connection with her academic work** rather than providing a service to the university. It held no employer-employee relationship existed. *Stewart v. Univ. of Louisville*, 65 S.W.3d 536 (Ky. Ct. App. 2001).

## V.  DISABILITY DISCRIMINATION

*Section 504 of the Rehabilitation Act of 1973, 29 U.S.C. § 794, prohibits discrimination against qualified individuals with disabilities in programs or activities receiving federal financial assistance. The Americans with Disabilities Act of 1990 (ADA), 42 U.S.C. § 12101, et seq., extends this protection to both private and public employees and prohibits discrimination against employees who are associated with disabled individuals.*

*The 2008 ADA Amendments addressed the term "disability" – defined as "a physical or mental impairment that substantially limits one or more major life activities" of an individual. "Disability" under the ADA is to be construed in favor of broad coverage "to the maximum extent permitted by the terms of this Act." The term "substantially limits" is to be interpreted consistently with congressional findings and purposes. U.S. Public Laws 110-325 (S. 3406), 110th Congress, Second Session. "ADA Amendments Act of 2008." 29 U.S.C. § 705, 42 U.S.C. §§ 12101-03, 12106-14, 12201, 12205a.*

*Guidance from the Equal Employment Opportunity Commission's ADA Enforcement Guide states that "if the employee's need for accommodation is not obvious, the employer may ask for reasonable documentation concerning the employee's disability and functional limitations."*

*In 2011, the U.S. Equal Employment Opportunity Commission (EEOC) issued regulations and interpretive guidance on the 2008 ADA Amendments. According to the EEOC guidance, the primary purpose of the 2008 ADA amendments was to make it easier for people with disabilities to obtain ADA protection. The EEOC states the primary issue in ADA cases should be whether an employer is meeting its legal obligations and whether discrimination has occurred, not whether an individual meets a qualifying definition of disability.*

*The guidance offers definitions of physical, mental and psychological impairment that include lists of qualifying impairments. Major life activities include caring for oneself, performing manual tasks, seeing, hearing, sleeping, walking, standing, speaking, breathing, learning, reading, concentrating, thinking, communicating, interacting with others and working.*

*The guidance indicates that it is unlawful for a covered entity to use qualification standards, employment tests or other selection criteria that screen out individuals with disabilities or classes of individuals with disabilities. A defense is offered in the guidance for employers who can show an individual's claimed impairment is both transitory and minor.* Federal Register, *Vol. 76, No. 58, Page 16978, March 25, 2011. 29 C.F.R. Part 1630.*

### A.  Liability

◆   *A Colorado federal court rejected a disability bias claim filed by a tenured professor who was excluded from campus for his disruptive behavior.*

The professor took medication for an anxiety disorder for several years. The university knew about the disorder and had granted accommodation requests, including a specific teaching schedule. During a meeting, the department chair asked the professor if he'd ever attempted suicide. In response, the professor said he'd never kill someone unless they were "truly evil" or "had Hitler's soul." After the meeting, the department chair conferred with other university officials. Because the professor had a history of threatening and disruptive behavior, the university banned him from campus until he underwent a violence assessment. He filed a disability discrimination complaint with the EEOC and went on to sue. To win, the professor had to show, among other things, that the university took an adverse action against him based on his disability. He failed to make that showing. **It was clear that** the school took the actions against the professor – at least in part – due to his disruptive and threatening behavior, the court held. It granted the university's motion to dismiss the claim. *Kaufman v. Univ. of Colorado at Boulder*, No. 15-cv-004-6-LTB-NYW, 2015 WL 7014440 (D. Colo. 11/12/15).

◆ *A federal district court in New York granted summary judgment against a university library clerk who said he was subjected to disability discrimination on the job.*

Court records indicated that a library clerk filled out an ADA Job Analysis Form when he was hired but did not include details about his disability. On the form, he asked for one accommodation, which was granted. When the clerk had been working at the university for about 10 years, his supervisor had concerns about ongoing deterioration of the clerk's job performance and his increasingly aggressive behavior at work. The university placed the clerk on a leave of absence and directed him to undergo a medical examination. Two independent medical professionals concluded that he was not able to perform his job duties. He was placed on sick leave with half pay. The following year, he was let go. He sued the university, claiming violations of the ADA and a laundry list of additional claims. The defendants filed a motion for summary judgment, and the court granted the motion. The court said the clerk's claims were time-barred. The only act alleged to have occurred within the limitations period was one negative evaluation. But he did not submit evidence showing that evaluation was biased. Instead, **the evidence showed he was terminated due to deteriorating behavior and job performance**. He failed to show that the employer's stated reasons for terminating him were pretextual. So the court rejected the claim that he was terminated based on his disability. The clerk also alleged an unlawful failure to accommodate his alleged disability. But no evidence in the record supported his accommodation claim, the court said. The school granted the only accommodation he ever requested. The motion for summary judgment was granted. *Brown v. State Univ. of New York*, No. 3:12-cv-411 (GLS/DEP), 2015 WL 729737 (N.D.N.Y. 2/19/15).

◆ *A federal district court refused to grant pretrial judgment to a university in a job applicant's disability discrimination claim.*

A man applied for two security positions. At the time, he had end-stage renal disease and was receiving dialysis treatments three times a week. The job postings for the positions said a "minimum requirement" for applicants was being able to work rotating shifts. While interviewing, the applicant disclosed his medical condition and his need to undergo the dialysis treatments. He did not get a job offer. He filed a charge of disability discrimination with the EEOC under the ADA, and the EEOC sued on his behalf. The school filed a motion for pretrial judgment, asserting that its failure to hire the applicant did not violate the ADA because he could not perform the essential job function of being able to work a three-shift schedule. The court denied the motion. It said that although the ability to work a rotating shift can be an essential job function, there was some question in this case regarding exactly what that requirement actually entailed. **The school did not show the applicant would be unable to perform rotating shift work as required.** As a result, it did not prove entitlement to pretrial judgment, so the motion was denied. *EEOC v. Howard Univ.*, No. 12-1186 (ABJ), 2014 WL 4828223 (D.D.C. 9/30/14).

◆   *A University of Illinois police officer who had a stroke did not show a federal court that the university discriminated against him based on disability.*

After suffering a stroke while off duty, the officer could not walk or care for himself. But he continued to improve to the point that the university stated in writing that he must return to work. The officer obtained medical clearance from the university health services department based on a cerebral angiogram showing his stroke-related injuries had healed. But he then refused to undergo a functional capacity examination and was not called back to work. After resigning, he found another job and sued the university. The court found the officer was not subjected to an adverse employment action because he had resigned and was not discharged. On appeal, the Seventh Circuit rejected the officer's argument that the university should have proposed a reasonable accommodation once he agreed to return to work. **In ADA accommodation cases, employees have a duty to trigger the interactive process by telling their employers of their needs for accommodations.** In any event, the officer had insisted he was fully recovered and could do his old job. In seeking reinstatement, he did not say he needed accommodations. The functional capacity evaluation was reasonable because it enabled the university to determine whether the officer could perform required duties. And he did not suffer an adverse job action because he had voluntarily resigned. *Pamon v. Board of Trustees of the Univ. of Illinois*, 483 Fed.Appx. 296 (7th Cir. 2012).

◆   *A Louisiana professor did not show an ADA violation when his request to limit faculty meetings to 20 minutes to accommodate his back pain was denied.*

The professor received poor evaluations for several years. Twenty years after being hired, he was subjected to a formal faculty performance review. A review panel found formal remediation was necessary. The professor asked the university to limit faculty meetings to 20 minutes to accommodate his chronic back pain. Instead, the university notified him it was initiating his termination for not cooperating with a remediation committee. After the professor was fired, he sued the university for violation of the Contracts Clause and his tenure rights. The court awarded pretrial judgment to the university, and he appealed.

On appeal, the U.S. Court of Appeals, Fifth Circuit, held the professor did not mention his constitutional and tenure claims in his brief and thus lost the right to appeal them. His ADA claims failed because his requests for a more accessible office were made so long before he filed suit that they were outside the statute of limitations. **An employee who challenges the denial of an accommodation must show why a requested accommodation is reasonable.** But the professor did not show his request to limit faculty meetings to 20 minutes was reasonable. As his ADA and other claims failed, dismissal was proper. *Windhauser v. Board of Supervisors for Louisiana State Univ. & Agricultural and Mechanical College*, 360 Fed.Appx. 562 (5th Cir. 2010).

◆   *A Connecticut community college did not discriminate against an assistant professor when it declined to renew her teaching contract.*

A year after being hired to teach computer courses, the professor had major surgery and her mother died. She told a supervisor she was under psychiatric care, but she did not provide a diagnosis or other details. The college denied the professor's requests for only lower-level class assignments and that she not be required to teach both day and evening classes. Students began to complain that she had "stopped teaching" and was relying on a student to facilitate class discussions. A supervisor assigned the professor a poor performance evaluation, saying she was unprepared for class. After the college did not renew the professor's contract, she filed a federal district court action accusing it of disability discrimination under the ADA and sex discrimination under Title VII. **The court noted she only vaguely alleged having a mental impairment, and she failed to show she had a disability as defined by the ADA.** There was enough evidence to show her contract was not renewed due to her poor job performance. As no reasonable jury could conclude the decision was motivated by sex discrimination, the court held for the community college.

On appeal, the U.S. Court of Appeals, Second Circuit, found no evidence that the professor had an impairment that met the ADA definition of disability. She also did not show she had any record of a qualifying disability. Since the professor did not demonstrate that her contract was not renewed because of a disability, the judgment for the community college was affirmed. *Mastrolillo v. State of Connecticut*, 352 Fed.Appx. 472 (2d Cir. 2009).

◆ *A counselor at an Arizona community college could proceed with an ADA claim, even though she threatened her department chair.*

The counselor suffered a brain injury in a car accident. The injury impaired her ability to regulate her emotional responses. When the college tried to discharge her, she filed a disability discrimination claim that was eventually settled. Months later, a new department chair reminded the counselor that she was to work 35 hours each week. After the meeting, the counselor became upset and threatened the chair. She then called an associate dean of student services to say she had experienced a breakdown. The college placed the counselor on leave and asked her to submit to fitness-for-duty examinations. One of the examining psychologists concluded she was unable to function as a counselor. As all open positions at the college involved interaction with students, the counselor's employment was terminated.

The counselor sued the college in a federal district court for ADA violations. Although the college argued no accommodations would permit her to serve as a counselor, the court held a jury could find that a job coach would enable her to do this work. While the college argued the counselor had violated its violence policy by threatening the department chair, the court said conduct resulting from a disability is "part of the disability" and not a separate basis for discharge. Pretrial judgment was not allowed on the termination claim. **As an examination to determine whether a threat will be carried out is consistent with business necessity, the college could require one.** *Menchaca v. Maricopa Community College Dist.*, 595 F.Supp.2d 1063 (D. Ariz. 2009).

◆ *The U.S. Supreme Court concluded that Congress exceeded its authority by allowing monetary damage awards against states in ADA cases.*

According to a 2001 U.S. Supreme Court decision, Congress did not identify a history and pattern of irrational employment discrimination against individuals with disabilities by the states when it enacted the ADA. For this reason, the states were entitled to Eleventh Amendment immunity from such claims. As a result, **two state employees were unsuccessful in their attempt to recover money damages under the ADA from their state employer for disability discrimination**. *Board of Trustees of Univ. of Alabama v. Garrett*, 531 U.S. 356, 121 S.Ct. 955, 148 L.Ed.2d 866 (2001).

◆ *A Harvard University staff assistant with bipolar disorder was permissibly discharged due to his egregious misconduct.*

The employee was diagnosed with bipolar disorder and sometimes had periods of mania on the job. He established a website where he criticized the pay scale. The employee updated his website at work on his personal laptop. Shortly after the employee created the website, he became severely manic. He was loud and animated as he told co-workers about Harvard's wage policies and invited them to view the website. In the university's main Museum lobby, he sang, clapped and danced to protest songs that were posted on his website. He was hospitalized for an episode of paranoia. Soon after that, staff members and police officers approached the employee and asked him to leave. When he refused, the officers arrested him, and the university later discharged him.

The employee sued Harvard in a state court for violating the ADA. Harvard relied on *Garrity v. United Airlines*, 421 Mass. 55 (1995), in which the state's highest court held if an employee's "egregious misconduct" is adverse to the interests of the employer and violates employer rules, the employee may not claim ADA protection. The court found the misconduct in this case was egregious and held for Harvard. On appeal, the supreme judicial court noted that its *Garrity* decision was consistent with the view adopted by the majority of courts facing the issue of egregious employer misconduct under federal law. This was so even though Congress only granted permission to employers to hold alcoholics to the same standard of conduct as other employees. **The court held disabled employees were not entitled to disability law protection if they engaged in egregious misconduct that would be sufficient to result in the discharge of a non-disabled employee.** *Mammone v. President and Fellows of Harvard College*, 446 Mass. 657, 847 N.E.2d 276 (Mass. 2006).

## B. Defenses

*In* Hosanna-Tabor Evangelical Lutheran Church and School v. EEOC, *below, the U.S. Supreme Court explained that there is a ministerial exception to the provisions of anti-discrimination laws, including Title VII and the ADA. This rule is rooted in the First Amendment rights of religious institutions to make decisions about the employment of those who carry out their missions.*

*To be covered by the ADA, an employee must have a disabling condition that substantially limits the ability to engage in a major life activity such as work. In 2008, Congress broadened certain ADA provisions to correct Supreme Court decisions that interpreted the Act differently than Section 504. Congress expected the ADA's definition of "disability" would be interpreted consistently with how courts were interpreting the definition of "handicapped individual" under Rehabilitation Act Section 504. Congress singled out* Sutton v. United Air Lines, Inc.*, 527 U.S. 471 (1999) and* Toyota Motor Mfg., Kentucky, Inc. v. Williams*, 534 U.S. 184 (2002), as cases in which the Supreme Court interpreted "substantially limits" more restrictively than Congress intended.*

◆   *A Louisiana federal judge dismissed the claim of a former employee who alleged a university discriminated against him on the basis of his disability.*

The employee was hired as a librarian. He suffered from manic and major depression – and warned his supervisor that his conditions might cause him to behave irrationally even though he was taking his medication. During a manic episode, the employee emailed his supervisor to falsely accuse the department director of sexual harassment. Realizing the next day what he'd done, the employee emailed the supervisor to explain he'd made the false accusation during a manic episode. He asked her to delete the email and forget all about it. Two weeks later, the university decided not to renew his contract. He filed a charge with the EEOC, and later sued under the ADA. But the court dismissed the case, finding Eleventh Amendment immunity bars it. **This immunity protects the state and its entities – which this college was – from lawsuits by citizens unless the state consents to the suit or an exception applies.** Determining the suit couldn't go forward, the court granted dismissed the claim. *Webster v. Board of Supervisors of the Univ. of Louisiana System*, No. 13-6613, 2015 WL 4459211 (E.D. La. 7/21/15).

◆   *The U.S. Supreme Court dismissed a suit against a Michigan Lutheran school based on a "ministerial exception" that exempts religious employers from liability under state and federal anti-discrimination laws.*

A Michigan Lutheran school teacher became ill and took a disability leave for what was diagnosed as narcolepsy. Later, the school discharged her. She sued it in a federal court for violating the ADA. The court held the First Amendment prohibited it from considering claims involving the employment relationship between a religious institution and a ministerial employee. In dismissing the case, the court held the teacher was a ministerial employee. On appeal, the U.S. Court of Appeals, Sixth Circuit, reversed the judgment, finding she was not a ministerial employee because she spent most of her school day teaching secular subjects and using secular textbooks. Though she led a chapel service, she did so only twice a year. Appeal reached the U.S. Supreme Court, which said there is a ministerial exception to bias laws rooted in the First Amendment. **A court order requiring a church to accept or retain a minister, or imposing liability for failing to do so, would intrude upon church governance and deprive churches of the power to select those who would preach their beliefs, teach their faiths and carry out their missions.** Declining to adopt a rigid formula for who may qualify as a "minister," the Court found significance in the teacher's title, which was "Minister of Religion, Commissioned." As a "called" employee, she had to complete extensive studies in church doctrine and ministry and become endorsed by the church synod and congregation. She could also claim an income tax break that was available only to ministers. In finding the teacher qualified for ministerial status, the Court noted her formal title of minister, the numerous requirements she performed to earn "called" status, and religious duties such as teaching religion and leading prayers and chapel services. As the teacher was covered by the ministerial exception, the Court reversed the judgment. *Hosanna-Tabor Evangelical Lutheran Church and School v. EEOC*, 132 S.Ct. 694, 181 L.Ed.2d 650 (U.S. 2012).

◆   *Georgia State University did not violate federal law by reducing the salary and later eliminating the position of a marketing director with a disability.*

After suffering a stroke, the director had to rely more on an administrative assistant to perform tasks that had become difficult for him. A budget reduction resulted in the layoff of the administrative assistant and a 20% reduction in the director's hours and salary. At his request, a part-time administrative assistant was provided for him. Soon, the director emailed an assistant dean and a human resources employee to complain that the reductions were made with knowledge that it would be hard for someone his age and with his disability to find a new job. He also met with the human resources employee and told him he believed the actions were related to his disability. A second round of budget cuts resulted in the elimination of the director's position, and he sued the university in a federal court. It held his request for a full-time administrative assistant was unreasonable. On appeal, the U.S. Court of Appeals, Eleventh Circuit, held the university did not unlawfully deny a disability-related job accommodation.

Although job restructuring was an available accommodation under federal disability laws, **the request for a full-time administrative assistant went beyond job restructuring and would have required the creation of a new position**. The court also held the director did not prove unlawful retaliation, as he could not show the budget cuts were a pretext. Similarly, the director could not show the elimination of his position was motivated by unlawful disability discrimination. As a result, the court held for the university. *Barton v. Board of Regents of the Univ. System of Georgia*, 478 Fed.Appx. 627 (11th Cir. 2012).

◆   *Generally, a seniority system takes precedence over ADA accommodation.*

In a case involving an airline employee with a bad back, who was seeking a mailroom position, **the U.S. Supreme Court held that as a general rule, an accommodation under the ADA is not reasonable if it conflicts with an employer's seniority rules**. However, employees may present evidence of special circumstances that make a "seniority rule exception" reasonable in a particular case. *US Airways, Inc. v. Barnett*, 535 U.S. 391, 122 S.Ct. 1516, 152 L.Ed.2d 589 (2002).

◆   *A federal court rejected a West Virginia university's defense that an employee could not pursue a disability action due to his own misconduct.*

A university information technology specialist had sleep apnea and sleep insomnia. He began to receive medical treatment and informed his supervisor and the human resources department. But the specialist was warned in writing about falling asleep on the job and eventually threatened with termination. The specialist responded by asking for accommodations, including a "doze alert" that would alarm him if his head tilted enough. After the accommodation was denied, the specialist sued the university in a federal district court for disability discrimination. According to the university, the specialist waited too long to ask for an accommodation and invoked it to excuse his prior misconduct. **The court agreed that the university was not required to excuse the specialist's past misconduct.** But the specialist had claimed that the university broke the law by rejecting his request for an accommodation. This claim was sufficient to survive pretrial dismissal. While it held for the specialist, the court held he would most likely not be qualified for his job under the law if he needed the "doze alert" to stay awake while at work. *Leschinskey v. Rectors and Visitors of Radford Univ.*, No. 7:11-cv-00189, 2011 WL 5029813 (W.D. Va. 10/24/11).

◆ *An Illinois college custodian did not show decisions not to promote and then to fire him were based on disability.*

The custodian worked for nine years as a part-time custodian at the college, despite having a mental impairment. He applied three times for full-time work without success. At a board of trustees meeting where new full-time custodial hires were expected to be approved, the custodian made a statement about college hiring practices and asked the board to delay the hiring decision until his application could be reviewed. Later, a supervisor issued the custodian's work evaluation and assigned him an overall rating of "unsatisfactory." The custodian filed an unsuccessful grievance and a disability discrimination claim with the U.S. Equal Employment Opportunity Commission (EEOC).

After six months on a correction plan, the college fired the custodian, and he filed a new grievance and EEOC complaint. An arbitrator reinstated him due to the college's failure to follow progressive discipline. The custodian sued the college in a federal district court for violating the ADA by denying him a promotion, firing him, and retaliating against him for addressing the board. The court held **the custodian's history of mediocre performance was a valid nondiscriminatory reason not to promote him**. He could not show retaliation because the supervisor who conducted the review testified he did not know about his board meeting comments. The court found the college used the same procedures it used for reviewing other part-time custodians and dismissed the custodian's ADA claims. *Dickerson v. Belleville Area Community College Dist. 522*, No. 08-716-GPM, 2010 WL 3835781 (S.D. Ill. 9/24/10).

◆ *A Florida professor's claim that he was discharged because his employer thought he was an alcoholic will not be dismissed prior to a trial.*

The professor began teaching as an adjunct professor and soon became a full-time associate professor. A few years later, he began missing meetings and showing signs of alcohol abuse. His divorce became final near this time. An associate dean arrived unannounced at the professor's residence and concluded he was under the influence of alcohol. The professor was placed on medical leave. The university told him he would be deemed to have resigned if he did not submit a leave of absence form and physician's certification by a specified date. It then discharged him after he did not submit the forms on time.

The professor sued the university under the Rehabilitation Act, claiming it discharged him because it "regarded" him as an alcoholic. Alcoholism can be a disability under the Rehabilitation Act when the individual claiming protection is not currently abusing alcohol. The court rejected the university's claim that pretrial judgment should be granted based on the professor's failure to actively participate on a dissertation review committee. A factual dispute existed as to whether active participation on the committee was an essential job function and as to whether he adequately performed it. **The court also rejected the university's argument that it accommodated the professor by placing him on leave and making its employee assistance program available to him.** These steps did not conclusively establish it met its duty to reasonably accommodate him. *Gardiner v. Nova Southeastern Univ.*, No. 06-60590 CIV, 2006 WL 3804704 (S.D. Fla. 12/22/06).

## C. Contagious Diseases

*In 1998, the U.S. Supreme Court held that a person with HIV was protected by the Americans with Disabilities Act (ADA), despite the fact that she was not yet exhibiting symptoms of the disease. Since HIV substantially impaired her ability to reproduce, she could not be excluded unless her condition presented a direct threat to the health and safety of others.* Bragdon v. Abbott, *524 U.S. 624, 118 S.Ct. 2196, 141 L.Ed.2d 540 (1998).*

◆ *The Supreme Court held that a person with a contagious disease was entitled to the protections of the Rehabilitation Act.*

A Florida elementary school teacher was discharged because of her continued recurrence of tuberculosis. She sued the school board under Section 504 of the Rehabilitation Act. A federal district court dismissed her suit, but the Eleventh Circuit held persons with contagious diseases fall within Section 504's coverage. The case then reached the U.S. Supreme Court, which held that **tuberculosis was a disability under Section 504**. The disease attacked the teacher's respiratory system and affected her ability to work. It would be unfair to allow an employer to distinguish between a disease's potential effect on others and its effect on the afflicted employee in order to justify discriminatory treatment. Accordingly, she was entitled to reinstatement or front pay if she could show that despite her disability, she was otherwise qualified for her job with or without a reasonable accommodation. *School Board of Nassau County v. Arline*, 480 U.S. 273, 107 S.Ct. 1123, 94 L.Ed.2d 307 (1987).

## VI. RETALIATION

### A. Generally

*Title VII prohibits an employer from retaliating against an employee for opposing an unlawful employment practice, or for making a charge, testifying, assisting, or participating in any manner in a discrimination investigation, proceeding or hearing. In* Robinson v. Shell Oil Co., *519 U.S. 337 (1997), the Supreme Court held a former employee could bring a retaliatory discrimination lawsuit against a former employer after he was given a negative employment reference following his filing of a discrimination complaint.*

◆  *A Wisconsin federal judge dismissed the retaliation claim of a professor who advocated for a student who complained about sexual harassment.*

A male professor lectured on "breach experiments" – provocations designed to display social norms by violating them so they can be studied. Demonstrating, the professor – in full view of the class – handed a female student a note that read, "Call me tonight" with his phone number. She didn't recognize the exchange as a demonstration. Upset, she sought out the plaintiff for advice. Advocating for the student, the plaintiff suggested to the dean and department chair that all faculty be informed of such experiments in the future. In response, the chair said that wasn't necessary. Then the chair circulated a memo to the department, outlining procedures to follow if a student had a problem with another professor. The plaintiff viewed the memo as a veiled public reprimand for helping the student. About 18 months later, the chair stepped down, but the plaintiff didn't get along with his replacement any better. So the dean wrote the plaintiff a letter of direction with five specific actions. She "flatly refused to accept any of [the dean's] directions." Instead, she filed a retaliation lawsuit. The court dismissed the claim, as the professor didn't show she suffered a "materially adverse action." The new policy's purpose was to provide a uniform procedure for addressing complaints – not to humiliate anyone, the court opined. **Moreover, "neither a bruised ego nor a lone instance of public humiliation constitutes actionable retaliatory conduct,"** the court held. So the university was entitled to judgment. *Burton v. Board of Regents of the Univ. of Wisconsin System*, No. 14-cv-274-jdp, 15-P-190, 2016 WL 1090676, (W.D. Wis. 3/17/16).

◆  *The Tennessee Supreme Court reinstated a jury's finding that a university retaliated against a housing worker that sued for bias.*

A Japanese-American employee worked in the housing department. He said his supervisor began acting cruelly after she found out the worker's mother was Japanese. She made him work beyond his medical restrictions for years. The employee said he had physical injuries that kept getting worse because of it. After an injury required back surgery, the employee filed an EEOC complaint alleging race and national origin discrimination. Then he filed a lawsuit. Later that same week, the employee was called in to work. Although his medical restriction was lifting 20 pounds occasionally, the employee was called in to unstop a drain that required lifting a 75- to 100-pound auger with a co-worker. As he worked on the drain, his leg went numb, so he left. The next day, the supervisor ordered the employee to finish the job. He added a retaliation claim to his suit. After a trial, the jury found for him only on the retaliation claim. It awarded him $3 million. An appeals court reversed, saying the worker didn't establish that the supervisor knew about the lawsuit, so there was no retaliation. The state's highest court reinstated the award, explaining that **the supervisor's deposition showed she was aware of the lawsuit. And the alleged retaliation occurred less than one week after the suit was filed**. The evidence supported the jury's verdict, so the high court reinstated it – but sent the case back for the appeals court to decide the school's claim that the jury's $3 million award was excessive. On remand, the appellate court found it was not. *Ferguson v. Middle Tennessee State Univ.*, No. M2012–00890–COA–R3–CV, 2015 WL 1186277 (Tenn. Ct. App. 3/11/15).

◆   *A tenured professor failed to state a valid Title VII retaliation claim, so an Oklahoma federal judge granted a motion to dismiss the case.*

A female professor didn't get along with a male colleague who was also a professor in the department. She claimed the co-worker growled at her and refused to allow her to ride the elevator with him on several occasions. She reported his behavior to the department chair every time it happened. When a tentative schedule of teaching assistant assignments was sent out, the professor realized she'd been assigned one teaching assistant for one of her courses – but not the second course she was assigned to teach. After she talked to the department chair, she expected to be given another teaching assistant. The bullying continued, and the employee again complained to the department chair about the co-worker's actions, saying he didn't treat male professors the way he treated her. She also complained to the dean. After meeting with the dean, the employee got a final schedule for the teaching assistant assignments. She was not assigned an assistant for the second scheduled course as she expected. She sued the board of regents for retaliation based on the assignment of just one teaching assistant. The board filed a motion for pretrial judgment. It said **the employee could not show a change in her employment status, as she'd been assigned one teaching assistant during the previous year with a similar class schedule**. Because the professor did not suffer an adverse action, the defense motion was granted. *Cox-Fuenzalida v. State of Oklahoma*, No. CV-12-1279-R, 2014 WL 1901061 (W.D. Okla. 5/13/14).

◆   *A Tennessee federal judge rejected the claim of an adjunct professor who alleged he was fired in retaliation for serving on a grand jury.*

The adjunct worked at two campuses – one in North Carolina and the other in Tennessee. In 2012, the professor was selected to serve on a county grand jury. The North Carolina jury-duty policy was to provide subs – but not pay – for part-time employees. But the Tennessee policy provided pay for jury service. The college decided to follow the Tennessee policy and paid the employee for jury time. Then the employee began to turn in time sheets with errors, including hours spent for "class prep time," which he wasn't entitled to. He was reprimanded but continued to make the same mistakes. **His time-sheet errors continued, with him recording fraudulent jury hours that didn't affect his teaching schedule.** He sued, claiming he was fired in retaliation for jury service. But the court found the college had a valid reason for termination. So the claim was dismissed. *Burton v. National College of Tennessee, Inc.*, No. 3:13-00149, 2014 WL 1334263 (M.D. Tenn. 4/2/14).

◆   *Finding an employee did not state a valid Title VII retaliation claim, a Connecticut federal judge dismissed the claim.*

Kimberley Warner worked as the therapist for the University of Connecticut (UC) Health Center. Another employee accused the doctor who was the supervisor of their department of making inappropriate sexual remarks. During the school's internal investigation, Warner was asked what she thought of the doctor's comments. She said she was shocked and insulted as a woman.

Four months later, Warner was transferred to a different department. Her pay, benefits, schedule and title were not affected. Warner also alleged the doctor who had been targeted by the investigation reduced her performance rating from "excellent" to "good" twice. This also had no tangible job effect. She filed a retaliation claim and sued the health center. The judge granted the health center pre-trial judgment for two reasons. First, **internal investigations not connected with an official EEOC proceeding are protected from retaliation by Title VII**. And second, Title VII prohibits employers from retaliating against an employee for opposing an unlawful employment practice. That wasn't the case here, so the claim failed. *Warner v. Univ. of Connecticut Health Center*, No. 311-CV-983(JCH), 2013 WL 3354428 (D. Conn. 7/3/13).

◆ *The Third Circuit held a New Jersey university faculty member could proceed with his discrimination and retaliation claims.*

The faculty member claimed he was passed over for promotion twice based on his race and Filipino national origin. He filed two race and national origin discrimination claims with a federal agency and added a retaliation claim to the second charge. A federal district court awarded pretrial judgment to the university. On appeal, the Third Circuit held the lower court should have looked at the evidence in the light most favorable to the faculty member. **He made a valid preliminary case of employment discrimination by showing he was qualified for the promotions, and that colleagues who were not Asian or Filipino were promoted.** And the faculty member produced evidence that at least one of the colleagues was less qualified than he was for the promotion. At this stage, he did not have to prove his case, he only had to raise doubts about the reasons given for denying a promotion. He did this by presenting testimony from promotions committee members who said they had not reviewed or could not remember reviewing his application. As a result, the court vacated the judgment and returned the case to the lower court for reconsideration under the correct legal standard and based upon all the evidence. *Andes v. New Jersey City Univ.*, 419 Fed. Appx. 230 (3d Cir. 2011).

◆ *A federal court refused to dismiss retaliation claims brought by a former dean at Gallaudet University, a higher education institution for deaf persons.*

According to the dean, many Gallaudet students and staff espoused "Deaf Culture," which includes a belief that deaf persons should use only American Sign Language (ASL) to communicate. While the dean used ASL, she used other methods such as hearing amplification and lip-reading. When Deaf students staged protests over the appointment of a new university president, the board of trustees revoked the appointment. According to the dean, the only basis for this was the perception that the new president wasn't "Deaf enough." She suggested the movement was biased and later said Gallaudet faculty, staff and alumni supported the protesters while she stood behind the president. The dean claimed her responsibilities were reduced and that she was excluded from administrative decision-making. She claimed university staff retaliated against her and spread lies about her. After the dean sued the university in a federal court for retaliation under state and federal law, Gallaudet sought dismissal.

The court allowed a retaliation claim under Section 601 of Title VII. **Section 601 does not explicitly prohibit retaliation – but the court held**

**Section 601 retaliation claims are implicitly allowed.** The court held the dean made a valid Title VII case by showing Gallaudet took adverse actions against her because of her advocacy for minority students. The court also found she stated a claim under the District of Columbia Human Rights Act, which prohibits retaliation for exercising civil rights, or for aiding or encouraging others to do so. The dean had supported a president whose appointment was revoked for what she alleged were discriminatory reasons. She also said that she suffered the same discrimination – being seen as not "Deaf enough." Finding the dean had stated valid retaliation claims, the court refused to dismiss the case. *Kimmel v. Gallaudet Univ.*, 639 F.Supp.2d 34 (D.D.C. 2009).

◆   *A Massachusetts general accounting director who complained about college financial practices could not claim retaliation under Title VII.*

The accounting director complained that a male co-worker's financial information was erroneous and in violation of state regulations. According to the director, illegal changes were made to the college's general ledger system. She said her supervisor retaliated against her for making these complaints and that instead of disciplining the co-worker, the supervisor discriminated against her and created a hostile work environment. The director took a leave of absence, claiming her supervisor had caused her to suffer a nervous breakdown. While she was on leave, an audit determined that her job performance was unsatisfactory. The college discharged the director, and she filed an administrative complaint for gender discrimination. She then filed a federal district court action against the college and some co-workers for gender discrimination and retaliation under Title VII. The court dismissed the case.

Appeal reached the U.S. Court of Appeals, First Circuit, which found the administrative complaint put the college on notice of possible gender discrimination. For this reason, the director's gender bias claim was reinstated. There is no individual liability under Title VII, so the lower court had properly disposed of the claims against the co-workers. **To prove her claim of unlawful retaliation under Title VII, the director had to show she opposed an unlawful employment practice under Title VII or participated in an investigation, proceeding or hearing under Title VII.** Since the financial improprieties she reported had nothing to do with Title VII, the court held this claim failed. *Fantini v. Salem State College*, 557 F.3d 22 (1st Cir. 2009).

◆   *No violation of Title VII occurred when a university employee was laid off after he complained that his supervisor was showing favoritism toward a lover.*

An Oklahoma State University (OSU) employee complained that his supervisor showed favoritism to a person he was having an affair with and then retaliated against him. After being laid off, he sued OSU in a federal district court for retaliation and age discrimination. OSU responded that the layoff was part of a restructuring. To prove retaliation, the court held the employee had to show he engaged in protected activity and suffered an adverse employment action as a result. However, he did not participate in a Title VII investigation, proceeding or hearing, and he could not show he opposed an unlawful employment practice. Since opposition to an affair is not protected conduct under Title VII, the employee could not proceed with his retaliation claim.

On appeal to the U.S. Court of Appeals, Tenth Circuit, the employee claimed he was subjected to a hostile work environment based on his reporting of the affair. The court held this was simply a re-hash of his invalid retaliation claim. **There was no evidence of a hostile work environment or unlawful discrimination.** As the supervisor's affair and favoritism were not enough to pursue a Title VII case, the court rejected the appeal. *Anderson v. Oklahoma State Univ. Board of Regents*, 342 Fed.Appx. 365 (10th Cir. 2009).

◆ *Two University of Denver professors did not show they were subjected to a hostile work environment or that they were retaliated against under Title VII.*

In their lawsuit against the university and several officials, the professors claimed retaliation after they engaged in more than 20 acts of protected conduct over a two-year period. They said they were subjected to public humiliation at a department meeting after they complained that they were treated unfavorably during a search for an assistant professor. The professors also said the Spanish section of their department was abolished after they complained about hostile work environment and discrimination. A federal district court dismissed the case, and the professors appealed to the U.S. Court of Appeals, Tenth Circuit.

**The court held that to prove retaliation, the professors had to show they engaged in protected activity resulting adverse employment action.** And there had to be a causal connection between the protected activity and the adverse employment action. The court held *Burlington Northern & Santa Fe Railway Co. v. White*, this chapter, required a showing that a reasonable person would have found the action was materially adverse in a way that dissuaded them from filing discrimination charges. The professors did not show this. The conduct they found humiliating consisted of colleagues rolling their eyes, laughing, snickering and making comments to one another while they talked. As this was insufficient to show they were subjected to an adverse action, the case was properly dismissed. **Title VII does not establish a workplace civility code.** *Somoza v. Univ. of Denver*, 513 F.3d 1206 (10th Cir. 2008).

◆ *A federal appeals court refused to disturb a verdict for a Grambling State University police chief who was fired after trying to hire a white job applicant.*

Grambling State University (GSU) is a historically black Louisiana institution. After reviewing the qualifications of four candidates for an assistant police chief position, he recommended a white applicant. A supervisor blocked the application, and the chief believed she was doing so based on race. Less than a week after the chief made a written inquiry about the status of the application, GSU fired him. He sued GSU in a federal district court for violations of Title VII and state law. GSU countered that the chief was discharged for not following proper hiring procedures, his rudeness at an interdepartmental meeting, and a harassment complaint by a co-worker.

A jury returned a unanimous verdict for the chief and awarded him $140,000 in compensatory damages. Appeal reached the U.S. Court of Appeals, Fifth Circuit, which upheld the compensatory damage award. **It found the chief's opposition to GSU's refusal to hire an applicant based on his race could be protected activity under Title VII.** There was also enough evidence for a jury to conclude GSU treated the applicant differently than others based on race. The compensatory damages award was justified, and the court held the lower court should have awarded the chief attorneys' fees. *Tureaud v. Grambling State Univ.*, 513 F.3d 1206 (5th Cir. 2008).

◆ *Actions taken against a Nebraska professor did not form the basis of a retaliation claim.*

The professor had worked at Creighton University for 10 years when a colleague filed a sexual harassment claim against her. A four-person committee investigated the charge and recommended discharging the professor. Instead, the university's president placed her on probation under close monitoring. She was forbidden from contact with her accuser and required to undergo a year of psychological counseling and training. The professor filed discrimination charges against Creighton, claiming she was placed on probation based on her national origin. She then sued the university in a federal district court, alleging 21 counts of retaliation. The court ruled for the university, and the professor appealed to the U.S. Court of Appeals, Eighth Circuit. **The court found none of the actions noted by the professor were harmful enough to constitute a "materially adverse" job action.** For example, the decision to alter her teaching schedule did not cause any significant harm. Nor was the professor's allegation that she received "the silent treatment" and was ostracized by other faculty members sufficient to show retaliation. As no link between the charge and alleged retaliation was demonstrated, the judgment was affirmed. *Recio v. Creighton Univ.*, 521 F.3d 934 (8th Cir. 2008).

◆ *The U.S. Supreme Court held the reassignment of a female to more arduous and dirtier work was evidence of retaliation by her employer.*

A Tennessee railway employee complained about her supervisor's sexually harassing comments. The company disciplined the supervisor but also transferred the employee to a less desirable position. A superior said her reassignment reflected complaints by co-workers that a "more senior man" should have the "less arduous and cleaner job of forklift operator." The employee filed a Title VII complaint, and the company suspended her without pay for insubordination. The employee sued, and the case reached the Supreme Court, which explained that Title VII's anti-retaliation provision was created to prohibit a wide variety of employer conduct intended to restrain employees in the exercise of protected activities. **Although Title VII does not create a general civility code for the workplace, the jury properly found that the reassignment and suspension amounted to retaliation.** The reassignment was "materially adverse" to the employee, who went unpaid for 37 days during which she was uncertain of her employment status. *Burlington Northern & Santa Fe Railway Co. v. White*, 548 U.S. 53, 126 S.Ct. 2405, 165 L.Ed.2d 345 (2006).

## B. Defenses

*In* Univ. of Tennessee v. Elliot, *478 U.S. 788 (1986), the Supreme Court rejected the Title VII defense that a former employee's federal court lawsuit had to be dismissed because it already had been resolved in an administrative hearing. The court held that a state administrative proceeding on a Title VII discrimination claim filed in state court could be appealed to the federal court system when the state proceeding remained unreviewed by state courts.*

◆   *A Pennsylvania university defeated an African-American wrestling coach's retaliation lawsuit by showing he punched a student.*

The coach joked about a wrestler who executed a move he considered comical. He said the student rushed toward him in a rage and that he punched the student in the mouth. Within a few days, the coach was fired, and he sued the university in a federal court for retaliation. As evidence of retaliation based on race, the coach asserted that the university's athletic director "kept a file on him." While the court found this to be true, it noted the file documented misconduct such as the coach's refusal to follow university and NCAA rules. **The court held the university offered a legitimate nonretaliatory reason for firing him that was not a pretext for unlawful retaliation.** On appeal, the Third Circuit affirmed the judgment for the university in a brief memorandum. *Heard v. Waynesburg Univ.*, 436 Fed.Appx. 79 (3d Cir. 2011).

◆   *An appeal of a verdict on a New York college vice president's retaliation claim led to a $400,000 reduction in a punitive damage award.*

The college fired the vice president days after she filed a sex discrimination complaint. She sued the college in a federal district court for sex discrimination and retaliation. A jury found the discharge was in retaliation for her sex discrimination complaint, and it awarded her $75,000 in compensatory damages and $425,000 in punitive damages. The college sought to overturn the judgment or obtain a new trial, arguing that its president had discharged the vice president before he learned she had filed her complaint. Therefore, the college claimed the action could not have been in retaliation for the complaint.

The court found enough evidence for the jury to find the president fired the vice president after he learned of the discrimination complaint. He did not ask her for her keys or other college property before she left. Nor did the college prove the firing was based solely on dissatisfaction with the vice president's job performance. Although the court upheld the verdict, it found the punitive damage award was excessive. **The reasonableness of a punitive damage award depends largely on the reprehensibility of a defendant's conduct.** In this case, there was no violence, threats or evidence of repeated misconduct. Under the circumstances, the most a jury could reasonably award in punitive damages was $25,000. *Norris v. New York City College of Technology*, No. 07-CV-853, 2009 WL 82556 (E.D.N.Y. 1/14/09).

◆   *A teaching assistant's retaliation claim failed because he did not engage in "protected activity" within the meaning of the law.*

An Iranian national began working as a graduate teaching assistant at a Missouri university while in a chemistry Ph.D. program. The student appealed a grade he received in an advanced inorganic chemistry course, accusing the professor of mismanaging the course and assigning grades capriciously. After a hearing, the grade was not changed. The teaching assistant later complained to a university international affairs office about compliance with Department of

Homeland Security regulations regarding foreign nationals. He also complained to the university affirmative action office about an investigation into the transmission of anonymous emails to a female student.

The chemistry department dismissed the teaching assistant without stating a reason, and he withdrew as a student. He sued the university and its officials in a federal district court for retaliation. The court held for the university, and the assistant appealed to the U.S. Court of Appeals, Eighth Circuit. **The court held that to prove retaliation, he needed to show he had engaged in a protected activity, and that the university took adverse action against him on that basis.** The court held the assistant did not engage in any "protected activity." His complaints regarding grades, Department of Homeland Security regulations and the student affairs office related to his status as a student, whereas his retaliation claim related to his status as an employee. Because none of the activities related to his status as an employee, the assistant could not prove his retaliation claim. The decision for university officials was affirmed. *Bakhtiari v. Lutz*, 507 F.3d 1132 (8th Cir. 2007).

◆   *The Eleventh Circuit reinstated a Florida academic advisor's Title VII retaliation claim.*

The advisor claimed his direct supervisor began making unwanted sexual advances soon after he was hired. He said he rejected the advances and the supervisor then overloaded him with work and verbally abused him. He claimed that when he applied for a promotion, the supervisor verbally attacked him in his office, spit in his face, and knocked papers out of his hands. The advisor filed a formal written sexual harassment complaint, called campus police and filed a protection order against her. The advisor later gave the dean a copy of the police report and protection order, then claimed she withdrew her recommendation for the promotion and discharged him for unprofessionalism. A federal district court held the university did not violate Title VII, and the advisor appealed. **The U.S. Court of Appeals, Eleventh Circuit, held a call to police might qualify as protected activity under Title VII.** *Scarbrough v. Board of Trustees Florida A&M Univ.*, 504 F.3d 1220 (11th Cir. 2007).

## C.  Causal Connection

*To prove unlawful retaliation, the courts insist upon some showing of a causal connection between protected activity taken by the employee and the employer's decision to take adverse employment action.*

◆   *The Fifth Circuit affirmed a Texas judge's decision to reject the retaliation claims of a professor whose contract wasn't renewed.*

Several co-workers had filed complaints about the professor's inappropriate conduct and unprofessional behavior. One incident led to a police report being filed. Meanwhile, the professor filed her own complaints, alleging gender discrimination and sexual harassment. The professor was demoted, and she filed a charge with the EEOC. The college agreed to settle. But the complaints didn't stop. Several students reported the professor for racial slurs, and staff complained about being bullied. The school notified the professor her contract would not be renewed. She sued, claiming the college retaliated against her for filing the EEOC charge. A Texas judge dismissed her claim, and the Fifth Circuit affirmed, noting **"the overwhelming number of documented, legitimate reason"** to fire her. *Austen v. Weatherford College*, 564 Fed.Appx. 89 (5th Cir. 2014).

◆ *The Second Circuit affirmed a New York court's ruling that held a former soldier's retaliation claim under the Uniformed Services Employment and Reemployment Rights Act (USERRA) failed.*

The soldier served in the army for seven years before he was hired as an electrician the college. He was also gay. There was no evidence that co-workers knew about his military service. One day, the employees were talking about the repeal of "Don't Ask, Don't Tell." During that conversation, one co-worker made several derogatory comments about gays. The employee reported the incident and asked to be transferred. He was – to a lower paying position. Then he sued, alleging the college retaliated against him in violation of USERRA. But the court dismissed the claim, as **he couldn't show the employee knew about his service or was harassing him due to anti-military bias**. He appealed, and the Second Circuit affirmed. *Lotta v. Univ. of Rochester*, 562 Fed.Appx. 11 (2d Cir. 2014).

◆ *A federal district court in New York rejected the Title VII and retaliation claims of an employee who was terminated.*

The employee filed bullying and harassment complaints against the department chair. Then he filed a complaint with the EEOC. It investigated and found no violations of the law. The employee filed suit, alleging several Title VII and retaliation claims for filing the EEOC complaint. The court dismissed the Title VII claims, as the employee did not claim the school took action against him on the basis of traits protected by Title VII, such as race, color, religion, sex or national origin. **The retaliation claim failed because there was no causal connection between the alleged conduct he complained of and his membership in a protected class.** So the claims were dismissed. *Johnson v. City Univ. of New York*, 48 F.Supp.3d 572 (S.D.N.Y. 9/8/14).

◆ *A grants manager of Hispanic ancestry was allowed to proceed with a federal court retaliation claim against Hawaii Pacific University (HPU).*

According to the grants manager, HPU denied her a promotion because of her Hispanic origin. About one month later, HPU conducted an investigation that determined she had falsely stated a former HPU director destroyed files and misrepresented paperwork for a grant. Asserting multiple violations of the HPU employee handbook, the university discharged the grants manager. She sued HPU in a federal district court for race discrimination and retaliation. The court dismissed the discrimination claim, but it held the retaliation claim should go forward. It held **the proximity in time between the complaint of discrimination and the initiation of the investigation was short enough to raise a question of possible retaliation**. Although HPU presented a valid, nonretaliatory reason to discharge the grants manager, her evidence cast doubt on the investigator's finding that she had lied about the former director destroying files. As the employee had cast doubt on one reason given for firing her, the court found further proceedings were necessary to consider her retaliation claim. *Graciano v. Hawaii Pacific Univ.*, No. 11-00432 SOM/KSC, 2012 WL 3029587 (D. Haw. 7/25/12).

◆   *A New Jersey court rejected a professor's claims that a dean and a department chair discriminated against him because of his Indian origin.*

In a state court action, the professor alleged that the dean of the university's School of Business and the chair of the Department of Economics violated the state Law Against Discrimination by discriminating and retaliating against him based on his national origin. He claimed the chair refused to switch a summer course with him and that the dean examined a request for travel expenses "minutely." And the professor claimed the dean gave him poor employment evaluations. A trial court ruled against him, finding he had failed to prove the basic elements of his discrimination and retaliation claims. On appeal, a state appellate court found the record indicated that the professor's department chair declined the request to switch summer courses because the chair's schedule was already set. **The professor did not prove a causal connection between an earlier suit and the decision to decline his request for a switch.** The court found no evidence that the dean retaliated against him through his employment evaluations. It held the dean used the same standards for all faculty members, and the professor did not suffer an adverse employment action in connection with the evaluations. *Kant v. Seton Hall Univ.*, No. L-8638-07, 2010 WL 4007642 (N.J. Super. Ct. App. Div. 10/13/10).

◆   *A Tennessee community college discharged an African-American professor in retaliation for accusing the college of unlawful discrimination.*

The professor complained of racial discrimination during his 25-year career and filed several complaints. The college received criticism from the students and colleagues about how the professor managed a psychology course. The department eventually let him go for unsatisfactory performance. He attempted to meet the requirements of a performance plan but was not given an entire term to complete it. The professor sued the college in a federal court, alleging it violated Title VII by opposing an unlawful employment practice. The court dismissed the action, but the U.S. Court of Appeals, Sixth Circuit, returned the case to the district court for further consideration. A jury awarded the professor $320,000, and the college appealed. When the case returned to the Sixth Circuit, it found sufficient evidence for a reasonable jury to have found the college unlawfully retaliated against him in violation of Title VII. **The professor presented ample evidence to support a causal connection between his termination and retaliation for his discrimination complaints.** Front pay was an appropriate way to compensate him for future loss. *Cox v. Shelby State Community College*, 194 Fed.Appx. 267 (6th Cir. 2006).

# CHAPTER EIGHT

## Intellectual Property

## I. COPYRIGHT LAW

*State and federal copyright laws protect original works of authorship by creating exclusive rights for the owner to make copies of the work, prepare derivative works, distribute copies of the work, and perform or display the work publicly. See 17 U.S.C. § 106. Copyright protection for an original work exists even if no copyright is registered. See 17 U.S.C. § 408(a). Registration is required in order to initiate a copyright infringement action. Employers are presumed to own the copyright to works prepared by their employees within the scope of their employment, unless a specific written agreement says otherwise.*

*For further background, including an informative fact sheet on fair use, see the website of the U.S. Copyright Office at http://copyright.gov/.*

### A. Fair Use

*Educators and others are entitled to make "fair use" of copyrighted works for the purposes described in 17 U.S.C. § 107. The statute lists four factors to assure such use is not for commercial purposes.*

*In* Stewart v. Abend, *495 U.S. 207 (1990), the U.S. Supreme Court held the primary factor in fair use cases is the effect that use will have on the work's potential market or value.*

17 U.S.C. § 107 states:

*The fair use of a copyrighted work, including such use by reproduction in copies ... for purposes such as criticism, comment, news reporting, teaching (including multiple copies for classroom use), scholarship, or research, is not an infringement of copyright. In determining whether*

*the use made of a work in any particular case is a fair use the factors to
be considered shall include –*

    *(1)  the purpose and character of the use, including whether such use is
        of a commercial nature or is for nonprofit educational purposes;*

    *(2)  the nature of the copyrighted work;*

    *(3)  the amount and substantiality of the portion used in relation to the
        copyrighted work as a whole; and*

    *(4)  the effect of the use upon the potential market for or value of the
        copyrighted work.*

◆   *The Eleventh Circuit reversed a decision favoring a school in a copyright
infringement case.*

    Three publishers sued a school, alleging it violated their copyrights via a
policy that let professors make digital excerpts of their books available to
students without permission or licenses. After the suit was filed, the school
instituted a policy that required professors to conduct their own fair use
analysis before posting an excerpt of a copyrighted work to the school's
E-Reserves. However, it continued its practice of posting excerpts without
seeking permission from the copyright owner. The district court concluded that
the school had violated the publishers' rights in five of 74 instances of alleged
infringement. In 26 instances, it said, the publishers did not establish a *prima
facie* case of infringement. It also decided that the fair use defense applied in
43 instances. The district court also concluded that the school defendants were
the prevailing parties in the case. As a result, it awarded their lawyers about
$2.8 million in attorneys' fees as well as nearly $86,000 in costs. Both sides
sought appellate review. The Eleventh Circuit reversed the ruling, explaining
**the district court used a flawed methodology to determine what
constituted "fair use."** When determining whether a use infringes copyright,
courts must consider four factors identified in the federal copyright act. The
district court assigned each of the four statutory factors equal weight. The
district court erred by using this mechanical "add up the factors" approach, the
appeals court said. Whether a particular use is a fair use is a highly
individualized inquiry, it explained, and in this case some factors weighed more
heavily on the fair use determination than others. Due to the district court's
failure to undertake a more holistic and qualitative analysis, its decision was
reversed. The case was remanded. *Cambridge Univ. Press v. Patton*, 769 F.3d
1232 (11th Cir. 2014).

◆   *A school must release course syllabi to a teacher quality group, a recent
Minnesota appellate court decision held.*

    The National Council on Teacher Quality (Council) is a nonprofit research
and advocacy education-reform institution. The Council asked the Minnesota
State Colleges and Universities (MSC) – an organization of the state's colleges
and universities – for copies of faculty-authored course syllabi. The request was
filed under the state's Government Data Practices Act, which generally
mandates that government data should be made public. MSU offered to let the
Council inspect the syllabi, but it declined to provide copies because it believed
doing so might violate the intellectual property rights of the authors and expose
MSC to liability.

The Council sued MSC, and a trial court ordered MSC to provide the copies the Council requested. The trial court agreed that the syllabi were the intellectual property of the authors, but it also decided the Council's proposed use of the requested materials constituted a "fair use" under copyright law. MSC appealed. The court explained the Data Practices Act cannot be construed to require the MSC to violate copyright law. The court also explained the Copyright Act gives copyright owners the exclusive right to control the reproduction and distribution of their materials. **However, reproduction and distribution for research purposes is not an infringement of copyright but instead is a lawful fair use.** The trial court's decision favoring the Council was affirmed. *National Council on Teacher Quality v. Minnesota State Colleges & Universities,* 837 N.W.2d 314 (Minn. Ct. App. 2013).

◆ *The Tenth Circuit rejected a university's claim that it was a fair use to make a student's dissertation available to the public in its libraries over his protests. Proceedings were needed on the student's claim that the university violated his exclusive right to distribution under copyright law.*

A University of New Mexico (UNM) Ph.D student complained to administrators his dissertation committee didn't give him needed feedback. He later explained a dissertation must be "fully reviewed and evaluated in its final form by the committee members and director before being officially approved and submitted; otherwise it is illegitimate and thus of no academic value."

The dissertation coordinator offered to proofread it, but the student claimed the dean of graduate studies "confiscated" the draft. Notified it had been deposited in a UNM library and also sent to ProQuest, UNM's dissertation publisher, the student contacted ProQuest. ProQuest returned the dissertation to UNM, but about four months later, the student discovered his dissertation had been made available to the public at two UNM libraries. His protests of copyright infringement and requests to return all copies of his dissertation were answered by UNM's lawyer, who explained UNM officials believed they had "an implied license to keep copies of the dissertation at the University Libraries and to catalog the work."

He sued to allege copyright violations. A federal court dismissed his case, but he appealed to the Tenth Circuit, which rejected UNM's fair use defense. Only the first fair use factor – purpose and character of use – weighed strongly in UNM's favor, as distributing a dissertation via university libraries is a non-commercial, educational purpose. The other factors weighed strongly in the student's favor: the nature of the work was an unpublished work; the amount to be used was the entire work; and **the student claimed the distribution of his work had completely deprived him of the value of his dissertation by preventing him from completing the dissertation review and defense process at another school while UNM listed it in its libraries' catalogs.** The student's claim of infringement of his exclusive right of distribution went back to the trial court for further proceedings. *Diversey v. Schmidly,* 738 F.3d 1196 (10th Cir. 2013).

◆ *A Massachusetts federal court refused to find file-sharing falls under the fair use exception to the Copyright Act.*

The "fair use exception" is a limit on the virtual monopoly a copyright holder has over a work. The exception allows a limited, free use of the work for a worthy public purpose, such as education that does not harm the copyright holder's market interest. A student shared music files he downloaded even after court decisions clarified that file-sharing is a copyright violation. Applying the four fair use factors and weighing the equities, the court declined to find the student had made fair use of the files. His purpose and the character of his use of the music was personal enjoyment. **The court found music should enjoy "robust copyright protections."** The court held the effect of the student's use of music would be destructive to the market. No one would purchase iTunes songs if they could get them for free. The court implored Congress to amend the statute to reflect the reality of file-sharing in the face of this case and thousands of suits like it. The record companies were entitled to a judgment, and the student had to pay $675,000 in damages. *Sony BMG Music Entertainment v. Tenenbaum*, 672 F.Supp.2d 217 (D. Mass. 2009).

◆ *A Missouri teacher was unable to convince a federal appeals court that his materials deserved the protection of U.S. copyright and patent laws.*

The teacher designed an "Out of Area Program" for use by teachers to respond to student disruptions. He claimed he developed and implemented the program during his employment with the school district. The teacher asserted the school district continued using materials he developed after it discharged him. He sued the district in a federal district court for patent and copyright infringement. The court dismissed the case, finding the teacher's program was a "business idea" that was excluded from federal copyright protection.

The teacher appealed to the U.S. Court of Appeals, Federal Circuit, which noted that **general concepts and ideas are beyond the protection of copyright law. Copyright law protects the expression of an idea, but not ideas themselves.** The court found a hall pass used at the school during the relevant time period had the same language as the teacher's program. The school's hall pass was not otherwise like the teacher's materials. The court found the limited use of similar functional language did not constitute copyright infringement, even if the district had deliberately copied it. Fragmentary words and phrases were not protected by copyright law. **Forms of expression directed solely at functional considerations did not exhibit the minimal level of creativity to warrant federal copyright protection.** The teacher failed to provide any evidence that he had been issued a U.S. patent, and he could not maintain a patent infringement action without one. As the district court had properly dismissed the case, its judgment was affirmed. *Clark v. Crues*, 260 Fed.Appx. 292 (Fed. Cir. 2008).

◆ *The U.S. Supreme Court has held that publishing companies must obtain permission from freelance writers before reusing their works.*

In 2001, the U.S. Supreme Court determined that permission was required for inclusion of freelancers' works in electronic databases. Copyright law allows publishers to reuse freelancers' contributions when a collective work, such as a magazine issue or an encyclopedia, is revised, but the Court said that **massive databases such as NEXIS do not fit within that provision of the law because they are not revisions of previously published collective works.**

The decision was the result of a lawsuit that was filed against New York Times Co., Newsday Inc., Time Incorporated Magazine Co., LEXIS/NEXIS and University Microfilms International, alleging violation of freelance writers' copyrights in articles they wrote that were included in complete issues of the publishers' products. *New York Times Co., Inc. v. Tasini*, 533 U.S. 483, 121 S.Ct. 2381, 150 L.Ed.2d 500 (2001).

◆   *A New York university defeated a media foundation's claims for copyright infringement and breach of contract.*

The parties contracted to produce public service announcements. The foundation alleged the university breached the contract by refusing to pay additional compensation as a condition of producing the announcements. It also contended the university violated federal copyright law by displaying copyrighted material at a fundraiser for a commercial purpose. The foundation sued the university in a federal district court for breach of contract and violation of the "fair use" provision of copyright law. The court allowed the case to go before a jury, and after a trial, it found for the university. The foundation appealed to the U.S. Court of Appeals, Second Circuit.

The court held the foundation breached the contract with the university by demanding extra compensation. To determine if the university satisfied the fair use requirements of 17 U.S.C. § 107, the court considered: 1) the purpose and character of the use, including whether such use is of a commercial nature or is for nonprofit educational purposes; the 2) nature of the copyrighted work; 3) the amount and substantiality of the portion used in relation to the copyrighted work as a whole; and 4) the effect of the use upon the potential market for or value of the copyrighted work. The court determined the fair use issue was properly presented to the jury. **Copyright law permits the reproduction or distribution of a copyrighted work as long as it is not done for commercial reasons.** The judgment was affirmed. *New York Univ. v. Planet Earth Foundation*, 163 Fed.Appx. 13 (2d Cir. 2005).

◆   *Forcing a university to disclose the identities of students accused of illegally downloading copyrighted music did not violate student privacy rights.*

Several recording companies filed a federal copyright infringement lawsuit against 14 University of Kansas students for illegally downloading copyrighted music files. The companies discovered the Internet protocol addresses used to access the files but were unable to discover the names of the students. A university log enabled identification of the students. A federal district court allowed the companies to subpoena the university for student names, addresses, telephone numbers, email addresses and media access control addresses.

The court noted the university was free to try to quash the subpoena and avoid disclosing the information. Two students moved to quash the subpoenas, claiming disclosure would violate their privacy rights and FERPA. The court rejected the claim that student privacy interests outweighed the companies' interest in discovering their identities. **A person who uses the Internet to download copyrighted music without consent is engaging in the exercise of speech only to a limited extent.** Disclosing student identities would not violate privacy rights because the companies made a preliminary showing of copyright infringement, and the request for identifying information was specific enough to lead to disclosure of appropriate information. There was no other way to gain access to the requested information, and identifying the students was essential to a successful copyright infringement claim. In any event, the students could not reasonably expect a great degree of privacy, as they opened their computers to others for file-sharing. While FERPA generally bars federally funded educational institutions from disclosing specified student records, otherwise protected information may be disclosed pursuant to a valid court order. In this case, the limited scope of the subpoenas made it unlikely that information relating to student identities would become public. Therefore, the court held disclosing the information would not violate their privacy. *Interscope Records v. Does 1-14*, 558 F.Supp.2d 1176 (D. Kan. 2008).

◆ *An Illinois professor could pursue her copyright claims against a publisher, but could not pursue claims against a college that formerly employed her based on how her books were used after being sold.*

The professor taught the course "Smart Foreclosure Buying" at City Colleges of Chicago. She authored a book of the same name, which she copyrighted and used as a text. When the professor stopped teaching the class, the college offered it with a new instructor, but still used the professor's initials in a catalogue. The professor advised the text's publisher by phone, letter and fax to stop printing the book, but it continued printing and selling the text, and stopped paying her royalties. The professor sued the college in a federal district court to force it to stop offering courses using her book or its title as a course name. She added federal copyright and trademark claims against the publisher and an instructor, claiming the college engaged in false advertising, fraud and deceptive business practices. The court held the professor did not state a valid claim, and she appealed to the U.S. Court of Appeals, Seventh Circuit.

The court reversed the decision to dismiss the copyright claims against the publisher, noting the professor said she had mailed the publisher a letter of termination. Although the publisher claimed it never got the letter, **oral licenses and terminations are generally allowed**. A jury could reasonably determine the publisher had some notice of the professor's intent to withdraw her consent to publish the text, especially since it stopped paying her royalties. Although it reversed the decision on the copyright claims against the publisher, the court affirmed the ruling with respect to the copyright claims against the new instructor and the college. The professor could not pursue claims based on how the books were used after they were sold. **Once a copy of a work has been sold, the buyer may use it as he pleases so long as he does not create a new copy or derivative work.** The court also found a valid claim for trademark violation against the college. Finally, the professor stated a valid claim against the college for false advertising, fraud and deceptive business practices based on the continued use of her initials in the course catalog. *Vincent v. City Colleges of Chicago*, 485 F.3d 919 (7th Cir. 2007).

◆ *The U.S. Court of Appeals for the First Circuit rejected a Tufts University visiting lecturer's claims based on the terms of a publishing contract.*

The lecturer had co-authored the second and third editions of an undergraduate textbook with a professor and director of the graduate nutrition program at another college. The third edition agreement assigned all present and future copyrights of the third and future editions to the book's publisher. The lecturer and professor contracted with the same publisher for a fourth edition that increased the lecturer's share of royalties from 25% to 40%.

The professor failed to meet deadlines set by the agreement, and the publisher suggested she assign more work to the lecturer. The professor refused, and the lecturer notified the publisher she was withdrawing from the project. She also stated her revisions could not be used without her permission. The publisher sent the lecturer an acknowledgement that she would receive 12.5% of the fourth edition royalties – half her compensation under the third edition agreement. She signed the acknowledgement, but later discovered her revisions were included in the fourth edition and that the professor was listed as its sole author. The lecturer copyrighted her revisions and brought a federal court complaint against the publisher and professor for copyright infringement and breach of contract. The court held the lecturer assigned her copyright interest under the fourth edition revisions. The publisher was not obligated to terminate its contract with the professor when she failed to meet her deadlines. The First Circuit affirmed the decision, holding the lecturer could not claim a copyright interest in her fourth edition revisions. She had "assigned … all present and future copyrights" of the third and future editions to the publisher. **The publisher was the sole copyright owner of the third edition and consequently the fourth "revised edition." There was no breach of contract by the publisher, because it had the option to extend the deadlines and did so for legitimate financial reasons.** *Zyla v. Wadsworth*, 360 F.3d 243 (1st Cir. 2004).

## B. Work-for-Hire

*Employers are presumed to own the copyright to works prepared by their employees within the scope of their employment, unless they have agreed otherwise in writing. See 17 U.S.C. § 201(a), also referred to as Section 201(b) of the Copyright Act of 1976. The work of independent contractors is considered "work for hire" under a written agreement for specially ordered or commissioned work used as a contribution to a collective work, part of a motion picture or other audiovisual work, a translation, supplementary work, compilation, instructional text, test or test answer, or an atlas.*

*Agency principles help determine whether a professor's work is covered by the work-for-hire doctrine. Section 228 of the Restatement (Second) of Agency deems a work to be "for hire" only if the work is of the type the faculty member was hired to create, was created substantially within the space and time limits of the job, and was motivated at least partly by a purpose to serve the university. Professors are expected to produce intellectual property in the scope of their employment, and those who conduct research, write and publish scholarly articles and create other forms of intellectual property receive better performance evaluations, more promotional opportunities and higher pay.*

◆ *A New York University (NYU) employee who helped design a logo selected as NYU's mascot could not overcome the "works made for hire" presumption.*

Although the employee began working for NYU as an equipment room aide, NYU also hired her as a graphic designer. Her artistic abilities were soon discovered, and she was invited to design a logo for use as the NYU mascot. For this work, the employee's compensation was doubled from $8 per hour to $16 per hour. When a final version of the logo emerged, she registered it with the U.S. Copyright Office, listing herself as the sole author. Although the employee claimed a supervisor reassured her that she would be compensated for use of the logo, NYU denied such conversations took place and maintained that the design had been a collaborative effort involving many NYU employees.

In a federal court, the employee sued NYU for copyright infringement. In pretrial activity, the court found that to prevail, she had to prove she owned a valid copyright and that NYU copied its constituent elements. Although the employee argued she owned the copyright because she registered it with the Copyright Office, the court held this only created a presumption of ownership. As NYU argued, **an employee's copyright is invalid if it was created within the scope of her employment**. This is known as the "works made for hire" exception to copyright ownership. In this case, the employee created the logo during the scope of her employment as a graphic designer. Evidence indicated NYU exerted control over her drafts of the logo and that she made changes on the basis of suggestions by NYU personnel. There was no written agreement assigning ownership to either party, and the works made for hire exception applied. Rejecting the employee's argument that creating the design was outside the scope of her duties as a graphic designer, the court held for NYU. *Fleurimond v. New York Univ.*, 876 F.Supp.2d 190 (E.D.N.Y. 2012).

◆ *Brown University retained its copyrights to photographs taken by a member of its staff under the "works-for-hire" doctrine.*

Brown University hired a full-time professional photographer to capture images of academic life and natural campus settings for its publications. He was also allowed to shoot pictures on his own initiative. The university purchased photographic equipment for him, arranged for student assistants, and provided him access to the university's darkroom. Brown's copyright policy contained a provision regarding the ownership of copyrightable materials.

After 24 years, Brown severed its relationship with the photographer as part of a reduction in force. He sued Brown in a federal district court, claiming ownership of 97 photographs in his possession. The court focused on the "Works Made for Hire" Section of the Copyright Act of 1976. The court explained that ownership rights of works by an employee typically vest with the employer. It held the photographs were "works for hire" owned by Brown. **The court distinguished between the photographs and the "faculty exception" from the works-for-hire rule.** Equitable considerations often mandate that a scholar retain the copyright to works, notwithstanding the works-for-hire doctrine. The faculty exception did not apply in this case because Brown officials often directed what images should be photographed. There was no document indicating a conveyance of ownership rights to the photographer. The language of the policy was too imprecise to support the photographer's claim of such a transfer. He did not think about copyright ownership in the photos until after his relationship with Brown was severed. As a result, the court held for Brown. *Foraste v. Brown Univ.*, 290 F.Supp.2d 234 (D.R.I. 2003).

◆ *The Supreme Court of Kansas held the work-for-hire doctrine did not prevent a state university and the employee association representing its faculty from entering into a memorandum of agreement on intellectual property rights.*

The university and Kansas Board of Regents proposed a policy to retain ownership and control over any intellectual property created by the faculty. The faculty association rejected the policy. The board responded it was not required to negotiate over the policy because intellectual property rights were not a "condition of employment." According to the board, the question of intellectual property rights was a management prerogative and was preempted by state and federal law. The board then adopted a policy giving some intellectual property rights to faculty, but without meeting and conferring with the association.

The state public employee relations board (PERB) held the university had no duty to meet and confer with the faculty association, because the subject was preempted by state and federal law. The case reached the Supreme Court of Kansas, which found neither state nor federal law preempted the subject of intellectual property from being included in a memorandum of agreement. **The work-for-hire doctrine was only a presumption regarding the ownership of copyrights, and it allowed parties to contract for particular ownership rights. The doctrine operated as a default provision, unless the parties agreed otherwise.** The court found Congress contemplated that parties could negotiate the ownership of a copyright. The federal Patent Act also allowed parties to assign patent ownership rights. Federal law did not preempt any kind of intellectual property rights from being covered by a memorandum of understanding or other written agreement. The court reversed the decision with directions to return the case to the PERB for further proceedings. *Pittsburg State Univ./Kansas National Educ. Ass'n v. Kansas Board of Regents/Pittsburg State Univ.*, 280 Kan. 408, 122 P.3d 336 (Kan. 2005).

## C. Standardized Tests

◆ *A federal court agreed with four educational testing agencies, including the College Entrance Examination Board, that the required disclosure of test questions under a New York law violated federal copyright law.*

New York education law requires college testing services to file copies of their test questions and statistical reports with the state education commissioner. A number of testing agencies claimed that the statute violated federal copyright law, and filed a lawsuit against the governor and other state officials. In view of the result in a similar case filed by the Association of American Medical Colleges, the parties entered into a stipulation under which the testing agencies disclosed questions for only some of the tests administered in the state and were allowed to administer a fixed number of undisclosed tests. The court then considered a motion by the agencies for temporary relief. The agencies argued that the compelled disclosure of the test questions violated federal copyright law and did not meet the fair use exception to federal copyright law. The state argued that **the public had an interest in ensuring the fairness and objectivity of standardized admission tests** and had a strong need to evaluate the scoring process. It also claimed that disclosure did not violate copyright laws because of the lack of any commercial purpose. **The court agreed with the testing agencies that the disclosure of test**

**questions violated federal copyright law** and issued a preliminary injunction. The court also found that the agencies were entitled to the presumption of irreparable injury that normally accompanies a showing of infringement. But because of the many factual issues existing in the case, the court issued an order preserving the status quo, under which only some tests administered in the state would be subject to the disclosure law pending further proceedings. *College Entrance Examination Board v. Pataki*, 889 F.Supp. 554 (N.D.N.Y. 1995).

Three of the testing agencies sought an order completely barring enforcement of the state law or alternative relief. A fourth agency submitted a statement indicating that it would comply with the order by disclosing three testing forms administered in New York during the test year and an additional form traditionally administered in the state in low-volume administrations.

The testing agencies asserted that the wording of the preliminary order would prevent the Graduate Record Examination (GRE) program from offering at least one administration in the state, and that the status quo provision of the order did not account for changing circumstances in testing from year to year. They further asserted that the preliminary order contravened **the principle in copyright infringement cases that the status quo sought to be preserved is the state of non-infringement**. The court held that the preliminary order struck the correct balance between competing interests, including that of the students who would take the examinations. There was no need to strictly comply with the rule that the status quo to be preserved is a state of non-infringement, since the parties had agreed by stipulation to provide for limited disclosure of test forms. The court modified the order to accommodate the GRE program's phase-out of paper and pencil administrations. *College Entrance Examination Board v. Pataki*, 893 F.Supp. 152 (N.D.N.Y. 1995).

◆ *New York's Standardized Testing Act requires testing agencies to file reports on standardized tests with the Commissioner of Education and also requires the filing of copyrightable test questions.*

The American Association of Medical Colleges (AAMC), a nonprofit educational association, sponsors a medical school testing program, the central feature of which is the MCAT exam. The AAMC holds copyrights in the MCAT test forms, test questions, answer sheets, and reports. When the state of New York enacted the Standardized Testing Act, requiring disclosure of this copyrighted information, the AAMC sued to enjoin the application of the act. It claimed that the Act was preempted by the federal Copyright Act and moved for pretrial judgment, which the court granted. The court found that the purpose and character of the use was noncommercial and educational, and that disclosure of the test questions would prevent their reuse.

The Second Circuit Court of Appeals found issues of fact precluded pretrial judgment. If the disclosure of material were considered "fair use," then there would be no Copyright Act violation. However, if the state act facilitated infringement, then the Copyright Act would preempt it. **Here, the state's goal of encouraging valid and objective tests was laudable, and there was a question of fact as to whether the test questions could be used again after being disclosed.** As a result, the fourth and most important fair use factor – the effect of the use upon the potential market for or value of the copyrighted work

– did not necessarily weigh in favor of the AAMC. The court remanded the case for further proceedings. *Ass'n of American Medical Colleges v. Cuomo*, 928 F.2d 519 (2d Cir. 1991).

## D.  Due Process Issues

◆  *A University of Texas professor will not keep a six-figure verdict he had won based on the loss of notebooks after he was ordered to clear out of his lab.*

After 24 years of work at the University of Texas at San Antonio (UTSA), a research professor was told he was not keeping his office space and laboratory in good order and that they created a safety hazard. Two years later, UTSA followed through on its warnings and advised him by letter that it was going to close his lab and clean it out. According to the professor, some of his notebooks were lost or destroyed during the cleanout process, and he sued UTSA and an administrator for due process violations, based on depriving him of his property without notice and a reasonable opportunity to be heard.

After the professor initiated a state court action, UTSA removed the case to a federal district court. It held for UTSA and the administrator, and the professor appealed to the U.S. Court of Appeals, Fifth Circuit. Although the court affirmed the judgment for UTSA, it returned a due process claim against the administrator to the district court for further consideration. The case was presented to a jury, which found the administrator had violated the professor's right to notice. The jury also found the professor had a property interest in the items in his lab. A verdict of $175,000 was awarded to him for the loss of his research notebooks. But following the verdict, the court granted the administrator's motion, finding the professor could not prevail under a due process claim because he did not have a protectable interest in the property that was lost. The case returned to the Fifth Circuit, which held the professor did not present enough evidence to show that he had a protectable property interest in notebooks that were lost in the cleanup. He argued he had a protectable property interest in his notebooks because they fell under an exception to the school's intellectual property policy applicable to "scholarly or educational materials." **But the court held the exception applies only to materials that are published, copyrighted or copyrightable.** In this case, the professor did not show the notebooks contained anything other than research data. For this reason, the judgment for the administrator was affirmed. *Stotter v. Univ. of Texas at San Antonio*, 369 Fed.Appx. 641 (5th Cir. 2010).

◆  *A tenured University of Michigan professor had an insufficient property interest in an idea to gain any protection of it as his intellectual property.*

In 1995, the professor wrote drafts for a design center in the university's Department of Aerospace Engineering. The drafts were revised by another professor and turned into an abstract. The first draft proposal listed two co-authors, and the second listed three others. The proposal identified a design center with resident visitors of different specialties, with a focus on Russian designers. The university obtained funding for the center and built it in 1999. The professor sued the university in the state court system asserting violation of his due process and intellectual property rights. The court held for the university, and he appealed. On appeal, the Court of Appeals of Michigan held the university had no fiduciary duty to the professor. A fiduciary relationship exists only "when there is confidence reposed on one side and a resulting superiority and influence on the other." The court disagreed with the professor's claim to a property interest in the design center. He prepared drafts for the center in 1995 with various others. The proposal indicated there were already programs for visiting designers. The university had previously hired retired designers to teach courses. The court held the protection of an idea under a property theory "requires that the idea possess property-like traits."

Moreover, **"ideas themselves are not subject to individual ownership or control. They do not rise to the level of property and are not in themselves protected by law."** The professor could not "own the idea" of a design center or a visiting designer program that already existed in other forms. The professor asserted the university's rules and policies made him "automatically the principal investigator" of the proposal. The court disagreed, finding no such rule or policy "promising or even hinting at how those benefits accrued to him." **In order to have a constitutionally protected interest, a person must have more than an abstract need or desire for it. There must be a legitimate claim of entitlement.** A party's unilateral expectation is insufficient to create a property interest protected by procedural due process. The court held that as the professor did not show any legitimate property interest in his idea, he could not allege a due process claim. *Kauffman v. Univ. of Michigan Regents*, No. 257711, 2006 WL 1084330 (Mich. Ct. App. 4/25/06). The Supreme Court of Michigan denied further review. *Kauffman v. Univ. of Michigan Regents*, 477 Mich. 911, 722 N.W.2d 823 (Mich. 2006).


## II.  PATENTS

*A patent is a legally protected property interest that gives the owner the right to exclude others from making, using, selling, offering for sale, or importing the invention covered by the patent. Patents generally run for a period of 20 years from the effective filing date of the patent application. To be patentable, an invention must be useful, new or novel, and non-obvious.*

*Unlike copyright law, there is no federal patent law provision on work-for-hire. Patent ownership is instead resolved by common law. The federal Patent Act also allows parties to assign patent ownership rights. In determining who owns the patent rights to an invention, courts look at the nature of the relationship between the inventor and the employer. Where the inventor is hired to invent something, the employer retains all patent rights; and where the inventor is hired under a general contract of employment, the inventor will retain ownership rights. However, most cases fall somewhere in between these two: for example, where a university hires a professor or a graduate student to teach and do research. The ambiguity this creates has led colleges and universities to enter into pre-employment assignments of intellectual property rights that specifically lay out the rights of both parties. Sometimes this is done by written agreement – other times, by use of a faculty handbook.*

*With respect to patent rights, professors usually are required to assign creations and patent rights to the colleges and universities that employ them in exchange for a percentage of the royalties. The issue becomes trickier when dealing with graduate students. Some universities require graduate students to assign patent rights, while others do not.*

*A number of states have enacted statutes to limit the extent to which employers can claim an interest in employee inventions. However, those statutes generally provide that if the employer provides resources, or if the invention relates to the employer's business, the employer can require assignment of intellectual property rights. It is only where the employer has no involvement at all that the employee can claim full rights to an invention.*

*Literal infringement refers to the misappropriation of all essential elements in a patent. Infringement under the doctrine of equivalents results when a device performs the same function as the patented device in substantially the same way to achieve the same result.*

## A.  Ownership and Inventorship

◆   *A federal court held the University of Massachusetts did not have to join an action filed by the University of Utah to name a Utah professor as an inventor or co-inventor of a "gene silencing process."*

Ribonucleic Acid (RNA) interference (RNAi), also known as "Gene silencing," is described as a process of great potential therapeutic value. It involves inserting a double-stranded RNA molecule into a cell to direct the destruction of messenger RNA before it can be translated into a protein. University of Utah officials sued research institutes, including the University of Massachusetts, asserting that a Utah professor should be named the sole or joint inventor on two patents directed to methods of preparing a particular type of double-stranded RNA molecule that could mediate RNAi. In a federal court, Utah requested an order correcting inventorship and a declaration of its rights that would require the research institutes to cease violating federal patent law.

In considering dismissal motions by the research institutes, the court held Massachusetts was not a necessary party. As other institutes and state officials would adequately represent its interests, Massachusetts was dismissed from the case. As for the merits of the claim, the court found **the complaint adequately stated that the Utah professor was the sole inventor of the patents at issue**. There was evidence that she had conceived the invention as a treatment for mammals, including humans. There was evidence that the Utah professor published an article explaining RNAi capabilities in mammals, which the other named inventors read and incorporated into their work. Since Utah presented a sufficient quantum of collaboration or connection with the other institutions to state a claim for joint inventorship, the court denied the dismissal motions. *Univ. of Utah v. Max-Planck-Gesellschaft Zur Forderung Der Wissenschaften E.V.*, 881 F.Supp.2d 151 (D.Mass. 2012).

◆   *Because an employment relationship alone is not sufficient to vest title to an employee's invention in the employer, Stanford University did not have exclusive patent rights to methodology in a joint venture with a company.*

In 1985, a small California research company began to develop methods to quantify blood-borne levels of HIV. Later, it began to collaborate with Stanford University to test the efficacy of new AIDS drugs. A doctor joined the university near that time and agreed to assign his "right, title and interest" in inventions resulting from his employment there. He conducted research at the company as part of the collaboration and signed an agreement by which he assigned his "right, title and interest" to it with respect to inventions made as a consequence of his working there. Along with employees of the company, the doctor devised a procedure for measuring the amount of HIV in a patient's blood.

Stanford secured three patents to the measurement process and received federal funding for the project. Roche Molecular Systems then acquired the company's assets and commercialized the HIV-quantification methodology developed at the company. Stanford sued Roche for patent infringement in a federal district court, and the case eventually reached the U.S. Supreme Court. The Court explained that the Bayh-Dole Act allocates rights in federally funded inventions between the federal government and federal contractors. In the Court's view, the Bayh-Dole Act did not automatically confer unilateral title to federal contractors. **Even though the doctor had developed the methods while working jointly for both Stanford and the company, Stanford did not have exclusive patent rights to the methodology.** Mere employment is not sufficient to vest title to an employee's invention in the employer. Roche was a co-owner of the procedure. Therefore, Stanford could not sue Roche for patent infringement. *Board of Trustees of Leland Stanford Junior Univ. v. Roche Molecular Systems, Inc.*, 131 S.Ct. 2188 (U.S. 2011).

◆  *Vanderbilt University was unable to show that two of its scientists contributed to the invention of an erectile dysfunction treatment and method.*

Vanderbilt sued ICOS Corporation in a Delaware federal district court, asserting that two of its scientists should be added as joint inventors of patented compounds and methods for treating erectile dysfunction. These included tadalafil, a PDE5 inhibitor, which is the active ingredient in Cialis. According to Vanderbilt, its scientists were among the first to discover PDE5 in the late 1970s, and they continued to work on related research. Vanderbilt retained ownership of the intellectual property under an underwriting and license agreement with Glaxo, Inc. Glaxo later assigned all its rights, title and interest in the patented compounds to ICOS. Vanderbilt then sought to correct inventorship of the patents in a federal district court. The court found no evidence that Vanderbilt scientists conceived of tadalafil's specific chemical structure. Vanderbilt appealed to the U.S. Court of Appeals, Federal Circuit.

According to the court, federal patent law permits joint inventorship by one or more inventors who are not physically working together. Each inventor needs to perform part of the task and make some contribution to the inventive thought and the final result. **For persons to be joint inventors, there must be some element of joint behavior, such as collaboration or working under common direction.** Vanderbilt could not counter ICOS' evidence that an ICOS researcher independently discovered the compounds to be tested for PDE5 inhibition. While Vanderbilt claimed ICOS' research was done more than 10 years after Glaxo did the same work, the court found no evidence of joint collaboration on the invention. Vanderbilt failed to present clear and convincing evidence that the ICOS researcher could not have independently identified the compound. Since the parties' stories were equally plausible and there was no clear and convincing evidence of joint invention, the judgment for ICOS was affirmed. *Vanderbilt Univ. v. ICOS Corp.*, 601 F.3d 1297 (Fed. Cir. 2010).

◆ *A federal district court was instructed to reconsider a case that originally appeared before it in 1997 to determine whether certain products infringed on patents under the doctrine of equivalents.*

The University of California (UC) and Abbott Labs claimed patents for inventions to improve methods for identifying and classifying chromosomes to detect abnormalities associated with genetic disorders, degenerative diseases and cancer. They sought to employ a staining technique to allow rapid and highly sensitive detection of chromosomal abnormalities in both metaphase and interphase cells using standard clinical and laboratory equipment. The patent claims were directed at blocking, selectively removing or screening repetitive sequences. UC and Abbott Labs, as the owner and exclusive licensee of the patents, sued a manufacturer in a federal district court for a preliminary order to prohibit it from manufacturing and selling certain products. The court held UC and Abbott could not prevail on a patent infringement claim based on limitations for "morphologically identifiable chromosome or cell nucleus," and "heterogeneous mixture of labeled unique sequence nucleic acid fragments." They also did not show their product met a blocking nucleic acid limitation under the doctrine of equivalents. The court later issued pretrial judgment to the manufacturer as to two of its products.

On appeal, the U.S. Court of Appeals, Federal Circuit, considered UC and Abbott's claim that the district court misconstrued the phrase "heterogeneous mixture of labeled unique sequence nucleic acid fragments." The manufacturer's products contained repetitive sequences found in prior art, while the patents referred to unique sequence fragments. The court found it was erroneous to characterize the patent as prior art. However, the lower court correctly found the products did not infringe upon a second patent, which employed a mixture including repetitive sequences. The original patent claim did not include the phrase "unique sequence." This was a response to three separate enablement rejections by a claims examiner. **The prosecution history demonstrated how the inventor intended to limit the invention.** The non-infringement judgment was affirmed as to the first patent. However, as to the second patent, the lower court improperly applied prosecution history to the "blocking nucleic acid" limitation. The court returned this claim to the lower court for reconsideration of whether the manufacturer had infringed the patent under the doctrine of equivalents. *Regents of Univ. of California v. Dakocytomation Cal., Inc.*, 517 F.3d 1364 (Fed. Cir. 2008).

◆ *A patent licensee could pursue claims against a competitor under the California unfair competition law and the Lanham Act, but not the Florida Deceptive and Unfair Trade Practices Act.*

Optivus Technology claimed to be the exclusive licensee of two proton beam therapy system patents. The University of Florida signed a non-binding letter of intent with Optivus regarding the proton beam therapy systems. After the letter expired, Florida considered other vendors and awarded a contract to Ion Beam Applications (IBA), which competed with Optivus in the same market. Optivus sued IBA in a federal district court for infringement of the patents. Loma Linda University Medical Center, as assignee of Optivus, became a party. Optivus added claims against IBA for unfair competition under California and Florida law, as well as violation of the Lanham Act. IBA counterclaimed against Optivus, seeking an order declaring the proton beam patents invalid in view of a neutron therapy facility in use at the University of Washington. The California unfair competition claim was based on the theory that IBA marketed a medical device that was not approved by the U.S. Food and Drug Administration (FDA). The district court refused to consider the California unfair competition law claim. The court held for IBA on the Florida Unfair Trade Act and Lanham Act claims, as well as a claim for intentional interference. The court found both patents invalid and ruled there was no patent infringement. Optivus appealed to the U.S. Court of Appeals, Federal Circuit.

The court agreed with Optivus that the district court should have ruled on the significance of an FDA letter. The district court had thus improperly dismissed the California state law unfair competition claim. The court considered the claim under the Florida Unfair Trade Act and noted the University of Florida had selected IBA as its vendor after the expiration of the letter of intent with Optivus. **At the time IBA was selected, only a "consumer" could bring a claim under the Florida Deceptive and Unfair Trade Practices Act.** For this reason, the district court properly awarded summary judgment to IBA on Optivus' Florida law claim. **The district court had found Optivus did not show a business relationship existed after the letter of intent expired.** The court of appeals found no error in this conclusion. Any business relationship between Optivus and Florida ended with the expiration of the letter. The court stated that to prevail on its Lanham Act claim, Optivus would have to show IBA made a false and material statement of fact that caused the University of Florida to award the contract to IBA. The court disagreed with the district court's findings in favor of IBA regarding false statements about financing. It reversed the judgment on the Lanham Act claim for further consideration of IBA's alleged statements. **The patent was invalid as obvious, in view of Washington's neutron therapy facility.** The patent for a safety system for a multi-room proton beam therapy facility was written with expansive, highly inclusive language. **As Loma Linda did not rebut this evidence, the judgment of patent invalidity was correct.** *Optivus Technology, Inc. v. Ion Beam Applications, S.A.*, 469 F.3d 978 (Fed. Cir. 2006).

◆   *A medical school student at a private New York university did not prove he contributed to a professor's patented treatment for glaucoma.*

The university owned a patent involving the use of prostaglandins in treating glaucoma. A long-time professor at the university was the named inventor of the patent. In 1980, the professor agreed to a proposal by the student to perform a one-semester ophthalmology research elective. He directed the student to begin his project by reviewing a faculty member's papers on prostaglandins and intraocular pressure (IOP). At the time, the professor had published several papers on the effects of prostaglandins on the IOP in animals such as rabbits and owl monkeys. The student conducted experiments in the lab that showed topical application of single doses of prostaglandin reduced IOP in rhesus monkeys and cats. After the student left the university, the professor conceived the patent while studying the effects of repeated prostaglandin application on the IOP in rhesus monkeys. He applied for the patent in 1982, and it was issued in 1986. When the student found out about the patent, he sued the university and professor in a federal district court, asking to be added as a co-inventor. The trial court granted summary judgment for the university and the professor. It found the student failed to present evidence of inventorship.

On appeal, **the U.S. Court of Appeals, Federal Circuit, held the student had to show he contributed to the conception of the invention in order to be considered one of the inventors of the patent**. The court found the student did not have an understanding of the claimed invention. He also did not discover that prostaglandins have an effect on IOP, or conceive of the idea of the use of prostaglandins to reduce IOP in primates. Furthermore, the student did not collaborate with the professor in developing a glaucoma treatment. **He simply carried out an experiment done previously by the professor on different animals.** The court held the student's contribution was insufficient to support his claim of co-inventorship and affirmed the judgment. *Stern v. Trustees of Columbia Univ. in the City of New York*, 434 F.3d 1375 (Fed. Cir. 2006).

◆  *A pharmaceutical company had to pay $54 million in damages for fraudulently obtaining a patent based on work by university researchers.*

Two University of Colorado researchers worked under an agreement with a pharmaceutical company. They discovered certain multivitamins were not supplying proper amounts of iron to pregnant women and published an article suggesting a reformulation to increase iron absorption. The researchers sent an advance copy to the doctor they had been working with at the company. The company then obtained a patent on the reformulation of the multivitamin without notifying the university. It copied and plagiarized portions of the article in the patent application. The university foundation sued the company in a federal district court for wrongfully obtaining the patent. The court found the company liable for fraudulent nondisclosure. It noted the company would have had to pay the university for the rights to the reformulation, and calculated the royalty rates at approximately $22 million. The court held the university could recover equitable damages for unjust enrichment of $23 million. It also ordered exemplary damages in the amount of $500,000 for each inventor, based on the company's "clandestine and deceptive conduct," and "fraud, malice, and willful and wanton misconduct." *Univ. of Colorado Foundation v. American Cyanamid Co.*, 216 F.Supp.2d 1188 (D. Colo. 2002).

The U.S. Court of Appeals, Federal Circuit, rejected the company's argument that the damage award for unjust enrichment created a state-based patent law that was inconsistent with the federal statutory scheme. The court held this was not the issue in this case. The unjust enrichment claim was based on the wrongful use of research and did not interfere with the federal patent scheme. The researchers satisfied state law requirements for unjust enrichment, as it would be unjust to allow the company to retain profits acquired through misconduct. **The district court had properly awarded damages based on incremental profits that were directly attributable to the misconduct. The court upheld the district court's findings establishing inventorship.** Clear and convincing evidence indicated the researchers were the sole inventors of the patent. Substantial evidence supported the damage award, including the award of exemplary damages, and the court affirmed the judgment for the researchers and university. *Univ. of Colorado Foundation v. American Cyanamid Co.*, 342 F.3d 1298 (Fed. Cir. 2003).

◆ *A university's patent policy validly required two researchers to assign all rights to their inventions to the university.*

The University of New Mexico's patent policy stated that all inventions developed during the course of research funded by the university or employment at the university belonged to the university. The policy also required the inventors to cooperate with the university in the patent process. Two researchers of chemical compounds completed work that led the university to submit 11 different patent applications regarding two compounds. The researchers assigned their rights in the patents to the university.

Two years later, the university submitted five continuation-in-part patent applications, and the researchers did not assign their rights under these applications to the university. When the university entered into a licensing agreement with a company regarding the two compounds, a dispute arose over the ownership of the patents. A New Mexico federal court assigned a special master, who concluded that the researchers had to assign their rights to one of the compounds to the university. With respect to the second compound, the court conducted a trial and determined that the university owned those patents as well. On appeal, the Federal Circuit largely affirmed. The researchers were to be listed as inventors, but **the university's patent policy, which was incorporated into the researchers' employment contracts, clearly made the university the owner of the patents**. *Regents of the Univ. of New Mexico v. Scallen*, 321 F.3d 1111 (Fed. Cir. 2003).

## B. Validity of Patents

*When competing applicants for a patent on the same invention cannot settle their differences privately, either party may seek to have the matter resolved by the U.S. Patent and Trademark Office via a procedure known as a patent interference proceeding. The purpose of these proceedings is to determine priority of invention between competing applicants. Sometimes, an applicant can ask that an interference proceeding be conducted even after the patent it seeks has been granted to another applicant.*

◆ *A patent claimed by a New York university was invalid because it did not comply with the written description requirement of federal patent law.*

Researchers at the University of Rochester developed a method for identifying a prostaglandin synthesis inhibitor. The university received two U.S. patents, one of which was based on a method that inhibited PGHS-2 prostaglandins. After four pharmaceutical manufacturers began using the method, the university filed a federal district court action against them for patent infringement. The court held the patent did not meet statutory written description requirements and merely described a theory, not an invention. The patent did not satisfy statutory enablement grounds, as it did not allow those skilled in the art to make and use the invention without undue experimentation.

The university appealed to the Federal Circuit. It held **the patent failed the written description requirement, as its description was "vague." It did not disclose the structure or physical properties of any compounds.** While it was not necessary for the university to describe the exact chemical compound of an inhibitor, its description of a non-steroidal compound that inhibits the activity of the PGHS-2 gene product was insufficient for statutory purposes. It would not provide a researcher, skilled in this area, with sufficient information to understand what it claimed to accomplish and how to perform the method. The court affirmed the judgment for the manufacturers. *Univ. of Rochester v. G.D. Searle & Co.*, 358 F.3d 916 (Fed. Cir. 2004).

◆   *A university and its licensee could not patent a discovery about the best time to harvest and eat certain vegetables.*

Johns Hopkins University owned three patents based in part on the discovery of the beneficial effects of harvesting and eating broccoli and cauliflower at the two-leaf stage, when they contain the highest levels of glucosinates and Phase 2 enzymes, which reduce the risk of developing cancer. The patents also contained a method for preparing the sprouts in order to increase their protective properties. The university licensed the patents to a company, then joined the company in a lawsuit against competitors for violating the patents. The defendants asserted that the portions of the patents that referred to the eating and growing of sprouts should be invalidated by prior art. A Maryland federal court ruled in favor of the defendants. On appeal, the Federal Circuit Court of Appeals noted that under 35 U.S.C. § 101, a patent can be obtained for inventing or discovering any new composition of matter or any new improvement thereof.

**The university and its licensee did not create a new kind of sprout or develop a new growing method.** They merely discovered that the vegetables contained glucosinates and Phase 2 enzymes (anti-cancer agents). Those elements were inherent in the sprouts. Since prior art unquestionably included growing, harvesting and eating the sprouts, the patents were invalidated to the extent they tried to protect that activity. The judgment was affirmed. *Brassica Protection Products, LLC v. Sunrise Farms*, 301 F.3d 1343 (Fed. Cir. 2002).

◆   *Inventions by a pharmaceutical concern and a university were separately patentable as their molecules had different chemical structures.*

Eli Lilly and Co. filed a reissue application surrendering a patent covering deoxyribonucleic acid (cDNA), a sequence code for human protein C. At the same time, Lilly filed a patent interference claim against the University of Washington concerning a university-held patent that also related to the sequence of human protein C. The university denied any interference, asserting the cDNA molecules had different chemical sequences. The Board of Patent Appeals and Interferences agreed, finding Lilly's invention was not the same as the university's. Lilly was dissatisfied with the board's ruling and moved to define the interfering subject matter by proposing two alternative constructions of the cDNA: a narrow construction and a broad construction. The board applied a two-part test and rejected Lilly's contentions. Regardless of whether the claim was construed as a genus or a species, Lilly's reissue application and the university's claim did not define the "same patentable invention." There was no interference-in-fact, and the matter was dismissed. Lilly appealed to the Federal Circuit, which explained that under 37 C.F.R. § 1.601(n), the "'same patentable invention' means that the one invention of one party anticipates or renders obvious the other party's invention."

Since the claimed interference involved genus/species inventions, it was unclear whether the genus claim or the species claim was invented first. **The court found it possible that both a genus claim and a species claim could be separate, patentable inventions. The director resolved the issue by presuming that both Lilly's invention and the university's invention were "prior art."** This meant that the university's invention was assumed to be prior art of Lilly's invention and vice versa. Although the court acknowledged Lilly's assertion that a one-way test should be applied, it was within the director's discretion not to accept it. The court upheld the use of the two-way test and affirmed the board's decision. *Eli Lilly & Co. v. Board of Regents of Univ. of Washington*, 334 F.3d 1264 (Fed. Cir. 2003).

## C. Defenses

*The Eleventh Amendment to the U.S. Constitution generally bars claims against state defendants. States can waive immunity from suit.*

◆   *A state university that voluntarily submits itself to the jurisdiction of the federal court system waives its Eleventh Amendment immunity.*

The University of Missouri filed an application for a patent of an unspecified invention. While the application was pending, a company filed an application to patent the same invention. The company's application proceeded more quickly, and it was granted while the university's remained pending. The university responded by instituting an interference proceeding. After a six-year interference proceeding, the U.S. Patent and Trademark Office held the company was not entitled to the patent. The university was awarded priority, and the office held it was entitled to the patent. The company appealed to a federal district court. The university moved for dismissal, arguing it was immune from suit in the federal courts under the Eleventh Amendment.

The district court agreed with the university, and the company appealed. The U.S. Court of Appeals, Federal Circuit, explained that a state does not waive its Eleventh Amendment immunity merely by participating in the federal patent system. In this case, however, the university asked the U.S. Patent and Trademark Office to conduct litigation-type activity, and it participated in that activity without claiming immunity. **When a state voluntarily submits itself to the jurisdiction of the federal court system, it waives its state immunity with respect to the claims raised.** In this case, an appeal to federal court was built into the U.S. Patent and Trademark Office proceeding by statute. Therefore, by instituting and participating in the proceeding, the university subjected itself to federal court jurisdiction. The appeals court reversed the decision and remanded the case for further proceedings. *Vas-Cath, Inc. v. Curators of the Univ. of Missouri*, 473 F.3d 1376 (Fed. Cir. 2007).

◆   *The Eleventh Amendment bars federal court lawsuits by private parties against states under the Patent Remedy Act and the Lanham Act.*

The Supreme Court held Congress overstepped its authority by enacting the Patent Remedy Act. It found no indication that the act was enacted under the authority of the Fourteenth Amendment. Rather, the legislation was authorized by Article I and thus improperly removed states' sovereign immunity. The case arose after College Savings Bank, which owned and marketed a patented investment methodology designed to finance the costs of college education, discovered that the state of Florida was selling a similar product. The bank brought separate actions against the state for patent infringement and false advertising under the Lanham Act. In the patent infringement action, the Court held Florida could not be sued without its consent where it engaged in interstate commerce. *Florida Prepaid Postsecondary Educ. Expense Board v. College Savings Bank*, 527 U.S. 627, 119 S.Ct. 2199, 144 L.Ed.2d 575 (1999).

In the false advertising action, the Court held that **the Trademark Remedy Clarification Act did not validly abrogate states' Eleventh Amendment immunity from a suit brought under the Lanham Act**. Although Congress may remove a state's sovereign immunity under Section 5 of the Fourteenth Amendment, there must be a property interest involved for it to do so. However, there was no property interest at stake in a false advertising suit under the Lanham Act. Further, the state of Florida had not constructively waived its immunity by engaging in interstate commerce. *College Savings Bank v. Florida Prepaid Postsecondary Educ. Expense Board*, 527 U.S. 666, 119 S.Ct. 2219, 144 L.Ed.2d 605 (1999).

## III. TRADEMARKS

*A trademark, defined at 15 U.S.C. § 1127, is any word, name, symbol or device, or any combination thereof used to identify and distinguish goods, including a unique product, from those manufactured or sold by others, and to indicate the source of the goods, even if the source is unknown.*

*Service marks are identical to trademarks in all respects except that they are intended to indicate the origin of services, rather than goods. Trade dress is defined as the total image of a product, and includes features such as size, shape, color, color combinations, texture, graphics or sales techniques.*

*Section 43(a) of the Lanham Act, 15 U.S.C. § 1125(a), creates a federal cause of action for unfair competition in interstate commercial activities. It forbids unfair trade practices involving infringement of trade dress, service marks or trademarks, even in the absence of federal trademark registration. See, for instance,* Two Pesos, Inc. v. Taco Cabana, Inc., *505 U.S. 763 (1992).*

*Under Section 43(a), civil liability exists in cases where a person "on or in connection with any goods or services, ... uses in commerce any word, term, name, symbol, or device, or any combination thereof, or any false designation of origin, false or misleading description of fact, or false or misleading representation of fact, which –*

*(A) is likely to cause confusion, or to cause mistake, or to deceive as*

*to the affiliation, connection, or association of such person with another person, or as to the origin, sponsorship, or approval of his or her goods, services, or commercial activities by another person, or (B) in commercial advertising or promotion, misrepresents the nature, characteristics, qualities, or geographic origin of his or her or another person's goods, services, or commercial activities ..."*

According to one court, the *"touchstone test" for a violation of Section 43(a) is the likelihood of confusion resulting from the defendant's adoption of a trade dress similar to the plaintiff's. See* Original Appalachian Artworks, Inc. v. Toy Loft, Inc., *684 F.2d 821 (11th Cir. 1982).*

◆ *A Georgia federal court dismissed a trademark infringement suit because the college failed to register the marks at issue.*

A private non-profit college owned several service mark registrations. Importantly, the marks were registered for use in connection with the provision of educational services but were not registered for use in connection with the sale of apparel or other related goods. An Internet-based business that sold customizable apparel and fan clothing began selling goods with the marks that belonged to the school. The college sued the company, alleging a violation of its trademark rights under the federal Lanham Act. The court explained, **although registration of a mark is evidence of the registrant's exclusive right to use it, the presumption of the right to exclusive use is limited to the goods or services specified by the holder of the mark in the registration**. The college could've stated a valid claim if it had shown it used the marks on apparel before the company did. It didn't make that showing so the claim was dismissed. *Savannah College of Art and Design, Inc. v. Sportswear, Inc.*, No. 1:14-CV-2288-TWT, 2015 WL 4626911 (N.D. Ga. 8/3/15).

◆ *An artist did not violate the Lanham Act by portraying University of Alabama uniforms in paintings, calendars and prints. But a court would have to decide whether he could continue making mugs and "mundane objects."*

Since 1979, the artist painted University of Alabama football scenes, portraying uniforms, helmets, jerseys and school colors. He reproduced paintings as prints, calendars, mugs and other articles. By 1995, the parties had entered into licensing agreements for some of the artist's works. In 2002, the university told the artist he would need permission to continue producing trademarked material. He stated that he needed no permission to "realistically portray historical events." In a federal action, the university sued the artist for breach of contract, trademark infringement and unfair competition. A court held the artist could produce paintings and prints, but it held the university was entitled to judgment regarding calendars, mugs and other "mundane products."

Appeal reached the U.S. Court of Appeals, Eleventh Circuit. As for the paintings, prints and calendars, the court rejected the university's argument that the licensing agreements prohibited the artist from making unlicensed portrayals of its uniforms. As the agreements were ambiguous, the court upheld the lower court judgment regarding the paintings and prints. Under the university's interpretation of a 1995 agreement, the artist "would need to perpetually obtain permission to paint any historically accurate scenes from

Alabama football games." Evidence indicated the parties did not intend that the artist's portrayal of uniforms in unlicensed paintings, prints and calendars would violate their licensing agreements. His **First Amendment interests in artistic expression outweighed any consumer confusion that might exist regarding university trademarks, so there was no Lanham Act violation**. But there was ambiguity in the licensing agreements regarding whether the artist needed permission to portray uniforms on mugs and other mundane items. As there was insufficient evidence about this aspect of the case, the lower court would have to engage in further fact-finding. *Univ. of Alabama Board of Trustees v. New Life Art, Inc.*, 683 F.3d 1266 (11th Cir. 2012).

◆   *A federal court denied an Indian tribe's action to stop the NCAA from ending the University of North Dakota's use of the "Fighting Sioux" nickname.*

In 1969, elders of the Standing Rock Tribe and one Spirit Lake elder ceremonially approved the use of the Fighting Sioux name by the University of North Dakota (UND). Later, the Standing Rock Tribe passed three resolutions requesting UND to stop using the name. In 2005, the NCAA prohibited Native American mascots, nicknames and images from championship events. UND and the state board of higher education sued the NCAA, which led to a settlement agreement under which UND could retain the name without sanctions if both tribes granted approval before November 30, 2010. But the Standing Rock Tribe never acted, and the state higher education board decided to retire the nickname. In a federal court, a Spirit Lake committee and elder sued the NCAA to enjoin any sanctions against UND for using the Fighting Sioux nickname. The action also sought non-economic damages of at least $10 million. After the court held for the NCAA, the committee and elder appealed.

The U.S. Court of Appeals, Eighth Circuit, held the committee and elder lacked standing to pursue the case. While they stated the NCAA's action would cause family turmoil, shame, humiliation, persecution and damage to Sioux youth self-esteem and educational opportunities, the court held this did not confer standing. Even if the court accepted the argument that the injury was sufficiently concrete and particularized, it was not shown that the NCAA acted with a discriminatory intent to "eradicate Sioux culture," as the committee and elder argued. **Nor did the court accept the claim that the NCAA interfered with a contract under the theory that a contract was created by the 1969 ceremony.** However meaningful the grant of the nickname may have been, there was no contract that could be enforced. Instead, the Tribes were free to withdraw their permission to use the nickname, and the state board was free to change it. As the ceremony was only a "statement of appreciation," it was not an enforceable contract. The judgment was affirmed. *Spirit Lake Tribe of Indians v. NCAA*, 715 F.3d 1089 (8th Cir. 2013).

◆   *A federal court rejected the University of South Carolina's bid to gain trademark rights in a mark resembling one that was already trademarked and was in use by the University of Southern California.*

The University of South Carolina filed an application to trademark its logo, which includes the letters "SC." South Carolina wanted to use the mark on hats, baseball uniforms, T-shirts and shorts. The University of Southern California opposed the registration of the mark, as it had previously registered a trademark that protects the letters "SC." It argued that allowing the proposed mark would create a likelihood of confusion. South Carolina filed a counterclaim seeking cancellation of Southern California's mark. South Carolina claimed the mark falsely suggested an association with the State of South Carolina. The Trademark Trial and Appeals Board refused to register South Carolina's proposed mark, finding it would create a likelihood of confusion among consumers. The board pointed out that the marks were identical and would appear on the same classes of goods and in the same channels of trade. South Carolina's counterclaim for cancellation of Southern California's mark was also rejected, as South Carolina did not show the initials "SC" are "uniquely and unmistakably associated" with South Carolina. On appeal, the U.S. Court of Appeals, Federal Circuit, held the evidence supported the board's conclusion.

**Allowing registration of the mark would create a likelihood of confusion, since the marks were the same and would appear on the same kinds of goods and in the same channels of trade.** The court upheld the decision to reject South Carolina's counterclaim for cancellation of Southern California's mark. To win, South Carolina had to show Southern California's mark was "unmistakably associated" with another person or institution. South Carolina did not make this showing, as "SC" refers to many entities other than the state of South Carolina. The initials "SC" do not uniquely point to the state of South Carolina. The Trademark Trial and Appeals Board's decision was affirmed. *Univ. of South Carolina v. Univ. of Southern California*, 367 Fed.Appx. 129 (Fed. Cir. 2010).

◆   *A state court rejected a Michigan State University football team manager's attempt to challenge a decision to have the Nike logo appear on team apparel.*

The manager claimed the appearance of the logos on the uniforms created confusion as to whether Michigan State student-athletes were personally endorsing Nike products. A state court held for the university, and the manager appealed on his state consumer protection act claim. The state court of appeals explained that he lacked standing to act as a private attorney general, as he did not suggest any injury from a deprivation of constitutional rights to himself or student-athletes at Michigan State. **The manager did not identify any student-athlete who objected to wearing the Nike logo.** The court also rejected his challenge under the state consumer protection act. As the manager did not identify any loss, the judgment was affirmed. *Sternberg v. Michigan State Univ.*, No. 281521, 2009 WL 131737 (Mich. Ct. App. 1/20/09).

◆   *A federal appeals court affirmed a decision for four major universities that sued an apparel manufacturer for federal trademark infringement.*

Louisiana State University, Ohio State University, the University of Oklahoma, and the University of Southern California held registered trademarks for their names and abbreviations. However, the institutions had no trademarks specifically relating to their color schemes. A clothing manufacturer sold T-shirts in color schemes and logos that were associated with the universities. Retailers displayed them alongside officially licensed merchandise, and the universities sued the manufacturer for trademark infringement. A federal district court found that even though the universities did not hold trademarks for their color schemes, the colors were associated with them closely enough to be entitled to trademark protection.

The manufacturer admitted it used the colors with the intent of identifying the universities. Since there was a likelihood of confusion regarding the source of the shirts, the court held the manufacturer violated the universities' trademark rights. A jury awarded the universities about $10,500 in actual damages and nearly $36,000 in lost profits. On appeal, the U.S. Court of Appeals, Fifth Circuit, found the universities established ownership of legally protectable marks. While they did not hold trademarks in their color schemes, each had acquired a "secondary meaning." **Secondary meaning occurs when the main reason for a mark is to identify the source of a product.** The universities had used their respective color schemes since the late 1800s, and they demonstrated a likelihood of confusion for consumers. The court rejected the manufacturer's argument that it made fair use of the color schemes and was not liable for trademark infringement. **The fair use doctrine does not apply when the use creates a likelihood of confusion.** *Board of Supervisors for Louisiana State Univ. Agricultural and Mechanical College v. Smack Apparel Co.*, 550 F.3d 465 (5th Cir. 2008).

◆  *A federal district court approved a settlement involving a university that included too much personal information on credit card receipts.*

University of Pittsburgh students who had purchased sporting event tickets over the Internet filed a federal district court action asserting they had been given receipts displaying more than the last five digits of their credit cards and/or card expiration dates. At the time, the practice violated the Fair and Accurate Credit Transaction Act (FACTA). The parties executed a settlement agreement that called for each class member to receive a ticket to one of two University of Pittsburgh football games. The court granted preliminary approval of the agreement. **Congress then amended the FACTA to eliminate a private cause of action based on a seller's inclusion of an expiration date on a receipt.** The amendment said a party could not be deemed to have been in willful noncompliance with the statute simply by virtue of printing an expiration date on a receipt. The amendment applied to transactions that occurred between specified dates. The court rejected the university's petition to vacate the settlement agreement, since it was a binding contract. The amendment did not apply to any action that became final after Congress acted. *Colella v. Univ. of Pittsburgh*, 569 F.Supp.2d 525 (W.D. Pa. 2008).

◆  *The University of Texas at Austin (UT) will be allowed to proceed with several trademark violation claims against an electric company that used several logos resembling UT's familiar longhorn steer logo.*

UT first requested that the company stop using the logo in 2002, claiming it had a longtime registered trademark depicting the silhouette of a longhorn steer. The owner refused, noting he had used the silhouette with certain embellishments since 1998. UT sued the company in a federal district court in 2006 for state and federal trademark claims. The court found UT correctly argued that its trademark and unfair competition claims should not be dismissed prior to further court activity. Trademark infringement occurs when a person, without consent, uses in commerce any reproduction, counterfeit, copy or imitation of a registered mark in connection with the sale, distribution or advertising of goods or services, when the use is likely to cause confusion or deception. **The court found that for both trademark infringement and unfair competition purposes, a "likelihood of confusion" means that confusion is probable, not just possible.** The court refused to dismiss the case at this early stage, finding UT showed a likelihood that the company logo suggested a UT affiliation or endorsement. However, the longhorn logo was not sufficiently famous to establish a basis for monetary relief based on federal dilution under the Lanham Act. The mark was not a household name, despite evidence of retail sales of UT products near $400 million in 2005-06. Only the claim based on federal dilution was dismissed. *Board of Regents of Univ. of Texas System v. KST Electric, Ltd.*, 550 F.Supp.2d 657 (W.D. Tex. 2008).

◆   *Texas Tech University won a $3.1 million judgment against a retailer who continued to sell unlicensed university merchandise after the termination of a longstanding contract between the parties.*

The retailer was one of 450 university licensees that sold a total of $8 million in licensed products annually. He failed to account for the university's share of royalties, and the license was terminated in 2003. However, the retailer continued selling unlicensed merchandise through 2005, when Texas Tech sued him in a federal district court for trademark infringement, unfair competition, breach of contract, trademark dilution and injury to business reputation.

The court held Texas Tech's marks were protectable under trademark law because they were distinctive and not functional. The color scheme of Texas Tech apparel and merchandise identified and distinguished it. The scheme was associated with the university since the 1920s. The products were easily recognized, and they signalled to the public that they were licensed by Texas Tech. The commercial impression created by the unlicensed products was identical to the impression created by the university's products. The strength of the marks was undeniable, and they deserved broad protection. In addition, the retailer sold licensed products right alongside unlicensed ones. Consumers were likely to be confused by the sales of similar goods at the same stores. Each of the factors regarding the potential confusion for consumers presented by the retailer's use of the trademarks weighed in favor of the university. Texas Tech was also entitled to judgment on the unfair competition claims. **Unfair competition occurs when an individual passes off the products of another by virtue of their substantial similarity.** The retailer clearly breached his contract with Texas Tech by continuing to sell licensed products after the contract was terminated. The Lanham Act permits the owner of a violated trademark to recover all the infringer's profits plus any damages and costs. Texas Tech showed the retailer's profits during 2004-05 totalled more than $2.8 million. The university was entitled to these profits as well as the royalties due under the contract. The court awarded the university a total of more than $3.1 million. *Texas Tech Univ. v. Spiegelberg*, 461 F.Supp.2d 510 (N.D. Tex. 2006).

◆ *The Nebraska Supreme Court denied an apparel store owner's claims against the University of Nebraska for wrongful use of a registered trade name.*

In late 1995, the Nebraska Athletic Department created an Authentic Shop, which would sell to the public apparel and equipment identical to that used by its teams and staff. That same year, the university's board of regents filed an application with the secretary of state to register the trade name "Husker Authentics" for licensed goods. But the university did not file necessary papers, and the registration was canceled without notice. Brent White, who had a license with the university, applied for registration of the trade name "Husker Authentics." Collegiate Licensing Company (CLC), the university's exclusive licensing agent, sent White a letter claiming he was in violation of his license agreement. The university then opened a store called Husker Authentic. Seven days later, White filed a petition requesting that the school be enjoined from using the disputed trade name. Later that month, White added a damages claim.

The university argued, among other things, that there had been a violation of common-law and statutory trade name and trademark rights. A state district court held White's registration had been improperly granted because he had not used the trade name prior to registration. White appealed. The Nebraska Supreme Court found the district court's decision to be correct, but on different grounds, citing the work the university had done in test-marketing the concept. It further concluded that this afforded the school the common-law right to the trademark and any subsequent registration was therefore invalid. **Because the university owned the common-law right to "Husker Authentics," White could not properly register the disputed trademark.** The lower court's cancellation of White's registration was upheld. *White v. Board of Regents of the Univ. of Nebraska*, 260 Neb. 26, 614 N.W.2d 330 (Neb. 2000).

# CHAPTER NINE

## Liability

## I.  NEGLIGENCE

*Negligence results from a failure to use reasonable or ordinary care. To impose liability on a person or an institution there must be a legal duty. This is determined by the foreseeability of the risk of harm that caused injury. If an injury is a foreseeable result of negligent or intentional conduct, a legal duty exists, and liability may follow. Once a duty on the part of the institution is shown, liability exists if there was a breach of that duty, an injury or loss caused by the breach, and some damages. A pattern of negligence by schools and colleges that shows conscious disregard for safety may be "willful misconduct," a form of intentional conduct discussed in Section II of this chapter.*

### A.  Duty of Care

◆  *A student failed to show an alleged breach of duty caused his injury, so a Washington appeals court affirmed a ruling to dismiss his negligence claim.*

The student took self-defense classes, where he performed exercises, drills and one-on-one exercises with an experienced student. In one class, the experienced student's knee struck the plaintiff's head while they were doing exercises. He didn't lose consciousness or "see stars." Later, he began to experience dizziness, memory problems and irritability. He went to his doctor, who diagnosed a concussion. The student sued the university, alleging negligence. The judge granted the university judgment without a trial. On appeal, the court affirmed. To state a valid claim, he had to show the university owed him a legal duty of care, breached the duty, and that breach was the cause of his injury. The student said the university should've provided protective gear. But he didn't show it was anything more than speculation that he was injured because he wasn't provided with protective gear. **As he couldn't show an alleged breach of duty caused his injury, his negligence claim failed.** *Perryman v. Bellevue College*, 192 Wash.App. 1030 (Wash. Ct. App. 2016).

◆　*A New York court refused to dismiss the claims of a high school student who was injured while taking a summer school chemistry lab at a university.*

The 17-year-old student had just completed her junior year of high school when she enrolled in the university's chemistry lab – which was for a mix of high school and college students. The student was injured when a pipette broke during a test. The class instructor was not present at the time, but a teaching assistant was in the room. The student sued, alleging negligence. The university asked the court to dismiss the claim, saying it had provided a lab manual with instructions. An expert testified that it was common practice for teaching assistants to oversee college chemistry labs. The crux of the university's argument was that its duty to supervise was limited to the duty owed to a college student. But the court rejected that argument – as **the class had a mix of high school and college students. As a result, the school had to exercise the same care that a reasonable parent would exercise under the same circumstances.** The school failed to conclusively show that the accident wasn't caused by inadequate supervision, so summary judgment wasn't appropriate, the court held. *Alban v. Cornell Univ.*, 48 Misc.3d 1062 (N.Y. Sup. Ct. 2015).

◆　*A California appeals court rejected a negligence claim against a university filed by a student who was stabbed by another student.*

The victim was working in a chemistry lab when she was stabbed by a fellow student. She suffered serious injuries and sued the school, alleging it failed to protect her from the attacker. When the court refused to grant judgment without a trial, the school appealed. The attacker had a history of mental health issues. He had been referred to the school's mental health services. University officials emailed the student to arrange a meeting to discuss concerns. That's when he attacked the student in the lab. She sued, arguing the university had a duty to protect her from a classmate's foreseeable attack. But the appellate court disagreed. **While K-12 schools have a duty to take reasonable measures to protect students from their peers, California courts have consistently held "an adult's affiliation with a college or university does not give rise to a similar duty,"** the court explained. The claim was dismissed. *The Regents of the Univ. of California v. Superior Court of Los Angeles County*, 240 Cal.App.4th 1296 (Cal. Ct. App. 2015).

◆　*An Arizona appeals court decided that the state board of regents was not liable in negligence for the death of a student in a study-abroad program.*

The student and 16 classmates spent a semester studying in China. The program included school-sponsored trips to various China cities, and the students were also free to organize their own trips. One of the students set up a trip to Mount Everest. The trip was not part of the study-abroad program, and no academic credit was awarded to students who took it. After flying from China to Tibet, the students drove to the Mount Everest base camp. There, the student developed altitude sickness and died. His mother filed a wrongful death negligence claim against the state of Arizona, the board of regents and the university in China. She said the defendants owed her son a duty of care as a result of the student-school relationship, and she also claimed public policy imposed a duty of care on them.

A trial court granted pretrial judgment, concluding that they did not owe the student a duty of care while he was on the trip to Tibet. His mother appealed. The appellate court affirmed the decision, agreeing that **the Tibet trip was an off-campus activity for which the defendants did not owe the student a duty of care**. The court pointed out that one of the students made arrangements directly with a Tibet-based tour company for the trip; the students paid the tour company either directly or through the student coordinator; the trip was not part of the study-abroad program; the defendants had no supervisory responsibility regarding the trip; and no faculty or staff made the trip. Because the defendants did not owe the student a duty of care, the ruling was affirmed. *Boisson v. Arizona Board of Regents*, 343 P.3d 931 (Ariz. Ct. App. 2015).

◆   *A New Jersey appeals court reversed a ruling that granted a college judgment without a trial in a personal injury case.*

One morning, a student fractured his ankle by slipping and falling on ice in a school parking lot. The area had been treated the day before, but temperatures plummeted overnight. As a result of the refreeze, more ice and slush accumulated. Two campus security officers saw the student sitting on the ground holding his ankle. They called an ambulance and called to report the hazard. Facilities employees arrived soon after the call to salt and sand the place where the student fell. The student filed a personal injury suit. To proceed with the claim, the student had to show the school's response to the dangerous condition was "palpably unreasonable." The school couldn't outline the actions it took to deal with the refreeze. The trial court inferred and presumed that the school had staff patrolling the grounds looking for weather-related problems – and found its response reasonable. The judge granted the school judgment without a trial, but an appeals court reversed. To grant pretrial judgment, the judge had to find the parties agreed on all the facts. Here, a dispute existed about the school's response to the overnight refreeze. **The appeals court returned the case to the trial court with instructions to get more information about steps the school took in responding to the plummeting weather conditions.** *Kavanaugh v. Camden County College*, No. L-970-12, 2014 WL 5343646 (N.J. Super. Ct. App. Div. 10/22/14).

◆   *A Michigan appellate court rejected the personal injury claim of a visitor who fell from a dorm's sixth-floor window.*

A student invited three friends to his dorm. Under dorm rules, the dorm's night receptionist required the guests to fill out visitor verification cards before allowing them to leave the outer vestibule and enter the dorm. Once in the student's dorm room, one guest fell from a sixth-floor window. She survived and filed a personal injury lawsuit, alleging the university violated its duty to repair and maintain the dorm. State law provided broad immunity from personal injury suits – but under an exception, schools had "the obligation to repair and maintain public buildings under their control when open for use by members of the public." The student claimed this exception applied because the vestibule was open to the public without restriction. The court granted judgment without a trial. **An appeals court affirmed the ruling, finding the fact that the vestibule was open didn't make the dorm open to the public.** The exception didn't apply so the suit couldn't proceed. *Pew v. Michigan State Univ.*, 859 N.W.2d 246 (Mich. Ct. App. 2014).

◆   *A student who was hurt was unable to convince a Massachusetts court that a negligently installed shower caddy was the cause of her injuries.*

A student with flu-like symptoms was injured in a dorm shower. She was facing a shower caddy on one of the shower walls. She passed out and fell, sustaining injuries to her forehead and left eye. No one saw her fall, and another student found her lying unconscious. Police were contacted, and the injured student was taken to a hospital. There was blood on the on/off water knob in the shower, but no blood was found anywhere else. The student sued, claiming her injury was caused by negligent installation of the shower caddy. The school filed a motion for pretrial judgment. The court granted the motion. **To prove her claim, the student had to show the shower caddy caused her injury.** She didn't. In fact, she admitted that she had no memory of how she hurt her eye, and she told her doctor that it was probably the on/off knob that caused her injury. Without evidence showing the shower caddy caused the injury, the court granted the school judgment. *Caffarella v. Bentley Univ.*, 31 Mass.L.Rptr. 595 (Mass. Super. Ct. 2014).

◆   *A federal district court rejected a student's claim that he was shot on campus as a result of the university's negligence.*

In September 2006, the Black Student Union – a registered student organization – hosted a back-to-school dance at Duquesne University. The student in this case attended the dance. When the dance ended at 2 a.m., the student walked to the dorms with some of his basketball teammates. One of his teammates began talking to a female, which angered a man in another group. There was a confrontation, and the student got shot. He sued, claiming his injuries were a result of the university's negligence. He claimed the school owed him a duty to provide better security relating to the event. **The court dismissed his claim, as the university did not have a duty to prevent the harm the student suffered.** As a general rule, there's no duty to prevent harm by third parties. Because the university had no duty to prevent this incident, the claim failed. *James v. Duquesne Univ.*, 936 F.Supp.2d 618 (W.D. Pa. 2013).

◆   *A student who was raped in her dorm room did not show the school was negligent, a federal Wisconsin court held.*

After a student was raped in her dorm room, she sued, alleging negligence. An expert witness would have provided testimony regarding security standards published by the International Association of Campus Law Enforcement Administrators. Part of the expert's testimony would've shown the basement door lacked a prop arm. But the district court held that the published safety standards were aspirational rather than mandatory and did not allow the expert's testimony. The court dismissed the student's claim, and she appealed. The U.S. Court of Appeals for the Seventh Circuit vacated the district court's ruling and remanded the case for further proceedings because some of the expert's testimony should've been allowed. On remand, the court determined **no evidence suggested the student's assailants entered her dorm through a basement door that lacked prop arms**. Therefore a finding that the assault was caused by the school's negligence would be based on speculation and conjecture. So the court ruled for the school. *Lees v. Carthage College*, No. 10-C-86, 2013 WL 5406447 (E.D. Wis. 9/24/13).

◆   *A Utah student had a "special relationship" with a dance team instructor that created a legal duty to protect her from injury during a team rehearsal.*

A dance team instructor told the student and her partner they were doing a lift incorrectly. He warned them they would have to cut the lift from their routine if they could not do it properly. When the partner tried to lift the student over his shoulder as instructed, he lost his footing and dropped her, causing her injury. A state court held the student accepted a risk of injury because she had the option of eliminating the lift from the routine. On appeal, the state court of appeals explained that Utah law does not generally recognize a special relationship between a college and its students. But the Utah Supreme Court created an exception to this rule in *Webb v. Univ. of Utah*. Under *Webb*, students relinquished some autonomy to their instructors based on expertise.

In this case, **a special relationship was formed if the student was injured by following an instructor's directive that fell "within the scope of the academic enterprise."** As the student was hurt during a team rehearsal, she was relying on her instructor during an academic enterprise and a special relationship existed. As a result, the college could be liable if a jury found the instructor did not use reasonable care in instructing her. A jury would have to decide if the instructor's conduct was reasonable and whether it caused injury. *Cope v. Utah Valley State College*, 290 P.3d 314 (Utah Ct. App. 2012).

◆   *Parents of a University of Kansas (KU) freshman who fell to his death from a ledge outside his seventh-floor dorm room were unable to hold KU liable.*

The student fell to his death after removing window screens and going onto a ledge to smoke a cigarette. His blood alcohol level at the time was .16. The parents filed a wrongful death suit in a state court against KU, saying the ledge presented a dangerous condition that the university should have corrected.

After the court awarded pretrial judgment to KU, the parents appealed. The Court of Appeals of Kansas explained that a "discretionary function exception" insulates government entities from liability when harm results from an entity's performance of, or failure to perform, a discretionary duty or function. While the parents argued that the exception did not apply because KU was obligated to use reasonable care to protect their son, the court disagreed. Any duty of KU did not require it to warn of known and obvious dangers such as stepping out onto the ledge. KU was not required to take any extraordinary steps to minimize the obvious risk of danger from going out onto the ledge. **Universities are not required to protect their students from their own reckless and negligent acts and are not insurers of student safety.** The court affirmed the judgment for KU. *Wellhausen v. Univ. of Kansas*, 40 Kan.App.2d 102, 189 P.3d 1181 (Kan. Ct. App. 2008).

◆ *The University of the District of Columbia was not liable for injuries sustained by a student who was attacked in an on-campus parking garage.*

Two assailants demanded money from the student, and one of them stabbed her in the face. She was able to escape, but the criminals were never apprehended. The student and her husband sued the university for negligence, claiming it should have taken safety precautions to prevent the attack. After a jury awarded $300,000 to the student and $100,000 to her husband, the case went before the District of Columbia Court of Appeals. It explained that a party may be held liable for negligence when there is a duty, a breach of that duty causing injury, and proof that the injury was proximately caused by the breach. **When injury results from an intervening criminal act, the injured party cannot recover for negligence unless the criminal act is so foreseeable that it creates a duty on the part of the defendant to guard against it.** This required some evidence that the university had "an increased awareness" that there was a risk of a violent, armed attack in its parking garage.

It was not enough to show there was a general possibility that a crime could occur in the garage. Although there was some evidence of crime on campus, none of the incidents involved a weapon, and none were committed in a parking garage or caused serious injury. Finding the university could not have foreseen the attack, the court held for the university. *Board of Trustees of Univ. of District of Columbia v. DiSalvo*, 974 A.2d 868 (D.C. Ct. App. 2009).

◆ *A Mississippi university was required to defend a negligence claim alleging it was liable for the rape of a 14-year-old girl on its campus in 1993.*

The student claimed she was raped by two 15-year-old boys on the campus of Jackson State University (JSU) during a National Youth Sports Program. As part of the program, JSU leased a bus and transported participating children from their homes to the JSU campus. Both boys had prior histories of trouble in the program. One had been expelled from the program for fighting, and the other had been threatened with expulsion for fighting on a bus and on campus. The girl was dropped off at the wrong location on campus, where both boys raped her in a restroom. The boys later pled guilty to raping her. Her parents sued JSU and its officials in the state court system for negligence. The court awarded judgment to JSU, but the Supreme Court of Mississippi returned the case to the trial court in 2000. It again granted judgment to JSU.

The case returned to state's highest court in 2007. **The court focused on the question of whether the rape was foreseeable to JSU officials. If it was, then the university could be held liable for negligence.** The court held that a reasonable juror might conclude JSU could have foreseen that, by leaving the girl and two boys unattended and unsupervised, JSU placed her in danger of "some violent act or impermissible sexual act." A jury could find that JSU knew there were 63 crimes reported on campus in the 10 months preceding the rape, including other rapes. It could also find JSU was on notice that the girl had been in the boys' restroom prior to the date of the rape, and that the boys who committed the rape had violent tendencies. The court remanded the case for trial. *Glover v. Jackson State Univ.*, 968 So.2d 1267 (Miss. 2007).

◆ *A Minnesota university was not liable for injuries to a cheerleader who injured her spine while participating in a pyramid stunt during a practice.*

The cheerleader fell and suffered a cervical spine fracture when the squad tried to perform a pyramid stunt. She later admitted she knew the stunt was risky, but felt pressured to attempt it. The cheerleader sued the university for negligence in a state court. The court found the university had no duty to protect her and held for the university. The cheerleader appealed to the Court of Appeals of Minnesota. **The court held that to prevail on her negligence claim, the cheerleader had to establish first that the university owed her a duty of care. A university is not required to guarantee student safety.**

The court found that courts in Utah, Indiana and Louisiana have found no special relationship exists between a university and a student-athlete. While the university handled some administrative tasks for cheerleading programs, it exerted minimal control over cheerleaders. The university did not provide a coach to direct practices or otherwise impose rules on participants. The court noted the university did not profit from cheerleading programs. The university was not in a position to protect the student and could not have been expected to do so. Nothing suggested the cheerleader was vulnerable. Because there was no special relationship in this case, the university did not owe her a duty of care, and the court affirmed the judgment. *Vistad v. Board of Regents of Univ. of Minnesota*, No. A04-2161, 2005 WL 1514633 (Minn. Ct. App. 6/28/05).

◆ *The Court of Appeals of Tennessee held a state university was not liable to a non-student actress who fell during a rehearsal.*

In a state court lawsuit, the actress claimed the university negligently failed to place glow tape on the edge of a darkened stage, causing injury. The Tennessee Claims Commission found the actress 100% at fault for her injuries. She appealed to the Court of Appeals of Tennessee, which agreed with her argument that theaters owed a duty to actors and actresses to exercise reasonable care. However, that did not make them liable for risks that could not be reasonably foreseen. **The court found the actress did not prove the university knew or should have known she would fall because no glow tape was on the edge of the stage.** Another cast member's complaint that glow tape should be placed on set pieces did not put the university on notice there was a dangerous condition in another part of the stage. The court held the actress failed to establish the state was negligent. *Fox v. State of Tennessee*, No. E2003-02024-COA-R3-CV, 2004 WL 2399822 (Tenn. Ct. App. 10/27/04).

## B. Premises Liability

*Generally, an institution may be held liable if it either knew or should have known about a defective condition on its property. But a landowner has no duty to protect visitors or even warn them about a condition that is obvious and not inherently dangerous. When an injured party's presence on property is not reasonably foreseeable, the property owner cannot be held liable for injury.*

*In* Agnes Scott College v. Clark, *273 Ga.App. 619, 616 S.E.2d 468 (Ga. Ct. App. 2005), the Court of Appeals of Georgia held an institution is generally not liable for the unforeseen criminal acts of a third party.*

◆   *West Virginia's highest court affirmed the dismissal of negligence and premises liability claims filed by a student who was hit by a car in a crosswalk.*

While crossing a busy road and listening to her iPod, a student was hit by a car in a crosswalk. The road belonged to the state – not the university. The student sued the university for negligence and premises liability. The trial court granted summary judgment to the school, and the student appealed, alleging the university was negligent as it failed to warn students about the dangerous condition of the crosswalk. Appeal reached the state's highest court, which affirmed the ruling. **The university had no legal duty to provide warnings, as it didn't own the crosswalk or the road**, the court explained. The student "failed to establish a duty owed by respondent to petitioners," the court concluded, so the ruling was affirmed. *Barb v. Shepherd Univ. Board of Governors*, No. 14-115, 2016 WL 143302 (W. Va. 1/8/16).

◆   *Maine's highest court revived a premises liability claim against a national fraternity that alleged a student was assaulted at a frat party.*

The woman attended a frat party where alcohol was served. There, she was allegedly sexually assaulted by a frat member. She reported him – and he was expelled from the fraternity. The woman sued the national fraternity and the alleged assaillant's chapter for negligence, premises liability and negligent infliction of emotional distress. The court dismissed the claims. On appeal, the premises liability claim was revived. The court held the national fraternity might have owed the woman a duty of care in connection with the chapter's hosting of a social event – especially since it's foreseeable that a sexual assault could happen at a frat party where alcohol is served. In addition, this national fraternity exercised significant control of the day-to-day activities of its local chapters by way of its constitution and bylaws, the court said. **It did more than just suggest standards; it enforced them "through constant monitoring, oversight and intervention,"** the court explained. More information was needed to determine whether the national fraternity breached a duty, so the premises liability claim was revived. *Brown v. Delta Tau Delta*, 118 A.3d 789 (Me. 2015).

◆   *A Florida appeals court affirmed a decision to dismiss the premises liability claim of a visitor who slipped and fell in a campus elevator.*

After a woman slipped and fell in an unidentified liquid on the floor of a campus elevator, she sued for damages. To state a valid claim, she had to show the university knew about the dangerous condition that caused the fall. She didn't provide evidence showing that, so the court granted the school judgment without a trial. On appeal, the ruling was affirmed because **she did not present facts showing how the school was liable for her fall**. She couldn't identify the liquid she slipped on or how long it had been there. She didn't show that anyone at school knew the liquid was on the elevator floor. The facts were insufficient to establish liability, so the ruling to dismiss was affirmed. *McCarthy v. Broward College,* 164 So.3d 78 (Fla. Dist. Ct. App. 2015).

◆ *A Georgia appeals court affirmed a ruling that dismissed a premises liability negligence claim filed by a visiting student of a nearby college.*

The visitor, a student and some friends were drinking at frat parties and bars in town. After the bars closed, the group walked toward campus and the student's dorm. They walked down a straight sidewalk. The area was not well lit – a street lamp wasn't working. The visitor stepped off the sidewalk and onto a landscaped area. When he did, he tripped on a flexible irrigation pipe and fell into an eight-foot-deep window well. The fall fractured his skull and damaged his right frontal lobe, and he spent six days in the hospital. A short time after the fall, his blood alcohol content was 0.243. He sued, claiming premises liability and negligent maintenance. A trial court dismissed the claim, and the visitor appealed, saying he was an "invitee," so the university owed him a greater duty of care than it owed a licensee. Not so, the appeals court held. **The visitor failed to provide evidence showing he had a business relationship with the owner that would make his presence mutually beneficial to both – an important distinction between invitees and licensees.** The decision for the school was affirmed. *Scully v. Board of Regents of the Univ. System of Georgia*, 332 Ga.App. 873 (Ga. Ct. App. 2015).

◆ *A New York appeals court affirmed the dismissal of a delivery driver's premises liability claim.*

A food service delivery driver arrived on campus to drop off an order. It had been raining earlier in the day, but the rain had stopped. The driver tried to pull a hand truck loaded with a 160-pound load up a removable metal ramp. He said he didn't notice any debris. He slipped and fell, sustaining injuries. Then he sued for damages. The trial court dismissed the case, and the driver appealed. The appeals court affirmed the ruling, as the school had never received complaints about the ramp and was not aware of any prior accidents involving the ramp. And because the driver admitted he fell only minutes after it rained and he hadn't seen any debris on the ramp, **no evidence showed the school created the condition that led to the fall or had notice of a problem with the ramp,** the appeals court said. The fact that a particular walking surface is wet as a result of recent rain does not, by itself, show that the walking surface constitutes a dangerous condition, the appeals court explained. The decision favoring the university was affirmed. *Ceron v. Yeshiva Univ.*, 126 A.D.3d 630 (N.Y. App. Div. 2015).

◆ *A Texas appeals court affirmed a ruling that allowed a student's premises liability claim to proceed.*

A waterline in the ceiling of a campus building broke and flooded a hallway. Two custodians were present when a student fell. One said, "My bad." The student was injured and sued for damages. The court refused to dismiss the claim, and the university appealed, claiming it was entitled to immunity. Under Texas law, a premises liability exception would apply if the school placed the water on the floor, knew the water was on the floor or the condition lasted long enough to give the school the opportunity to discover the flooded hallway. Depositions of several university employees indicated **the school knew about the water an hour before the student fell and was still attempting to clean it up at the time of her fall**. That was enough to allow the claim to proceed, so the court affirmed the ruling. *Texas State Technical College v. Monique Washington*, No. 10-15-00089-CV, 2015 WL 5474881 (Tex. Ct. App. 9/17/15).

◆    *The Eleventh Circuit affirmed the dismissal of a student's premises liability claim.*

The student was hired to take videos and photos at a fashion show. In connection with the events, a temporary concert stage was built in an arena on campus. While performing the work, he fell from the stage. He was knocked unconscious, and he later said that his first recollection of the fall came to him either while he was on the way to the hospital or after he got there. He sued, claiming the school negligently failed to make sure the stage was safely constructed. The court granted pretrial judgment, and on appeal, the Eleventh Circuit affirmed. **The court noted that a plaintiff cannot rely solely on speculation to prove what caused a fall.** But the record was nothing more than speculation. The student couldn't remember what happened, and witnesses could only guess about why or how the fall occurred. So the decision was affirmed. *Atakora v. Franklin*, 601 Fed.Appx. 764 (11th Cir. 2015).

◆    *A New York appeals court refused to dismiss a negligence claim that was filed by the family of a student who died after falling from an off-campus cliff.*

Two students left their fraternity and began walking to another. They began running on a trail behind the fraternity house. One stopped, but the other kept going. He ran off the trail and over a split-rail fence. He continued through the woods, where he overran the edge of a gorge. He fell 200 feet to his death. At the time of his death, the student's blood alcohol level was 0.167%. There was also evidence he had smoked marijuana. His parents sued, claiming the university was negligent. The school filed a motion for pretrial judgment, saying it was entitled to statutory immunity on the negligence claim because the student was hiking when he fell. The court rejected this argument, saying there was no evidence that the students were on the trail for hiking. **The court explained the school had a duty to "take reasonable precautions to prevent accidents which might foreseeably occur as the result of dangerous terrain on its property."** The court needed more information to determine whether the school did enough to maintain the premises in a reasonably safe condition. So the case had to move forward. The university appealed, saying it had no duty to warn the student because the dangers presented by the gorge were open and obvious. However, **the university did not show the conditions at the cliff's edge, and a question of fact existed as to whether it was open and obvious**. More information was needed to determine the adequacy of the warnings and safety measures taken. So the decision to deny the university's motion was affirmed. *King v. Cornell Univ.*, 119 A.D.3d 1195 (N.Y. App. Div. 2014).

◆   *A federal court in New York refused to dismiss claims that a university's negligence contributed to a student's suicide.*

Cornell's campus has seven bridges spanning two large gorges located on or near the campus. One of the bridges connects the area where freshmen live to the main academic area on campus, and freshman Bradley Ginsburg crossed it every day. In mid-February of 2010, Ginsburg jumped to his death from the bridge. His father filed a lawsuit against the city of Ithaca (which owns the bridge his son used) and Cornell (which owns the property on both sides of the bridge). He claimed that the defendants should have designed, built and maintained the bridge in a way that would have prevented foreseeable suicide attempts. The defendants filed a motion for pretrial judgment.

First, the court concluded that a fact issue was present as to whether Cornell could be held liable, as Cornell provided assistance and input during the design phase of a bridge reconstruction project. It also paid for and installed temporary fencing and permanent netting that was later installed. Ithaca had a duty to design and maintain the bridge in a reasonably safe condition, and Cornell may have had such a duty as well. The issue was whether any suicide attempt from the bridge was foreseeable. A jury would have to decide the scope of the duty to keep the bridge safe. Finally, the court rejected the defendants' argument that they were entitled to pretrial judgment because the bridge was not in a dangerous or defective condition when Ginsburg jumped from it. In addition, a 2012 article co-authored by four Cornell administrators noted that the eventual addition of fences and nets was "essential" and filled "a gap in Cornell's comprehensive suicide prevention approach." The court concluded that **fact issues existed as to whether: Cornell exercised enough control over the bridge to make it liable for injuries caused by a bridge hazard, a suicide attempt was foreseeable enough to impose a duty on the defendants to prevent an attempt, and the bridge was in a reasonably safe condition when Ginsburg jumped from it.** The motion for pretrial judgment on the premises-liability-based wrongful death claims and personal injury claims was denied. *Ginsburg v. City of Ithaca*, 3 F.Supp.3d 243 (N.D.N.Y. 2014).

◆   *A Kentucky appeals court found the college has state-law immunity to a student's negligence claim based on stepping on glass in the grass on campus.*

A student at the Ashland Community and Technical College (ACTC) was walking on campus when she injured her foot by stepping on a piece of glass hidden in the grass. She sued, alleging the college breached its duty to provide a reasonably safe premise for student. ACTC asked the court to dismiss the suit on the basis of governmental immunity. The student argued ACTC waived its immunity by purchasing liability insurance. The court denied the motion to dismiss. The college appealed, and the appellate court reversed. The appellate court explained that **Kentucky's highest court has clearly held that purchasing liability insurance doesn't constitute a waiver of immunity**. Under Kentucky law, a state agency has immunity to negligence claims based on the agency's performance of "governmental functions" – acts integral to state government. Agencies don't have immunity for negligence claims based on its performance of "proprietary functions" – acts that aren't integral to state government and can generally be performed for profit by private persons or businesses. Kentucky law specifies that one of the purposes of the university and college system in Kentucky is to provide instruction in residence. The court wrote, "As maintaining the campus premises is integral to providing higher education by any community college in Kentucky, ACTC is clearly performing a governmental function in maintaining its campus and is thus shielded by governmental immunity from tort claims related thereto." The appeals court remanded the case with instructions to dismiss the suit on the ground of the governmental immunity. *Ashland Community and Technical College v. Steele*, No. 2013-CA-000812-MR, 2014 WL 1155790 (Ky. Ct. App. 3/21/14).

◆ *Since a freezing rain storm was still ongoing when a campus visitor slipped and fell, he couldn't sue the school for not having cleared away the ice.*

A prospective student was scheduled to take a college entrance exam. She and her father left the house early because freezing rain was expected and the roads were likely to be icy. When they arrived on campus, the wintry storm continued. When they reached the entrance, the father slipped and fell. His injuries eventually required shoulder surgery. He sued for personal injury, but the trial court found the circumstances meant the college didn't owe him a legal duty under Minnesota law to clear the walkway, and an appellate court affirmed. To state a valid negligence claim, the father had to show the school owed him a duty of care but breached it and the breach was the cause of his injury. The general rule in Minnesota is that a city must exercise reasonable care to maintain its sidewalks and streets in a safe condition. However, as a 1958 state case explained the "ongoing storm rule," city entities aren't negligent if they wait until a freezing rain or sleet storm is over "and a reasonable time thereafter before removing ice and snow from its outside entrance walk, platform or steps." The rule exists because it isn't reasonable to expect the removal of freezing precipitation while it's still falling. **Based on the weather, no rational judge or jury could find the freezing rain had stopped, and a reasonable time had elapsed before the man's fall.** That meant the school did not have a duty to have cleared the walkways of ice – and the trial court was right to grant pretrial judgment. *Larson v. Saint Paul College*, No. A13-1171, 2014 WL 1125592 (Minn. Ct. App. 3/24/14).

◆ *A New York appellate division court dismissed a negligence action by a college banquet guest, finding it was based on purely speculative claims.*

During the banquet, the guest walked from a lavatory to the kitchen at least four times to talk to staff members. On his final trip, he slipped and fell. Later, the guest said he saw soapy water from dishwashing machines near the area where he fell. He sued the college in a state court for personal injury, claiming the college knew about a dangerous condition that caused his injury. The trial court held for the college. On appeal, a state appellate division court found that to prevail, the college had to show it maintained the premises in a reasonably safe condition and was not aware of water on the floor at the time of the fall. There was evidence that college wait staff had walked over the area of the fall without incident and without seeing any water. A supervisor explained that a college policy required wait staff to immediately attend to spills, slippery surfaces or liquid on the floor. Evidence indicated that college staff members routinely checked on dishwashing machines and had regular safety meetings. In the court's view, no evidence supported the guest's claim that there was water near the place of the fall due to negligence. **The guest's claim that the college created a danger of injury was based on speculation, not evidence.** As the trial court had ruled correctly, the judgment was affirmed. *Flahive v. Union College*, 952 N.Y.S.2d 821 (N.Y. App. Div. 2012).

◆  *A South Carolina court upheld a jury verdict rejecting liability for negligence in a case filed by a parent who fell on university property.*

The University of South Carolina leased an undeveloped island primarily for sea turtle research. The parent of a university intern was injured when she slipped on the stairs of a beach house and broke her ankle. She later sued the university in a state court for negligent design, construction and maintenance of the stairs. At trial, the judge explained to the jury the difference between an invitee and a licensee in a premises liability case. The jury was instructed to determine which category best fit the parent while she was on the island. The judge also told the jury that a state law limiting landowner liability applied.

After the jury returned a verdict for the university, the parent appealed to the state court of appeals, arguing the judge should have decided she was an invitee. **Invitee status would have triggered a higher duty of care on the part of the university.** According to the court, there was enough evidence for the jury to conclude she was a licensee, not an invitee. The judge did not commit error by leaving this question for the jury. The court rejected the claim that the judge, and not the jury, should have determined if the landowner liability statute applied. As the parent's other challenges to the jury instructions were not properly preserved for review, the judgment was affirmed. *Harris v. Univ. of South Carolina*, 706 S.E.2d 45 (S.C. Ct. App. 2011).

◆  *A New York college was denied pretrial dismissal in a slip-and-fall case due to evidence that it may have known about a defective condition in a shower.*

A New York woman and her friend visited the campus at Skidmore College to participate in a reunion planning meeting. They were assigned to stay in an on-campus apartment. The woman turned on a bathroom shower and stepped away while waiting for the water to heat up. When she returned to the bathroom, she slipped and fell on the floor, breaking her wrist. She sued the university in a state court for negligence, asserting that the showerhead had a clog that caused it to spray water over the top of the shower curtain and onto the floor. She claimed the defective showerhead led to the slippery floor and her fall. She also said the college made things worse by negligently applying a soap or polish to the surface of the floor. After the court entered pretrial judgment against her, an appellate division court reversed the decision. It found **the woman had presented evidence that the college either knew or should have known about the defective condition**. *Anderson v. Skidmore College*, 94 A.D.3d 1203, 941 N.Y.S.2d 787 (N.Y. App. Div. 2012).

◆  *An Ohio university was not liable for injuries to an elevator repairman because it did not control the building where he was hurt at the time of injury.*

An elevator repairman working in a Cleveland State University dormitory that was undergoing renovation was hurt when the elevator malfunctioned and fell eight stories. He sued the university in state court for negligence. The university asserted that it did not maintain, operate or control the dormitory on the day he was injured. Instead, it had leased the dormitory to a developer and did not possess or control it on the date of the injury. The case reached the Court of Appeals of Ohio, which stated the general rule is that **a lessee who manages and controls an elevator in a leased building is responsible for injuries caused by defects**. An exception says that owners can be held responsible if the defective condition existed at the time of the transfer of control and possession to the lessee. In this case, the elevator was not defective when the university transferred possession of it to the developer, and the university could not be held liable for the injuries. *Matteucci v. Cleveland State Univ.*, No. 10AP-576, 2011 WL 1744117 (Ohio Ct. App. 5/3/11).

◆   *A New York appellate court held City University of New York (CUNY) was properly granted pretrial judgment in a personal injury lawsuit.*

A visitor to the CUNY campus said she was injured going down steep steps that separated an upper patio from a lower patio. She also said it was the only available exit, meaning special rules of the New York City administrative code applied. CUNY sought pretrial judgment on the ground that the condition of the steps was open, obvious and not inherently dangerous. The court denied the motion and CUNY appealed. A state appellate division court held that in New York, landowners have a duty to maintain their premises in a reasonably safe manner. **But a landowner has no duty to protect visitors against or warn them about a condition that is both obvious and not inherently dangerous.** That was the case here. As CUNY breached no duty to the visitor, she could not hold it liable. The court also found that the administrative code provision concerning building exits did not apply to outdoor stairways. *Losciuto v. City Univ. of New York*, 80 A.D.3d 576 (N.Y. App. Div. 2011).

◆   *Boston University (BU) was not responsible for the death of a student who was struck by a train after she trespassed onto a railroad yard near campus.*

The student and a friend apparently gained access to the rail yard through a hole in a fence. They were struck from behind by a commuter train and killed. In a state court case against BU and several other entities, the student's parents asserted various tort claims. They included a contract claim against BU trustees premised on the theory that BU's website and police handbook obligated it to protect its students from harm. The court rejected the tort claims, finding no duty of care was owed the student. According to the court, any reasonable person could see that the rail yard was "an inherently forbidding place." **Where a danger is open and obvious, a landowner does not have a duty to warn of the danger**, because it is not reasonably foreseeable that a person exercising reasonable care will fall victim. Nor was there any duty to remedy the risk posed by the yard, because the risk was "blatant and unequivocal" and could be easily avoided by a reasonable person. Both students were trespassing at the time they were killed, and state law made their presence on the tracks a criminal offense. Finally, the court held no reasonable jury could find BU breached a contractual duty to provide a safe environment. For this reason, BU was entitled to judgment on the contract claim. *Shattuck v. Trustees of Boston Univ.*, 27 Mass.L.Rptr. 288 (Mass. Super. Ct. 2010).

◆   *A woman who fell on a college campus could not recover damages because the college did not have notice of a dangerous condition where she fell.*

The woman was catering an event at the college when she slipped and fell in a restroom. She claimed she did not remember falling, but she said she heard others say the floor was slippery and that there was "something" on it. College employees examined the floor and found the texture of the tile in front of the sink smoother than the rest of the floor. When the woman sued the college in a state court, her expert witness offered the opinion that the college had maintained a hazardous condition due to the presence of glassware polish on the tile floor. The court entered an order that barred the woman's expert from testifying about the alleged existence of a foreign substance on the floor, since this was based on speculation. The court then awarded judgment to the college. On appeal, the court explained that **an expert cannot offer a mere conclusion. Instead, the expert must provide the "why and wherefore" of his opinion.** In this case, the conclusion that a foreign substance contributed to the fall was speculation. The lower court permissibly barred the expert from testifying that a foreign substance contributed to a slippery condition, and the college was entitled to judgment. *Byrd v. Salem Community College*, L-172-06, 2009 WL 2015128 (N.J. Super. Ct. App. Div. 7/14/09).

◆   *Morehead State University was not liable for injuries sustained by a blind student who slipped and fell on candy on the floor of an on-campus restroom.*

Four witnesses testified that pieces of candy the size of marbles were "strewn everywhere" on the restroom floor after the student fell. There was no evidence indicating how the candy got on the floor. A cleaning staff of 63 employees was responsible for maintaining 44 campus buildings. The building where the fall took place was cleaned twice a day. A maintenance worker testified that the bathroom where the fall took place was inspected and cleaned before the accident. A hearing officer dismissed the case, and appeal reached the Court of Appeals of Kentucky. It found substantial evidence supporting the decision for the university. **Evidence showed the restroom was cleaned before and after the fall. There was enough evidence to support a conclusion that the university reasonably maintained the property,** justifying a decision for the university. *Glass v. Morehead State Univ.*, No. 2008-CA-001018-MR, 2009 WL 2192739 (Ky. Ct. App. 7/24/09).

◆   *A Tennessee university could be liable for injuries contractors sustained while performing repairs on the school's premises.*

A maintenance supervisor discovered a malfunctioning switchgear in an electrical equipment cabinet and called in outside help when he discovered unusually high voltage was present. He told the contractor's service manager that high voltage was present but did not relay this information to the two contractors who arrived to fix the problem. The two men began to work on the equipment and were injured when a high-voltage arc of electricity generated a flash of light and ball of fire. Both men sued the university in the state court system for negligence, claiming it misstated the voltage. They also faulted the university for failing to provide warning signs and failing to maintain its electrical equipment. The case reached the Supreme Court of Tennessee.

**The court explained that a premises owner who hires an independent contractor and offers information regarding the repair has a duty to make sure the information is accurate.** If the university employees told the contractors that the equipment carried only 480 volts, the university had a duty to make sure that information was correct. The university was also potentially liable to the contractors on a theory of negligent misrepresentation. Under that theory, a person or entity that supplies false information to others with respect to business transactions can be liable for losses suffered as a result of reliance on the information. Since a disputed issue remained as to whether university employees supplied false information to the contractors about the voltage in the equipment, the case was returned to a lower court for additional proceedings. *Bennett v. Trevecca Nazarene Univ.*, 216 S.W.3d 293 (Tenn. 2007).

◆  *A Texas student could not rely on a university safety manual to prove the university knew about the dangerous condition that caused his fall.*

While walking to a class on campus, the student tripped on a water hose and broke his knee. In his state court negligence lawsuit, the university claimed immunity under the state tort claims act. Under the act, the university was not liable for injuries caused by a premises defect unless it knew about a dangerous condition on its premises and failed to warn others about it. The court rejected the student's claim that a university safety manual, which required walking areas to be kept unobstructed, created a fact issue about whether the university had knowledge of the condition that caused his fall. A trial court agreed and denied the university's motion for summary disposition. The state appeals court affirmed the judgment, but **the Supreme Court of Texas held the manual was not evidence that the university knew about the hazard that caused the fall**. While the manual warned of the danger created when flexible cords were placed across paths of travel, it did so while discussing indoor safety. Nothing in the manual suggested that the hose created an unreasonable risk of harm. As a result, the lower court decisions were reversed, and the case was dismissed. *Univ. of Texas-Pan American v. Aquilar*, 251 S.W.3d 511 (Tex. 2008).

◆  *An Indiana college did not owe the parent of a student any duty to exercise reasonable care because he was not an "invitee" under state law.*

The parent slipped on some loose gravel on a campus walkway while walking toward a restroom. He severely injured his left arm and sued the college for negligence. A state court held for the college. On appeal, the Court of Appeals of Indiana explained that a landowner's duty in negligence cases depends on the legal status of the visitor. The duty owed varies depending on whether the visitor is an invitee, a licensee or a trespasser. The highest duty of care is owed to invitees, who are owed a duty of reasonable care. Licensees are those who enter premises for their "own convenience, curiosity or entertainment." The duty owed to licensees is the duty not to "willfully or wantonly" injure them or to "increase [their] peril." The law offers the least protection to trespassers. The court held that under the circumstances, "no reasonable person could conclude Ivy Tech extended an invitation" to the parent to use its public restrooms. **As a licensee, the parent needed to prove the college willfully or wantonly injured him or increased his peril.**

However, he did not even allege that the college did so. Because the parent was aware of the loose gravel and it was not a latent danger, the judgment was affirmed. *Gilpin v. Ivy Tech State College*, 864 N.E.2d 399 (Ind. Ct. App. 2007).

◆ *A Utah student failed to produce expert testimony showing her fall was caused by defective stairs, defeating her negligence action.*

The student and her husband sued the university for negligence and loss of consortium, saying the student's fall was caused by a failure to maintain the stairs. They did not present any expert testimony and relied primarily on the student's account. A state trial court held an affidavit and report from a university emergency response team were admissible under state rules of evidence. It also held expert testimony was needed to prove causation. The Court of Appeals of Utah said the state rules of evidence took precedence in this case. The reviewing court also affirmed the finding that expert testimony was needed to show a causal link between the allegedly defective stairs and the injury. Only in "the most obvious cases" are plaintiffs excused from proving causation via expert testimony. **Without the benefit of expert testimony, a fact-finder would need to resort to speculation regarding what really caused the injury.** The trial court's decision for the university was affirmed. *Fox v. Brigham Young Univ.*, 176 P.3d 446 (Utah Ct. App. 2007).

◆ *The Court of Appeals of Mississippi held a university was not liable for a visitor's shooting of a student on campus.*

One evening, three non-students entered the university campus in a car. They were not asked to log in as required by a university policy. The non-students rode around the campus, threw beer bottles at students and became involved in a number of fights. One of the non-students drew a gun and shot into a crowd that had gathered to watch the fighting. A bullet hit a student and he underwent surgery to remove it. The student sued the university in a state trial court for negligence. The court held he could not prove a connection between alleged reckless disregard of the log-in policy by campus police officers and the shooting. The student appealed to the Court of Appeals of Mississippi, contending that had the police conducted log-in procedures, they would have become suspicious and would not have admitted the non-students. The court disagreed. It emphasized that because the log-in procedures did not require a search for weapons, the outcome would have been the same. **The court agreed with the trial court that the student failed to prove a causal connection between the police officers' conduct and his injuries.** As a result, the court affirmed the judgment for the university. *Johnson v. Alcorn State Univ.*, 929 So.2d 398 (Miss. Ct. App. 2006).

◆ *A Maryland university was not negligent when it assigned a student to live with a roommate who had a prior record of fighting.*

The student was in the process of moving out of the room when the roommate accused him of breaking a fish tank. The roommate hit the student in the jaw, requiring him to undergo surgery and have his mouth wired shut. The student sued the university for negligence. The case went before a jury. The student presented evidence of the roommate's disciplinary history at the university. He had been involved in fights with other students. The university suspended the roommate and allowed him to return only after he completed a conflict resolution counseling program. The case reached the Court of Appeals of Maryland, which held **the university could not have reasonably foreseen what happened**. The roommate had no history of violence under similar circumstances. Even the student did not believe the roommate was dangerous, he knew about the roommate's prior incidents and did not ask for a new room or roommate. The university was entitled to judgment. *Rhaney v. Univ. of Maryland Eastern Shore*, 388 Md. 585, 880 A.2d 357 (Md. 2005).

◆  *The Supreme Court of Montana held a state university was liable for injuries to a child who fell on library stairs.*

The child slipped between the stairway balusters of a second-story open stairwell and fell approximately 20 feet to the concrete floor. He suffered three skull fractures from the fall. The mother sued the state in a Montana trial court, alleging negligence. The court found the state had a duty of care to the child and breached that duty, so it was liable for the fall. The state appealed to the Supreme Court of Montana. **The court held the state had a duty to maintain the balcony and staircase at the university library so they were safe for ordinary public use.** The court found the risk of falling was foreseeable because the state knew the distance between the staircase balusters was 11 to 12 inches. As the state failed to cure, remove or warn the public about the stairway defect, the court affirmed the judgment. *Henricksen v. State of Montana*, 84 P.3d 38 (Mont. 2004).

## C.  Defenses

### 1.  Immunity

*State laws preclude liability in many tort cases against public institutions. Such laws confer immunity on public entities unless they cause injury through conduct that is willful, wanton or grossly negligent.*

◆  *A Michigan appeals court found a university was entitled to immunity in a personal injury lawsuit.*

A pedestrian fell while walking along a walkway between a building exit and a parking lot on the community college campus. When she fell, she was close to the parking lot and was about 80 feet from the building's exit. The woman sued to recover for her injuries, and the college filed a motion for summary judgment, saying it was entitled to immunity. The trial court denied the motion, and the college appealed. A state appeals court reversed, explaining that under the state's government tort liability act, governmental agencies are generally immune from tort liability when engaged in the exercise or discharge of a governmental function. An exception applies if someone gets hurt due to a dangerous or defective condition of a public building, but only if the agency knew about the defect and failed to correct it. The woman argued that the public buildings exception to the general rule of immunity applied, **but the appeals court disagreed because the dangerous condition alleged by the woman was not an allegedly dangerous or defective condition of the building itself.**

Since the facts did not show the walkway was connected to the building, the exception did not apply and the college was entitled to immunity. *Standen v. Alpena Community College*, No. 12-005047, 2014 WL 6957497 (Mich. Ct. App. 12/9/14).

◆ *A man who was hurt while riding his bicycle on the campus of a Texas state university could not sue the university to recover for his injuries.*

Officials at the University of Texas at Austin (UT) closed off some areas of the campus to prepare for a football game. Workers stretched a metal chain across an entrance and placed an eight-foot orange-and-white barricade in front of the chain. While riding a bicycle on campus, the man crashed into the chain as he tried to avoid the barricade, suffering injuries. He sued UT for premises liability. As a state entity, UT would be immune to his claims unless he could show his injury resulted from either a premises defect or what Texas law refers to as a "special defect." After the trial court granted partial pretrial judgment to the man. On appeal, the court explained that state entities are not immune to tort claims that arise from premises defects or "special defects." In this case, **the condition that led to injury was not a special defect, such as an excavation or road obstruction**. Road users in the normal course of travel turn back or take another route when a barricade tells them a roadway is closed. The chain did not pose a threat because ordinary users would not have moved past the barricade. UT had closed the road and had no reason to know the chain was dangerous to users. There was no evidence that UT had any prior reports of injuries or accidents at the site of injury. As a result, the man failed to show the chain was a premises defect within the meaning of the state law, and the case was dismissed. *Univ. of Texas at Austin v. Hayes*, 327 S.W.3d 113 (Tex. 2010).

◆ *A spectator who slipped and fell in front of a stadium at the University of Texas could not recover damages for her injuries.*

The spectator was hurt when she slipped and fell on a removable drainage trench cover. The metal cover was slippery at the time of the fall because of rain. The spectator sued the university in a state court, claiming the trench cover was a premises defect. Under the tort claims act, state entities are immune from claims based on discretionary decisions. Despite an engineer's statement that the metal cover was used as the result of a discretionary design decision, the court refused to dismiss the case. The Court of Appeals of Texas held that the university had immunity if incorporating the cover into the sidewalk was a discretionary act. **A "discretionary act" requires the exercise of judgment and occurs when "the law does not mandate performing the act with such precision that nothing is left to discretion or judgment."** The engineer's statement established that the decision to place the cover in the sidewalk was discretionary. As a result, the university had state tort act immunity from the lawsuit. *Univ. of Texas v. Amezquita*, No. 03-06-00606-CV, 2009 WL 1563533 (Tex. Ct. App. 6/4/09).

◆ *A woman who was injured when she fell down a flight of stairs at Texas Southern University (TSU) could proceed with her lawsuit.*

The woman fell down stairs in an area where a work order had recently been issued to repair a loose handrail. A supervisor had signed off on the work order. The woman sued TSU in a state court for negligence. TSU responded by claiming state law immunity, but the court denied pretrial dismissal. TSU appealed to the Court of Appeals of Texas. It explained that state agencies such as TSU were immune from suit unless immunity was waived. An exception to immunity exists when a condition of personal or real property causes personal injury, or when an injury is caused by a premises defect. **To prove liability on a premises defect theory, the woman had to show TSU would be liable under the circumstances if it were a private person.** According to the court, she met this requirement by producing evidence that work orders were created for the handrail and that repairs were made to it. Since there was enough evidence to go forward with the claims, the judgment was affirmed. *Texas Southern Univ. v. Gilford*, 277 S.W.3d 65 (Tex. Ct. App. 2009). In 2010, the Supreme Court of Texas denied a petition to further review the case.

◆ *A personal injury action by the grandparent of a University of Michigan (UM) student was barred by state law immunity.*

The grandparent fell from a chair tethered to a riser in a UM auditorium after she watched a student performance. She sued the university in a state court, claiming the riser should have had guard rails to help prevent patrons from falling. The court noted **the state governmental immunity law provides a broad grant of immunity from tort liability to government agencies when they perform governmental functions**. The court found a public building exception barred UM's claim to immunity. On appeal, the Court of Appeals of Michigan explained that the public building exception does not allow claims based on design defects. In this case, the grandparent claimed her injuries were caused by design defects. Therefore, the public building exception did not apply, and immunity barred her claims. *Hetherington v. Univ. of Michigan Regents*, No. 07-000036-MZ, 2009 WL 692444 (Mich. Ct. App. 3/17/09).

◆ *Immunity barred a claim by a Michigan community college student who tripped and fell over an electrical floor socket in a campus lab.*

In a state court lawsuit against the community college, the student asserted negligent maintenance of a dangerous and defective condition, failure to keep the floor free of improperly raised, protruding floor-mounted electrical boxes, and creation of a dangerous condition by failing to properly repair and/or maintain the premises. Under Michigan law, community colleges and other government entities are immune to such claims unless an exception applies. A state court held the public building exception applied since there was a claim based on a failure to properly repair or maintain public buildings. After the court denied the college's motion for summary disposition, appeal reached the Court of Appeals of Michigan. It reversed the judgment, finding that in reality, **the student was asserting a design defect claim**. Public building exception language relating to "dangerous or defective conditions" did not remove the requirement for claims to allege failure to repair and maintain premises. As a design defect was alleged, the court reversed the judgment. *Collins v. Oakland County Community*, No. 282351, 2009 WL 794686 (Mich. Ct. App. 3/26/09).

◆ *A Michigan university had immunity from liability for injuries to a high school student who fell and was injured at a university football stadium.*

The student participated in a band camp sponsored by her high school that was held on the campus of Central Michigan University (CMU). While watching a band performance at CMU's football stadium, she left her seat to use a restroom. She tripped and fell while walking up some steps, injuring her hand and wrist. The student sued CMU for negligence in a state court. The court held for CMU, finding it had government immunity under state law. On appeal, the state appeals court agreed that the university was immune and that no statutory exception applied. An exception requiring government agencies to repair and maintain public buildings did not apply. The band camp was not open to the public, so the stadium was not a "building" under the law. A proprietary function exception to immunity was also inapplicable, as there was no government activity designed to produce a profit in this case. CMU merely allowed the high school to use its facilities, and fees it charged the high school covered costs only. **Since neither exception applied, the university was immune to the student's suit, and the judgment was affirmed.** *Williams v. Cent. Michigan Univ.*, No. 276445, 2008 WL 942268 (Mich. Ct. App. 4/8/08).

◆ *A Texas recreational use statute barred claims by a bicyclist who was injured while riding on a university campus.*

Water from an oscillating sprinkler knocked the bicyclist to the ground, injuring her. She sued the university in state court for gross negligence. The university claimed immunity under the state tort claims act, which applied to claims arising out of discretionary decisions. It also asserted the claim was barred by the state recreational use statute. The court denied the university's motion to dismiss the case, and the university appealed. The Supreme Court of Texas held the state tort claims act did not bar the claim, as it was based on the university's implementation of a policy decision to irrigate its campus. However, **the claim was barred by the state's recreational use statute**. That law limited the liability of landowners who open their property to recreational use by immunizing them from claims unless there was gross negligence or intent to cause injury. As the bicyclist could not show the university intended to injure her or was grossly negligent, the lower court's ruling was reversed. *Stephen F. Austin State Univ. v. Flynn*, 228 S.W.3d 653 (Tex. 2007).

◆ *A Kentucky university was immune to a claim of negligence in the case of a student who was assaulted, raped and set on fire in her dormitory room.*

Three days after being brutally attacked in her dorm room at Western Kentucky University, the student died from her injuries. Two men who were not residents of the dorm were later charged in the case. The administrators of the student's estate filed negligence claims in a suit against the university in state court. The court dismissed the case, and the state appeals court affirmed the judgment. The case reached the Supreme Court of Kentucky.

The court explained that governmental immunity extends to state agencies that perform governmental functions. At the same time, immunity does not extend to state agencies that are not created to perform a governmental function. Officials of state agencies can also be entitled to immunity if the agency itself is immune to suit. When sued in their official capacities, these officials enjoy the same immunity as the state agency. The university operated the dorm as part of its statutory duty to provide college instruction, and therefore it was not performing a proprietary function. **As the dormitory operation was a discretionary function, the university was entitled to immunity.** Because the claims against the university were barred by immunity, the claims against the officials in their official capacities were also barred. *Autry v. Western Kentucky Univ.*, 219 S.W.3d 713 (Ky. 2007).

◆    *A Kansas state university was immune from liability in a case filed by a student who slipped and fell on an icy crosswalk.*

The student stated it was snowing lightly at the time of her fall. She testified that snow that had fallen earlier had been pushed off the crosswalk. She thought the snow had probably refrozen to form ice. The university had 13 landscaping employees responsible for snow removal. Most of them started work at 6:30 a.m. and were instructed to begin their shifts by walking the campus in search of any hazardous conditions needing immediate attention. Employees were to sprinkle ice melting compound on hazardous spots, remove the ice, or report the problem to a manager.

The student stated the employees negligently failed to inspect and treat the crosswalk on the morning she fell, and sued the university in a state court. The court granted summary judgment to the university, finding it was immune from liability under the Kansas Torts Claims Act. The student appealed to the Court of Appeals of Kansas. **The court agreed with the university that the only exception to state immunity is injury caused by an employee's affirmative act. By contrast, an employee's failure to act has no bearing on liability.** As the student did not allege any affirmative act by a university employee, the court held the university was immune from liability under the act and affirmed the judgment. *Owoyemi v. Univ. of Kansas*, 91 P.3d 552 (Kan. Ct. App. 2004).

◆    *A New Jersey state university was entitled to charitable immunity.*

A student at Montclair State University fell down an amphitheater staircase on campus, fracturing his ribs and elbow. He spent several days in the hospital and sued the university for damages. The university asserted that it was immune under the New Jersey Charitable Immunity Act, and a trial court agreed. Because the student was a "beneficiary" under the act, the university was entitled to charitable immunity. The appellate division court reversed that decision, but the New Jersey Supreme Court reinstated the trial court's ruling. Here, the university was formed for a nonprofit purpose; it was organized for educational purposes; and it was promoting those goals at the time the student (beneficiary) was injured. **Nothing in the act required that an entity be a private nonprofit institution in order to qualify for charitable immunity.** As a result, the public university was entitled to have the lawsuit against it dismissed. *O'Connell v. State of New Jersey*, 795 A.2d 857 (N.J. 2002).

## 2. Assumption of Risk

*Assumption of risk is an affirmative defense to negligence. If the defense is proven, the claimant cannot recover on a negligence claim. To prove the defense, a university or college must show the claimant had knowledge of the risk, appreciated the risk, and voluntarily confronted it. Because the risk of injury is inherent and obvious in many sports, assumption of risk often bars recovery in negligence actions brought by student-athletes.*

*Institutions may further limit their liability in this area by requiring students to sign waivers and releases prior to engaging in hazardous activities. In* Lemoine v. Cornell Univ., *769 N.Y.S.2d 313 (N.Y. App. Div. 2003), a New York Appellate Division, held that clearly stated release language pointing out the dangers of rock climbing barred negligence claims against a university.*

◆ *An employer's "hold harmless" agreement was sufficient to insulate a private Idaho university from liability in a negligence lawsuit.*

An employer scheduled a team-building exercise for its employees and held the event at the university. The program included a wall-climbing activity. The employer instructed its employees to sign a hold harmless agreement before participating. According to the agreement, the university, "its members, directors, administrators, representatives, officers, agents, employees, and assigns" were released from any and all present or future claims as the result of any injuries that might occur during the program. While on the climbing wall, an employee fell and was badly hurt. He sued the university in the state court system for negligence. The court held for the university, and the employee appealed. The Supreme Court of Idaho rejected his assertion that a disadvantage in bargaining power between him and his employer made the agreement unenforceable. In addition, **the language of the release clearly stated that the hold harmless clause applied to negligence and covered any loss or damage he might incur from participating in the program**. For this reason, the judgment for the university was affirmed. *Morrison v. Northwest Nazarene Univ.*, 152 Idaho 660, 273 P.3d 1253 (Idaho 2012).

◆ *A New York court summarized the general rule that voluntary athletic participants assume the commonly appreciated risks of a sporting activity.*

A freshman pitcher on Clarkson University's baseball team was hit by a line drive during an indoor practice. He was not using a protective screen. He sued the university in a state court, which held that he had assumed the obvious risk of getting hit by a line drive. On appeal, a state appellate division court noted the pitcher was an experienced baseball player who had encountered line drives hit at him some 50 to 100 times in the past. Moreover, the court found he had seen the conditions prior to stepping to the mound and engaging in the activity of pitching without a screen. Finding **the pitcher understood the risk of playing without a protective screen** and was not compelled to pitch without one, the court held the university was entitled to judgment. *Bukowski v. Clarkson Univ.*, 86 A.D.3d 736, 928 N.Y.S.2d 369 (N.Y. App. Div. 2011).

◆ *A New York appeals court allowed a student to proceed with a claim that his college was liable for his hand injury at the college fitness center.*

The student was hurt when 140 pounds on a jammed weight machine suddenly dislodged and fell onto his hand. He sued the college in the state court system. The college argued it could not be held liable because it did not have notice of any dangerous condition. But a college custodian admitted that jamming had been a recurring problem with the machine, which had been repaired several times. The court denied the college's request for pretrial judgment. On appeal, a state appellate division court found evidence that the college was on notice that the machine created a danger. There were relevant factual issues regarding whether an accessory weight was being used at the time of injury. There was a possibility that use of the accessory weight caused the jam that led to injury. **There would have to be further consideration of the college's claim that the student ignored a warning label on the machine by placing his hand underneath the weights.** This created the possibility that comparative fault principles applied. Since further consideration of the facts was warranted, the trial court's decision was affirmed. *Beglin v. Hartwick College*, 67 A.D.3d 1172, 888 N.Y.S.2d 320 (N.Y. App. Div. 2009).

◆ *A Georgia student who ran across a street to join a fight voluntarily assumed a risk of injury.*

A Morris Brown College student was killed after being struck on the head with a glass bottle during a fight. His parents sued the college in the state court system for wrongful death. The trial court denied judgment to the college. On appeal, the Court of Appeals of Georgia explained that **adults of ordinary intelligence are deemed to be aware that they risk injury to themselves when they voluntarily join a fight**. Even when a person enters an altercation with the intention of breaking it up, he is responsible for any injury he suffers. In this case, the student ran across a street to voluntarily join a fight that had already begun. Under a state law doctrine known as "the rescue doctrine," individuals may recover for their injuries even though they assumed a risk of harm – but only if the injured party was acting to rescue someone from harm and the rescue was made necessary by another party's negligence. The court held that the rescue doctrine did not apply in this case, because the student chose to interject himself into the fight. As he assumed the risk of injury, the judgment against the college was reversed. *Cornelius v. Morris Brown College*, 299 Ga.App. 83, 681 S.E.2d 730 (Ga. Ct. App. 2009).

◆ *The parent of a Maryland student was unable to pursue a negligence case because she assumed the risk of injury by trying to cross an icy parking lot.*

The parent drove to the university to deliver gas money and other supplies to her daughter after about 22 inches of snow had fallen in the vicinity. As soon as she drove into the parking lot near her daughter's dormitory, she noticed it had not been cleared of ice and snow. Although the parent made it to her daughter's room safely, she fell and broke her leg in the icy lot while returning to her car. She sued the university in state court for negligent failure to clear the lot of snow and ice. She also claimed negligent hiring, training and supervision based on the failure of university employees to clear the lot in a timely manner. A Maryland trial court held the parent voluntarily assumed the risk of injury by walking on the snow and ice. The state court of special appeals reversed the decision, finding that a jury should decide whether to bar her negligence claim.

On appeal, the Court of Appeals of Maryland held the parent had voluntarily assumed the risk of injury when she chose to cross the icy lot. There was no evidence that the parent was forced to confront the danger of walking on ice and snow against her will. She understood she was taking a chance when she chose to cross the lot. **It was clear that a person of normal intelligence would have understood the risk presented. In assumption of risk cases, the claimant relieves the defendant of its duty of care by voluntarily choosing to encounter a known risk.** For that reason, the university's failure to clear the lot was irrelevant. The decision against the university was reversed. *Morgan State Univ. v. Walker*, 397 Md. 509, 919 A.2d 21 (Md. 2007).

◆   *A Rhode Island university was not liable for injuries to a student who fell while walking at night on campus.*

The student lived in a university dormitory. He fell while on an unlighted pathway on an unpaved embankment on the side of a road on campus. The student sued the university in a state trial court for negligence. The case was heard by a jury. It ruled in favor of the university. The student filed a motion for a new trial. After the court denied the motion, he appealed to the Supreme Court of Rhode Island. The student argued the trial court overlooked evidence about defects in the asphalt where he fell. He also claimed the area was commonly used by students. The court held the trial court judge had properly reviewed the evidence and assessed the credibility of the witnesses. The judge had found the student was not credible. The court agreed with the trial court's finding that the student tripped on crumbled asphalt, not a defect in a campus walkway. **The trial court made a well-supported finding that the area of the fall was not an existing pathway and the student could have used an existing route instead of the one he chose.** The judgment for the university was affirmed. *Candido v. Univ. of Rhode Island*, 880 A.2d 853 (R.I. 2005).

### D.  Damages

*Damage awards generally reflect the nature of the injury and the conduct of the parties. Compensatory damages compensate an injured party for his or her injuries such as medical expenses or pain and suffering. Punitive damages, on the other hand, are not designed to compensate for loss. Instead, they punish the offending party because of the party's willful and wanton conduct.*

◆   *Georgia's highest court dismissed the personal injury suit of a student who suffered ankle injuries in a campus parking lot.*

The student tripped and fell over a pothole. She suffered a broken ankle and torn tendons. She sued. Under state law, plaintiffs must provide the state a notice of a personal injury claim before filing the suit. Otherwise, the state has sovereign immunity. As part of the notification, plaintiffs are required to specify the amount of loss being claimed "to the extent of the claimant's knowledge and belief and as may be practicable under the circumstances." The student filed the notice and stated the amount of her loss was "yet to be determined as she is still incurring medical bill and does not yet know the full extent of her injury." The state asked the student to provide copies of her medical bills, medical reports and verification of any lost wages. She didn't provide the documentation and later rejected a $10,000 settlement offer. She filed suit, and **the legal battle went all the way to the state supreme court,**

**which dismissed her suit as she did not specify the amount of her loss as required by law**. Because she did not fulfill the requirements, the state had sovereign immunity and the case had to be dismissed. *Board of Regents of Univ. System of Georgia v. Myers*, 764 S.E.2d 543 (Ga. 2014).

◆ *A Louisiana appeals court rejected a student's attempt to increase the amount of damages she was awarded after she fell on a wet hallway floor.*

After slipping and falling on a wet floor, student Betty Issac complained of back and knee pain. The college paid for her medical treatment, including physical therapy. After undergoing treatment, Issac sued the college to seek damages for her injuries. As evidence was reviewed, some of Issac's claims looked sketchy. The court awarded a total of $1,500 for pain and suffering. Issac appealed, contending the award of damages was "abusively low." **The only way an award can be disturbed is if the trial court abused its discretion in the determination. The court reviewed the testimony and noted many inconsistencies in Issac's testimony regarding her treatment and pain.** In light of all the evidence, the trial court didn't abuse its discretion when it rendered an award of $1,500, so the decision was affirmed. *Issac v. Remington College*, 114 So.3d 636 (La. Ct. App. 2013).

◆ *An Ohio appeals court found an injured security guard may be able to make a viable negligence claim against a university.*

A security guard was on patrol at a university when he slipped and fell on a wet floor. There were no "wet floor" signs, according to the guard. He hit the back of his head on the bottom step, fracturing two vertebrae. He sued, claiming negligence. The trial court dismissed the claim, but on appeal, the decision was reversed and remanded. **Under Ohio law, "open and obvious" is an objective standard – so for the danger of slipping to be open and obvious, it had to be so to a reasonable person.** Some facts – such as the presence of "wet floor" signs – were disputed, so the court needed more info to determine if the school was liable. *Trowbridge v. Franciscan Univ. of Steubenville*, No. 12 JE 33, 2013 WL 6859024 (Ohio Ct. App. 12/23/13).

◆ *A Louisiana student who was injured on campus increased the amount of her personal injury recovery by appealing to the state court of appeal.*

A Louisiana university held an event at a ballroom for students to finalize the details of their graduation ceremony. Vendors were allowed to sell products and services on a three-tier stage in the ballroom. A student fell and was seriously injured as she left the station of one of the vendors. She later sued the state through the board of supervisors for the University of Louisiana in a state court for negligence. A jury decided the university was 66% at fault in causing the fall. It awarded the student more than $100,000 for her injuries. On appeal, the state argued the evidence did not support the jury's finding that an unreasonably dangerous condition existed at the time of the fall. The Court of Appeal of Louisiana found **a university employee who was responsible for setting up and supervising student union activities acknowledged that the stage created a trip hazard**. Even though he was aware of the hazard, he did not take steps to reduce or eliminate it, such as by roping off certain areas or posting warning signs. Based on the testimony of the school employee and the student, the court held she met her burden to prove her case. It also noted that she had developed back and wrist problems, and it pointed to her husband's testimony that "she ceased to be her jovial self." In light of this evidence, the court increased the amount awarded for past, present and future pain and suffering by $85,000. *Antley v. State of Louisiana*, No. 10-316, 2010 WL 3903816 (La. Ct. App. 10/6/10, review denied 1/7/11).

◆ *A New York court preserved a $4 million verdict for a student who was injured when she fell into an open manhole on a college campus.*

The student stepped into an open manhole at 1:00 a.m. one morning and hurt her right leg. About three weeks after the fall, she experienced swelling and pain. She eventually was diagnosed with blood clots in both legs. In a state court action for negligence, a jury found negligence by the college had caused the student's injuries. The court substantially reduced a multi-million dollar verdict to reflect future pain and suffering in the amount of $1.5 million and future medical expenses of $3.36 million. The college appealed to a New York Appellate Court,which found enough evidence for a jury to conclude that the fall caused a recurrence of the student's underlying medical condition.

The award of $3.36 million for future medical expenses was supported by testimony indicating the student would need to take blood-thinning medicine for the rest of her life, at a cost of about $5,000 per month. Since the college did not show these estimates were inaccurate, the award for future medical expenses was upheld. The court also upheld the decision to award $300,000 for past pain and suffering. But the $1.5 million awarded for future pain and suffering was not justified. After the student was released from a hospital, she was able to walk, exercise and go to the gym. **While she endured some long-term limitations and effects from the fall, her injuries were not debilitating, permanent or life-changing, and did not justify an award of $1.5 million.** A new trial on damages for future pain and suffering was required, unless the student agreed to accept only $450,000 for her future pain and suffering. *Nolan v. Union College Trust of Schenectady*, 51 A.D.3d 1253, 858 N.Y.S.2d 427 (N.Y. App. Div. 2008).

◆ *A Louisiana university was liable for failing to protect patrons from getting hit by foul balls when they entered a baseball park.*

A visitor went to a baseball game held on a university baseball field. She was struck in her right eye by a foul ball near the ticket booth along the third-base side of the field. The visitor suffered a fracture and permanent ocular blindness resulting in permanent 10/200 vision in her right eye. She sued the university in a state trial court for negligence. The court awarded the visitor $485,000, and the university appealed to the Court of Appeal of Louisiana. The court explained that ballpark owners cannot be held responsible for every foul ball in common areas. There are certain areas of a ballpark where protection is required. One such area is the main entrance, where people have to enter to buy a ticket. **The university could have reasonably anticipated there would be foul balls in the main entrance area.** There was sufficient evidence to support the jury's finding that the baseball park presented an unreasonably dangerous condition to those who entered and that the university had notice of the defect. The court affirmed the judgment. *Reider v. Louisiana Board of Trustees for State Colleges and Universities*, 897 So.2d 893 (La. Ct. App. 2005).

◆   *The Court of Appeals of Ohio held a university was liable for injuries to an operations manager of a mobile production unit.*

The manager got hurt when he was on the campus setting up for television coverage of a basketball game. He spoke to a university representative, who told him to run cables beside two large air conditioning units. The units were housed inside a dimly lit brick enclosure. Based on what the university representative told him, the manager thought the power was on the other side of the enclosure. He tossed the cable over a wall and over one of the air conditioner units, but it fell short. The manager entered into the darkness, took two steps and fell into a large pit. He injured his head, wrist and elbow. After two surgeries, the manager got a staph infection. He sued the university for negligence in a state trial court. The court found the university had breached its duty of care to the manager and caused his injuries. The university appealed, arguing expert medical testimony was required to establish a connection between the manager's original injuries and the staph infection. The court of appeals disagreed. Expert testimony is needed only where the internal complexities of the body are at issue. The court found the staph infection was not internal or elusive, so the trial court needed to focus only on the location and nature of the infection to determine a connection. A court could sufficiently understand the infection and its connection to the surgery without expert medical testimony. **The court also rejected the university's contention that the operations manager played a part in getting hurt by stepping into the brick enclosure.** It was unclear whether a university representative lulled him into a false sense of safety by directing him to the area without warning him of the danger of the pit. The court affirmed the judgment. *Dixon v. Miami Univ.*, No. 04 AP-1132, 2005 WL 3316963 (Ohio Ct. App. 12/8/05).

## II.  INTENTIONAL CONDUCT

*Institutions may be found liable for the intentional acts or omissions of their personnel. Courts have found colleges and universities liable for intentional acts of third parties on or near campuses. In those cases, courts may find the institution should have foreseen the potential for misconduct.*

### A.  Instructor Misconduct

◆   *Five graduate students had no valid claim for infliction of emotional distress based on an Illinois university program director's misconduct.*

The students said a clinical exercise physiology program director touched their breasts, kissed them, trapped them, and suggested that they have group sex. According to the students, their complaints to university officials about the director went unheeded. They filed a multi-count federal court lawsuit against the director and university, and the university sought dismissal of claims for intentional infliction of emotional distress and punitive damages. The court stated that an intentional infliction of emotional distress claimant must show conduct that was extreme and outrageous, emotional distress so severe that no reasonable person could be expected to endure it, and offensive actions taken with a substantial certainty that severe emotional distress would result.

In this case, **any failure by the university to respond adequately to the complaints against the director was not outrageous enough to support a claim of intentional infliction of emotional distress**. Nor could any such failure be said to have been done with knowledge or substantial certainty that it would cause severe emotional distress. As the students did not state valid claims against the university for intentional infliction of emotional distress, and punitive damages were not available, the court dismissed the claims. *Krumlauf v. Benedictine Univ.*, No. 09 C 7641, 2010 WL 1418579 (N.D. Ill. 4/7/10).

◆ *A Tennessee court rejected a battery claim filed by a student against her instructor, who forcibly removed her from a nursing class.*

The student learned she would be removed from the program because of a D grade. She said a vice president of student affairs eventually phoned her to say her grade appeal had been granted. Based on this assurance, the student went to class on the first day of the semester. She said that when she got to class, the instructor asked her why she was there and then physically removed her from the room. In a state court lawsuit against the instructor and other university officials, the student asserted claims of battery, conspiracy to commit battery, and intentional infliction of emotional distress. The court dismissed the case, and the student appealed. The Court of Appeals of Tennessee rejected the student's battery claim. **Not every touching without consent amounts to a battery. Certain classes of employees, including police officers and teachers, "are expected to touch people at times in order to direct their movements."** In this case, the alleged touching of the student by the class instructor was not offensive enough to constitute a battery.

The instructor apparently believed the student was not supposed to be in his class. The student did not say she was injured as a result of the contact. Since her conspiracy claim was premised on the meritless battery claim, it failed as well. There was no evidence supporting the student's claim that the instructor had conspired with university administrators to keep her out of the classroom. An emotional distress claim failed, as it was based on conduct that was not extreme or outrageous. *Runions v. Tennessee State Univ.*, No. M2008-01574-COA-R3-CV, 2009 WL 1939816 (Tenn. Ct. App. 7/6/09).

## B. Employee Misconduct

◆ *A federal district court dismissed a vicarious liability claim against Penn State University, finding coach Jerry Sandusky was not acting within the scope of his employment when he sexually abused one of his victims.*

In 1998, Doe was an 11-year-old. Sandusky invited the boy to work out with him at Penn State's football facility. There, the boy claims he was sexually abused by Sandusky. The boy's mother confronted Sandusky, who admitted there was contact with the child. In spite of the admission, a district attorney declined to press charges, and the school allowed Sandusky to stay on campus. More than 10 years later, Sandusky was convicted of 45 counts of criminal sexual assault. Doe sued Penn State, Sandusky and his charity. Claims against the school included vicarious liability, negligence and civil conspiracy. At the district court, Penn State filed a motion to dismiss the vicarious liability and civil conspiracy claims. It said it wasn't vicariously liable for Sandusky's abusive actions because they fell outside the scope of his employment. **Employers are liable for tortious acts of employees if the acts were committed within the scope of employment and within the general scope of the employer's authority.** Relying on four previous relevant rulings, the court concluded that Sandusky's abuse fell outside the scope of employment. The court dismissed the vicarious liability claim, but it refused to dismiss the civil conspiracy claim, finding Doe had submitted a plausible claim. That claim – along with others not addressed at this time – will move forward. *Doe 6 v. Pennsylvania State Univ.*, 982 F.Supp.2d 437 (E.D. Pa. 2013).

◆   *A federal court delayed its consideration of a civil action arising from the Jerry Sandusky sex abuse case pending the conclusion of criminal proceedings.*

After Penn State assistant football coach Jerry Sandusky was found guilty and sentenced for sexual abuse, a student charged him and other Penn State officials of violating his First, Fourth and Fourteenth Amendments rights in a federal court civil action. He also alleged state-law claims of premises liability, negligence, conspiracy, intentional infliction of emotional distress and sexual assault. The court found his complaint closely resembled the criminal charges against the officials. Their trials were not expected to begin until 2014. **Among the factors in favor of granting a stay was a risk of exposing the officials to self-incrimination for their criminal cases.** As the requested stay would not harm the public interest, it was granted. *Doe v. Pennsylvania State Univ.*, No. 1:12-CV-2068, 2013 WL 593415 (M.D. Pa. 2/14/13).

◆   *A New York student could proceed with a Fourth Amendment claim against college officials based on an incident in which she was involuntarily committed.*

An international honors student lived in an off-campus apartment. She told a college security officer that her roommates were defaming her on the Internet. The student also revealed that she suspected her landlord had installed a hidden camera in her bedroom. The security officer called the college honors academy coordinator and an assistant professor who also served as the school psychologist. The professor asked the student a series of questions about whether she had a history of mental illness, whether she ever heard voices and whether she ever thought about suicide. The professor and coordinator prevented her from leaving the office and then called an ambulance to transport her to a psychiatric hospital. As a result, the student was involuntarily committed for two weeks, which prevented her from taking her final exams. She later sued the college and several officials, alleging violation of her rights under the Fourth Amendment, among other claims. A federal court held that her Fourth Amendment claim could proceed to a trial even though no police were involved in her detention and transport to the hospital. But **the professor and coordinator could not be held liable for her involuntary commitment**

**because neither was involved in the decision to commit her for inpatient treatment and evaluation**. *Eze v. City Univ. of New York at Brooklyn College*, No. 11-CV-2454 (JG)(CLP), 2011 WL 6780652 (E.D.N.Y. 12/27/11).

## C. Third-Party Misconduct

*In* Wheeler v. Ohio State Univ., *below, an Ohio court stated the general rule that "ordinarily no duty exists to prevent a third person from harming another unless a 'special relationship' exists between the actor and another." A special relationship may arise if the institution knows (or should have known) that a danger is present. Institutions cannot be held liable for unforeseen actions by third parties and are not the insurers of student safety.*

◆ *An Alabama federal judge granted a university judgment, finding it had no legal duty to protect a student from third-party violence.*

After a verbal altercation, a group of locals who were not students followed a group of students back to their dorm. A street fight broke out, and a campus police officer broke things up. The locals drove away. After the officer went off in pursuit of the locals, the dorm director allowed the students to go outside to sit on the porch. A few minutes later, shots were fired. One student was shot in the abdomen. The shooter's identity was unknown. The victim sued the college for negligence, but the judge dismissed the claim. To find the college had a duty to protect the student from third-party violence, **the judge had to find the criminal activity was foreseeable, the college had enough knowledge about it to have prevented it, and the crime was probable enough to require the college to act**. That test wasn't met. The court found a shooting was not a foreseeable consequence of "a brawl in which no weapons were observed." Additionally, Alabama courts have refused to find liability for third-party violence when the identity of the violent third party is unknown. The court dismissed the claim. *Emery v. Talladega College*, No. 1:14-CV-880-VEH, 2016 WL 880038 (N.D. Ala. 3/8/16).

◆ *The U.S. Court of Appeals for the Fourth Circuit found Duke University did not intentionally inflict emotional distress on a student who was raped.*

When the student reported being raped, she said a Duke official issued a statement downplaying her report and suggesting she was at fault. The statement was broadcast nationwide, and the student claimed Duke discredited her report because she was a white woman accusing a black man of rape at a time when Duke was mired in negative press regarding its handling of an earlier rape case. According to the student, Duke did not adequately investigate the incident, and she said she was not allowed to register for the courses she wanted. In a federal court, the student sued Duke for negligence, infliction of emotional distress, hostile educational environment, and breach of contract. The court found some of the negligence claims were untimely. But the student could pursue a claim based on a letter from Duke stating she had withdrawn from the university, as it was within the relevant three-year limitations period. She could proceed with an intentional infliction of emotional distress claim, which was based on the charge that Duke suggested she was responsible for her own rape. On appeal, the Fourth Circuit looked at her claim for intentional infliction of emotional distress and found **the dean's letter outlining Duke's transfer policy contained nothing that should cause her to suffer severe emotional distress associated with the rape**. At the time the letter was sent, the student had no intention of returning to Duke. So the court dismissed the claim. *Rouse v. Duke Univ.*, 535 Fed.Appx. 289 (4th Cir. 2013).

◆ *Concluding that Virginia Tech had no duty to protect students from the gunman who shot dozens of people during the 2007 attack, Virginia's highest court eradicated a jury verdict favoring two of the shooter's victims.*

In mid-April of 2007, the police department at Virginia Tech received a call about an incident in a dorm. Campus police arrived on the scene and found two gunshot victims. Initially, the authorities thought they were dealing with a domestic homicide because there were no signs of forced entry. When they learned the boyfriend was a gun enthusiast, they moved quickly to find him. By that time, Seung-Hui Cho had moved to another part of campus, where he shot many more victims. All told, 32 were killed and another 17 were injured. Erin Peterson and Julia Pryde were among those who died during Cho's second attack. The administrators of their estates sued Cho's estate, the Commonwealth of Virginia and many others. The suit claimed the victims died because the Commonwealth breached its duty to warn them about the danger of criminal attacks by third parties. By the time the case went to jury, the Commonwealth was the sole defendant. The jury returned a verdict of $4 million in favor of the victims' families. To comply with state tort laws, each award was reduced to $100,000. The Commonwealth appealed to the state's highest court, which explained there's generally no duty to warn or protect another from criminal acts committed by a third person. An exception to the rule is if there's a special relationship, which is determined on a case-by-case basis. In this instance, the school reasonably believed that the initial phase of the shooting spree was a domestic incident. **Based on police's limited information, it wasn't known or reasonably foreseeable that students in a second location were in danger. So the exception didn't apply**, which meant the school had no duty to protect those killed or injured during the second phase of Cho's attack. The court entered final judgment in favor of the school. *Comwlth. v. Peterson*, 749 S.E.2d 307 (Va. 2013).

◆ *Ohio State University avoided liability to a student who said classmates assaulted her, because it was not aware of any prior assaults or threats.*

The student was injured when a classmate pushed her chair forward from behind. She was not sure who pushed her, but she reported what happened to the university's chief student life officer. The university moved two classmates suspected of pushing the student to another area of the classroom. In addition, arrangements were made for the student and classmates to attend different laboratory classes. But the student claimed one of the classmates continued to harass her afterward, asserting that race may have been a factor. She sued the university in the state court system. The case reached the Court of Appeals of Ohio, which found the assault that caused the student's injuries was not reasonably foreseeable. For this reason, **the court held the university did not**

**breach any duty of ordinary care by failing to protect her from being assaulted, and it could not be liable for her injuries.** *Wheeler v. Ohio State Univ.*, No. 11AP-289, 2011 WL 6147619 (Ohio Ct. App. 12/8/11).

◆ *A Tennessee court affirmed a $300,000 judgment for a student who was attacked while walking to her dorm.*

To get to her dorm, the student had to go down a stairwell in a parking garage. When she got to the bottom of the steps, she was attacked by a man who hit her on the head with a brick. The student suffered severe injuries, including permanent brain damage. Her family filed a state claims commission action against the university for negligently creating or maintaining a dangerous condition. The claims commissioner found the university created a dangerous condition by failing to provide and maintain adequate lighting on the steps. He awarded the student $300,000 – the maximum amount available. The case reached the Court of Appeals of Tennessee, which upheld the award. There was enough evidence to support a finding that the lighting on the stairwell was inadequate, creating a dangerous condition. In addition, **the history of crime near the garage justified a finding that the attack was foreseeable**. A university expert testified that there were 55 thefts at the garage in 2001-02. The university had breached a duty of care to the student, and the court affirmed the commission's decision. *Smith v. State*, No. E2007-00809-COA-R3-CV, 2008 WL 699062 (Tenn. Ct. App. 3/17/08).

◆ *A Massachusetts university was not liable for the murder of a student in his off-campus apartment because the risk of injury to him was not foreseeable.*

The student leased the apartment where he was murdered from a private landlord. On the day of the murder, another tenant let the perpetrators into the building. The student's estate sued the university for wrongful death and negligence. The court granted the university's motion for pretrial judgment on grounds that **the university had no duty to provide security for the student or to prevent his murder. Although there had been four burglaries at the building in the six months before the murder, there was no evidence that they involved violence or that any other violence occurred in the building.** The building was privately owned and managed, and the university was not in the best position to take the steps needed to ensure the student's safety. *Doyle v. Gould*, 22 Mass.L.Rptr. 373 (Mass. Super. Ct. 2007).

◆ *The Supreme Court of Texas held a state university was not liable for the stabbing of a student actor during a school play.*

The university had no theater curriculum, but it offered a voluntary student drama club whose members received no grades or class credit for participating. The club director and his wife told actors to use a real knife in a play, in violation of a university policy prohibiting deadly weapons on campus. During the second performance of the play, an actor missed a stab pad worn by the student and drove the knife into the student's chest, puncturing his lung. The student sued the university in a Texas court, alleging the university was liable for his injuries. The court held for the student, and the university appealed. The state court of appeals reversed the decision, finding the director, his wife, and faculty advisors were not "employees" under the Texas Tort Claims Act. For that reason, the university was protected by governmental immunity. The Supreme Court of Texas found the advisors were university employees under the act. But the director and his wife had no employment contract with the university. **The university had only a minimal degree of control over them that did not indicate employee status. The court held the university was protected from liability by governmental immunity.** It reversed the judgment. *Texas A&M Univ. v. Bishop*, 156 S.W.3d 580 (Tex. 2005).

◆ *Lawsuits filed against Texas A&M after a tragic bonfire accident were allowed to continue by a federal appeals court.*

In 1999, a bonfire stack collapsed on the campus of Texas A&M University, killing 12 students and injuring 27 others. A university special commission report exonerated university officials, finding that their actions did not rise to the level of deliberate indifference. However, numerous lawsuits arose, alleging violations of 42 U.S.C. § 1983 under a state-created danger theory. A federal district court dismissed the lawsuits, but the Fifth Circuit reversed and remanded the case. The court held **the record supported a finding of deliberate indifference**. The plaintiffs presented evidence that university officials allowed the bonfire stack to increase over the years to a pile of burning trash weighing more than 3 million pounds.

A university official had described the stack as the "most serious risk management activity at the university." Nevertheless, university officials did not use their authority to control the stack's building or destruction. The plaintiffs even asserted that the university encouraged students to add to the stack as a "marketing tool to lure prospective students" and to gain alumni donations. Based on all this evidence, the Fifth Circuit found that the plaintiffs established their Section 1983 claim. The district court's decision was reversed, and the case was remanded. *Scanlon v. Texas A&M Univ.*, 343 F.3d 533 (5th Cir. 2003).

◆ *An Alabama district court found a state university was not liable for the murder of a freshman residing in a dormitory.*

The student was a freshman at the university and lived in a dormitory room. A stranger entered the dormitory without authorization and murdered her in her room. Her parents sued the university in a federal district court for civil rights violations. They argued the student's relationship with the university was involuntary, such that it had a "special relationship" to her. This meant the university would have a duty to protect her from violence by a third party. The parents argued this relationship arose from a university requirement that all freshmen live on campus. The court disagreed. The student voluntarily attended the university and was not in its custody. She was able to retain her liberty and therefore had no special relationship to the university. The court also rejected the parents' due process claim based on deliberate indifference to a risk of serious injury to the student. **The university did not know about or disregard a risk to the student's health and safety.** The court found the university was entitled to qualified immunity and dismissed the case. *Griffin v. Troy State Univ.*, 333 F. Supp.2d 1275 (D. Ala. 2004).

◆ *The University of Maine may have been negligent in failing to prevent a sexual assault that occurred in one of its dorms.*

A student participated in a pre-season summer soccer program at the University of Maine. The university allowed participating students to live on campus during the program. The student stayed in a dorm and attended a fraternity party, after which a young man offered to escort her back to her dorm. When she reached her room, the man followed her in and sexually assaulted her. The student and her parents sued the university for negligence and breach of an implied contract. The court granted pretrial judgment to the university. On appeal, the Supreme Judicial Court of Maine reversed the dismissal of the negligence claim. It found that the university owed a duty of care to the student. Under Maine law, **a business (such as the university) has a duty to protect its "invitees" from reasonably foreseeable danger**.

**A sexual assault in a college dormitory is foreseeable** and is one of the reasons the university went through the trouble of establishing safety measures in the dorms. In this case, the student had never seen or met with the resident assistant on her floor; there were no group meetings offering instruction on rules and regulations regarding safety within the dorms; and there were no signs posted in the dorms informing residents who should or should not be allowed in. The negligence claim was allowed to proceed, but the court affirmed the dismissal of the contract claim. *Stanton v. Univ. of Maine System*, 773 A.2d 1045 (Me. 2001).


## III. BREACH OF CONTRACT

*Colleges and universities can be liable for breach of contract even where they have immunity from lawsuits for negligence or other torts. In order for a contract to exist, there must be some enforceable promise, not just general representations of the kind typically found in student handbooks.*

◆ *South Carolina's supreme court held a state university breached an agreement with a season ticket holder when it sought to require him to pay a seat license fee.*

The season ticket holder elevated his status to "Lifetime Full Scholarship," which meant he'd get preferred seating at basketball and football games. To obtain the status, the ticket holder purchased a $100,000 life insurance policy and made the school the beneficiary. He had to pay the premium for eight years. After that time, the insurance policy had not matured to ensure the face value. In a new contract, the school required the ticket holder to pay $500 per year. Several years later, the school added an additional seat license fee of $325 per year. The ticket holder sued alleging the school breached the agreement. The case went before the state's highest court, which ruled against the university. **The court reasoned that by requiring the ticket holder to pay the seat license fee, the university tried to impose an additional term that the ticket holder never agreed to.** The university was required to let the ticket holder buy tickets without paying the licensing fee, the court ruled. *Lee v. Univ. of South Carolina*, 407 S.C. 512 (S.C. 2014).

◆   *A man who fell from a climbing wall on a university campus could not sue the school for negligence because the release he signed was binding, a Texas state appeals court decided.*

The student was climbing a wall on campus when he fell and suffered ankle and back injuries. Before he climbed the wall, he signed a release from liability. The front page of the form stated that by signing the form, the student agreed to give up his right to sue for any injuries he might sustain climbing the wall, "however caused." The back page of the form included a list of safety rules, including one that said a university employee had to make sure the climber's knot and harness buckle were fastened properly. A witness to the accident confirmed no university employee checked the climber's equipment. A trial court issued a ruling for the university, and the student appealed, arguing the release did not bar his lawsuit because the school did not follow the safety policies listed on the back of the form. The appeals court rejected his arguments, saying he effectively conceded that the release purported to relieve the university of liability for all personal injury claims. The student argued that the university's failure to check his equipment constituted a material breach of the release or a failure to satisfy a precondition of the release contract. The appeals court rejected these arguments. **The safety policies on the back of the form were not part of the agreement to release the university from liability on the front of the form, the court said. The separate sides of the release document were separate agreements, it reasoned.** The form did not condition the release from liability on the performance by the university of any duty, and it did not include a promise on the part of the university to follow safety policies as consideration for the contract, the court ruled. The language of the release explicitly stated that the consideration for the release was the climber's opportunity to climb the wall, the court said. So the trial court's decision was affirmed. *Benavidez v. Univ. of Texas-Pan American*, No. 13-13-00006-CV, 2014 WL 5500469 (Tex. Ct. App. 10/30/14).

◆   *A Tennessee restaurant owner, who claimed she lost revenue because she closed shop for two nights based on incorrect information, was unable to pursue a breach of contract claim against a private university.*

Informed that the sidewalk in front of her two Nashville restaurants would be closed for a 2008 presidential debate at Belmont University (BU), the owner closed her restaurants for that evening. After it turned out the sidewalks were not closed, the restaurant owner sued BU and the local government in the state court system, seeking reimbursement for lost revenue and alleging negligent misrepresentation. The court held for BU, and the owner appealed to the Court of Appeals of Tennessee. It held that to claim negligent misrepresentation under Tennessee law, the owner had to show she relied on information that was false and not carefully communicated about a past or present fact. But the court found the information about the planned sidewalk closing was a representation of a future event. At the time, it was only a "present intention" – and could not be a present fact. The breach of contract claim failed because the restaurant owner could not show she and the restaurants were intended beneficiaries of an indemnification agreement between a local government agency and BU. A third-party beneficiary is someone for whose benefit the contract was entered.

**Though not a party to the contract, a third-party beneficiary has a legal right to sue if the contract is breached.** But this contract was only for the benefit of the local government agency and BU. Tennessee Law only recognized citizens as third-party beneficiaries to a government contract if a contract specified this. This contract contained no such specification. As both of the restaurant owner's claims failed, the court affirmed the judgment. *Int'l Market and Restaurant, Inc. v. Belmont Univ.*, No. M2010-00005-COA-R3-CV, 2010 WL 4514980 (Tenn. Ct. App. 11/9/10).

◆ *Representations to incoming students in a university's medical department brochure were not sufficiently definite to form an enforceable contract.*

A Massachusetts Institute of Technology student overdosed on Tylenol with codeine during her freshman year. She was hospitalized and admitted to a psychiatric hospital for one week. While receiving treatment there, the student revealed she suffered from mental health problems and had cut herself when she was in high school. A psychiatrist at the university's mental health services department diagnosed the student with adjustment disorder. He recommended further therapy when she returned for her sophomore year. When the student returned after summer break, she told a dean she was thinking about suicide.

The dean sent her to the mental health department for an immediate assessment. The psychiatrist stated the student had passive suicidal ideation, but he did not believe she was at risk of hurting herself. Her mental health problems resurfaced about five months later. The psychiatrist decided the student should be admitted for observation at the university infirmary. After she was examined, she was allowed to return to the dorm. Shortly thereafter, the student died from self-inflicted thermal burns. Her parents sued the university in a state court, asserting representations in the university's medical department brochure and in its medical department bylaws created an enforceable contract. **The court held the representations in the brochure and bylaws were only generalized representations of the purpose and medical services available to the school community. Such statements are not definite and are too vague to form an enforceable contract.** There was no evidence of specific promises made by the university. The court held there was no contract and awarded the university pretrial judgment. *Shin v. Massachusetts Institute of Technology*, 19 Mass. L. Rptr. 570 (Mass. Super. 2005).

◆ *The U.S. Supreme Court held that the doctrine of substantial performance applied to contracts in an academic setting.*

An overweight Rhode Island student joined a college nursing program in her sophomore year. During her junior year, the college began pressuring her to lose weight. She received a failing grade in a clinical nursing course, for reasons related to her weight rather than her performance. By school rules, the failing grade should have resulted in expulsion from the program. However, the college offered her a contract that allowed her to stay in the program if she lost at least two pounds per week. She failed to lose the weight, was asked to withdraw from the program, and transferred to another nursing program. She sued the college in a federal district court, alleging that it had violated the

Rehabilitation Act and that it had breached an implied contract to educate her. She was awarded damages for breach of contract. The jury determined that the student had substantially performed her obligations under the contract so as to enable her to prevail on her claim against the college. Appeal reached the U.S. Supreme Court. The Supreme Court held that the court of appeals should have reviewed the case *de novo* (as if hearing it for the first time). The appellate court should not have deferred to the district court's determination of what state law would be. Instead, **it should have examined the doctrine of substantial performance to ascertain whether it ought to be applied to a contract in an academic setting**. The Court reversed and remanded the case. *Salve Regina College v. Russell*, 499 U.S. 225, 111 S.Ct. 1217, 113 L.Ed.2d 190 (1991).

## IV. INSURANCE

*Insurance policies may provide coverage for both first- and third-party claims. Third-party claims generally involve liability policies and lawsuits for negligence by employees. Unless an exclusion in the policy specifically exempts a claim from coverage, an insurer may be required to defend and indemnify the policyholder in any lawsuit arising from an injury to a third party.*

◆ *Insurers were obligated to defend and indemnify a New York college that was sued by a man who was injured at a volleyball tournament.*

The man was hurt when a referee's platform collapsed. He sued the college and the tournament sponsor for his injuries. The college asserted cross-claims against the sponsor, which was obligated to indemnify the college by contract. Although the college was listed as an additional insured party on the sponsor's liability policies, the insurers denied a request by the college for defense and indemnification. The college sued the insurers in a state court, which held for the college, ruling that the sponsor had contracted to defend and indemnify it. The insurers were also required to defend and indemnify the college.

On appeal, a state appellate division court noted that the injured party had settled his case for $75,000. Despite the settlement, the case was not moot because the settlement reserved the right to pursue an appeal regarding the college's responsibilities. **The court found the parties had expressly agreed that the sponsor would indemnify the college against all claims for damages based on injuries during the tournament.** The fact that the college was named as an additional insured on the policy created a duty on the part of the insurers to provide a defense. The ruling was affirmed. *Balyszak v. Siena College*, 63 A.D.3d 1409, 882 N.Y.S.2d 335 (N.Y. App. Div. 2009).

◆ *The Third Circuit held a private college's breach of contract claim against its insurance carrier could proceed to trial.*

The college purchased a policy that covered repairs necessary to return property to pre-fire condition. It bought a separate "Ordinance and Law Endorsement" that covered loss to the undamaged portion of a building if it had to be fixed to comply with any ordinance or law. The insurance carrier denied coverage for fire damage caused to the upper floors of a dormitory. The college sued the carrier in a federal district court for breach of contract, contending the endorsement provided coverage for repair and renovation costs required by the Americans with Disabilities Act (ADA). It asserted that the endorsement covered numerous accessibility upgrades made to the building because they had to be done to comply with the ADA. The court held the protections of the ADA did not apply to dormitory space on the second, third and fourth floors of the building. It found they were akin to apartments. The court held for the carrier, and the college appealed to the Third Circuit. It held the repairs to the dormitory were alterations within the meaning of the ADA because they included remodeling, renovation or reconstruction. **The court agreed with the college's contention that because dorms are part of boarding colleges, they are places of education.** The ADA prohibited denying disabled students reasonable accommodations that would allow them to live in its dorms. The court held the ADA applied to all four floors of the dormitory. It reversed the judgment. *Regents of Mercersburg College v. Republic Franklin Insurance Co.*, 458 F.3d 159 (3d Cir. 2006).

◆ *A liability insurer did not have to defend a university accused of fraud.*

A Florida university did not disclose in its catalog that its physical therapy program's accreditation status was probationary. When the applicable accrediting organization withdrew the program's certification, students who had enrolled in the program became ineligible for a physical therapy licensing examination. They sued the university in a state court for breach of contract, fraud, and violation of the Florida Deceptive and Unfair Trade Practices Act. The university sought to have its liability insurer defend and indemnify it in the action, but the Florida District Court of Appeal held for the insurer. Here, **the insurance policy covered any bodily injury caused by an occurrence, and defined "occurrence" as an accident**. However, the students were alleging intentionally fraudulent conduct by the university, not anything accidental. Fraud in the inducement could not be accidental. The university would have to defend itself in the action. *Barry Univ. v. Fireman's Fund Insurance Co. of Wisconsin*, 845 So.2d 276 (Fla. Dist. Ct. App. 2003).

◆ *A North Dakota university was entitled to coverage for flood damage in a case that reached the state's supreme court.*

After a record rainfall, the Red River flooded, and the city of Grand Forks shut down two sanitary sewer lift stations that serviced the University of North Dakota campus. As a result, water entered 22 campus buildings through the sewer system and damaged boiler and machinery equipment. The university's insurer denied coverage on the grounds that the sewer backup actually was caused by flooding, which was excluded by the policy. The university asserted that the damage was caused instead by the sewer backup, and that the policy therefore provided coverage. In the lawsuit that followed, a jury ruled in favor of the university, finding that the flood was not the efficient proximate cause of the damage. (Efficient proximate cause is the predominating cause of the loss, though not necessarily the last act in the chain of events, nor the triggering cause of the loss.) **The jury determined that the sewer backup, not the flood, was the efficient proximate cause of the damage.** The North Dakota Supreme Court affirmed, noting that the jury had properly considered the evidence before finding that the sewer backup caused the loss. Accordingly, the court upheld the jury's award of $3.35 million to the university. *Western National Insurance Co. v. Univ. of North Dakota*, 643 N.W.2d 4 (N.D. 2002).

◆ *An insurer had to contribute to a Colorado university's defense costs.*

A Colorado professor sued a university in state court for denial of tenure, wrongful termination, defamation and breach of contract, among other claims. Eighteen months later, she filed a second lawsuit against the university in federal court, but chose not to include the defamation claim. The lawsuits were consolidated in federal court, and a question of insurance coverage then arose – namely, which insurer (primary or excess) had to pay the costs of defending the university. The primary insurer was held to have the responsibility for defending the first lawsuit because of the defamation claim – the only claim it was potentially liable for paying. **The excess insurer had to contribute $50,000 to the second lawsuit** (where no defamation claim was presented and the primary insurer could not be liable) even though the two cases were consolidated. Here, even though the cases were consolidated and the primary insurer had the primary obligation to defend the lawsuit, the second lawsuit retained its separate identity for purposes of allocating defense costs. *Farmington Casualty Co. v. United Educators Insurance Risk Retention Group, Inc.*, 36 Fed.Appx. 408 (10th Cir. 2002).

◆ *A Missouri medical school could not obtain reimbursement from its insurer for a settlement.*

The medical school agreed to buy land from an energy company that it intended to convert into a parking lot. Before the sale closed, the school's contractor began working on the site, struck and ruptured an underground storage tank, and caused the release of coal tar wastes. The company sued the school and contractor for negligence and trespass, and the school's insurer initially defended it. It withdrew from the defense after a federal court concluded it had no duty to defend. That decision was later reversed. After a court found that the contractor had not trespassed because it had implied permission to work on the site, a settlement was reached. The school then sued its insurer for indemnification. A federal court ruled in favor of the insurer, and the Eighth Circuit affirmed. Here, the policy excluded environmental contamination claims, and the contractor was found not to have trespassed (the only claims for which the insurer could have been liable). Thus, **even though the insurer breached its duty to defend the school, it did not have to indemnify the school for the settlement**. *Royal Insurance Co. of America v. Kirksville College of Osteopathic Medicine*, 304 F.3d 804 (8th Cir. 2002).

◆ *City University of New York (CUNY) did not have to compensate Carnegie Hall Corporation for damages resulting from a student fall at graduation.*

CUNY's licensing agreement with Carnegie Hall allowed CUNY to use the hall for the 1994 graduation ceremony of the university's technical college. The agreement required CUNY to obtain comprehensive general liability insurance to cover any claims arising out of the event, but CUNY never obtained the required coverage. During the ceremony, a graduating student fell on a staircase and sued Carnegie Hall for failing to keep the staircase in a reasonably safe condition. The hall's insurance company ultimately paid $41,987 in settlement fees and defense costs. Carnegie Hall and the insurance company sued CUNY for reimbursement because the university failed to get insurance coverage, as mandated by the license agreement. A state appellate division court held neither Carnegie Hall nor the insurer had any basis for recovery against CUNY. Carnegie Hall had no ground to seek damages from CUNY because it did not incur any financial loss – its insurer paid the expenses related to the student's lawsuit. In addition, **the insurer was not entitled to recover settlement and defense costs. It was not a party to the license agreement, and it did not claim to be a third party to the agreement.** Therefore, any basis for recovery was based on its status as the subrogee of Carnegie Hall. New York's high court previously has ruled that recovery for the breach of a contract requiring the purchase of insurance is limited to the cost of obtaining substitute coverage, and not defense costs. The case was dismissed. *Carnegie Hall Corp. v. City Univ. of New York*, 729 N.Y.S.2d 93 (N.Y. App. Div. 2001).

## V. PRIVATE INSTITUTIONS

*Like their public counterparts, private colleges and universities are liable for negligence if they breach a legal duty. In most situations, institutions have a duty to exercise only "reasonable care" in their activities. A claimant in a tort case must show a legal duty, breach of the duty that proximately caused an injury, and damages. Institutions organized exclusively for religious, charitable, or educational purposes may claim charitable immunity.*

*In* Bloom v. Seton Hall Univ., *704 A.2d 1334 (N.J. Super. Ct. App. Div. 1998), a New Jersey court held nonprofit corporations, societies or associations organized exclusively for religious, charitable, or educational purposes could not be held liable for negligence under the state charitable immunity statute, where the injured party was a beneficiary of the works of the nonprofit corporation, society or association. But in* Mooring v. Virginia Wesleyan College, *514 S.E.2d 619 (Va. 1999), the Supreme Court of Virginia denied charitable immunity to a professor who was not acting on behalf of a charitable institution at the time he injured a beneficiary.*

◆ *A Pennsylvania court held alumnae of a formerly all-female college lacked standing to seek review of the school's decision to go coeducational.*

The private school was founded in 1869 as a women's college. Its charter said the school's purpose was "to promote the education of young women in literature, science and the arts." That changed in 2013, when the board of trustees voted to go coed. It amended its articles of incorporation to reflect the change. Four alumnae challenged the change in court. The department asked the court to dismiss their petition for review, saying the alumnae lacked standing to appeal its decision. The court agreed. To establish standing to appeal a decision of a government agency, the alumnae had to show they had a direct interest in the matter and were aggrieved by the agency's decision. They didn't meet this test. The challengers graduated more than 30 years before the events at issue took place. Further, they aren't directly affected by whether the school is single sex or coeducational. **A person's status as a graduate of a** school does not confer standing to challenge changes in the school's "practices, structure or governance," the court said. The petition for review was dismissed. *Tishok v. Dep't of Educ.*, 133 A.3d 118 (Pa. Commw. Ct. 2016).

◆ *A Missouri federal court dismissed a laundry list of claims filed by a student who graduated from a private college.*

The student graduated from a private college in 2013. She had a variety of problems during her last two years of classes. She told the school she was "suffering from a possible terminal illness." After she graduated, she retained an on-campus job. When she continued to have problems, the university terminated her employment. She alleged several claims, including negligence. She claimed the school had a duty to assist her after she made it aware of her alleged illness. Among other things, she said the school should have checked on her well-being on a daily basis. But the court noted that **she only vaguely alleged that she had a "possible terminal illness" – and no such duty was triggered by her ambiguous statement**. That claim – and the others – were dismissed. *Gillis v. Principia Corp.*, 111 F.Supp.3d 978 (E.D. Mo. 2015).

◆ *A federal district court judge in Pennsylvania rejected a claim that a private college should be held liable for the death of a man who suffered a cardiac arrhythmia while playing basketball in a college's gym.*

The man was playing basketball in the gym where his son was a student. While playing, the man had a heart attack. Someone called 911, and an ambulance took him to a hospital. The school's public safety office did not respond before local police. The man died. Nine years later, his wife sued the college and others under 42 U.S.C. § 1983. She said the 911 call necessarily would have been routed through the school's public safety office, and she alleged that the office did not respond quickly enough. The college and other defendants filed a motion to dismiss, arguing that the claims raised were time barred. The court held that even if the complaint stated a valid claim under Section 1983, it would've been time barred. **Section 1983 does not have its own statute of limitations, the court said, and courts are to borrow an analogous statute of limitations from the state where the cause of action arose.** In Pennsylvania, the limitations period for this Section 1983 claim was two years. The wife filed the suit nine years after her husband died. The defense motion was granted. *Mast v. Lafayette College*, No. 13-4161 2015 WL 409774 (E.D. Pa. 1/30/15).

◆ *A California state court ordered a private university to pay damages to a transgender female student who was banned from university businesses open to the public.*

A religious private university ran businesses that were open to the public. The student, a pre-operative transgender female, was admitted on a merit scholarship. On her application, she listed her gender as "female." When the school became aware of the student's transgender status, it said the student misrepresented herself as a female. It expelled the student and banned her from all university properties. She sued, alleging the university breached the state's Unruh Civil Rights Act. That law protects all persons from discrimination in "all business establishments" – including private businesses. The court found that as a values-based, religious, non-profit educational institution, the "on-campus educational program is not subject to the act as a matter of law" – **but the same was not true of its operations not based on religion or values and open to the public.** They were subject to the law as business establishments. The court granted the university judgment on the challenge to the student's expulsion. But it held the school illegally excluded the student from its business establishments due to her transgender status. It awarded her $4,000 in statutory damages on that claim. *Cabading v. California Baptist Univ.*, No. RIC1302245 (Super. Ct. Cal. 7/11/14).

◆ *The Mississippi Supreme Court held an arbitrator, not a court, had to consider a challenge to the validity of enrollment contracts.*

Virginia College (VC) is a private chain of institutions that offers online study options. VC enrollment and tuition agreements for surgical technology students had an arbitration clause. Thirty-one surgical technology students sued VC in a Mississippi court, claiming it falsely represented to them that its program was or would be accredited for appropriate professional licensure. VC asked the court to compel the students to arbitrate their claims, but the court held the enrollment contract and arbitration clause were both invalid because VC had fraudulently induced the students to sign them. On appeal, the Mississippi Supreme Court held the claims had to be arbitrated. Arbitration agreements are severable from a contract in which they might appear. **Under established law, courts leave challenges to the validity of a contract to an arbitrator.** Since the students did not claim VC fraudulently induced them to enter the arbitration agreement, their claim had to be heard by an arbitrator. *Virginia College LLC v. Blackmon*, 109 So.3d 1050 (Miss. 2013).

◆ *A federal district court upheld an Alabama college's decision to expel a student who sent a series of harassing messages to college officials.*

The student sent anonymous letters to a college vice president and the college president. The letters included harassing and threatening language. After an investigation, the student admitted writing the letters. The president decided to expel her immediately. She sued the college for First Amendment and due process violations, negligence, and breach of contract. The court rejected the First Amendment and due process claims. **As the college was a private institution, it could not be subjected to constitutional liability.** The court found no breach of contract based on student handbook violations. The handbook was not a binding contract, and it had language declaring it was subject to revision at the discretion of the college. Even if the handbook was considered a contract, it allowed for the immediate expulsion of students who engaged in conduct that might violate the law. As college officials were confident that the student's conduct could be prosecuted, the court held in its favor. *Cook v. Talladega College*, 908 F.Supp.2d 1214 (N.D. Ala. 2012).

◆ *A New York court rejected a personal injury claim because evidence showed a sidewalk where a pedestrian slipped and fell had been regularly shoveled.*

A pedestrian slipped and fell on a sidewalk on a university campus. He claimed that the fall took place during a snowstorm, and he had a meteorologist prepare a statement that the ice that caused the fall was there before the storm. A state court held for the university, and appeal went to a state appellate division court. In the court's view, no evidence supported the meteorologist's statement. **A building custodian testified the area of the fall was shoveled and salted at least twice per weekday during the relevant time.** Based on this evidence, the court affirmed the judgment for the university. *Rand v. Cornell Univ.*, 91 A.D.3d 542, 937 N.Y.S.2d 49 (N.Y. App. Div. 2012).

◆  *Under New York law, students could not be liable for injuries to another student at a party unless it was foreseeable that she would get drunk.*

A 19-year-old Ithaca College sophomore drank alcohol at a party. She then fell from a balcony and was seriously hurt. Her parents sued Ithaca in a state court, claiming the college was liable because the balcony and railings were unsafe and negligently designed. Ithaca sought contribution from five students who shared the apartment and from the architect who designed the balcony and railings. The college claimed the injuries were caused, at least in part, by the fact that the students who hosted the party supplied the student with alcohol. The trial court denied pretrial judgment to a student who had provided alcohol. But another who did not know the student was at the party until after the accident avoided liability. On appeal, a New York Appellate Division Court affirmed the judgment. Under state law, the students could not be liable unless it was foreseeable that someone at the party would get drunk, engage in a fight, and cause an injury. That showing was not made. **There was no common law claim based on negligent provision of alcohol to underage drinkers.** *O'Neill v. Ithaca College*, 56 A.D.3d 869, 866 N.Y.S.2d 809 (N.Y. App. Div. 2008).

◆  *Private institutions must exercise reasonable care to protect students from foreseeable criminal or dangerous acts by third persons.*

A New York private college student was punched in the face by a classmate during a classroom altercation. He sued the college in the state court system for negligently failing to prevent the attack. The court held for the college, and the student appealed. The New York Supreme Court, Appellate Division, held that to prove negligence, there must be a breach of a legal duty that proximately caused damages. **The court noted that colleges generally have no duty to shield students from dangers presented by other students.** However, **they must exercise reasonable care to protect students from reasonably foreseeable criminal or dangerous acts committed by others**, including other students. In this case, the college did not breach any duty, because the injury was the result of a "sudden, unexpected, and unforeseeable act." The attack was not foreseeable, so the college's failure to prevent it was not negligent. The judgment was affirmed. *Luina v. Katharine Gibbs School New York, Inc.*, 830 N.Y.S.2d 263 (N.Y. App. Div. 2007).

◆  *A private Connecticut university was not liable for harassment of a student based on his religion.*

The student attended a doctoral program in management systems. He claimed one of his professors suggested he adopt some Chinese heritage and culture, and that another remarked that he had a "mind like a computer." The student told the professor his mental abilities came from God. The professor responded, "It doesn't come from God, it comes from David, from the Jewish religion." A third professor allegedly made a remark about the student being Catholic. The student claimed several other faculty members also harassed him, delayed his presentation of his doctoral thesis, and prevented him from taking classes. He sued the university, claiming it violated state and federal laws when it harassed him based on his religion. The student alleged the university violated his federal civil rights, as protected by 42 U.S.C. § 1983. **The university argued it was a private entity that could not be sued for federal civil rights violations.** The student contended that as the university received some federal funding, the court should further determine if its acts or decisions would be considered functions of the state. The court agreed with the university and granted its motion for summary judgment. *Martin v. Univ. of New Haven*, 359 F.Supp.2d 185 (D. Conn. 2005).

◆   *A Vermont university was liable for over $2 million in damages for hazing.*

A five-year veteran of the Navy enrolled in the Military College of Vermont of Norwich University under a Navy Reserve Officer Training Corps scholarship. He lasted for only 16 days, during which he was subjected to, and observed, repeated instances of hazing by upperclassmen. After withdrawing from school, he sued the university for assault and battery, infliction of emotional distress and negligence, asserting that it was vicariously liable for the actions of the upperclassmen. A jury returned a verdict in the student's favor, awarding him almost $500,000 in compensatory damages and $1.75 million in punitive damages. The Supreme Court of Vermont affirmed the compensatory damage award against the university, but reversed the award of punitive damages, finding no evidence of malice on the university's part. Here, **the university had charged the upperclassmen with "indoctrinating and orienting" the student**. As a result, this was not a simple case of student-on-student hazing for which the university could not be held liable. Because the upperclassmen were acting as agents of the university, it breached its duty of care toward the student. The court also found that the nearly $500,000 in compensatory damages awarded by the jury was not clearly erroneous. *Brueckner v. Norwich Univ.*, 730 A.2d 1086 (Vt. 1999).

◆   *An errors and omissions policy did not provide a private Texas college coverage for losses caused by a board member's misrepresentations.*

A Texas Christian College purchased a "school leaders errors and omissions" policy that insured it against wrongful acts committed by directors and officers of the school. Subsequently, a member of the board of trustees convinced the board to invest $2 million of its endowment funds in a company that accepted accounts receivable as security for short-term loans. However, he did not disclose that the company had a negative net worth, that he was a 49% owner of the company, or that he also was a salaried employee of the company.

When the investment failed, the college obtained the board member's resignation, then sued him and his company for misrepresentation of certain facts and for making false statements. The college obtained a judgment against the board member for $1.8 million and against the company for $2 million. Unable to collect on the judgments, it sought to collect under its errors and omissions policy. The insurer denied coverage under the "fraud or dishonesty" exclusion and the "personal profit or advantage" exclusion. A Texas federal court held that the two exclusions applied to bar coverage, and the college appealed to the Fifth Circuit, which affirmed as **the exclusion for "any claim arising out of the gaining in fact of any personal profit or advantage to which the Insured is not legally entitled" applied to bar coverage**. Here, the board member clearly gained a personal advantage by his company's receipt of the $2 million in endowment funds from the college. Despite the fact that the board member did not ultimately make a profit, he did gain a personal advantage by his wrongful acts. As a result, the insurer had no obligation to pay out under the policy. *Jarvis Christian College v. National Union Fire Insurance Co.*, 197 F.3d 742 (5th Cir. 1999).

◆ *A New York college could declare an alumnus "persona non grata" and bar him from campus.*

Over the course of his nine years at a college, a student exhibited disruptive behavior on campus and began receiving psychiatric treatment. His mother allegedly warned a nurse that he might act violently at his graduation ceremony, and security guards questioned him shortly before the ceremony began. However, the ceremony took place without any trouble. A month later, the student was declared "persona non grata" by the college and was barred from the campus. He eventually sued the college and the nurse. A state court ruled for the defendants, and the New York Supreme Court, Appellate Division, affirmed. Here, **since he had graduated, he was no longer a student and was not entitled to due process as a result of the college barring him from campus**. Further, his claims against the nurse could not succeed because he could not show that she breached a duty to keep information confidential. *Godinez v. Siena College*, 733 N.Y.S.2d 262 (N.Y. App. Div. 2001).

# CHAPTER TEN

## University Operations

## I. GOVERNMENT REGULATION

### A. Public Records and Freedom of Information

*Enacted in 1966, the federal Freedom of Information Act (FOIA) 5 U.S.C. § 552, provides that any person has a right, enforceable in court, to obtain access to federal agency records, except as protected by an exemption such as law enforcement, personnel records and other confidential items. States have analogous freedom of information and data practices acts that govern the disclosure of government data and create procedures for requesting records.*

◆ *Connecticut's highest court affirmed a ruling that held reports concerning grievances filed against a state-system higher ed employee are matters of public record.*

A university's orthopedic surgeon filed a grievance against the chairman of the orthopedic department. The health center's appeals committee and the university's president emeritus wrote reports in response to the grievance. The surgeon requested copies of both documents under the state's Freedom of Information Act. The university denied the request, saying it fell under an exception for a "record of the performance and evaluation of a faculty or professional staff member" of a unit of the state system of higher education. The issue reached the state's highest court, which affirmed the reports were public records for two reasons for two reasons. First, the court's own precedent of strictly limiting exceptions to the Freedom of Information Act; and second, legislative history surrounding this exception. Among other things, the records showed lawmakers enacted the exception in response to student organizations' efforts to gain access to student evaluations of faculty. The court determined the exception was only intended to protect faculty and professional staff in the state's system of higher ed institutions from having their performance reviews and student evaluations made available to the public. **There was no evidence that lawmakers intended to give that protection to reports about a grievance.** So the supreme court affirmed the lower court's decision that the reports were public records. *Lieberman v. Aronow*, 319 Conn. 748 (Conn. 2015).

◆ *Connecticut's highest court denied a freedom of information act request for databases containing information that could be considered trade secrets.*

A private individual sought database information from the University of Connecticut relating to season ticket buyers, subscribers, individual event ticket buyers, library donors and others. The university claimed the information was exempt from disclosure under the state's freedom of information act. It said the databases were trade secrets that qualified for an exemption for "contact and/or other information related to students." A state commission found the databases were not "customer lists" protected by the trade secret exemption. The commission held the university was not required to disclose the library list with respect to people who had requested anonymity or information that would personally identify students, it said the university otherwise had to comply with the request. Appeal reached the Supreme Court of Connecticut.

The court held the university could create a trade secret that was entitled to an exemption under the state's freedom of information act. **The state law definition of "trade secrets" focused on the nature and accessibility of the information, not whether the entity holding the information was engaged in a trade.** In fact, there was no requirement that an entity be engaged in a trade before claiming entitlement to the trade secret exemption. As the information sought in this case met the statutory criteria for trade secrets, a lower court ruling denying the request for access was affirmed. *Univ. of Connecticut v. Freedom of Information Comm'n*, 303 Conn. 724, 36 A.3d 663 (Conn. 2012).

◆ *The Florida public records law did not shield the NCAA from disclosing to the media documents from investigation reports it kept on a secure website.*

Florida State University (FSU) learned that staff members gave improper assistance to student-athletes. It conducted an investigation, then turned over its findings to the NCAA. Months later, the NCAA issued FSU a formal notice of allegations to initiate disciplinary proceedings for the reported misconduct. An NCAA committee issued an infractions report and imposed penalties for academic misconduct, including the forfeiture of some games. To prepare an appeal, FSU lawyers viewed documents posted on a secure NCAA website. The Associated Press (AP) sought disclosure of the NCAA documents in a state court action. A state court held for the AP, finding the documents were "public records" as they were received by a state agency and not exempt under federal laws (they contained no information directly related to a student).

A Florida District Court of Appeal noted Chapter 119 had a public policy of keeping public records open for personal inspection and copying. It held **the Public Records Law applied to documents maintained on a computer in the same way that it would apply to those kept in a file cabinet**. A document may qualify as a public record if it was prepared by a private party, if it was received by the government and used in the transaction of public business. The term "received" referred to examination of a document on a remote computer, as had taken place in this case. The requested documents did not reveal the identity of any student, so federal law did not prohibit disclosure. Since the documents were "received" by FSU lawyers in connection with public business, the Public Records Law applied, and the documents had to be disclosed. *NCAA v. Associated Press*, 18 So.3d 1201 (Fla. Dist. Ct. App. 2009).

◆ *Two Wisconsin veterans could not proceed with a court challenge to a proposal to change the name of a university football stadium.*

In 1945, the city of La Crosse chose the name Veterans Memorial Stadium for the football facility at the University of Wisconsin-La Crosse (UWL). Between 2000 and 2005, the name of the facility was changed three times. The veterans said the 2000 and 2001 name changes violated Wisconsin's open meetings and public records laws and UWL policies. They claimed the changes resulted from "malfeasance" by UWL's board of regents. A state circuit court dismissed the case, finding that the veterans failed to show they had suffered any injury and thus lacked standing to pursue their claims.

The Court of Appeals of Wisconsin agreed with the trial court that the veterans lacked standing to challenge the name change. **To have standing, or the legal right to bring an action, a party must show he has suffered an injury or has been threatened with an injury as a result of the other party's conduct.** In addition, the injury must be to a legally protectable interest. The veterans did not allege any direct personal injury as a result of the name changes. Their concern that the name changes did not sufficiently honor veterans was not a "direct personal injury" that gave them the right to bring an action against UWL. The court affirmed the judgment for UWL. *Nedvidek v. Kuipers*, No. 2006AP3077, 747 N.W.2d 527 (Table), 2008 WI App. 51, 2008 WL 516781 (Wis. Ct. App. 2/28/08). The Supreme Court of Wisconsin dismissed a later appeal. *Nedvidek v. Kuipers*, 766 N.W.2d 205 (Wis. 2009).

◆ *A Michigan university police report had to be reviewed by a trial court judge in chambers to consider if parts of it were exempt from public disclosure.*

Three men were arrested in connection with an assault on the campus of Michigan State University (MSU). A news organization asked MSU for a copy of its police incident report related to the incident. The request was filed under the state freedom of information act (FOIA). The organization had already published a story with the names of three men who were arrested for the assault, but it wanted additional information from the report, such as personally identifiable information relating to victims, witnesses, and police officers. The report also included photographs and statements from the responding officers and others. MSU officials denied the request, saying disclosure would violate individual privacy rights and interfere with the law enforcement investigation.

The case reached the Michigan Court of Appeals, which held MSU did not show FOIA privacy and law enforcement exemptions applied. It held the trial court had wrongfully failed to review the report to decide if parts of it could be separated and disclosed without violating privacy rights or interfering with the investigation. Appeal reached the Supreme Court of Michigan, which held that unless a FOIA exemption provided otherwise, the relevant time to consider was when the public body asserted the exemption. **The passage of time and the course of events after asserting a FOIA exception did not affect whether a public record was initially exempt from disclosure.** This part of the appeals court decision was reversed, and the case was returned to the trial court. Upon return to that court, the judge was to inspect the police incident report in chambers to determine what information was exempt from disclosure, to make particularized findings regarding disclosure or nondisclosure, and to separate any exempt material from nonexempt material. *State News v. Michigan State Univ.*, 481 Mich. 692, 753 N.W.2d 20 (Mich. 2008).

◆  *A federal district court found a Montana student had no constitutional right to his school transcripts and or continued enrollment at a state university.*

A sophomore at Montana State University (MSU) enrolled in a program that would enable him to study in England. After leaving his studies in England early, officials at the school in England informed officials at MSU that he had left without completing his exams and that he owed rent at his residence hall. MSU responded by suspending the student for the remainder of the summer term, terminating his financial aid, and placing a hold on all of his academic records. After his grievance was denied, he sued university officials in federal court, claiming they unconstitutionally deprived him of his property interest in continued enrollment and transcripts without due process. A federal magistrate judge recommended dismissing the case. The court adopted the recommendation. **Legal precedent established that a student has no property interest in a transcript, which is owned by the school and not the student.** As to the other claim, there is no clearly established right to continued enrollment. Summary judgment was granted to the university officials. *Comer v. Meyers*, No. CV-06-65 BURFC, 2007 WL 1810684 (D. Mont. 6/20/07).

◆  *Massachusetts' highest court held incident reports and other documents held by a private university police department were not "public records."*

A student newspaper asked two municipal police departments and Harvard University's police department for all records related to certain incidents listed on the university department's weekly log of complaints, including incident reports and correspondence. The municipal police departments supplied the documents to the newspaper, but the university asserted it did not have to comply with the public records law because it was not a public entity.

The newspaper asked a state court for an order requiring the university to release the documents. The court dismissed the case, ruling that private university officers were not governmental employees. Accordingly, documents they made or received were not "public records." The newspaper appealed to the Supreme Judicial Court of Massachusetts, arguing the appointment of some university officers as special state police officers or deputy sheriffs vested them with broad police powers. Under this theory, they were subject to public records law requirements. **The court held the university records were not covered by the state public records law and did not have to be disclosed.** The judgment for Harvard was affirmed. *Harvard Crimson v. President and Fellows of Harvard College*, 445 Mass. 745, 840 N.E.2d 518 (Mass. 2006).

◆ *The Supreme Court of Iowa held a state university could not shield its financial records from public view by outsourcing certain university functions.*

University financial records were managed by a private nonprofit foundation that had been incorporated by the university in 1958. In 2002, the university and foundation renewed an elaborate service agreement. In the agreement, the university expressed its desire to engage the expertise of the foundation as an independent contractor to provide advice, coordination, and assistance in fundraising, development, and in the operation, accounting and fund investment management of those areas.

A group of citizens sought a state court order to view university tax and financial records under the Iowa Freedom of Information Act, I.C.A. § 22.1, *et seq.* The act creates a public right to view governmental records. The court held the foundation was not a government body under the act, so its documents were not "public records." On appeal, the Supreme Court of Iowa stated "public records" included documents or other information belonging to the state, school corporation, or nonprofit corporation whose facilities are supported with property tax revenue, and relate to the investment of public funds. **The court held the foundation was performing a government function through the contract with the university, so its records were subject to public disclosure.** It said a government body may not outsource its functions to a private corporation and then keep the information from the public. In executing the service agreement, the university, a government body, contracted away its ability to raise money and manage its finances to what was assumed to be a nongovernment body. The university had attempted to do indirectly what it could not do directly – avoid disclosure of what would otherwise be public records. The court held the act prevented this result and reversed the judgment. *Gannon v. Board of Regents of State of Iowa*, 692 N.W.2d 31 (Iowa 2005).

## B. Aliens and Immigration

*A federal immigration law, 8 U.S.C. § 1623, bars the states from providing "any postsecondary education benefit" to illegal aliens "on the basis of residence within a state" – unless U.S. citizens are also eligible for the benefit. Another federal law, 8 U.S.C. § 1621, generally makes illegal aliens ineligible for state or local public benefits. In* Martinez v. Regents of the Univ. of California, *this chapter, the Supreme Court of California upheld a state law provision making illegal aliens eligible for an in-state tuition rate as long as they satisfied certain criteria. These are: attendance at a high school in the state for at least three years, graduation from a high school in the state, registration at an accredited California higher education institution, and an affidavit indicating the intention to seek legalized immigration status.*

◆ *Florida regulations denying in-state tuition rates to children of undocumented residents were held invalid under the Equal Protection Clause.*

A Florida law disqualified from resident status any dependent child whose parents were not state residents. Any dependent child who could not show his or her parents were in the country legally was disqualified from resident status under a state regulation. Five high school graduates who were born in the U.S. and resided in Florida sued state officials under the Equal Protection Clause. Although they could not provide proof of their parents' federal immigration status, they were not aliens. According to the state, the classification was needed to prevent the loss of $200 million a year in tuition revenue. The court rejected this argument, finding that the state would not be required to offer in-state tuition to all U.S. citizens. The state could still distinguish between in-state and out-of-state residents. **By classifying the students as aliens, the state created a second tier of citizenship that depreciated the historic values of citizenship.** The court found the classification was not reasonably related to any state interest in ensuring that in-state tuition rates were provided only to those who intended to stay in Florida. The state's definition of "legal resident" and the state regulation violated the Equal Protection Clause. *Ruiz v. Robinson*, 892 F.Supp.2d 1321 (S.D. Fla. 2012).

◆ *A New York university that disenrolled a Nigerian engineering student after his arrest by federal agents had to provide him with his official transcript.*

The university disenrolled the student after U.S. State Department special agents arrested him on campus because they suspected that he had fraudulently obtained his F-1 student visa. The university never conducted a hearing into the matter, but it deemed the charges against him to be true. The expulsion led to the student's deportation and cut short his higher education. He sought a copy of his official transcript to help him continue his education elsewhere, but the university refused to provide it on the grounds that he owed various fees. When the student sued the university for due process violations, a federal district court held in his favor. However, a hearing would not benefit him because he could not presently re-enter the country. As a result, **the court ordered the university to provide the student with his official transcripts, despite the fact that withholding them was not related to the due process violation**. The university also had to convene a new hearing, when and if he was ever able to re-enter the United States and request one. *Oladokun v. Ryan*, No. 06 cv 2330(KMW), 2011 WL 4471882 (S.D.N.Y. 9/27/11).

◆ *A foreign student was unable to obtain relief in a federal court action asserting constitutional violations when her name was accidentally removed from a Utah university's international student list.*

The student sued Weber State University in a federal court, claiming a computer glitch caused the removal of her name from the university's list of international students. She raised several state law and constitutional claims, asserting her legal status to be a student in the U.S. had been accidentally taken away. A federal magistrate judge found the university was immune from suit because it was an arm of the state of Utah. **The student's constitutional claim failed because she did not assert discrimination by any individual**, and her claim of cruel and unusual treatment failed because the case did not involve prison officials or penological responsibilities. Since the court lacked jurisdiction over the state law claims, the case was recommended for dismissal. A federal district court adopted the recommendation, and the student appealed to the U.S. Court of Appeals, Tenth Circuit. It affirmed the district court's decision, concluding that the student had failed to identify any reversible error. *Sethunya v. Weber State Univ.*, 382 Fed.Appx. 793 (10th Cir. 2010).

◆   *The Supreme Court of California upheld a state law allowing illegal aliens to pay in-state tuition rates at state public universities and colleges.*

A number of out-of-state U.S. citizens sued the Regents of the University of California in a state court, alleging a state law allowing illegal aliens to pay in-state tuition rates violated federal immigration law. After the court dismissed the case, the state court of appeal reversed the judgment, finding the state law was preempted by federal law and that the citizens could pursue Equal Protection and Privileges and Immunities challenges. On appeal, the Supreme Court of California found the state law conditioned in-state tuition to those who had attended a California high school for at least three years, graduated from a high school in the state and met certain other requirements. According to the court, the state law did not violate 8 U.S.C. § 1623, which is a federal immigration law. Section 1623 bars the provision of education benefits to illegal aliens only when a benefit was provided on the basis of state residence.

**The court found California was not providing an education benefit to illegal aliens on the basis of state residency**, but was offering in-state tuition rates based on satisfaction of the other criteria. The court also found the state law did not violate 8 U.S.C. § 1621. While that section generally made illegal aliens ineligible for state or local public benefits, it also said **states may enact laws negating the ineligibility and extending benefits to illegal aliens**, as California had done. The court found no legal authority for a Privileges and Immunities Clause claim by the citizens asserting a privilege "of being treated no worse than an illegal alien in the distribution of public benefits." The court rejected the citizens' other arguments and reversed the judgment. *Martinez v. Regents of the Univ. of California*, 50 Cal.4th 1277, 241 P.3d 855 (Cal. 2010).

◆   *A Muslim scholar was entitled to further consideration of a claim that he was improperly denied a visa without an opportunity to show he did not knowingly support an organization that gave support to terrorist groups.*

The federal Immigration and Nationality Act (INA) makes an alien who has afforded material support to terrorist organizations ineligible for a visa. The American Academy of Religion and the American Association of University Professors sued the Department of Homeland Security in a federal court, challenging the exclusion of a well-known Muslim scholar who shuns violence and has spoken out against terrorism and radical Islam. However, the U.S. revoked his visa because he admitted making donations to an organization that supported terrorist groups. This was a direct violation of the INA. Finding the government excluded him for legitimate reasons, the court held for the U.S.

The organizations appealed to the U.S. Court of Appeals, Second Circuit, arguing that the visa was improperly rejected in violation of a First Amendment right to hear the scholar's views. The court upheld a statutory provision making contributors to terrorist organizations ineligible for visas. **A knowledge requirement provision of the INA required a consular officer to find that the scholar knew his contributions provided material support to a terrorist organization, and to confront him and afford him an opportunity to deny this.** Since the record did not establish that the consular officer who denied the visa confronted the scholar with the claim that he knowingly gave support to Hamas, the court returned the case to the district court. The scholar would be entitled to an opportunity to demonstrate by clear and convincing evidence that he did not know he was supporting a terrorist organization. *American Academy of Religion v. Napolitano*, 573 F.3d 115 (2d Cir. 2009).

◆   *A federal court ordered the University of Pittsburgh to retain a research assistant while she pursued administrative charges of unlawful discrimination.*

The research assistant worked at the university until her supervisor told her that her contract would end due to insufficient funding. If the contract ended on the stated date, the research assistant's visa would expire and she would be forced to return to Russia. She claimed that the decision to end her employment was motivated by national origin discrimination. To support this claim, she noted that her supervisor had hired and/or retained similarly situated Korean employees while non-renewing her contract. A federal district court granted the research assistant's request for an injunction and ordered the university to retain her while she filed administrative charges of discrimination. She showed a reasonable probability of succeeding on the merits of her discrimination claim since she was let go while similarly situated Korean employees were retained. **In addition, if relief was denied, she would either have to return to Russia voluntarily or be subject to immediate deportation.** *Karakozova v. Univ. of Pittsburgh*, No. 09cv0458, 2009 WL 1652469 (W.D. Pa. 6/11/09).

◆   *The Supreme Court struck down a university policy that restricted an alien's right to acquire domicile in a state and thus qualify for in-state tuition.*

The University of Maryland's student fee schedule policy denied students whose parents held nonimmigrant alien visas in-state status, even if they were domiciled in the state, thus denying them preferential fee and tuition schedules. The U.S. Supreme Court found the policy to be in violation of the Supremacy Clause of the U.S. Constitution. The Court stated that the university's policy conflicted directly with the will of Congress as expressed in the Immigration and Nationality Act of 1952. In passing the Immigration and Nationality Act, Congress explicitly decided not to bar nonimmigrant aliens, such as these, the right to acquire domicile in the United States. **The university's policy denying these aliens "in-state" status, solely on the basis of their immigration status, amounted to a burden not contemplated by Congress** in admitting them to the United States. Thus, the University of Maryland's student fee schedule, as applied to these aliens, was held to be unconstitutional. *Toll v. Moreno*, 458 U.S. 1, 102 S.Ct. 2977, 73 L.Ed.2d 563 (1982).

◆ *The right to rebut a presumption of nonresidence extends even to aliens with visas living in state.*

The University of Maryland granted "in-state" tuition status only to students domiciled in Maryland, or, if a student was financially dependent on the student's parents, to students whose parents were domiciled in Maryland. The university also could deny in-state status to individuals who did not pay the full spectrum of Maryland state taxes. The university refused to grant in-state status to a number of students, each of whom was dependent on a parent who held a "G-4 visa" (a nonimmigrant visa granted to officers and employees of international treaty organizations and members of their immediate family). The university stated that the holder of a G-4 visa could not acquire Maryland domicile because the holder was incapable of showing an essential element of domicile – the intent to live permanently or indefinitely in Maryland.

After unsuccessful appeals at the administrative level, the students brought a class action lawsuit in federal court seeking declaratory and injunctive relief. The students alleged that university policy violated the Equal Protection Clause. A federal district court granted relief, stating that the G-4 visa could not create an irrebuttable presumption of nondomicile. On appeal, the U.S. Supreme Court stated that the case was controlled by the principles announced in *Vlandis v. Kline*, this chapter, that **when a state purports to be concerned with domicile, it must provide an individual with the opportunity to present evidence bearing on that issue**. Federal law allows aliens holding a G-4 visa to acquire domicile in the United States. However, the question of whether such domicile could be acquired in Maryland was a question of state law. Since no controlling precedent had been decided by the state's highest court, the Supreme Court declined to rule and certified the question to the Maryland Court of Appeals for resolution. *Elkins v. Moreno*, 435 U.S. 647, 98 S.Ct. 1338, 55 L.Ed.2d 614 (1978).

## C.  Residency and Tuition Issues

*State laws creating favorable in-state tuition rates are valid insofar as they create a presumption of residency based on reliable indicators. However, an inflexible or improperly applied presumption is open to challenge.*

◆ *A state appeals court upheld a determination that a student was not a resident of Wisconsin for purposes of determining her tuition rate.*

The student was born in Illinois and lived there with her parents until she enrolled at a Wisconsin state university. During the summers, she lived and worked in Illinois. She paid nonresident tuition rates. After she graduated, she moved into a house in Wisconsin. She commuted to Illinois for work twice a week. She filled out an application for the university's pharmacy school. She applied as a nonresident and listed an Illinois address as her permanent home address. After her first year in the program, she tried to change her status from nonresident to resident for tuition purposes. An appeals committee twice rejected her application for in-state status. A court upheld the committee's determination, and the student filed an appeal. The appeals court explained that pursuant to a relevant Wisconsin statute, the determinative factor in deciding residency – and entitlement to in-state tuition rates – is whether the person has intended, for the prior 12 months, to establish and maintain a permanent home in the state. Although the student filed income taxes, registered to vote, owned a car and had a driver's license in Wisconsin, **that wasn't enough, the court held, explaining that she also maintained substantial ties with Illinois – working there and visiting frequently**. The record adequately supported the committee's decision that the student did not meet her burden of showing residence in Wisconsin for the requisite 12 months. The decision was affirmed. *Lukanich v. Board of Regents of the Univ. of Wisconsin System*, 359 Wis.2d 268 (Wis. Ct. App. 2014).

◆  *A New York appeals court reversed a ruling that dismissed the claims of a student who was wrongfully denied tuition reimbursement after being terminated from a study abroad program.*

The student was enrolled in a London-based program offered by a state-side university. He did not complete the program. The school said the student voluntarily withdrew more than four weeks into the semester. That meant he wasn't entitled to tuition reimbursement. The student claimed a London-based employee of the school sent him a letter telling him his student status in the program was being terminated and he needed to sign a particular form. The form apparently indicated that he was being placed on "voluntary medical leave." When parents sued to recover tuition, the school balked. At the trial level, the school filed a motion to dismiss. The trial court granted the motion, and the student appealed. The appeals court found the school did not conclusively establish the student voluntarily withdrew. And **there were questionable circumstances surrounding the form.** As a result, the appeals court decided that the case could proceed. The trial court's ruling was reversed. *Uddin v. New York Univ.*, 47 Misc.3d 38 (N.Y. App. Div. 2014).

◆  *Because her enrollment agreement included a clause requiring arbitration of any disputes, a student could not proceed with her claim that she was illegally denied financial aid assistance.*

When the student enrolled at the school, the agreement included a clause that stated "any disputes, claims or controversies" would be resolved by way of arbitration. The arbitration provision specifically mentioned that disputes relating to financial aid were subject to arbitration. The student initially enrolled in a three-credit course. She claimed the school told her those hours were enough to qualify her for federal financial aid and a stipend. However, she claimed she was later told that under federal regulations, she needed to take at least four credits to be eligible. She filed suit, alleging the school wrongfully refused to disburse her financial aid. The school denied it promised the student financial aid. **It argued the dispute could not proceed in court because it was subject to arbitration.** The court dismissed the student's claim, as the dispute was subject to arbitration. *Grasty v. Colorado Technical Institute*, No. 13 CV 3221, 2014 WL 3937889 (N.D. Ill. 8/12/14).

◆  *Purchasing a home in Vermont was not enough to establish residency, so a student was not entitled to the in-state tuition rate at a state university.*

A student moved to Vermont from out of state and enrolled at the University of Vermont. He planned to earn an undergraduate degree there and then enter the university's medical school. For the first three years, he paid the out-of-state tuition rate. Then he applied for in-state tuition, saying he'd decided to stay in Vermont. The application was denied. He reapplied a second and third time, and both requests were denied. He reapplied a fourth time and produced evidence of residency, such as showing banking and financial relationships with the state, being registered to vote in the state and paying taxes to the state. He also claimed he had become financially independent, noting that he'd purchased a home. His fourth application was denied. The trial court upheld the school's ruling that the student had established a domicile in the state, but only for the purpose of attending the university. The student appealed, and the state's highest court upheld the decision, saying the state legislature authorized the school to set rules for in-state tuition rates, and it pointed out that **the standard of proof for eligibility for in-state tuition is higher than the standard for proving domicile**. The evidence also supported that he wasn't financially independent. His father was a co-buyer on the home the student purchased. So he didn't provide enough evidence to meet the high bar set by the state school's requirements to be eligible for in-state tuition. *Roberts v. Univ. of Vermont*, 70 A.3d 1058 (Vt. 2013).

◆  *A student who failed to show she had established residency in Oregon was not entitled to the in-state tuition rate at a state university.*

An Oklahoma student moved to Oregon at the age of 22, at a time when she was financially independent. More than a year later, she enrolled at a state university and sought to qualify for the in-state tuition rate. Her request was denied by a university committee, which found she was not a resident of Oregon for tuition purposes. The state board of education upheld the determination, ruling that to prove residency, students must establish and maintain a domicile in Oregon for at least 12 straight months and be primarily engaged in activities other than those of being a college student. A state circuit court then held the second requirement for establishing entitlement to the in-state tuition rate was unconstitutional, as it created an irrebuttable presumption against residency for students who attended school in the state within 12 months of moving there.

On appeal, the Court of Appeals of Oregon found **the student did not give up her residency in Oklahoma and failed to establish and maintain a domicile in Oregon for at least 12 straight months**. It held reviewing courts should not address constitutional challenges when a case can be resolved otherwise. In this case, the court held the circuit court should have affirmed the board's decision on the domicile issue. The judgment was reversed, and the case was returned to the lower court with instructions to reinstate the board's decision. *Deatherage v. Pernsteiner*, 239 Or.App. 161, 243 P.3d 865 (Or. Ct. App. 2010). The Supreme Court of Oregon denied review in *Deatherage v. Pernsteiner*, 249 Or. 664, 249 P.3d 1282 (Or. 2011).

◆   *A state court upheld a determination by Florida Atlantic University (FAU)*
*that a student did not qualify for resident tuition rates.*

After graduating from a Michigan high school, the student went to Florida
to attend a community college. Three years later, she transferred to FAU. After
a year at FAU, the student took steps to qualify as a resident of the state for in-
state tuition rates. She obtained a Florida driver's license and executed a
declaration of domicile. FAU denied the student's application to reclassify her
as a Florida resident for tuition purposes, and she commenced a state court
action against FAU. A Florida district court of appeal explained that a student
seeking to qualify for resident tuition rates must show Florida residency for the
previous 12 months, and that Florida is the student's permanent domicile. In
this case, there was sufficient evidence to support FAU's conclusion that
residency in Florida was merely incident to the student's school enrollment.

Although the student had been in the state for the previous 12 months, she
did not produce enough evidence to show she intended to reside in Florida
permanently. **She did not own real property in the state or have a vehicle
registered there, and she did not work there on a full-time basis.** In
addition, the student did not get her Florida driver's license or execute a
declaration of domicile until just a month before she applied for residency
reclassification. When she initially applied to FAU in 2007, she said she was
not a Florida resident. This statement contradicted the student's later claim that
she intended to become a resident in 2005. There was enough evidence to
support FAU's decision, and the court affirmed it. *Hallendy v. Florida Atlantic
Univ.*, 16 So.3d 1057 (Fla. Dist. Ct. App. 2009).

◆   *A student did not present sufficient evidence of residence to overcome a*
*presumption that he was in the state just to attend law school.*

The student completed a graduate degree program in Indiana, then moved
to Virginia. During his first year at a Virginia law school, he paid an out-of-state
tuition rate while taking steps to establish residency in Virginia. He registered
his car in Virginia, obtained a state driver's license, and registered as a voter.
Before the start of his second year, the student asked the school to reclassify
him as a state resident. While over a year had passed since he moved to the
state, the law school said he failed to prove he had established and maintained
a Virginia domicile for a year before the start of his second year.

The student's internal appeals failed, but a state circuit court reversed its
decision. The case reached the Virginia Supreme Court. The court held that to
qualify for in-state tuition in Virginia, students must prove they have been
domiciled in the state for at least a year and have abandoned any previous
domicile. Importantly, **the law specifies that an out-of-state student who
attends school in Virginia is presumed to be in the state for the purpose of
attending school and not a resident of the state.** Students cannot prove they
have become Virginia residents simply by "performing acts which are auxiliary
to fulfilling educational purposes" or acts that are "required or routinely
performed by temporary residents." State law sets out a number of factors to be
considered in determining whether a student has established residency for
tuition purposes, including income taxes, driver's license, motor vehicle
registration, voter registration, employment, property ownership, sources of

financial support, military records and employment offers following graduation. After reciting these factors, the court found the university had reasonably concluded the student was in Virginia primarily to attend law school. *George Mason Univ. v. Floyd*, 654 S.E.2d 556 (Va. 2008).

◆ *Arizona's highest court refused to address a constitutional challenge to the state's decision to substantially raise tuition rates at state universities.*

The Arizona Constitution requires state universities to provide instruction "as nearly free as possible," and provides for the state board of regents to set tuition and fees. The board approved a request from state universities to increase tuition rates by over 39% for the 2003-2004 academic year. Four students at the University of Arizona sued the board and the state legislature to challenge the increase, saying it violated the "as nearly free as possible" constitutional provision. A state court dismissed the claims, finding the board and legislature had state law immunity. The case reached the Arizona Supreme Court, which held the case presented a nonjusticiable political question that was not suited for resolution by the judicial branch. **Decisions about setting university tuition were entrusted by the state's constitution to other government branches, and there were no manageable standards a state court could apply to determine whether tuition was being provided "as nearly free as possible."** As neither case law nor statutes provided adequate guidance, the supreme court held the case had been properly dismissed. *Kromko v. Arizona Board of Regents*, 216 Ariz. 190, 165 P.3d 168 (Ariz. 2007).

◆ *A Maryland state university's presumption against in-state residency for all students who depended upon out-of-state sources did not violate equal protection principles. However, university administrators may not have applied the presumption in a constitutional manner.*

Four students who were enrolled in professional and post-graduate degree programs at a state university sued the university board of regents in a state court, claiming the board violated their constitutional rights by refusing to classify them as in-state residents. This decision denied them a substantial tuition reduction offered to Maryland residents, which the students claimed was a violation of equal protection principles. The university system presumed that students who were not financially independent were residing in the state primarily for the purpose of attending a college or university, if they remained financially dependent upon a nonresident. A state court held for the board and the students appealed to the Court of Special Appeals of Maryland.

The court stated no single definition could mechanically determine a person's domicile. The most important factors for determining domicile were where a person actually lived and where he or she voted, although a number of other factors also had weight. **The court held the university system's presumption was valid. The source of a student's financial support was related to the issue of residence.** However, there was evidence that some administrators did not allow students to challenge the presumption by treating the financial dependency presumption as irrebuttable. **The absence of uniformity in standards or criteria under the tuition policy violated equal protection principles.** The students were in the state during the time they attended the university, and each satisfied many other traditional domicile factors. The court vacated the lower court order for the board and remanded the case for further activity. *Bergmann v. Board of Regents of the Univ. System of Maryland*, 167 Md. App. 237, 892 A.2d 604 (Md. Ct. Spec. App. 2006).

◆   *The Court of Appeals of Kansas held that a student who moved to Kansas to attend law school could not claim resident tuition status.*

The student, who was born in England, came to Kansas in May 1999 and moved to Colorado in July 1999. He lived there until March 2002. He signed a contract to build a house in Kansas, contingent on his acceptance to the law school there. He was accepted, and he and his wife finalized the purchase of a house in Kansas in June 2002. The university denied the student's application to be reclassified as a Kansas resident for the 2003 fall semester. The residence committee denied his appeal. A state court agreed, and the student appealed.

The court of appeals noted several state law factors determined if a student was a Kansas resident. **These included a continuous presence in Kansas, employment in the state, payment of resident income taxes, reliance on in-state sources of financial support, commitment to an education program indicating an intent to remain permanently, and owning a home in Kansas.** The committee found the purchase of the house was contingent on the student's acceptance to the law school. This did not demonstrate an intent to remain in Kansas permanently. All of the other factors could be considered routinely performed by temporary residents of Kansas. The court found the committee's decision supported by substantial competent evidence and affirmed the judgment. *Lockett v. The Univ. of Kansas, Residence Appeals Committee*, 33 Kan. App.2d 931, 111 P.3d 170 (Kan. Ct. App. 2005).

◆   *State residency requirements for favorable tuition rates are subject to the due process right of students to present evidence about their residency.*

Connecticut required nonresidents enrolled in the state's university system to pay tuition and other fees at a higher rate than state residents. It also created an irreversible and irrebuttable statutory presumption that if the legal address of a student, if married, was outside the state at the time of application for admission or, if single, was outside the state at some point during the preceding year, the student remained a nonresident as long as the student remained enrolled in Connecticut schools. Two resident students, one married, one single, challenged the presumption, claiming it violated the Fourteenth Amendment's guarantee of due process and equal protection. A panel upheld the students' claim. The U.S. Supreme Court held that **the Due Process Clause does not permit states to deny a student the opportunity to present evidence that the student is a bona fide resident of the state, and thus entitled to in-state tuition rates**, on the basis of an irrebuttable presumption of nonresidence. Such a presumption is not necessarily true, and the state had alternatives in making residency determinations. *Vlandis v. Kline*, 412 U.S. 441, 93 S.Ct. 2230, 37 L.Ed.2d 63 (1973).

## D. Zoning and Land Use

◆  *A Rhode Island municipal ordinance was upheld in the face of a constitutional challenge by university students and others.*

A resort town attempted to keep disturbances by college students to a minimum by passing an ordinance making it a public nuisance to "conduct a gathering" of at least five people in a way that "constitutes a substantial disturbance of the quiet enjoyment of private or public property in a significant segment of the neighborhood, as a result of conduct constituting a violation of law." The ordinance authorized police to post a bright orange sticker at the front of any residence found to have hosted an "unruly gathering." Further offenses called for fines of up to $500. The University of Rhode Island's Student Senate, a group of students and a group of landlords sued the town in a federal district court to challenge the constitutionality of the ordinance. After the court held for the town, the students appealed to the U.S. Court of Appeals, First Circuit.

First, the court held that the ordinance was not preempted by the state landlord and tenant act. Next, it rejected a procedural due process claim, which was focused on the posting of orange stickers on a dwelling before a hearing was held. The court found this did not result in harm to any legally recognized liberty or property interest. **An asserted right of association did not encompass purely social gatherings**, and the ordinance did not reach a substantial amount of constitutionally protected conduct. As a result, the court rejected a claim that the ordinance was overbroad. While it used vague terms like "substantial disturbance" and "significant segment of the neighborhood," when viewed in context, the court found it clearly indicated the conduct it banned. The district court's decision to uphold the ordinance was affirmed. *URI Student Senate v. Town of Narragansett*, 631 F.3d 1 (1st Cir. 2011).

◆  *The Supreme Court of Vermont upheld the state environmental court's approval of a college building project over the objections of several neighbors.*

The college proposed to renovate an existing building in Burlington and build a new 18,000 square-foot building on the same lot to create 49 new student rooms that could house 94 students. A development review board conditionally approved the project and neighbors appealed to the Vermont Environmental Court. After a hearing and a site visit, the court approved the application with conditions, finding the project satisfied city density and setback requirements. On appeal, the Supreme Court of Vermont considered a claim by the neighbors that the lower court order had permitted a project exceeding the city's maximum allowable density and setback requirements.

The court deferred to the city's approach of treating each group of four dormitory rooms as a "single dwelling unit." Using this approach, the court upheld the environmental court's conclusion that the project complied with city density requirements. While neighbors complained that the lot was not a "corner lot" and thus violated setback requirements, the court disagreed. It found that **the neighbors sought to have the court "rewrite the zoning ordinances to declare that large lots cannot be corner lots under the City's definition of that term."** Since the lot was a "corner lot" as defined by the city, the environmental court did not commit error in allowing the project with conditions. *In re Champlain College Maple Street Dormitory*, 186 Vt. 313, 980 A.2d 273 (Vt. 2009).

◆   *A New Jersey court rejected claims that a zoning board improperly approved a university's plan to build a dormitory in a residential area.*

A group of neighbors objected to the construction of a three-story dormitory at Monmouth University. The local board of adjustment granted several variances for the project, which was planned in an area zoned for low-density residential uses. The neighbors sued Monmouth in the state court system, claiming several board members should have been disqualified from the application based on their financial or personal involvement with the university. The court upheld the decision, and the neighbors appealed.

A New Jersey appellate division court acknowledged that **the state Municipal Land Use Law has a conflict of interest provision that bars board of adjustment members from acting on any matter on which they have any personal or financial interest**. But none of the board members in this case came within the scope of this law. Some members were alumni of the university, but they were inactive and did not contribute substantially to Monmouth. No board members or any of their family members were currently students at the university. As none of the connections noted by the neighbors could reasonably be expected to impair the independence or objectivity of a board member, the judgment was affirmed. *Hughes v. Monmouth Univ.*, 394 N.J. Super. 193, 925 A.2d 741 (N.J. Super. Ct. App. Div. 2007).

◆   *The Court of Appeals of North Carolina upheld a decision to grant a university's request for an order to close a road running along its property.*

The university asked the Town of Chapel Hill to close part of Laurel Hill Road to promote safety, unify the grounds of the North Carolina Botanical Garden, and provide better teaching and visitor experiences. The town council adopted an order to permanently close a section of the road. A nearby property owner filed a state court petition to vacate the order. The court dismissed the petition and affirmed the order of the town council. The owner appealed to the Court of Appeals of North Carolina. He contended the trial court erred in failing to conduct an evidentiary hearing and in refusing to allow him to present evidence at the hearing on his petition.

The court noted the owner did not contest the procedures at the town hearing and did not contend the trial court violated other applicable local requirements. **The town held three public hearings on the proposed road closing in two months. Those hearings were the proper place for the owner to present evidence, not the trial court.** The court affirmed the judgment upholding the town's decision. *Houston v. Town of Chapel Hill*, 177 N.C.App. 739, 630 S.E.2d 249 (N.C. App. 2006). The state's highest court denied review in *Houston v. Town of Chapel Hill*, 639 S.E.2d 449 (N.C. 2006).

◆   *A federal district court upheld a District of Columbia zoning board order concerning a campus plan.*

The District zoning board approved the university's campus plan for 2000-2010, but imposed conditions including a cap on student enrollment. The university had already admitted a substantial number of its students for the next semester. The order also directed that if the university failed to meet a requirement to house 70% of buildings on campus, it would be barred from erecting nonresidential buildings on campus while it was noncompliant. A federal district court granted the university's request to prevent enforcement of the order. The board then issued a corrected final order that also imposed a cap on housing with certain housing requirements for undergraduates. The university amended its federal district court complaint to include a due process claim. The court found the board's order was not rationally related to its legitimate purpose and violated due process. The U.S. Court of Appeals, D.C. Circuit, reversed in part, noting that **the zoning board did not violate the university's substantive due process rights by imposing the housing restrictions**. Since students are not a suspect class deserving of heightened protections, the board's zoning regulations would be constitutional if they were rationally related to a legitimate governmental interest. Preservation of the residential character of an adjoining neighborhood was a legitimate governmental interest, and the zoning restrictions were upheld. *George Washington Univ. v. Dist. of Columbia*, 318 F.3d 203 (D.C. Cir. 2003).

The case returned to the district court, which found the final order did not deprive the university of all economic benefits. The university did not show the order diminished the property value. The court held the order did not interfere with the university's reasonable investment-backed expectations because it knew the property was subject to regulation. Because of the potential impact on the neighborhood, the court held the board's order advanced a common good or public purpose. The conditions imposed by the order did not constitute a taking of property, and the complaint was dismissed. *George Washington Univ. v. Dist. of Columbia*, 391 F.Supp.2d 109 (D.D.C. 2005).

◆ *A Massachusetts zoning board's density regulation was invalid as applied to a college campus under state law.*

Boston College (BC) applied to the Newton Board of Aldermen for special permits to construct three buildings. It also sought an exemption from the parking requirements of a local zoning ordinance. The purpose of the construction project was to provide additional space for academic functions, faculty offices and dining facilities. The board denied the application, and BC sued the board in a state court, alleging violation of the Dover Amendment, a state law barring zoning ordinances that prohibit or restrict the use of land for educational purposes. The court held the board unreasonably applied its dimensional and density regulations to the building project, but was reasonably justified in denying a parking waiver. The parties appealed.

The Court of Appeals of Massachusetts noted that **a municipality could reasonably regulate parking, open spaces, and buildings used for educational purposes**. The floor area ratio density requirement of the local zoning ordinance was invalid as applied to the BC middle campus. The entire middle campus was "nonconforming" under the ordinance, with the practical result that enforcement would require BC to always secure a special permit to construct any building there. Strict compliance with the density requirement would thwart an "educational use" and was invalid. The trial court correctly found the denial of a waiver for more parking spaces was unreasonable. The court affirmed the decision. *Trustees of Boston College v. Board of Aldermen of Newton*, 793 N.E.2d 387 (Mass. App. Ct. 2003).

## E.  State and Local Regulation

*In* Valley Forge Christian College v. Americans United for Separation of Church and State, *454 U.S. 464, 102 S.Ct. 752, 70 L.Ed.2d 700 (1982), the Supreme Court explained that Courts were not available to taxpayers to vent generalized grievances about government conduct or spending. Litigants were entitled to bring a lawsuit only by showing some actual or threatened injury. As a result, the Court held a Pennsylvania taxpayer group lacked standing to challenge a governmental sale of surplus property to a religious college.*

◆  *An Indiana appeals court held a private university's police department was subject to the state's public records act – but the university, itself, was not.*

An ESPN reporter made a public records request to the university's police department. It named 275 student-athletes and asked for incident reports in which they were named as victims, suspects or reporting parties. The police department refused to fulfill the request. ESPN sued, alleging the private university's police department qualified as a public agency subject to the public records act – so had to produce the records. A trial court backed the university police department, but an appeals court reversed. Citing precedent from the U.S. Supreme Court and other states – plus the **"danger that the public will be denied access to important public documents"** if a private agency exercising a public function wasn't held accountable under the public records act – the court found the university police department had to comply with the public records act. But it found the university, apart from its police department, was not required to. The appeals court remanded the case to determine which records must be produced. *ESPN, Inc. v. Univ. of Notre Dame Security Police Dep't*, 50 N.E.3d 385 (Ind. Ct. App. 2016).

◆  *Ohio's highest court held a private university's campus police department had to produce records requested by the editor of a student-run website.*

The editor mailed a letter to the university's chief of police. In it, she asked for criminal reports of anyone whose cases were referred to a local court. The school's vice president and dean of student affairs denied the request. The editor sued to compel production of the records. The court explained that under a state public records act, the term "public records" are "records kept by any public office." In addition, "public office" includes "any ... organized body ... established by the laws of this state for the exercise of any function of government." The school argued its police department was not a "public office" because the school is not a public entity. But **a private corporation can be deemed a public office under the law when it performs a governmental function**, the court explained. The fact that the school is private did not bar a finding that its police department was a public office, the court said. As a result, it was required to comply with the public records act even though it is a private institution. The court ordered the school to produce the documents. *State v. Banaszak*, 142 Ohio St.3d 535 (Ohio 2015).

◆ *A state appeals court in Florida found a state university cannot ban students from keeping guns in their cars on campus.*

A student wanted to have her gun with her on the way to and from school. She planned to leave the weapon in her car while she was on campus. But the school banned the storage of weapons in vehicles located on campus. The student, joined by an organization of gun owners, sued, claiming the school lacked the authority to enforce such a regulation.

Florida law generally barred the possession of guns on school property unless they were part of school-sponsored events. However, it also provided exceptions to the general ban – including one that specifically said guns could be kept in private conveyances as long as they were "securely encased." The state law also specified its provisions regarding the lawful carrying of firearms were to be liberally construed. The exception also gave "school districts" the ability to ban guns for purposes of student and campus parking privileges. The trial court denied the plaintiff's motion for a preliminary injunction and granted the defense's motion to dismiss. The student appealed. The appeals court reversed, explaining **the university was a "school" under the law, but not a "school district." The state university system was organized very differently than the state's public school district system**, the court explained. So the case was remanded for further proceedings. *Florida Carry, Inc. v. Univ. of Florida*, 133 So.3d 966 (Fla. Dist. Ct. App. 2013).

◆ *Oregon's State Board of Higher Education lacked authority to create a rule prohibiting firearms on university property, as this was a legislative matter.*

The state board of higher education adopted a rule penalizing anyone who used or possessed firearms on institutionally owned or controlled property without express authorization. A firearms group challenged the rule, asserting that the board had exceeded its statutory authority in creating it. According to the challengers, the state legislature had the exclusive authority to regulate firearms. The case reached the Court of Appeals of Oregon, which agreed with the group that the board's rule exceeded its authority under state law. **The board had only the general authority to control and manage its property.** This general authority did not extend so far as to regulate an area that was specifically reserved to the state legislature by statute. As a result, the court invalidated the board's rule. *Oregon Firearms Educ. Foundation v. Board of Higher Educ.*, 264 P.3d 160 (Or. Ct. App. 2011).

◆ *Virginia's highest court upheld a regulation banning possession of firearms inside school buildings and at educational events.*

A non-student patronized George Mason University (GMU) resources and libraries. He objected to a GMU regulation prohibiting weapons possession on campus in academic office buildings, student housing, dining facilities, and from on-campus sporting, entertainment and educational events. In a state court action, the non-student claimed the regulation violated the Second Amendment and a corresponding provision of the Virginia Constitution. A state trial court held the regulation was consistent with the requirements of the state and federal Constitutions. It relied on a U.S. Supreme Court ruling that said local laws can legally forbid the carrying of firearms in "sensitive places" such as schools.

On appeal, the Supreme Court of Virginia held the right to carry a firearm is not unlimited. Second Amendment jurisprudence does not ban laws that bar the carrying of firearms in "sensitive places." GMU had some 30,000 students. Another 50,000 high school and elementary students attended GMU summer camps, and 130 attended a preschool on campus. **There was no question that the university qualified as a "sensitive place" under the Supreme Court's ruling.** The regulation did not impose a total ban of weapons on campus, and it was tailored to keep weapons out of places where people congregate and are most vulnerable. As the university was a "sensitive place" and its firearms regulation did not violate the Second Amendment or the corresponding state constitutional provision, the court held for the university. *DiGiacinto v. Rector and Visitors of George Mason Univ.*, 281 Va. 127, 704 S.E.2d 365 (Va. 2011).

◆   *Wisconsin taverns that banned drink specials in response to pressure from municipal officials could claim immunity in an antitrust suit.*

Concerned about binge drinking by its students, officials at the University of Wisconsin, Madison pressured city officials to prohibit taverns from using weekend drink specials to lure customers. When officials threatened to pass an ordinance that would ban the practice by all taverns, a group of tavern owners announced at a news conference that they were giving in to the demands and would no longer offer drink specials. Some students at the University of Wisconsin accused the taverns of unlawful price-fixing and brought a state court antitrust action against them. The court held that the antitrust claim was barred based on the city's public health and safety concerns.

Appeal reached the Supreme Court of Wisconsin, which held the taverns were immune to the antitrust claim. **When legislators enacted the antitrust law, they intended to permit municipalities to take anti-competitive actions.** It was reasonable to find the regulation was intended to supersede competition in alcohol sales. Cities can regulate alcohol, as long as doing so serves an important public interest. Municipal immunity extended to the taverns because it was essentially the city that was responsible for the taverns' decision to "voluntarily" end the weekend drink specials. Since the lower courts correctly held for the taverns, the court affirmed the judgment. *Eichenseer v. Madison-Dane County Tavern League*, 748 N.W.2d 154 (Wis. 2008).

◆   *A Texas law violated the First Amendment by requiring private postsecondary schools to obtain a certificate of authority or accreditation before granting degrees or using the name "seminary."*

In an effort to stop "diploma mills," Texas passed a law that barred schools from using the words "college," "university," "seminary" and other specified terms in their names unless they first obtained a certificate of authority from the state. The law also restricted the designations schools could use regarding educational attainment. HEB Ministries, Inc., which operated a school it called the Tyndale Theological Seminary and Bible Institute, was assessed an administrative penalty of $173,000 for violating the state law. In response, it sued the state for a declaratory judgment that the law violated the Establishment Clause and the Free Exercise Clause of the First Amendment.

An intermediate court ruled for the state, and HEB Ministries appealed. The Supreme Court of Texas held **the state law violated the Establishment Clause by requiring private postsecondary institutions to obtain a certificate of authority or accreditation before granting degrees or using the word "seminary" in their names.** In addition, the law violated the Free Exercise Clause because it forced a party to either comply with state standards and compromise its religious mission or forgo the use of restricted terms. The decision of the intermediate court was reversed. *HEB Ministries, Inc. v. Texas Higher Educ. Coordinating Board*, 235 S.W.3d 627 (Tex. 2007).

◆   *The Court of Appeal of California held a community college was required to perform an environmental study before moving a campus shooting range.*

The college proposed a new site for a shooting range used for firearms courses offered in its criminal justice programs. It obtained approval by county and city governments, but a report indicated high levels of lead contamination at the new site. A public interest group alleged violation of state Environmental Quality Act requirements for an environmental study. A state superior court disagreed, finding the site change was not a "project" under the act.

The Court of Appeal of California stated that under the act, **a "project" is defined as "an activity which may cause either a direct physical change in the environment, or reasonably foreseeable indirect physical change in the environment" by a person or agency receiving public funds.** Even though dismantling and removing the range would be accomplished incrementally, these actions were all part of a single project. The college argued the lead abatement aspect of the move was exempt from the act, as the cleanup would cost less than $1 million. The court held that while lead abatement was exempt, this did not relieve the college of its responsibility to conduct an initial study of the project. **The decision was reversed and remanded with instructions for an environmental study.** *Ass'n for a Cleaner Environment v. Yosemite Community College Dist.*, 10 Cal.Rptr.3d 560 (Cal. Ct. App. 2004).

### F. Licensing

◆   *Wyoming's amended Private School Licensing Act did not violate the rights of a private educational institution.*

A Wyoming corporation offered post-secondary degrees to students in 17 international learning centers. It operated under a license granted in 2003. In 2006, amendments to the Private School Licensing Act significantly changed state licensing requirements. Prior to the change, institutions could obtain licensure by paying fees and posting a bond. Under amended law, all private post-secondary institutions had to become accredited within five years unless they obtained a good cause extension. The amended law imposed minimal standards for institutions and provided for state investigation and evaluations to implement state rules. An emergency rule required all private post-secondary degree-granting institutions to submit applications to the state and provide proof of an application for accreditation from an association approved by the

U.S. Department of Education. The corporation attempted to renew its license under the old law, but the department rejected its application.

Appeal reached the Supreme Court of Wyoming, which denied each of the corporation's constitutional claims. There was no differentiation among new state regulations, as the corporation argued, defeating an equal protection claim. As the lower court found, the new law did not create classes of institutions that were accredited or not. Instead, the law required all trade, correspondence, distance education, technical, vocational, business or other private schools to be accredited. There was no improper delegation of legislative authority based on the requirement of accreditation by an approved association. The amended law was not so vague as to be constitutionally void. The court held that **the state had authority to regulate private institutions under its police powers**. As none of the corporation's arguments had merit, the court held for the department. *Newport Int'l Univ. v. State of Wyoming, Dep't of Educ.*, 186 P.3d 382 (Wyo. 2008).

◆ *The Michigan Department of Education could deny a license to operate to the owner of a trade school teaching casino gambling.*

A Michigan resident applied to the proprietary school unit of the department of education for a license to operate a private trade school teaching casino gambling. The board denied his application because gaming was considered criminal behavior in Michigan. The applicant appealed to a Michigan trial court. The trial court reversed, and the board of education appealed to the Court of Appeals of Michigan. The court of appeals noted that public policy did not completely prohibit casino gambling as evidenced by the legislature's decision to legalize millionaire parties and to allow casino gambling on Indian reservations. On further appeal, the Supreme Court of Michigan reversed. It adopted the dissenting opinion from the lower court, which stated that **licensing the proposed school would violate public policy**. If the school were allowed to teach casino gambling, it would be teaching behavior that was currently defined as illegal under Michigan law. *Michigan Gaming Institute v. State Board of Educ.*, 547 N.W.2d 882 (Mich. 1996).

◆ *A corporation that provided review courses for nursing school graduates had to pay an annual renewal licensing fee for each location.*

The corporation offered courses that prepared nursing school graduates for state certification exams. It operated at five different locations in the state. The review courses were held in hotel meeting rooms, college auditoriums or hospital conference rooms. The California legislature modified the Private Postsecondary and Vocational Education Reform Act to increase the annual renewal fee for nondegree-granting institutions from $225 to a range of $600 to $1,200, depending on size. The corporation made a single $1,200 payment but refused to make a separate payment for each of its course sites.

A lawsuit arose, and a California trial court found that a separate fee could be charged for each location. The California Court of Appeal, First District, noted that because the corporation's educational sites were 50 miles from corporate headquarters and were held in places such as hotel conference rooms, they were neither branches nor satellites subject to separate annual fees under the act. However, since the legislature provided that each site be inspected by the governing council, the court inferred a legislative intent to require separate annual fees for each site. **As long as the governing council used some "reasonable method" of estimating the administrative costs of the entire program, its annual fee interpretation was reasonable.** Thus, the court of appeal required the corporation to pay an annual fee for each site. *RN Review for Nurses, Inc. v. State*, 28 Cal.Rptr.2d 354 (Cal. Ct. App. 1994).

◆ *A board for community colleges should have provided an occupational school with a hearing prior to terminating the school's license.*

A private Colorado occupational school was licensed to do business by the State Board for Community Colleges and Occupational Educations. A new statute revised licensing requirements, and the school was required to renew its license. The board's vice president rejected the school's application because it had not employed an independent accountant or utilized accepted accounting procedures as required by the new statute. The school filed a 42 U.S.C. § 1983 action in a Colorado district court against the vice president and the board. It alleged that both had failed to provide a hearing prior to terminating the school's license and had failed to provide an impartial tribunal.

A trial court determined that neither the board nor its vice president could be sued under 42 U.S.C. § 1983 and dismissed the case. The Colorado Court of Appeals found that the board was a state regulatory body that was entitled to immunity from suits for damages. Next, the court determined that **the vice president's failure to grant the school a pre-deprivation hearing was not a clear violation of its constitutional rights**. The vice president, therefore, had immunity on the claim for damages under Section 1983. However, the board's refusal to grant the school a pre-deprivation hearing potentially violated its statutory rights. On remand, the school could sue for injunctive relief. *National Camera, Inc. v. Sanchez*, 832 P.2d 960 (Colo. Ct. App. 1991).

## G.  Desegregation

◆ *A longstanding court battle to end racial segregation in Alabama colleges and universities could not be used to force changes in state K-12 funding.*

The suit was filed in 1981, when a group of black citizens claimed the state perpetuated a segregated university system. They said admissions standards at historically white institutions disqualified disproportionate numbers of black applicants. The citizens claimed historically black institutions were plagued by unfair funding and facility policies. In 1991, a federal district court ordered the state to encourage greater racial integration at its colleges and universities. Four years later, it entered a decree that ordered numerous additional changes to the state's higher education policies. Among other things, it required more flexible admissions policies and increased integration of faculty and administration at all state colleges and universities. The court also required the state to increase its funding of historically black institutions. Over the next eight years, the state and the plaintiffs "worked tirelessly" to make the changes required by the court. From 1990-2004, the state increased its annual funding of higher education by $340 million. During this time, undergraduate and graduate degrees awarded to black students increased by over 96%. In 2009, the plaintiffs filed a motion to require the state to provide better funding for K-12 schools. They sought an order invalidating property tax limitations imposed by the state constitution.

The plaintiffs said a funding crisis in the state's K-12 schools resulted in segregation at its colleges and universities. The district court denied the motion, and the plaintiffs appealed. On appeal, the U.S. Court of Appeals, Eleventh Circuit, explained that the case had always been about segregation in the state's higher education system. The plaintiffs' motion was about reforming the state's K-12 school funding system. Because the motion raised a claim relating to school finance rather than desegregation, it could not be pursued. The plaintiffs tried to link the inadequacy of K-12 funding with segregation at higher levels by proposing a chain of causation. Property tax limitations resulted in underfunded public schools, leading to the diversion of higher education funds to lower education. This diversion resulted in higher tuition rates and decreased black student enrollment at state colleges and universities. **Under *U.S. v. Fordice*, below, race-neutral state policies governing higher education can be challenged under the Constitution if they are traceable to a system of segregation.** The court found the asserted relationship between the underfunding of the state's K-12 schools and segregation in Alabama colleges and universities was too attenuated and based on too many unpredictable premises. The judgment for the state was affirmed. *Knight v. Alabama*, 476 F.3d 1219 (11th Cir. 2007).

◆   *Where a state perpetuates policies and practices that can be traced to a segregative system and that have segregative effects, the policies will be considered unconstitutional unless there is sound educational justification for them and it is not practical to eliminate them.*

Mississippi maintained a dual system of public education at the university level – one set of universities for whites, and another set for blacks. In 1981, the State Board of Trustees issued "Mission Statements" to remedy this, classifying the three flagship historically white institutions (HWI) as "comprehensive" universities, redesignating one of the historically black institutions (HBI) as an "urban" university and characterizing the rest as "regional" institutions. However, the universities remained racially identifiable. A federal court found that state policies need merely be racially neutral, developed in good faith, and not contribute to the racial identifiability of each institution. It held that Mississippi was currently fulfilling its duty to desegregate. The U.S. Court of Appeals, Fifth Circuit, affirmed.

On appeal, the U.S. Supreme Court held that the district court had applied the wrong legal standard in ruling that Mississippi had brought itself into compliance with the Equal Protection Clause. **If a state perpetuates policies and practices traceable to its prior dual system that continue to have segregative effects, and such policies are without sound educational justification and can be practicably eliminated, the policies violate the Equal Protection Clause.** This is true even if the state has abolished the legal requirement that the races be separated and has established neutral policies. The proper inquiry is whether existing racial identifiability is attributable to the state. Applying the proper standard, several surviving aspects of Mississippi's prior dual system were constitutionally suspect. First, the use of higher minimum ACT composite scores at the HWIs, along with the state's refusal to consider high school grade performance was suspect. Second, the unnecessary duplication of programs at HBIs and HWIs was suspect. Third, the mission statements' reflection of previous policies to perpetuate racial separation was suspect. Finally, the state's policy of operating eight universities had to be examined to determine if it was educationally justifiable. *U.S. v. Fordice*, 505 U.S. 717, 112 S.Ct. 2727, 120 L.Ed.2d 575 (1992). On remand, a federal court **entered a remedial decree prohibiting the state from maintaining remnants of the prior segregated system** and mandating specific relief in areas of admissions and funding. However, the court refused to order the relief requested by the complaining parties, which would significantly increase the number of African-Americans accepted for regular admission at state universities. The complaining parties claimed that the district court order's reliance on a summer remedial program to boost African-American admissions was inappropriate, and the parties appealed to the Fifth Circuit. The court held the district court's order affirming the elimination of many remedial courses had to be reconsidered, along with its finding that use of college entrance scores as a criterion for scholarships was not traceable to the illegal system of segregation. The court remanded for clarification the status of a proposal to merge two universities to eliminate unnecessary program duplication, as well as questions of increasing the other-race presence at two HBIs and issues of accreditation and funding. The court affirmed many aspects of the district court decision as consistent with the *Fordice* decision, significantly affirming its decision to maintain admissions standards that ensured educational soundness. *Ayers v. Fordice*, 111 F.3d 1183 (5th Cir. 1997).

## II.  ACCREDITATION

*Regional and other accrediting institutions have been sued by private schools upon withdrawal of accreditation. The cases suggest: 1) actions of accrediting institutions do not constitute "state action" triggering due process requirements, 2) a school may maintain a breach of contract lawsuit against an accrediting institution if the institution fails to follow its own rules and procedures, and 3) if an accrediting institution's procedures are fair, its decision to revoke accreditation will likely be upheld.*

### A.  Grants of Accreditation

◆  *Where an accreditation foundation's denial of accreditation to a college of art and design was supported by substantial evidence, it did not qualify as arbitrary or unreasonable.*

In 1995, Savannah College of Art & Design sought accreditation for its interior design program from the Foundation for Interior Design Education Research. Although a team of evaluators' report generally praised the program, it recommended the denial of accreditation. The foundation's board of trustees accepted the recommendation. Savannah College appealed, and a second on-site evaluation also recommended denial of accreditation for poor student achievement. Believing it had been treated unfairly, Savannah turned to the foundation's appeals panel, which determined that the denial of accreditation was supported by substantial evidence and consistent with other schools' accreditation reports. After the college threatened legal intervention, the foundation sued for a declaration that its decision to reject accreditation was lawful. In response, the college filed counterclaims against it. A federal court granted pretrial judgment to the foundation and dismissed all of the counterclaims. The school appealed to the Sixth Circuit.

**The court held the foundation's denial of accreditation was neither arbitrary nor discriminatory.** Savannah College argued that the foundation's method of evaluation deviated from the usual evaluative process and was therefore discriminatory. The court agreed that the process in this case differed, but to the college's favor. The foundation would not normally send a second evaluation team, but it did so in this case to ensure fairness. Savannah's final argument claimed the foundation acted arbitrarily because the college's interior design program closely resembled other accredited programs. The court disagreed and affirmed the judgment, finding the foundation's decision was based on substantial evidence. *Foundation for Interior Design Educ. Research v. Savannah College of Art & Design*, 244 F.3d 521 (6th Cir. 2001).

◆ *A federal court refused to force the American Bar Association (ABA) to provisionally accredit a law school.*

After a religious university acquired a non-accredited law school, it applied for provisional accreditation from the ABA. The ABA rejected the application. The following year, the university applied again, and again was rejected. A group of graduates, students and instructors then sued the ABA seeking a preliminary injunction to force provisional accreditation. The university also filed a third application for provisional accreditation. A Florida federal district court refused to grant the injunction, finding no evidence that irreparable harm would befall the plaintiffs if the injunction was not granted. While the third application was pending, **graduates still could be admitted to practice in other states, and they could seek a waiver of the 12-month rule on sitting for the Florida Bar Exam** from the state supreme court. *Staver v. American Bar Ass'n*, 169 F.Supp.2d 1372 (M.D. Fla. 2001).

◆ *An Oregon law allowing certain schools to be exempted from requirements that out-of-state schools were not exempted from, was struck down.*

A private Washington university with a branch campus in Oregon was accredited by the Northwest Association of Schools and Colleges (NASC). Following NASC accreditation, the Oregon Office of Educational Policy and Planning (OEPP) continued to review non-Oregon schools every three years. The statute provided that "no school … shall confer … any degree … without first having submitted the requirements for such degree to the [OEPP] and having obtained the approval of the director." However, an amendment exempted Oregon schools in good standing with the NASC from OEPP review. The university filed suit in an Oregon circuit court, seeking a declaration that the statute violated the Commerce Clause. The circuit court held for the university and severed a portion of the amendment. The court of appeals affirmed but invalidated the exemption in its entirety. The Oregon Supreme Court allowed the university's petition for review solely on the issue of remedy.

The university contended that the entire amendment had been improperly invalidated. The supreme court disagreed, ruling that the statute as severed was not capable of being executed in accordance with legislative intent. The legislature had intended both to continue the exemption from OEPP authority for Oregon schools that were members of the NASC and to remove the exemption from OEPP authority for out-of-state schools, even if those schools were NASC members. However, the dominant intent of the amendment was to ensure that Oregon branch campuses of the out-of-state schools had the same level of faculty and facilities as their main campuses. **As partial severance would subject these out-of-state schools to lesser scrutiny, the court ordered the amendment severed in its entirety.** The court of appeals' ruling was affirmed. *City Univ. v. Office of Educ. Policy*, 885 P.2d 701 (Or. 1994).

## B.  Claims of Fraud

◆  *Filing a suit that involves* "qui tam" *claims under the False Claims Act (FCA), an instructor tried to convince an Indiana federal judge that the school's mandatory non-disparagement agreement resulted in defrauding the federal student aid program.*

*Qui tam* is part of a Latin phrase that means: "One who sues on behalf of the King as well as for himself." In a *qui tam* action, a government informer gets a share of the claim if the target has to pay a penalty. The FCA imposed steep penalties for fraudulently claiming money from the federal government. National College (NC) was a for-profit higher ed institution for adults seeking post-secondary programs and degrees. David Hoffman worked for NC for a year and a half as an instructor. NC required all faculty to sign a confidentiality agreement, in which faculty, while employed and for a year after leaving, agreed not to "criticize, ridicule" or make disparaging or derogatory statements about anything connected with NC to anyone. The long list of "anyone" in the agreement included regulators. Hoffman balked at the agreement and refused to sign it. NC fired him. Hoffman brought a *qui tam* action against NC under the FCA. **To state a valid FCA claim, Hoffman had to state the "who, what, when, where and how: the first paragraph of a news story."** He didn't. As he didn't state valid claims or provide the required specifics, the court dismissed his case. *U.S. ex rel. Hoffman v. National College*, No. 3:12CV-237-TLS, 2013 WL 3421931 (N.D. Ind. 7/8/13).

◆  *A Georgia court refused to certify a class action by students who alleged fraud by a private university, because it found their claims required a case-by-case review.*

According to the students, the education they received was "not worth the cost." They claimed the university engaged in fraudulent recruiting practices. Although the university was continuously accredited during the time in question, the students asserted that the accreditation was obtained through false representations including inflated employment rates for university graduates. They filed a state court action against the university and its parent corporation, seeking damages because they had paid tuition and incurred loans but were unable to find employment in their respective fields of study. The court found no reason to certify the case as a class action, and on appeal, the Court of Appeals of Georgia agreed. **The students had introduced a great deal of individualized evidence that required a case-by-case review.** For this reason, the court found their claims not suitable for class certification. As determining whether each student was adversely affected by some aspect of the university's operation would "require a separate mini-trial," the court affirmed the judgment denying class certification. *Diallo v. American Intercontinental Univ.*, 301 Ga.App. 299, 687 S.E.2d 278 (Ga. Ct. App. 2009).

◆ *A law school graduate who could not take a bar exam after attending an unaccredited Massachusetts law school could not proceed with fraud claims.*

At the time of the student's admission, the school was not accredited by the American Bar Association (ABA). This meant graduates could not sit for a state bar examination. Upon learning that the ABA was recommending a provisional accreditation, the school sent prospective students a letter expressing confidence that accreditation was forthcoming. But a disclaimer was included in the law school catalogue, which stated that it did not represent it would be approved prior to the graduation of any matriculating student. The ABA denied the school accreditation near the time the student enrolled.

Further attempts to gain accreditation failed, and the student was unable to transfer to another school. He graduated but was unable to sit for a state bar examination due to the school's lack of accreditation. The student sued the school for fraudulent misrepresentation in a federal district court. The case reached the U.S. Court of Appeals, First Circuit, which held that to prevail, **the student had to show he relied on a false representation and acted on it to his detriment. He also had to show his reliance on the false statement was reasonable.** But the student did neither. His claim that he relied on statements regarding accreditation was contradicted by his transfer attempt after the school indicated its difficulties gaining accreditation. The student's transfer application strongly suggested he did not believe the assurances regarding accreditation. Even if the student did rely on the statements of assurance regarding the school's chances at accreditation, reliance was not reasonable. As a result, the court affirmed a lower court judgment for the law school. *Rodi v. Southern New England School of Law*, 532 F.3d 11 (1st Cir. 2008).

## C.  Withdrawal of Accreditation

◆ *A Pennsylvania immunity statute did not block claims against a community college that lost its certification.*

Students attending a police training program at a Pennsylvania community college learned the college had lost its certification and that their credits were jeopardized. A group of students filed a lawsuit against the college for breach of contract, breach of warranty, and violation of the state Unfair Trade Practices and Consumer Protection Law (UTPCPL). According to the community college, the UTPCPL did not apply to local governmental entities, and it was immune to any UTPCPL claim. The court denied pretrial judgment for the community college on the UTPCPL claims. It held the immunity statute was intended to block claims based in tort, not contract claims such as the ones the students were advancing. Appeal reached the Supreme Court of Pennsylvania, which agreed with the students that the governmental immunity afforded by the statute did not extend to all statutory causes of action. Instead, **the court held the statute granted immunity based on conduct that caused "injury to a person or property."** These terms indicated to the court an intent to grant immunity with respect to tort claims. As a result, the court returned the case to the trial court for further proceedings. *Meyer v. Community College of Beaver County*, 606 Pa. 539, 2 A.3d 499 (Pa. 2010).

◆ *A small college in Tennessee failed in its attempt to reverse an accrediting agency's decision to remove its accreditation.*

Hiwassee College lost its accreditation by the Southern Association of Colleges and Schools (SACS) based on its troubled financial condition. The college sued the SACS in a federal district court, claiming that SACS failed to meet its own requirements relating to removal of accreditation. It asserted that SACS denied it due process of law under the Higher Education Act (HEA) and the Due Process Clause of the Fifth Amendment. The court held the SACS was entitled to judgment as a matter of law, and the college appealed.

The U.S. Court of Appeals, Eleventh Circuit, held the college could not bring a claim against SACS under the HEA statute. **Nothing indicated Congress intended to create a private right of action in the HEA. The court held the SACS was not a government actor and therefore was not required to comply with Fifth Amendment due process requirements.** Nor did SACS fail to meet any common law duty to provide the college with due process in connection with the accreditation decision. The college never asserted that it was in compliance with the agency's accreditation criteria. The judgment was affirmed. *Hiwassee College, Inc. v. Southern Ass'n of Colleges and Schools*, No. 07-13033, 2008 WL 1701694 (11th Cir. 4/14/08).

## III.  CONSTRUCTION AND OUTSIDE CONTRACTS

◆ *A federal district court refused to find an American university breached a contract to enter into an affiliation agreement with an Israeli college.*

In 1994, the college began partnering with American institutions to offer courses at a campus in Israel. It began a search to replace New England College. The search led it to Southern New Hampshire University (SNHU), which initially decided not to go forward with the affiliation. Two years later, negotiations proceeded to a point where the parties signed affiliation and academic supervision agreements. The agreements outlined the responsibilities of each party with respect to curriculum, faculty, admission criteria and other details. They also outlined contractual obligations. The president of SNHU signed the documents, and the Israeli college president then signed them. Five months later, SNHU's president decided not to move ahead with the affiliation. The college then sued SNHU for breach of contract in a federal district court.

SNHU claimed that the parties had a memo of understanding but not a contract. The court denied the college pretrial judgment. **There were disputed facts about what happened at meetings leading up to the signing of the two documents, and it was unclear whether an agreement to enter into a binding contract was conditioned on SNHU's completion of due diligence.** *Israel College-Educational Horizons, Ltd. v. Southern New Hampshire Univ.*, No. 05-cv-392-JD, 2008 WL 187606 (D.N.H. 1/17/08).

◆ *A university that did a thorough environmental impact evaluation of a construction project did not have to file an environmental impact statement with New York state officials.*

A New York state university planned five separate campus housing projects, including a 116-unit building for which it filed a full environmental assessment form that was supported by an environmental site assessment report. A lawsuit nevertheless ensued, seeking to compel the university to file an environmental impact statement and seeking a temporary injunction to prevent construction until such statement was filed. The New York Supreme Court, Appellate Division, ruled that the university did not have to file an environmental impact statement because its thorough study of the environmental effects of construction concluded that there would not be an adverse impact on wetlands, cultural resources, groundwater, air quality, solid waste, removal of vegetation, wildlife or open space such that the project should be stopped. **In light of the university's thorough evaluation, the project could proceed.** *Forman v. Trustees of State Univ. of New York*, 757 N.Y.S.2d 180 (N.Y. App. Div. 2003).

◆ *Alaska's highest court held a state university was entitled to money from a contractor who underbid a project and then sought to recoup its losses as additional work.*

The University of Alaska solicited bids for fixing a drainage problem involving an access road and gravel pad surfaces at a research facility. **It accepted the lowest bid but then experienced problems with the contractor.** The contractor first obtained a one-week extension, then sought approval for extra materials, extra work and the payment of additional money. The university rejected the claims. When the contractor failed to finish the project on time, the ground froze, and it was unable to complete the project. Both the university and the contractor sought financial reimbursement, and a hearing officer determined that the contractor underbid the project, then sought to recover its losses as additional work. However, the university also owed some additional monies to the contractor. The case reached the Supreme Court of Alaska, which largely upheld the hearing officer's determinations. It refused, however, to grant the university liquidated damages because the university had entered into an agreement with the contractor's bonding company regarding the hiring of another contractor to finish the project. *Lakloey, Inc. v. Univ. of Alaska*, No. 5-9690, 2002 WL 1732561 (Alaska 2002).

◆ *West Virginia's highest court set forth five factors to be used in determining whether a construction project is a public project.*

West Virginia University and the West Virginia University Foundation (a private, nonprofit corporation) began planning and developing a layout for the construction of a building to be known as the University Services Center. After a bidding process, a developer agreed to build the center at its own cost and risk. The foundation would then purchase the site and lease the building to the university. When an affiliation of construction trades sued for a declaration that the proposed construction was a public project governed by state wage and competitive bidding laws, the university and the nonprofit foundation moved for pretrial judgment. A state court granted the motion, finding that the foundation was not a state agency, and its connection to the university did not convert the construction into a public project.

On appeal, the West Virginia Supreme Court of Appeals listed five factors to be used in determining whether a construction project is a public project. It held **the lower court record was not sufficiently developed to determine whether public funds had been used on the project**. Further, the building was now completed, and there was no indication of wage violations. *Affiliated Construction Trades Foundation v. Univ. of West Virginia Board of Trustees*, 557 S.E.2d 863 (W. Va. 2001).

◆ *A university could not recover from a contractor for an explosion and fire several years after the construction of a power plant.*

The University of Colorado contracted with a construction company to build a co-generation power facility on its Boulder campus. The contract contained a provision stating that **acceptance of the work would constitute a release of all claims against the company** and also contained a 12-month warranty period. However, the university purchased an extended five-year warranty from the subcontractor that furnished the gas turbine engines for the facility. After the facility had been in operation for three and a half years, a combination of events caused a backup in one engine, resulting in an explosion and fire. The university sued the contractor and subcontractor for breach of contract, breach of warranty, negligence and strict liability. A state court ruled for the defendants, and the Colorado Court of Appeals affirmed. Here, the contractor's warranty and the release clearly protected it from liability. Also, with respect to the subcontractor, the jury's ruling was not unsupported by the evidence. *Regents of the Univ. of Colorado v. Harbert Construction Co.*, 51 P.3d 1037 (Colo. Ct. App. 2001).

◆ *The U.S. Supreme Court held a choice of law clause in a construction contract entered into by Stanford University superseded arbitration rights found in the Federal Arbitration Act.*

An electrical contractor contracted with a California university to install conduits. The contract contained a clause in which the parties agreed to arbitrate disputes relating to the contract. The contract also contained a choice-of-law clause that stated that it would be governed by the law of the place of the project's location. A dispute arose concerning overtime compensation, and the contractor made a formal request for arbitration. The university sued the contractor in a California trial court for fraud and breach of contract. **The contractor claimed that it was entitled to arbitration under the contract and the Federal Arbitration Act (FAA).** The court granted the university's motion to stay arbitration under a California statute that permits a stay when arbitration is the subject of pending court action. The contractor appealed to the California Court of Appeal, which affirmed the trial court's decision. The court of appeal acknowledged that although the contract affected interstate commerce, the California statute applied because of the contractual choice-of-law clause. The California Supreme Court denied the contractor's petition for discretionary review, but the U.S. Supreme Court agreed to hear its appeal.

On appeal, the contractor reiterated its argument that the court of appeal's ruling on the choice-of-law clause deprived it of its federally guaranteed right to arbitration under the FAA. The Supreme Court ruled that **the FAA did not confer a general right to compel arbitration. Rather, it guaranteed the right to arbitrate according to the manner provided for in the parties' contract.** The court of appeal had correctly found that the contract incorporated California law. The FAA was not undermined by the state law that permitted a stay of arbitration. The Court affirmed the court of appeal's decision for the university. *Volt Information Sciences v. Board of Trustees of Leland Stanford Junior Univ.*, 489 U.S. 468, 109 S.Ct. 1248, 103 L.Ed.2d 488 (1989).

## IV.   CAMPUS SAFETY AND SECURITY

### A.   Search and Seizure

*The Fourth Amendment to the U.S. Constitution prohibits unreasonable searches and seizures by states, including state institutions of higher education. A "seizure" does not occur every time police stop and question a person. Officers may use reliable reports from staff to make investigatory stops.*

◆ *A Missouri appeals court determined a university police officer's warrant for a professor's home lacked probable cause – so the drugs found in the search couldn't be used as evidence against the professor.*
During an interview for the school newspaper, a student interviewer told an officer that a faculty member posted on Facebook that he was going to climb the campus bell tower and shoot students. The officer got a warrant to search the newspaper's office and found the identity of the faculty member who posted the threat. He posted the comment in response to a colleague's status about how the start of the semester was going. In part, he posted "[b]y October, I'll be wanting to get up to the top of the bell tower with a high powered rifle – with a good scope, and probably a gatling gun as well." The professor admitted others didn't seem amused. He later deleted his comments. The next day an administrator called the officer to report a rumor about the professor saying he had a bomb on campus. The university officer talked to the professor, who responded flippantly, "Yesterday they thought it was a gun. Today I've brought a bomb." The officer arrested the professor. He admitted making the remark, but insisted it was a joke. The officer also obtained a warrant to search the professor's home for firearms. Instead, officers found marijuana. Charged with two felony drug charges, the professor asked the court to quash the search warrant and exclude the evidence against him. A trial court did – and an appeals court affirmed. **To be valid, the warrant had to be supported by probable**

**cause to believe that the search would reveal either criminal contraband or the evidence of a crime.** The officer acknowledged he got the warrant to assess the professor's ability to commit a violent crime. The appeals court rejected the argument that finding firearms would have gone toward proving the professor made a terroristic threat or a false bomb report. Having weapons wasn't illegal, wasn't evidence of a crime, and had no bearing on whether the professor made a bad joke as opposed to a threat, the court explained. *State v. Rouch*, 457 S.W.3d 815 (Mo. Ct. App. 2014).

◆  *The U.S. Court of Appeals for the Seventh Circuit upheld a ruling that a university did not violate the Fourth Amendment rights of a student.*

Indiana University student housing contracts allowed university personnel to enter dorm rooms to perform safety inspections. During a routine health and safety inspection, two resident specialists saw a clear tube of what looked like marijuana in plain view on a desk in a student dorm room. They called university police, who saw the container on the desk and detected a strong odor of marijuana. An officer entered the room and confiscated the container. When a resident specialist continued on with the safety inspection, she found what looked like a large marijuana plant inside a closet. She told one of the officers, who re-entered the room and saw the plant. The officer then obtained a search warrant. After further searching the room, the officer seized an additional 89 grams of marijuana and assorted drug-related paraphernalia.

The student was arrested, and two days later he was suspended from school. He sued the university in a federal court, claiming the search violated his Fourth Amendment rights. The court disagreed, finding the resident specialists went into his room solely to perform a health and safety inspection, not to gather evidence for a criminal proceeding. Once the specialists lawfully entered his room and saw marijuana, they were justified in allowing access by the university police. The student appealed. The appellate court said the **"in-your-face flagrancy" of the student's violation of school rules and criminal law required the school to take immediate remedial action**. So the court rejected the student's appellate arguments and upheld the ruling in favor of the school. *Medlock v. Trustees of Indiana Univ.*, 738 F.3d 867 (7th Cir. 2013).

◆  *A Texas student was unable to show a search by University of Texas at San Antonio (UTSA) campus police violated his constitutional rights.*

A UTSA officer smelled marijuana in an apartment. From the hallway, he saw marijuana on a table in a room. The officer conducted a protective sweep of the apartment. In a bedroom, he saw drug paraphernalia and a lockbox. After the student's parents arrived, the student consented to a search. Police found a handgun, ammunition, a stun gun, cocaine and $517. In criminal proceedings, the UTSA officer said he saw marijuana on a table in the student's room from the hallway. In response, the student said this would have been impossible. But photographs showed it was possible to see the table from where the officer stood. The student was convicted of possession with intent to deliver cocaine. On appeal, he argued the evidence seized from the search should have been suppressed and excluded from the case. But the Court of Appeals of Texas held that **the jury was entitled to determine which witnesses were the most**

**believable**. Marijuana odor alone might not have been enough to justify a warrantless search. The court held it would defer to the jury verdict, as the jury had relied on the testimony it found the most believable. *Clark v. Texas*, No. 04-10-00540-CR, 2012 WL 3025685 (Tex. Ct. App. 7/25/12).

◆  *A Pennsylvania university avoided liability for civil rights violations based on the security stop of a high school student who resembled a criminal suspect.*

Temple University officers stopped a high school student who fit the description of a shooting suspect. They took him to the police station, where he was arrested and charged with attempted murder, aggravated assault and firearms offenses. He spent time in jail and missed his senior prom and graduation. After the student was cleared, he sued the university for violation of his constitutional rights under the Fourth and Fourteenth Amendments. Among other things, he claimed that Temple University officers intentionally provided false information to the Philadelphia Police Department and failed to investigate his alibi. A federal court dismissed the lawsuit, holding that **Temple University was a municipal subdivision that could not be held responsible for the conduct of its employees on vicarious liability grounds**. The student did not allege that the Temple officers acted at the direction of a Temple official or pursuant to a policy or custom. *Franks v. Temple Univ.*, No. 11-879, 2011 WL 1562598 (E.D. Pa. 4/26/11).

◆  *A community college in New Mexico did not violate the constitutional rights of a former student when it briefly detained him.*

After being disenrolled by the college, the student went to the financial aid office, where he got into a heated argument with an employee. Before he left campus, several officials detained him and questioned him about the argument. After the questioning, the student left campus without further incident. He sued the community college and several officials in a federal district court for Fourth Amendment violations. He added a breach of contract claim based on the decision to disenroll him. The court dismissed the complaint, finding no unreasonable seizure. The student appealed to the U.S. Court of Appeals, Tenth Circuit. According to the court, **the brief detention was reasonable under the circumstances**. Thus, the district court had properly dismissed the Fourth Amendment claim. The court also affirmed the district court's decision to decline jurisdiction over the state law contract claim. *Reyes v. Cent. New Mexico Community College*, 410 Fed.Appx. 134 (10th Cir. 2011).

◆  *A mentally disabled African-American woman did not prove she was unlawfully excluded from a Northwestern University library.*

Although not affiliated with the university, the woman used its law school library to research disability law. After the law school revoked her permission to use its facilities, she researched elsewhere. The woman accused a student in a computer lab of assaulting her, and she was escorted from the building. Later, she claimed campus security told her to leave another library. In a federal district court action against Northwestern, the woman claimed race and disability discrimination under federal laws. After the court dismissed her case, she appealed to the U.S. Court of Appeals, Seventh Circuit. It found the claims relied on laws requiring proof of differential treatment based on race or disability. **But as the woman did not allege any facts that could reasonably lead to the belief that the university excluded her on either basis, the district court was correct in dismissing the action.** *Gillard v. Northwestern Univ.*, 366 Fed.Appx. 686 (7th Cir. 2010).

◆ *A "seizure" does not occur every time police stop and question a person. Officers may rely on trustworthy reports from staff to make investigatory stops.*

An African-American library patron was using a computer in a library at the New Jersey Institute of Technology. An assistant librarian called the security department to report him for taking a stapler. The patron agreed to answer questions by the police and let them search his bag. After they did not find the stapler, the patron left the building. He sued the officers, institute and library staff in a federal district court for constitutional rights violations. The court held for the institute and staff, and the patron appealed to the U.S. Court of Appeals, Third Circuit. While he admitted consenting to the questioning and the search of his bag, he claimed the consent was invalid because one officer failed to inform him that he had a right to refuse the search. The court found no such requirement. The patron's consent was valid, as the investigation lasted only seven minutes, took place in public, and was not threatening or intimidating. The district court had properly held that no jury could have found a Fourth Amendment violation. The U.S. Supreme Court has held a seizure does not occur every time police approach someone to ask a few questions.

The court found the patron obviously did not feel coerced or threatened into remaining in the library or responding to questions. After the brief search of his bag, he walked out of the library without responding to the officer's request for his name. In any event, **officers may rely on a trustworthy secondhand report and need not base an investigatory stop on personal observation**. The court rejected the patron's additional arguments and affirmed the judgment. *Only v. Cyr*, 205 Fed.Appx. 947 (3d Cir. 2006).

◆ *The U.S. Supreme Court held a school search must be reasonable at its inception, and not overly intrusive under the circumstances.*

A New Jersey high school teacher found two girls smoking in the lavatory in violation of school rules. She brought them to the assistant vice principal's office where one of the girls admitted smoking in the lavatory. The other denied even being a smoker. The assistant vice principal then asked the latter girl to come to his private office, where he opened her purse and found a pack of cigarettes. As he reached for them he noticed rolling papers and decided to thoroughly search the entire purse. He found marijuana, a pipe, empty plastic bags, a substantial number of one dollar bills and a list of "people who owe me money." He then turned her over to the police. After a juvenile court hearing, the girl was found delinquent. Appeal reached the U.S. Supreme Court.

The Supreme Court held the search did not violate the Fourth Amendment. When police conduct a search, they have to meet the probable cause standard. But school officials are held to the lower "reasonable suspicion" standard. In determining the reasonableness of a search, the search must be justified initially by reasonable suspicion. Second, the scope and conduct of the search must be reasonably related to the circumstances that gave rise to the search, and school officials must take into account the student's age, sex and the nature of the offense. **The Court upheld the search of the student in this case because the initial search for cigarettes was supported by reasonable suspicion.** The discovery of the rolling papers then justified the further searching of the purse since such papers are commonly used to roll marijuana cigarettes. The "reasonableness" standard was met by school officials in these circumstances. *New Jersey v. T.L.O.*, 469 U.S. 325, 105 S.Ct. 733, 83 L.Ed.2d 720 (1985).

## B.  Other Police Matters

*To help assure campus security, some of the states have empowered state universities and their campus police to exercise their authority off campus.*

◆   *A Massachusetts federal judge refused to dismiss a grand jury indictment that charged a student with one count of making a bomb threat.*

A professor found a poem "Invictus" – the same one Timothy McVeigh, the Oklahoma City bomber, chose as his last words – scrawled on a bathroom wall. Under it, a warning urged an evacuation of the building at a specific time. The professor notified campus police. Meanwhile, faculty across campus also contacted police about pages of a manifesto that had been placed under office doors. It was written by a killer in Norway, whose bombing and shooting attack left 77 dead. The building was evacuated and searched. Nothing was found. An investigation led police to a student who had posted sympathetic comments about the Norwegian killer. The student was subpoenaed to provide fingerprints. He did, and they matched the latent fingerprints found on the pages in the manifesto. A grand jury indicted the student on one count of making a bomb threat. The student asked the court to dismiss the indictment, arguing that the grand jury had insufficient evidence to indict him. The court refused, saying that **"the content of the manifesto, together with the poem and warning to evacuate" was enough to constitute a threat under the law.** The court refused to dismiss the indictment. *Comwlth. v. Forts*, 33 Mass.L.Rptr. 73 (Mass. Super. Ct. 2015).

◆   *A Kentucky appeals court affirmed a jury verdict that found a former student guilty of obstructing governmental operations by using threats to hinder a multi-agency active shooter drill at a community college campus.*

A community college, a local police department and a nearby medical center teamed up to conduct an active shooter drill. An actor was hired to play the part of the shooter. Professors and other staff told students about the drill months in advance. On the day of the drill, one student walked into the college library wearing coveralls, military-style boots, a camouflage jacket and sunglasses. He approached other students, telling them if someone came in with a gun, he would shoot that person first. Outside the library, he told another student he would shoot anyone who came onto campus with a weapon because he wouldn't go out like a coward. The students reported his strange behavior and remarks. Given all the armed people on campus, the security director notified the police. Officers were about to be debriefed – but were told instead to report back to campus. After an investigation, the student was charged with obstructing governmental operations. A jury found him guilty and fined him $500. He appealed, but the conviction was upheld. He had **threatened to shoot any armed person coming through a door when he knew an actor with a weapon would be coming through doorways on campus pursued by multiple armed officers**. *Skuljan v. Comwlth.*, No. 2014-CA-000261-MR, 2016 WL 930160 (Ky. Ct. App. 3/11/16).

◆   *The Fifth Circuit affirmed a Texas court ruling that dismissed the due process claims of a former professor who alleged campus police made false and stigmatizing statements about her.*

A professor was terminated when the research funding that paid for her job came to an end. The school cancelled the professor's email and told her to turn in her office keys and ID badge. The professor petitioned another employee to reinstate her. Then the professor hand-delivered a grievance letter to the school. Concerned about the terminated professor's mental state, university police were called. The police department issued a Crime Alert Bulletin that included the professor's photo and description, designated her as an ex-employee and "suspicious person" with "no official business on property," and banned her from campus. A few weeks later, the professor's former supervisor had the ban lifted so she could help him onsite for no pay. She asked the school take down the Crime Alert Bulletin and clear her name. It didn't. The professor sued, alleging a violation of her due process rights due to false and stigmatizing statements. A Texas federal judge dismissed her case for failure to state a claim, and the Fifth Circuit affirmed. To state a successful claim, the professor had to show the stigmatizing charges were made against her in connection with her discharge. The Fifth Circuit found **they were instead made due to her perceived emotional instability and her enigmatic presence at UT after her termination**. As the professor failed to state a valid claim, the Fifth Circuit found the judge was right to dismiss her suit. *Jingping Xu v. Univ. of Texas M.D. Anderson Cancer Center,* 595 Fed.Appx. 341 (5th Cir. 2014).

◆   *An Illinois appeals court threw out the conviction of a man who purportedly violated the protection order of a female student.*

A student took out an order of protection against a man under the Illinois Domestic Violence Act of 1986. Section A of the order of protection said the man had to stay at least 1,000 feet from the woman's home, school and any other specified place. Section B prohibited him "from entering or remaining" on school property while she was there. One day a university police officer saw the man on campus and pulled him over for a registration violation. When the officer ran a check on the man's license, the protection order came up. The man was arrested for violating the protection order. At trial, the man argued the protection order only required him to stay away from the school when the woman he'd been ordered to stay away from was on campus – and the state hadn't offered any evidence that she was at the school at the time. The prosecutor argued that only Section B stipulated the man couldn't come on campus while the woman was there – Section A clearly stated he had to stay 1,000 feet from the school. The judge agreed and found the man violated the order. He appealed, and the appellate court reversed. Under the Illinois Domestic Violence Act, a court could order a person to stay away from a petitioner and to stay away from the petitioner's school when the petitioner was present – **but the act didn't give a court authority to order a person to stay away from a petitioner's school when the petitioner wasn't at the school**. No evidence showed the woman was on campus when the man was there, so the prosecutor didn't prove him guilty beyond a reasonable doubt of violating the protection order. So the conviction was overturned. *People v. Gabriel*, 25 N.E.3d 698 (Ill. App. Ct. 2014).

◆   *A California federal judge dismissed claims against three university police officers in connections with an "occupy" protest – but excessive force claims against one other officer were allowed to proceed.*

Thousands of participants held a protest at a university. Officers arrived to take the tents down. Participants who brought the suit alleged officers "forcefully attacked" them, pushing and jabbing them with batons, putting some in headlocks and "yanking people out by their hair and arresting them." By 4 p.m., police had cleared the tents and retreated. The protesters erected more tents. The university notified protesters that they could stay – but they had to take the tents down. They didn't. Officers in riot gear came back at 10 p.m. and allegedly became more brutal by hitting protestors on the head with batons. Protesters sued to allege rights violations including excessive force and false arrest. The court dismissed the charges against three officers. The protesters knew their identities and believed they'd responded with excessive force. The protesters could have – but didn't – name them as defendants in the suit within the two-year statutory time limit. But the court refused to dismiss another officer from the suit. **In his case, the protesters contend that they were able to identify the officer as the person who struck some of them only after a video analysis. Also, they say they were only able to ascertain his supervisory role over other officers as a result of the video analysis plus documents that were disclosed as part of the lawsuit.** Two-year statutory time limit hadn't passed since the protesters learned the officer's identity, so the claim could proceed. *Felarca v. Birgeneau*, No. 11-cv-05719-YGR, 2014 WL 7140262 (N.D. Cal. 12/12/14).

◆   *University police did not use excessive force in connection with a parking ticket to a contractor who was working at the school, a federal South Carolina court ruled.*

A contractor parked his truck in an area of a university parking garage. During a lunch break, he noticed that he had been given a parking ticket. He saw a university police officer riding his bike in the vicinity and asked if he had written the ticket. The contractor said the officer said, "No, but [I have] the authority to do so." Then the contractor turned his radio back up and began to eat his lunch. He claimed the officer yelled at him, ordered him to get out of the truck and unholstered his weapon when he didn't comply. The contractor called 911, and the operator told him to follow the officer's instructions. The contractor was arrested, charged with breach of the peace and taken to jail. He was later found not guilty of the charge. The contractor sued the officer and the university, alleging false arrest and use of excessive force. The court rejected the false arrest claim, accepting the officer's determination that there was probable cause to place the contractor under arrest because he displayed an "aggressive and uncooperative" attitude. It also noted the contractor didn't comply with the order to get out of the truck. The court rejected the excessive force claim, as the officer said it looked like the contractor was reaching for something in his truck. **Officers could use guns in connection with a seizure if they reasonably believed it was required to protect their safety**, the court said. So the claims were dismissed. *Alexander v. Bolin*, No. 3:13-cv-01722-TLW, 2014 WL 4656384 (D.S.C. 9/17/14).

◆ *A New York appeals court dismissed a personal injury suit filed by a cab driver who was assaulted by students.*

A cab driver took students to their campus. When they arrived, the students disputed the fare. The argument turned physical, and the cab driver was injured. A campus security guard was on the scene but did nothing to break up the fight. The driver sued the student, the school, the security guard and the security firm that contracted the guard for personal injury. The school, the security guard and the security firm asked the court to grant judgment without a trial. The trial court granted judgment to the school. The security guard and the security firm appealed. The appellate court held that the security guard and the security firm should've been granted judgment, too. The relationship between the school and the security firm was contractual – and the contract only required the firm to supply an unarmed guard. **The contract didn't say the guard would protect campus visitors from attack or injury**, the court explained. So all three parties were dismissed from the suit. *Ramirez v. Genovese*, 117 A.D.3d 930 (N.Y. App. Div. 2014).

◆ *A man who was arrested for trespassing on campus didn't state valid claims, but could have an opportunity to rewrite and refile his claim, a Vermont federal judge ruled.*

A local resident was sitting outside the library of the University of Vermont (UVM) when an officer tried to serve him with a complaint that was allegedly filed by the man's daughter. The man refused to sign the service papers and walked away from the officers. A few days later, the man went back to the UVM library, where he was arrested for trespassing. He spent two days in jail. The man sued, claiming UVM's police unlawfully arrested him and humiliated him in public. **The court dismissed the unlawful arrest claim, but found the "humiliation" allegations might indicate a valid constitutional claim.** So the judge gave the man 30 days to rewrite and refile his claim. *Lamore v. Vermont*, No. 2:12-cv-59-FL, 2013 WL 3560969 (D. Vt. 7/11/13).

◆ *Massachusetts' highest court overturned a ruling to suppress the evidence connected to a campus police officer's stop of a driver charged with reckless driving and driving under the influence on campus.*

The lower court had found the officer exceeded his authority under state law, but the high court disagreed. **Massachusetts state law said state police could appoint higher ed institution's employees as "special state police officers [who] ... shall have the same power to make arrests as regular police officers for any criminal offense committed in or upon lands or structures owned, used or occupied" by the college or university.** The court denied the suppression request. *Comwlth v. Smeaton*, 465 Mass. 752 (Mass. 2013).

◆ *Because a secret service agent didn't have a student in custody when he questioned her, he wasn't required to give her* Miranda *warnings.*

Christine Wright-Darrisaw was a student at Monroe Community College (MCC) in New York. Investigating a threat against the President of the United States, the U.S. Secret Service suspected Wright-Darrisaw was behind the threat. Special Agent Joel Blackerby went to MCC to talk to Wright-Darrisaw. When Blackerby arrived on campus, he notified MCC security about his suspicions and asked campus police to escort him to Wright-Darrisaw's class. The student was called out of class. In the hall, Blackerby introduced himself as a Secret Service agent who was investigating a threat against the president. The interview took place in the hallway just outside of class and lasted about 30 minutes. Blackerby asked if he could search Wright-Darrisaw's car. She said no and ended the interview. Blackerby thanked her for her time and told her she was free to go. She was later indicted for threatening to kill the president and making false statements to a federal officer. Wright-Darrisaw asked the court to suppress the statements she made to Balckerby during the interview. But the court found **she wasn't in custody during the interview, so** *Miranda* **warnings weren't required** and her motion was denied. *U.S. v. Wright-Darrisaw*, No. 12-CR-6117-FPG, 2013 WL 3456950 (W.D.N.Y. 7/9/13).

◆ *A state court upheld a Texas university's policy regarding access to its library by outsiders.*

A police officer observed a suspicious person leaving a university library. The officer questioned the man, who provided a false name and had no identification. The officer saw what looked like an ID card in the man's front pocket. It was a card he carried to identify him as a registered sex offender. The officer arrested the man for providing false identification. As per university policy, the officer issued a written trespass warning. The man didn't appeal. Three years later, the warning was still in effect when the officer again encountered the man on campus. The officer arrested the man for criminal trespassing. At trial, the man argued the original trespass warning violated his right to due process and it was unconstitutionally vague. The trial court denied the man's motion to dismiss the indictment. He was sentenced to 30 days in jail and ordered to pay a $250 fine. He appealed, asserting the criminal trespass statute was unconstitutional because it deprived him of his interest in the school's public library. The court determined the policy was clear, and it left the officer with no discretion, so it wasn't vague. The court also explained that **the man didn't have a fundamental right to use the library. The school wasn't required to make its facilities equally available to students and non-students.** Nor was it required to grant free access to all its facilities and buildings. The trial court's judgment was affirmed. *Sanderson v. State of Texas*, No. 06-13-00092-CR, 2013 WL 6255228 (Tex. Ct. App. 12/4/13).

◆   *In a groundbreaking decision, a New York appeals court affirmed the state's unlawful surveillance statute could be used to criminally punish a former student for secretly recording consensual sex acts.*

Michael Piznarski and "A" were enrolled at the same university. They began dating in the fall. The following March, Piznarski used a digital camera to secretly record A performing oral sex on him. After the couple split, Piznarski contacted A on Facebook, insinuating he planned to post the video online and identify her in a post. He threatened to do so – unless she had sex with him again and let him record it. She did, but then reported the incident to police. After obtaining a search warrant, police found videos of A and another female student on Piznarski's computer. He was charged and convicted of unlawful surveillance in the second degree and coercion in the second degree. He served time in prison for the conviction. He appealed, but the appellate court affirmed the convictions. Under New York law, a person was guilty of unlawful surveillance in the second degree when he or she "intentionally uses or installs" a recording device to record a person in an intimate situation without their knowledge. Piznarski argued the statute didn't apply to a person filming a consensual sex act. The court rejected this argument, **citing a Governor's memorandum that said one circumstance that made the law necessary was that there was no other legal recourse for women whose partners had videotaped sex acts without their consent "and are now showing them to friends" and posting them online**. So the convictions were affirmed. *People v. Piznarski*, 977 N.Y.S.2d 104 (N.Y. App. 2013).

◆   *Nebraska's highest court rejected a former employee's claim that a university unlawfully deprived him of his right to his good name when it circulated an email to other workers.*

In 2009, student Paul Potter began working on a full-time temporary basis in the Communications and Information Technology Department at the University of Nebraska. The school did a background check on Potter, and it knew that in 2004 he was charged with burglary, battery and stalking. It also knew he was on probation due to a conviction for driving under the influence. Potter began to have performance issues at work, and the school considered terminating his employment. Pursuant to procedure, the school completed a "threat assessment" in relation to the potential termination. The school's assessment noted Potter's history of "getting upset" at work, a decrease in sociability and his criminal record. On July 20, 2010, two police officers arrived at Potter's place of work and took him away because he had missed a court date and a bench warrant had been issued. With that, the school finalized its decision to terminate Potter, and it sent an email to staffers saying they should lock their door and call for help if they saw Potter in the workplace. Thereafter, Potter's employment with the school was terminated by mail. He sued, claiming deprivation of a liberty interest in his good name without due process. Nebraska's highest court rejected his claim. It determined that **the school made a good-faith judgment about how best to protect its employees**

**and students**. A decision favoring the school was affirmed. *Potter v. Board of Regents of the Univ. of Nebraska*, 844 N.W.2d 741 (Neb. 2014).

◆   *A rule that gave West Virginia University (WVU) campus police too much discretion to issue trespassing forms was held unconstitutional.*

A person wearing a trench coat disturbed others at the WVU student union building because of his mannerisms and because he sat down with a yellow bag near his feet. Campus officers detained the person, searched him, and forced him to empty his pockets. Though nothing inappropriate was found, the officers issued him a "trespassing form" that said he had "interfered with the peaceful or orderly operations" of the university. The person was escorted from the campus and told he would be arrested if he returned. He sued WVU officials in a federal court for constitutional violations. The court held **WVU's trespassing policy was unconstitutionally vague because it was based on a state law that provided for the removal of individuals from campus based on no standards at all**. There were no guidelines or standards for issuing the forms. In addition, the failure to provide an appeal process for the trespassing forms violated due process. The court granted the person's motion for pretrial judgment and declared the trespassing policy unconstitutional. It barred WVU from enforcing the policy, but declined to rule on the issue of damages pending its receipt of further information. *Williams v. West Virginia Univ. Board of Governors*, 782 F.Supp.2d 219 (N.D. W. Va. 2011).

◆   *The arrest of a job applicant by California university campus police did not violate his rights because he matched the description of a criminal suspect.*

A sergeant in the university police department was called by a Florida sheriff's investigator about a suspect wanted in Florida for aggravated battery with a deadly weapon. After contacting a university department, the sheriff confirmed that a person matching the description of the Florida suspect had applied for employment at the university. The applicant had the name and birth date of the suspect, was the same race and gender, had the same hair color and eye color, and was similar in height and weight to the suspect. Based on this information, the sergeant orchestrated an arrest. The applicant later sued the university, sergeant and others in a federal district court. The court applied an objective standard to determine if there was probable cause for the arrest. This involved determining whether a reasonable officer would believe the applicant was the same person named in the warrant based on information available to the sergeant at the relevant time. **The court found the sergeant reasonably believed he was arresting the right person, defeating the false arrest and negligence claims.** *Garcia v. Univ. of California at Los Angeles*, No. CV 09-8193-R, 2010 WL 3814551 (C.D. Cal. 9/27/10).

◆   *A federal court ordered a Pennsylvania state university to let a student take her finals pending the completion of her challenge to drug possession charges.*

University police officers arrested the student after discovering 12 ecstasy pills in her dorm room. At a disciplinary hearing a month later, the university refused to let a lawyer represent her. The only witness at the hearing was the university police chief, who read out the arresting officer's report. The student declined to cross-examine him, called no witnesses and did not testify on her own behalf. The hearing body recommended immediate suspension, academic probation, a drug and alcohol evaluation, and a ban from campus housing. The student sued the university and its president in a federal district court for due process violations. The court granted her request for a preliminary order preventing her expulsion and allowing her to attend classes and take exams. **The court found the university violated her due process rights by refusing to let her attorney speak for her at the hearing.** Since this could lead to a one-sided hearing and wrongful discipline, the court ordered the university to let the student take her finals. *Coulter v. East Stroudsburg Univ.*, No. 3:10-CV-0877, 2010 WL 1816632 (M.D. Pa. 5/5/10).

◆  *A federal district court rejected a man's claim that Marquette University safety officers violated his rights when arresting him for aggravated battery.*

Marquette University Department of Public Safety (DPS) officers assisted the Milwaukee police in arresting the man for aggravated battery. He claimed a DPS employee and Milwaukee police officers held him "hostage" for about two hours and placed him in a "bogus" lineup. After the man was convicted for aggravated battery, he sued the DPS in a federal district court for false imprisonment and violation of his due process rights. **The court explained that to prevail, the man had to show an intentional deprivation of a constitutionally protected right "under color of state law."** He further had to show any constitutional deprivation was caused by an official DPS policy, ordinance, or regulation. A single employee who was not named as a party was the only person from DPS who had anything to do with the arrest. As the claims were insufficient to hold the DPS or any employees liable, DPS received pretrial judgment. *Scott v. Marquette Univ. Dep't of Public Safety*, No. 06-C-0384, 2009 WL 2240234 (E.D. Wis. 7/27/09).

◆  *A Florida university did not violate a student's due process rights when it relied on an unsworn police report as a basis for imposing discipline on him.*

The student asserted the use of the police report in his disciplinary hearing violated his due process rights. He said the police report was unsworn hearsay evidence and that its use violated the university's code of student conduct. The court held the use of an unsworn report did not violate this code provision, which applied only to witnesses who testified at disciplinary hearings. Since the challenged evidence related to a report and not to witness testimony, there was no violation of the code provision. Even though hearsay evidence was used, the court held the student was given all the process he was due. **He was confronted with the report and had a chance to rebut the charges against him.** Also, the student made no attempt to call witnesses or present evidence. He refused to answer questions and relied on his right not to incriminate himself. Under the circumstances, there was no due process violation. *Heiken v. Univ. of Cent. Florida*, 995 So.2d 1145 (Fla. Dist. Ct. App. 2008).

## C. Liability

*University police officers sometimes have to make split-second decisions under stressful conditions. Because of the discretionary nature of their work,*

*the law gives officers immunity from civil liability when they act in good faith.
But immunity was denied to officers who used pepperballs to disperse a crowd.*

◆   *A former student violated a court order when he sent Facebook "friend"
requests to an instructor and other personnel at his school, a court decided.*

After a student made threatening comments aimed at staff and faculty, the
university filed a lawsuit asking the court to ban him from the school's
campuses. The suit further asked the court to issue an order prohibiting him
from communicating with school faculty or other school employees. Soon after
the case was filed, the parties entered into a court-sanctioned stipulation. It
banned the student from campus and from initiating communication with
faculty, staff, employees or students. But the student didn't stick to the
agreement. After sending two cease-and-desist letters, the school asked the
court to find the student in violation of the stipulation after he called the school
president, sent an email to an instructor, sent Facebook "friend" requests to the
school's director of nursing, a clinical coordinator and a nursing instructor,
called an employee on her cell phone, posted threatening and annoying posts
on Facebook, protested outside the school, and sent a harassing letter to the
nursing director. The court found the student violated the stipulation, as calling,
emailing and sending "friend requests" constituted "initiating communication."
**Having found that he violated the stipulation, the court considered the
appropriate sanction. Noting that no actual damages were demonstrated,
it levied a fine of $250 against him and directed the school to submit a
statement of reasonable attorneys' fees.** Finally, the court granted the
school's request that the student be ordered to stay at least 100 yards away from
the school. *St. Paul's School of Nursing, Inc. v. Papaspiridakos,* 984 N.Y.S.2d
634 (N.Y. Sup. Ct. 2014).

◆   *The parents of a student who was killed by a university police officer could
not proceed with their negligence and injunctive relief claims against the
university's chief of police.*

In October 2012, Gilbert Collar was a student at the University of South
Alabama. According to his parents, he was talking outside a dormitory with
other students late one night when he "was given a substance that is believed to
have included illegal drugs." He removed his clothing and began to run around,
eventually making his way to the university's police station. At the police
station, he began hitting a door. An officer came out of the station with his gun
drawn. Collar began to advance on the officer, and the officer shot and killed
him. Collar's parents said a baton or pepper spray could have been used instead
of the fatal shot. The parents sued the school, the officer, the university's chief
of police and others. In one count of the complaint, they sought injunctive relief
in the form of requiring specific training and equipment (including Tasers) for
university police. They also claimed negligence and said excessive force was
used. After the university gained dismissal of the claims against it based on
state immunity, the chief of police filed a similar motion to dismiss. The trial
court denied his motion, and the chief sought review.

Alabama's highest court granted the police chief's petition for relief. As to
the parents' claim for injunctive relief, the chief of police asserted that the

request for injunctive relief was essentially an impermissible claim for monetary damages that did not fall within any exception to statutory immunity. The court granted the chief of police's request to dismiss the claim for injunctive relief, but not on the basis he urged. Instead, it determined that the parents lacked standing to pursue the claim for injunctive relief. **To have standing, the parents had to show that granting their requested injunctive relief would remedy the injury they suffered.** However, neither additional police training nor the provision of Tasers to officers would remedy the injury they suffered. As a result, they lacked standing to pursue their claims for injunctive relief. The reviewing court also determined that the negligence claim against the chief of police in his official capacity should be dismissed. It was well-established that actions for damages against state agents in their official capacities were barred under state law. The petition filed by the chief of police was granted. *Ex parte Aull,* 149 So.3d 582 (Ala. 2014).

◆ *Negligence – but not constitutional – claims went forward against a public Iowa university based on its officers' failure to protect a woman from suffering permanent damage from exposure to the cold.*

On a December night in 2011, when the temperature was below zero, a woman fell, suffered a head injury and managed to lose her shoes. Dana Jaeger, a male UNI peace officer, found her. The woman said Jaeger and other officers put her in a police car that wasn't adequately heated and failed to give her any covering for her feet. She says they then took her to the county jail, where she still wasn't provided appropriate care for her feet – so she wound up with permanent damage from exposure to the freezing conditions that night. She sued, claiming negligence. Her suit alleged UNI and Officer Jaeger were deliberately indifferent to "obvious and serious medical risks" in violation of the Eighth and Fourteenth Amendments and that UNI had policies, customs or habits of providing inadequate medical care in violation of the Eighth and Fourteenth Amendments. The UNI defendants asked the court to dismiss the claims against them. The court dismissed the constitutional claims because UNI (as a state entity) and Jaeger (as a state official acting in his official capacity) had immunity to them. **It refused to dismiss the negligence claim against UNI, but substituted the state for Officer Jaeger in that claim as Iowa's Tort Claims Act required.** Only a negligence claim went forward against the university, but the woman alleged constitutional claims against the county and its sheriff. Those claims proceeded. *Kellner v. Univ. of Northern Iowa,* No. 14-CV-2004-LRR, 2014 WL 855831 (N.D. Iowa 3/5/14).

◆ *University of California at Davis (UCD) police faced constitutional liability after shooting pepperballs into a crowd of partygoers.*

Police responded to a gathering of about 1,000 people at an apartment complex. When some of the people started rocking a car and setting off bottle rockets, a property owner asked the police to disperse the crowd for trespassing. Municipal police called UCD police for backup. Officers in riot gear moved through the crowd, but the partygoers did not disperse. When officers shot pepperballs, a student was hit in the eye. He lost visual acuity, eventually lost his athletic scholarship and withdrew from UCD. In a federal court, the student sued UCD for seizing him in violation of his civil rights. The case reached the U.S. Court of Appeals, Ninth Circuit, which held it was not relevant that the injury was inadvertent. In the court's opinion, **the incident was an unreasonable Fourth Amendment seizure because the police used unjustified force**. It held the general disorder of the complex could not be used to legitimize the use of pepperballs against non-threatening individuals. As a result, the court held university police officers were not entitled to pretrial judgment. *Nelson v. City of Davis*, 685 F.3d 867 (9th Cir. 2012).

◆ *North Carolina's highest court rejected an arrestee's argument that a private university could not maintain campus police officers.*

A Davidson College campus police officer pulled over a speeding vehicle that was weaving on roads near campus and, after administering two alcohol tests, arrested the driver for reckless driving and driving while impaired. The driver later filed a motion to suppress the evidence against her, asserting that since Davidson was a religiously affiliated college, it should not have campus police officers or there would be a violation of the Establishment Clause. When the case reached the state supreme court, it held that the evidence could be used against the driver. **The state's Campus Police Act (CPA) had a secular purpose and did not foster excessive state entanglement with religion.** The CPA provided substantial protections to ensure neutrality and guard against excessive church-state entanglement. In particular, the CPA made it clear officers could only enforce secular laws – not campus policies or religious rules. As a result, the court denied the driver's challenge. *State v. Yencer*, 365 N.C. 292, 718 S.E.2d 615 (N.C. 2011).

◆ *A New York federal court dismissed a student's federal claims against New York University (NYU) for making a false police report about him.*

A university security employee accused the student of stealing a wallet in a locker room. Although the student denied this, the employee called NYU's public safety administrator, who in turn called municipal police. A municipal police officer arrested and jailed the student. After the student was acquitted of all charges, he accused NYU of refusing to let him return as a student. He sued NYU in a federal court. The court found the federal claims were all based on conclusory allegations and did not state necessary facts. The race discrimination claim failed because the student did not claim he was mistreated because of his race. There was no evidence that NYU conspired with the police to frame him, defeating the conspiracy claim. **The court dismissed all the federal claims against NYU as they were based on conclusory allegations.** *Johnson v. City of New York,* 669 F.Supp.2d 444 (S.D.N.Y. 2009).

◆ *An Oregon public university did not violate the First Amendment by expelling a student who threatened a university administrator.*

The student kept guns and ammunition in his dorm room and told acquaintances that he wanted to kill or hurt an assistant director of residence life. University officials told the assistant director about the comments and recommended that he and his family move off campus for a few days. The assistant director followed the recommendation and also obtained a restraining order against the student. The school then held a hearing at which a committee recommended expulsion for violating the student conduct code and standards relating to residence housing. The university adopted the recommendation, and the student sought court review, claiming the expulsion violated his free speech rights. **The court held that it was reasonable for school officials to expel him since the threats disrupted university activities.** *Hagel v. Portland State Univ.*, 228 Or.App. 239 (Or. Ct. App. 2009).

◆   *A student identified as a safety threat was properly dismissed from a Pennsylvania nurse anesthesia program.*

The university said the student constantly needed assistance, and nurse anesthetists who supervised him said he had clinical performance issues. The university placed the student on probation and later dismissed him from the program for jeopardizing the health or safety of patients. He sued the university in a federal district court for breach of contract and related claims. The court rejected the student's claim that his contract called for progressive discipline prior to dismissal from the program. **A university handbook separately provided that it could dismiss any student who jeopardized the safety or welfare of a patient.** There was no evidence that the student was dismissed for any reason other than patient safety. The court upheld the action. *Kimberg v. Univ. of Scranton*, No. 3:06cv1209, 2009 WL 222658 (M.D. Pa. 1/29/09).

◆   *The criminal prosecution of a temporary instructor charged with making email and phone threats to college personnel was allowed to proceed.*

Based on his poor job performance, the college decided not to renew the temporary instructor's contract. But he continued to threaten faculty and administrators. The college responded by barring him from campus. However, the instructor sent several emails and made phone calls in which he threatened to kill faculty and administrators, as well as members of their families. Threats were made to professors, a department chairman, the vice president of the college, and the dean of the college. After the FBI executed a search warrant at the instructor's residence and seized evidence relating to the case, a grand jury indicted him on nine counts of transmitting an interstate email threat to kill or injure another person. It also indicted him on three counts of interstate threats via telephone. The instructor sought dismissal, claiming the indictment did not sufficiently allege that he transmitted a "true threat," as the applicable statute required. **The court found a "true threat" exists if the recipient is familiar with the context of the communication and would interpret it as a true threat.** Each count of the indictment in this case met the test. *U.S. v. Li*, 537 F.Supp.2d 431 (N.D.N.Y. 2008).

◆   *A Florida court held that in an emergency, a university can exclude a student and provide a hearing afterward to protect the campus.*

A graduate of Florida Atlantic University (FAU) returned to FAU for a graduate program but was dismissed for receiving a failing grade. She then enrolled in continuing education classes. Faculty members became fearful of the student, saying she made veiled threats. FAU issued a "no trespass warning" that barred her from campus. The student was arrested three times for violating the warning and was convicted of trespassing. After several more incidents, the student was banned from FAU indefinitely. She sued FAU in a state court, claiming it violated her due process rights. The court held for FAU, and the student appealed. A Florida District Court of Appeal found that due process protection can extend to interests in specific benefits created by state laws or state university rules and policies. It was a mistake for the trial court to rule the student had no interest in continued enrollment. FAU could not permanently deprive her of access to its campus without notice and an opportunity for a hearing. **However, the court recognized that in emergencies, a university can exclude a student and provide a hearing afterward.** *Lankheim v. Florida Atlantic Univ.*, 992 So.2d 828 (Fla. Dist. Ct. App. 2008).

◆   *A Connecticut college did not violate a student's due process rights as he received notice and a chance to be heard regarding the charges against him.*

The university held a disciplinary hearing, after which a hearing officer found the student had stalked a female classmate. He was suspended for 15 months, barred from student activities and prevented from earning credits. After an unsuccessful internal appeal, the student filed an action in state court, seeking an order that would require the university to reinstate him as a full-time student in good standing. The court found he was entitled to the requested order only if he could show the suspension proceeding did not meet due process requirements. He failed to make this showing as he could not prove a violation of any due process rights. **There is no fundamental right to attend college. The student received notice of the charges against him, and neither the form nor content of the notice prejudiced his ability to defend the charges.** As he was not denied due process with respect to the university's procedures, the court denied his request for a preliminary injunction. *Danso v. Univ. of Connecticut*, 50 Conn.Supp. 256, 919 A.2d 1100 (Conn. Super. Ct. 2007).

# CHAPTER ELEVEN

## School Finance

## I.  PUBLIC ASSISTANCE TO SCHOOLS

### A.  Federal Funding

#### 1.  Compliance

*The U.S. government distributes funds to higher education institutions under Title IV of the Higher Education Act (HEA), 20 U.S.C. § 1094, to assist with the costs of secondary education. In order to receive federal funds under the HEA, institutions must enter into Program Participation Agreements with the U.S. Department of Education. In doing so, the institutions agree to various statutory, regulatory, and contractual requirements. Among these requirements is a recruiter-incentive compensation ban, which prohibits institutions from paying recruiters "incentive payments" based on the number of students they enroll. This provision was considered by a District of Columbia federal court.*

◆  *A former instructor alleged a university lied about legal compliance, but a Florida federal judge dismissed his claim.*

Kaplan University (KU) operated online distance learning programs in the U.S. as a subsidiary of Kaplan Higher Education Corporation (KHEC). To receive federal student financial aid funds, both KU and KHEC had to enter a Program Participation Agreement (PPA) with the U.S. Department of Education to certify they'd comply with specified laws. In 2004 and 2007, KU's PPA specified it would comply with Section 504 of the Rehabilitation Act and its regulations. Employee Judy Gillespie filed a complaint with the Office for Civil Rights (OCR), accusing KU of disability bias and failure to comply with Section 504. After OCR investigated, KU signed a resolution agreement – not admitting wrongdoing but agreeing to take specific steps to bring its programs into full compliance. Within two years, OCR notified KU that it had fully complied with the resolution agreement. But Gillespie brought a *qui tam* action to allege KU, KHEC and Kaplan, Inc., violated the False Claims Act (FCA) by falsely certifying they were in compliance with the Rehabilitation Act and its regulations – and therefore wrongfully received federal funds.

Qui tam is the first part of a Latin phrase that means: "One who sues on behalf of the King as well as for himself." In a *qui tam* action, a government informer gets a share of the penalty if there is one. Kaplan defendants asked the court to dismiss the claim. It did. To win an FCA claim, Gillespie had to show the defendants submitted a false claim while knowing the claim was false. That wasn't the case here. The FCA "was not meant to punish honest mistakes or … mere negligence," the court explained. **"It was meant to reach the situation where an individual has 'buried his head in the sand' and failed" to attempt to fix problems.** In this instance, the defendants proved the opposite by showing they had staff responsible for guaranteeing legal compliance and they acted diligently. So the claim failed. *U.S. ex rel. Gillespie v. Kaplan Univ.*, No. 09-20756-CIV, 2013 WL 3762445 (S.D. Fla. 7/16/13).

◆   *In December 2012, a federal appeals court held a group of religious colleges could not challenge the federal Affordable Care Act's requirement that employers provide health insurance coverage for contraceptives.*

In separate federal court actions, Wheaton College and other religious institutions challenged the Affordable Care Act's mandate that group health plans and health insurers cover preventive care and screenings for women. This has been defined by the U.S. Health Resources and Services Administration (HRSA) to mean plans must cover contraception. But the HRSA acknowledged that requiring coverage for contraceptives might interfere with the religious beliefs of some employers. In March 2012, federal agencies implementing the law announced that they would create a rule that would not require cost-sharing for contraceptives among all participants in religious employers' health plans.

A federal district court dismissed the cases, finding the colleges lacked standing. On appeal, the U.S. Court of Appeals, District of Columbia Circuit, held the claims by the religious colleges were not ripe for court review, noting the federal government's indication that **a rule relating to contraceptive coverage requirements was forthcoming**. *Wheaton College v. Sebelius*, 703 F.3d 551 (D.C. Cir. 2012).

*Note: In July 2015, the federal government issued final regulations concerning the Coverage of Certain Preventive Services Under the Affordable Care Act. See 180 Fed. Reg. 41318-41347. It maintains an accommodation for religious nonprofits, extends it to some closely held for-profits, and provides alternative notice provisions.*

◆   *A conservative advocacy group lacked standing to enforce the Solomon Amendment on behalf of its student-members in a federal court.*

Under the Solomon Amendment, a college or university can lose federal funds if the U.S. Secretary of Defense determines the institution does not allow military recruiting on campus on terms at least equal to those allowed other employers. The Young America's Foundation (YAF) informed the Secretary of Defense that some students and faculty prevented or disrupted military recruiting at the University of California at Santa Cruz (UCSC) and prevented YAF members from meeting with military recruiters at campus job fairs. When the Secretary took no action under the Solomon Amendment, the YAF asked a federal court to order him to withhold funds from UCSC. The court dismissed the case, and the YAF appealed to the U.S. Court of Appeals, D.C. Circuit. The court held the YAF lacked standing to bring the action. Organizations may sue to enforce the rights of members if at least one member has the right to bring the lawsuit on her own behalf. But since none of these member-students did, the YAF lacked standing. **The YAF could not demonstrate that ordering the Secretary of Defense to withhold funds from UCSC would provide student-members greater access to military recruiters** at job fairs. *Young America's Foundation v. Gates*, 573 F.3d 797 (D.C. Cir. 2009).

◆   *Federal assistance may be conditioned on compliance with federal law.*
    Section 12(f) of the Military Selective Service Act denied federal financial assistance under Title IV of the Higher Education Act to male students between the ages of 18 and 26 who did not register for the draft. Applicants for assistance were required to file a statement with their institutions attesting to their compliance with the Selective Service Act. A group of students who had not registered for the draft sued the selective service system to enjoin enforcement of Section 12(f). A federal district court held that the act was a bill of attainder (a law that imposes a penalty on a group of people without a trial) because it singled out an identifiable group that would be ineligible for Title IV aid based on their failure to register. The court also held that the compliance requirement violated the Fifth Amendment. On appeal, the Supreme Court rejected the claims that the law was a bill of attainder and upheld the law.
    The law clearly gave non-registrants 30 days after receiving notice of ineligibility for federal financial aid to register for the draft and thereby qualify for aid. Furthermore, the bill of attainder prohibition in the Constitution applies only to statutes that inflict punishments on specified groups or individuals such as "all Communists." The Court also held that the denial of aid based on these requirements was not "punishment." The Court stated that **if students wish to further their education at the expense of their country, they cannot expect the benefits without accepting their fair share of governmental responsibility**. Finally, the law did not violate the Fifth Amendment because there was nothing forcing students to apply for federal aid. *Selective Service System v. Minnesota Public Interest Research Group*, 468 U.S. 841, 104 S.Ct. 3348, 82 L.Ed.2d 632 (1984).

◆   *A federal law that cuts off financial aid to students convicted of drug-related offenses did not violate the Fifth Amendment.*
    A federal statute located at 20 U.S.C. § 1091(r) cuts off federal grant, loan or work assistance to any student who is convicted of an offense involving the sale or possession of a controlled substance. A student advocacy group sued the U.S. Department of Education Secretary, claiming the law was unconstitutional

because it punished them criminally a second time for the same offense in violation of the Double Jeopardy Clause of the Fifth Amendment.

A federal district court rejected the group's arguments. On appeal, the U.S. Court of Appeals, Eighth Circuit, analyzed whether punishment imposed by the statute was civil or criminal in nature. **The fact that the law suspended eligibility and did not impose penalties, and the fact that an administrative agency determined eligibility indicated that Congress intended a civil sanction, not a criminal one.** The court also found the statute's scheme was not so punitive that it could be deemed to levy a criminal penalty. Application of the relevant factors weighed in favor of a finding that the statute did not impose criminal punishment. Therefore, there was no violation of the Double Jeopardy Clause, and the judgment was affirmed. *Students for Sensible Drug Policy Foundation v. Spellings*, 523 F.3d 896 (8th Cir. 2008).

◆   *The Supreme Court held a violation of Title IV of the Higher Education Act may be shown without proving specific intent to injure or defraud.*

A private, nonprofit technical school in Indiana participated in the Guaranteed Student Loan (GSL) program authorized by Title IV of the Higher Education Act. The program required the school to make refunds to the lender if a student withdrew from school during a term. If the school failed to refund loans to the lender, the student – and if the student defaulted, the government – would be liable for the full amount of the loan. The treasurer of the school conferred with the school's owners and initiated a practice of not making GSL refunds. As a result, the school owed $139,649 in refunds. After the school lost its accreditation, a federal grand jury indicted the treasurer for "knowingly and willfully misapplying" federally insured student loan funds in violation of 20 U.S.C. § 1097(a). A federal district court dismissed the indictment because it lacked an allegation that the treasurer intended to injure or defraud the U.S. The Seventh Circuit reinstated the prosecution, and the U.S. Supreme Court affirmed the decision. The Court held Section 1097(a) did not require the specific intent to injure or defraud. **If the government can prove the defendant misapplied Title IV funds knowingly and willfully, that is sufficient to show a violation of Section 1097(a).** *Bates v. U.S.*, 522 U.S. 23, 118 S.Ct. 285, 139 L.Ed.2d 215 (1997).

## 2. Government Authority

*To participate in HEA Title IV programs and accept federal funds, a postsecondary institution must satisfy several statutory requirements. These requirements are intended to ensure that participating schools actually prepare their students for employment, such that those students can repay their loans.*

◆   *Months after the University of Phoenix (UP) paid $78.5 million to settle a case charging the institution with breaching HEA student aid requirements, two former employees filed a new case stating that UP fraud was continuing.*

To participate in federal student loan programs, an institution must agree not to base compensation for admissions staff on the number of students they enroll or financial aid awards they obtain. In December 2009, UP paid $78.5

million to settle a lawsuit alleging it had violated this provision. About nine months later, two former UP admission counselors filed a new action in a federal court against UP, alleging it was still committing the same offenses.

Both the U.S. government and the state of California intervened in the case, alleging UP violated federal and state false claims acts. Former UP admission counselors said UP's policies would continue to disguise the unlawful practice of basing salaries on enrollment numbers. The court found the prior case was not a bar to the second action. It held the first case was no longer "pending," as it had been settled. UP also argued the suit was blocked by a federal rule that an action based on already-disclosed allegations or transactions is barred unless the person bringing the action was an original source of the information. **The court held the employees in the present case based their action on the claim that UP adopted procedures to cover up a continuation of the fraud.** As a result, the court held the case could proceed. *U.S. ex rel. Hoggett v. Univ. of Phoenix*, No. 2:10-cv-02478-MCE-KJN, 2013 WL 875969 (E.D. Cal. 3/7/13).

◆ *A federal court challenge to 2009 HEA Title IV regulations governing compensation practices in higher education, state authorization requirements for institutions of higher learning, and distance education will proceed.*

In 2009, the U.S. Department of Education (DOE) proposed new HEA regulations to address concerns that its regulations governing several areas of Title IV administration were lax. The DOE's 2010 regulations concerned state authorization, compensation, misrepresentation, and other statutory requirements. One regulation required states to authorize specific institutions by name, and to maintain a process to review and act upon complaints concerning these institutions. Another rule required institutions offering distance or correspondence education (including online courses) to obtain state authorization. One regulation eliminated a "safe harbor" provision for compensation practices to eliminate incentive payments.

An association representing private colleges sued the DOE's secretary in a federal court to challenge certain requirements of the 2010 regulations. The federal court upheld the provision regarding compensation and misrepresentation by higher education institutions. The federal court also found the group lacked standing to challenge the regulation regarding state authorization of institutions. It also upheld the provision on distance education. On appeal, the U.S. Court of Appeals, District of Columbia Circuit, upheld the compensation regulations. But it sent two aspects of the compensation issue to the lower court for further consideration. While the challengers had standing to bring a lawsuit challenging the school authorization regulation, the court upheld it as valid. **A challenge to a distance education regulation was struck down because it was "not a logical outgrowth of the Department's proposed rules."** *Ass'n of Private Sector Colleges and Univ. v. Duncan*, 681 F.3d 427 (D.C. Cir. 2012).

◆ *A private college was not covered by the Privacy Act because participation in a student financial assistance program did not make it a federal agent.*

An Illinois student's father died, and her mother was unable to comply with her college's requests for verification of income. As a result, she did not receive federal financial aid for one school year. The college allowed the student to register for classes and treated her tuition as an "unpaid debt." Although she qualified for federal aid, the college's financial aid office refused to issue her funds because she was not in good standing. The student's mother then took out private loans to cover her tuition. The student completed the requirements for her bachelor's degree that year – but the college refused to grant her a degree because her tuition for the previous year remained unpaid.

The student and her mother sued the college and the U.S. Department of Education (DOE) in a federal district court for violating the federal Privacy Act. **The court found the Privacy Act is intended to protect citizens from the improper disclosure of personal information by government agencies.** The court awarded pretrial judgment to the college because it is not a government agency. The DOE was also entitled to judgment because it had not maintained the financial information in this case. Instead, the college kept it. The court rejected the argument that the college was a DOE agent that could be held liable for record-keeping. *Lengerich v. Columbia College*, 633 F.Supp.2d 599 (N.D. Ill. 2009).

◆   *A private university did not meet the eligibility requirements for student financial assistance programs under Title IV of the Higher Education Act.*

In 1991 and 1992, the DOE found the university system, Sistema Universitario Ana G. Mendez, was not eligible for Title IV programs dealing with Pell grant programs. As a result of the DOE's finding, **the university system was responsible for refunding to the federal government $1,712,540 in student grant funds** that were disbursed from 1989 to 1991. The secretary of education's determination was based on the fact that the university system failed to license its additional campuses. When filling out its Title IV application forms, the university system did not report these campuses under the "additional locations" section. It also failed to obtain prior approval from the Puerto Rico Commission on Higher Education for most of the satellite locations. The university system filed an administrative challenge, but a DOE administrative law judge affirmed its $1.7 million liability. The university system appealed to a federal district court, which reversed the administrative decision, finding the satellite campuses were licensed. However, it also found that the certifications did not necessarily constitute legal authorization under the Higher Education Act. On remand, the DOE determined that the certifications did not constitute legal authorization. The district court affirmed.

The university system then asked the U.S. Court of Appeals for the First Circuit to determine whether the Higher Education Act gives the secretary of education the final word on whether a university program is legally authorized by a state under the act and is therefore eligible for Title IV funding. The First Circuit held that **the Higher Education Act does not explicitly give either the secretary of education or the states the exclusive right to determine "legal authorization."** However, the court reasoned that it is not impermissible or unreasonable to allow the secretary to make that determination. The DOE's finding of liability was affirmed. *Sistema Universitario Ana G. Mendez v. Riley*, 234 F.3d 772 (1st Cir. 2000).

## B. State Funding

◆ *A Wisconsin federal judge refused to order the University of Wisconsin (UW) to fund a conservative student group from student fees.*

UW student fees funded registered student organizations. "Collegians for a Constructive Tomorrow-Madison" (CFACT) missed an application deadline for funding set by the student services finance committee (SSFC), and the application was rejected. CFACT appealed, arguing its conservative viewpoint was the real reason SSFC denied it eligibility. After a student government panel upheld the decision, CFACT filed a federal district court action against UW, alleging denial of equal access to UW's student activity fee forum based on its viewpoint. The court denied the organization's request for a preliminary order requiring UW to fund it. It found a limited pool of money for student groups meant both sides faced equal harm. **Denying the injunction would hinder the group's ability to convey its expressive message on campus, but granting it would cause the same harm to other student groups.** UW successfully refuted the claim that SSFC granted eligibility to other groups that missed the deadline. The court denied the injunction. *Collegians for a Constructive Tomorrow-Madison v. Regents of Univ. of Wisconsin System*, 698 F.Supp.2d 1058 (W.D. Wis. 2010).

◆ *The New York Supreme Court, Appellate Division, held that the state could review a nonpublic educational institution's certification of a student's eligibility for a state grant.*

A New York private college accepted and certified a group of students who had previously attended a local community college as eligible for state Supplemental Tuition Assistance Program (STAP) grants. The STAP grants provided tuition assistance to New York students whose educational deficits were so great that they would not be considered admissible to a college-level program. The state denied the college's request for STAP award, and a New York trial court affirmed the denial. On appeal by the college, the appellate division court held that **the state had both the authority and the obligation to review a nonpublic educational institution's certification of a student's eligibility for a STAP grant**. The regulatory scheme did not contemplate awards to students with successful college experience who had previously received funds pursuant to the Tuition Assistance Program. The appellate court affirmed the trial court's denial of STAP funds. *Touro College v. Nolan*, 620 N.Y.S.2d 558 (N.Y. App. Div. 1994).

◆ *A university could not maintain a race-based scholarship program where past discrimination did not justify it.*

The University of Maryland maintained a merit scholarship program open only to African-American students. It alleged that the program redressed prior constitutional violations against African-American students by the university, which had formerly been segregated by law. A student of Hispanic descent attempted to obtain a scholarship under the program, but was denied on the basis of his race. He filed a lawsuit against the university and a number of its officials in the U.S. District Court for the District of Maryland. The court granted summary judgment to the university, and the student won reversal from the U.S. Court of Appeals, Fourth Circuit. On remand, the parties again filed cross motions for summary judgment, and the district court again awarded summary judgment to the university.

The case was again appealed to the court of appeals. It determined that the district court had improperly found a basis in the evidence for its conclusion that a remedial plan of action was necessary. It also had erroneously determined that the scholarship program was narrowly tailored to meet the goal of remedying past discrimination. The court had misconstrued statistical evidence presented by the parties and had erroneously found a connection between past discrimination and present conditions at the university. **The reasons stated by the university for maintaining the race-based scholarship – underrepresentation of African-American students, low retention and graduation rates and a negative perception among African-American students – were legally insufficient.** The court reversed the summary judgment order for the university and awarded summary judgment to the student. *Podberesky v. Kirwan*, 38 F.3d 147 (4th Cir. 1994).

## C.  Student Default

*Section 523(a)(8) of the U.S. Bankruptcy Code does not allow the discharge of student loans in bankruptcy. However, a bankruptcy court may permit the discharge of student loan debt if the student can show it would impose an undue hardship to repay the loans. In addition to the test for "undue hardship," a bankruptcy court may consider exceptional circumstances that strongly suggest a continuing inability to repay, such as a disability, and a student's failure to take advantage of forebearances or deferments.*

*The bankruptcy code does not define "undue hardship," and the courts have struggled with its meaning. In the case of* In re Frushour, *433 F.3d 393 (4th Cir. 2005), the U.S. Court of Appeals, Fourth Circuit, held that having a low-paying job does not in itself cause undue hardship, especially when the debtor has not tried to get a job that pays more. Government-backed student-loan debt is ordinarily not discharged in Chapter 7 proceedings.*

◆ *A bankruptcy court held that a student was not entitled to have his student loans discharged.*

The student completed a bachelor's degree program in computer network administration and a master's degree program in organizational leadership. Despite the degrees, he could not find work in his field. Instead, he earned money as a part-time tutor and a handyman. For the next five years, his gross income was well under $10,000 per year. His student loan debt was more than $100,000. He lived with his stepsister, drove a 1999 Pontiac and received food stamps from the state. He asked the bankruptcy court to discharge his student loans. Under the Bankruptcy Code, educational loans are to be discharged only if they impose an undue hardship on the borrower.

To prove an undue hardship, one thing the borrower had to show was that this state of affairs was likely to persist for a significant portion of the repayment period. The court said the student didn't. **He was only 33, so the**

**court was not convinced his lack of employment was likely to continue indefinitely.** The court said Owens was "at the front end of his working years." The Department of Education and the school also argued that the student did not satisfy another requirement: good-faith efforts to repay the debt. To support this argument, the Department of Education and university pointed out that he didn't pay back any part of the loans and did not apply for an income-contingent payment plan. **The court concluded that the student did not show that he made a good-faith effort to repay the loans.** Because he did not meet the two requirements, he was not entitled to have his loans discharged. The Department of Education and the university were entitled to judgment. *In re Owens*, 525 B.R. 719 (Bkrtcy. C.D. Ill. 2015).

◆ *A federal district court in Michigan rejected a former student's claim that his student loan was voidable because he was a minor when he obtained it.*

The student signed a note for a student loan. A decade later, the student filed a court complaint. In it, he sought a declaration that the loan he obtained was voidable at his option because he was underage when he signed the note. He also sought to recover damages under the federal Truth in Lending Act (TILA). The university filed a motion to dismiss the case. The court rejected the student's claim under the TILA because **student loans issued under Title IV of the Higher Education Act were exempt from the protections of the TILA**. Further, the Higher Education Act specifically provided that an infancy defense could not be used with respect to loans issued under the act, the court explained. The motion to dismiss was granted. *Bush v. Northern Michigan Univ.*, No. 2:14-CV-43, 2014 WL 1952267 (W.D. Mich. 5/15/14).

◆ *An African-American student at a South Carolina technical college did not convince a federal court that his financial aid was withheld based on race.*

The student claimed in his federal lawsuit that the college held back financial aid money because of his race. He asked for an order requiring the college to pay him $5 million in damages for pain and suffering. He also asked the court to order the college to provide him with "passing grades of (C) and above." A magistrate judge recommended that his complaint be dismissed, and a federal court adopted the magistrate judge's recommendation. In ruling for the technical college, **the student failed to allege that the financial aid disbursement policy applied only to him or only to members of his racial group**. *Logan v. Greenville Technical College*, No. 6:11-467-TMC, 2011 WL 5082230 (D.S.C. 10/26/11).

◆ *A disabled student borrower's request to have her student loan debt discharged was rejected by a federal appeals court.*

A former Illinois college student took out federal loans totalling $13,250. She later defaulted on them and filed a series of applications with the U.S. Department of Education (DOE) to discharge her debt on the basis of her disability. Although the former student produced letters from her physician declaring her inability to work, the DOE denied the application for discharge.

When the student sought judicial review of the denial, her doctors provided 10 years of medical records. Based on the new evidence, the court sent the case back to the DOE. But the DOE found her physician failed to explain why she was completely unable to work, and the DOE again denied discharge. A federal district court upheld the decision, and appeal went before the U.S. Court of Appeals, Seventh Circuit. It found that **to discharge a student loan debt on the basis of disability, the student had to show she was "permanently and totally disabled."** To do so, she had to establish she was unable to work because of an injury or illness that was expected to continue indefinitely or result in death. The student did not meet this standard. Her physician provided few details about her condition, and the DOE was not required to accept his conclusory assertions. *Boutte v. Duncan*, 348 Fed.Appx. 151 (7th Cir. 2009).

◆ *An Ohio court reversed a decision that excused a suspended student from repaying student loan funds he had received.*

The student compiled a history of using profanity and raising his voice when calling the university's financial aid office. He received repeated warnings about his behavior. The university approved a financial aid package on the assumption that the student would be taking a certain number of courses. When officials learned he would not be taking all the classes, his financial aid was decreased. The student called the financial aid office and used profanity. He told a financial aid office employee that "if he could reach through the phone, he would slap her." Shortly after his outburst, the student received a student loan check of $2,600. The university suspended him for misconduct.

The student's appeal was denied, and the university adjusted his account and sued him in a state court to recover $1,700 of the financial aid it gave him. He said he was not required to pay back the money because the suspension was unjust. The court agreed, saying the university had "demanded full payment for classes never given." The university appealed to the Court of Appeals of Ohio, which reversed the judgment. It found **the student had undisputedly received a loan check and spent the money**. Some of the funds were used to purchase a computer. Under the circumstances, the trial court abused its discretion, and the case was returned to it for more proceedings. *Franklin Univ. v. Ickes*, 181 Ohio App.3d 10, 907 N.E.2d 793 (Ohio Ct. App. 2009).

◆ *A Wisconsin university violated federal law by denying a transcript to a teacher whose tuition debt had been discharged in a bankruptcy proceeding.*

An art teacher stopped making payments midway through the first year of her master's degree program. By the time she completed the program, she owed the university over $6,000 in tuition. A federal bankruptcy court discharged this debt. During and after the bankruptcy proceeding, the university denied the teacher's requests for a copy of her transcript. **Under the U.S. Bankruptcy Code, creditors cannot take actions to collect a debt until a bankruptcy proceeding ends.** The code also bars creditors from taking action to collect debts that have been discharged. The teacher said the university violated both provisions when it denied her requests for her transcript. A bankruptcy judge ordered the university to provide the teacher a copy of her transcript, and to pay her damages and attorneys' fees. On appeal, **the U.S. Court of Appeals, Seventh Circuit, said students have a right to receive copies of their transcripts**. It found a right to receive a transcript "is essential to a meaningful property right in grades." Finding the university violated the Bankruptcy Code by refusing to provide the teacher with a copy of her transcript, the court affirmed the judgment. *In re Kuehn*, 563 F.3d 289 (7th Cir. 2009).

◆   *A New York court rejected a graduate's claim that a college wrongfully intercepted his state tax refunds to recoup money he owed for tuition.*

A college intercepted the graduate's state tax refunds after obtaining a civil court judgment against him for failing to pay his tuition. He filed a state court action to force the return of the intercepted refunds. The graduate claimed he had already paid back his student loans and did not owe more tuition. He claimed the college failed to apply the intercepted refunds to his loans. After a trial, the court dismissed the case, and the graduate appealed. On appeal, a New York Appellate Division Court agreed with the lower court's decision that the case was meritless. The judgment authorizing interception of the graduate's state tax refunds was obtained in a suit to recover sums previously awarded to him as federal Pell grants and state awards. **Those sums were used to pay his tuition, and the college was obligated to repay them to state and federal agencies.** As a result of this obligation, the college was entitled to recoup tuition amounts, which the graduate did not pay. The graduate failed to show the civil court judgment that served as the basis for intercepting the funds was not properly entered. As a result, the court affirmed the judgment for the college. *Onitiri v. CUNY*, 55 A.D.3d 808 (N.Y. App. Div. 2008).

◆   *A Utah college graduate was not entitled to have about $88,000 in student loan debt discharged during bankruptcy proceedings.*

The graduate had a degree in Middle East studies and formerly worked as an interpreter. As a single parent, she did not apply for a job for over 10 years, and received $1,100 per month in government benefits. When the graduate filed for bankruptcy, she asked the court to discharge her student loan debt. A bankruptcy court instead held the debt was not dischargeable in bankruptcy because requiring her to repay it would not impose an undue hardship on her.

A federal district court affirmed the decision. The graduate appealed to the U.S. Court of Appeals, Tenth Circuit, arguing she had medical conditions precluding full employment. But the only evidence she offered regarding her condition was her own testimony, and she admitted that no doctor had ever told her she was unable to work. **Instead, the court focused on her failure to apply for a job in more than 10 years and her failure to repay any portion of the debt when she received lump sums of cash.** Her decision to use $1,000 of that money for dance lessons and $4,000 of it for orthodontic work indicated she did not act in good faith. In addition, she had turned down an opportunity to consolidate her student loan debt. Because the graduate failed to meet the applicable test, the court affirmed the denial of her request for discharge of her student loan debt. *In re Roe*, 295 Fed.Appx. 927 (10th Cir. 2008).

◆   *The U.S. Department of Education could intercept a 67-year-old disabled Washington man's Social Security benefits to offset a delinquent student loan.*

The man failed to repay federally reinsured student loans he incurred between 1984 and 1989 under the Guaranteed Student Loan Program. The loans were reassigned to the Department of Education, which certified the debt to the U.S. Department of Treasury through the Treasury Offset Program. The U.S. began withholding a portion of the man's Social Security benefits to offset his debt, part of which was over 10 years delinquent. He sued the U.S. in a federal district court, alleging the offset was barred by the 10-year statute of limitations contained in the Debt Collection Act of 1982. The federal district court dismissed the case, and the U.S. Court of Appeals, Ninth Circuit, affirmed. The U.S. Supreme Court agreed to review the case.

The Court noted the Debt Collection Act permits U.S. agency heads to collect an outstanding debt by "administrative offset." However, Section 407(a) of the Social Security Act limits the availability of benefits to offset a debt. The Court explained that the Higher Education Technical Amendments of 1991 "sweepingly eliminated time limitations as to certain loans." This included the student loans in this case. The Debt Collection Improvement Act of 1996 clarified that, notwithstanding any other law, including Section 407, all payments due under the Social Security Act were subject to offset. **The Court held the Debt Collection Improvement Act clearly made Social Security benefits subject to offset. Moreover, the Higher Education Technical Amendments removed the 10-year limit that would otherwise bar an offset of Social Security benefits.** The Court rejected the man's argument that Congress could not have intended in 1991 to repeal a statute of limitations as they concerned Social Security benefits that were not made available for offset until 1996. Congress does not need to foresee all the consequences of a statutory enactment. It was also unnecessary for Congress to explicitly mention Section 407 in the Higher Education Technical Amendments. The Debt Collection Improvement Act gave the U.S. the authority to use Social Security benefits to offset debts. The retention of the 10-year limit on debt collection in the Higher Education Technical Amendments did not apply in all contexts, including this administrative offset. It affirmed the judgment for the U.S. *Lockhart v. U.S.*, 546 U.S. 142, 126 S.Ct. 699, 163 L.Ed.2d 557 (2005).

◆   *A federal court denied a Pennsylvania law school graduate's request to have her student debt discharged in bankruptcy.*

At the time of her bankruptcy filing, the graduate had accumulated over $150,000 in student loan debt and repaid only $622. She was 36 years old, in good health and earning more than $51,000 a year. The graduate sought discharge of her student loan debt on grounds of undue hardship. **The court found the graduate failed to show she would be unable to maintain a minimal standard of living if she had to repay the debt.** Her net income at the time of the proceedings exceeded her monthly expenses by almost $500. In addition, she had the option of reducing her expenses. The court noted that the graduate had indulged in luxuries beyond her basic needs. She was young and healthy, and she had marketable skills. Therefore, she did not show she would be unable to repay her student loans in the future. As the graduate's efforts to repay her student loan debt had been "negligible," her request to discharge the debt was denied. *Johnson v. Access Group*, 400 B.R. 167 (M.D. Pa. 2009).

◆ *A husband and wife who failed to make a good-faith effort to repay their student loans could not discharge their student loan debt.*

The couple received student loans in connection with their studies at several North Carolina universities. The husband had a degree in information systems and obtained work as a programmer. He was later laid off, then went to work at a home improvement store. The store fired the husband because of "excessive daytime sleepiness." The wife worked as a music teacher at a middle school. In 2002, 2003 and 2004, the couple earned about $75,500, $78,300 and $64,100, respectively. In December 2004, they asked a court to discharge their student loan debt in connection with their ongoing bankruptcy proceedings. At the time, they had a combined total debt of about $120,500. The bankruptcy court considered whether they showed they would not be able to maintain a minimum standard of living if they had to repay the loans; whether their current state of financial affairs was likely to continue for a significant part of the loan repayment period; and whether they made a good-faith effort to repay the loans.

The court found that the pair satisfied each part of the test, and it discharged their student loan debts. The case reached the U.S. Court of Appeals, Fourth Circuit, which determined the couple did not make a good-faith effort to obtain employment and maximize their income. The wife did not work during the summer, and the husband did not show that his medical condition completely prevented him from working. The monthly budget they submitted to the court showed $75 for Internet service, $80 for cell phones, $60 for satellite television and $68 for a YMCA membership. In the three months prior to their bankruptcy filing, the couple spent a combined total of $4,600 on consumer expenditures. These expenditures were not necessary to maintain a minimal standard of living and were evidence that the couple did not make a good-faith effort to minimize expenses. **The record also showed the pair failed to make loan payments for a period of time when they were financially able to do so, and they did not adequately pursue loan consolidation options.** The decision to discharge the student loan debt was reversed. *In re Mosko*, 515 F.3d 319 (4th Cir. 2008).

◆ *A debtor was not required to present expert medical evidence to support his claim for discharge of his student loans due to his medical condition.*

The student accumulated nearly $95,000 in student loan debt while earning master's degrees from Saint Louis University. His student loans became due while he underwent chemotherapy for Hodgkin's disease. The treatments made him too weak to work, and he was approved for economic hardship deferments in 2000 and 2001. The student filed for bankruptcy and was then diagnosed with vascular necrosis. The condition caused him to suffer severe pain in his hips, shoulders and knees. He underwent two shoulder surgeries and began taking multiple pain medications. He also expected to undergo surgery on both hips and his other shoulder. The student was the only witness at his bankruptcy proceeding, where he said he performed computer jobs that required him to do nothing more than move a computer mouse with his left hand. In addition, he claimed his condition was getting worse. The bankruptcy court considered records indicating the student had a monthly income of $868 and monthly expenses of $3,575. Based on the evidence presented, the bankruptcy court found it would be an undue hardship for him to repay his student loans.

The creditor sought review by the U.S. Court of Appeals, Sixth Circuit. It argued the student was required to provide expert medical evidence showing his condition was likely to last throughout the repayment period of the loans. It also claimed he had failed to show he made a good-faith effort to repay his loans. **The court rejected the argument that expert medical evidence was needed to show entitlement to discharge.** Under the circumstances, requiring corroborating medical evidence would only serve to place an additional, unnecessary burden on the student. His account of his medical status and history was not disputed. The court also rejected the argument that the student did not make a good-faith effort to repay the loans based on his failure to apply for a particular repayment option. *In re Barrett,* 487 F.3d 353 (6th Cir. 2007).

## II.  ESTABLISHMENT CLAUSE ISSUES

*The Establishment Clause of the First Amendment prohibits Congress from making any law respecting an establishment of religion. It was construed by the U.S. Supreme Court through the 1980s as prohibiting financial assistance by government agencies to religious schools and colleges.*

*In 1997, the Court decided* Agostini v. Felton, *521 U.S. 203, 117 S.Ct. 1997, 138 L.Ed.2d 391, an important private school finance case in which the Court abandoned the presumption that the presence of public employees on parochial school grounds creates a symbolic union between church and state that violates the Establishment Clause. Under* Agostini, *government assistance to private schools must not result in government indoctrination or endorsement of religion. The recipients of government assistance must not be defined by reference to their religion, and the assistance must not create excessive entanglement between church and state.*

◆   *A federal appeals court ruled a university's women's studies program was not a religion and did not violate the Establishment Clause.*

An attorney filed a class-action lawsuit against several New York State education officials, the U.S. Department of Education and the U.S. Secretary of Education to challenge the provision of public funding to Columbia University. The suit claimed the school's women's studies program amounted to a "modern-day religion," and said the funding was used to "promote and favor the religion Feminism while inhibiting other contradictory viewpoints." The allegations in this action mirrored those presented by the attorney in an earlier – and unsuccessful – suit, in which the court ruled he did not have standing to pursue such claims. The court also dismissed this recent claim. The attorney filed a motion to vacate and amend his complaint – as he had two new plaintiffs. The appellate court refused. A motion to vacate was appropriate when there was an intervening change in law, new evidence, the need to correct an error or the need to prevent manifest injustice. **New plaintiffs were not the same thing as new evidence**, so the district court's ruling was affirmed. *Hollander v. Members of Board of Regents of Univ. of New York*, 524 Fed.Appx. 727 (2d Cir. 2013).

◆ *State appropriations for a pharmacy school at a Baptist college and a scholarship program violated the Kentucky Constitution.*

Kentucky legislators appropriated $10 million to build a pharmacy school building on the campus of a Baptist college. In the same budget bill, $1 million was appropriated for a pharmacy scholarship program to benefit students who attended a four-year higher education institution located in a designated area encompassing the site of the new school. Taxpayers sued the governor, university and others in a state court, claiming the appropriations violated the state constitution. The court declared both appropriations unconstitutional.

On appeal, **the Supreme Court of Kentucky explained that Section 189 of the state constitution bars any portion of any tax raised or levied for educational purposes to aid any church, sectarian or denominational school**. Since the university was "precisely the type of school referenced in Section 189," the appropriation was unconstitutional. The court rejected a claim that Section 189 violated the First Amendment. Construing Section 189 to ban the pharmacy school appropriation did not constitute illegal viewpoint discrimination. The court also rejected an argument that Section 189 violated the Equal Protection Clause. The scholarship program violated the state constitution because it was intended only for students who would attend the new pharmacy school. It was "special legislation" that violated Section 59 of the Kentucky Constitution. By restricting scholarships to those who would attend a particular school, the legislature failed to treat all members of the relevant class equally. As a result, the judgment for the taxpayers was affirmed. *Univ. of Cumberlands v. Pennybacker*, 308 S.W.3d 668 (Ky. 2010).

◆ *Colorado violated the Establishment Clause by denying scholarship funding to state colleges it deemed to be "pervasively sectarian."*

Colorado provided scholarships to in-state students who attended private colleges except for those that were "pervasively sectarian." Some confusion existed among state officials regarding eligibility criteria. When the state law provision excluding pervasively sectarian schools was enacted in 1977, U.S. Supreme Court precedents indicated the states could not provide financial aid to pervasively sectarian schools. But the Supreme Court modified its Establishment Clause jurisprudence in cases such as *Agostini v. Felton*, above.

Colorado never repealed the statutory provision that barred funding to pervasively sectarian schools, and state officials determined Colorado Christian University (CCU) was "pervasively sectarian." CCU filed a federal district court challenge to the denial of its application for public funding, claiming religious Free Exercise, Establishment Clause and Equal Protection violations. The court held for state officials, and CCU appealed to the U.S. Court of Appeals, Tenth Circuit. **The court explained that the Establishment Clause permits "evenhanded funding" of education through student scholarships.** Federal law did not require the state to discriminate against CCU with respect to funding, and it also prevented the state from permissibly doing so. Instead, religions must be treated neutrally and without discrimination or preference by the state. **Making scholarships available to students who attended "sectarian" but not "pervasively sectarian" schools discriminated among religious institutions.** Proof of discriminatory intent was not required to invalidate the challenged provision as unconstitutional. The state law required intrusive judgments by officials relating to questions of religious belief or practice. This type of entanglement between government and religion violated the Establishment Clause, requiring reversal of the judgment for state officials. *Colorado Christian Univ. v. Weaver*, 534 F.3d 1245 (10th Cir. 2008).

◆   *An Arkansas city bond issue to finance a Christian university building project was upheld as a neutral benefit available to any entity seeking funding.*

An Arkansas city issued bonds to fund building projects at a private Christian university. Before issuing the bonds, a local housing board required the university to agree that the facilities being financed would not be used for sectarian instruction or religious worship. The university agreed to repay the bonds and all expenses, operate and maintain the financed facilities as a four-year, degree-granting institution, and maintain its nonprofit status. After the city approved the bonds, several residents sued the university in a federal district court for constitutional violations. They claimed the bond issue violated the Establishment Clause and provisions of the Arkansas Constitution.

The court held the city did not act to advance or inhibit religion. The bond issue had a secular purpose and did not have the effect of advancing or inhibiting religion. There was no risk that issuing the bonds would result in any religious indoctrination, and no evidence supported the residents' claim that the bonds had the primary effect of promoting or fostering religion. Moreover, no evidence showed government funds were being used for religious purposes. The tax benefits of the bonds were neutrally available. Issuance of the bonds did not create an excessive entanglement with religion. The bonds were issued to finance buildings that were to be used for the nonsectarian purpose of buildings for higher education. **The court cited U.S. Supreme Court decisions indicating that the government may provide aid to religiously affiliated institutions of higher learning.** The court also concluded that the issuance of the bonds did not violate the state constitution. *Gillam v. Harding Univ.*, No. 4:08-CV-00363BSM, 2009 WL 1795303 (E.D. Ark. 6/24/09).

◆   *The U.S. Supreme Court approved of the state of Washington's choice to exclude devotional theology candidates from a state scholarship program.*

Washington law created the Promise Scholarship Program, which made state funds available to qualified students for their educational costs. To be eligible, students had to meet certain performance standards and income limits, and enroll at least half-time in an eligible postsecondary institution in the state. The program excluded scholarships for theology majors, but students who attended religiously affiliated schools could still obtain scholarships so long as they did not major in theology and the institution was accredited. A student who received a Promise Scholarship enrolled as a double major in pastoral ministries and business at a private Christian college. A college financial aid administrator advised him he could not use the scholarship to pursue a devotional theology degree and could only receive program funds by certifying he would not pursue a theology degree. The student sued state officials in a federal court for violating the Free Exercise, Establishment, Speech and Equal Protection Clauses. The U.S. Supreme Court held **the program was not a state expression of disfavor against religion**, as the student argued. The program did not impose civil or criminal sanctions on any type of religious service or rite.

**There was no Free Exercise Clause violation, as the program did not require students to choose between their religious beliefs and a government benefit.** The state had only chosen not to fund a distinct category of instruction. The training of ministers was essentially a religious endeavor that could be treated differently than training for other callings. There was no evidence of state hostility toward religion. **The program permitted funding recipients to attend pervasively religious schools, and nothing in its text or the state constitution suggested anti-religious bias.** The state interest in denying funds to theology majors was substantial, and the program placed only a minor burden on recipients. *Locke v. Davey*, 540 U.S. 712, 124 S.Ct. 1307, 158 L.Ed.2d 1 (2004).

◆ *A federal appeals court held taxpayers could not sue to force a Catholic university to repay federal funds it received for a teacher quality initiative.*

The federal Department of Education (DOE) awarded the University of Notre Dame a one-time, $500,000 grant for a program called Alliance for Catholic Education. The program trained and placed teachers in underserved Catholic schools. Two private taxpayers sued the secretary of the DOE to block payment of the grant money, claiming it would violate the Establishment Clause. But they did not file a motion for a preliminary injunction, and by the time the district court heard the case the money had already been paid. As a result, the district court dismissed the case as moot. On appeal to the U.S. Court of Appeals, Seventh Circuit, the taxpayers agreed any request for injunctive relief was moot. But they argued they could still seek to force Notre Dame to repay the money by having the court order the DOE to seek recoupment.

The court rejected the taxpayers' argument on the basis that it was up to the DOE to decide whether to file an enforcement action to recoup the money. The DOE's decision was not judicially reviewable. However, the district court could order Notre Dame to repay the money if the disbursement violated the Establishment Clause. In the meantime, the U.S. Supreme Court made it clear in *Hein v. Freedom from Religion Foundation, Inc.*, 127 S.Ct. 2553 (U.S. 2007), that **taxpayers who claim a congressional appropriation violates the Establishment Clause can sue for injunctive relief only**. When the Notre Dame case later reached the Supreme Court for review, the Court vacated the decision and returned it to the Seventh Circuit for reconsideration. On remand, the appeals court held the district court had properly dismissed the case as moot. *Laskowski v. Spellings*, 546 F.3d 822 (7th Cir. 2008).

◆ *Missouri's highest court held the city of St. Louis could constitutionally fund the construction of an arena at a Jesuit university.*

St. Louis University's philosophy is "to teach young men and women ... to follow their Judeo-Christian conscience." The president is a Jesuit, as are nine of its 42 trustees. However, the university is not owned or controlled by any church. When the university decided to construct a new 13,000-seat arena, it sought financial assistance from the city under a state law that authorizes the provision of assistance to encourage urban renewal. Since the proposed site for the arena was in a blighted area, the city authorized funding for the project. The

Masonic Temple Association of St. Louis filed a federal court action against the city, claiming it violated the establishment clauses of the state and federal constitutions by providing public aid to a religious institution.

After Masonic's suit was dismissed, the university filed a state court action, seeking a declaration that the funding was valid. The court granted summary judgment for the university. On appeal, the Supreme Court of Missouri rejected the argument that university bylaws proved it was a religious institution. **Mere affiliation with a religion does not prove a college or university is controlled by a religious creed.** Although they clearly indicated a religious affiliation, neither the bylaws nor the university's mission statement showed the school was controlled by a religious creed. The university convinced the court that its primary mission was education and not indoctrination. Moreover, the purpose of the arena was not to advance religion. Instead, its purpose was to provide a venue for secular student and community events in a blighted area of the city. Because Masonic did not show the university was controlled by a religious creed, the city did not violate the state constitution. *Saint Louis Univ. v. Masonic Temple Ass'n of St. Louis*, 220 S.W.3d 721 (Mo. 2007).

◆   *The U.S. Supreme Court held the First Amendment did not prevent the state of Washington from providing financial assistance directly to an individual with a disability attending a Christian college. However, the Supreme Court of Washington held on remand that the assistance violated the state constitution.*

A visually impaired Washington student sought vocational rehabilitative services from the Washington Commission for the Blind pursuant to state law. The law provided that individuals with visual disabilities were eligible for educational assistance to enable them to "overcome vocational handicaps and to obtain the maximum degree of self-support and self-care." However, because the plaintiff was a student at a Christian college intending to pursue a career of service in the church, the Commission for the Blind denied him assistance. The Washington Supreme Court upheld this decision on the ground that the First Amendment to the U.S. Constitution prohibited state funding of a student's education at a religious college. The U.S. Supreme Court took a less restrictive view of the First Amendment and reversed the Washington court. The operation of Washington's program was such that the Commission for the Blind paid money directly to students, who could then attend the schools of their choice. The fact that the student in this case chose to attend a religious college did not constitute state support of religion because "the decision to support religious education is made by the individual, not the state." The First Amendment was therefore not offended. *Witters v. Washington Dep't of Services for the Blind*, 474 U.S. 481, 106 S.Ct. 748, 88 L.Ed.2d 846 (1986).

On remand, the Washington Supreme Court reconsidered the matter under the Washington State Constitution, which is far stricter in its prohibition on the expenditure of public funds for religious instruction than is the U.S. Constitution. **Vocational assistance funds for the student's religious education violated the state constitution because public money would be used for religious instruction.** The court rejected the student's argument that the restriction on public expenditures would violate his right to free exercise of religion. The court determined that the commission's action was constitutional under the Free Exercise Clause because there was no infringement of the student's constitutional rights. Finally, denial of the funds to the student did not violate the Fourteenth Amendment's Equal Protection Clause because the commission had a policy of denying any student's religious vocational funding. The classification was directly related to the state's interest in ensuring the separation between church and state as required by both state and federal constitutions. The court reaffirmed its denial of the student's tuition. *Witters v. State Comm'n for the Blind*, 771 P.2d 1119 (Wash. 1989).

◆  *For more than a generation, courts have analyzed Establishment Clause cases under the framework established by the following decision.*

In *Lemon v. Kurtzman*, the Court invalidated Rhode Island and Pennsylvania statutes that provided state money to finance the operation of parochial schools. The Rhode Island statute provided a 15% salary supplement to parochial school teachers who taught nonreligious subjects using public school teaching materials. The Pennsylvania statute authorized payment of state funds to parochial schools to help defray the cost of teachers' salaries, textbooks and other instructional materials. Reimbursement was limited, however, to the costs of secular subjects, which also were taught in the public schools. The Supreme Court evaluated the Rhode Island and Pennsylvania programs using its **three-part test: First, the statute must have a secular legislative purpose; second, its principal or primary effect must be one that neither advances nor inhibits religion; finally, the statute must not foster "an excessive government entanglement with religion."**

Applying this test to the two state programs in question, the Court held that the legislative purpose of the programs was a legitimate, secular concern with maintaining high educational standards in both public and private schools. The Court did not reach the second inquiry because it held that the state programs failed under the third inquiry. The Rhode Island salary supplement program excessively entangled the state with religion because of the highly religious nature of the Catholic schools that were the primary beneficiaries of the program. The teachers who received the salary supplements provided instruction in classrooms and buildings containing religious symbols such as crucifixes. In such an atmosphere, even a person dedicated to remaining religiously neutral probably would allow some religious content to creep into the ostensibly secular instruction. Similar defects were found in the Pennsylvania program. The Court also observed that in order to ensure that the state-funded parochial school teachers did not inject religious dogma into their instruction, the state would be forced to extensively monitor the parochial school classrooms. This would result in excessive state entanglement with religion. Consequently, **the salary supplement programs were held to violate the Establishment Clause of the First Amendment**. *Lemon v. Kurtzman,* 403 U.S. 602, 91 S.Ct. 2105, 29 L.Ed.2d 745 (1971).

◆  *The Supreme Court held that the "secular side" of a college could be distinguished from sectarian programs, making it permissible for a state to provide funding to a religiously affiliated college's secular side.*

The state of Maryland enacted a program that authorized annual, noncategorical grants to religiously affiliated colleges. The program was challenged by taxpayers who alleged that state money was being put to religious uses by the schools, which had wide discretion in spending the funds.

The Supreme Court held that 1) no state aid at all may go to institutions that are so "pervasively sectarian" that secular activities cannot be separated from sectarian ones, and 2) if secular activities can be separated out, they alone may be funded. The colleges involved in this case were not found to be pervasively sectarian even though they were affiliated with the Catholic Church. The Court held that the "secular side" of the colleges could be separated from the sectarian and found that **state aid had only gone to the colleges' secular side**. It was admittedly somewhat difficult to ensure that the colleges and the Maryland Council for Higher Education would take care to avoid spending state funds on religious activities, but the Court expressed its belief that those entities would spend the money in good faith and avoid violating the First Amendment. *Roemer v. Board of Public Works*, 426 U.S. 736, 96 S.Ct. 2337, 49 L.Ed.2d 179 (1976).

◆    *The Supreme Court held that the receipt of Higher Education Facilities Act funds by four religious colleges did not violate the Establishment Clause.*

The Higher Education Facilities Act of 1963 contained an exclusion for any facility used for sectarian instruction or as a place of religious worship or any facility that is used primarily as part of a school divinity department. Federal education officials had powers to enforce the statute for a 20-year time period during which they could seek to recover funds from violators. A group of Connecticut taxpayers filed a federal district court action against government officials and four religious colleges that received Higher Education Facilities Act funds, seeking an order against the release of funds to sectarian institutions that used federal funds to construct libraries and other facilities. The court held the act did not have the effect of promoting religion.

The U.S. Supreme Court reviewed the case and held that the statute had been carefully drafted to ensure that no federal funds were disbursed to support the sectarian aspects of these institutions. **The four colleges named as defendants in this case had not violated any of the restrictions in the statute, as they had placed no religious symbols in facilities constructed with the use of federal funds, and had not used the facilities for any religious purposes.** There was no evidence that any of the colleges maintained a predominantly religious atmosphere, and although each of them was affiliated with the Catholic Church, none excluded non-Catholics from admissions or faculty appointments, and none of them required attendance at religious services. The receipt of funds by the colleges did not violate the Establishment Clause. The Court held, however, that the 20-year limit on federal oversight created the potential for religious use of the facilities after the 20 years expired. Because of the risk of use of the facilities for advancing religion, the court invalidated this portion of the legislation. *Tilton v. Richardson*, 403 U.S. 672, 91 S.Ct. 2091, 29 L.Ed.2d 790 (1971).

◆    *A Tennessee city development board could issue tax-exempt bonds to a sectarian university for a building project without violating the Constitution.*

A Christian university began a renovation project and sought $15 million in low-interest loans from the Industrial Development Board for Nashville, Tennessee. The board approved the loan and issued tax-exempt bonds to the university. A group of taxpayers sued, asserting that the bond issuance impermissibly benefited a religious university in violation of the Establishment Clause. A federal court ruled that the university was so pervasively sectarian that no state aid could go to it. The Sixth Circuit Court of Appeals reversed, noting that **the tax-exempt bonds did not violate the Establishment Clause**. First, public funds were not used to issue the bonds; the university had to arrange for private financing; and bond purchasers only had recourse against the university. Second, the bonds were issued in a neutral manner to nonprofit organizations. Third, the bonds advanced the secular objective of promoting economic development. The university was entitled to receive the tax-exempt bonds. *Steele v. Industrial Development Board of Metropolitan Government of Nashville*, 301 F.3d 401 (6th Cir. 2002).

◆ *A Wisconsin program allowing unrestricted telecommunications access grants to sectarian schools and colleges violated the Establishment Clause.*

A 1997 Wisconsin law created the Technology for Education Achievement (TEACH) Board, which administered the Education Telecommunications Access program. The TEACH board approved access for data lines and video links under a heavily subsidized program in which both public and private schools participated. A taxpayer group objected to the program on constitutional grounds because $58,873 of the program's annual total of over $1.9 million was awarded to nine religiously affiliated Wisconsin schools and private colleges. The taxpayers sued state education officials, including the TEACH board, challenging the program as unconstitutional.

The case reached the Seventh Circuit. It noted that **the Wisconsin law violated the Establishment Clause. In the absence of any restriction on the expenditure of public funds by the schools, the expenditures had a primary effect that advanced religion.** The subsidies could easily be used for maintenance, chapels, religious instruction, or connection time to view religious websites. The law did not bar schools from using the grants for these and other constitutionally impermissible purposes. Because direct aid from the government to a sectarian institution in any form is invalid, the court held the direct subsidies to religious schools were unconstitutional. *Freedom From Religion Foundation, Inc. v. Bugher*, 249 F.3d 606 (7th Cir. 2001).

## III.  PRIVATE SCHOOL TAXATION

*In* Camps Newfound/Owatonna, Inc. v. Town of Harrison, Maine, *520 U.S. 564, 117 S.Ct. 1590, 137 L.Ed.2d 852 (1997), the Supreme Court found no reason why nonprofit status should exempt a private entity from laws regulating commerce, including local property tax laws.*

### A.  Federal Income Taxation

◆ *The U.S. Supreme Court upheld a federal regulation requiring colleges and universities to make employment tax payments on behalf of employees who are normally scheduled to work at least 40 hours a week.*

Under federal law, no Federal Insurance Contributions Act (FICA) employment tax payments are due for "service performed in the employ of ... a school, college, or university" if the service is "performed by a student who is enrolled and regularly attending classes [at the school]." In 2004, the U.S. Treasury Department clarified an implementing regulation said the exemption did not apply to those who normally worked at least 40 hours a week for a school. The department cited medical residents as an example of employees who were not exempt. Medical school graduates typically worked 50-80 hours a week in a medical residency program offered through the Mayo Foundation of Medical Education and Research, the Mayo Clinic and the University of Minnesota. The programs lasted from three to five years, and residents received annual stipends of $41,000 to $56,000 with health and malpractice insurance and vacation time. Mayo sued the federal government to recover a refund of FICA tax it had withheld and paid on resident stipends. It claimed the residents were exempt under the statute and asserted that the regulation was invalid.

A federal district court held for Mayo, and after an appeals court reversed the judgment, the case reached the U.S. Supreme Court. The Court found the relevant statute did not define the term "student" or address whether medical residents were subject to FICA. But it held the regulation was a reasonable interpretation of the statute. **The Court rejected Mayo's argument that the Treasury Department should have to determine what each resident does and why before deciding whether the exemption applied.** The Court affirmed the decision upholding the regulation. *Mayo Foundation for Medical Educ. and Research v. U.S.*, 131 S.Ct. 704, 178 L.Ed.2d 588 (U.S. 2011).

◆  *A strong public policy against racial discrimination was held sufficient to deny tax-exempt status to an otherwise qualified private college.*

Section 501(c)(3) of the Internal Revenue Code (IRC) provides that "corporations ... organized and operated exclusively for religious, charitable ... or educational purposes" are entitled to tax-exempt status. The Internal Revenue Service routinely granted tax exemption under IRC Section 501(c)(3) to private schools regardless of whether they had racially discriminatory admissions policies. In 1970, however, the IRS concluded it could no longer grant tax-exempt status to racially discriminatory private schools because such schools were not "charitable" within the meaning of Section 501(c)(3). In *Bob Jones Univ. v. U.S.*, two private colleges whose racial admissions policies were allegedly rooted in their interpretations of the Bible sued to prevent the IRS from interpreting the federal tax laws in this manner. The Supreme Court rejected the colleges' challenge and upheld the IRS's interpretation.

The Court's ruling was based on a strong federal public policy against racial discrimination in education. **Because the colleges were operating in violation of that public policy, the colleges could not be considered "charitable" under Section 501(c)(3). Thus, they were ineligible for tax exemption. The Court held that in order to fall under the exemption of Section 501(c)(3) an institution must be in harmony with the public interest.** It also held that the denial of an exemption did not impermissibly burden Bob Jones' alleged religious interest in practicing racial discrimination. *Bob Jones Univ. v. U.S.*, 461 U.S. 574, 103 S.Ct. 2017, 76 L.Ed.2d 157 (1983).

## B. State and Local Taxation

◆  *A Maryland local tax on admissions and amusements did not apply to gate receipts from Johns Hopkins University lacrosse games, because the funds were used exclusively for educational purposes.*

Maryland law authorizes counties and municipalities to impose admissions and amusement taxes. But no admissions and amusement taxes may be imposed by a county or municipality on gross receipts that are used exclusively for charitable, educational, or religious purposes. Johns Hopkins University earned substantial revenue from its men's lacrosse program. It paid an admissions and amusement tax to the comptroller of the treasury for several years. The university then sought a refund from Baltimore City, asserting it was entitled to the exception for receipts used exclusively for an educational purpose. The Maryland Tax Court granted the university's request for a refund, and the comptroller appealed to the Court of Special Appeals of Maryland.

The court considered evidence that lacrosse game revenues were used to cover the costs of games and to contribute to the maintenance of the field and surrounding jogging track. The comptroller had already deemed the university field exempt from real property tax, and the university was exempt from federal tax under 26 U.S.C. § 501(c)(3). The court found substantial evidence to support the tax court's conclusion that receipts from the lacrosse games were used exclusively for an educational purpose. **The evidence showed that gross receipts were used to benefit the university, intercollegiate athletes, other non-participating students, and spectators.** About 50% of university students were involved in athletics of some sort. The field was used by all students and their families for commencement exercises, and it was also used by some students for ROTC and intramural games. As intramural athletic contests had always been treated by the Maryland taxing authorities and the Tax Court as "educational" in purpose, the court affirmed the judgment for the university. *Comptroller of Treasury v. Johns Hopkins Univ.*, 186 Md.App. 169, 973 A.2d 256 (Md. Ct. Spec. App. 2009).

◆  *Office space leased by a bank from a university was exempt from property taxation because it was used for a "school purpose."*

The University of Delaware contracted with a bank to develop a student identification card that could also be used as a debit card for services. The university provided office space to the bank for the project. The local land use department discontinued the university's property tax exemption for the space and assessed taxes on it. A county board of assessment review upheld the assessment, but its decision was reversed by a state superior court, which found the space was used for a school purpose under state law.

The Supreme Court of Delaware noted the term "school purpose" was undefined by 9 Del. C. Section 8105. Under that section, college or school property used for educational or school purposes was not subject to taxation. The court rejected the county's argument that Section 8105 must be read narrowly. Statutes exempting educational institutions from taxation are generally "construed more liberally than other tax exempting statutes." The trial court had correctly determined the bank served a "school purpose." The court held "school purposes" included use of school-owned property that contributed to the legitimate welfare, convenience, and/or safety of the school community or its members. The judgment was affirmed. *New Castle County Dep't of Land Use v. Univ. of Delaware,* 842 A.2d 1201 (Del. 2004).

◆   *A university's bus service was not entitled to a credit for fuel taxes for its campus bus service.*

An Ohio public university owned a campus bus service that provided free transportation within the university campus. It also transported disabled students to and from the airport, and serviced the city of Kent and neighboring townships. However, it did not operate under a contract with the city or any other regional transit authority. When it applied for reimbursement of motor vehicle fuel taxes, claiming eligibility for the credits because its buses were transit buses, the tax commissioner and the Board of Tax Appeals ruled that its buses did not meet the statutory definition of "transit buses." The Supreme Court of Ohio upheld that determination. Here, even though the buses benefited non-students as well as students, **the bus service did not meet the requirement that it be operated by or for a municipal corporation**. The bus service was not entitled to the tax reimbursement. *Campus Bus Service v. Zaino,* 786 N.E.2d 889 (Ohio 2003).

◆   *A city was allowed to proceed in its lawsuit against a Catholic university for back taxes.*

The city of Scranton and its school district sued the University of Scranton, a Roman Catholic institution, for payment of back business privilege and/or mercantile taxes since 1995. The city asserted that the university gained income in those years from the sale of books and food, from parking lot revenue and from other sources. Since those income-generating activities took place in the city, the university ought to have to pay mercantile taxes. The university sought to dismiss the suit, **asserting that it was a charitable institution under the state's Purely Public Charity Act**, and the court of common pleas agreed. However, the Pennsylvania Commonwealth Court reversed, finding issues that required the lawsuit to proceed. As a result, the university had to answer the city's complaint. *School Dist. of City of Scranton v. Univ. of Scranton,* No. 2345 C.D. 2001, 2002 WL 876980 (Pa. Commw. Ct. 2002).

◆   *An office building owned by teaching doctors of Midwestern University did not qualify for real estate tax exemptions.*

The primary activities taking place at the property constituted billing, collection, data processing, accounting, administration, management, payroll and related functions for the physician group. When a state court held that the physician group did not qualify for the "charitable purposes" or "school" exemptions under Illinois law, appeal reached the Appellate Court of Illinois. **Under Illinois law, a property entitled to an exemption must be used exclusively for charitable purposes and owned by a charitable organization.** Here, the group failed to meet either requirement. The Appellate Court did not allow the group to use its relationship with the university to cast itself as a charitable organization. No patient care, medical research or instructional classes took place on the property. *Midwest Physician Group, Ltd. v. Dep't of Revenue of Illinois*, 711 N.E.2d 381 (Ill. App. Ct. 1999).

◆ *A university could not claim tax-exempt status for a parking garage or parts of a building leased to for-profit companies.*

A university owned a four-story building with an attached parking garage, and leased space to five tenants. Two tenants were nonprofit organizations, and the other three tenants were for-profit companies. The Board of Tax Appeals found that the building and the land under it were exempt from taxation, but the garage and land under it were not. The Cleveland Board of Education filed a notice of appeal, wanting the whole property to be taxed. The Supreme Court of Ohio affirmed the Board of Tax Appeals decisions regarding the tax exemption for the space leased by the two nonprofit organizations, and the non-tax-exempt status of the garage and the land under it. It reversed exemptions given to the university for the space held by the for-profit tenants and vacant areas in the building. **The garage did not qualify for tax-exempt status because it was not an essential and integral part of the university's or nonprofit tenants' charitable and/or educational activities.** *Case Western Reserve Univ. v. Tracy*, 84 Ohio St.3d 316, 703 N.E.2d 1240 (Ohio 1999).

◆ *Land used by a seminary for recreational purposes and as a buffer zone was exempt from taxation.*

A North Carolina county reviewed several parcels of land owned by a seminary and determined that they were not eligible for tax exemptions because they were not used for educational or religious purposes. After the state property tax commission held that exemptions applied to three parcels, the county appealed. The North Carolina Court of Appeals affirmed the decision in favor of the seminary. **Although the land was used essentially for recreational purposes, and as a buffer between the campus and commercial development surrounding the campus, it served to provide and maintain a relaxed campus atmosphere.** Further, the seminary's attempt to rezone one of the parcels for commercial development so that it could sell the land for a profit was a planned future use, which did not change the present exempted use of the land. *In the Matter of Southeastern Baptist Theological Seminary*, 135 N.C.App. 247, 520 S.E.2d 302 (N.C. Ct. App. 1999).

◆ *The Commonwealth Court of Pennsylvania held that property owned by the private college in the following two cases was tax exempt because the college was a public charity under state law and the property was regularly used for the purposes of the college.*

A Pennsylvania nonprofit private college owned a house occupied by its grounds crew leader. The college charged the grounds crew leader a discounted rent that averaged about 70% of the fair market value. In exchange for the discount, the grounds crew leader agreed to be available on a 24-hour basis to respond to emergencies and nighttime calls. He was allegedly called to campus after-hours six times in both 1991 and 1992 for snow and ice removal, and to remove fallen tree limbs. The Delaware County Board of Assessment Appeals determined that the house was not exempt from property taxes. On appeal by the college, a Pennsylvania trial court reversed, finding the house exempt from taxation. A local public school district appealed the finding to the Commonwealth Court of Pennsylvania.

Article VIII of the **Pennsylvania Constitution provides that the general assembly can exempt real property of public charities "regularly used for the purposes of the institution."** Section 204 of the General County Assessment Law exempts all college property "necessary for the occupancy and enjoyment of the same." The commonwealth court stated that the college need not prove that the property was absolutely necessary to its needs for the exemption to apply. Rather, it was required to show only that it had a reasonable need for the property. Here, emergency personnel were essential to the college community. The grounds crew leader was able to respond much quicker to an emergency than personnel who were living off campus. The college properly chose to forgo the additional rental revenues to provide these needed services. Further, the alleged infrequency of emergency situations did not render the house incidental to the college's purposes. **Because emergency services were directly related to the proper functions of the college, the trial court did not err in concluding that the house was tax exempt.** *In re Swarthmore College*, 645 A.2d 470 (Pa. Commw. Ct. 1994).

The college also owned a large house designed for entertaining. The college's vice president for alumni development lived in the house rent-free and was not charged for utilities. The house was used for meetings, special events, receptions and to entertain potential donors from whom one-third of the college's yearly income was derived. The county Board of Assessment Appeals determined that the house was not exempt from property taxes. The Commonwealth Court of Pennsylvania stated that the **college was not required to prove that the property was absolutely necessary to its needs for the exemption to apply. Rather, it was required to show only that it had a reasonable necessity for the property.** Here, the vice president was required to live in the house, use it to cultivate personal relationships with donors, and utilize it for numerous college functions. These uses were directly related to the proper functions of the college. Consequently, the vice president's house was tax exempt. *In re Swarthmore College*, 643 A.2d 1152 (Pa. Commw. Ct. 1994).

◆   *The Court of Appeal of Louisiana held that state law does not require private colleges to substantiate their tax-exempt status except as set forth by the state legislature.*

A Louisiana church operated a private university that offered a variety of secular undergraduate and graduate programs. The Louisiana Board of Regents notified the university that it had failed to complete and submit the required licensure application and was therefore in violation of state law. Consequently, it sought to close the school. **Although degree-granting institutions were generally required to be registered and licensed by the board, institutions granted a tax exemption under the Internal Revenue Code were exempted from these requirements.** Previously such private universities were required to supply only basic information to obtain a license. The state attorney general filed suit in a Louisiana trial court, seeking to enjoin the church's operation of the university based on its noncompliance with the board's procedural requirements. The trial court found that because the Internal Revenue Code does not require churches to obtain recognition of their exempt status, the board was prohibited from requiring the organization to do so. It denied the state's request for injunctive relief, and the state appealed.

The Court of Appeal of Louisiana affirmed the decision, noting that the state legislature chose to defer to federal law in this procedural area. Federal law, pursuant to the Internal Revenue Code, granted churches automatic exempt status without the necessity of paperwork. Absent a contrary directive from the state legislature, the court refused to read additional requirements into the law. *Ieyoub v. World Christian Church*, 649 So.2d 771 (La. Ct. App. 1994).

## IV. PRIVATE ASSISTANCE TO SCHOOLS

*Generally, when private parties donate money to schools, they have to be careful to specify how that money will be used or the schools will be able to put the money into their general operating funds. Colleges and universities often rely on financial boosters to support their athletic programs. But when questions arise as to how money is being raised and spent, relationships between booster organizations and schools can go sour. In the following case, an Iowa court rejected a college's claim that the head of a booster club mishandled funds and engaged in other unauthorized activities.*

◆   *The departure of a prominent researcher from a university led to a dispute regarding whether donors could authorize a transfer of donated materials.*

A highly respected urologist and researcher had worked at Washington University, a private institution in Missouri, since 1976. His area of specialty was prostate cancer, and he performed thousands of surgeries and spearheaded research activities. The urologist was particularly interested in the genetic basis of prostate cancer, and he focused his research efforts in this area. In 1983, he began collecting samples of biological materials consisting of blood and tissue that were removed during surgery. The storage facility he helped create for biological samples eventually became the largest of its kind in the world. Donors who became research participants by allowing their samples to be used were required to complete an informed consent form, which used the term "donation" to describe the transfer of biological samples from the participant to a university physician or medical technician. The forms also specified that participants agreed to waive any claim to donated body tissues. In early 2003, the urologist accepted a new position at Northwestern University. Soon after he arrived there, he sent a letter to donors, asking them to release their samples to him. Washington University filed a federal court lawsuit seeking a declaration that it owned them and was not required to honor any transfer request. The urologist filed a counterclaim, seeking a declaration that the donors had a right to transfer their samples to him. The court held Washington owned the samples. It also found that neither the urologist nor the donors had an ownership interest in them, and that none of the urologist's forms transferred their ownership.

The U.S. Court of Appeals for the Eighth Circuit affirmed the district court's ruling, finding the donors did not retain an ownership interest allowing them to transfer the samples to a third party. **All of the donors transferred their samples to the university as gifts.** The university established that a gift was made by showing the donors intended to make a gift. The samples were delivered by the donors, and the university accepted them. The consent form and brochure language supported the conclusion that the sample transfers were gifts, and the university retained "absolute possession" over them, while at Washington. The urologist signed agreements acknowledging the university's ownership of the samples. Although he claimed that the donors retained an ownership interest, he also regularly ordered the destruction of donated samples to create more storage space. This activity was inconsistent with his claim that the donors retained an ownership interest. In addition, both federal and state regulations bar the return of donated body tissue and blood to donors. *Washington Univ. v. Catalona*, 490 F.3d 667 (8th Cir. 2007).

◆ *Members of nonprofit organizations are not liable for the debts of an organization unless they engage in intentional misconduct.*

Over the course of his long tenure as a benefactor, Charles Talbot personally donated more than $45,000 and helped raise more than $97,000 for Indian Hills Community College. Talbot approached the school to discuss the creation of a more formal tax-exempt booster club in 2001. The school told Talbot it would need to endorse such a move, but he went ahead and formed a nonprofit corporation without asking for approval. The relationship between Talbot and the school began to sour. The president told the group they needed to run the booster club funds through a school-audited account, but the group refused to do so. They also refused to provide the college access to the club's financial records. In April 2004, the college sued Talbot and the booster club in a state court. The suit accused Talbot and the club of conversion, and it claimed he had engaged in unauthorized acts. The trial court held for Talbot, relying on state law immunity for members of nonprofit organizations and corporations. On appeal, the Court of Appeals of Iowa held the trial court had correctly applied state law immunity provisions to block the college's claims.

**Members of nonprofit organizations were not liable for debts or obligations of the organization unless they engaged in intentional misconduct, knowingly violated the law, or derived an "improper personal benefit" from a transaction.** There was no showing that any actions taken by Talbot were illegal or inappropriate Therefore, he could not be held liable for any of the allegedly improper actions taken on behalf of the booster club. The trial court decision against the college was affirmed. *Indian Hills Community College v. Indian Hills Booster Club*, No. 06-0392, 734 N.W.2d 486 (Table), 2007 WL 911890 (Iowa Ct. App. 3/28/07).

◆ *Vanderbilt University could not change the name of its dormitories in violation of an agreement with a donor organization.*

In 1905, trustees of the Peabody Education Fund voted to direct $1 million to create a permanent endowment for a college of higher education for teachers in the southern states. Trustees of the college voted to buy several properties adjacent to Vanderbilt University. The United Daughters of the Confederacy (UDC) entered into a contract with college trustees to raise $50,000 to construct the women's dorm on the new campus. In return for the gift, the college had to allow female descendants of Confederate soldiers nominated by the UDC to live in the dorm rent-free. In 1927, the college and UDC entered into a second contract specifying that a Confederate Memorial Hall be constructed on the campus. From 1935 until the late 1970s, female descendants of Confederate soldiers nominated by the UDC lived in the dorms rent-free. The college started experiencing financial difficulties. To raise money, college trustees leased two dorms, including Confederate Memorial Hall, to Vanderbilt. When the college's financial situation became worse, it merged with Vanderbilt. A year after the renovation of Confederate Memorial Hall, some Vanderbilt students, faculty and staff expressed dissatisfaction with the building name. They emphasized demographic changes over the years. The chancellor of Vanderbilt decided to change the name to "Memorial Hall" without consulting the UDC. The UDC sued Vanderbilt in a state court for breach of contract. The court awarded summary judgment to Vanderbilt. It found it impractical and unduly burdensome for Vanderbilt to continue to perform the terms of the contract. The UDC appealed to Court of Appeals of Tennessee.

Vanderbilt argued it already had substantially fulfilled its obligations because it had allowed many women to live in the dorms rent-free over the years and had kept the building's original name for almost 70 years. Moreover, the university should no longer be obligated to keep the name because it would be inconsistent with laws prohibiting racial discrimination. **The court held the intent of the UDC was for the funds to be a conditional gift. Generally, if the university failed to comply with the conditions, the donor would recover the gift.** However, since the value of a dollar was different now from when the money was given, returning the gift would be unfair to the UDC. The court held that as Vanderbilt had refused to abide by the conditions of the gift, the present value of the gift must be returned, or the university would have to agree to abide by the conditions. The court reversed the judgment and returned the case to the trial court to calculate the gift's present value. *Tennessee Division of United Daughters of the Confederacy v. Vanderbilt Univ.*, 174 S.W.3d 98 (Tenn. Ct. App. 2005).

◆   *The Court of Appeals of Kentucky denied a claim to property by a college under a property owner's will.*

A Kentucky property owner bequeathed property to a relative. However, the will stated that if the relative died without children, the property was to pass to the relative's younger sister and her heirs. The will also provided Georgetown College would receive the proceeds from the sale of 71 acres of farmland, to be used to fund a permanent endowment at the college. Any additional money would be paid to the college for the endowment fund. Both the relative and her sister died without children. A state court distributed $1.3 million from the estate in three equal shares to the sister's heirs, finding the college was only covered under a specific item in the will. The state appeals court rejected the college's argument that the devises to the sisters were substitutional. **When the property owner died, the court explained, the interest in her property vested in the sister's heirs. The college's reasoning**

**would lead to a finding that the property owner had died without heirs.** As this result was disfavored, the court affirmed the judgment for the heirs. *Georgetown College v. Alexander*, 140 S.W.3d 6 (Ky. Ct. App. 2003).

◆   *A university hospital could not get money bequeathed to another institution even though a condition of the will was illegal.*

A doctor associated with the Keswick Home in Baltimore provided for four annuitants in his will and, after the death of the last of them, directed that the remainder of his estate (nearly $29 million) go to the Keswick Home for the acquisition or construction of a new building in his name for "white patients who need[ed] physical rehabilitation." If Keswick found the bequest unacceptable, the money was to pass to the University of Maryland Hospital to be used for physical rehabilitation. A lawsuit developed over the funds, with the university hospital arguing that the illegal racial restriction required the money to be awarded to it. A trial court agreed, but the Maryland Court of Appeals reversed. It excised the illegal condition attached to the will and awarded the money to Keswick. *Home for Incurables of Baltimore City v. Univ. of Maryland Medical System Corp.*, 797 A.2d 746 (Md. 2002).

# APPENDIX A

## UNITED STATES CONSTITUTION

*Provisions of Interest to Higher Educators*

## ARTICLE I

Section 1. All legislative Powers herein granted shall be vested in a Congress of the United States, which shall consist of a Senate and House of Representatives.

* * *

Section 8. The Congress shall have Power To lay and collect Taxes, Duties, Imposts and Excises, to pay the Debts and provide for the common Defence and general Welfare of the United States; but all Duties, Imposts and Excises shall be uniform throughout the United States;

To borrow money on the credit of the United States;

To regulate Commerce with foreign Nations, and among the several States, and with the Indian Tribes;

To establish an uniform Rule of Naturalization, and uniform Laws on the subject of Bankruptcies throughout the United States;

* * *

To promote the Progress of Science and useful Arts, by securing for limited Times to Authors and Inventors the exclusive Right to their respective Writings and Discoveries;

* * *

To make all Laws which shall be necessary and proper for carrying into Execution for the foregoing Powers, and all other Powers vested by this Constitution in the Government of the United States, or in any Department or Officer thereof.

* * *

Section 9. * * * No Bill of Attainder or ex post facto Law shall be passed.

* * *

Section 10. No State shall * * * pass any Bill of Attainder, ex post facto Law, or Law impairing the Obligation of Contracts, or grant any Title of Nobility.

## ARTICLE II

Section 1. The executive Power shall be vested in a President of the United States of America. * * *

## ARTICLE III

Section 1. The judicial Power of the United States, shall be vested in one supreme Court, and in such inferior Courts as the Congress may from time to time ordain and establish. The Judges, both of the supreme and inferior courts, shall hold their Offices during good Behaviour, and shall, at stated Times, receive for their Services a Compensation, which shall not be diminished during their Continuance in Office.

Section 2. The judicial Power shall extend to all Cases, in Law and Equity, arising under this Constitution, the Laws of the United States, and Treaties made, or which shall be made, under their Authority; - to all Cases affecting Ambassadors, other public Ministers and Consuls; - to all Cases of admiralty and maritime Jurisdiction, - to Controversies to which the United States shall be a party; - to Controversies between two or more States; - between a State and Citizens of another State; - between Citizens of different States; - between Citizens of the same State claiming Lands under the Grants of different States, and between a State, or the Citizens thereof, and foreign States, Citizens or Subjects.

* * *

## ARTICLE IV

Section 1. Full Faith and Credit shall be given in each State to the public Acts, Records and judicial Proceedings of every other State. * * *

Section 2. The Citizens of each State shall be entitled to all Privileges and Immunities of Citizens in the several States.

* * *

Section 4. The United States shall guarantee to every State in this Union a Republican Form of Government, and shall protect each of them against Invasion; and on Application of the Legislature, or of the Executive (when the Legislature cannot be convened) against domestic Violence.

## ARTICLE V

The Congress, whenever two thirds of both Houses shall deem it necessary, shall propose Amendments to this Constitution, or, on the Application of the Legislatures of two thirds of the several States, shall call a Convention for proposing Amendments, which, in either Case, shall be valid to all Intents and Purposes, as part of this Constitution, when ratified by the Legislatures of three fourths of the several States, or by Conventions in three fourths thereof, as the one or the other Mode of Ratification may be proposed by the Congress; Provided that no Amendment which may be made prior to the Year One thousand eight hundred and eight shall in any Manner affect the first and fourth Clauses in the Ninth Section of the first Article; and that no State, without its Consent, shall be deprived of its equal Suffrage in the Senate.

## ARTICLE VI

\* \* \*

This Constitution, and the Laws of the United States which shall be made in Pursuance thereof; and all Treaties made, or which shall be made, under the Authority of the United States, shall be the supreme Law of the Land; and the Judges in every State shall be bound thereby, any Thing in the Constitution or Laws of any State to the Contrary notwithstanding.

The Senators and Representatives before mentioned, and the Members of the several State Legislatures, and all executive and judicial Officers, both of the United States and of the several States, shall be bound by Oath or Affirmation, to support this Constitution; but no religious Test shall ever be required as a Qualification to any Office or public Trust under the United States.

\* \* \*

## AMENDMENT I

Congress shall make no law respecting an establishment of religion, or prohibiting the free exercise thereof; or abridging the freedom of speech, or of the press; or the right of the people peaceably to assemble, and to petition the Government for a redress of grievances.

\* \* \*

## AMENDMENT IV

The right of the people to be secure in their persons, houses, papers, and effects, against unreasonable searches and seizures, shall not be violated, and no Warrants shall issue, but upon probable cause, supported by Oath or affirmation, and particularly describing the place to be searched, and the persons or things to be seized.

## AMENDMENT V

No person shall be held to answer for a capital, or otherwise infamous crime, unless on a presentment or indictment of a Grand Jury, except in cases arising in the land or naval forces, or in the Militia, when in actual service in time of War or public danger; nor shall any person be subject for the same offence to be twice put in jeopardy of life or limb; nor shall be compelled in any criminal case to be a witness against himself, nor be deprived of life, liberty, or property, without due process of law; nor shall private property be taken for public use, without just compensation.

## AMENDMENT VI

In all criminal prosecutions, the accused shall enjoy the right to a speedy and public trial, by an impartial jury of the State and district wherein the crime shall have been committed, which district shall have been previously ascertained by law, and to be informed of the nature and cause of the accusation; to be confronted with the witnesses against him; to have compulsory process for obtaining witnesses in his favor, and to have the Assistance of Counsel for his defense.

## AMENDMENT VII

In Suits at common law, where the value in controversy shall exceed twenty dollars, the right of trial by jury shall be preserved, and no fact tried by jury, shall be otherwise re-examined in any Court of the United States, than according to the rules of the common law.

## AMENDMENT VIII

Excessive bail shall not be required, nor excessive fines imposed, nor cruel and unusual punishments inflicted.

## AMENDMENT IX

The enumeration in the Constitution, of certain rights, shall not be construed to deny or disparage others retained by the people.

## AMENDMENT X

The powers not delegated to the United States by the Constitution, nor prohibited by it to the States, are reserved to the States respectively, or to the people.

## AMENDMENT XI

The Judicial power of the United States shall not be construed to extend to any suit in law or equity, commenced or prosecuted against one of the United States by Citizens of another State, or by Citizens or Subjects of any Foreign State.

\* \* \*

## AMENDMENT XIII

Section 1. Neither slavery nor involuntary servitude, except as a punishment for crime whereof the party shall have been duly convicted, shall exist within the United States, or any place subject to their jurisdiction.

Section 2. Congress shall have power to enforce this article by appropriate legislation.

## AMENDMENT XIV

Section 1. All persons born or naturalized in the United States, and subject to the jurisdiction thereof, are citizens of the United States and of the State wherein they reside. No State shall make or enforce any law which shall abridge the privileges or immunities of citizens of the United States; nor shall any State deprive any person of life, liberty, or property, without due process of law; nor deny to any person within its jurisdiction the equal protection of the laws.

\* \* \*

Section 5. The Congress shall have power to enforce, by appropriate legislation, the provisions of this article.

# APPENDIX B

## Subject Matter Table of United States Supreme Court
## Cases Affecting Higher Education

*Note: Please see the Table of Cases (located at the front of this volume)
for Supreme Court cases reported in this volume.*

### Academic Freedom

*Univ. of Pennsylvania v. EEOC*, 493 U.S. 182, 110 S.Ct. 577, 107
L.Ed.2d 571 (1990).
*Minnesota State Board for Community Colleges v. Knight*, 465 U.S. 271,
104 S.Ct. 1058, 79 L.Ed.2d 299 (1984).
*Epperson v. Arkansas*, 393 U.S. 97, 89 S.Ct. 266, 21 L.Ed.2d 228 (1968).
*Sweezy v. State of New Hampshire*, 354 U.S. 234, 77 S.Ct. 1203,
1 L.Ed.2d 1311 (1957).

### Activity Fees

*Board of Regents of Univ. of Wisconsin System v. Southworth*, 529 U.S.
217, 120 S.Ct. 1346, 146 L.Ed.2d 193 (2000).

### Affirmative Action

*Fisher v. Univ. of Texas at Austin*, 136 S.Ct. 2198 (U.S. 6/23/16).
*Schuette v. Coalition to Defend Affirmative Action*, 134 S.Ct. 1623
(U.S. 2014).
*Fisher v. Univ. of Texas at Austin*, 133 S.Ct. 2411, 186 L.Ed.2d 474
(U.S. 2013).
*Grutter v. Bollinger*, 539 U.S. 306, 123 S.Ct. 2325, 156 L.Ed.2d
304 (2003).
*Gratz v. Bollinger*, 539 U.S. 244, 123 S.Ct. 2411, 156 L.Ed.2d
257 (2003).
*Regents of Univ. of California v. Bakke*, 438 U.S. 265, 98 S.Ct. 2733, 57
L.Ed.2d 750 (1978).

### Arbitration

*Volt Information Sciences v. Board of Trustees of Stanford Univ.*, 489
U.S. 468, 109 S.Ct. 1248, 103 L.Ed.2d 488 (1989).

### Athletics

*NCAA v. Smith*, 525 U.S. 459, 119 S.Ct. 924, 142 L.Ed.2d 929 (1999).
*NCAA v. Tarkanian*, 488 U.S. 179, 109 S.Ct. 454, 102 L.Ed.2d 469
(1988).
*NCAA v. Board of Regents of Univ. of Oklahoma*, 468 U.S. 85, 104 S.Ct.
2948, 82 L.Ed.2d 70 (1984).

## Collective Bargaining

*Cent. State Univ. v. American Ass'n of Univ. Professors, Cent. State Univ. Chapter,* 526 U.S. 124, 119 S.Ct. 1162, 143 L.Ed.2d 227 (1999).

*NLRB v. Yeshiva University,* 444 U.S. 672, 100 S.Ct. 856, 63 L.Ed.2d 115 (1980).

## Criminal Activity

*Bates v. U.S.,* 522 U.S. 23, 118 S.Ct. 285, 139 L.Ed.2d 215 (1997).

## Desegregation

*U.S. v. Fordice,* 505 U.S. 717, 112 S.Ct. 2727, 120 L.Ed.2d 575 (1992).

*Bob Jones Univ. v. Simon,* 416 U.S. 725, 94 S.Ct. 2038, 40 L.Ed.2d 496 (1974).

## Discrimination in Admissions

*Texas v. Lesage,* 528 U.S. 18, 120 S.Ct. 467, 145 L.Ed.2d 347 (1999).

*Cannon v. Univ. of Chicago,* 441 U.S. 677, 99 S.Ct. 1946, 60 L.Ed.2d 560 (1979).

*DeFunis v. Odegaard,* 416 U.S. 312, 94 S.Ct. 1704, 40 L.Ed.2d 164 (1974).

## Employee Searches

*O'Connor v. Ortega,* 480 U.S. 709, 107 S.Ct. 1492, 94 L.Ed.2d 714 (1987).

## Employees and Due Process

*Gilbert v. Homar,* 520 U.S. 924, 117 S.Ct. 1807, 138 L.Ed.2d 120 (1997).

*Cleveland Board of Educ. v. Loudermill,* 470 U.S. 532, 105 S.Ct. 1487, 84 L.Ed.2d 494 (1985).

*Perry v. Sindermann,* 408 U.S. 593, 92 S.Ct. 2694, 33 L.Ed.2d 570 (1972).

*Board of Regents of State Colleges v. Roth,* 408 U.S. 564, 92 S.Ct. 2701, 33 L.Ed.2d 548 (1972).

## Employment Discrimination

*Vance v. Ball State University,* 133 S.Ct. 2434, 186 L.Ed.2d 565 (U.S. 2013).

*Univ. of Texas Southwestern Medical Center v. Nassar,* 133 S.Ct. 2517, 186 L.Ed.2d 503 (U.S. 2013).

*Edelman v. Lynchburg College,* 535 U.S. 106, 122 S.Ct. 1145, 152 L.Ed.2d 188 (2002).

*Raygor v. Regents of Univ. of Minnesota,* 534 U.S. 533, 122 S.Ct. 999, 152 L.Ed.2d 27 (2002).

*Board of Trustees of the Univ. of Alabama v. Garrett,* 531 U.S. 356, 121 S.Ct. 955, 148 L.Ed.2d 866 (2001).

*Kimel v. Florida Board of Regents*, 528 U.S. 62, 120 S.Ct. 631, 145 L.Ed.2d 522 (2000).

*Univ. of Pennsylvania v. EEOC*, 493 U.S. 182, 110 S.Ct. 577, 107 L.Ed.2d 571 (1990).

*Carnegie-Mellon Univ. v. Cohill*, 484 U.S. 343, 108 S.Ct. 614, 98 L.Ed.2d 720 (1988).

*St. Francis College v. Al-Khazraji*, 481 U.S. 604, 107 S.Ct. 2022, 97 L.Ed.2d 749 (1987).

*Univ. of Tennessee v. Elliot*, 478 U.S. 788, 106 S.Ct. 3220, 92 L.Ed.2d 635 (1986).

*Burnett v. Grattan*, 468 U.S. 42, 104 S.Ct. 2924, 82 L.Ed.2d 36 ((1984).

*Patsy v. Board of Regents of State of Florida*, 457 U.S. 496, 102 S.Ct. 2557, 73 L.Ed.2d 172 (1982).

*Delaware State College v. Ricks*, 449 U.S. 250, 101 S.Ct. 498, 66 L.Ed.2d 431 (1980).

## Federal Funding

*Rumsfeld v. Forum for Academic and Institutional Rights, Inc.*, 547 U.S. 47, 126 S.Ct. 1297, 164 L.Ed.2d 156 (2006).

*Selective Service System v. MPIRG*, 468 U.S. 841, 104 S.Ct. 3348, 82 L.Ed.2d 632 (1984).

## Federal Funding for Religious Institutions

*Valley Forge Christian College v. Americans United for Separation of Church and State*, 454 U.S. 464, 102 S.Ct. 752, 70 L.Ed.2d 700 (1982).

*Roemer v. Board of Public Works of Maryland*, 426 U.S. 736, 96 S.Ct. 2337, 49 L.Ed.2d 179 (1976).

*Hunt v. McNair*, 413 U.S. 734, 93 S.Ct. 2868, 37 L.Ed.2d 923 (1973).

*Tilton v. Richardson*, 403 U.S. 672, 91 S.Ct. 2091, 29 L.Ed.2d 790 (1971).

*Lemon v. Kurtzman*, 403 U.S. 602, 91 S.Ct. 2105, 29 L.Ed.2d 745 (1971).

*Flast v. Cohen*, 392 U.S. 83, 88 S.Ct. 1942, 20 L.Ed.2d 947 (1968).

## FERPA

*Gonzaga Univ. v. Doe*, 536 U.S. 273, 122 S.Ct. 2268, 153 L.Ed.2d 309 (2002).

## Freedom of Religion

*Locke v. Davey*, 540 U.S. 712, 124 S.Ct. 1307, 158 L.Ed.2d 1 (2004).

*Rosenberger v. Rector and Visitors of Univ. of Virginia*, 515 U.S. 819, 115 S.Ct. 2510, 132 L.Ed.2d 700 (1995).

## Freedom of Speech

*Lane v. Franks*, 134 S.Ct. 2369. 189 L.Ed.2d 312 (U.S. 2014).

*Garcetti v. Ceballos*, 547 U.S. 410, 126 S.Ct. 1951, 164 L.Ed. 2d 689 (2006).

Board of Regents of Univ. of Wisconsin System v. Southworth, 529 U.S. 217, 120 S.Ct. 1346, 146 L.Ed.2d 193 (2000).

Rosenberger v. Rector and Visitors of Univ. of Virginia, 515 U.S. 819, 115 S.Ct. 2510, 132 L.Ed.2d 700 (1995).

Board of Trustees of the State Univ. of New York v. Fox, 492 U.S. 469, 109 S.Ct. 3028, 106 L.Ed.2d 388 (1989).

Connick v. Myers, 461 U.S. 138, 103 S.Ct. 1684, 75 L.Ed.2d 708 (1983).

Papish v. Board of Curators of Univ. of Missouri, 410 U.S. 667, 93 S.Ct. 1197, 35 L.Ed.2d 618 (1973).

Keyishian v. Board of Regents of Univ. of State of New York, 385 U.S. 589, 87 S.Ct. 675, 17 L.Ed.2d 629 (1967).

## Intellectual Property

Florida Prepaid Postsecondary Educ. Expense Board v. College Savings Bank, 527 U.S. 627, 119 S.Ct. 2199, 144 L.Ed.2d 575 (1999).

College Savings Bank v. Florida Prepaid Postsecondary Educ. Expense Board, 527 U.S. 666, 119 S.Ct. 2219, 144 L.Ed.2d 605 (1999).

## Labor Relations

Lehnert v. Ferris Faculty Ass'n, 500 U.S. 507, 111 S.Ct. 1950, 114 L.Ed.2d 572 (1991).

Minnesota State Board for Community Colleges v. Knight, 465 U.S. 271, 104 S.Ct. 1058, 79 L.Ed.2d 299 (1984).

NLRB v. Yeshiva Univ., 444 U.S. 672, 100 S.Ct. 856, 63 L.Ed.2d 115 (1980).

NLRB v. Catholic Bishop of Chicago, 440 U.S. 490, 99 S.Ct. 1313, 59 L.Ed.2d 533 (1979).

## Racial Discrimination

Fisher v. Univ. of Texas at Austin, 136 S.Ct. 2198 (U.S. 6/23/16).

Schuette v. Coalition to Defend Affirmative Action, 134 S.Ct. 1623 (U.S. 2014).

Fisher v. Univ. of Texas at Austin, 133 S.Ct. 2411, 186 L.Ed.2d 474 (U.S. 2013).

Grutter v. Bollinger, 539 U.S. 306, 123 S.Ct. 2325, 156 L.Ed.2d 304 (2003).

Gratz v. Bollinger, 539 U.S. 244, 123 S.Ct. 2411, 156 L.Ed.2d 257 (2003).

Bazemore v. Friday, 478 U.S. 385, 106 S.Ct. 3000, 92 L.Ed.2d 315 (1986).

Regents of the Univ. of California v. Bakke, 438 U.S. 265, 98 S.Ct. 2733, 57 L.Ed.2d 750 (1978).

**Recognition of Student Organizations**

> *Christian Legal Society Chapter of the University of California, Hastings College of the Law v. Martinez,* 561 U.S. 661, 130 S.Ct. 2971, 177 L.Ed.2d 838 (2010).
>
> *Iron Arrow Honor Society v. Heckler,* 464 U.S. 67, 104 S.Ct. 373, 78 L.Ed.2d 58 (1983).
>
> *Widmar v. Vincent,* 454 U.S. 263, 102 S.Ct. 269, 70 L.Ed.2d 440 (1981).
>
> *Healy v. James,* 408 U.S. 169, 92 S.Ct. 2338, 33 L.Ed.2d 266 (1972).

**Religious Rights**

> *Zubik v. Burwell,* 136 S.Ct. 1557, 194 L.Ed.2d 696 (U.S. 2016).
>
> *Wheaton College v. Burwell,* 134 S.Ct. 2806, 189 L.Ed.2d 856 (U.S. 2014).
>
> *Hosanna-Tabor Evangelical Lutheran Church and School v. EEOC,* 132 S.Ct. 694, 181 L.Ed.2d 650 (U.S. 2012).

**Residency**

> *Toll v. Moreno,* 458 U.S. 1, 102 S.Ct. 2977, 73 L.Ed.2d 563 (1982).
>
> *Elkins v. Moreno,* 435 U.S. 647, 98 S.Ct. 1338, 55 L.Ed.2d 614 (1978).
>
> *Vlandis v. Kline,* 412 U.S. 441, 93 S.Ct. 2230, 37 L.Ed.2d 63 (1973).

**School Liability**

> *Regents of Univ. of California v. Doe,* 519 U.S. 425, 117 S.Ct. 900, 137 L.Ed.2d 55 (1997).

**Sex Discrimination**

> *U.S. v. Virginia,* 518 U.S. 515, 116 S.Ct. 2264, 135 L.Ed.2d 735 (1996).
>
> *Mississippi Univ. for Women v. Hogan,* 458 U.S. 718, 102 S.Ct. 3331, 73 L.Ed.2d 1090 (1982).
>
> *Cannon v. Univ. of Chicago,* 441 U.S. 677, 99 S.Ct. 1946, 60 L.Ed.2d 560 (1979).

**Sexual Violence on Campus**

> *U.S. v. Morrison,* 529 U.S. 598, 120 S.Ct. 1740, 146 L.Ed.2d 658 (2000).

**Student Dismissals**

> *Salve Regina College v. Russell,* 499 U.S. 225, 111 S.Ct. 1217, 113 L.Ed.2d 190 (1991)
>
> *Regents of Univ. of Michigan v. Ewing,* 474 U.S. 214, 106 S.Ct. 507, 88 L.Ed.2d 523 (1985).
>
> *Board of Curators of Univ. of Missouri v. Horowitz,* 435 U.S. 78, 98 S.Ct. 948, 55 L.Ed.2d 124 (1978).
>
> *Papish v. Board of Curators of Univ. of Missouri,* 410 U.S. 667, 93 S.Ct. 1197, 35 L.Ed.2d 618 (1973).
>
> *Jones v. State Board of Educ. of State of Tennessee,* 397 U.S. 31, 90 S.Ct. 779, 25 L.Ed.2d 27 (1970).

## Student Loans

*United Student Aid Funds, Inc. v. Espinosa*, 559 U.S. 260, 130 S.Ct. 1367, 176 L.Ed.2d 158 (2010).

*Central Virginia Community College v. Katz*, 546 U.S. 356, 126 S.Ct. 990, 163 L.Ed.2d 945 (2006)

*Lockhart v. U.S.*, 546 U.S. 142, 126 S.Ct. 699, 163 L.Ed.2d 557 (2005).

## Student Privacy

*Gonzaga Univ. v. Doe*, 536 U.S. 273, 122 S.Ct. 2268, 153 L.Ed.2d 309 (2002).

*Department of Air Force v. Rose*, 425 U.S. 352, 96 S.Ct. 1592, 48 L.Ed.2d 11 (1976).

## Student Searches

*Washington v. Chrisman*, 455 U.S. 1, 102 S.Ct. 812, 70 L.Ed.2d 778 (1982).

*Zurcher v. Stanford Daily*, 436 U.S. 547, 98 S.Ct. 1970, 56 L.Ed.2d 525 (1978).

## Student Suspensions

*U.S. v. Morrison*, 529 U.S. 598, 120 S.Ct. 1740, 146 L.Ed.2d 658 (2000).

*Board of Curators of Univ. of Missouri v. Horowitz*, 435 U.S. 78, 98 S.Ct. 948, 55 L.Ed.2d 124 (1978).

*Jones v. State Board of Educ. of State of Tennessee*, 397 U.S. 31, 90 S.Ct. 779, 25 L.Ed.2d 27 (1970).

*Norton v. Discipline Committee of East Tennessee State Univ.*, 399 U.S. 906, 90 S.Ct. 2191, 26 L.Ed.2d 562 (1970).

## Students With Disabilities

*Univ. of Texas v. Camenisch*, 451 U.S. 390, 101 S.Ct. 1830, 68 L.Ed.2d 175 (1981).

*Southeastern Community College v. Davis*, 442 U.S. 397, 99 S.Ct. 2361, 60 L.Ed.2d 980 (1979).

## Taxation

*Mayo Foundation for Medical Educ. and Research v. U.S.*, 562 U.S. 44, 131 S.Ct. 704, 178 L.Ed.2d 588 (2011).

*Bob Jones Univ. v. U.S.*, 461 U.S. 574, 103 S.Ct. 2017, 76 L.Ed.2d 157 (1983).

*Bob Jones Univ. v. Simon*, 416 U.S. 725, 94 S.Ct. 2038, 40 L.Ed.2d 496 (1974).

# The Judicial System

In order to allow you to determine the relative importance of a judicial decision, the cases included in *Higher Education Law in America* identify the particular court from which a decision has been issued. For example, a case decided by a state supreme court generally will be of greater significance than a state circuit court case. Hence a basic knowledge of the structure of our judicial system is important to an understanding of higher education law.

Almost all the reports in this volume are taken from appellate court decisions. Although most education law decisions occur at trial court and administrative levels, appellate court decisions have the effect of binding lower courts and administrators so that appellate court decisions have the effect of law within their court systems.

State and federal court systems generally function independently of each other. Each court system applies its own law according to statutes and the determinations of its highest court. However, judges at all levels often consider opinions from other court systems to settle issues that are new or arise under unique fact situations. Similarly, lawyers look at the opinions of many courts to locate authority that supports their clients' cases.

Once a lawsuit is filed in a particular court system, that system retains the matter until its conclusion. Unsuccessful parties at the administrative or trial court level generally have the right to appeal unfavorable determinations of law to appellate courts within the system. When federal law issues or constitutional grounds are present, lawsuits may be appropriately filed in the federal court system. In those cases, the lawsuit is filed initially in the federal district court for that area.

On rare occasions, the U.S. Supreme Court considers appeals from the highest courts of the states if a distinct federal question exists and at least four justices agree on the question's importance. The federal courts occasionally send cases to state courts for application of state law. These situations are infrequent and, in general, the state and federal court systems should be considered separate from each other.

The most common system, used by nearly all states and also the federal judiciary, is as follows: a legal action is commenced in district court (sometimes called trial court, county court, common pleas court or superior court) where a decision is initially reached. The case may then be appealed to the court of appeals (or appellate court), and in turn this decision may be appealed to the supreme court.

Several states, however, do not have a court of appeals; lower court decisions are appealed directly to the state's supreme court. Additionally, some states have labeled their courts in a nonstandard fashion.

In Maryland, the highest state court is called the Court of Appeals. In the state of New York, the trial court is called the Supreme Court. Decisions of this court may be appealed to the Supreme Court, Appellate Division. The highest court in New York is the Court of Appeals. Pennsylvania has perhaps the most complex court system. The lowest state court is the Court of Common Pleas. Depending on the circumstances of the case, appeals may be taken to either the Commonwealth Court or the Superior Court. In certain instances the Commonwealth Court functions as a trial court as well as an appellate court. The Superior Court, however, is strictly an intermediate appellate court. The highest court in Pennsylvania is the Supreme Court.

While supreme court decisions are generally regarded as the last word in legal matters, it is important to remember that trial and appeals court decisions also create important legal precedents. For the hierarchy of typical state and federal court systems, please see the diagram below.

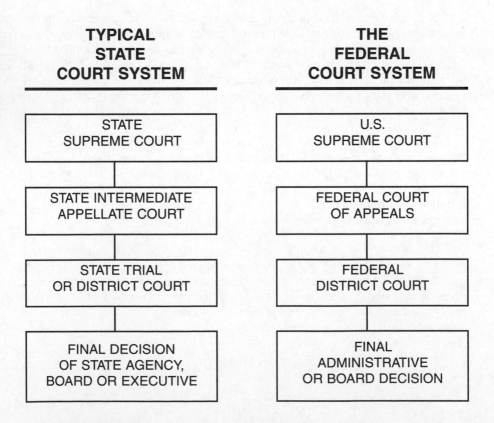

Federal courts of appeals hear appeals from the district courts that are located in their circuits. Below is a list of states matched to the federal circuits in which they are located.

First Circuit — Puerto Rico, Maine, New Hampshire, Massachusetts, Rhode Island

Second Circuit — New York, Vermont, Connecticut

Third Circuit — Pennsylvania, New Jersey, Delaware, Virgin Islands

Fourth Circuit — West Virginia, Maryland, Virginia, North Carolina, South Carolina

Fifth Circuit — Texas, Louisiana, Mississippi

Sixth Circuit — Ohio, Kentucky, Tennessee, Michigan

Seventh Circuit — Wisconsin, Indiana, Illinois

Eighth Circuit — North Dakota, South Dakota, Nebraska, Arkansas, Missouri, Iowa, Minnesota

Ninth Circuit — Alaska, Washington, Oregon, California, Hawaii, Arizona, Nevada, Idaho, Montana, Northern Mariana Islands, Guam

Tenth Circuit — Wyoming, Utah, Colorado, Kansas, Oklahoma, New Mexico

Eleventh Circuit — Alabama, Georgia, Florida

District of Columbia — Hears cases from the U.S. District Court for the District of Columbia.

Federal Circuit — Sitting in Washington, D.C., the U.S. Court of Appeals, Federal Circuit, hears patent and trade appeals and certain appeals on claims brought against the federal government and its agencies.

# How to Read a Case Citation

Generally, court decisions can be located in case reporters at law school or governmental law libraries. Some cases also can be located on the Internet through legal websites or official court websites.

Each case summary contains the citation, or legal reference, to the full text of the case. The diagram below illustrates how to read a case citation.

case name (parties)　　case reporter name and series　　court location

*Jones v. Temple Univ.,* 622　　Fed.Appx.　131　　(3d Cir. 2015).

volume number　　first page　　year of decision

Some cases may have two or three reporter names, such as U.S. Supreme Court cases and cases reported in regional case reporters as well as state case reporters. For example, a U.S. Supreme Court case usually contains three case reporter citations.

first reporter　　　　　　third reporter

*U.S. v. Lopez,* 514 U.S. 549, 115 S.Ct. 1624, 131 L.Ed.2d 626 (1995).

second reporter

The citations are still read in the same manner as if only one citation has been listed.

Occasionally, a case may contain a citation that does not reference a case reporter. For example, a citation may contain a reference such as:

case name　　year of decision　　first page　　date of decision

*Gordon v. LaSalle Univ.,* No. 14-3056,　2015　WL　1736962　(E.D. Pa. 4/16/15).

court file number　　WESTLAW[1]　　court location

The court file number indicates the specific number assigned to a case by the particular court system deciding the case. In our example, the Eastern District of Pennsylvania court has assigned the case of *Gordon v. LaSalle Univ.,* the case number of "14-3056" which will serve as the reference number for the case and any matter relating to the case. Locating a case on the Internet generally requires either the case name and date of the decision, and/or the court file number.

---

[1]WESTLAW® is a computerized database of court cases available for a fee.

Below, we have listed the full names of the regional reporters. As mentioned previously, many states have individual state reporters. The names of those reporters may be obtained from a reference law librarian.

**P.**          **Pacific Reporter**
                Alaska, Arizona, California, Colorado, Hawaii, Idaho,
                Kansas, Montana, Nevada, New Mexico, Oklahoma,
                Oregon, Utah, Washington, Wyoming

**A.**          **Atlantic Reporter**
                Connecticut, Delaware, District of Columbia, Maine,
                Maryland, New Hampshire, New Jersey, Pennsylvania,
                Rhode Island, Vermont

**N.E.**        **Northeastern Reporter**
                Illinois, Indiana, Massachusetts, New York, Ohio

**N.W.**        **Northwestern Reporter**
                Iowa, Michigan, Minnesota, Nebraska, North Dakota,
                South Dakota, Wisconsin

**So.**         **Southern Reporter**
                Alabama, Florida, Louisiana, Mississippi

**S.E.**        **Southeastern Reporter**
                Georgia, North Carolina, South Carolina, Virginia,
                West Virginia

**S.W.**        **Southwestern Reporter**
                Arkansas, Kentucky, Missouri, Tennessee, Texas

**F.**          **Federal Reporter**
                The thirteen federal judicial circuits courts of appeals
                decisions. *See The Judicial System, p. 509* for specific
                state circuits.

**F.Supp.**     **Federal Supplement**
                The thirteen federal judicial circuits district court
                decisions. *See The Judicial System, p. 509* for specific
                state circuits.

**Fed.Appx.**   **Federal Appendix**
                Contains unpublished decisions of the U.S. Circuit Courts
                of Appeal.

**U.S.**        **United States Reports**
**S.Ct.**       **Supreme Court Reporter** ⟩ U.S. Supreme Court Decisions
**L.Ed.**       **Lawyers' Edition**

# GLOSSARY

**Ad Valorem Tax** - In general usage, a tax on property measured by the property's value.

**Age Discrimination in Employment Act (ADEA)** - The ADEA, 29 U.S.C. § 621, *et seq.*, is part of the Fair Labor Standards Act. It prohibits discrimination against persons who are at least 40 years old, and applies to employers that have 20 or more employees and that affect interstate commerce.

**Americans with Disabilities Act (ADA)** - The ADA, 42 U.S.C. § 12101, *et seq.*, was signed into law on July 26, 1990. Among other things, it prohibits discrimination against a qualified individual with a disability because of that person's disability with respect to job application procedures; the hiring, advancement or discharge of employees; employee compensation; job training; and other terms, conditions and privileges of employment. The act also prohibits discrimination against otherwise qualified individuals with respect to the services, programs or activities of a public entity. Further, any entity that operates a place of public accommodation (including private schools) may not discriminate against individuals with disabilities.

**Bill of Attainder** - A bill of attainder is a law that inflicts punishment on a particular group of individuals without a trial. Such acts are prohibited by Article I, Section 9, of the Constitution.

**Bona fide** - Latin term meaning "good faith." Generally used to note a party's lack of bad intent or fraudulent purpose.

**Claim Preclusion** - (see *Res Judicata*).

**Class Action Suit** - Federal Rule of Civil Procedure 23 allows members of a class to sue as representatives on behalf of the whole class provided that the class is so large that joinder of all parties is impractical, there are questions of law or fact common to the class, the claims or defenses of the representatives are typical of the claims or defenses of the class, and the representative parties will adequately protect the interests of the class. In addition, there must be some danger of inconsistent verdicts or adjudications if the class action were prosecuted as separate actions. Most states also allow class actions under the same or similar circumstances.

**Collateral Estoppel** - Also known as issue preclusion. The idea that once an issue has been litigated, it may not be re-tried. Similar to the doctrine of *Res Judicata* (see below).

**Due Process Clause** - The clauses of the Fifth and Fourteenth Amendments to the Constitution which guarantee the citizens of the United States "due process of law" (see below). The Fifth Amendment's Due Process Clause applies to the federal government, and the Fourteenth Amendment's Due Process Clause applies to the states.

**Due Process of Law** - The idea of "fair play" in the government's application of law to its citizens, guaranteed by the Fifth and Fourteenth Amendments. Substantive due process is just plain *fairness*, and procedural due process is accorded when the government utilizes adequate procedural safeguards for the protection of an individual's liberty or property interests.

**Employee Retirement Income Security Act (ERISA)** - Federal legislation that sets uniform standards for employee pension benefit plans and employee welfare benefit plans. It is codified at 29 U.S.C. § 1001, *et seq.*

**Enjoin** - (see Injunction).

**Equal Pay Act** - Federal legislation that is part of the Fair Labor Standards Act. It applies to discrimination in wages that is based on gender. For race discrimination, employees paid unequally must utilize Title VII or 42 U.S.C. § 1981. Unlike many labor statutes, there is no minimum number of employees necessary to invoke the act's protection.

**Equal Protection Clause** - Fourteenth Amendment clause that prohibits a state from denying any person equal protection of the law – for example, by treating people differently on the basis of race. The U.S. Supreme Court has interpreted the Due Process Clause of the Fifth Amendment to require the federal government to provide equal protection.

**Establishment Clause** - The clause of the First Amendment that prohibits Congress from making "any law respecting an establishment of religion." This clause has been interpreted as creating a "wall of separation" between church and state. The test now used to determine whether government action violates the Establishment Clause, referred to as the *Lemon* test, asks whether the action has a secular purpose, whether its primary effect promotes or inhibits religion, and whether it requires excessive entanglement between church and state.

**Ex Post Facto Law** - A law that punishes as criminal any action that was not a crime at the time it was performed. Prohibited by Article I, Section 9, of the Constitution.

**Exclusionary Rule** - Rule from the 1961 U.S. Supreme Court decision, *Mapp v. Ohio*, that prohibits the state from using evidence obtained by an unconstitutional search or seizure against a criminal defendant at trial.

**Fair Labor Standards Act (FLSA)** - Federal law that deals with child labor, minimum wage, overtime and employer record-keeping.

**42 U.S.C. §§ 1981, 1983** - Section 1983 of the federal Civil Rights Act prohibits any person acting under color of state law from depriving any other person of rights protected by the Constitution or by federal laws. A vast majority of lawsuits claiming constitutional violations are brought under Section 1983. Section 1981 provides that all persons enjoy the same right to make and enforce contracts as "white citizens." Section 1981 applies to employment contracts. Unlike Section 1983, Section 1981 is not limited to those acting under color of state law. These sections do not apply to the federal government, though the government may be sued directly under the Constitution for any violations.

**Free Exercise Clause** - The clause of the First Amendment that prohibits Congress from interfering with citizens' and institutions' rights to the free exercise of religion. Through the Fourteenth Amendment, it also has been made applicable to the states.

**Injunction** - A court order that requires a person or institution to do (or stop doing) something. (See Preliminary Injunction.)

**Issue Preclusion** - (see Collateral Estoppel).

**Jurisdiction** - The power of a court to determine cases and controversies. The Supreme Court's jurisdiction extends to cases arising under the Constitution and under federal law. Federal courts have the power to hear cases where there is diversity of citizenship or where a federal question is involved.

**Labor Management Relations Act (LMRA)** - Federal labor law that preempts state law with respect to controversies involving collective bargaining agreements. The most important provision of the LMRA is Section 301, which is codified at 29 U.S.C. § 185.

**Mill** - In property tax usage, one-tenth of a cent.

**National Labor Relations Act (NLRA)** - Federal legislation that guarantees employees the right to form and participate in labor organizations. It also prohibits employers from interfering in employees' exercise of their rights under the NLRA – such as to band together regarding common workplace concerns – and thus applies even in workplaces that aren't unionized.

**Negligence per se** - Negligence on its face. Usually, the violation of an ordinance or statute will be treated as negligence per se because no careful person would have been guilty of it.

**Occupational Safety and Health Act (OSHA)** - Federal legislation that requires employers to provide a safe workplace. Employers have both general and specific duties under OSHA. The general duty is to provide a workplace that is free from recognized hazards that are likely to result in serious physical harm. The specific duty is to conform to the health and safety standards promulgated by the Secretary of Labor.

**Overbroad** - A law (or policy at a public higher ed institution) is overbroad if it prohibits not only things that it's permitted to prohibit but also First Amendment rights of speech, press or assembly.

*Per Curiam* - Latin phrase meaning "by the court." Used in court reports to note an opinion written by the court rather than by a single judge or justice.

**Preemption Doctrine** - Doctrine that states that when a federal and a state law attempt to regulate the same thing, federal law trumps state law. Based on the Supremacy Clause of Article VI, Clause 2, of the Constitution.

**Preliminary Injunction** – A court order that typically orders a person or institution to do something (for example, let a dismissed student attend classes) or not do something (for example, forbid students to protest in front of a campus building) while a lawsuit concerning the challenged act proceeds.

**Prior Restraint** - Restraining a publication before it is distributed. In general, constitutional law doctrine prohibits government from exercising prior restraint.

*Pro Se* - Latin for "on one's own behalf." A person handling a court matter without a lawyer is acting *pro se*.

**Remand** - The act of an appellate court in returning a case to the original court for further action.

**Remedies** - There are two general categories of remedies, or relief: legal remedies, which consist of money damages, and equitable remedies, which consist of a court mandate that a specific action be prohibited or required. For example, a claim for compensatory and punitive damages seeks a legal remedy; a claim for an injunction seeks an equitable remedy. Equitable remedies are generally unavailable unless legal remedies are inadequate to address the harm.

*Res Judicata* - Latin phrase that means a thing has already been decided. In law, it refers to a prohibition against relitigating a claim that has been validly resolved by another court.

**Section 504 of the Rehabilitation Act of 1973** - Section 504 prohibits discrimination on the basis of disability. The law applies to public or private institutions that receive federal financial assistance. It provides: "No otherwise qualified individual ... shall, solely by reason of her or his disability, be excluded from" participating in any program or activity, denied its benefits or be subjected to discrimination.

**Section 1981 & Section 1983** - (see 42 U.S.C. §§ 1981, 1983).

**Sovereign Immunity** - The idea that the government cannot be sued without its consent. It stems from the English notion that the "King could do no wrong." This immunity from suit has been abrogated in most states and by the federal government through legislative acts known as "tort claims acts."

**Standing** - The judicial doctrine that states that in order to maintain a lawsuit a party must have some real interest at stake in the outcome of the trial.

**Statute of Limitations** - A statute of limitation provides the time period in which a specific cause of action may be brought.

**Summary Judgment** - Also referred to as a pretrial judgment or a judgment without a trial. Similar to dismissal. Where there is no genuine issue as to any material fact and all that remains is a question of law, a judge can rule in favor of one party or the other without first holding a trial. In general, summary judgment is appropriate when the plaintiff has not stated a valid legal claim.

**Supremacy Clause** - Clause in Article VI of the Constitution that states that federal legislation is the supreme law of the land. This clause is used to support the Preemption Doctrine (see above).

**Title VI, Civil Rights Act of 1964 (Title VI)** - Title VI prohibits racial discrimination in federally funded programs. This extends to admissions, financial aid, and virtually every aspect of the federally assisted programs in which private schools are involved. Codified at 42 U.S.C. § 2000d.

**Title VII, Civil Rights Act of 1964 (Title VII)** - Title VII prohibits discrimination in employment that's based on race, color, sex, national origin, or religion. It applies to any employer having 15 or more employees.

**Title IX** - Enacted as part of the Education Amendments of 1972, Title IX prohibits sexual discrimination in any school program or activity receiving federal financial assistance. Codified at 20 U.S.C. § 1981, *et seq.*

**U.S. Equal Employment Opportunity Commission (EEOC)** - The EEOC is the government entity that is empowered to enforce Title VII (see above) through investigation and/or lawsuits. Private individuals alleging discrimination must complete administrative remedies within the EEOC before they are allowed to pursue a lawsuit under Title VII.

**Vacate** - The act of annulling the judgment of a court either by an appellate court or by the court itself. The Supreme Court generally will vacate a lower court's judgment without deciding the case itself, and remand the case to the lower court for further consideration in light of some recent controlling decision.

**Void-for-Vagueness Doctrine** - A judicial doctrine based on the Fourteenth Amendment's Due Process Clause. In order for a law that regulates speech, or any criminal statute, to pass muster under the doctrine, the law must make clear what actions are prohibited or made criminal. Under the principles of the Due Process Clause, people of average intelligence should not have to guess at the meaning of a law.

**Writ of Certiorari** - The device used by the Supreme Court to transfer cases from the appellate court's docket to its own. Since the Supreme Court's appellate jurisdiction is largely discretionary, it need only issue such a writ when it desires to rule in the case.

# INDEX